THE JOHN HARVARD LIBRARY

Bernard Bailyn

Editor-in-Chief

UNION PAMPHLETS
OF THE CIVIL WAR

1861–1865

Edited by Frank Freidel

VOLUME II

THE JOHN HARVARD LIBRARY

The Belknap Press of Harvard University Press

Cambridge, Massachusetts

1967

John Harvard Library books are edited at the Charles Warren
Center for Studies in American History, Harvard University.

CONTENTS

VOLUME II

CONTENTS

UNION PAMPHLETS OF THE CIVIL WAR

1861–1865

Pamphlet 23

The Great Union Meeting. Held at Indianapolis, February 26th, 1863. Speeches of Andrew Johnson, of Tennessee, Gen. Samuel F. Carey, of Ohio, and Others.

Indianapolis, 1863

[As a means of building lagging morale, Union supporters in cities throughout the North upon occasion held great mass meetings. These functioned as a wartime counterpart not only to the political rallies, but perhaps even the revivals, of peacetime. Many of the largest mass meetings were held in Eastern cities like New York, but they were effective also in the Middle West. In this era when the size of the audience was limited to the unamplified range of the human voice, no one speaker could make himself audible to the huge crowds. Consequently several orators at once would speak from different bunting-decked stands, or in various assembly halls. Patriotic poets would make their way from one stand to another, to fill interludes with their doggerel. The proceedings were solemnly recorded and often later appeared in pamphlet form. This pamphlet reporting the meeting at Indianapolis on February 26, 1863, is particularly interesting because Indiana was a state which had been carried by the Democrats in the previous election and anti-war sentiment was strong there. Also it is notable that the main speaker was Andrew Johnson, for the moment a hero to the Radical Republicans, who came to regard him so differently after he became President a little more than three years later. Johnson (1808–1875), a Democrat and the spokesman for small farmers of the South, had been governor of Tennessee from 1853 to 1857 when he entered the United States Senate. Among all the Southern senators, he alone remained in the Senate when his state seceded, and became active along with Radical Republicans on the Joint Committee on the Conduct of the War. Early in 1862, President Lincoln appointed him military governor of Tennessee, the position he held when he participated in the Indianapolis mass meeting. General Samuel Fenton Carey (1814–1900), long a temperance lecturer, was a successful army recruiter during the Civil War. In 1868 he was the only Republican member of the House of Representatives to vote against President Johnson's impeachment. The poet at this rally, Thomas Buchanan Read (1822–1872), was

one of the most popular of the era; he published several volumes of
verse but is remembered only for "Sheridan's Ride."]

NEVER before in this State, or any other, have we witnessed a
demonstration of popular feeling so magnificent in its proportions,
and so impressive in its enthusiasm, as the great Union meeting
yesterday. Nothing in any party campaign will compare with it.
There was more than party at stake, and more than party devotion
responded. The country is in peril and the people came out to
encourage and hold up the hands of those whose courage must
save it. It was the voice of the people crying to the army: "Be of
good cheer, your friends have not forsaken you." There was no
element of party in it. It was a broad, bold, noble assertion of the
right of the nation to save itself. The spirit that animated it was as
glorious as its own strength was invincible. It looked as if the
foundations of the popular deep were broken up, and a deluge of
indignant feeling had risen to sweep from the earth all treason and
disaffection. No man could see it and not feel how miserable and
mean is the cause that could deny itself to such support. But we
must spare comment for to-day.

THE CROWD.

All day Wednesday crowds were coming in, giving warning,
though insufficient, as it proved, of the immense gathering that they
preceded. At night there was not a spare bed in the city in any
hotel, nor in many private houses, and hundreds had to sit up all
night in hotel parlors sleeping in chairs, or how they could, or not
sleeping at all. Many ladies who arrived on late trains were unable
to procure any resting place at all. Yesterday morning early the
streets seemed sown with people, though not a train had yet arrived of the many from which the real crowd was expected. The
sky was damp with the promise of rain, which was speedily fulfilled,
but the crowd still poured along, and gathered thicker every
minute. There was every indication of a most unpleasant and disheartening day, but the trains came in lengthened out for hundreds
of yards and loaded with people. The whole State seemed to be
emptying itself into the city, and the clouds, without any seeming

about it, were emptying themselves into the streets. It was an outpouring and downpouring together. By nine o'clock it was almost
impossible to cross the streets for the mud, or pass along them for
people. An endless procession streamed along towards the State
House square, where even then there was a far larger crowd collected than attended the Butternut meeting last July. In spite of
the dismal weather gay flags floated from many a building, and
they didn't droop, even for the rain, but sailed out boldly as if
they felt that they were representing an occasion that demanded
their full beauty. Over the windows of the police office a magnificent
evergreen arch, decorated with flags, was erected, but we did not
notice any other attempt at this kind of display. — At 10 o'clock the
clouds broke away, and the sun came out. And then the crowd
swelled faster than ever. The promise of a pleasant day seemed to
be answered by a fresh burst of people, and a faster whirl of huge
excursion trains. When we reached the State House yard the entire
eastern side from Washington street to Market was full, and it
was almost impossible to get near the main stand. Still the long
procession poured through the gate, and stray streams were leaping
in cataracts over the fence in fifty places. The band of the 18th
Regulars came along directly playing superbly, and the crowd that
followed was so thick that many thought a procession had really
been formed up the street of the remnant that still remained out
of the yard. The band mounted a stand prepared for them to the
right of the main stand, and entertained as many as could
hear with some of their finest airs. Two beautiful new flags, one
belonging to the 9th Indiana, were fastened to the main stand, and
showed their glorious stars and stripes in as brilliant a sun, and as
balmy an air, as any in all that sunny South where their authority
is reviled. The day seemed to have become enchanted with a crowd
that *wouldn't* be put out by any sort of weather, and showed its
prettiest face, though it changed capriciously several times before
dark. By this time the ceremony of the reception of Gov. Johnson
was expected. But it was speedily whispered about, till all knew
it, that Gov. Morton would not be able to make the reception
speech. An accidental fall during the night, while waiting upon a
sick child, had severely bruised and sprained his shoulder and knee,
and his doctors had forbidden him to go out. We heard many an

expression of disappointment at the failure to see him. "If we could only have *seen* him, we would have been satisfied," was a constant exclamation. It told better than many a formal declaration how he has endeared himself to all true men by his exertions in behalf of our soldiers.

About half past 10 o'clock Gov. Johnson entered the yard, accompanied by Governor Wright, who readily accepted the hospitable duty, so well known to his own career as Governor, of receiving Gov. Johnson. The band struck up "Hail to the Chief," and in a cloud of music and cheering they made their way through the thick mass to the stand. Some minutes were passed in introductions and other attendant ceremonies, and then, as the main ceremony was about to begin, Major Frybarger's guns began thundering all round the city. From every direction came the roaring of artillery, now in regular rapid explosions, and again in irregular bursts that crashed through the clear sky like a drove of thunderbolts on a stampede. Sections of batteries had been placed at a dozen different points, near and far, around the State House, and the gunners seemed to let themselves out in making just as much noise, and as fast, as they could. There could be no speech making while that lasted, but it stopped in five minutes or so, and the ceremonies proceeded. At this time the sight of the crowd was a memory for a life time. We can't describe it. We never saw such an one before, and we doubt if any one else ever did, at least in Indiana. There could hardly have been less than 15,000 people in one solid block, with faces upturned to the stand, as if their bodies were one huge chunk on which faces had been glued, like shells on a fancy basket, as thickly as they could stick. The whole number in attendance on the meeting was fully 25,000, and, measured by the old exaggerated standard of party campaigns, was at least 75,000. We put it moderately and reasonably at 25,000.

ORGANIZATION.

The Convention was called to order by Hon. H. C. Newcomb, who nominated Gov. Joseph A. Wright for President.

Gov. Wright returned his thanks for the honor conferred upon him in appropriate remarks.

On motion of Hon. H. C. Newcomb, the following additional officers were nominated:

Hon. Caleb B. Smith, of Marion.
Hon. Charles H. Test, of White.
Col. H. B. Carrington, 18th Regulars.
James H. McNeeley, of Vanderburg.
Lieut. Col. Timberlake, 81st Ind.
Major I. B. Glover, 38th Ind.
Joseph Devin, of Gibson.
Hon. Cyrus M. Allen, of Knox.
Col. B. F. Mullen, 35th Ind.
Hon. T. C. Slaughter, of Harrison.
Robert Barnes, of Vanderburg.
Lieut. Col. J. A. Keith, 21st Ind.
Col. Ben Spooner, 83d Ind.
Lieut. Col. J. F. Cheek, 7th Ind.
W. H. Dixon, of Clark.
Col. Silas Colgrove, 27th Ind.
Gen. Ebenezer Dumont.
Col. A. D. Streight, 51st Ind.
Col. C. C. Hines, 57th Ind.
Gen. Milo S. Hascall.
Hon. Henry Secrest, of Putnam.
Hon. John A. Matson, of Putnam.
Hon. Harvey D. Scott, of Vigo.
Lieut. Col. J. E. Balfe, 35th Ind.
Hon. Samuel A. Huff.
Hon. Charles W. Cathcart, of Laporte.
Col. W. T. Spicely, 24th Ind.
Hon. W. S. Smith, of Allen.
Hon. W. M. Clapp, of Noble.
Col. Thos. J. Harrison, 39th Ind.
Major J. D. Evans, 39th Ind.

E. H. Barry, of Marion.
Henry Crawford, of Floyd.
F. M. Thayer, of Vanderburg.
C. E. Fuller, of Fulton.

The throne of Grace was addressed by Bishop E. R. Ames, of the M. E. Church.

On motion of Hon. H. C. Newcomb a committee of one from each Congressional District on resolutions was appointed as follows:

COMMITTEES ON RESOLUTIONS.

John Ingle, Jr., of Vanderburg.
Thos. Slaughter, of Harrison.
N. T. Hauser, of Bartholomew.
Col. Ben. Spooner, of Dearborn.
Jehu T. Elliott, of Henry.
H. C. Newcomb, of Marion.
D. E. Williamson, of Putnam.
W. C. Dougherty, of Boone.
Chas. H. Test, of White.
Wm. S. Smith, of Allen.
Col. Thos. J. Harrison, of Howard.

RECEPTION SPEECH OF GOV. WRIGHT.

In introducing Gov. Johnson, Gov. Wright said:

I have the pleasure of introducing to you a statesman whose name is familiar throughout the land, a personal and political friend, Gov. Andy Johnson, of Tennessee. Twenty years ago last December he had met him in the halls of Congress as a representative from Tennessee. Since then, as her Governor and her Senator, he had commanded the respect and confidence of every man North and South. He is a proper representative of that State to talk to you at this terrible hour of our national crisis. He was also a representative of one of the features of our free institutions, rising from a poor boy to the highest position, learning us that the humblest may equal the wealthiest in position. The question now is, whether wealth shall rule the country, or merit and talent. To every man who heard him to-day, whether he pushes the plane or follows the plow, the question comes home, whether you have a right to protection from the Government, and to participate in it. — Gov. Johnson comes from the South, as a representative of your Government, and tells you that he is for the Union, the whole Union, and nothing but the Union. While regretting that our worthy Governor was not present to do this duty, and while, as Executive of this State, he had introduced, on former occasions, distinguished statesmen, he had never in his life felt the emotions he now did in presenting to them a statesman cradled in the State where Jackson is entombed, and a Democrat who knows what Democracy is. Nor could he refrain from mentioning the fact that a few months ago, when Nashville was threatened by Bragg, and its surrender was advised by military men, Gov. Johnson, with his iron will, avowed that he would not abandon Nashville till its Capitol was in ruins, and himself buried by its fall. I present him to you and ask you to receive him with open arms.

Gov. Johnson was received with outbursts of applause, and replied as follows:

GOV. JOHNSON'S SPEECH.

Fellow-citizens of the State of Indiana, and I think I have a right to call you fellow-citizens. Although an inhabitant of another State, I claim to be a citizen of the United States, and recognize each and every one of you as a fellow-citizen, who claims citizenship under the broad panoply of this Union of ours. In presenting myself to you, it is with no ordinary degree of embarrassment. I find an audience far beyond my capacity to address, so far as my voice is concerned, nor have I strength to present the subject as I wish. Another cause of embarrassment is that I appear before you in the midst of a civil war, a revolution, which is calculated to interest each one of you. If any had come expecting oratory they would be disappointed. For in presenting myself to this concourse of people, if I know my own mind, it will be for the purpose of making a lodgment in your hearts of the truth on the great questions which have agitated the nation, and involved it in civil war.

When we look around, what condition do we find the country in? Just the other day all was peaceful, happy and prosperous. All portions of the country vied with each other in their professions of their desire for the common good. The great contest seemed to be between the advocates of the various parties and creeds, in pronouncing eulogies on their several States. Each one uttered eulogies on the blessings which had flowed upon this people under the Constitution of the United States since the formation of the Government. What has transpired or taken place in so short a period of time, as to make it necessary for one portion of your countrymen to commence a war of disintegration in the nation?

It has been contended by some in high places, and some in places not so high, that one portion of our fellow citizens had been deprived of their rights. Let me ask this sea of upturned faces before me to lay aside their prejudices — to forget that they ever belonged to the respective parties of the country — let me ask them what rights have been lost in the United States since the formation of the Constitution? Has any right been given up, or any right been taken away? I care not what party any man belongs to, can he put his finger on any one constitutional right which has been lost? Why, then, this crusade on the Constitution and the institutions under it?

As I remarked on a former occasion, I do not appear here as a partisan; but I have not given up my political creed in the slightest degree. I have neither come here, or been elsewhere, to revoke a single political principle which I espoused at the commencement of my public life. I stand where I have always stood, an uncompromising Democrat. I stand to-day, as the advocate of the great Democratic principle of self-government, that the people are the great source of political power. In later years I have come to the conclusion that the Union of these States was a fixed principle of Democracy. Hence, we simply adhere to the principles of self-government, and of the people as the source of power, when we talk of the Constitution and of all laws enacted under it as obligatory on those who live under it. This is Democracy. This is where I stand. It is a true doctrine that the Government was made for the convenience of man, and not man for the Government; just as the shoe is made for the foot, not the foot for the shoe.

One of the first ideas I learned in connection with government was that the soul of liberty was the love of law. What liberty have you without the Constitution or laws? Take away law, and you have vice and anarchy rampant. With law we have liberty. It protects the weak against the strong, virtue against vice. This is a part of my Democracy.

But, my countrymen, what has brought this condition upon us? I will illustrate the question by reference to the history of party politics. We have been divided into political parties — Whig and Democratic — and, latterly, Republican and Democratic. Whichever party was dissatisfied with the result of an election appealed to the people. Whatever the issue, banks or tariffs, or latterly the issues between the Democratic and Republican parties, there was waving over all the stars and stripes. All parties vied in their fealty to the Constitution and devotion to the banner of our country. Let me ask my Republican friends and my Democratic friends whether the contest has not been as to which would best promote the prosperity of the Union and preserve its existence? On all public measures the contest was whether the policy of either party would best preserve the Union and prosperity of the States. All agreed in the supremacy of the Constitution and Union of States. What are we doing about this matter now? These defenders of the South profess to find reasons for the men for whom they sympathize.

At the last election Lincoln, Bell, Douglas and Breckinridge were candidates, and they all professed to be strongly devoted to the Union. I made speeches for John C. Breckinridge, for the same reason I would have spoken for Douglas, had I been living in a free State, because he was the strongest man there, and by supporting him we hoped to beat the candidate of the Republican party. This is the truth, and I will not lie about it. We repudiated all idea that Breckinridge was a disunionist. Each party was especially devoted to the country. To satisfy my Democratic friends that he was a professed Unionist, I will read to you a few extracts from his speeches. We all know how parties divide, some going one way, some another, and we had as well admit it as honest men that thousands of them have their sympathies based on old party biases. If we were deceived is it any reason why we would turn traitors? He deceived me then — that was his fault. If he deceives me now it would be my fault. If God forgives me for advocating the claims of one who turned traitor. I pledge this assembly that I will never again be guilty of a like offense.

(Gov. Johnson quoted passages from Breckinridge's speeches, which he had used during the campaign to prove him a devoted Union man, referring to his speech on the occasion of the removal from the old Senate chamber to the new, when he prophesied that the execration of mankind would rest on any one who attempted to disrupt the Union. They were used by his advocates to convince the people that he was the most devoted Union candidate.)

Now, what has transpired since the Presidential election to make the Union so odious, and the Constitution so inefficient and illy calculated to benefit the country? What has been done to destroy the Union of the States? Can any one tell? Let me ask my Republican and Democratic friends, in the language of soberness and truth, to-day, do you believe if John C. Breckinridge had been elected, could we not have stood this Constitution and this Union at least four years longer? (Cries of "We do.")

The question resolves itself into this. One party was in power, and after the election it saw the sceptre of the Union had gone from it. For, even looking to the expiration of Lincoln's term of four years, there was, even if Mr. Lincoln was not re-elected, other organizations coming up to retain the power from them, and they knew it. Now, they said, is the time to strike and make the slavery question a pretext to unite the Southern States. We see to-day, in this terrible war, what it ended in. Let me ask this audience to-day, if we are to have a civil war after every election, because one party or the other is defeated, what are we coming to? Look at Mexico, torn with internal dissension, too feeble to resent foreign oppression. What is it to end in? Anarchy, loss of property, of life, and of national prosperity and honor.

What is our true policy? Because Mr. Lincoln beat us, and was elected under the forms of law, he was entitled to come into power and try his policy, and if the country prospered we ought to submit to it like men. If it was a bad administration we could oppose, as in the past we had that of others. That being so, let me ask every Democrat in the State of Indiana, and every Democrat in the Southern Confederacy, where was the danger of wrong when Mr. Lincoln came into power? Let me be heard on this point a few moments. On the 4th day of March, 1861, he came into power. A new Congress came in. In the House was a majority of Representatives against him. In the Senate there was a majority of six against him. There could be no danger from his administration. He must bring his Cabinet about him, whose nomination must be confirmed by the Senate. If he attempted to bring into power men opposed to the interests of any one section, they had the power to reject them. He could not make a Cabinet without their consent. We had it in our power to make the whole Cabinet to suit ourselves. — Where was the danger, then, from his administration? He could not send out a foreign minister without our consent. Every treaty he made must be submitted to us for ratification. Nor could he appoint Consuls. Nor draw his own salary unless we appropriated it for him. Hence, you see, there was on the part of these men a fixed determination to break and destroy the government. This is no new thing. I will read you one or two extracts from Southern papers, to show you how disunion has been going on from time to time. There was a determination to break up the government, and the great difficulty was making an excuse for it.

Governor Johnson then read from the Montgomery (Ala.) Daily Advertiser, which said that "it was no precipitate rebellion." They could have staid in the Union and arrested every unfriendly measure. One of their organs says "it has not been a precipitate revolution, but with coolness and deliberation has been thought of for forty years. For ten years this has been the all-absorbing question." I will read nothing further to show that it was their design in 1860 that the Union should be broken up. I might introduce other authorities.

In proof of what I am now saying I may quote an extract from a letter of General Jackson on the disunion movement of South Carolina in 1832. Let me ask Jackson Democrats, if there are any here, to hear him speak on this occasion. He now sleeps in a tomb which was, but a short time since, in the Southern Confederacy. I was told that, when they took possession of that county, they marched out to his tomb and attempted to plant the stars and bars upon it. On that occasion an old Jackson Democrat remarked: "By the Eternal God, I expected to see Jackson jump out of his grave!" Though he now sleeps in the grave, if it were possible to communicate with the dead, and if he could foresee the condition of to-day, I have sometimes thought he would turn over in his tomb, burst it asunder, and, extending that long arm and that long finger, declare: "The Federal Union — it must be preserved!" (Immense applause.)

Governor Johnson then quoted his comments on the schemes of Calhoun, in which he proved that the very tariff which was made a pretext for nullification was protective to the coarse wools of the South, and was a mere pretext, and closed with this prophesy: "The next pretext will be the negro, or the slavery question."

Have we not come to it? Is the Constitution changed? I think not. What rights have the South lost? ("None!") Who can tell? Do you not see that the establishment of a Southern Confederacy was their real object? Jackson's prophesy has been followed out to the very letter.

Who commenced the war — this damnable struggle to destroy the people's rights? The South. Who struck the first blow, fired the first gun, shed the first blood? It is a matter of history that a delegation from Virginia urged the attack upon the Federal forts at Charleston, as a spur for Virginia to revolt. They knew that in fifteen days Anderson and his gallant band in Fort Sumter would be out of food. But so fearful were they that these men would not be starved to death, or into a surrender, they opened fire on Fort Sumter, on this wretched garrison, and kept it up for three days, so incessantly that they were compelled to fall on their faces and wet their blankets to keep from suffocation. The surrender was communicated to Jeff. Davis at Montgomery. He could not speak in response to the news, but his Secretary did. It was, in substance:

"The first blow has been struck. Who can tell where it will end? Before May the Confederate flag shall be floating on the Capitol at Washington and on Congress Hall at Philadelphia."

They at once raised men and levied taxes. Mr. Lincoln came into power, administering the Constitution like an honest man, and, loving my country, I determined to sustain him. Because he called for men to defend the Constitution and the laws, he has been denounced as a usurper and a despot. If he had not called on you when your country was in peril would not the same armies have been raised by the South, and the revolution gone on? What sort of a Government would you have had to-day? Would it not have been a military despotism? You complain of the great wrong he has done, of arrests, &c. If I have any complaint to make, it is that President Lincoln has not done more to crush the rebellion. Has Lincoln violated the Constitution and trampled the law under foot? Who commenced the war? Did not the South? — Somehow these sympathizers forget that Davis and his piratical crew have violated the Constitution. They can see only the blunders of the party in power, but they have not a word of disapproval for the total annihilation of the Constitution at the South. They can't see any wrong there, but it is all here. They are attempting to build up a party on the blunders and the imputed crimes of the present Administration. Let me say here, if you want to build up a party on the ruins of the Administration party, you build upon a foundation of sand, which will be washed from under it. You must re-establish the Democracy in power on the basis of the restoration of the Union and the enforcement of the laws. That is what I intend to do.

It has been called a high crime to subjugate a State and to enforce the laws. Without law you can have no legislature, no State. Has a State a right to secede? Settle the question, they say, by peaceable secession and reconstruction. This is impossible. This government cannot be divided without bloodshed. Where will you divide it? Where will you draw the line? Who shall have the territories? Such are the questions which arise when you attempt to divide the Union. It cannot be done. The framers of the Constitution designed that it should be perpetual. — That instrument contains principles which are fundamental to all government, immutable, emanating from Deity himself. We are engaged in a long war, but we shall come out triumphant. Neither this nor succeeding generations shall destroy our rights. They had their origin in a seven years' war, in which our fathers spent their treasure and offered up their lives. So now, brave men of Indiana, your sorrows will return like bread cast upon the waters.

Gov. Johnson then referred to the history of the Constitution, as following after the Articles of Confederation which were to form a perpetual Union, and the Constitution in its preamble sets forth that it is "to form a more perfect Union." It could be adapted to any change in the condition of man, by amendments to the Constitution, and was adapted to all coming time.

Let the idea be kept in mind. We have civil war and revolution. Why not have sought their remedy in the mode pointed out in the Constitution? But no, that must be destroyed, and the destruction of this Government must go with it. They wanted a separation of the States, and then reconstruction. They knew that reconstruction could not follow separation. I hold to the theory that no State can secede. The Union was to be perpetual. Separation dissolves all bonds, and restores the Union to its original elements. What State, what Government, could stand this result? To illustrate: you form a State government, pass laws, and impose penalties for crime. Each man assents to it. But suppose some one commits murder, and is arraigned for it, and should then notify you that he had seceded, and was no longer bound by your laws. He was a sovereign. Do you not think the other sovereigns would punish him? A man builds a house in a city; it is his property and he burns it down, on the principle that he can dispose of his own property as he pleases, without regard to the rights of others, and so burn down a block, or the city. Recognize such a principle, and you have no government but anarchy, and I repudiate the doctrine, *in toto coelo,* that a State has a right to secede, without reference to its effect on the other States. Hence I am for the Union. I intend to stand by the Union so long as I live, and shed my heart's blood, if needed, as a libation for its preservation.

There can be no government unless the laws are enforced. What is the language of the sympathizers with Southern rebels? "I am for the Constitution as it is, and the Union as it was." They are giving the enemies of the Union aid and comfort by their clamor. When these cringing, fawning, sycophantic set of fellows, are talking about dividing the Union, a Northwestern Confederacy, peace, armistice, etc., they laugh at you, and hold you in utter contempt. No terms will suit them better than the acknowledgment of their independence.

Let me ask the rebel sympathizers of Indiana, why you are sympathizing with them — why your bowels of compassion yearn for them. Why, you forget the Union men, then? You will not sympathize with us, but you would compromise with traitors. (Never.) Union men of those sections of country, whose necks rest beneath the iron heel of power, ask you to carry out the Constitution. I do not demand it for them, as a privilege, but demand it of you as a right, that the traitors of this rebellion shall be put down. Why? Because "the United States SHALL — not *may* — guarantee to every State in the Union a republican form of government." I call on the sympathizers here, I demand, in the name of the Constitution as it is, protection and support, and the guaranty of a republican form of government, for the Union men of the South. And, pardon me for my remarks. I ask, in the name of the Constitution, for the relief of that portion of the people in my State east of the Cumberland mountains, who, not excepting yourselves, are the most loyal people of the Nation, because they have dared to be loyal in the face of death — while some of you have been loyal, because you have not dared to be otherwise. We are loyal in our principles, and we have dared to speak and maintain them. I demand of the sympathizers a morsel of their sympathy, for the Union men of the South. You answer, "Compromise." What will you do with your humble speaker, and those who have stood by him? I suppose these sympathizers, like the rebels, want to see me hung.

The redemption of that brave people has been postponed long enough. I notify the people of Indiana, that, if the effort is not made soon, I will come to Ohio, Indiana and Illinois, and plead with you for a chosen band of men to go with me and redeem East Tennessee. (Cheers.)

Talk about being tired of the war! I know it is terrible, and realize its horrors, but these are incidents of a civil war. The ruin that has come, the blood that has been shed, are upon the heads of those who precipitated this civil war, and not on ours. You who have brought on this war, have forced this ruin, set brother against brother, orphaned these children, widowed these wives, and filled the land with mourning — you have done all this, — and let me ask you rebel sympathizers to lift up your hands and see if they are not crimsoned with the blood of the victims of the rebellion? Whether it comes sooner or later, justice will come. The slower its pace, the surer is its blow. It will come, if we live; and if not living, when we are dead. Sooner or later, justice will overtake those whose hands are crimsoned with blood.

Tired of an eighteen months' war? Your fathers fought for seven years to establish this government, and you are tired of fighting eighteen months to defend it. So far as I am concerned, I am ready to fight seven years, thirty years, and would not stop then. What is a war of thirty years, when you look at the vast results to flow from it down the sea of time, in laying the foundation of a government which will live in future ages, and revolutionize the governments of the world? — Nothing. You are laying the foundation of a government which will endure while the sun rises and sets. I say, to-day, not from impulse, but from cool reflection, if my life was spared 700 years, I would fight on and fight ever. I would war against this Southern aristocracy as long as the Moors did against the Spaniards 700 years ago.

Governor Johnson also referred to the gallantry of Paul Jones, who refused to surrender when his ship was sinking, but answered "I am just getting ready to fight." He also quoted from the Knoxville Register an editorial article, in which the rebellion was despaired of, unless dissensions at the North weakened the Union armies. The editor remarked that the *quasi* rebellious attitude of the Governors of New York and New Jersey had produced demoralization in Burnside's army, just as the same attitude of their sympathizers in the Northwest had prevented the advance of Rosecrans' army.

The effect of a compromise would give strength to the rebels.

You have commenced the demoralization here. An armistice will increase it. When divided, one half contending against the other, they would turn their invading armies on us and conquer the North. The very state of the war indicates the speedy suppression of the rebellion. If we prosecute the war, with the advance of the armies of the Mississippi, it would soon be opened, East Tennessee occupied by Rosecrans, and the great railroad artery of the South cut by our armies; a close blockade of Galveston, Mobile, Charleston, and other ports — would confine the rebellion so narrowly that it would die in its own feeble struggles.

Why has not this been done? Lincoln has made some blunders, but that is no reason for attacking the government. He is not perfect, but I sustain him in putting down the infamous rebellion, and in every other measure which is right. We are not committed to his blunders. When the government is saved by the suppression of the rebellion, and we have a government to quarrel in, we can quarrel as to whether Lincoln is right or wrong. Let us save the government first.

An armistice! The constitution as it is, and the Union as it was! I assure you as Jackson did about the tariff, it is a mere pretext for giving up to the rebellion. A compromise is the last thing they want. They want to divide, and then conquer the whole. What will you put in your compromise? That each State shall regulate its own domestic institutions? That is spurious coin. After Jeff Davis and other Senators had left Congress, Mr. Corwin, a Republican, proposed an amendment to the constitution providing that slavery should not be interfered with by any amendment to the constitution hereafter. It passed Congress by a two-thirds vote, and now waits adoption by the Legislatures of three-fourths of the States to become a part of the constitution. If they wanted a compromise to secure slavery from legislation, why did they not accept it?

Has any slave State adopted the amendment? Why did not Jeff. Davis urge Mississippi to adopt the amendment? It is nearly two years since it passed Congress, and not a seceded State has adopted the guaranty. They did not want it, because they wanted to get their rights — Southern rights. Another case in point was the organization of the territories. In the acts organizing them, the territorial legislatures were prohibited from impairing the rights of the people. This prevented any action against slavery in all the territory, then unorganized, of the United States. This proves that they wanted to separate from the other States, or conquer them. They had no desire for compromise, and had lost faith in man's capability to govern himself, and desired to establish an aristocratic form of government.

In support of this Gov. Johnson referred to the Southern papers, the Richmond Examiner, DeBow's Review, and to the utterances of such men as Isham G. Harris, and the Rhetts and others, that they were our masters. This piratical King, Jeff. Davis, to be my master? Isham G. Harris to be my master? Instead of being my master he should not be my slave. The time has arrived in connection with the down-trodden people of the South, when the tyrant's rod should be broken and the captive set free. Though a Southern man I am a citizen of the United States, and because a man lives at the South is no reason why he should be opposed to any one at the North.

Born and raised in the South, I have been a slave owner, having owned ten slaves. I obtained my Southern rights. The rebels stole my negroes, turned my invalid wife and children into the street, and made my house a barracks for "Butternuts" to lie sick in. That's my Southern rights, and if such are the rights to be awarded us when the Southern Confederacy is extended over us, I pray to be relieved from such a fate.

Great ado has been made about negroes. Let that be as it may, is that any reason why we should oppose our Government, and go croaking about and appealing to a squeamish sympathy in the country. I have lived among negroes, all my life, and I am for this Government with slavery under the Constitution as it is, if the Government can be saved. I am for the Government without negroes, and the Constitution as it is. I want to be understood on this question. I am for the government of my fathers, if it is being carried out according to the principles of the Constitution.

If, as the car of State moves along, the negroes get in the way let them be crushed. If they keep out of the way let them remain where they are. I am for the Government and all measures necessary to maintain it. Is not this Government, the giant embodiment of the principles of human liberty, worth more than the institution of slavery? It is but as the dust in the balance. Some persons in the free States have an idea that if King Cotton didn't rule, they cannot sell a mule or a bushel of corn, but this Government would go on were the cotton plant lost to the world. And when you come to think of it, that by raising a little more wool and flax and hemp — [cries of "that's what's wanted"] — you may withhold the article of cotton from the markets of the world, and they would be supplied without a ripple upon commercial waters, they will go on with or without cotton, and whether cotton or negroes continue in the United States, the Government will continue to remain. I am for the Government of my fathers with negroes. I am for it without negroes. Before I would see this Government destroyed I would see every negro back in Africa, and Africa disintegrated and blotted out of space.

Then let us defend this great fabric of human liberty, and the time will come when this nation will be the great centre of the world, the great guiding star to other nations in government, religion, science and arts, the great centre from which an influence and principle will radiate. Is this not worth battling for? Let us go on with this great experiment of Democracy.

The time has come and is now upon us when we are assured by Southern leaders and their sympathizers that we have an institution that is more powerful than the government itself. When any institution, whether banks or the aristocracy of wealth, or any other combination of capital, asserts that the government has no right to agitate its claims, and shakes it to its centre, then the government must put it down. If the institution of slavery denies the government the right of agitation, and seeks to overthrow it, then the government has a clear right to destroy it.

I look upon these principles of free government as the powerful means of elevating mankind to a higher state of civilization. I look upon our system of religion as advancing man in his spiritual nature. And when we go on, as it were, in these two parallel lines of progress, then we shall pass beyond the church and political systems, and we shall secure harmony, "peace on earth and good will to all men."

I will hold to the government as the palladium of our liberties, and cling to it as the mariner clings to the last plank when the waves are surging over him. If the government is to be overthrown, I do not want to survive it. If the government is to be entombed in the tomb of nation, let me be buried with it. Let us stand together with those brave Indianians, some of whom are in hospitals, some in new made graves, and others battling in the field. Indiana has erected a monument for herself. Her reputation will be inscribed on the highest pinnacle of fame. Will you disgrace it by withholding your aid and encouragement?

Will you deny that your soldiers' blood has been shed in a glorious cause? If you do you are unworthy fathers and mothers. Who will turn his back upon his blood? [Cries of "traitors!"] Yes, traitors, none but traitors. For him who sleeps in the grave, let him know that he has fallen in a glorious cause, and water his grave with tears, and, if need be, to crown the war with success, you should shed your own blood and spend your last dollar.

Gov. Johnson concluded by returning his thanks to his fellow-citizens. He made special mention of the ladies. At the South he said it to their shame they had unsexed themselves, and exerted more influence for the rebellion than the men. He believed that at the North the ladies had it in their power to wield an influence that would materially aid the Union cause. It was better to be a brave soldier's widow than a coward's wife.

Gov. Johnson then retired amid vociferous cheering, and when Gov. Wright proposed nine cheers for Gov. J., they were given with a will, the united tribute of esteem of 25,000 freemen of Indiana for the noble Governor of Tennessee.

REMARKS OF READ, THE POET.

After Gov. Johnson, T. Buchanan Read, the poet, was introduced by Gov. Wright, and was warmly greeted. He said:

My Countrymen: I do not come before you as an orator. (Turning to Gov. Johnson.) I am no orator, as Brutus is, else would I put tongues into the wounds of this bleeding nation which should cry aloud for vengeance. I am not a politician; I am, I hope, only a patriot, and I have endeavored to write some patriotic verses. While I have a patriotic pulse in my heart, that impulse shall find expression upon my lips, and I would that they might be words of fire. He wisely spake who said, "let me but write the songs of a nation, and let who will enact the laws." I have not the vanity to suppose that I can write the songs of this nation, but I am one who is willing to do his best towards filling the air with patriotic lays, for there are babbling lips that should be filled with song, lest they breathe treason unaware.

When this unnatural rebellion broke out I was five thousand miles from here. I was standing among the ruins of the old Republic of Rome, my feet white with the dust of the palace of the Caesars — all Italy at that moment was clamoring for Union, from Alps to Aetna past me rolled the cry — that one word Union woke that antique land, and led her sons to triumph or the grave. At that same moment I fancied the setting sun blushed as it went sinking into the west over a nation nearly one half of which was clamoring for disunion. Could I remain there under such circumstances? No! My heart would have ceased to beat. I gave up everything to return to do the little I could for my country. What is painting worth among the ruined chambers of a nation? What would poetry be worth among the broken temples of human liberty?

If God has given me the power of song I will lift my voice in this cause — it is my country's cause — it is God's cause. If need be I will go like the Poet Koerner with my war songs on my lips and my sword in my hand. I propose giving you one of those war songs.

The poet then read a poem, written, as he said, for a fourth of July celebration in Rome, entitled "THE DEFENDERS."

It was received with immense applause. Mr. Read then said: "My countrymen, I feel deeply on this subject. My father fought for this country. — This accursed rebellion has caused the death of my brother and my two nephews. — I have a right to feel deeply, nay, bitterly, and in the bitterness of my feeling, I wrote the following poem."

Mr. Read then read "THE OATH," every stanza of which was enthusiastically applauded and subscribed to.

THE OATH

BY THOMAS BUCHANAN READ.

HAMLET — Swear on my sword.
GHOST (below) — *Swear!* (Shakespeare.)

Ye freemen, how long will ye stifle
  The vengeance that justice inspires?
With treason how long will ye trifle
  And shame the proud name of your sires?
Out, out with the sword and the rifle
  In defense of your homes and your fires.
The flag of the old Revolution
  Swear firmly to serve and uphold,
That the treasonous breath of pollution
  Shall tarnish one star on its fold.
     Swear!
And hark, the deep voices replying
From graves where your fathers are lying,
    "*Swear, oh, swear!*"

In this moment who hesitates, barters
  The rights which his forefathers won,

He forfeits all claim to the charters
    Transmitted from sire to son.
Kneel, kneel at the graves of our martyrs
    And swear on your sword and your gun:
Lay up your great oath on an altar
    As huge and as strong as Stone-henge
And then with sword, fire and halter,
    Sweep down to the field of revenge,
            Swear!
And hark, the deep voices replying
From graves where your fathers are lying,
      "Swear, oh, swear!"

By the tombs of your sires and brothers,
    The host which the traitors have slain,
By the tears of your sisters and mothers,
    In secret concealing their pain,
The grief which the heroine smothers
    Consuming the heart and the brain,—
By the sigh of the penniless widow,
    By the sob of her orphans' despair
Where they sit in their sorrowful shadow,
    Kneel, kneel every freeman and swear.
        Swear!
And hark the deep voices replying
From graves where your fathers are lying.
      "Swear, oh, swear!"

On mounds which are wet with the weeping
    Where a Nation has bowed to the sod.
Where the noblest of martyrs are sleeping.
    Let the winds bear your vengeance abroad;
And your firm oaths be held in the keeping
    Of your patriots' hearts and your God.
Over Ellsworth, for whom the first tear rose,
    While to Baker and Lyon you look —
By Winthrop, a star among heroes,
    By the blood of our murdered McCook,
        Swear!
And hark, the deep voices replying
From graves where your fathers are lying.
      "Swear, oh, swear!"

At the conclusion of the reading, Gov. Wright offered this sentiment: "I want every soldier to take these stripes and lash every traitor in the land." (Immense cheering.)

GEN. CAREY'S SPEECH.

Gen. Samuel F. Carey, of Ohio, was next introduced. He said the enemies of free institutions had said that there was no power in free government to put down rebellion.

It was not so. Monarchists knew that the success of a free government would be the signal for their downfall, and hence it was that all the monarchical governments of the old world sympathized with the Southern rebellion. We had been heretofore in the habit of considering Benedict Arnold as the prince of traitors, but of late he had been so far surpassed that he ought to be considered a patriot in comparison to modern traitors. Gov. Johnson had truly said that the principle that underlaid the opposition to our government at the South was hostility to popular sovereignty. He read an extract from DeBow's Review, showing that the hostility of Southern aristocrats to the Yankees was based upon the fact that they held all labor to be degrading, and that the Yankees belonged to the working classes. Every neighborhood of the West contained a small sprinkle of Yankees, and many of them had been the pioneers that had opened up this beautiful country. He spoke of Yankee characteristics, and said "If you would put one out upon the ocean with nothing but a pen-knife and a shingle, he would whittle out some way to get on shore." There were diversities of interest in all sections of the Union, and it was these diversities that made unity, and without them we could not exist. The North could not get along without the South, nor the South without the North.

Speaking of traitors at home, he said they were not known by the color of their skin, nor the complexion of their coats. There were negroes in Indiana who were loyal, and there were also white men who were worse than such negroes, for their hearts were blackened with treason. These latter complained loudly that arbitrary arrests had been made, but for one, the only complaint he had to make was that there had been too few arrests.

(The proceedings were interrupted at this point by the firing of a salute of one hundred guns by a park of artillery stationed in the Arsenal grounds, the rapidity of whose firing was the occasion of much cheering by the assembled thousands.)

General Carey proceeded: If a man were setting fire to your house, would you go and get out a warrant to arrest him, or would you take hold of him and arrest him yourself? — The same rule would apply where men were attempting to destroy the government. Gen. Lew. Wallace, in defending Cincinnati, had declared martial law, and made many arbitrary arrests. In enforcing the draft arbitrary arrests were made. Yet what patriot could say this was not right. One Edson B. Olds of Ohio made a speech urging the squirrel hunters to remain at home, and not go to Cincinnati to aid in its defense, and he was arrested and sent to Fort Lafayette. This arrest had been denounced by a portion of the Indiana press as arbitrary and tyrannical. It was not, and had Olds had his dues he ought to have been hanged, for he believed in the doctrine that the shortest road to hell was the best for all traitors.

When members of a conspirators' secret order were brought into Court and called upon to divulge the secrets of the order and plead that by so doing they would criminate themselves, it furnished the best evidence that a conspiracy existed. When men met in school houses and organized conspiracies, the loyal people should exercise that reserved right belonging to all men to protect themselves, and without waiting for Courts, should apply the proper remedy at once. The suppression of disloyal newspapers and estopping them from the privileges of being sent through the mails was a right the government had to exercise in its defense, and the government was justifiable in all it had done in that respect.

There was no difficulty in determining who were traitors. If any man was so God-forsaken as to go into a secret order and there take an oath against his country, he should not be believed under oath, and his own opinion was that all such could be guilty of committing the worst crimes known to society, for they had already committed the foulest of crimes: treason to their country.

How were you going to punish such men, when they went into the Courts and plead that they could not be compelled to criminate themselves? He would "arbitrary arrest" all of them, and call upon the people to sustain him, and he believed the people would sustain any man in such a course.

There was another way by which traitors could be distinguished. Those men who went around crying: "this is an abolition war," were all of that class. They didn't believe the South could be subjugated. For one he believed that it would not only be subjugated, but that every slave holder would be exterminated forever, before the Union would be given up. He denied that this Government had ever made war against the institution of slavery. On the other hand it had been the special object of the protecting care of the Government. We had tried, even during this war to save the nation without injuring slavery. The army in the past had been used to protect the property of rebel slaveholders, but he thanked God that day was now over.

The historical fact was that the government had tried in every way to save slavery during the progress of the war. There never was such an exhibition of moderation on the part of a government towards those in rebellion against it. He spoke of the condition of the government when Mr. Lincoln came into power, and what followed. His calling out 75,000 volunteers was declared by traitors to be the exercise of a despotic power. So it was when he suspended the writ of habeas corpus. Gen. Jackson had done the same thing, but they had forgotten this patriotic act of the old hero. Gen. Carey defended the President's conduct in this matter as patriotic and wise, and such as was demanded by the condition of the times. It was not a dangerous exercise of power. The outcry made against Mr. Lincoln was for the purpose of deceiving voters, and not with a view to accomplish any good results.

Another cry now heard throughout the land was that the government was being bankrupted. The wish, in such case, was father to the thought. They wished the government to become bankrupt. The government had no money when the war began, nor men, but both had been supplied. The men who had confidence in their country had confidence in "green backs," and those who desired its destruction were afraid of the national currency.

The impression existed at the South that we were about "played out" up North; that there existed 90,000 Knights of the Golden Circle in Indiana, 85,000 in Ohio and 100,000 in Illinois. But there were men and women enough to save the country, notwithstanding the opposition of traitors. He would wage this war until the country became desolated, and all the achievements of our fathers blotted out, and the American name forgotten, before he would give up the Union. He cared not what instruments were used to kill off rebels. He would take mules and put upon their feet steel heels and toes and train them to kick rebels to death. He would arm negroes for the same reasons. He would answer the question, "what are you going to do with the negroes?" by saying "it's time enough to talk about that when the war's over." He believed, however, that as the negro loved the Southern sun they would flock to that region if slavery was blotted out. He had always been in favor of prosecuting this war without reference to the negro, believing that the white race were interested in determining the question as to whether white men were to become slaves or not. There were six million Southern white men who were degraded socially and treated as slaves by a Southern aristocracy. He believed the races ought to be separated — how, he could not say. The country of the Amazon may be reserved by Providence for an African republic. But if this could not be done, he was for cleaning out South Carolina and turning it over to the exclusive use of the negroes.

No matter what it might cost in money or in blood, the preservation of this government would be purchased cheap enough if we could only hand it down to posterity undivided, in all its purity and integrity.

He alluded to the bravery of Indiana soldiers, and said they had shed more glory upon the State than all it had cost. Yet there were men in Indiana who encouraged these soldiers to desert, and the swiftest and surest punishment for them would be to hang them on the first tree that came handiest. He was for carrying on the war, not only until the rebels were subjugated, but until they were wholly exterminated, if that were necessary, to secure our own liberties.

A Northern sympathizer was worse than a Southern rebel. They had but two rights: one was to die, and the other to be damned. They had undertaken a big job in endeavoring to alienate the West from New England, and would fail. Nor could they alienate us from the Union men of the South. Andrew Johnson was worth more to us than all the rebels of the South, and we would not give him up.

This was a contest between the two systems of civilization — the aristocracy and the working classes. One reason why Andrew Johnson could not be anything but a loyal man was because he had earned his bread by the sweat of his brow. The Northern theory was that educated labor was the best of all labor. The Southern idea was the reverse of this.

He believed that were it not for the discouragement shown by traitors at the North we could raise a million more of men. We could do it anyhow. We had men enough, money enough and spirit enough to crush out the rebellion, and he hoped the Government would be strong enough to sustain the people in their wishes in this behalf.

The laboring masses everywhere were in sympathy with us in this conflict, while those who loved tyranny were in sympathy with the Southern Confederacy. He believed that when the war ended a higher order of civilization would be inaugurated, and it would probably be the last war in this country, as it would settle all doubtful issues forever and place our Republic upon an enduring basis.

He concluded by warning his fellow citizens to watch the scorpions in their midst, and clean them out. (Cheers.)

The report of the Committee on Resolutions was made by Charles H. Test immediately after the conclusion of the speech of General Carey. It was read so clearly and well that it could be heard all over the crowd, and was received with the most deafening cheers. The resolutions against any compromise or armistice; demanding that the Legislature should leave untouched the constitutional powers of the Governor; pledging the meeting to the support of the families of soldiers; and denouncing the traitors at home who attempt to discourage the soldiers, were each received with three tremendous cheers. At the conclusion Gov. Wright put the question "All in favor of the resolutions hold up the right hand," and the uprising of hands was an astonishing sight. It looked like a new growth of crowd on the top of the lower one, and every hand held up a hat, and every voice below cheered as if cheering was the only thing it had done from childhood. All previous shouting was tame to it. Never were resolutions so heartily and unanimously adopted, and we may add, never did resolutions better deserve it.

RESOLUTIONS

WE, the loyal people of the State of Indiana, in Mass Convention assembled, at the Capitol Square, in the city of Indianapolis, on the 26th day of February, 1863, do resolve:

1. That our attachment to the Federal Union is unabated; and that we will adhere with unflinching devotion to the National cause. That we believe the safety of the country and the preservation of our liberties depend upon the perpetuity of the Union; and that we view every proposition of compromise with rebels, on any other

basis than that of unqualified submission to the laws and the National authority, as wholly inadmissible, and fraught with the most dangerous consequences to the country.

2. That we desire "that no effort which inspires a reasonable hope of success in restoring the Union as it was under the Constitution, shall be omitted; and being solemnly impressed with the conviction that arms alone" are adequate to the accomplishment of that end, we will heartily support the government in a vigorous prosecution of the war until the rebellion is crushed; and that we deprecate all truckling armistices and juggling conventions with traitors in arms, as weak inventions of the enemy; that a cessation of hostilities for a single day would only serve to strengthen the foe and weaken ourselves, and would be a base surrender of all the advantages we have gained in the pending struggle; and that such a proposition cannot be entertained by loyal men for one moment.

3. That the highest interests of Indiana "demand the perpetuation of the Union," and not only that the great Valley of the Mississippi, from its source to its mouth, but all the States of this Union, from the eastern border of Maine to the Gulf, and from the Atlantic to the Pacific, shall remain under one government and one flag, and that *the* government and *the* flag of our fathers.

4. That the attitude of the gallant soldiers of Indiana, in the various armies of the Republic, in view of the disloyal propositions which have been introduced into the Legislature of our State, challenges our admiration and excites our gratitude. The voices that come to us over mountain and river, and from many bloody fields, in the ringing accents of patriotism, evince the high resolve of our citizen soldiery to sustain the government of their fathers, and to restore the supremacy of the flag of the Republic over every foot of the soil embraced in the Federal Union.

5. That we believe that in every measure which President Lincoln has adopted for the maintenance of the Union and the restoration of the national authority he has been actuated by the highest patriotism and the most loyal devotion to the interests of the people, and we pledge ourselves to a hearty support of the Administration in all its measures for the suppression of the rebellion.

6. That our distinguished Governor, Oliver P. Morton, is entitled to the gratitude of the people of Indiana for his patriotic and untiring efforts in behalf of the cause of the country, for his able admin-

istration of the affairs of the State, civil and military, and for his devotion to the comfort and welfare of the Indiana troops; that to his energy, foresight and patriotism, so gloriously sustained by the conduct of our soldiers in the field, are we indebted for the proud position which our beloved State now occupies amongst her loyal sisters; that in behalf of our soldiers, as well as for the honor and safety of the State, we demand of the General Assembly that they pass no law or measure depriving the Governor of any of the powers or prerogatives granted him by the Constitution, or hitherto accorded to his office by law or custom.

7. That the loyal people of Indiana are determined to maintain their allegiance to the National Government at all hazards; that they will never submit to the withdrawal of the State of Indiana from the Union, nor to the formation of a Northwestern Confederacy; that experience has shown that peaceable disintegration of any portion of the Union is impossible, and we adjure the people of our loyal State to rebuke, in such terms as will need no repetition, all men who strive to sow discord between different States, or who speak of a re-construction of the Government by leaving any State or section out of the Union.

8. That resistance to law is revolutionary in its tendency, and that any attempt to embarrass the Government in the execution of the Revenue, Conscription, or any other law of the United States, will be promptly met and suppressed by the loyal people of Indiana.

9. That to our distinguished guest, Gov. Andrew Johnson, of Tennessee, we tender our heartfelt thanks for his firm and patriotic adherence to the national cause; that we hold up his example of faithful loyalty to the young men of Indiana as worthy of their imitation, and we tender, through Governor Johnson, to his oppressed and persecuted loyal fellow-citizens of Tennessee our sympathies in their afflictions, and our hope that their day of deliverance may speedily come.

10. That the miscreants in our midst who attempt to create dissatisfaction in the ranks of our gallant soldiers, and induce them to desert the colors made glorious by their valor on repeated battlefields, are meaner traitors than the armed rebels of the South; that they are entitled to, and will receive the scorn of all honorable men; that they are more dangerous enemies to the soldier than the armed hosts in his front, inasmuch as the latter strike only at the

life of the soldier, while the former seek the destruction of his honor and self-respect, which to the true soldier are dearer than life.

11. That we pledge ourselves, collectively and individually, to look to and provide for the comfort and support of the wife and family of the soldier who is absent in the field battling for the restoration of the Government.

Gov. Wright being loudly called upon, declined, saying that he had spoken oftener than any man in the State, and others were here, who could entertain them better than he. He therefore introduced Hon. Chas. W. Cathcart, who was, perhaps, a stranger to many of those present, and who was a Democrat from principle, one who would never recognize a party organization as paramount to the support of his country, no matter who was President.

Mr. Cathcart followed in an excellent address, which was enthusiastically cheered throughout. We regret we have no space to give a report of it.

SECOND STAND.

At the second stand Hon. Charles Case was the first speaker. We failed to hear the opening of his speech, but he discussed four leading points after we came up. 1st, Northwestern Confederacy and separation from New England; 2d, Suspension of the habeas corpus; 3d, The singular vehemence of the Copperheads against everything done by our government, and their silence as to everything done by the rebels; and 4th, the immense stake which the sacrifices already made have given the people of the North in the successful prosecution of the war. He was followed by Hon. W. S. Smith, of Fort Wayne, the Union candidate for Superintendent of Public Instruction last fall. He was dubbed "Pop Gun Smith" by the Butternuts, but the Union men have found a better name. They call him "Parrott Gun Smith," and the way he made the bones crack, and the blood fly in his speech was good proof that the latter was the better name.

Several other speakers followed. Matthew R. Hull, Capt. Ben S. Nicklin of the artillery, and Parke Dewey of Minnesota, formerly of this State, a son of the lamented Judge Dewey of our Supreme Bench, a lawyer of unusual talent and high standing, capable of attaining any position, and a private in a Minnesota regiment.

He was followed by Capt. John H. Farquhar, who closed the

exercises at that stand. We believe there were one or two other speakers at this stand, but we were unable to hear them.

At the Third Stand Hon. John A. Matson was appointed President, and upon the stand beside him were Generals Kimball and Hascall, and the eloquent Henry Secrest. Gen. Kimball was introduced by Mr. Matson.

GENERAL KIMBALL'S SPEECH.

He said, — Indianians, I am proud of my native State. I never was so proud before of being born on the soil of Indiana. I never was so rejoiced as I am to witness this great outpouring of her patriotic people. I want to be with the army, but I am glad to be here. I am glad to see this demonstration of your purpose to put down the traitors at home who are encouraging this unholy rebellion. This vast crowd says to treason "Thus far shalt thou go, and here shalt thy waves be stayed." (applause.) It is written that the "seed of the woman shall bruise the head of the serpent," and you are proving its truth to-day. (Laughter and applause.) I have no soft words for traitors, and those who cry peace, and discourage the army, who would end this war otherwise than by the crushing of the rebellion, are traitors. (Applause, and cries of "that's so.") When I fight, I fight to win, (Cries of "good") and I fight now to preserve the constitution. I stand upon the constitution. I care for nothing else. The constitution is my watchword and my battle cry, and shall be as long as God gives me strength or power to lift my arm in its defence. (Applause.) The rebels are fighting to destroy that constitution, and I loathe those who lend them encouragement at home. Of all mean, miserable, despicable, dirty, crawling — (The rest was lost in a storm of cheering, but it is not hard to guess where this destructive shower of grape shot was aimed.) Indiana should give no countenance to such. Her name is too glorious in this war, and her services too great, to allow her to lower herself by such a course. To you belongs the honor of keeping that name still glorious. If you cannot support and sustain your soldiers while fighting for the government, the cause is lost, and Indiana and the government will fall together. But let Indiana keep bravely up to her gallant soldiers, support them, and encourage them, and both will surely be saved. I love Indiana. I was born on her soil, but dearly as I love her I love the Union more. (Great applause.) He then alluded to the treasonable course of the Butternuts and said if they don't like the government, let them go South where they can find one they do like, and then if they will only take arms in their hands we will whip them too. (Tremendous cheering.) He discussed briefly the emancipation proclamation, and declared that the pretense of the Copperheads that it had changed the aspect or character of the war in any respect was false.

His speech was singularly in harmony with the feeling of the crowd, and contained a great deal of solid sense, and fervid patriotism.

He was followed by General Hascall, and he by Hon. Henry Secrest of Greencastle, one of the ablest orators of the State, and one of the great leaders of the Union movement.

NIGHT MEETINGS.
MASONIC HALL.

The immense crowd of the day left over a huge crowd for the night, which wasn't half satisfied with the dozen speeches it had got, and wanted more. It was announced that Hon. Sam. Galloway, of Ohio, and Col. R. W. Thompson, of this State, would speak at Masonic Hall, and Gov. Wright at the Hall of the House. At 7 o'clock we went down to Masonic Hall and found a large crowd outside the door, who appeared to be waiting for the opening of the room. We soon found a better reason. We pushed on half way up the stairs, and were actually forced back by the overflow of the Hall, already packed and jammed full. Hundreds had come away, and the stairs were crowded with others, singing out as they pressed down the steps, "It's no use, you can't get in." "You couldn't drive a man in there with a pile-driver." "Who's speaking?" "Dick Thompson, and he's doing it gloriously, but you can't get an inch of room to listen." We concluded to back out and let Col. Thompson's speech speak for itself, since his reputation and its eloquence left us no other chance. Getting back to the pavement again we found that the crowd outside were resolved not "to give it up so," and had somehow got up word to the inside that they wanted a speaker outside. Rev. J. H. Lozier, the Brownlow of Indiana, the witty, eloquent and earnest Chaplain of the 37th regiment, who brought up the resolutions and votes of the Indiana troops in the army of the

Cumberland to our Legislature, had been sent out, and was just getting his hat off for a speech. At this moment we glanced over the crowd in the street, and it was monstrous. Nearly across the street, and half the length of the square up and down, it reached, filling pavement, gutter and all in a compact mass. It was four times as large at least as the crowd in the hall. No room in the city would have held half of it. And yet the hall was still as tightly crammed as ever, and Gov. Wright had the Hall of the House as tightly packed as it would hold. Verily the Union men are great on big meetings.

MR. LOZIER'S SPEECH.

In an off-hand, unclerical, but decidedly popular style, and in a clear, distinct voice, that seemed to punch the words out, each one by itself, like bullets, Mr. Lozier began, and after a brief introductory allusion to the circumstances of his appearance, said he felt an inch bigger every way to-day. The demonstration was one that would carry joy to the heart of the soldier, who for months had bowed his head in discouragement before the disloyalty at home. It was a blow the copperheads would feel, and to strike copperheads had been his business for some time past. It was written that "the seed of the woman should bruise the head of the serpent," and he, as a Methodist preacher, was licensed to strike the serpent wherever he could find it. (Laughter.) But if any body doubted that authority, he came as the emissary of the Army of the Cumberland, and *that* was authority nobody could doubt for killing the animal anywhere. (Laughter.) — What kind of animals these copperheads were, he illustrated by relating an incident of his speech, in some town up North, a few days since. In the course of the speech, he said he challenged any man to place his finger on the clause, section or article of the Constitution which the President had violated. He waited for an answer. Nobody spoke for some moments. Finally, a man away back by the door said, "I can give you an instance." "Name it, sir, name it," — "Why, he has — he has — he has violated the *corpus christi!*" (Uproarious laughter.) — The poor fellow did not even know the name of the thing his leaders had been trying to mislead him about. He was driving at the habeas corpus, and supposed it was all right when he got anything with a "corpus" in it. (Laughter.)

The speaker next alluded to Senator Cobb's assault upon the army. That Senator had said that "there was a trick in the adoption of the resolutions sent up by the Army of the Cumberland. A Brigadier General had written so to him." The "trick" was this: A certain Colonel commanding a brigade had refused to let his Indiana regiment vote on the resolutions. The speaker, in discharge of his duty as a member of the committee to collect the votes, came to that regiment to get its vote. The Adjutant, whom he first met, said the *regiment wanted to vote,* but the Colonel wouldn't allow it. When the Colonel came in he said "his regiment had not voted and should not." And that was all the "trick" there was in the matter. (Cries of "Name that officer." "Who is he?" "Turn him out!") It was Colonel Caldwell, of the 81st Indiana. (Tremendous shouts and cries of derision.)

The speaker said further in regard to Mr. Cobb, that it would be a good thing for him and his copperhead friends to go to the army, and clean out one of these regiments they entertain such a contempt for. (Laughter, and cries of "Let them try it.") He would find that every individual soldier would prove a "Little Giant Corn and *Cobb* Crusher." (Uproarious cheering and laughter.) These copperheads had proclaimed from every stump and every dry-goods box during the past fall, that the majority of the army were Democrats. Their organs asserted it, their speakers swore to it, and they all declared it. Yet when the Legislature meets, they decide it is *unconstitutional for the soldiers to vote.* (This lick "brought down the house," if that phrase can be applied to a crowd out doors. The cheering lasted so long that we feared the speaker would not get started again.) He had taken down the names of every one of the men who voted that the soldiers could not vote, and he meant to make them household words in the army. (Cheers. — "That's right." "Remember them.")

We have not space to follow the speaker through his long succession of telling blows, but we must conclude with his conclusion. — "Fellow citizens: I don't know who you are, but you came up here from all parts of the State. I want you when you go home to sit down and write to your son, or brother, or nephew in the army, what you saw here today. Tell your neighbors who have gone home to do so too. I tell you it will send a thrill of joy through the soldier's heart such as he has not felt for months. (Cheering and cries

of 'we will,' 'we'll attend to it.') Another thing: You pledged yourselves to-day in the resolutions you adopted to support the families
of soldiers. The knowledge that you will stick to that pledge will
encourage the soldier more than anything you can do. Let me tell
an incident, for an illustration and example:

A few weeks since, the farmers living on the Hillsboro pike in
Wayne county, met and agreed that the next Saturday every one
of them that could would go to Richmond with a load of wood, and
whatever else, in the way of support, he could give, for the families
of absent soldiers. Well, Saturday came, and with it came a long
procession of *forty-five wagons* loaded with wood, and on the top
of every load a sack of flour or potatoes. About *two thousand pounds
of flour,* and potatoes in proportion, were thus contributed. The next
week the farmers on the Boston pike, not to be outdone, went into
Richmond with *seventy-five* loads of wood, *more than two thousand
pounds* of flour, and potatoes, meat and other things in proportion.
On next Saturday the farmers on Newton pike take their turn, and
the Lord only knows how much they *will* give. And there are six
more pikes to come in yet! (The cheering at this point was something terrific. It fairly made the buildings around quiver.) That's
the way old Wayne is doing. Now I want you to see if you can't do
so too. (Cries of "Yes, yes!" and one voice: "We'll *resolve ourselves
into turnpikes all over!*" which capital hit was as vociferously
cheered as the speaker had been before.) — With a few words
more, the speaker closed, and was asked who he was, by hundreds
of men, "We want to know you," "Who are you?" "I am the Chaplain of the 37th Indiana regiment." "Three cheers for the Chaplain
of the 37th." And they came with a will. The speaker returned his
thanks for the compliment, and said he hoped to deserve it by his
efforts for the soldiers and the country, and retired.

Col. A. D. Streight, of the 51st, was called out next, and spoke
ably and well, but our space is too entirely used up to allow us to
notice it further to-night.

THE MEETING AT REPRESENTATIVE HALL

Was opened by Governor Wright's introducing T. Buchanan
Read, who recited two or three appropriate selections from his
poems.

Governor Wright then addressed the meeting. He said that when he looked over the vast assemblage of to-day, when Governor Johnson was addressing the people, he was satisfied that the hearts of the people were right, and that a reaction was going on in the land that two-penny politicians little dreamed of. He had had the pleasure of taking by the hand a Democratic Governor from a slave State, who had acted with him heretofore in party contests, and had introduced him to the people.

He wished to know whether he was to be hereafter denounced as an Abolitionist? The difficulty with some was that they could not distinguish the difference between the importance of their Government and the temporary ruler thereof. Party prejudice had more to do with controlling the opinions of men than reason, and it was unfortunate for the country that demagogues knew this, and acted only upon that rule. One argument with them was that abolition and secession were twin heresies. But this was not so, for the remedy for the one was the ballot, and for the other bullets and bayonets.

Jeff. Davis never dared to declare that this was a revolution, nor that any rights had been lost under the Constitution, but claimed that our Government was but a confederacy, and not a compact, and that States had the right to withdraw from it. Our Constitution was a written compact between States as binding as the marriage relation was to the husband and wife. If States had committed acts inconsistent with the Constitution the remedy was the ballot box, and not secession.

Referring to the suspension of the writ of habeas corpus, and the arrests, about which so much complaint has been made, he said the Constitution gave the President ample power to suspend the writ of habeas corpus in time of rebellion. The question was now in the Supreme Court, and should it decide that the President had such power, those complaining gentlemen who had claimed that the power only belonged to Congress would feel exceeding cheap.

He said that no greater falsehood had been circulated than that the government had attempted and was attempting to bring negro labor in competition with white labor. Mr. Lincoln's doctrine was to colonize the negroes, and the absence of every negro by colonization made more room for the white man.

The cry of abolition was used by bad men to create prejudice in the minds of the ignorant and prevent them from reasoning on this question. But the sober second thought was at work, and many who had voted with the opposition to the Administration in the belief that that party would do more to prosecute the war than all others were beginning to get their eyes open and to see which way they were drifting.

Congress had said that this war had been commenced by the acts of the rebels, and it was the duty of the people to sustain it. But four voted against this declaration in the two houses of Congress, and three of them were in the rebel army, and the other ought to be there. When Fort Sumter was struck the Constitution and Union were struck, and it was every man's duty to resist such acts of war, or leave the country. Wrangling, now, while we had a disunited republic, was wrong and destructive to unity of action in support of the country. It should be postponed until after the war. There had been no candidate for Congress on the Democratic ticket last summer that did not claim that it was right to work negroes on fortifications, but they could not bring themselves up to the second step, to use negroes as soldiers, if necessary. But he predicted that no man could get a thousand votes in 1864 who had not been willing to use every instrument that could be had to put down this rebellion.

These politicians were feeling for public opinion. They had introduced resolutions in that very Hall about an armistice, peace conventions, &c., in the early part of the session. They dare not pass such resolutions now, for public sentiment would not endorse such action, and they could not afford to face the music.

Six months ago they denied the existence of Knights of the Golden Circle, but now they refuse to appoint a committee to investigate the existence of such order. There can never be peace in this country while secret organizations exist in communities into which men went and took oaths against their country. Nine-tenths of the men who had joined these associations had been misled into them, and they would get out of them. They were doing it now. And he believed that when men went into Court and refused to tell what they knew of such organizations, they should be sent off to Fort Warren. Tennessee went out of the Union through the influence of these organizations. He had charged last summer that such societies existed, and that if they thought proper to do so they would attempt to take this State out of the Union. — No man was to be trusted who joined these societies. If they could agree to commit the highest known crime — treason — they could be induced to commit every crime known to society.

In conclusion, he said he had faith that this government would be preserved. He had no fears of foreign intervention so long as large armies were in the field contesting against one another. No government had ever put down rebellion in two years. He considered it a matter of wonder that so much had been done in twenty-two months. We had done what no other nation had been able to accomplish — keep up an almost perfect blockade. — We had a million of men under arms, and the stars and stripes now wave over two-thirds of the territory of the slave States. We had either to subdue them or they must subdue us. There could be no compromise or armistice. If compromise was wanted by the South let them send members to Congress and submit their case to the proper tribunal. It was your duty to stand by your brave boys who were in the field fighting your battles. — Don't send them armistice resolutions or seek to disgrace them by ignominious compromise. If twenty millions could not conquer eight millions his prayer was that there might be none of us left to bear the shame that would follow such a confession.

Gov. Wright then read a letter from our Consul at Frankfort-on-the-Maine, saying that the middle classes were sympathising with the Union cause, and stating that large quantities of lint, linen and socks for our wounded had been contributed by them, and that 25,000 Germans stand ready to volunteer to aid us in crushing out this rebellion.

We were not loyal enough. If we would come forward and offer up our wealth in aid of our government it would do more to bring about peace than all else. He closed by appealing to all present to do all they could to save their country in this the hour of its peril. Gov. Wright was frequently interrupted during his remarks by the cheering of the audience.

Col. H. B. Carrington was then introduced, who said he appeared before them as a soldier who had taken an oath to support his government against all opposers whatsoever, whether such opposers were in the field or elsewhere. He alluded to the obstacles thrown in the way of our army at the outset, the lack of arms, &c., and how those obstacles had been overcome. He believed this to be a war for the world. It was the law of God that the right must rule. And he conscientiously believed that the working out of this rule would be to not only strengthen our own government, but to shed a radiating light over all the other nations of the world by which the downtrodden people could see their way to liberty.

He contended that it was right, just, proper and politic to use the slaves of rebels to aid our army in destroying rebels. It would result in the saving of thousands of lives.

As to secret societies organized to thwart and overthrow the government, he would say that so long as he was military commandant of Indiana, he would consider it his duty to break up such lodges and bring their members to judgment. His oath as a soldier required this of him, and when he could not do this, he would lay his commission at the feet of the President. (Cheers.)

Hon. James Wilson, of Crawfordsville, next addressed the meeting in a neat, eloquent and patriotic effort, during which he was loudly applauded.

CONCLUSION

AN IMPRESSIVE SCENE

On Thursday night, the meeting at Masonic Hall, concluded the proceedings of the great Union Convention. T. Buchanan Read, the Poet, opened the meeting by the recitation of two or three of his thrilling patriotic poems, and Hon. R. W. Thompson and Hon. Sam Galloway continued them with speeches that roused a pitch of enthusiasm such as was never before witnessed in any meeting in this State. Every sentence was cheered, and what is better every sentence deserved it. — The audience had become so full of the occasion, and the glorious cause that created it, that they threw off all the reserve and coolness of manhood, and shouted with delight like boys. At the close of Galloway's speech, which was one of his very best, and that is saying a great deal, a scene occurred which put a fitting climax on the enthusiasm, and closed most gracefully and imposingly the extraordinary spectacle of the day. Governor Wright, who had come over from the State House meeting, and miraculously got upon the platform somehow, came forward and said that "a venerable gentleman in the audience desired to see our distinguished guest, Governor Johnson, having come a long distance to enjoy that pleasure, and failed so far." — Gov. Johnson rose at this remark and came forward on the platform amid a tempest of cheering, continued till any lungs less inspired by enthusiasm would have given out, and said "he did not arise to make a speech, but to make an apology for not making one. It would be readily perceived that his voice was in no condition to say anything, but he must take advantage of the opportunity to declare that this was the proudest and happiest day of his life. He then alluded to the extraordinary changes produced by our great national struggle, men of life-long contrarieties of opinion finding themselves side by side, and former enemies made friends by the power of a great common cause, and said that it afforded him unspeakable satisfaction to meet here two distinguished gentlemen with whom he had always differed in politics, (Thompson and Galloway,) as well as the distinguished gentleman with whom he had always politically agreed (Governor Wright). Their hearts now beat in unison for the great cause in which all were engaged. In conclusion of this glorious day's proceedings, he asked the satisfaction of taking the two distinguished gentlemen, his former opponents, by the hand, in the presence of this immense assembly." As the Governor made this last remark he stepped forward and grasping with one hand a hand of Mr. Thompson, and with the other that of Mr. Galloway, the three stood for a moment overpowered by their feelings; then, as if by a common impulse, *threw their arms round each other,* and the audience, worked up to a pitch of feeling hardly less intense than that of the distinguished gentlemen, broke into shouts and cries of joy, cheers, and stormy applause, very generally moistened with tears, too, which actually shook the building. Such another scene was never witnessed in a political meeting. It was a natural, irrepressible outburst of feeling, and made many a wet eye among the sturdy patriots, who were little used to the "melting mood." The iron old Andy Johnson, who had faced rebel pistols, and endured rebel persecution, had seen his property destroyed, and his family turned into the streets, without a tear, crying like a boy with the delight of an occasion so grateful to his patriotic soul, was a sight to remember for a life time. For many minutes the audience was a wild sea of joyful commotion, utterly indescribable, which only subsided on the announcement of the propriety of providing means to distribute the report of the speeches and proceedings of the meeting among the soldiers and the people. On this subject the following resolution was offered by Col. John W. Ray, and unanimously adopted:

Resolved, that when the Union men in attendance at this meeting return to their various counties, that each person consider himself a committee of one to raise funds and forward the same to James Blake, sr., in this city, for the purpose of defraying the expense of printing a large edition of the speeches and proceedings of to-day's meeting for gratuitous circulation among the Indiana soldiers now in the field.

The following lines were sent to us to be read at the Union meeting on Thursday, but failed to reach us till it was too late to use them as desired:

INDIANA
BY THOMAS B. LONG

All hail! Indiana, proud State of the brave!
    For nobly thy valor hath purchased renown —
Thy deeds shall be blazened from wave unto wave,
    Thy star shall be brightest in Liberty's crown!
The sons of thy soil in their might have appeared
    Wherever the Union's bright flag was unfurled,
With the valor of Spartans — for ages revered —
    And have written their deeds on the scroll of the world.
Their track in the carnage of battle is traced,
    'Till thy honor is bright as the face of the day,
For the blot that the traitor so wrongfully placed,
    Has been washed with the blood of his legions away.

Thy heroes are numbered like sands on the shore —
    Like the leaves of the forest when autumn appears —
And still, when our country demands them, shall more
    Fall blessed in our mem'ries, embalmed in our tears.
Their blood has enriched every soil of our land,
    Where battle has waved its dread standard on high,
And the names of that gallant and glorious band,
    With the names of the blest, are enrolled in the sky.
Thy honor, proud State, is untarnished again;
    Thy glory endured in their valor to-day,
For the traitor's accursed and infamous stain
    Has been washed with the blood of his legions away.

Oh! long may thy glory and honor endure,
    Enshrined in the pages of history's tomes,

In the songs of the bard and in music inure,
    'Till their halo shall gleam o'er our hearths and our homes
And whenever a foe, from at home or afar,
    Shall threaten our sisterhood's honor and name,
May thy glory still shine, like a new-risen star,
    And thy thousands respond to the calling of fame.
Then hail Indiana! proud State of the free!
    Thy name is as bright as the sun light to-day,
For the slander the traitor once breathed against thee
    Has been washed with the blood of his legions away!
    Terre Haute, Indiana.

The following poems were among the number recited by T. Buchanan Read, at the great Union Convention.

THE BRAVE AT HOME
BY T. BUCHANAN READ.

The maid who binds her warrior's sash,
    With smile that well her pain dissembles,
The while beneath her drooping lash
    One starry tear drop hangs and trembles;
Though Heaven alone records the tear,
    And Fame shall never know her story,
Her heart has shed a drop as dear
    As e'er bedewed the field of glory.

The wife who girds her husband's sword,
    'Mid little ones who weep or wonder,
And bravely speaks the cheering word,
    What though her heart be rent asunder,
Doomed nightly in her dreams to hear
    The bolts of death around him rattle,
Hath shed as sacred blood as e'er
    Was poured upon the field of battle.

The mother who conceals her grief,
    While to her breast her son she presses,
Then breathes a few brave words and brief,
    Kissing the patriot brow she blesses;
With no one but her secret God
    To know the pain that weighs upon her,
Sheds holy blood as e'er the sod
    Received on Freedom's field of honor.

THE FLAG OF THE CONSTELLATION
T. BUCHANAN READ.
Air — "Sparkling and Bright."

The stars of morn on our banner borne,
　With iris of Heaven are blended
The hand of our sires first mingled those fires,
　And by us they shall be defended.
Then hail the true, Red, White and Blue,
　The flag of the Constellation,
It sails as it sailed by our forefather's hailed,
　O'er battles which made us a nation.

What hand so bold as strike from that fold,
　One star or one stripe of its bright'ning,
For him be those stars, each a fiery Mars,
　And each stripe be as terrible lightning.
Then hail the true, Red, White and Blue,
　The flag of the Constellation,
It sails as it sailed by our forefathers hailed,
　O'er battles which made us a nation.

Its meteor form shall ride the storm,
　Till the fiercest of foes surrender,
The storm gone by it shall gild the sky,
　A rainbow of peace and of splendor.
Then hail the true, Red, White and Blue,
　The flag of the Constellation,
It sails as it sailed by our forefathers hailed,
　O'er battles which made us a nation.

Peace, to the world, is our motto unfurled,
　Tho' we shun not the field that is gory;
At home or abroad, fearing none but our God,
　We will carve our own pathway to glory!
Then hail the true, Red, White and Blue,
　The flag of the Constellation,
It sails as it sailed by our forefathers hailed,
　O'er battles which made us a nation.

Pamphlet 24

Copperheads Under the Heel of an Illinois Farmer.
New York, 1863

[In the early months of 1863, Unionists were especially worried by alleged disloyalty in the Middle West. There was striking concrete evidence in Illinois where the Democrats in control of the legislature, although protesting their abhorrence of secession, tried to avoid voting war appropriations and argued resolutions calling for an armistice. Finally Governor Richard Yates prorogued the legislature. Evidence of Eastern concern was the publication in New York City of the patriotic retort to the Copperheads delivered by a wealthy farmer in the Illinois State Senate in February, 1863. The farmer, Isaac Funk of Bloomington, a former Whig, was a notable cattle feeder. In 1854 he had sold a single lot of 1400 head of cattle.[1] The publisher was Frank Moore (1828–1904), who throughout the war and for several years thereafter issued, section by section, a massive compilation, *The Rebellion Record* (1861–1868).[2]]

On the last day of the Illinois Legislature, in February, 1863, Mr. Funk, a Senator from McLean County, delivered a speech, which is thus described and reported by the Springfield correspondent of the Chicago *Tribune:*

A great sensation was created by a speech by Mr. Funk, one of the richest farmers in the State, a man who pays over three thousand dollars per annum taxes towards the support of the Government. The lobby and gallery were crowded with spectators. Mr. Funk rose to object to trifling resolutions, which had been introduced by the Democrats to kill time and stave off a vote upon the appropriations for the support of the State Government. He said:

Mr. Speaker, I can sit in my seat no longer and see such by-play going on. These men are trifling with the best interests of the country. They should have asses' ears to set off their heads, or they are traitors and secessionists at heart.

I say that there are traitors and secessionists at heart in this

---

[1] [Arthur C. Cole, *The Era of the Civil War, 1848–1870* (Centennial History of Illinois, Chicago, 1922), 83, 150.]

[2] [Randall and Donald, *The Civil War and Reconstruction,* 299.]

Senate. Their actions prove it. Their speeches prove it. Their gibes and laughter and cheers here nightly, when their speakers get up to denounce the war and the administration, prove it.

I can sit here no longer and not tell these traitors what I think of them. And while so telling them, I am responsible, myself, for what I say. I stand upon my own bottom. I am ready to meet any man on this floor in any manner, from a pin's point to the mouth of a cannon, upon this charge against these traitors. [Tremendous applause from the galleries.]

I am an old man of sixty-five; I came to Illinois a poor boy; I have made a little something for myself and family. I pay three thousand dollars a year in taxes. I am willing to pay six thousand, aye, twelve thousand, [great cheering, the old gentleman striking the desk with a blow that would knock down a bullock, and causing the inkstand to fly in the air,] aye, I am willing to pay my whole fortune, and then give my life, to save my country from these traitors that are seeking to destroy it. [Tremendous applause, which the Speaker could not control.]

Mr. Speaker, you must please excuse me; I could not sit longer in my seat and calmly listen to these traitors. My heart, that feels for my poor country, would not let me. My heart, that cries out for the lives of our brave volunteers in the field, that these traitors at home are destroying by thousands, would not let me. My heart, that bleeds for the widows and orphans at home, would not let me. Yes, these traitors and villains in this Senate [striking his clenched fist on the desk with a blow that made the Senate ring again] are killing my neighbors' boys now fighting in the field. I dare to say this to these traitors right here, and I am responsible for what I say to any one or all of them. [Cheers.] Let them come on now, right here. I am sixty-five years old, and I have made up my mind to risk my life right here, on this floor, for my country. [Mr. Funk's seat is near the lobby railing, and a crowd collected around him, evidently with the intention of protecting him from violence, if necessary. The last announcement was received with great cheering, and I saw many an eye flash and many a countenance grow radiant with the light of defiance.]

These men sneered at Colonel Mack a few days since.[3] He is a

---

[3] Hon. A. W. Mack delivered a powerful speech in the Senate of Illinois, on the thirteenth of February, in opposition to the Armistice Resolutions of the "Copperheads."

small man, but I am a large man. I am ready to meet any of them in place of Colonel Mack. I am large enough for them, and I hold myself ready for them now and at any time. [Cheers from the galleries.]

Mr. Speaker, these traitors on this floor should be provided with hempen collars. They deserve them. They deserve hanging, I say, [raising his voice, and violently striking the desk;] the country would be the better of swinging them up. I go for hanging them, and I dare to tell them so, right here to their traitorous faces. Traitors should be hung. It would be the salvation of the country to hang them. For that reason I must rejoice at it. [Tremendous cheering.]

Mr. Speaker, I beg pardon of the gentlemen in this Senate who are not traitors, but true loyal men, for what I have said. I only intend it and mean it for secessionists at heart. They are here in this Senate. I see them gibe, and smirk, and grin at the true Union men. Must I defy them? I stand here ready for them, and dare them to come on. [Great cheering.] What man, with the heart of a patriot, could stand this treason any longer? I have stood it long enough. I will stand it no more. [Cheers.] I denounce these men and their aiders and abettors as rank traitors and secessionists. Hell itself could not spew out a more traitorous crew than some of the men that disgrace this Legislature, this State, and this country. For my-self, I protest against and denounce their treasonable acts. I have voted against their measures; I will do so to the end. I will denounce them as long as God gives me breath; and I am ready to meet the traitors themselves, here or any where, and fight them to the death. [Prolonged cheers and shouts.]

I said I paid three thousand dollars a year taxes. I do not say it to brag of it. It is my duty, yes, Mr. Speaker, my privilege, to do it. But some of these traitors here, who are working night and day to put their miserable little bills and claims through the Legislature, to take money out of the pockets of the people, are talking about high taxes. They are hypocrites as well as traitors. I heard some of them talking about high taxes in this way, who do not pay five dol-lars to the support of the Government. I denounce them as hypo-crites as well as traitors. [Cheers.]

The reason they pretend to be afraid of high taxes is, that they do not want to vote money for the relief of the soldiers. They want to embarrass the Government and stop the war. They want to aid the secessionists to conquer our boys in the field. They care about high taxes! They are picayune men, any how, and pay no taxes at all, and never did, and never hope or expect to. This is an excuse of traitors. [Cheers.]

Mr. Speaker, excuse me. I feel for my country, in this her hour of danger, from the tips of my toes to the ends of my hair. That is the reason I speak as I do. I can not help it. I am bound to tell these men to their teeth what they are, and what the people, the true loyal people, think of them. [Tremendous cheering. The Speaker rapped upon his desk, apparently to stop it, but really to add to its volume, for I could see by his flushed cheek and flashing eye that his heart was with the brave and loyal old gentleman.]

Mr. Speaker, I have said my say. I am no speaker. This is the only speech I have made, and I do not know that it deserves to be called a speech. I could not sit still any longer and see these scoundrels and traitors work out their hellish schemes to destroy the Union. They have my sentiments; let them, one and all, make the most of them. I am ready to back up all I say, and I repeat it, to meet these traitors in any manner they may choose, from a pin's point to the mouth of a cannon. [Tremendous applause, during which the old gentleman sat down, after he had given the desk a parting whack, which sounded loud above the din of cheers and clapping of hands.]

I never before witnessed so much excitement in an assembly. Mr. Funk spoke with a force of natural eloquence, with a conviction and truthfulness, with a fervor and pathos which wrought up the galleries, and even members on the floor, to the highest pitch of excitement. His voice was heard in the stores that surround the square, and the people came flocking in from all quarters. In five minutes he had an audience that packed the hall to its utmost capacity. After he had concluded, the Republican members and spectators rushed up and took him by the hand to congratulate him. The Democrats said nothing, but evidently felt the castigation they were receiving most keenly, as might be seen from their blanched cheeks and restless and uneasy glances.

Robert Dale Owen

The Future of the North-West: In Connection with
the Scheme of Reconstruction Without New
England. Addressed to the People of Indiana.
(Loyal Publication Society, No. 1)

New York, 1863

[Robert Dale Owen, the Indiana reformer, feared in the winter of 1863 that the friends of peace-at-any-price in his state would accept Confederate overtures to reconstruct the Union leaving out the New England states. He had no evidence that this was the intent of the Confederate leaders beyond some vague remarks allegedly made at the time of the secession crisis, nor was there any indication that Indiana Democrats would welcome such a compromise. Yet at the instigation of the Radical Republican governor, Oliver P. Morton, he wrote a pamphlet outlining the purported proposal and exhorting his fellow Indianans not "to unite your fate with a slave empire." At the suggestion of Parke Godwin of the New York *Evening Post,* the newly founded Loyal Publication Society issued Owen's warning as its first pamphlet. The Union League of Philadelphia issued it as its sixth publication. It was widely circulated and taken seriously in the East, but in Indiana where several Republican newspapers published it without comment, it attracted little attention. Owen (1801–1877), long a notable reformer and publicist, had helped found the New Harmony community and had served as a Democrat in both the Indiana legislature and Congress. During the Civil War he served as an unofficial assistant to Governor Morton, and temporarily was an assistant secretary of war in Washington.[1]]

MORE than a third of a century since, I found a home, Citizens of Indiana, among you. Kindly you received me. Largely have you bestowed on me your confidence. I owe to you honorable station

[1] [Richard W. Leopold, *Robert Dale Owen, A Biography* (Cambridge, 1940), 357–359.]

and a debt of gratitude. Let me endeavor, now in your hour of danger, to repay, if in part I may, that debt.

On the future of our country clouds and darkness rest. We are engaged in a war as terrible as any which history records; an outrage on civilization, if it be not God's agency for a great purpose. All good citizens earnestly desire its termination. The fervent longing of every Christian man and woman is for the restoration of peace.

To this righteous desire there are addressed, especially here in our North-West, certain proposals of compromise and accommodation. Shall we take counsel as to what these are worth? Can we reason together on a subject of interest more vital to ourselves and to our children?

But before we scan the future, let us glance at the past. Ere we advance, let us determine where we stand, and ascertain how we came hither. Looking back on our steps throughout the last two years, let us, in a dispassionate spirit, by the aid of authentic and unimpeachable documents, very briefly examine the causes, underlying a stupendous national convulsion, which have resulted in the present condition of things.

The secession ordinance passed the Convention of South Carolina, December 20, 1860. The next day, December 21, the Convention adopted the "Declaration of Causes," justifying secession. In language plain as can be desired are these causes set forth. They all center in one complaint, Northern encroachment on slavery; there *is* no other cause alleged.

What proof of such encroachment is offered? First, the allegation that "for years past" fourteen Northern States, among which Indiana is named, "have deliberately refused to fulfill their Constitutional obligations" (as regards the fugitive-slave-law) by "enacting laws which either nullify the acts of Congress or render useless any attempt to execute them." But if you have looked through our statute-book, you know that no such law then existed, or ever existed, there. That solemn Declaration, inaugurating a war as fearful as ever desolated a nation, is based, so far as regards our State, on a statement either ignorantly or wilfully false.

If, in regard to any of the other States named, there be truth in the allegation; — if, in any one or more of these, there existed then, a state law nullifying or rendering nugatory a Constitutional provision; — none knew better than these South Carolinians what their easy, peaceful, effectual remedy was: — an appeal to the Supreme Court. That Court has sovereign control over all unconstitutional laws. Had the South no chance of justice — of more than justice — before the Supreme Court of the United States? Be the Dred Scott decision the reply!

A thing, to be credited, must have some semblance of common sense. Will any man believe that the citizens of South Carolina — who would find it difficult to prove that by the unconstitutionality of State laws at the North they had lost twenty slaves since their State first joined the Union — will any sane man believe that South Carolina sought to break up that Union for cause so utterly trivial as that?

No! far deeper must we search for the true cause. It is plainly set forth in the latter paragraphs of the Declaration, in which the Convention speaks, not of any special laws, but of "the action of the non-slaveholding States."

It declares that these States have "denied the rights of property established in fifteen of the States and recognized by the Constitution;" that they "have denounced as sinful the institution of slavery;" that they "have united in the election of a man to the high office of President of the United States whose opinions and purposes are hostile to slavery;" who declares that "the Government cannot endure permanently half slave, half free," and that "the public mind must rest in the belief that slavery is in the course of ultimate extinction." And it winds up by this assertion: "All hope of remedy is rendered vain by the fact that the public opinion of the North has invested a great political error with the sanctions of a more erronious religious belief."

These South Carolinian sentiments, afterward endorsed by every seceding State, are doubtless, in substance, sincere. They may be received as the secession creed. Though loosely worded they are intelligible. Taken in connection with the steadily-progressing increase, disclosed each ten years by the census, of population and Congressional votes and consequent political influence in the Free States as compared with the Slave, they disclose, beyond question, the true cause of the gigantic insurrection that has made desolate so many domestic hearths, and spread war and devastation where peace and tranquillity used to reign.

It is, of course, not true, that the Northern States, as States, have denied the rights of Southern property, or denounced slavery as sinful. The Convention could only mean that certain citizens of these States had expressed such sentiments; or as they afterward phrase it, that public opinion in the North had given the sanction of religion to a great political error.

I pray you to remark that the South secedes from the Union *because of these opinions.* She will not remain in fellowship with States in which such opinions are expressed. She holds that men ought not to be allowed to say or to write that slavery is sinful, or that religion does not sanction it. She hangs those who say or write such things within her own borders.[2] To satisfy her, such opinions must be suppressed also among us. But the Constitution provides that "Congress shall make no law abridging the liberty of speech or of the press." Here is a difficulty. How shall we of the North satisfy a slaveholding South, unless we not only surrender the dearest of a freeman's rights, but also either violate the Constitution, or else amend it so that free thought and free speech shall be among past and forgotten things?

But these outspoken sentiments are not our only offense. We are accused of having elected a President "whose opinions and purposes are hostile to slavery;" and who believes that "slavery is in the course of ultimate extinction."

Because of the election of such a President, the slaveholders of the South secede. They do not wait to see what he will do. They secede before he is inaugurated. They secede, then, not because of his acts, but because of his opinions.

His opinions on the subject of slavery; the same opinions which, for a century past, have been spreading and swelling into action throughout the civilized world; the same opinions which have taken practical form and shape — which have become law — till not a Christian nation in Europe, Spain alone excepted, stands out against them. Look at the array of names! England led the way. In 1834 she emancipated all her slaves. King Oscar of Sweden followed her

---

[2] "Let an abolitionist come within the borders of South Carolina, if we can catch him we will try him, and notwithstanding all the interference of all the Governments on earth, including the Federal Government, we will hang him." — *Senator Preston, in debate in U.S. Senate, January,* 1838.

"If chance throw an abolitionist into our hands, he may expect a felon's death." — *Senator Hammond of South Carolina, in Senate,* 1836.

example in 1846. Then came Denmark in 1847; France, in 1848; Portugal, in 1856; the vast empire of Russia, in 1862. Finally, with nearly thirty years' experience in English colonies and fifteen years' experience in those of France before her eyes, plain, practical, unimaginative Holland, by a vote in her Chambers of forty-five to seven, gave freedom, with compensation, to her forty-five thousand slaves; to take effect on the first of July next.

And our offense in Southern eyes — an offense so grievous that it is held to justify insurrection and its thousand horrors — our unpardonable sin is, that we have elected a President whose opinions regarding negro servitude are those of all Christendom; whose belief that "slavery is in the course of ultimate extinction," is but the plain inevitable deduction from the last thirty years' history of the civilized world.

Observe, I pray, that in thus setting forth the causes which produced this fratricidal war, I have let the South speak for herself. Nor have I cited against her vagrant opinions, carelessly expressed by her citizens. I have quoted, word for word, from her solemn deliberate "Declaration of Causes;" that document which is to Secessiondom, what the Declaration of Independence was to the United States. Out of her own mouth I have condemned her.

Yet I am not assuming to sit in judgment on her motives. I but show you where the difficulty lies, and how deep-sunk and radical it is. Opinions (she declares) stand in the way. Based on a religious sentiment, these opinions render vain (she says) all hope of remedy; for her Government is founded on opinions diametrically the reverse. And I show you further, that in this she stands alone among the nations calling themselves civilized. Alexander H. Stephens, whom, in February, 1861, she named her Vice President, with commendable frankness admits that she does so. In Savannah, the Mayor presiding, Mr. Stephens, addressing an immense crowd on the 21st of March following his election, spoke thus: "Slavery is the natural and moral condition of the negro. This, our new Government, is the first, in the history of the world, based upon this great physical, philosophical, and moral truth." [3]

[3] Speech of Mr. Stephens as reported in the *"Savannah Republican."* It is thence copied into *"Putnam's Rebellion Record,"* vol. i., document 48, pp. 44 to 49. The *Republican,* in publishing this address, says: "Mr. Stephens took his seat amid a burst of enthusiasm and applause, such as the Athenaeum has never displayed within its walls in the memory of the oldest inhabitant."

Alone she stands! the first government, in the history of the world, founded on the principle — "Slavery is good; slavery is moral; slavery is just;" the only people in all the eighteen centuries since Christ preached justice and mercy, who rose in rebellion because, among their brethren, His religion was appealed to in favor of that emancipation which, within the last thirty years, England, and France, and Sweden, and Denmark, and Portugal, and Russia, and Holland, have all conceded — a tribute to Christian civilization.

Thus, then. Opinions not carried out in practice — opinions unfavorable to slavery expressed in the North, and held by the President elect — the same opinions that are entertained and have been acted upon by almost every civilized nation — these, according to Southern declaration, were the immediate causes of the war: opinions, not acts; the acts were all the other way.

Inaugurated on the 4th of March, 1861, Abraham Lincoln expressly reassumed, in his Message, the ground occupied by himself, and by a large majority of his supporters, before the election. "I have no purpose" (said he), "directly or indirectly, to interfere with the institution of slavery in the States where it exists." He went much further. Alluding, in the same Message, to an amendment to the Constitution, which had passed Congress on the 28th of February, to the effect that no amendment shall ever be made to the Constitution authorizing Congress to interfere with slavery in any State, the President said: "I have no objection to its being made express and irrevocable."

This was the first act: an offer sanctioned by Congress, endorsed by the President, so to amend the Constitution, that never, while the world lasted, should the power be given to Congress, by any subsequent amendment, to interfere with slavery.

The scene when, on Mr. Corwin's motion, this amendment passed, is recorded in the newspapers of the day. "As the vote proceeded, the excitement was intense, and on the announcement of the result, the inexpressible enthusiasm of the members and the crowded galleries found vent in uproarious demonstrations. All feel that it is the harbinger of peace." [4]

Was it the harbinger of peace? Did this concession — bordering surely on humiliation — a promise, as to slavery, never through all time to amend our acts no matter how we may change our opinions

[4] N.Y. *Commercial,* February 28, 1861.

— did this unheard-of concession to the slave interest conciliate the South, or arrest her action? It passed by, like the idle wind. State after State seceded. Security against the encroachment alleged to be intended — the amplest within the bounds of possibility — had, indeed, been offered; but the remedy did not reach the case. Opinions remained unchanged; and the rebellion was against opinions. Men in the North still said that human servitude was sinful. The President still believed that "slavery is in the course of ultimate extinction." No fraternity with such men! No obedience to such a President!

And yet this President, in the same Inaugural from which I have quoted, pushed forbearance to the verge of that boundary beyond which it ceases to be a virtue. "The Government" (he said to the Secessionists already in arms against lawful authority) — "the Government will not assail you. You can have no conflict without being yourselves the aggressors." And in mild but cogent terms he reminded them of his and their relative situations, and of the final necessity which his position imposed upon him. "You have no oath" (he said) "registered in Heaven to destroy the Government: while I have the most solemn one to preserve, protect, and defend it."

He spoke to the deaf adder. As if they *had* sworn before God to destroy the Government under which, for eighty years, they had enjoyed prosperity and protection, they became the aggressors. Unassailed by that Government, they opened fire, on the memorable twelfth of April, from the batteries of Charleston, on Fort Sumter.

The echo of that cannonade reverberated throughout the Union. The North rose up, like a strong man from sleep. It needed not the President's Proclamation, issued three days thereafter, to call men forth. In advance of that call, the farmer had left his plow in the furrow; the mechanic had deserted his workshop. The People had taken the war in hand.

Such were the causes of this rebellion; such were the acts on either side.

What have been the results? The war, as wars in their commencement always are, was popular. Men engaged in it, as in a new and stirring enterprise men are wont to do, with enthusiasm. Unmingled successes, a prompt and triumphant termination — these, as always happens, were confidently anticipated. But the usual checkered fortunes of war attended our arms; now a victory, now a defeat. The contest was protracted. Visionary hopes of speedy triumph faded away. Then came revulsion of feeling, sinking of spirit. There never was a protracted war in this world, no matter how successful in the end, without just such a reaction. How did the souls of our revolutionary fathers, sore tried, sink within them, year after year — how often did Washington himself despair — before the final victory that heralded American Independence! England is still one of the greatest nations of the world, proud, powerful, prosperous; yet, during her five years' Peninsular war (in Spain against Napoleon) the depression in England was almost beyond example. At the commencement of that war the people accepted it with acclamation. Opposite parties in Parliament vied with each other in their zeal to vote men and money. Before a year had passed, how changed was the scene! The retreat and defeat at Corunna (the Bull Run of that year's campaign) plunged the nation in despair. Nothing was talked of but the stupid blunders of the Government, its absurd and contradictory orders, its gross ignorance of the first principles of war. Croakers spoke loudly of the folly of any attempt to check the progress of the French arms in Spain. Universal distrust seized the public mind. The Ministry kept their places with extreme difficulty. But England's *pluck* bore her through. She spent four hundred and fifty millions a year, bought gold at thirty per cent premium to pay her troops, persevered to the end — and conquered: yet not till her Government stocks, ordinarily at 90, had come to stand habitually at 65; nay, before Napoleon was finally conquered, had fallen to 53 (payable in depreciated paper), and had been negotiated by the Chancellor of the Exchequer at that rate.

Nor let it be imagined that it was the uninformed masses alone who despaired. The greatest men shared the doubt whether England was not tottering to her destruction. Sir Walter Scott wrote to a friend: "These cursed, double cursed news from Spain have sunk my spirits so much that I am almost at disbelieving a Providence. There is an evil fate upon us in all we do at home or abroad." A letter of Sir James Mackintosh is still more gloomy. "I believe, like you" (he writes to a friend at Vienna), "in a resurrection, because I believe in the immortality of civilization; but a dark and stormy night, a black series of ages, may be prepared for our posterity before the dawn of a better day. The race of man may reach the promised land, but there is no assurance that the present generation will not perish in the wilderness." [5]

Such is the dark valley, shadowed by despondency, through which even the most powerful nation, once engaged in a great contest of life and death, must consent to travel ere it emerges to the light. If we were not prepared to traverse its depths — if we have not courage to endure even to the end — we ought never to have entered upon the gloomy road at all. Many good men thought, at the outset, that the wiser course was to let the deluded South go in peace. A thousand times better to have done this than to falter and look back now, false to the great task we have undertaken, recreant to the solemn purpose on which we have lavished millions of treasure, to which we have set the seal of our best blood. That which might have been graceful concession two years since, would be base submission to-day.

Base and unavailing! What are the proposals now, rife throughout the North-West, among the friends of peace-at-any-price? Worst devise of feeble or faithless heads, busily echoed by thousands of faint hearts, embodied in public resolutions, trumpeted through hundreds of newspapers, what is the favorite project, long matured in secret, that is urged upon you to-day by the enemies of the war and of the Administration that conducts it?

Of vast import is that project, yet a few words suffice to state it. The greatest of human changes can be expressed in one word — Death!

The project is, to reconstruct the Union, leaving out the New England States.

This plan is spoken of as a compromise. The South, abandoning her avowed intention to erect a separate purely slave-holding Confederacy, is to consent to receive into her fellowship a portion of the Northern States. The Northern States, in return, are to abandon six of their number; those six in which the opinions against which the war is waged chiefly prevail.

But this plan is no after-thought — no compromise whatever. It has been in the minds and intentions of the Southern leaders from the very commencement of the rebellion.

[5] A pamphlet by C. J. Stillé, on this subject, giving many more details, is well worth studying. Its title is, *"How a free people conduct a great war."* Published by Collins, Philadelphia.

I vouch for the truth of the following: Early in January, 1861, a few days after South Carolina had seceded, and before any other State had followed her example, Senator Benjamin, of Louisiana, said to one of the Foreign Ministers: "A great revolution has commenced. It will end in the separation from the Union either of the slave States or of New England."

Within a few days of the same time, before Jefferson Davis had left Washington, Mrs. Davis, conversing with a friend from Pennsylvania, who had been lamenting a probable separation, replied, in substance: "Do not afflict yourself. We shall not separate from Pennsylvania, nor New York, nor New Jersey; they, like the North-West, are our natural allies."

It was the original plan, abandoned for a time, when the entire North rose in arms; unavowed even now; yet secretly fomented and sanctioned ever since the elections seemed to result adversely to the Administration, and since meetings and newspapers, calling themselves Democratic, have been sending forth, to an enemy in arms, words of sympathy and comfort.

Well might such a plan be the first choice of the secessionists! Well may they intrigue with the North-West to favor and adopt it now! Far better for them than a mere Southern Confederacy, never was a more specious nor a more daring device to uphold a sinking cause!

Look at it, I pray you; not vaguely or hastily, but carefully, and in all its practical details. In the Senate, *thirty* Southern votes to *twenty-two* Northern; in the House, *ninety* Southern votes to *a hundred and thirteen* Northern. One House hopelessly gone; while twelve votes changed would give a Southern majority in the other. And when has Congress seen the day when twice twelve votes could not have been had from Northern Representatives for any measure the South saw fit to propose?

Just North enough in the scheme to afford protection and support to slavery; and *not* North enough to exert over it the slightest influence or control.

Plausible, too! "You have a majority in one House, and we in the other. What can be more fair?"

But mark the workings of the plan! A free State applies for admission. The Bill must pass the Senate. Will it pass? Slaveholders have to decide that question. Will they relinquish the balance of power which they hold in their grasp? While they retain their reason, never! A slave State for every free State admitted; that will be the rule. The controlling majority in the Senate, therefore, perpetual!

Think, next, of the nominations by the President — a President, of course, who believes in the justice, and in the perpetual duration of negro slavery — for none other will be suffered to take his seat; nominations of Cabinet officers; of Foreign Ministers and Consuls; of Judges of the Supreme Court; of Generals in the army; of men to all lucrative Post-offices; of Registers and Receivers, and all the long list of other nominations to offices in the gift of the President and confirmatory by the Senate. Will the name of one man pass the ordeal who thinks human servitude a sin or an evil, or who believes that "slavery is in the course of ultimate extinction?"

It will be a Senate requiring a political test for office that would have excluded Washington, if proposed for Brigadier-General, or Jefferson, if nominated as a member of the Cabinet. For Washington, on the 9th of September, 1786, wrote to John F. Mercer, of Maryland: "It is among my first wishes to see some plan adopted by which slavery in this country may be abolished by law." [6] And Jefferson, in his "Summary View of the Rights of British America," originally published in August, 1774, said: "The abolition of domestic slavery is the great object of desire in these Colonies, where it was, unhappily, introduced in their infant state;" [7] while, eight years later, in his "Notes on Virginia," he falls into that "erroneous religious belief" which, according to the South Carolina Declaration, renders hopeless all remedy for the grievances of the South. Adverting to a possible conflict, in the future, between slave and slaveholder, he says: "The Almighty has no attribute which can take side with us in such a contest." [8]

If this view of revolutionary opinions should happen to surprise you, it will be because you are less accurately informed on the subject than the Vice President of the insurrectionary States. Let Mr. Stephens have credit for the honesty with which, in the address from which I have already quoted, he made this confession: "The prevailing ideas entertained by Jefferson and most of the leading

[6] *Sparks' Washington,* vol. ix., p. 159.
[7] *Jefferson's Works,* vol. i., p. 135.
[8] *Jefferson's Writings,* vol. viii., p. 404.

statesmen, at the time of the formation of the old Constitution, were, that the enslavement of the African was in violation of the laws of nature; that it was wrong in principle, socially, morally, and politically." The "ultimate extinction" heresy, too, was shared by these men, as Mr. Stephens thus reminds us: "Slavery was an evil they knew not well how to deal with; but the general opinion of the men of that day was, that, somehow or other, in the order of Providence, the institution would be evanescent, and pass away." [9]

Reconstruct the Union without New England, and no man who shares these revolutionary sentiments, — no man who believes as Washington and Jefferson believed, — can ever reach the Presidential chair, or ever receive, from the occupant of that chair, any office, at home or abroad, civil or military, of any importance whatever.

The vast patronage of the Government — the tens of millions annually in its gift — would become a gigantic bribe. Its demoralizing influence in calling forth professions of a money-getting creed, would be immense.

But well would it be if this wholesale premium on hypocrisy were the only evil, or the worst evil, which a South-controlled Congress would bring upon us. What laws would such a Congress pass?

The characteristic political doctrine universally asserted throughout the South is this: "The Constitution provides that 'the citizens of each State shall be entitled to all privileges and immunities of citizens in the several States.' Therefore all citizens are entitled, wherever they may reside, to equal rights of property. Neither the Federal Government nor a State has a right to discriminate between different kinds of property, legally held. It is unconstitutional to declare by law that any legally held property *is* property in one portion of the Union, and is *not* property in another. It is equally unconstitutional for the Federal Government, or for any State, to pass laws which shall prohibit the transfer of any legally held property from one portion of the Union to another; or to enact that any one species of property legally used in any one State or Territory may not be used in another.

"But slaves are property: as absolutely and legally articles of merchandise (though differing in kind) as horses, or cattle, or flocks

[9] Address of A. H. Stephens, reported, as stated in a previous note, in the "*Savannah Republican.*"

of sheep; property righteously as well as legally held; property the holding of which is based on a great physical, philosophical, and moral truth, and is sanctioned by religion.

"Therefore, wherever one citizen may lawfully take or use his cattle and horses and flocks of sheep, another citizen may lawfully take and use his slaves. To prohibit him from so doing is a moral wrong, as well as an unconstitutional act." [10]

That is the openly-avowed doctrine and demand of the South. Individual exceptions to such opinions there are, of course, in the slave States, just as, in the free States, men are found who believe that slavery is enjoined by morality and sanctioned by religion. But the official declarations of the South prove, and no honest slaveholder will deny, that I have here fairly and candidly stated the leading article, never to be relinquished, of their political creed.

Upon this doctrine was based that claim of the South to equal rights of settlement in the Territories, the expected denial of which was one of the chief incentives to this war. But it is evident that if the doctrine be tenable at all, it applies as justly to a State as to a Territory. An Indianian may buy a Kentucky farm and settle thereon with all his movable property. Shall a Kentuckian be forbidden to settle, in like manner, on a farm in Indiana, unless he shall first sell the most valuable movable property he possesses?

It is not more certain that the earth will continue to revolve around the sun, than that the South, while slaveholding, will persevere, whenever and wherever she obtains the political ascendency, in asserting and enforcing by law what she regards as her political rights in this matter.

Choose, then, farmers of Indiana! citizens of the North-West! Strike off twenty-nine votes from the northern majority of the House. Abandon, by the cession of twelve votes more, your present majority in the Senate. Consent to the dismemberment of your country. Relinquish for ever to the South the balance of legislative

---

[10] If any man doubt that this *is* the claim maintained by the South, and short of which she will never be satisfied, let him read the *note* on the last page of this pamphlet, on recent legal opinions and decisions touching slaves.

These afford conclusive proof that the South, with the power in her hands, would declare null and void, because in violation of the Constitution of the United States, the provision in the Constitution of Indiana excluding negroes. Should we tolerate a similar provision excluding our horses and cattle from Kentucky? A State cannot, without the consent of Congress, even lay a duty on property brought within her limits from another State; far less, of course, can she exclude it altogether.

power. Do this, if you will. But bear in mind, that on the day you assent to the scandalous compact, you will have virtually repealed that noble ORDINANCE to which the North-West owes not freedom only, but a social and commercial prosperity far outstripping that of any slave-tilled State. Bear in mind that on that day you will have to decide, which of two alternatives you will advise your sons to select; — to regard honest labor as unbecoming a gentleman, or to take their chance of working in sight of the overseer, side by side with the slave.

Do all this, if good it seem to you. I make no argument against it. Facts, not counsels, are what I offer you. I but seek to shed daylight on the slaveholders' project; to show you, beforehand, what it is you are invited to do.

The invitation is, to unite your fate with a slave empire; not an empire part free and part slave, but an empire *all* slave; an empire in every portion of which slavery will be permitted by law, and restricted as to the number of slaves by soil and climate alone. The invitation is to become, yourselves, part and parcel of such an empire; to enter into fellowship with those who, not content to legalize slavery, canonize it also; regard it as philosophical, commend it as moral, extol it as religious: who adopt it as the cornerstone of the social edifice and the basis of the political system.

The invitation is, to ignore, or to defy, the public sentiment of Christendom. The invitation is to stand still, or sink back, while all other civilized nations advance. An eminent writer, alluding to certain ancient collegiate foundations of Europe, declared that they were not without their use to the historian of the human mind: immovably moored to the same station by the strength of their cables and the weight of their anchors, they served to mark the rapidity of the current with which the rest of the world was borne along. Is such to be the fate and the vocation of America, once proud, powerful, freedom-loving? Is God's mighty current of Progress to sweep past her, as she lies paralyzed, weighted down, rock-stranded, by her political sins?

This invitation is given on conditions. The first is, that throughout this slave empire, no man shall be allowed to deny the "great physical, philosophical, and moral truth", now first recognized, upon which the new Government is founded; namely, that slavery is the natural and moral condition of the African negro. No man is to be permitted, on pain of punishment, to argue that slavery is sinful, or that religion condemns it. We are required to go back to the spirit of those days when it was held to be seditious to question, by speech or writing, the idea on which the existing Government was based; to the Tudor and Stuart age of England: the only difference being that while under the old English rule, it was punishable as sedition to question the right divine of Kings, under the new Southern rule, sedition is to be punished when it questions the right divine of slavery. It will be a remarkable experiment, in the nineteeth century, to establish a government upon a principle which will not bear question, or suffer an argument touching its truth or its merits. The despotism of Naples recently went down, crushed by the difficulties and the odium of maintaining, in these modern days, a similar state of things.

The second condition demanded of us is, that the North, before it is admitted to Southern fellowship, shall cast off six of her States; thus curtailing her power and her possessions by the surrender of nearly one-fifth of her population and more than one-fifth of her wealth.

And here discloses itself the Hercules foot of this most audacious scheme. Think of proposing to Great Britain, that she should set Scotland adrift, or to France that she should detach and abandon all Normandy! When was dismemberment ever dreamed of or demanded, except by a victor from a prostrate foe?

And will no other demands be made based on the same relative condition of the contracting parties? The Southern insurrection will have cost its authors a thousand millions, at the least. Can any man doubt that the North, once entrapped into this base compact, will be held to pay her full share of that stupendous sum? — not only to accept as justifiable an insurrection against lawful authority, but to pay what that insurrection cost? And will nothing be included in that cost but the bare expenses of the war? Is it not certain, beyond possible doubt, that there will be thousands upon thousands of claims for damages — for plantations ruined, for dwellings destroyed, for cotton burnt, for hundreds of thousands of slaves lost — from every Southern State that has been reached by our arms? and that these claims will amount to hundreds of millions, exceeding probably the war expenses themselves? On whom is to be imposed the enormous tax that is to pay for these ravages of war? On whom but on those who inflicted them? And when such a tax is levied and paid by you, what acknowledgment can be imagined more practically conclusive of the admission that the so-called insurrection was no insurrection at all, but, on the contrary, a noble war for liberty and independence, just in its inception, triumphant in its result?

Their hewers of wood and drawers of water we should become; the recorders of their edicts; the submissive agents to execute their good pleasure!

And if we yield now, so should we be! If with half the territory constituting the Slave States virtually in our possession, we accept at the hands of armed enemies the very plan they themselves had chalked out before a cannon was fired, richly shall we deserve our fate! Under such a plan the insurgents would not merely have secured their own independence: conquerors over us, they would have mastered ours. Have we mercy to expect? Woe to the vanquished!

Let there be no self-deception. If we are to do this thing, let us look it honestly in the face, and make plain to ourselves what it is we are doing. We give up; we surrender; we acknowledge (twenty millions against six) *that we are beaten*. Yet that is a trifle: the bravest may be defeated; the holiest cause may fail. But we, if we take this step, must consent to repentance as well as to submission. Before the world we must confess our sins. Before the world our acts must declare, that from the first, we were in the wrong and the South in the right. Before the world our acts must declare, that a thousand millions have been squandered — that a hundred thousand brave men have sunk from the battle-field to the grave — all in a disgraceful warfare, all in an iniquitous cause.

And the retrospect, when this war, thus stigmatized as aggressive and faithless, is brought to a shameful close! The scene, when the thinned ranks of a hundred Indiana regiments, whose gallant deeds, untarnished by a single disgrace, have been till now the pride and boast of their State — the scene of bitter humiliation, when these brave and war-worn men shall return — to find themselves degraded from patriots to marauders; their labors counted but an outrage, their wounds a disgrace; shall return, to hear their dead comrades spoken of as mercenaries hired by the oppressor, and justly overtaken by the oppressor's fate; shall return, to find the war-made widow pensionless, the soldier's orphan cast helpless on the mercy of the world!

And then the scene — it may be far more terrible yet — when Indiana, base and craven, shall put forth her hand attempting to sign the compact of degradation!

Attempting to sign! Will the attempt ever be consummated? In peace, without bloodshed, without the hand of brother raised against brother, of father against son — never! Until Indiana shall have shared a worse fate than Missouri or Kentucky, or Virginia; until her fields shall be desolate, her cities spoiled, her substance wasted; until we shall have learned, by sickening experience, the nightly terrors, the daily horrors of civil war — never! Will the men who have stood firm while shot and shell decimated their ranks, turn cowards on their return to their native State, and patiently suffer it? So sure as God lives, never — never!

Let Indiana, belying the courage she has shown on the battle field, casting from her the last remnant of self-respect, false to her constitutional obligations, blind to a future of abject servility, deaf alike to the warnings of revolutionary wisdom and to the voice of Civilization speaking to-day in her ears — let Indiana, selling Freedom's birthright for less than Esau's price, resolve to purchase Southern favor by Northern dismemberment and the world-wide contempt that would follow it — but let her know, before she enters that path of destruction, that her road will lie over the bodies of her murdered sons, past prostrate cabins, past ruined farms, through all the desolation that fire and sword can work. Let her know, that before she can link her fate to a system that is as surely doomed to ultimate extinction as the human body is finally destined to death, there will be a war within her own borders to which all we have yet endured, will be but as the summer's gale, that scatters a few branches over the highway, compared to the hurricane that plows its broad path of ruin, mile after mile, leaving behind, in its track, a prostrate forest, harvest crops uprooted, and human habitations overthrown.

But the hurricane is of God's sending. Whether the tempest of war, from which He has hitherto mercifully preserved our State, shall now sweep over it, as it has swept over the ill-fated Southern border, depends, Citizens of Indiana, upon you. Courage, prudence, patriotism will avert it. Faint-heartedness and folly will bring it down upon our heads. If it come, God help the present generation that has to endure it! God help our children after us, to whom we bequeath a North-West steeped in scandalous dependence, so long as she submits to her masters, and a prey to a second civil war, so soon as she awakes to her true condition, and draws the sword once more, to redeem the errors of the past!

ROBERT DALE OWEN.

March 4, 1863.

NOTE, *as to recent legal opinions and decisions touching slavery.* — The direct question whether slaves brought by their masters to reside in a Free State become free — in other words, whether a State law be constitutional which declares free all slaves, not fugitives, who may come within the limits of the State, — has never been brought before the Supreme Court.

But in the Dred Scott case the opinion delivered by the Court was based on principles, the practical application of which appears to establish the right of an owner of slaves to their "service and labor" throughout life, no matter where that life may be spent.

Chief Justice Taney, in that opinion, declares: That negroes imported from Africa, were "brought here as articles of merchandise;" that in every one of the thirteen colonies which formed the Constitution of the United States, "a negro of the African race was regarded as an article of property, and held and bought and sold as such," and that, at the time the Constitution was adopted, the negro was "treated as an ordinary article of merchandise and traffic, whenever a profit could be made by it." As such Chief Justice regards him.

Dred Scott, the plaintiff in this case, a slave owned in Missouri by Dr. Emerson, had been taken by his owner into Illinois, kept there two years, then kept two years in a Territory of the United States north of the Missouri Compromise line, while that Compromise was in force, and had then been brought back to Missouri.

The Court, after reciting that "Scott was a slave when taken into the State of Illinois *and there held as such*," decided that when brought back to Missouri he remained a slave, inasmuch as "his *status*, as free or slave, depended *on the laws of Missouri, not of Illinois.*"

So also of his residence in a Territory declared free by a law of the United States. The Court held the law to be unconstitutional and void, because the Constitution recognizes a slave as property, and "makes no distinctoin between that property and any other." And the Court decides that Scott cannot be liberated under such a law.

Though the question did not come before the Court for decision, whether Scott could have been held for life as a slave in Illinois, yet it is a fair inference from the above, that that question also would be decided in the affirmative. Either Scott, while residing with Dr. Emerson in Illinois, was his slave or he was not. If his slave, as the words of Chief Justice Taney would imply, then slaveholders may hold their slaves to service and labor in a Free State. If not his slave, he was a freeman. But if a freeman, how could any law of Missouri be held again to reduce him to slavery?

In the Lemmon case (before the New York Court of Appeals, January, 1860), in which the question came up, whether slaves owned by a Virginian in transit through the State of New York became free, the Court decided (five against three) in favor of the slaves. But the arguments of the counsel (O'Conor) assigned by the State of Virginia for the slaveowner, clearly indicate the character and extent of Southern claims in this matter, and the principles upon which these are based. He said: "Property in African negroes is not an exception to any general rule. Upon rational principles it is no more local or peculiar than any other property." And he argued that a State has the same right to declare a wife who might be brought within its limits to be "free from all obligations of that condition," as to declare the same thing of a slave.

It is to be conceded that no Court has yet made a decision in conformity with the claims here put forth, on behalf of Virginia. But can the nature and extent of the rights demanded by the South be doubted or misunderstood? And whenever a Senate with a perpetual Southern majority shall have the control of nominations for Judges of the Supreme Court, is it not morally certain that the decision, in the premises, of Judges thus selected will be in favor of Virginia's claims?

————————◆◆◆◆◆————————

Pamphlet 26

Edward N. Crosby and S. F. B. Morse

The Letter of a Republican, Edward N. Crosby, Esq.,
of Poughkeepsie, to Prof. S. F. B. Morse,
Feb. 25, 1863, and Prof. Morse's Reply, March 2d,
1863. (Papers from the Society for the Diffusion
of Political Knowledge. No. 4)

New York, 1863

[In the fourth of the pamphlets of the Society for the Diffusion of Political Knowledge, the Society's prime mover, Samuel F. B. Morse, aired his full views upon the war issues — constitutional questions, his suspicion that the British were intriguing to perpetuate disunion, and above all, his fervent belief that Negroes belonged in slavery because they were inherently inferior to whites. He mustered a startling pair of supporters for his racist arguments, linking President Lincoln and Vice-President Alexander H. Stephens of the Confederacy. Lincoln, he pointed out, had bluntly advised a delegation of free Negro leaders in August, 1862, that they emigrate, since they could never live on a basis of equality among the white race. Stephens had asserted that the cornerstone of his new government "rested upon the great truth that the negro is not equal to the white man" — hence slavery was the Negro's natural and moral condition. Morse purportedly was not only replying to the criticisms of a Poughkeepsie friend, but also to an attack upon him in the New York *Evening Post* written by David Dudley Field (1805–1894), a lawyer famous for his efforts to codify both municipal and international law. Field, long an anti-slavery Democrat, was a Republican during the Civil War.]

LETTER FROM EDWARD N. CROSBY, ESQ.

Troy, Feb. 25th, 1863.

Prof. S. F. B. Morse:

My Dear and Respected Sir: I have read with deep interest the letter in the N. Y. Evening *Post* of the 19th inst., addressed to you by Mr. D. D. Field. Its general tenor harmonizes with views which I have long coveted the privilege of expressing to you, but which have been repressed by a constitutional feeling of respect for eminence and seniority, and a fear of even seeming officiously to intrude. But, as Mr. Field suggests, your fame has become a national inheritance, and this alike is a motive and an apology for a jealous care on the part of your fellow-citizens as to aught that may impair its lustre. It is the omissions, however, rather than the contents of Mr. Field's sensible and temperate letter that prompt me to speak. While appealing to you on many high grounds, still he fails to reach the highest from which the subject is to be viewed. And I trust it is not assuming too much for one who is not only an admiring fellow-countryman and a near neighbor, but also a Christian friend, to discuss this matter with you from the Christian's stand-point. And what, may I ask, appears to you the sufficient reason for a Christian citizen to ally himself with others, for the extreme and radical purpose of undermining or paralyzing the power of the Government at a crisis when unanimity of support is so plainly essential, not only to the welfare but to the very life of the nation?

There are many, alas! who from ignorance or passion, persistently confound all the immense party, which came into being and into power only on the grand purpose of resisting Southern aggression, with the extremest radicalism and infidelity of the Garrison stamp. They would thus justify themselves in an indiscriminate and reckless hostility to the policy of the Government. I can, of course, find in this fact no explanation of the deliberate action of one of your principles and intelligence. Some may say that "the war on our part is unrighteous and, therefore, unworthy of support." But the rebels began it. To this it may be said: "The provocations offered them were such as greatly to diminish if not remove their criminality in thus beginning it." These assertions, though easily refuted, might require a discussion both long and foreign somewhat to my purpose. But it may be said that "the war though righteous is waged by unrighteous methods, such as confiscation and more particularly emancipation." If, however, it is a legitimate function of our Government to destroy the fabric of the Southern Confederacy, *à fortiori*, is it not justified in removing that which their own highest authorities pronounce to be the *cornerstone* of that fabric? Moreover, though this position is as palpably untenable as the two previously stated, yet supposing it to be a sincere Christian conviction, inasmuch as these methods must be objected to rather as inexpedient than as morally and legally unjustifiable, should not another Christian conviction, that of duty to the "powers that are ordained of God," prevent any disposition to resist or thwart the Government? But I would fain suppose that rather than either of the above, the grounds of your political views and action have been an earnest desire for peace, and an abomination of war, and its attendant horrors. In both of these feelings I claim the fullest sympathy with you, and yet I can not possibly construct upon them a fulcrum for unfriendly action against our Government.

I have seen in the progress of events much to criticise and regret in the Administration, but I feel assured that as far at least as our President is concerned, the errors have been those of the judgment, and are compatible with a pure integrity and a high-toned patriotism. Horrible too as war is, we are to remember that it may yet be a worthy means to a worthy end. God has certainly in his word more directly and repeatedly given his sanction to it, than he has to slavery. But what is the legitimate, the inevitable tendency of such unfriendly demonstrations as those to which you were persuaded to give countenance at Delmonico's, and which have had a fuller but natural development in Connecticut and elsewhere? We are not left to theories for a reply. Facts show that while the rebel leaders insultingly spurn all pusillanimous overtures of conciliation, they also exult over them as evidences of divided counsels and increasing feebleness at the North. They are thereby emboldened to declare themselves utterly implacable, except by success in their own ruinous plans. What then should be our necessary logic, our irresistible inference? Certainly patriotism and a wise appreciation of the worthy end and the abundant means committed to us would decide at once. Let us by united and courageous effort show the rebels that their success is perfectly hopeless. May I venture to speak a word also as to the "*personnel*" in these matters? Mr. Field says that he knows personally nearly all of those who were associated with you at Delmonico's, and implies very plainly that they borrowed from your presence a respectability for which they could make no becoming return. It was on a previous public occasion, that I saw, with no slight regret, your good name published, as appearing on the same platform with the characterless —— , the infamous —— , and the pitiable ———. Can it be that the purest and most patriotic measures draw to their advocacy such persons, while they fail to attract the innumerable host who dissent, and whose patriotism and probity you can not but heartily commend?

The high estimate I have formed of your Christian character, confirmed and increased by my intercourse with ———, has encouraged me to speak with the more freedom, and with the hope that it will be received in the same kindly spirit which has prompted it.

Yours most sincerely and respectfully,

EDWARD N. CROSBY.

PROF. MORSE'S REPLY.

NEW-YORK, March 2d, 1863.

MY DEAR SIR: Yours of the 25th of February is received, and I take in good part, what you say, written, however, wholly under misconception of my opinions, my position, and the objects for which the Society for the Diffusion of Political Knowledge has been organized. I know from your estimable character that your intention and motives were of the most benevolent kind in addressing me, and in reply, I shall make a few remarks, I trust in the same kindly spirit, while on the subjects you introduce I use perfect plainness of speech.

Your letter touches on many topics, upon some of which I have, for years, bestowed much study, and it may be that a frank discussion of them at a time when the public mind is alive to such discussions, may be useful in eliciting truth. Fundamental difference of opinion is often more seeming than real, perhaps from the inherent imperfection of language itself, in conveying our real thoughts to another's mind, or through some defect of intellect or education in not using perspicuous language. If due weight were given to a consideration of this kind, there would be less of that asperity of remark upon others' misconceptions, which in this day of excitement deforms the popular style. Mere difference of opinion, honestly entertained, is entitled to that forbearance which is denied to brazen-faced, persistent falsehood.

I can account for your [view?] of the purpose of our Society, as well as of many other topics upon which you have written, only on the presumption that you ground your remarks on the assumed truth of the egregiously false and impudent representations of an unprincipled reporter of the *Evening Post*. If this was the source of your information, you might as well look for truth respecting Bible doctrine, from Voltaire or Thomas Paine. Are you not aware that the pretended report of the incipient meeting at Delmonico's which led to the formation of our Society, is a tissue of falsehoods from beginning to end, exposed and refuted in numerous journals? Of how many falsehoods, persistently repeated, must a journal be convicted before its statement of facts shall be received with suspicion? I need not say to you that the admission into the *Evening Post* of such a grossly abusive report, while entertaining as I have hitherto, for its senior editor, so much personal respect, (however much I may differ from him politically,) is a source of deep mortification to me.

MR. FIELD'S LETTER.

Mr. Field's letter addressed to me was probably indited under the influence of impressions made by that same infamous report, and while I have no complaint of want of courtesy on his part towards me personally, I saw nothing in its general tenor of sufficient importance to require any answer from me. Though addressed to me, it was evidently addressed to the public through me, and I was used only as a convenient mode of addressing the public. So far as any thing he said required notice, that notice was taken of it by several journals. I enclose you clippings from two which happen to be at hand. Whatever personal regard I have for Mr. Field and for his highly respectable family connections, the state of the country compels me to waive all consideration of social relations, in treating of its political condition. His views and mine on the subject of the policy of the Administration are antipodal, and in view of his reported action in the Peace Congress, in connection with some of his radical associates, to which action can be traced the present awful condition of the country, since it was in their power (if I have been rightly advised) to have averted the war, I cannot but look upon his and their political course as laying upon them a weight of responsibility which I would not have upon my conscience for a thousand worlds.

CHRISTIAN STAND-POINT.

You desire "to discuss the subject from the Christian's stand-point." I accede to this the more readily since that is precisely the stand-point from which I have always endeavored to view the whole field of controversy. On Bible truth, therefore, I am ready to plant every position I take.

Did it not lead me into too long a discussion for a letter like this, a discussion starting from a point too far back, even from fundamental theological principles, I should like to establish with you this stand-point impregnably on the Bible. This will have to be done ere the perverted Christian mind of the country can be disabused of the ruinous fallacies which have turned aside the incumbents of so many pulpits from their legitimate duty of allaying the fierce passions of men, through the tranquillizing influences of the gospel of peace, and changed them into impassioned political orators, whose exasperating harangues have added fuel to the already raging fires of a ferocious and desolating fanaticism.[1] Such a discussion, important as it is, must be in abeyance.

I proceed to answer your question: "What appears to you the sufficient reason for a Christian citizen to ally himself with others for the extreme and radical purpose of undermining or paralyzing the power of the Government at a crisis when unanimity of support is so plainly essential not only to the welfare but to the very life of the nation?"

---

[1] "*Politics* and the *pulpit* are terms that have little agreement. No sound ought to be heard in the church but the healing voice of Christian charity. The cause of *civil liberty* and *civil Government* gains as little as that of *religion*, by this confusion of duties. Those who quit their proper character to assume what does not belong to them, are, for the greater part, ignorant both of the character they leave and of the character they assume. Wholly unacquainted with the world in which they are so fond of meddling, and inexperienced in all its affairs, on which they pronounce with so much confidence, *they have nothing of politics but the passions they excite.* Surely the church is a place where one day's truce ought to be allowed to the dissensions and animosities of mankind." — BURKE: *Reflections on French Revolution,* vol. i. p. 460.

"I have something also to the *divines,* though brief, to what were needful, not to be *disturbers of the civil affairs;* being in hands better able, and more belonging, to manage them; but to study harder, and to attend the office of good pastors, knowing that he whose flock is least among them has a dreadful charge, not performed by mounting twice into the pulpit with a formal preachment huddled up at the odd hours of a whole lazy week, but by incessant pains and watching, in season and out of season, from house to house, over the souls whom they have to feed. Which, if they well considered how little leisure would they find to be *the most pragmatical sidesmen of every popular tumult and sedition.*" — MILTON: *Treatise on Tenure of Kings,* etc.

GOVERNMENT AND ADMINISTRATION.

I will analyze the component parts of your question. You assume, without any warrant, that my purpose is to "undermine and paralyze the power of the Government." You appear to have fallen into the prevalent error of confounding the *Government* with the *Administration* of the Government. You are too sensible not to see that they are not the same. The word *Government* has indeed two meanings, and in order to rescue the subject from ambiguity allow me to say that the ordinary meaning of Government, in free countries, is, that form of fundamental *rules* and *principles* by which a nation or state is governed, or by which *individual members* of a body politic are to *regulate their action.* Government is in fact a *Constitution* by which the rights and duties both of *citizens* and *public officers* are *prescribed* and *defined.* If the word sometimes has a secondary or more limited meaning synonymous with *Administration* of public affairs, then *"the Government"* is metonymically used for *Administration,* and should not be confounded with the original and true signification of the term *Administration,* which means the *persons collectively* who are intrusted with the execution of the laws, and with the superintendence of public affairs.

Opposition to the *Administration* then, is not opposition to the *Government;* the former may not only be utterly destroyed without affecting the health of the Government, but it may be, and constantly is, thought to be necessary, in the opinion of the supreme power, *the People,* to destroy the Administration in order to preserve the life of the Government. This is in accordance not only with the theory of our institutions, but with the daily practice of the people. Every change of Administration at every election, Federal, State, or municipal, great or small, exemplifies this great truth. The Government remains intact, unscathed, while the Administration is swept out of existence.

In the light of this explication, you must perceive that so far from "allying myself with others for the purpose of undermining and paralyzing the power of the Government," the very purpose of our Society is to uphold and strengthen the Government, by diffusing among the people, such a knowledge of the principles upon which it is founded, that it shall not be in the power of any Administration, whether weak or wicked, to work its injury.

I yield to no man, in hearty *loyalty to the Government,* nor in obedience also to the Administration in all its *constitutional* measures, whatever may be my private opinion of their wisdom. You mistake me if you suppose I have any "radical purpose of undermining or paralyzing" any of its legal measures. If I think them unwise, I shall use my constitutional liberty to say so, and if the Administration transcends the power intrusted to it by the People, I shall endeavor to point out their error, not in a contumacious or unkind spirit, but nevertheless firmly. To the standard of the *Constitution, and the Union* under it, of all the United States I shall cling as the only *political* hope of the country, our only defence against anarchy and despotism.

WHAT MUST WE SUPPORT?

But you say "unanimity of support is essential to the very life of the nation." Support of what? Laws and acts subversive of the Government? Laws and acts in direct and palpable contravention of the Constitution? Laws and acts outside of the Constitution? Where in the fundamental law of the Government, the Constitution, does the President, one of the administrators of the Supreme Law, find his authority for his *emancipation proclamation?* Where for his usurpation of the power to suspend the *habeas corpus?* Where for the confiscation acts? Where for his authority to arrest and incarcerate citizens? These are all acts of the *Administration,* not of the *Government;* they are acts subversive of the Government; acts that are "paralyzing and undermining" the Government; acts that are dividing the people of the North, alarming them for the safety of the Constitution, the Government, and arousing them to call their servants, the Administrators, to account.

It is on such a confounding of terms as this, of *government* and *administration,* that you charge "extreme and radical purposes" upon those who rally in support of the Government.

NECESSITY FOR OUR SOCIETY.

You must excuse me, dear sir, if I say that your letter, to so great an extent based upon the popular fallacies of the day, is itself a proof of the necessity of just such a Society as we have formed; because if minds like yours, intelligent, reflective, ingenuous, and conscientious, are so much at fault on the fundamental principles of our institutions, what must be inferred of the minds of others less intelligent, who imbibe their opinions, and mould their actions, from the prejudiced and befogged intellects controlling the fanatical avenues to public opinion?

CHARACTER OF ABOLITIONISM.

By the manner in which you allude to the "extreme radicalism and infidelity of the Garrison stamp," I am glad to find we have a common stand-point from which to view a portion of the field. Look at that dark conclave of conspirators, freedom-shriekers, Bible-spurners, fierce, implacable, headstrong, denunciatory, Constitution and Union haters, noisy, factious, breathing forth threatenings and slaughter against all who venture a difference of opinion from them, murderous, passionate advocates of imprisonments and hangings, bloodthirsty, and if there is any other epithet of atrocity found in the vocabulary of wickedness, do they not every one fitly designate some phase of radical abolitionism?

DISTINCTION BETWEEN ABOLITIONISTS AND REPUBLICANS IMPOSSIBLE.

But you would have us make a distinction between these "radicals and infidels of the Garrison stamp," and the "immense party which," as you say, "came into being and into power only on the grand purpose of resisting Southern aggression."

Waiving the question you raise of the existence of any *Southern Aggression,* (previous to the last Presidential Election,) making resistance necessary on the part of the North, I ask you how can any distinction be made, between parties in close alliance, carrying out together and sustaining the same policy? Did not the Republican party, (in whose ranks I recognize many excellent, intelligent, conscientious men,) did not, I say, that party, in the full consciousness of the diabolical character of that "radical and infidel" faction, form a political alliance with it for the purpose of obtaining the power which they now hold? The expectation in forming the coalition was doubtless that you would be able to control the numerically smaller wing of the alliance. You thought this possible; I did not. So soon as it was apparent that such an alliance had been formed, I predicted that the abolition wing would control the whole; and if the party thus formed were successful, the hopes of the country for Peace and Union would be wrecked; for it is the very nature of fanaticism to leaven the whole lump. Was I not right? I ask you now to look at the state of the country. Is it not true that the abolition element has acquired the control of that "immense party" of which you speak? Are you not advocating and supporting the abolition policy of the Administration? Is it not true that these very "radicals and infidels of the Garrison stamp," whom you justly loathe, have framed and passed the most offensive abolition measures that tinge the whole policy of the Administration? So notorious is this fact, that to ask is to answer the question. These then, are the men with whom I find you affiliated. May I not appropriately quote your own question, and ask: "Can it be that the purest and most patriotic measures draw to their advocacy such persons, while they fail to attract the innumerable host who dissent," etc.? But I will not do you the injustice thus to judge you by the standard by which you would judge me, for your standard is defective. Every one of any experience in political movements is aware that on both sides, in party excitements, there is every possible variety of character associating together, not because of other or general affinities, but for the single purpose of carrying a common measure, in which all feel more or less interest. Their several interests in that common measure may be as diverse as possible; some from high principle, some for the triumph of an opinion, some to obtain office, some to obtain money. It is not, therefore, safe to characterize a cause by the character of some few who may be loud and forward in advocating it. Bad men may promote a good cause for bad ends. It is safest to judge of a cause on its own merits.

EMANCIPATION PROCLAMATION AND THE CORNER-STONE.

I am sorry to find you defending the President's *emancipation proclamation*. It is a measure which I have considered from the moment of its promulgation, unwise, unconstitutional and calamitous, productive of evil and only evil, a measure that, more than any other, has tended to divide the counsels of the North, and unite the South, and render the restoration of the national Union next to hopeless. Your defense of it rests on a fallacy. You say "If it is a legitimate function of our Government to destroy the fabric of the Southern Confederacy, *à fortiori*, is it not justified in removing that which their own highest authorities pronounce to be its *corner-stone?*" To answer your question intelligently, it is necessary to know the nature of that *corner-stone,* before we can pronounce whether the Government would be justified in removing or attempting to remove it. If the stone should happen to be a *providential fixture,* unalterable in its very nature by any thing that man can do, a condition of a *physical character,* not to be affected by any act of man, you will agree with me, that the Government would not be justified in making any such necessarily abortive and quixotic attempt. I presume from your question you have adopted the prevalent misunderstanding of a passage in Mr. Stephens's speech at Savannah, in which he speaks of the *corner-stone* of the Confederate Government. You assume that this corner-stone is *slavery,* and so our Government is justified in its measures to destroy slavery. Although a great multitude both in Europe and America entertain this stereotyped error, and it has within a few days been twice reiterated in the late non-intervention report of the Senate Committee of Foreign Relations, yet it is none the less an egregious misapprehension of Mr. Stephens's remark, and a false assumption that the Confederate Government has adopted any such corner-stone. In the first place if Mr. Stephens had made such an announcement in his speech, (which he has not,) that would not constitute law for the Government. We do not look for the authority of the fundamental law of a government in a casual speech of any members of its administration, not even from the President, but in the fundamental law itself, in its written officially accepted Constitution. Now, there is not one word in the Constitution of the Confederacy that gives color to any such idea as slavery being the corner-stone of the Government; on the contrary, Section IX. Article I. clearly repudiates it. For if slavery is the adopted corner-stone of their Government, common-sense suggests, that in their fundamental law they would and should use every effort to strengthen and support it, and yet they forbid in that section and article that very policy which would give strength and permanency to such a corner-stone. Mr. Stephens, however, *has made no such declaration,* yet he is quoted every where as the source whence this wide-spread erroneous apothegm has proceeded. It may be well to ventilate this matter more thoroughly.

THE CORNER-STONE IS THE INEQUALITY OF THE TWO RACES.

Let us learn what Mr. Stephens actually did say. His language is this: "The foundations of our new Government are laid, its corner-stone rests upon" — what? slavery? no, "upon the *great truth* that *the negro is not equal to the white man,* that slavery" which he then defines to be, "subordination to the superior race, is his natural and moral condition. This our new Government is the first in the history of the world based upon this great physical, philosophical, and moral truth." This language could not be applied to slavery. It would be a strange misapplication of terms to call slavery a physical, philosophical and moral truth. He had just been stating to his hearers that the ideas prevalent at the time our Federal Constitution was formed "rested upon the assumption of the *equality of the races.*" This proposition he declares to be unsound, and that the new Government was founded upon exactly the opposite idea. The error on one side which he combats is *the assumed equality of the races.* The opposite truth which he propounds is the physical, philosophical and moral truth, that *the two races are not equal,* and the inference he draws from this truth is that this physical difference determines the *status* of the inferior race. I confess I can not see how to escape that conclusion, except by denying the *inequality* of the races; by denying that there is this *physical differ-ence* between them, for if there is this difference, then one race of necessity is superior, and the other inferior, and if the two *physically unequal* races are compelled to live together in the same community, the superior must govern the inferior. Can you avoid this conclusion?

THE CORNER-STONE CAN NOT BE REMOVED.

What prospect of success then is there, of any attempt to remove such a corner-stone? Who has constituted the two races physically different? There can be but one answer, it is God. To attempt, therefore, a removal of this corner-stone, which infinite wisdom has laid in the fabric of human society, is of so presumptuous a char-acter, that few should be rash enough to undertake it. The *physical inequality of the races* then is this corner-stone, and not Slavery. Slavery, which is a *Government,* must be, in some form, the necessary resultant of this fact, and if you can remove the corner-stone, to wit, the *physical inequality of the races,* you may thus destroy slavery; but since the "Ethiopian can not change his skin," nor can any earthly power do it for him, so long as the two races exist together in the same community, you may change the master, or the relative position of the races, but one or the other will still be dominant. Slavery in America can only be abolished by *separating the races.* Is it worth while to attempt to remove a corner-stone which God has laid?

The reasoning of Mr. Stephens has an apposite parallel in the reasoning of the elder Adams, on the Theory of Government, as given in his "Life by his grandson, C. F. Adams, the accomplished representative of our Government to the Court of St. James.

"Unlike most speculators on *the theory of Governments,* Mr. Adams begins by assuming *the imperfection of man's nature,* and introducing it at once as an element with which to compose his edifice.

"He finds *the human race impelled by their passions* as often as guided by their reason, sometimes led to good actions by scarcely corresponding motives, and sometimes to bad ones rather from inability to resist temptation than from natural propensity to evil. This is the *Corner-stone* of his system."

Let us put Mr. Adams' theory in the language of Mr. Stephens. "The foundations of Civil Government are laid, its corner-stone rests upon the great truth that *man has an imperfect nature,* that *the human race is impelled by their passions,* that, therefore, *subordination* of the *inferior* to the *superior,* inherent in the very nature of Government, is man's natural and moral condition. Civil Government is based upon this great physical, philosophical and moral truth." Would it be just to accuse Mr. Adams of basing Government on *Slavery,* as the corner-stone, because he admits the necessity of the *subordination* of *the inferior to the superior?* In other words, to make him utter the absurdity, that *"Government is the corner-stone of Government"?*

PRESIDENT LINCOLN AND MR. STEPHENS

PROCLAIM THE SAME CORNER-STONE.

Perhaps you may think I have adopted Southern views on this point, and that the inequality and physical differences of the two races are altogether Southern dogmas. I need not cross the Potomac to find the same great truth proclaimed in a quarter entitled to respect, and by one who politically outranks the Vice-President of the Confederacy, to wit, the President of the United States.

You will recollect the interview, on August fourteenth, 1862, between a committee of colored men and President Lincoln, invited by him, to hear what he had to say to them. His object in summoning them before him was to persuade them to *emigrate,* and he bases his argument to them on the very corner-stone declared by Mr. Stephens, to wit, the physical difference or inequality of the two races. President Lincoln's plan was to *separate the races.*

"You and we," said he to them, "are different races. We have between us a *broader difference* than exists between almost any other two races. Whether it is right or wrong, I need not discuss, but this *physical difference* is a great disadvantage to us both, as I think. Your race are suffering, in my judgment, the greatest wrong inflicted on any people. But even when you cease to be slaves, you are far from being placed on an equality with the white race. On this broad continent not a single man of your race is made the equal of a single man of ours. Go where you are treated the best, and the ban is still upon you. I do not propose to discuss this, but to present it as a *fact* with which we have to deal. I can not alter it if I would. It is a *fact* about which we all feel and think alike, I and you."

THEIR DIFFERENT MODES OF DEALING WITH THE CORNER-STONE.

Thus you perceive that both President Lincoln and Mr. Stephens are in perfect accord in accepting and acting upon the same great truth. President Lincoln accepts the *physical inequality* of the two races, as completely as Mr. Stephens, for where there is a *broader difference* than exists between almost any other two races, it would be absurd to say they are *equal,* especially when the President justly adds that this difference is *physical,* that is, grounded in the original constitution of each race. The only difference between the President of the United States and Mr. Stephens is in the use to which they put this physical, philosophical and moral truth, this corner-stone. Mr. Stephens proposes it in his Savannah speech, as the basis of the new government; Mr. Lincoln adopts it as the basis of his plan of separating the races, because of this physical difference.

Mr. Stephens takes the stone, as a whole, upon which he would construct a government. Mr. Lincoln would split the stone and drag the parts asunder. Mr. Stephens accepts the fact and adjusts his fabric to it. Mr. Lincoln also accepts the fact, and is perplexed with inextricable difficulties in his attempts to dispose of the two portions of the common corner-stone.

THE PRESIDENT'S PERPLEXITIES IN DEALING WITH THE CORNER-STONE.

It is well to notice these perplexities of the President's mind as they are manifested in his singular interview with this colored delegation. The great truth of the physical difference of the two races is so palpable that he can not controvert it, and he frankly declines to make the attempt, yet, while accepting the fact, he more than doubts the wisdom of the fact itself by raising the singular question of *right and wrong* upon its existence, and thus (no doubt unconsciously) impugns the wisdom of the Creator, for who but God could ordain a *physical* difference in the two races? The raising of the question, therefore, whether a *physical* fact is "right or wrong," as if there were two sides to such a question, directly implicates the wisdom of the Creator. The President, too, while declining to discuss this question of right and wrong, actually decides it to be wrong, by declaring it to be a "disadvantage to both" races, in his opinion. The plain good sense of most of the remarks of the President in this interview, and the collisions of thought in his own breast which he discloses, where truths and doubts come into constant conflict, point to some great radical disturbing error, not in the President's mind alone, but pervading the popular mind on the subject of African slavery every where.

THE GREAT ERROR OF THE WORLD ON SLAVERY.

The great fallacy, so rife throughout the world, that *slavery is the cause of our national troubles,* rests on the almost universal persistent closing of the eyes to this fact of the physical difference between the two races. Slavery is not the cause of the sectional war, but a blind and mad resistance to a physical condition which God has ordained and which man is, in vain, attempting to subvert.

THE CORNER-STONE DULY ACKNOWLEDGED,
SOLVES THE VEXED QUESTION OF SLAVERY.

Take your stand on this great acknowledged fact that the African and white races are physically different, follow out this truth to its logical result, and the question of slavery, or subordination of the inferior to the superior race, is clearly solved in all its phases.

Do you ask how?

First: We must accept as a fixed fact that ordinance of God which he has decreed, that the two races are *physically different,* and not complicate the fact, with any modifications, drawn from the prevalent visionary, infidel notions of an *equality* which has no existence, nor make any vain attempt to fix upon the mere relation of superior and inferior, or of rulers and ruled, moral or religious qualities which God in his word has not fixed to the relation.

Second: We must leave to each and every State in the Union where the two races exist together, whether in larger or smaller proportions, unmolested control over any adjustment of their relations to each other.

Third: In the kindly spirit of the Fathers of 1787, which they brought to the construction of our priceless Constitution, we should refrain from embittering the relations of the two races by an irritating busybodyism, a meddlesome interference with the manner in which the duties belonging to their relation to each other are or are not fulfilled, and taking the Apostle's counsel "to be quiet and mind our own business."

These three directions carried out in a Christian spirit faithfully, would restore the Union on the only basis on which it can ever be restored. Whether enlightened reason can make its voice heard in this din of warring passions and interests, so that its "Peace be still," can calm the storm that is desolating us, is a question I will not pretend to answer. It is to the true, sober, Christian sentiment of the country when disenthralled from its entanglement with the delusive socialistic and infidel theories of the day, that we look with any hope for our national salvation.

I have dwelt at some length on this one point because of its paramount importance. It is a noticeable and gratifying circumstance that our President and the Vice-President of the Southern government are in accord on a fundamental principle. Union of opinion on one point, especially if that point be fundamental, is hopeful, and prophetic of further conciliation, perhaps pacification in the future. The great *physical* fact of the *broad difference* of the African and white races, which the President so justly and openly recognizes, lies at the root of the whole controversy respecting slavery. Let us, then, study the condition of things resulting from this truth in the light of an intelligent Christian philosophy, not viewing it through the distorted medium of Abolition spectacles, but with the clear vision of an eye spiritually enlightened, and a temper of heart which accepts a Providential fact with humility, recognizing the highest wisdom in all God's ordinances, however mysterious to us, endeavoring to adapt our ways to his facts, not his facts to our ways. In that temper of heart you will clearly discern that this providential arrangement of conditions in human society has for its end a purpose of infinite and eternal good to both races, a purpose clearly discerned in the light of gospel truth, but wholly obscured in the smoke with which a proud but shallow infidel philosophy, a false Christianity, and pretentious humanitarianism have enshrouded the whole subject.

PROBABLE ENGLISH INTRIGUE TO PREVENT RE-UNION.

One word on your remark that the South "spurns all overtures of conciliation." When, where, and by whom have any overtures been made[;] where, and by whom have they been spurned? If you take the intemperate speeches, the passionate flings in editorial and anonymous articles, in the Southern journals, as the exponents of the real sentiments of the Southern masses, are these the safe bases upon which to found your remarks? If so, by parity of reasoning, the Southern masses should take the "radical and infidel" ravings of the "Garrison stamp" which are their counterpart in the speeches, editorials, and anonymous articles of our newspapers. We have been accustomed to condemn the South for its false judgment of Northern sentiment, because formed from just such radical sources. These are very unsafe sources of information on each side in exciting times like these, on which to found intersectional sentiment. Let me hint at one latent danger from relying on such undiplomatic sources of information. Glance for a moment at the attitude of England towards the United States. We there see two well-defined parties, neither of them friendly to us as a nation, one the cotton interest siding with the South, and the other her abolition coteries siding with the North, and so, England, balancing herself adroitly between these two parties in her own island, safe from any dangerous collision between them, harmful to herself, through her administration can give aid in our deplorable strife to the one section or to the other, or to both, to prevent conciliation, as best may serve the great political purpose of England, *the permanent Division of the United States.* Keeping within the bounds of a quasi-neutrality, England can, on the one hand, furnish the South with munitions of war, and privateers to prey on Northern commerce, and on the other can get up abolition demonstrations at Exeter Hall and elsewhere, to strengthen and encourage the fanatical element of the North, as the vicissitudes of our unnatural war, manifest, in the one or the other section, any abatement of that ferocity of hate which she has for so long a period engendered and sedulously promoted as the sure means of accomplishing her political purpose of *permanent separation.*[2] Is it an unreasonable supposition that English emis-

[2] Let me ask your attentive reflection upon such indications of English designs and desires as the following. In an able article on the American Revolution, in the *Edinburgh Review* of Oct., 1862, the reviewer says: "We therefore say, without hesitation, that we wish the war to cease, and the *independence of the South to be established.*"

Lord Campbell, in the House of Lords on the 4th of August, 1862, said: "It is not too much to say that *no class* or *party* in the country any longer desires to see the reconquest of the South and the *reconstruction of the Union.*" The reviewer says: "At the outset of the struggle the tendency was strong in England to side with the North. On the other hand, *many felt undoubted satisfaction at the breaking up of that great democratic Government, whose institutions had been held up to them by their own reformers as a model of perfection,*" etc. The reviewer puts the question: "Is it the interest of the civilized world, and *especially of our own country* (England), that the American Union should be restored?" And he answers it by saying: "It can scarcely be said that the relations of the *American Union* to Europe, *and to England in particular,* have been so satisfactory *as to make us anxious for its continuance.*"

Further on he says: "The feeling in England is not founded on a desire of vengeance or personal retribution on any one, for insults which we have received. It rests on a much more *calm* and *rational* basis — that is to say, on the conviction *that the unity of the Government at Washington alone made the blow tell; it is hoped that when that unity is gone,* all insults of the kind, if not so impolitic as to be avoided altogether, *will at least be harmless,* and of *no consequence to England.*" In another place: "The independence of the South *would open new markets for our manufactures,* without the previous restrictions of *Federal tariffs.*

These extracts, from the most intelligent exponents of public opinion in England, could be multiplied to any extent. I give one or two only from the *North British Re-*

saries at the South, supported from the "secret service fund," are the authors of those assumed spurnings of conciliatory overtures which you look upon as coming from the Southern heart? While this supposition, natural in the light of her past history, is not only *possible* but *probable*, I need better evidence than has yet appeared that the Southern masses, the great conservative body of the Southern people are really Disunionists. There is evidence on the contrary, that Union sentiment exists in the South, and would show its existence and activity, were it not stifled by the *unconstitutional* means which Northern, in alliance with English abolitionism, have brought to bear, to kill it.

I stop rather abruptly, possibly to my disadvantage, for I am compelled to leave untouched points perhaps necessary to prevent misapprehension. There is, however, a sentence in your letter, which I can not pass unnoticed, grounded, it appears, upon a remark of Mr. Field, casting an imputation upon the respectability and purity of intention of those associated with me in the effort to diffuse political knowledge. What Mr. Field may have said under the influence of that mendacious report of the *Post*, or what he may think of their characters, becomes of consequence only through your reïteration of his opinion. I notice it, therefore, (since you are in actual ignorance as well of the persons who were present, as of their social and moral position,) to say that neither could their respectability be enhanced, nor my own diminished by my association with them. I can not close without thanking you for your frank letter

---

view of February, 1862: "Most Englishmen, and ourselves among the number, have arrived at the conclusion, not only that the Secessionists *will* succeed in their enterprise, but that *this success will,* eventually *be of the most signal service to humanity, to civilization, and to the cause of universal and enduring peace.*"

Again: "We entertain, then, no doubt that the *dissolution of the Union* is an *accomplished and irreversible fact,* and one of the very *greatest* facts of our day. We can see *no grounds* on which the *continuance of that Union should be desired by any wise or good man.*"

Again: "That the independence of the South and *the dissolution of the great Republic* are accomplished and irreversible facts, seems to us undeniable. *The nation* founded by Washington *is severed* — the *Union* contrived by his wisdom, and consecrated by his name, is *at an end.* We have now to ask what beauty there was in it that we should have longed for its continuance? What sacred purpose did it serve that we should deplore its end?"

These are specimens only indicating the bias of English sentiment, and showing that the English Government looks with exultation on the success of its plot of dividing our Union. Is this then the time for *persistence in unconstitutional* acts which must inevitably create further rendings and divisions?

and expressions of neighborly and friendly interest, which I cordially reciprocate.

Truly, with respect and high personal esteem, your friend and neighbor,

SAMUEL F. B. MORSE.

Pamphlet 27

Henry Carey Baird

General Washington and General Jackson
on Negro Soldiers. (Union League, No. 3)

Philadelphia, 1863

[Following the promulgation of the Emancipation Proclamation, Republicans in the North pressed strongly against a reluctant public opinion for the enlistment of Negroes in the Union army. In the earlier stages of the war there had been much resistance to the use of Negro troops; even President Lincoln thought it would be "productive of more evil than good." As the need for men became acute in 1862, several commanders began on their own initiative to enroll Negroes; in August, 1862, the War Department sanctioned Negro troops. President Lincoln authorized their use in his final Emancipation Proclamation and by March, 1863, had come to regard them as "very important, if not indispensable." Nevertheless there remained considerable Northern prejudice against their use. In 1862, George Livermore (1809–1865), a wool merchant and book collector, wrote a lengthy research paper demonstrating that a large number of the founders of the republic had favored the emancipation of slaves and the use of Negroes as soldiers. He read the paper before the Massachusetts Historical Society and published it as a 184-page pamphlet under the imprint of the New England Loyal Publication Society. Livermore included much data on the service of Negroes in the Revolutionary Army, and as an appendix printed General Andrew Jackson's proclamation praising the Negro troops who had fought in the Battle of New Orleans. Other publication societies made frequent use of the quotations in Livermore's paper in numerous pamphlets citing precedents for the use of Negroes and hailing their heroic exploits. Thus Henry Carey Baird (1825–1912), a publisher and writer on economics, assembled a pamphlet for the Union League, quoting Generals Washington, Jackson, and Nathaniel P. Banks. He included a poem hailing the bravery of Negro troops, "The Second Louisiana" by George Henry Boker (1823–1890), secretary of the Union League, a playwright especially known for his *Francesca da Rimini*, and a writer of lyric verse.[1]]

---

[1] [Randall and Donald, *Civil War and Reconstruction*, 391–395; George Livermore, *An Historical Research Respecting the Opinions of the Founders of the Republic on*

WE are in the midst of a great war for the existence of free institutions.

No one can be so blind as not to see that the triumph of the Confederacy would insure the overthrow of rational liberty.

In the heart of the Rebel States there exist four millions of an oppressed race, who would gladly aid us in the war we are carrying on, but from regard to the feelings and interests of our enemies we have hitherto refused their assistance.

That we should have hesitated so long to accept and secure the cooperation of these people, shows a degree of forbearance unequalled in history.

There certainly does exist at this time a strong prejudice in the minds of many against employing Negroes as soldiers, but the following extracts from authentic documents will show that this prejudice is unfounded, and that our wisest and best men, our bravest and most patriotic generals, our Washington, and our Jackson, did not hesitate to solicit, to employ, and to reward the military services of Negroes in the War of the Revolution, and again, within the memory of many of us, in our last war with England.

If our fathers in 1812, and our grandfathers in 1776, did not hesitate to put muskets into the hands of Negroes, why should we? If Washington and Jackson thought it no disgrace to lead Negroes to battle, why should any officer now hesitate to follow their example?

George Livermore, Esq., has lately published "An Historical Research respecting the Opinions of the Founders of the Republic on Negroes as Slaves, as Citizens, and as Soldiers." As its size and scarcity prevents its general circulation, the following extracts have been taken from his work to bring the views of our ancestors relative to the policy of Negro enlistments before the public.

Bancroft in his History of the United States, vol. vii., p. 421, speaking of the Battle of Bunker Hill, says: "Nor should history forget to record, that as in the army at Cambridge, so also in this gallant band, the free Negroes of the colony had their representatives. For the right of free Negroes to bear arms in the public

---

Negroes as Slaves, as Citizens, and as Soldiers (New England Loyal Publication Society, Boston, 1863). Cf., Anonymous, *Opinions of the Early Presidents and of the Fathers of the Republic, Upon Slavery, and Upon Negroes as Men and Soldiers* (Loyal Publication Society No. 18, New York, 1863).]

defence was at that day as little disputed in New England as their other rights. They took their places, not in a separate corps, but in the ranks with the white men; and their names may be read on the pension-rolls of the country, side by side with those of other soldiers of the Revolution."

Major Samuel Lawrence served through the war of the Revolution. "At one time he commanded a company whose rank and file were all Negroes, of whose courage, military discipline and fidelity he always spoke with respect. On one occasion, being out reconnoitering with this company, he got so far in advance of his command that he was surrounded, and on the point of being made prisoner by the enemy. The men, soon discovering his peril, rushed to his rescue, and fought with the most determined bravery till that rescue was effectually secured." — *Memoir of William Lawrence, by Rev. S. K. Lothrop, D.D., pp. 8, 9.*

On the 23d of October a Committee of Conference, "to consider the condition of the army, and to devise means for its improvement," agreed that Negro soldiers be rejected altogether. But notwithstanding this action of the Committee of Conference, Washington, on the 31st of December, 1775, wrote from Cambridge to the President of Congress as follows: — "It has been represented to me that the free Negroes who have served in this army are very much dissatisfied at being discarded. As it is to be apprehended that they may seek employ in the ministerial army, I have presumed to depart from the resolution respecting them, and have given license for their being enlisted. If this is disapproved of by Congress, I will put a stop to it." — *Sparks' Washington,* vol. iii., pp. 218, 219.

On the 16th of January, 1776, Congress decided "That the free Negroes, who have served faithfully in the army at Cambridge, may be re-enlisted therein, but no others." — *Journals of Congress,* vol. ii., p. 26.

General Thomas, in a letter to John Adams, says:

I am sorry to hear that any prejudices should take place in any southern colony with respect to the troops raised in this. I am certain the insinuations you mention are injurious, if we consider with what precipitation we were obliged to collect an army. In the regiments at Roxbury, the privates are equal to any that I served with in the last war; very few old men and in the ranks very few boys. Our fifers are many of them boys. We have some Negroes; but I look on them, in general, equally serviceable with other men for fatigue; and in action many of them have proved themselves brave.

I would avoid all reflection, or any thing that may tend to give umbrage; but there is in this army from the southward a number called riflemen, who are as indifferent men as I ever served with. These privates are mutinous, and often deserting to the enemy; unwilling for duty of any kind; exceedingly vicious; and I think the army here would be as well without as with them. But to do justice to their officers, they are, some of them, likely men. — *M. S. Letter, dated 24th October,* 1775.

The following is an extract from the journal of a Hessian officer, dated October 23d, 1777:

From here to Springfield, there are few habitations which have not a Negro family dwelling in a small house near by. The Negroes are here as fruitful as other cattle. The young ones are well foddered, especially while they are still calves.

Slavery is moreover very gainful. The Negro is to be considered just as the bond servant of a peasant. The Negress does all the coarse work of the house, and the little black young ones wait on the little white young ones. *The Negro can take the field instead of his master; and, therefore, no regiment is to be seen in which there are not Negroes in abundance; and among them are ablebodied, strong and brave fellows.* — *Schloezer's Briefwechsel,* vol. iv., p. 365.

We next give an extract from an act of the "*State of Rhode Island and Providence Plantations, in General Assembly. February Session,* 1778.

Whereas, for the preservation of the rights and liberties of the United States, it is necessary that the *whole powers of Government should be exerted* in recruiting the Continental battalions; and whereas His Excellency, Gen. Washington, hath inclosed to this State a proposal made to him by Brigadier-General Varnum, to enlist into the two battalions, raising by this State, such slaves as should be willing to enter into the service; and whereas history affords us frequent precedents of the *wisest,* the *freest,* and *bravest* nations having liberated their slaves and enlisted them as soldiers to fight in defence of their country; and also whereas, the enemy, with a great force, have taken possession of the Capitol and a great part of this State; and this State is obliged to raise a very considerable number of troops for its own immediate defence, whereby it is, in a manner, rendered impossible for this State to furnish recruits for the said two battalions without adopting the said measure so recommended:

"*It is Voted and Resolved,* That every able-bodied *Negro, Mullato,* or *Indian* man slave in this State, may enlist into either of the said two battalions, to serve during the continuance of the present war with Great Britain; that every slave so enlisting shall be entitled to and receive all the bounties, wages, and encouragements allowed by the Continental Congress to any soldier enlisting into their service.

"*It is further Voted and Resolved,* That every slave so enlisting, shall, upon his passing muster before Col. Christopher Green, be immediately discharged from the service of his master or mistress, and be absolutely FREE, as though he had never been incumbered with any kind of servitude or slavery."

The Negroes enlisted under this act were the men who immortalized themselves at Red Bank.

Arnold, in his "History of Rhode Island," vol. ii., pp. 427, 428, describing the "Battle of Rhode Island," fought August 29th, 1778, says: "A third time the enemy, with desperate courage and increased strength, attempted to assail the redoubt, and would have carried it, but for the timely aid of two Continental battalions despatched by Sullivan to support his almost exhausted troops. It was in repelling these furious onsets, that the newly raised *black regiment,* under Col. Green, distinguished itself by deeds of desperate valor. Posted behind a thicket in the valley, they three times drove back the Hessians, who charged repeatedly down the hill to dislodge them."

On March 29th, 1779, we find in the Secret Journals of Congress, vol. i., pp. 107–110:

Resolved, That it be recommended to the States of South Carolina and Georgia, if they shall think the same expedient, to take measures immediately for raising three thousand able-bodied Negroes.

That the said Negroes be formed into separate corps, as battalions, according to the arrangements adopted for the main army, to be commanded by white commissioned and non-commissioned officers.

After other provisions for their organization the last section provides, "That every Negro who shall well and faithfully serve as a soldier to the end of the present war, and shall then return his arms, *be emancipated,* and receive the sum of fifty dollars."

Washington, Hamilton, General Greene, General Lincoln, and Colonel John Laurens were warm friends of this measure.

That the "Mother of Statesmen" also enlisted Negroes during the War of the Revolution, and emancipated them for their services, is shown by the heading of a law passed by the General Assembly of Virginia, in 1783, entitled "*An Act directing the Emancipation of certain Slaves who have served as soldiers in this State, and for the emancipation of the slave Aberdeen.*" — *Hening's Statutes at Large of Virginia,* vol. xi., pp. 308, 309.

In the navy, Negroes have always been entered on the ship's books without any distinction. The following extract from a letter of Commodore Chauncey gives his views on this subject. "I regret that you are not pleased with the men sent you by Messrs. Champlin and Forrest; for to my knowledge a part of them are not surpassed by any seamen we have in the fleet; and I have yet to learn that the color of the skin, or the cut and trimmings of the coat, can affect a man's qualifications or usefulness. I have nearly fifty blacks on board of this ship, and many of them are among my best men."

In 1814 the State of New York passed "An Act to authorize the raising of two regiments of men of color; passed October 24, 1814."

In conclusion we offer the proclamation and address of General Andrew Jackson to the Negroes.

Headquarters 7th Military District.
MOBILE, *September* 21, 1814.
To THE FREE COLORED INHABITANTS OF LOUISIANA:

Through a mistaken policy you have heretofore been deprived of a participation in the glorious struggle for national rights in which our country is engaged. This no longer shall exist.

As sons of freedom, you are now called upon to defend our most inestimable blessing. As Americans, your country looks with confidence to her adopted children for a valorous support, as a faithful return for the advantages enjoyed, under her mild and equitable government. As fathers, husbands, and brothers, you are summoned to rally around the standard of the Eagle, to defend all which is dear in existence.

Your country, although calling for your exertions, does not wish you to engage in her cause without amply remunerating you for the services rendered. Your intelligent minds are not to be led away by false representations. Your love of honor would cause you to despise the man who should attempt to deceive you. In the sincerity of a soldier and the language of truth I address you.

To every noble-hearted, generous freeman of color, volunteering to serve during the present contest with Great Britain, and no longer, there will be paid the same bounty in money and lands, now received by the white soldiers of the United States, viz.: one hundred and twenty-four dollars in money, and one hundred and sixty acres of land. The non-commissioned officers and privates will also be entitled to the same monthly pay and daily rations, and clothes, furnished to any American soldier.

On enrolling yourselves in companies, the major-general commanding will select officers for your government from your white fellow-citizens. Your non-commissioned officers will be appointed from among yourselves.

Due regard will be paid to the feelings of freemen and soldiers. You will not, by being associated with white men in the same corps, be exposed to improper comparisons or unjust sarcasm. As a distinct, independent battalion or regiment, pursuing the path of glory, you will, undivided, receive the applause and gratitude of your countrymen.

To assure you of the sincerity of my intentions, and my anxiety to engage your invaluable services to our country, I have communicated my wishes to the Governor of Louisiana, who is fully informed as to the manner of enrolment, and will give you every necessary information on the subject of this address.

ANDREW JACKSON, *Major-General Commanding.*
Niles's Register, vol. vii., p. 205.

At the close of a review of the white and colored troops in New Orleans, on Sunday, December 18th, 1814, General Jackson's address to the troops was read by Edward Livingston, one of his aides, and the following is the portion addressed:

To the men of Color. — Soldiers! From the shores of Mobile I collected you to arms, — I invited you to share in the perils and to divide the glory of your white countrymen. I expected much from you; for I was not uninformed of those qualities which must render you so formidable to an invading foe. I knew that you could endure hunger and thirst and all the hardships of war. I knew that you loved the land of your nativity, and that, like ourselves, you had to defend all that is most dear to man. But you surpass my hopes. I have found in you, united to these qualities, that noble enthusiasm which impels to great deeds.

Soldiers! The President of the United States shall be informed of your conduct on the present occasion; and the voice of the Representatives of the American Nation shall applaud your valor, as your general now praises your ardor. The enemy is near. His sails cover the lakes. But the brave are united; and if he finds us contending among ourselves, it will be for the prize of valor, and fame, its noblest reward. — *Niles's Register,* vol. vii., pp. 345, 346.

Such are some of the views of our ancestors in regard to the employment of Negro soldiers. Is it not the duty of every loyal man to give a careful consideration to these facts?

By utilizing this element the Government can secure the services of 700,000 able-bodied men, acclimated to and familiar with the seat of war, and at the same time strike the Rebels a vital blow. Will not posterity hold to a severe account the statesman who would neglect to use so powerful a force for the suppression of the Rebellion?

Pamphlet 28

John H. Hopkins

Bible View of Slavery. (Society for the Diffusion of Political Knowledge, No. 8)

New York, 1863

[Unwilling to accept the disintegration of slavery in the wake of the Emancipation Proclamation, conservatives in the North continued to defend the institution. Slavery remained untouched in the border states which had not seceded, and in Confederate territory already occupied by the Union army before January 1, 1863. Gradually slavery was abolished in the District of Columbia, and by state action in every border state but Kentucky and Delaware, but it was not until January, 1865, that sufficient votes were mustered in Congress to launch the Thirteenth Amendment abolishing slavery. By December, 1865, it was ratified and in effect. Meanwhile, in 1863 and 1864, the pamphlet war over slavery continued. The Society for the Diffusion of Political Knowledge in the spring of 1863 issued a curious pro-slavery pamphlet. Its author was by no means opposed to emancipation. In 1851, John Henry Hopkins (1792–1868), first Protestant Episcopal bishop of Vermont, delivered a lecture at Buffalo on "Slavery: Its Religious Sanction, Its Political Dangers, and the Best Mode of Doing It Away." Hopkins declared that the Bible sanctioned slavery, but that abolition was urgently important and should be accomplished by fraternal agreement. His arguments in the years following, particularly during the Civil War, were reiterated and excerpted in pamphlets and periodicals. They were most widely distributed in *The Bible View of Slavery*, which failed to lay stress on abolition.]

THE word "slave" occurs but twice in our English Bible, but the term "servant," commonly employed by our translators, has the meaning of slave in the Hebrew and the Greek originals, as a general rule, where it stands alone. We read, however, in many places, of "hired servants," and of "bondmen and bondmaids." The first were not slaves, but the others were; the distinction being precisely the same which exists in our own day. Slavery, therefore, may be defined as *servitude for life, descending to the offspring*. And this kind of bondage appears to have existed as an established institution in all the ages of our world, by the universal evidence of history, whether sacred or profane.

This understood, I shall not oppose the prevalent idea that slavery is an evil in itself. A *physical* evil it may be, but this does not satisfy the judgment of its more zealous adversaries, since they contend that it is a *moral* evil — a positive *sin* to hold a human being in bondage, under any circumstances whatever, unless as a punishment inflicted on crimes, for the safety of the community.

Here, therefore, lies the true aspect of the controversy. And it is evident that it can only be settled by the Bible. For every Christian is bound to assent to the rule of the inspired Apostle, that "sin is the transgression of the law," namely, the law laid down in the Scriptures by the authority of God — the supreme "Lawgiver, who is able to save and to destroy." From his Word there can be no appeal. No rebellion can be so atrocious in his sight as that which dares to rise against his government. No blasphemy can be more unpardonable than that which imputes sin or moral evil to the decrees of the eternal Judge, who is alone perfect in wisdom, in knowledge, and in love.

With entire correctness, therefore, your letter refers the question to the only infallible criterion — the Word of God. If it were a matter to be determined by my personal sympathies, tastes, or feelings, I should be as ready as any man to condemn the institution of slavery, for all my prejudices of education, habit, and social position stand entirely opposed to it. But as a Christian, I am solemnly warned not to be "wise in my own conceit," and not to "lean to my own understanding." As a Christian, I am compelled to submit my weak and erring intellect to the authority of the Almighty. For then only can I be safe in my conclusions, when I know that they are in accordance with the will of Him, before whose tribunal I must render a strict account in the last great day.

I proceed, accordingly, to the evidence of the sacred Scriptures, which, long ago, produced complete conviction in my own mind, and must, as I regard it, be equally conclusive to every candid and sincere inquirer. When the array of positive proof is exhibited, I shall consider the objections, and examine their validity with all the fairness in my power.

The first appearance of slavery in the Bible is the wonderful prediction of the patriarch Noah: "Cursed be Canaan, a *servant of servants* shall he be to his brethren. Blessed be the Lord God of Shem, and Canaan *shall be his servant.* God shall enlarge Japhet, and he shall dwell in the tents of Shem, and Canaan *shall be his servant.* (Gen. 9: 25.)

The heartless irreverence which Ham, the father of Canaan, displayed toward his eminent parent, whose piety had just saved him from the deluge, presented the immediate *occasion* for this remarkable prophecy; but the actual *fulfillment* was reserved for his posterity, after they had lost the knowledge of God, and become utterly polluted by the abominations of heathen idolatry. The Almighty, foreseeing this total degradation of the race, ordained them to servitude or slavery under the descendants of Shem and Japhet, doubtless because *he judged it to be their fittest condition.* And all history proves how accurately the prediction has been accomplished, even to the present day.

We come next to the proof that slavery was sanctioned by the Deity in the case of Abraham, whose three hundred and eighteen bond servants, born in his own house, (Gen. 14: 14,) are mentioned along with those who were *bought with his money,* as proper subjects for circumcision. (Gen. 17: 12.) His wife Sarah had also an Egyptian slave, named Hagar, who fled from her severity. And "the angel of the Lord" commanded the fugitive to *return to her mistress and submit herself.* (Gen. 16: 9.) If the philanthropists of our age, who profess to believe the Bible, had been willing to take the counsel of that angel for their guide, it would have preserved the peace and welfare of the Union.

The third proof that slavery was authorized by the Almighty occurs in the last of the Ten Commandments, delivered from Mount Sinai, and universally acknowledged by Jews and Christians as THE MORAL LAW: "Thou shalt not covet thy neighbor's house, thou shalt not covet thy neighbor's wife, nor his *man-servant, nor his maid-servant,* nor his ox, nor his ass, nor any thing that is thy neighbor's." (Exod. 20: 17.) Here it is evident that the principle of *property —* "any thing that is thy neighbor's" — runs through the whole. I am quite aware, indeed, of the prejudice which many good people entertain against the idea of *property* in a human being, and shall consider it, in due time, amongst the objections. I am equally aware that the wives of our day may take umbrage at the law which places them in the same sentence with the slave, and even with the house and the cattle. But the truth is none the less certain. The husband has a real *property* in the wife, because she is bound, for life, to serve and to obey him. The wife has a real *property* in her husband, because he is bound for life to cherish and maintain her. The *character* of property is doubtless modified by its design. But whatever, whether person or thing, the law *appropriates* to an individual, becomes of necessity his *property*.

The fourth proof, however, is yet more express, as it is derived from the direct rule established by the wisdom of God for his chosen people, Israel, on the very point in question, namely:

"If thou buy a Hebrew servant, six years shall he serve, and in the seventh year he shall go out free for nothing. If he came in by himself, he shall go out by himself. If he were married, then his wife shall go out with him. If his master have given him a wife, and she have borne him sons or daughters, *the wife and the children shall be her master's, and he shall go out by himself.*" (Exod. 21: 2–4.) Here we see that the separation of husband and wife is positively directed by the divine command, in order to secure the property of the master in his bond-maid and her offspring. But the husband had an alternative, if he preferred slavery to separation. For thus the law of God proceeds: "If the servant shall plainly say, I love my master, my wife, and my children; I will not go out free; then his master shall bring him unto the judges; he shall also bring him to the door or unto the door-post; and his master shall bore his ear through with an awl, and *he shall serve him forever.*" (Exod. 21: 5, 6.) With this law before his eyes, what Christian can believe that the Almighty attached immorality or sin to the condition of slavery?

The treatment of slaves, especially as it regarded the degree of correction which the master might administer, occurs in the same chapter, as follows: "If a man smite his servant or his maid with a rod, and he die under his hand, he shall be surely punished. Notwithstanding if he continue a day or two, *he shall not be punished; for he is his money.*" (Exod. 21: 20, 21.) And again, If a man smite the eye of his servant or the eye of his maid, that it perish, he shall let him go free for his eye's sake. And if he smite out his man-servant's tooth, or his maid-servant's tooth, he shall let him go free for his tooth's sake." (Exod. 21: 26, 27.) Here we see that the master was authorized to use corporal correction toward his slaves, within certain limits. When immediate death ensued, he was to be punished as the judges might determine. But for all that came short of this, the loss of his property was held to be a sufficient penalty.

The next evidence furnished by the divine law appears in the peculiar and admirable appointment of the Jubilee. "Ye shall hallow the fiftieth year, and proclaim liberty throughout all the land to all the inhabitants thereof: it shall be a Jubilee unto you, and *ye shall return every man unto his possession, and ye shall return every man to his family.*" (Lev. 25: 10.) This enactment, however did not affect the slaves, because it only extended to the Israelites who had "a possession and a family," according to the original distribution of the land among the tribes. The distinction is plainly set forth in the same chapter, namely:

"If thy brother that dwelleth by thee be waxen poor, and be sold unto thee, thou shalt not compel him to serve as a bond servant, but as a hired servant and as a sojourner he shall be with thee, and shall serve thee unto the year of Jubilee, and then shall he depart from thee, both he and his children with him, and shall return unto his own family, and unto the possession of his fathers shall he return. For they are my servants which I brought forth out of the land of Egypt, they shall not be sold as bondmen. *Both thy bondmen and bondmaids, which thou shalt have, shall be of the heathen that are round about you; of them shall ye buy bondmen and bondmaids.* Moreover, of the children of the *strangers that do sojourn among you, of them shall ye buy, and of their families that are with you, which they begat in your land,* and they shall be your possession. And ye shall take them as an *inheritance for your children after you,* to inherit them for a possession; THEY SHALL BE YOUR BONDMEN FOR EVER; but over your brethren, the children of Israel, ye shall not rule one over another with rigor. For unto me the children of Israel are servants; they are my servants whom I brought forth out of the land of Egypt: I am the Lord your God." (Lev. 25: 40–46, with v. 55.)

The distinction here made between the temporary servitude of the Israelite and the perpetual bondage of the heathen race, is too plain for controversy. And this express and positive law furnishes the true meaning of another passage which the ultra abolitionist is very fond of repeating: "Thou shalt not deliver unto his master the servant which is escaped from his master unto thee: he shall dwell with thee, even among you, in that place which he shall choose, in one of thy gates where it liketh him best: thou shalt not oppress him." (Deut. 23: 15, 16.) This evidently must be referred to the case of a slave who had escaped from a *foreign heathen master*, and can not, with any sound reason, be applied to the slaves of the Israelites themselves. For it is manifest that if it were so applied, it would nullify the other enactments of the divine Lawgiver, and it would have been an absurdity to tell the people that they should "buy bondmen and bondmaids of the heathen and the stranger, to be their possession and the inheritance of their children for ever," while, nevertheless, the slaves should be at liberty to run away and become freemen when they pleased. It is the well-known maxim, in the interpretation of all laws, that each sentence shall be so construed as to give a consistent meaning to the whole. And assuredly, if we are bound to follow this rule in the legislation of earth, we can not be less bound to follow it in the legislation of the Almighty. The meaning that I have adopted is the only one which agrees with the established principle of legal construction, and it has invariably been sanctioned by the doctors of the Jewish law, and every respectable Christian commentator.

Such, then, is the institution of slavery, laid down by the Lord God of Israel for his chosen people, and continued for fifteen centuries, until the new dispensation of the Gospel. What change did this produce? I grant, of course, that we, as Christians, are bound by the precepts and example of the Saviour and his apostles. Let us now, therefore, proceed to the all-important inquiry, whether we are authorized by these to presume that the Mosaic system was done away.

First, then, we ask what the divine Redeemer said in reference to slavery. And the answer is perfectly undeniable: HE DID NOT ALLUDE TO IT AT ALL. Not one word upon the subject is recorded by any of the four Evangelists who gave His life and doctrines to the world. Yet slavery was in full existence at the time, throughout Judea; and the Roman empire, according to the historian Gibbon, contained sixty millions of slaves, on the lowest probable computation! How prosperous and united would our glorious republic be at this hour, if the eloquent and pertinacious declaimers against slavery had been willing to follow their Saviour's example!

But did not our Lord substantially repeal the old law, by the mere fact that he established a new dispensation? Certainly not, unless they were incompatible. And that he did not consider them incompatible is clearly proved by his own express declaration. "Think not," saith he, "that I am come to destroy the law or the prophets. I am not come to destroy, but to fulfill." (Matt. 5: 17.) On that point, therefore, this single passage is perfectly conclusive.

It is said by some, however, that the great principle of the Gospel, love to God and love to man, necessarily involved the condemnation of slavery. Yet how should it have any such result, when we remember that this was no new principle, but, on the contrary, was laid down by the Deity to his own chosen people, and was quoted from the Old Testament by the Saviour himself? And why should slavery be thought inconsistent with it? In the relation of master and slave, we are assured by our Southern brethren that there is incomparably more mutual love than can ever be found between the employer and the hireling. And I can readily believe it, for the very reason that it is a relation for life, and the parties, when rightly disposed, must therefore feel a far stronger and deeper interest in each other.

The next evidence which proves that the Mosaic law was not held to be inconsistent with the Gospel occurs in the statement of the apostles to St. Paul, made some twenty years, at least, after the establishment of the first Christian church in Jerusalem. "Thou seest, brother," said they, "how many thousands of Jews there are who believe, *and they are all zealous of the law.*" (Acts 21: 20.) How could this have been possible, if the law was supposed to be abolished by the new dispensation?

But the precepts and the conduct of St. Paul himself, the great apostle of the Gentiles, are all sufficient, because he meets the very point, and settles the whole question. Thus he saith to the Ephesians: "Servants, (in the original Greek, *bond servants* or slaves) "be obedient to them that are your masters, according to the flesh, with fear and trembling, in singleness of your hearts, as unto Christ. Not with eye service, as men-pleasers, but as the servants of Christ, doing the will of God from the heart, with good will doing service, as to the Lord, and not unto men, knowing that whatsoever good thing any man doeth, the same shall he receive of the Lord, whether he be bond or free. And ye masters, do the same things unto them, forbearing threatening, knowing that your Master also is in heaven, neither is there any respect of persons with him." (Eph. 6: 5–9.)

Again, to the Colossians, St. Paul repeats the same commandments. "Servants," (that is, *bond servants* or slaves) "obey in all things your masters according to the flesh, not with eye service, as men-pleasers, but in singleness of heart, fearing God." (Col. 3: 22.) "Masters, give unto your servants that which is just and equal, knowing that ye also have a Master in heaven." (Col. 4: 1.)

Again, the same inspired teacher lays down the law in very strong terms, to Timothy, the first Bishop of Ephesus: "Let as many servants as are under the yoke," (that is, the yoke of bondage,) "count their own masters worthy of all honor, that the name of God and his doctrine be not blasphemed. And they that have believing masters, let them not despise them because they are brethren, but rather do them service because they are faithful and beloved, partakers of the benefit. These things teach and exhort. *If any man teach otherwise, and consent not to wholesome words, even the words of our Lord Jesus Christ, and to the doctrine which is according to godliness, he is proud, knowing nothing, but doting about questions and strifes of words, whereof cometh envy, strife, railings, evil surmisings, perverse disputings of men of corrupt minds and destitute of the truth, supposing that gain is godliness.* From such withdraw thyself. But godliness with contentment is great gain. For we brought nothing into this world, and it is certain we can carry nothing out. And having food and raiment, let us be therewith content." (1 Tim. 6: 1–8.)

Lastly, St. Paul, in his Epistle to Philemon, informs him that he had sent back his fugitive slave, whom the apostle had converted to the Christian faith during his imprisonment, asking the master to forgive and receive his penitent disciple. "I beseech thee for my son Onesimus," saith he, "whom I have begotten in my bonds, which in time past was to thee unprofitable, but now profitable to thee and to me, whom I have sent again: thou therefore receive him that is mine own bowels, whom I would have retained with me, that in thy stead he might have ministered unto me in the bonds of the gospel. But without thy mind would I do nothing, that thy benefit should not be as it were of necessity, but willingly. For perhaps he therefore departed for a season, that thou shouldst receive him forever, not now as a servant, but above a servant, a brother beloved, specially to me, but how much more to thee, both in the flesh and in the Lord. If thou countest me therefore a partner, receive him as myself. If he hath wronged thee or oweth thee aught, put that on mine account. I Paul have written it with mine own hand. I will repay it; albeit I do not say to thee how thou owest unto me thine own soul besides." (Ep. to Philemon 5: 10, 19.)

The evidence of the New Testament is thus complete, plainly proving that the institution of slavery was not abolished by the Gospel. Compare now the course of the ultra abolitionist with that of Christ and his inspired apostle. The divine Redeemer openly rebukes the sanctimonious Pharisees, "who made void the law of God by their traditions." He spares not the wealthy, infidel Sadducees. He denounces the hypocritical Scribes, who "loved the uppermost rooms at feasts and to be called of men, Rabbi, Rabbi." He calls the royal Herod "that fox," entirely regardless of the king's displeasure. He censures severely the Jewish practice of divorcing their wives for the slightest cause, and vindicates the original sanctity of marriage. He tells the deluded crowd of his enemies that they are "the children of the devil, and that the lusts of their fathers they would do." He makes a scourge of small cords, and drives the buyers and sellers out of the temple. And while he thus rebukes the sins of all around him, and speaks with divine authority, he proclaims himself the special friend and patron of the poor — preaches to them his blessed doctrine, on the mountain, by the seaside, or in the public streets, under the open canopy of heaven — heals their diseases, partakes of their humble fare, and, passing by the rich and the great, chooses his apostles from the ranks of the publicans and the fishermen of Galilee. Yet he lived in the midst of slavery, maintained over the old heathen races, in accordance with the Mosaic law, and uttered not one word against it! What proof can be stronger than this, that he did not regard it as a sin or a moral evil? And what contrast can be more manifest than this example of Christ on the one hand, and the loud and bitter denunciations of our anti-slavery preachers and politicians, *calling themselves Christians*, on the other? For they not only set themselves against the Word of God in this matter, condemning slavery as the "monster sin," the "sum of all villainies," but — strange to say — they do it in the very name of that Saviour whose whole line of conduct was the very opposite of their own!

Look next at the contrast afforded by the inspired Apostle of the

Gentiles. He preaches to the slave, and tells him to be obedient to his master for Christ's sake, faithful and submissive, as a main branch of religious duty. He preaches to the master and tells him to be just and equal to his slave, knowing that HIS Master is in heaven. He finds a fugitive slave, and converts him to the Gospel, and then sends him back again to his old home, with a letter of kind recommendation. Why does St. Paul act thus? Why does he not counsel the fugitive to claim his right to freedom, and defend that right, if necessary, by the strong hand of violence, even unto death? Why does he not write to his disciple, Philemon, and rebuke him for the awful sin of holding a fellow-man in bondage, and charge it upon him, as a solemn duty, to emancipate his slaves, at the peril of his soul.

The answer is very plain. *St. Paul was inspired, and knew the will of the Lord Jesus Christ, and was only intent on obeying it.* And who are we, that in our modern wisdom presume to set aside the Word of God, and scorn the example of the divine Redeemer, and spurn the preaching and the conduct of the apostles, and invent for ourselves a "higher law" than those holy Scriptures which are given to us as "a light to our feet and a lamp to our paths," in the darkness of a sinful and polluted world? Who are we, that virtually blot out the language of the sacred record, and dictate to the Majesty of heaven what he shall regard as sin, and reward as duty? Who are we, that are ready to trample on the doctrine of the Bible, and tear to shreds the Constitution of our country, and even plunge the land into the untold horrors of civil war, and yet boldly pray to the God of Israel to bless our very acts of rebellion against his own sovereign authority? Woe to our Union when the blind become the leaders of the blind! Woe to the man who dares to "strive against his Maker!"

Yet I do not mean to charge the numerous and respectable friends of this popular delusion with a willful or conscious opposition to the truth. They are seduced, doubtless, in the great majority of cases, by the feelings of a false philanthropy, which palliates, if it can not excuse, their dangerous error. Living far away from the Southern States, with no practical experience of the institution, and accustomed, from their childhood, to attach an inordinate value to their personal liberty, they are naturally disposed to compassionate the negro race, and to believe that the slave must be supremely wretched in his bondage. They are under no special inducement to "search the Scriptures" on this particular subject, nor are they in general, I am sorry to say, accustomed to study the Bible half as much as they read the newspapers, the novel and the magazine. There they find many revolting pictures of slavery, and they do not pause to ask the question whether they are just and faithful. Perhaps a fugitive comes along, who has fled from his master, and who, in justification of himself, will usually give a very distorted statement of the facts, even if he does not invent them altogether. And these good and kind-hearted people believe it all implicitly, without ever remembering the rule about *hearing both sides* before we form our opinion. Of course, they sympathize warmly with the poor, oppressed African, and are generously excited to hate the system of slavery with all their heart. Then the eloquent preacher chooses it for the favorite topic of his oratory. The theme is well adapted to rouse the feelings, and it is usually by no means difficult to interest and gratify the audience, when the supposed sins of others, which they are under no temptation to commit, are made the object of censure. In due time, when the public mind is sufficiently heated, the politician lays hold of the subject, and makes the anti-slavery movement the watchword of party. And finally the Press follows in the wake of the leaders, and the fire is industriously fanned until it becomes a perfect blaze; while the admiring throng surround it with exultation, and fancy its lurid light to be from heaven, until the flames begin to threaten their own security.

Such has been the perilous course of our Northern sentiment on the subject of slavery. The great majority, in every community, are the creatures of habit, of association and of impulse, and every allowance should be made for those errors which are committed in ignorance, under a generous sympathy for what they suppose to be the rights of man. I can not, however, make the same apology for those who are professionally pledged to understand and inculcate the doctrines of the Bible. On that class of our public instructors, the present perilous crisis of the nation casts a fearful responsibility. Solemnly bound by their sacred office to preach the Word of God, and to follow Christ and his apostles, as the heralds of "peace and good-will to men," they seem to me strangely regardless, on this important subject, of their highest obligations. But it is not for me to judge them. To their own Master, let them stand or fall.

I have promised, however, to notice the various objections which have been raised in the popular mind to the institution of Southern slavery, and to these I shall now proceed.

First on this list stand the propositions of the far famed Declaration of Independence, "that all men are created equal; that they are endowed by their Creator with certain unalienable rights; that among these are life, liberty, and the pursuit of happiness." These statements are here called "self-evident truths." But with due respect to the celebrated names which are appended to this document, I have never been able to comprehend that they are "truths" at all. In what respect are men "created equal," when every thoughtful person must be sensible that they are brought into the world with all imaginable difference in body, in mind, and in every characteristic of their social position? Notwithstanding mankind have all descended from one common parent, yet we see them divided into distinct races, so strongly marked, that infidel philosophers insist on the impossibility of their having the same ancestry. Where is the equality in *body* between the child born with the hereditary taint of scrofula or consumption, and the infant filled with health and vigor? Where is the equality *in mind* between one who is endowed with talent and genius, and another whose intellect borders on idiocy? Where is the equality in *social position* between the son of the Esquimaux or Hottentot, and the heir of the American statesman or British peer?

Neither am I able to admit that all men are endowed with the *unalienable* right to life, liberty and the pursuit of happiness, because it is manifest that since "sin entered into the world and death by sin," they are all *alienated*, forfeited and lost, through the consequences of transgression. Life is *alienated* not only by the sentence of the law, but by innumerable forms of violence and accident. Liberty is *alienated* not only by imprisonment, but by the irresistible restraints of social bondage to the will, the temper, the prejudices, the customs, or the interests of others; so that there is hardly an individual to be found, even in the most favored community, who has really the liberty of word and action so confidently asserted as the *unalienable* right of all men. And as regards the "pursuit of happiness," alas! what multitudes *alienate* their right to it, beyond recovery, not only in the cells of the penitentiary, but in the reckless indulgence of their appetites and passions, in the disgust arising from ill-chosen conjugal relations, in their associations with the profligate and the vile, in the pain and suffering of sickness and poverty as the results of vice, in the ruin of the gambler, the delirium of the drunkard, the despair of the suicide, and in every other form of moral contamination!

If it be said, however, that the equality and unalienable rights of all men, so strongly asserted by this famous Declaration, are only to be taken in a *political* sense, I am willing to concede that this may be the proper interpretation of its intended meaning, but I can not see how it removes the difficulty. The statement is that "all men are *created equal*," and that, "the CREATOR has endowed them with these *unalienable* rights." Certainly if the authors of this celebrated document designed to speak only of *political* rights and *political* equality, they should not have thus referred them to the act of creation, because it is perfectly obvious that, since the beginning of human government, men have been created with all imaginable inequality, under slavery, under despotism, under aristocracy, under limited monarchy, under every imaginable form of political strife and political oppression. In no respect whatever, that I can discover, has the Almighty sent our race into the world with these imaginary rights, and this fanciful equality. In his sight the whole world is sinful, rebellious, and lying under the just condemnation of his violated laws. Our original rights, whatever they might have been, are all forfeited and gone. And since the fall, mankind have no *rights* to claim at the hand of the Creator. Our whole dependence is on his *mercy and compassion*. And he dispenses these according to his sovereign will and pleasure, on no system of equality that any human eye can discover, and yet, as every Christian must believe, on the eternal principles of perfect benevolence, in union with impartial justice, and boundless knowledge, and wisdom that can not err.

Where, then, I ask, did the authors of the Declaration of Independence find their warrant for such a statement? It was probably judicious enough to call their propositions "self-evident truths," because it seems manifest that no man can prove them. To estimate aright the vast diversity among the races of mankind, we may begin with our own, the highly privileged Anglo-Saxon, which now stands at the head, although our ancestors were heathen barbarians only two thousands years ago. From this we may go down the descending scale through the Turks, the Chinese, the Tartars, the Japanese, the

Egyptians, the Hindoos, the Indian tribes, the Laplanders, the Abyssinians, the Africans, and how is it possible to imagine that God has made them all *equal!* As truly might it be said that all the trees of the forest are equal — that all the mountains, and seas, and rivers are equal — that all the beasts of the fields are equal — that all the birds of the air are equal. The facts rather establish the very contrary. The Deity seems to take pleasure in exhibiting a marvelous wealth of power through the rich variety of all his works, so that no two individuals of any species can be found in all respects alike. And hence we behold a grand system of order and GRADATION, from the thrones, dominions, principalities and powers in heavenly places, rank below rank, to man. And then we see the same system throughout our earth displayed in the variety of races, some higher, some lower in the scale — in the variety of governments, from pure despotism to pure democracy — in the variety of privilege and power among the subjects of each government, some being born to commanding authority and influence, while others are destined to submit and obey. Again, we behold the system continued in the animal creation, from the lordly lion down to the timid mole, from the eagle to the humming bird, from the monsters of the deep to the sea-star in its shell. The same plan meets us in the insect tribes. Some swift and powerful, others slow and weak, some marshaled into a regular government — monarchy in the bee-hive, aristocracy in the ant-hill, while others, like the flies, have no government at all. And in perfect harmony with this divine arrangement, the inanimate creation presents us with the same vast variety. The canopy of heaven is studded with orbs of light, all differing in magnitude, all differing in radiance, and all yielding to the sovereign splendor of the sun. The earth is clothed with the most profuse diversity of vegetation, from the lofty palm down to the humble moss. The mineral kingdom shines with gold, silver, iron, copper, and precious stones, in all conceivable forms and colors. From the mammoth cave down to the minutest crystal — from mountains of granite down to the sand upon the shore, all is varied, multiform, unequal, yet each element has its specific use and beauty, and the grand aggregate unites in the sublime hymn of praise to the wisdom, the goodness, and the stupendous resources of that ineffable Power which produced the whole.

This brief and most inadequate sketch of the order of creation

may serve at least to show that the manifest inequality in the condition of mankind is no exception to the rule, but is sustained by
all analogy. It is the will of God that it should be so, and no human
sagacity or effort can prevent it. And the same principle exists in
our political relations. We may talk as we please of our equality in
political rights and privileges, but in point of fact, there is no such
thing. Amongst the other civilized nations it is not even pretended.
None of the great galaxy of European governments can have a better
title to it than England, yet who would be so absurd as to claim
political equality in a land of monarchy, of hereditary nobles, of
time-honored aristocracy? The best approach to political equality
is confessedly here, and here only. Yet even here, amidst the glories
of our universal suffrage, where is it to be found? Political equality,
if it means any thing, must mean that every man enjoys the same
right to political office and honor; because the *polity* of any government consists in its *system of administration,* and hence it results,
of necessity, that those who can not possibly be admitted to share
in this administration, have no *political equality* with those who can.
We do, indeed, say that the *people are sovereign.* But every one
knows, full well, that the comparative few who are qualified to take
the lead, by talent, by education, by natural tact, and by a con-
junction of favoring circumstances, are practically *sovereigns over
the people.* The man who carries a hod gives his vote for the
candidate. The candidate himself can do no more, so far as it
concerns the mere form of election. Are they therefore politically
equal? Who formed the party to which the candidate belongs? Who
ruled the convention by which his name was put upon the list? Who
arranged the orators for the occasion? Who subsidized the Press?
Had the poor hodman any share in the operation, any influence,
any voice whatever? No more than the hod which he carries. Can
any human power ever manufacture a candidate out of *him?* The
notion would be preposterous. Where then is his political equality?
Even here, in our happy land of universal suffrage, how does it
appear that *"all men are born equal"?* The proposition is a sheer
absurdity. All men are born *unequal,* in body, in mind, and social
privileges. Their intellectual faculties are unequal. Their education
is unequal. Their associations are unequal. Their opportunities are
unequal. And their freedom is as unreal as their equality. The poor
are compelled to serve the rich, and the rich are compelled to serve

the poor by paying for their services. The political party is compelled to serve the leaders, and the leaders are compelled to scheme and toil, in order to serve the party. The multitude are dependent on the few who are endowed with talents to govern. And the few are dependent on the multitude for the power, without which all government is impossible. From the top to the bottom of the social fabric, the whole is thus seen to be *inequality* and *mutual dependence.* And hence, although they are free from that special kind of slavery which the Southern States maintain over the posterity of Ham, yet they are all, from the highest to the lowest, in bondage quite as real, from which they can not escape — the *slavery of circumstances,* called, in the ordinary language of the world, NECESSITY.

I have been, I fear, unreasonably tedious in thus endeavoring to show why I utterly discard these famous propositions of the Declaration of Independence. It is because I am aware of the strong hold which they have gained over the ordinary mind of the nation. They are assumed by thousands upon thousands, as if they were the very doctrines of divine truth. And they are made the basis of the hostile feeling against the slavery of the South, notwithstanding their total want of rationality. Yet I do not wonder that such maxims should be popular. They are admirably calculated to gratify the pride and ambition so natural to the human heart, and are therefore powerful incentives in the work of political revolution. It was for this purpose, I presume, that they were introduced in that famous document, which publicly cast off the allegiance of the colonies to the British crown. And the same doctrines were proclaimed a few years later, in a similar service, by the French Directory, in the midst of a far more terrible revolution. *Liberty, equality, and fraternity* — THE RIGHTS OF MAN, were then the watchwords of the excited populace, while their insane leaders published the decree of Atheism, and a notorious courtesan was enthroned as the goddess of reason, and the guillotine daily massacred the victims of democratic fury, till the streets of Paris ran with blood.

I do not state this fact because I desire to place the revolutions in the Colonies and in France on the same foundation, with respect to the *spirit* or the *mode* in which they were conducted. God forbid that I should forget the marked features of contrast between them! On the one side, there was religious reverence, strong piety, and pure disinterested patriotism. On the other, there was the madness of atheism, the brutality of ruffianism, and the "reign of terror" to all that was good and true. In no one mark or character, indeed, could I deem that there was any comparison between them, save in this: that the same false assumption of human equality and human rights was adopted in both. Yet how widely different was their result on the question of negro slavery! The American revolution produced no effect whatever on that institution; while the French revolution roused the slaves of their colony in St. Domingo to a general insurrection, and a scene of barbarous and cruel butchery succeeded, to which the history of the world contains no parallel.

This brings me to the last remarks which I have to present on this famous Declaration. And I respectfully ask my readers to consider them maturely.

First, then, it seems manifest, that when the signers of this document assumed that "*all men* were born equal," they did not take the negro race into account at all. It is unquestionable that the author, Mr. Jefferson, was a slaveholder at the time, and continued so to his life's end. It is certain that the great majority of the other signers of the Declaration were slaveholders likewise. No one can be ignorant of the fact that slavery had been introduced into all the colonies long before, and continued to exist long after, in every State save one. Surely then, it can not be presumed that these able and sagacious men intended to stultify themselves by declaring that the negro race had rights, which nevertheless they were not ready to give them. And yet it is evident, that we must either impute this crying injustice to our revolutionary patriots, or suppose that the case of the slaves was not contemplated.

Nor is this a solitary example, for we have a complete parallel to it in the preamble to the Constitution, where the important phrase, "We, the people of the United States," must be understood with the very same limitation. Who were the people? Undoubtedly the free citizens who voted for the Constitution. Were the slaves counted as a part of that people? By no means. The negro race had no voice, no vote, no influence whatever in the matter. Thus, therefore, it seems perfectly plain that both these instruments must be understood according to the same rule of interpretation. The slaves were not included in the Declaration of Independence, for the same reason precisely that they were not included amongst the "people" who adopted the Constitution of the United States.

Now it is the established maxim of the law, that every written document must be understood according to the *true intent* of the parties when it was executed. The language employed may be such that it admits of a different sense; but there can be only one *just* interpretation, and that is fixed unalterably by the apparent meaning of its authors at the time. On this ground alone, therefore, I respectfully contend that the Declaration of Independence has no claim whatever to be considered in the controversy of our day. I have stated, at some length, my reasons for rejecting its famous propositions, as being totally fallacious and untenable. But even if they were ever so "self-evident," or capable of the most rigid demonstration, the rule of law utterly forbids us to appeal to them in a sense which they were not designed to bear.

In the second place, however, it should be remembered that the Declaration of Independence, whether true or false, whether it be interpreted legally or illegally, *forms no part of our present system.* As a great historical document, it stands, and must ever stand, prominent before the nations of the world. But it was put forth more than seven years anterior to the Constitution. Its language was not adopted in that Constitution, and it has no place whatever in the obligatory law of the United States. When our orators, our preachers, and our politicians, therefore, take its propositions about human rights and human equality, and set them up as the supreme law, overruling the Constitution and the acts of Congress, which are the *real law* of the land, I can not wonder enough at the absurdity of the proceeding. And I doubt whether the annals of civilized mankind can furnish a stronger instance of unmitigated perversity.

Thirdly, and lastly, I am utterly opposed to those popular propositions, not only because I hold them to be altogether fallacious and untrue, for the reasons already given, but further, because their *tendency* is in direct contrariety to the precepts of the Gospel, and the highest interests of the individual man. For what is the unavoidable effect of this doctrine of human equality? Is it not to nourish the spirit of pride, envy, and contention? To set the servant against the master, the poor against the rich, the weak against the strong, the ignorant against the educated? To loosen all the bonds and relations of society, and reduce the whole duty of subordination to the selfish cupidity of pecuniary interest, without an atom of respect for age, for office, for law, for government, for Providence, or for the word of God?

I do not deny, indeed, that this doctrine of equality is a doctrine of immense power to urge men forward in a constant struggle for advancement. Its natural operation is to force the vast majority into a ceaseless contest with their circumstances, each discontented with his lot, so long as he sees any one else above him, and toiling with unceasing effort to rise upon the social scale of wealth and importance, as fast and as far as he can. There is no principle of stronger impulse to stimulate ambition in every department. And hence arises its manifold influence on the business, the enterprise, the commerce, the manufactures, the agriculture, the amusements, the fashions and the political strifes of our Northern people, making them all restless, all aspiring, and all determined, if possible, to pass their rivals in the race of selfish emulation.

But how does it operate on the order, the stability, and the ultimate prosperity of the nation? How does it work on the steadfast administration of justice, the honor and purity of our public officers, the quiet subordination of the various classes in the community, the fidelity and submission of domestics, the obedience of children, and the relations of family and home? Above all, how does it harmonize with the great doctrines of the Bible, that the Almighty Ruler appoints to every man his lot on earth, and commands him to be satisfied and thankful for his portion — that we must submit ourselves to those who have the rule over us — that we should obey the laws and honor the magistrates — that the powers that be are ordained of God, and he that resisteth the power shall receive condemnation — that we may not covet the property of others — that having food and raiment, we should be therewith content — that we must avoid strife, contention and railing accusations, and follow peace, charity, and good will, remembering that the service of Christ is the only perfect freedom, and that our true happiness depends not on the measure of our earthly wealth, on social equality, on honor, or on our relative position in the community, but on the fulfillment of our personal duty according to our lot, in reliance on His blessing?

I have no more to add, with respect to this most popular dogma of human equality, and shall therefore dismiss it, as fallacious in itself, and only mischievous in its tendency. As it is the stronghold of the ultra-abolitionist, I have devoted a large space to its examination, and trust that the conclusion is sufficiently plain. Happily it forms no part of our Constitution or our laws. It never was intended to apply to the question of negro slavery. And it never can be so applied without a total perversion of its historical meaning, and an absolute contrariety to all the facts of humanity, and the clear instruction of the Word of God.

The next objection to the Slavery of the Southern States, is its presumed *cruelty*, because the refractory slave is punished with corporal correction. But our Northern law allows the same in the case of children and apprentices. Such was the established system in the army and the navy, until very lately. The whipping-post was a fixed institution in England and Massachusetts, and its discipline was administered even to free citizens during the last century. Stripes, not exceeding forty, were appointed to offenders in Israel by divine authority. The Saviour himself used a scourge of small cords when he drove the money-changers from the temple. Are our modern philanthropists more merciful than Christ, and wiser than the Almighty?

But it is said that the poor slaves are treated with *barbarity*, and doubtless it may sometimes be true, just as soldiers and sailors, and even wives and children, are shamefully abused amongst ourselves, in many instances. It is evident, however, that the system of slavery can not be specially liable to reproach on this score, because every motive of interest as well as moral duty must be opposed to it. The owner of the horse and the ox rarely treats his brutes with severity. Why should he? The animals are his property, and he knows that they must be kindly and carefully used, if he would derive advantage from their labor. Much more must the master of the slave be expected to treat him with all fairness and affection, because here there are human feelings to be influenced, and if the servant be not contented and attached, not only will he work unwillingly, but he may be converted into an enemy and an avenger. When the master is a Christian, the principles of the Gospel, as laid down by St. Paul, will operate, of course, in favor of the slave. But even when these are wanting, the motives of interest and prudence remain. And hence

I can not doubt that the examples of barbarity must be exceedingly few, and ought to be regarded, not as the general rule, but as the rare exceptions. On the whole, indeed, I see no reason to deny the statement of our Southern friends, that their slaves are the happiest laborers in the world. Their wants are all provided for by their master. Their families are sure of a home and maintenance for life. In sickness they are kindly nursed. In old age they are affectionately supported. They are relieved from all anxiety for the future. Their religious privileges are generously accorded to them. Their work is light. Their holidays are numerous. And hence the strong affection which they usually manifest toward their master, and the earnest longing which many, who were persuaded to become fugitives, have been known to express, that they might be able to return.

The third objection is, that slavery must be a *sin*, because it leads to *immorality*. But where is the evidence of this? I dispute not against the probability and even the certainty that there are instances of licentiousness enough among slaveholders, just as there are amongst those who vilify them. It would be a difficult, if not an impossible task, however, to prove that there is more immorality amongst the slaves themselves, than exists amongst the lower class of freemen. In Sabbath-breaking, profane cursing and swearing, gambling, drunkenness and quarreling — in brutal abuse of wives and children, in rowdyism and obscenity, in the vilest excesses of shameless prostitution — to say nothing of organized bands of counterfeiters, thieves and burglars — I doubt whether there are not more offenses against Christian morality committed in the single city of New-York than can be found amongst the slave population of all the fifteen States together. The fact would rather seem to be that the wholesome restraints of slavery, as a general rule, must be, to a great extent, an effectual check upon the worst kinds of immorality. And therefore this charge, so often brought against it, stands entirely unsupported either by positive proof or by rational probability.

The fourth objection is advanced by a multitude of excellent people, who are shocked at the institution of slavery, because it involves the principle of *property in man*. Yet I have never been able to understand what it is that so disgusts them. No slaveholder pretends that this property extends any farther than the *right to the labor of the slave*. It is obvious to the slightest reflection that slavery can not bind the intellect or the soul. These, which properly constitute the MAN, are free, in their own nature, from all human restraint. But to have a *property in human labor,* under some form, is an essential element in all the work of civilized society. The toil of one is pledged for the service of another in every rank of life; and to the extent thus pledged, both parties have a *property* in each other. The parent especially has an established *property* in the labor of his child to the age of twenty-one, and has the further power of transferring this property to another, by articles of apprenticeship. But this, it may be said, ends when the child is of age. True; because the law presumes him to be then fitted for freedom. Suppose, however, that he belonged to an inferior race which the *law did not presume to be fitted for freedom at any age,* what good reason could be assigned against the continuance of the property? Such, under the rule of the Scriptures and the Constitution of the United States, is the case of the negro. God, in his wisdom and providence, caused the patriarch Noah to predict that he should be the *servant of servants* to the posterity of Japhet. And the same almighty Ruler, who alone possesses the power, has wonderfully adapted the race to their condition. For every candid observer agrees that the negro is happier and better as a slave than as a free man, and no individual belonging to the Anglo-Saxon stock would acknowledge that the intellect of the negro is equal to his own.

There have been philosophers and physiologists who contended that the African race were not strictly entitled to be called *men* at all, but were a sort of intermediate link between the baboon and the human being. And this notion is still maintained by some at the present day. For myself, however, I can only say that I repudiate the doctrine with my whole heart. The Scriptures show me that the negro, like all other races, descends from Noah, and I hold him to be a MAN AND A BROTHER. But though he be my *brother,* it does not follow that he is my *equal.* Equality can not be found on earth between the brothers even in one little family. In the same house, one brother usually obtains a mastery over the rest, and sometimes rules them with a perfect despotism. In England, the elder brother inherits the estate, and the younger brothers take a lower rank, by the *slavery of circumstances.* The eldest son of the royal family is in due time the king, and his brothers forthwith become his subjects. Why should not the same principle obtain in the races of mankind, if the Almighty has so willed it? The Anglo-Saxon race is king, why should not the African race be subject, and subject in that way for which it is best adapted, and in which it may be more safe, more useful, and more happy than in any other which has yet been opened to it, in the annals of the world?

I know that there may be exceptions, now and then, to this intellectual inferiority of the negro race, though I believe it would be very difficult to find one, unless the intermixture of superior blood has operated to change the mental constitution of the individual. For all such cases the master may provide by voluntary emancipation, and it is notorious that this emancipation has been cheerfully given in thousands upon thousands of instances, in the majority of which the gift of liberty has failed to benefit the negro, and has, on the contrary, sunk him far lower, in his social position. But no reflecting man can believe that the great mass of the slaves, amounting to nearly four millions, are qualified for freedom. And therefore it is incomparably better for them to remain under the government of their masters, who are likely to provide for them so much more beneficially than they could provide for themselves.

The difference then, between the power of the Northern parent and the Southern slaveholder, is reduced to this, namely, that the master has a *property in the labor of his slave for life,* instead of having it only to the age of twenty-one, because the law regards the negro as being always a child in understanding, requiring a superior mind to govern and direct him. But, on the other hand, the slave has just as really a *property for life in his master's support and protection,* and this property is secured to him by the same law, in sickness and in health, in the helplessness of old age, as well as in the days of youthful vigor, including, besides, a comfortable maintenance for his wife and family. Can any rational judgment devise a fairer equivalent?

The fifth objection, which often meets the Northern ear, proceeds from the overweening value attached, in our age and country, to the name of liberty, since it is common to call it the dearest right of man, and to esteem its loss as the greatest possible calamity. Hence we frequently find persons who imagine that the whole argument is triumphantly settled by the question: *"How would you like to be a slave?"*

In answer to this very puerile interrogatory, I should say that whether any condition in life is to be regarded as a loss or an advantage, depends entirely on circumstances. Suppose, for example, that the Mayor of New-York should ask one of its merchant princes: "How would you like to be a policeman?" I doubt whether the question might not be taken for an insult, and some words of indignation would probably be uttered in reply. But suppose that the same question were addressed to an Irish laborer, with what feelings would he receive it? Assuredly with those of gratitude and pleasure. The reason of the difference is obvious, because the employment which would be a degradation to the one, offers promotion and dignity to the other. In like manner, slavery, to an individual of the Anglo-Saxon race, which occupies so high a rank in human estimation, would be a debasement not to be thought of with patience for a moment. And yet, to the Guinea negro, sunk in heathen barbarism, it would be a happy change to place him in the hands of a Southern master. Even now, although the slaves have no idea of the pagan abominations from which their forefathers were taken, it is notorious that they usually value their privileges as being far superior to the condition of the free negroes around them, and prefer the certainty of protection and support for life to the hazards of the liberty on which the abolitionist advises them to venture. How much more would they prize their present lot, if they understood that, were it not for this very institution of slavery, they would be existing in the darkest idolatry and licentiousness among the savages of Africa, under the despotic King of Dahomey, destitute of every security for earthly comfort, and deprived of all religious hope for the world to come!

If men would reflect maturely on the subject, they would soon be convinced that liberty is a blessing to those, and only those, who are *able to use it wisely*. There are thousands in our land, free according to law, but so enslaved to vice and the misery consequent on vice, that it would be a mercy to place them, supposing it were possible, under the rule of some other will, stronger and better than their own. As it is, they are in bondage to Satan, notwithstanding their imaginary freedom; and they do his bidding, not merely in the work of the body, but in the far worse slavery of the soul. Strictly speaking, however, the freest man on earth has no *absolute liberty,* for this belongs alone to God, and is not given to any creature. And hence it is the glory of the Christian to be the *bond servant* of the divine Redeemer who "bought us to himself with his own precious blood." The *service of* CHRIST, as saith the Apostle, is "the only *perfect freedom."* All who refuse that service, are slaves of necessity to other masters; slaves to Mammon; slaves to ambition; slaves to lust; slaves to intemperance; slaves to a thousand forms of anxious care and perplexity; slaves at best to pride and worldly decorum, and slaves to circumstances over which they have no control. And they are compelled to labor without ceasing under some or all of these despotic rulers, at the secret will of that spiritual task-master, whose bondage does not end at death, but continues to eternity.

The sixth objection arises from the fact that slavery separates the husband from the wife and the parents from the children. Undoubtedly it sometimes does so, from necessity. Before we adopt this fact, however, as an argument against slavery, it is only fair to inquire whether the same separations do not take place, perhaps quite as frequently, amongst those who call themselves free. The laboring man who has a large family is always obliged to separate from his children, because it is impossible to support them in his humble home. They are sent to service, therefore, one to this master and another to that, or bound as apprentices, as the case may be, and thus the domestic relations are superseded by strangers, for the most part beyond recovery. So among the lower orders, the husbands are separated from their wives by the same necessity. How many, even of the better classes, have left their homes to seek their fortune in the gold regions! How many in Europe have abandoned their families for Australia, or the United States, or the Canadas! How many desert them from pure wickedness — a crime which can hardly happen under the Southern system. But above all, how constantly does this separation take place amongst our soldiers and sailors, so that neither war nor foreign commerce could be carried on at all without it! All these are borne by *freemen,* under the *slavery of circumstances.* Is it wise to declaim against this necessity in one form, when we are forced to submit to it in so many other kinds of the same infliction?

There is only one other argument which occurs to me, requiring notice, and that is based upon the erroneous notion that the laws of God, under the Mosaic dispensation, allowed polygamy as well as slavery; and, therefore, it is inferred that the legislation of the Old Testament is of no authority upon the subject, but as the Gospel did away the first, so also it should do away the other.

The facts here are misunderstood, and the inference is without any real foundation. Let us look at the matter as it is explained by the Saviour himself. "The Pharisees came to him, tempting him, and saying unto him: Is it lawful for a man to put away his wife for every cause? And he answered and said unto them: Have ye not read that he which made them at the beginning made them male and female; and said, for this cause shall a man leave father and mother and shall cleave to his wife, and they twain shall be one flesh? Wherefore they are no more twain, but one flesh. What therefore, God hath joined together let no man put asunder. They say unto him: Why did Moses then command to give a writing of divorcement, and put her away? He saith unto them: Moses, because of the hardness of your hearts, suffered you to put away your wives, but from the beginning it was not so. And I say unto you, Whosoever shall put away his wife, except it be for fornication, and shall marry another, committeth adultery, and whoso marrieth her that is put away, doth commit adultery." (Matt. 19: 3–9.)

Now, here our Lord plainly lays down the original law of marriage, referring expressly to Adam and Eve, one man and one woman, declared to be *one flesh,* and adding the command, *What God hath joined together let no man put asunder.* But it is evident that polygamy must, of necessity, interfere with this divine union. The *twain* can no longer be *one flesh,* when another wife is brought between them, because the new wife must deprive the former one of her exclusive rights and privileges, and the husband destroys the very unity which God designed in joining them together. The doctrine of our Saviour, therefore, restores the law of marriage to its original sanctity, and the apostles, accordingly, always speak of the wife in the singular number, in no instance appearing to contemplate the possibility of the Christian having more wives than one, while, in the case of a bishop, St. Paul specifies it as an essential condition that he shall be "the husband of one wife." (1 Tim. 3: 2.)

But how had the chosen people been allowed for so many centuries to practice polygamy, and divorce their wives for the slightest cause? Our Lord explains it by saying that *Moses* suffered them to put away their wives "because of the hardness of their hearts." The special questions addressed to him by the Pharisees, did not, indeed, refer to polygamy, but only to the liberty of divorce, for at that time it should seem that the practice of polygamy had well nigh ceased in *Judea,* and it is certainly not countenanced by the Jewish laws at this day. The principle, however, is precisely the same in the two cases. Dissatisfaction with the present wife and desire for another, were the cause of action in both; and when the husband did not wish to be burdened by the murmurs or the support of his old companion, he would naturally prefer to send her away, in order to make room for her successor. We see, then, how readily this facility of divorce became the mode in which the Jews of that day sought for the gratification of their capricious attachments, instead of the more expensive and troublesome system of polygamy. And hence our Lord applied the remedy, where it was specially required, by forbidding divorces unless for the weightiest cause, such as adultery. Yet this was no change in the divine arrangement, which had been the same from the beginning. He expressly declares, on the contrary, that the latitude assumed by the Israelites was an *indulgence granted by Moses,* on account of "the hardness of their hearts." And this is a very different thing from an authoritative decree of the Almighty.

It is surely therefore manifest, from this language of our Saviour, that God had never given any direct sanction to polygamy. Doubtless, as we must infer from many parts of the Old Testament, it had become common among the Israelites, who, supposing themselves justified by the case of Jacob, had probably adopted it in so many instances that Moses did not think it safe or prudent to put it down, lest worse evils might follow, unless he was constrained to do so by the positive command of the Almighty. All that can be truly stated, therefore, is, that *no such positive command* was given, and the Deity left the human law-giver to use his own discretion in the matter.

Such is the aspect of this question, according to the statement of our Lord, which must be conclusive to every Christian. And hence we may perceive, at once, that the case is in no respect parallel to that of slavery. For here the Almighty caused his favored servant Noah to predict that the posterity of Ham should be the servants of servants, under the descendants of Shem and Japhet. He recognized the bondman and the bondmaid in the ten commandments. He laid down the positive law to Israel that they should buy the children of the heathen that were round about them, and of the strangers who dwelt in their land, to serve them and their families forever. The Saviour, when he appeared, made no allusion to the subject, but plainly declared that he had not come to destroy the law. The first church of believers in Jerusalem were all "zealous" for the law. And St. Paul preached obedience to the slaves among the Gentile churches, and sent a converted slave back to his Christian master.

Where, then, is the resemblance between these cases? In the matter of divorce and polygamy, the Deity is silent, leaving them to the discretion of Moses, until the Messiah should come. But in regard to the slavery of Ham's posterity, he issues his commands distinctly. And the Saviour disclaims the intention to repeal the laws of his heavenly Father, while he asserts the original design of marriage, and his inspired Apostle gives express sanction to slavery, and speaks of the one husband and the one wife, in direct accordance with the word of his divine Master. Here, therefore, it is plain that the cases are altogether unlike, and present a contrast, rather than a comparison.

We know that the doctrine of the primitive church was in harmony with this, for polygamy was never permitted, nor divorces for trifling causes, while slavery was allowed, as being perfectly lawful, so long as the slave was treated with justice and kindness. The ancient canons sometimes advert to the mode in which slaves might be corrected. Bishops and clergy held slaves. In later times, bondmen and bondmaids were in the service of convents and monasteries. And no scruple was entertained upon the subject until the close of the last century, when the new light burst forth which now dazzles the eyes of so many worthy people, and blinds them not only to the plain statements of Scriptures, but to the interests of national unity and peace.

Thus, then, I have examined the various topics embraced in your inquiry, and the conclusion which I have been compelled to adopt must be sufficiently manifest. The slavery of the negro race, as maintained in the Southern States, appears to me fully authorized both in the Old and the New Testament, which, as the written Word of God, afford the only infallible standard of moral rights and obligations. That very slavery, in my humble judgment, has raised the negro incomparably higher in the scale of humanity, and seems, in fact, to be the only instrumentality through which the heathen posterity of Ham have been raised at all. Out of that slavery has arisen the interesting colony of Liberia, planted by slaveholders, to be a place of refuge for their emancipated bondmen, and destined, as I hope, to be a rich benefit, in its future growth and influence, to Africa and to the world. I do not forget, and I trust that I do not undervalue, the missionary work of England and our own land, in that benighted continent. But I believe that the number of negroes Christianized and civilized at the South, through the system of slavery, exceeds the product of those missionary labors, in a proportion of thousands to one. And thus the wisdom and goodness of God are vindicated in the sanction which his word has given, and the sentence originally pronounced on Canaan as a curse has been converted into a blessing.

I have now gone over the whole ground covered by your kind application, and would only here repeat that on the question of slavery, which lies at the root of all our present difficulties, I have obeyed the rule of conscience and of duty, in opposition to my habits, my prejudices, and my sympathies, all of which would tend strongly to the other side. I need hardly say that I am no politician. More than forty years have elapsed since I ceased even to attend the polls. But as a Christian, I am bound to accept the doctrine of the apostles for my guide. And as a citizen, I am bound to sustain the Constitution of the United States, and defend those principles of law, and order, and friendly comity, which every State should faithfully regard in its relations to the rest. Nor is this the first time that I have expressed my opinions. In a lecture at Buffalo, published in 1850, and again in a volume entitled *The American Citizen,* printed by Pudney & Russell, in 1857, I set forth the same views on the subject of slavery; adding, however, a plan for its gradual abolition, whenever the South should consent, and the whole strength of the Government could aid in its accomplishment. Sooner or later, I believe that some measure of that character must be adopted. But it belongs to the slave States themselves to take the lead in such a movement. And meanwhile, their legal rights and their natural feelings must be respected, if we would hope for unity and peace.

In conclusion, I would only say, that I am perfectly aware how distasteful my sentiments must be, on this very serious question, to the great majority of my respected fellow-citizens, in the region where divine Providence has cast my lot. It would assuredly be far more agreeable if I could conscientiously conform to the opinions of my friends, to whose ability, sincerity, and zeal I am ready to give all just commendation. But it would be mere moral cowardice in me to suppress what I believe to be the truth, for the sake of popularity. It can not be long before I shall stand at the tribunal of that Almighty and unerring Judge, who has given us the inspired Scriptures to be our supreme directory in every moral and religious duty. My gray hairs admonish me that I may soon be called to give an account of my stewardship. And I have no fear of the sentence which He will pronounce upon an honest though humble effort to sustain the authority of His WORD, in just alliance with the Constitution, the peace, and the public welfare of my country.

With the fervent prayer that the Spirit of Wisdom, unity, and fraternal kindness may guide our National Congress, the Legislatures of the several States, and the sovereign will of our whole people, to a happy accommodation of every existing difficulty,

I remain, with great regard,

Your faithful servant in Christ,

JOHN H. HOPKINS,
Bishop of the Diocese of Vermont.

Pamphlet 29

To Churchmen.
New York, 1863

[Bishop Hopkins' *Bible View of Slavery* served as a focal point of Northern religious attack on slavery, either through direct refutation or involved scriptural argument. The Union League juxtaposed passages of Hopkins' with shocking passages from Fanny Kemble's widely-read *Journal of a Residence on a Georgian Plantation*. Most of the attacks were overflowing with solemn fervor, but the learned historian Henry C. Lea demonstrated in another Union League pamphlet that slavery was not the only institution that could be defended with the scriptures. His pamphlet was the *Bible View of Polygamy* (Union League No. 62, Philadelphia, 1863). The satire that follows also appeared, masquerading as a publication of the Society for the Diffusion of Political Knowledge.[1]]

THE following Memorial is reported to have been laid before the "General Council" of the Bishops, Clergy and Laity, of the Protestant Episcopal Church in "The Confederate States of America," held in St. Paul's Church, Augusta, Georgia, November 22d, 1862. It is understood to have been referred to a Select Committee, (of which that truly apostolic man, Bishop General Polk is Chairman,) with instructions so to revise the Prayer Book as to free it from all traces of Abolitionism, and also to consider and report on the expediency of a corrected Southern version of the Old and New Testaments — especially the latter.

This proposed Revision of the Prayer Book is of great and obvious interest to Churchmen, North as well as South. For when our present political misunderstandings shall have been arranged by judicious concession under the guidance of wise and patriotic

---

[1] [Some serious refutations were: *The Views of Judge Woodward and Bishop Hopkins on Negro Slavery at the South, Illustrated from the Journal of a Residence on a Georgian Plantation by Mrs. Frances Anne Kemble (Later Butler)* (Union League No. 48, Philadelphia, 1863); Henry Drisler, *"Bible View of Slavery," By John H. Hopkins, Bishop of the Diocese of Vermont, Examined* (Loyal Publication Society No. 39, Part I, New York, 1863); Louis C. Newman, *Bible View of Slavery Reconsidered* (Loyal Publication Society No. 39, Part II, New York, 1863).]

statesmen like Mr. Fernando Wood, Mr. James Brooks, and the Honorable Mr. Toucey, of Connecticut, the great question will still remain to be solved, How shall we restore the unity of the Church, now alas! divided? The first step toward this blessed result will obviously be the prompt and cheerful adoption of such changes and improvements in the Ritual and Order of the Church as our Southern brethren may think expedient. We should begin to familiarize ourselves with the alterations they are said to contemplate, and thus learn to approve, and at last to love, the Prayer Book as conformed to Southern institutions.

For the peace of Jerusalem, Northern Churchmen will surely consider without passion or prejudice any trifling changes in the Liturgy which their Southern brethren may desire. They will especially strive to free themselves from any unreasonable bias growing out of a mere popular clamor against "Treason," "Rebellion," and "Schism." St. Ambrose says, "*Humanum est errare*," and St. Clement of Alexandria declares very forcibly, that "*Communis populus est sicut asinus præsertim in Rebus Politicis et Ecclesiasticis.*" Hence Churchmen will consider the very prevalence and general currency of these loose charges as at least presumptive evidence that they are unfounded. It is obvious, moreover, that persons of respectability, (to say nothing of High Tone and Chivalric Impulses, sanctified by the soundest church principles,) could never have incurred the guilt of schism, treason and rebellion, except under the pressure of irresistible provocation, or for some other satisfactory reason. Faith and charity would oblige us to assume the existence of such sufficient provocation, even were it undiscoverable by mere unaided human intellect. But it is in truth painfully apparent that THE SOUTH WOULD NEVER HAVE SECEDED BUT FOR THE EXISTENCE OF THE NORTHERN STATES.

None but a fanatical abolitionist will dare to deny this great fact. Surely, therefore, we have been to blame, and should be ready, with all diligence, to humble ourselves before those we have thus offended, striving to out-do them only in the fruits of charity and lowliness of spirit, and holding ourselves always ready to concede whatever they ask of us, for the sake of Peace, Concord, and Christian Unity.

We should bear in mind, also, that when Mr. Brooks and Mr. Wood shall have re-established the Union by inviting our Southern brethren to bring their colored boys and girls to New York and Boston under the guaranty of Northern laws, we shall find these calumniated but truly generous men abounding in magnanimity. Though they will, of course, expect and require our Prayer Book to be corrected in conformity with theirs whenever its services are administered to any of their "people," they will doubtless permit us to retain it with but little change, for use in our own churches and among persons of unquestionable Caucasian descent. It will only be necessary that we have two Prayer Books, which may be designated respectively as Black and White, or as the "Liturgy of Light," and the "Liturgy of Darkness," a concession so trifling that no Churchman or Patriot can hesitate over it for a single instant. The mulatto race are not yet sufficiently powerful to maintain their right to a third, or Yellow Prayer Book, but their rapid increase and multiplication in the sunny homesteads of Alabama and the Carolinas may yet render a "Yellow-covered Liturgy" indispensable.

Head-quarters of the Society for
the diffusion of Political Knowledge,
   DELMONICO's, Feb. 14, 1863.

MEMORIAL

To the General Council of the Protestant Episcopal Church in the Confederate States of America:

RIGHT REVEREND AND REVEREND FATHERS AND BRETHREN: — We pray leave to address you on a subject of the profoundest interest to our beloved Church.

The inscrutable decrees of Providence have committed to us the charge in things spiritual, as well as temporal, of the colored biped mammalia, now several millions in number, who are domiciled among us. You know with what pious vigilance and devout fidelity our Zion has cherished and protected these black and yellow lambs of the flock, striving ever to keep them from going astray, and to make them daily more abundant in good works. We have indeed labored without ceasing, and not wholly in vain, to make those thus entrusted to our Christian rule, good and faithful servants; sparing no means that could promote this our godly endeavor. To keep them unspotted from an unbelieving world, we have denied ourselves the happiness of sharing with them our stores of profane knowledge, and have made it a felony to teach them to read. That they might not be hindered in running the race that is set before them, we have forbidden them to cumber themselves with worldly goods, and to retain even the fruits of their daily labor, and we have ourselves borne the added burden without complaining. The task of mortifying the flesh and bringing it into subjection, which even the great Apostle of the Gentiles was compelled to perform for himself, we have taken off their hands and performed for them. That they might learn not to set their hearts on things of this world (which passeth away like a shadow), we have ordained that their domestic ties should be transient, and that they, with or without their wives and children, be kept in free circulation as the basis of trade. And we have labored generally, in the spirit of Christian love, to assimilate them to that order of created beings which is commended in Holy Writ as superior even to the favored people of old, for that "it knoweth its master."

And thus we may say, without boasting, that the Christian graces of humility, long-suffering, and submission to wrong (so difficult of attainment), are nowhere manifested on a larger scale than by this generation, though by nature stiff-necked and untractable. And it is indeed a blessed thought that these biped millions, who might at this day have been herding with their families around them, in contented degradation,

> Where Afric's sunny fountains
> Roll down their golden sands,[2]

and bowing down before Mumbo-Jumbo, or Baal, or that hideous idol, Boo-Ghoo-Boo, now sit where the light of Evangelical truth and Apostolic order shines on those who own them, and where they are daily taught that all help in adversity comes from God alone, and not from man.

But to make the system of the Church more self-consistent and harmonious, and to adapt her ministrations to these tender lambs of her flock and to Southern Churchmen, we hold certain changes in her liturgy and discipline to be indispensable.

Our attention to this subject was first awakened in 1856 by the introduction, (during a session of the general convention of the old "Protestant Episcopal Church in the United States of America,"

[2] Wm. Gilmore Simms.

from which unclean and infidel body we have seceded,) of a "Canon," absurdly mis-called "of Discipline," so ignorantly and mischievously framed (we would fain believe without actual malignity of purpose), that, under its proposed provisions, a dozen or more mulatto (not to say negro) communicants, if unfortunately eye-witnesses of the commission of a crime by a deacon or presbyter, might actually have been admitted to testify to the fact, and thus to subvert the whole social and political fabric of Virginia or South Carolina. Though this insane and unchristian novelty (which disturbed our peace) was promptly rejected by a unanimous Southern vote, the mere fact that it was put forward filled us with gloomy forebodings, and entitled us to demand of the Church securities for the future, and such changes in her Ritual and Order as should suit both to Southern institutions. Can it be doubted that communicants not credible under oath require a special Liturgy?

It is to be observed that the *whole* Prayer Book is intended for homogeneous congregations of responsible beings capable of forming domestic ties and enjoying personal rights. It is, therefore, as a whole, unfit for congregations where the front pews *own* the free sittings — assemblages composed in varying proportions of two classes of Christians, one of which bought the other yesterday and may sell it to-morrow.

But waiving this for the present, certain prominent details require immediate change.

For example, the promise and vow of the marriage service: "I, M., do take thee, N., to be my wedded husband, to have and to hold . . . *till death doth us part*," is a mockery when uttered by one of this beloved but subordinated race. We cannot bear thus to put unreal words into the mouths of those so dear to us. It should be amended to read: "till death, or my owner, his executors, administrators, or assigns, do us part." So, too, the demand: "Wilt thou, ——, keep thee only unto him so long as ye both shall live?" and the answer, "I will," should be improved by adding to the words "I will," some form of *protestando,* reserving the legal rights of the owner, present or future, of either party, with which the voice of the Church expressed in the service seems to conflict. This apparent conflict is still more painfully conspicuous when the officiating clergyman is required to say: "Those whom God hath joined together, *let no man put asunder.*" Volumes of fanaticism and unbelief are latent in these few words. If the officiating clergyman himself own either the bride or bridegroom, this declaration may be considered (most unreasonably, but still with some plausibility,) as in some sense estopping him from any future exercise of his rights as a Christian and a patriarch, even at considerable pecuniary loss. In every case he is thus made the mouthpiece of a revolutionary doctrine that blasphemes the rights of property, and distinctly implies the existence of that Anti-Christian fiction, a "Higher Law." Such profane utterances may suit the atmosphere of other communities, rank with Fourierisms and Freeloveisms, and every social corruption. But no Church that openly proclaims them can flourish within *our* borders.

Another remedy is submitted, which may allow of our leaving this service (so touching and beautiful when used in its proper place,) unchanged for the present. Since the Church hath inherent power to loose as well as to bind, your Honorable Body may, in its wisdom, create and establish a fourth subordinate order of the Ministry, specially to exercise the function of loosing, and to administer the Rite of Divorce from time to time, with due solemnity, to colored couples who have been married in the usual form. This fourth order might be styled that of sub-Deacon, Acolyte, Exorcist, *Hastiarius*, or simply *Auctioneer*. Any person experienced in the duties of that useful calling, and "apt and meet for his smartness and godly conversation to exercise that ministry duly for the edifying of the Church," might be ordained by the Bishop for this particular office, to which other minor duties might judiciously be added. For these, useful hints may lawfully be borrowed from another and ancient branch of the Church; and we refer to the "Discipline of the Order of Flagellants" (*Disciplina et Regula Ordinis Flagellantium, 4to., Romae*, 1567), as embodying practical suggestions of much value. A suitable "Form of ordaining Auctioneers" to administer the blessed sacrament of divorce should stand in the Prayer-book immediately after that for ordaining Deacons. A tasteful symbolism would dictate the presentation of a hammer to the candidate by the Bishop (as the New Testament is delivered to the newly ordained Deacon), with the solemn words, "Take thou authority to divorce colored persons in the Church at public or private sale, for cash or on credit, and also to knock them down if thou be thereto licensed by the Bishop himself." There should be also an appropriate and very brief service introductory to such sales, concluding with a suitable exhortation to the parties.

The rite of Confirmation, or laying on of hands, also needs regulation. For the avoiding of scandal, persons of the African denomination must be sternly repelled from that ordinance. The peace of Jerusalem may be disturbed if Episcopal hands are still to be brought into physical contact with the heads of these dear children of the Church, except in the way of paternal chastisement. Whatever benefit these black but precious vessels may derive from Confirmation would be far outweighed by the damage the Church would sustain if a chivalric and impulsive public should visit one of her chief ministers with the indignity of tar and feathers for demeaning himself to administer it.

The Litany too, contains phrases that tend to mischief — the prayers, for instance, to be delivered "from hardness of heart and contempt of Thy Word and commandments," and that "all Christian rulers and magistrates may have grace to execute justice and maintain truth." Properly understood, these are, of course, prayers that we may not fall into the delusion of imagining ourselves bound to mitigate the severity and brutality (falsely so called) of our eminently humane and evangelical "Slave Code," and that the civil authority may be strengthened to maintain and develop it to the end of time. But these supplications have been known to stir up distressing doubts and misgivings in diseased and over sensitive consciences. The prayer for "all who are desolate and oppressed" is so manifestly liable to perilous misconstruction that its use can no longer be tolerated.

The service for the burial of the dead needs comparatively little change to adapt it to Southern institutions. But in the passage "Forasmuch as it has pleased Almighty God, in his wise providence, to take out of the world the soul of *our deceased brother,*" &c., the last quoted three words are unmeaning, offensive to our instincts, and in conflict with the great fundamental ideas of our social system. "This deceased biped," or "this defunct individual black man," or words to that effect, should be substituted. In the solemn offices of religion, aught unreal should be studiously avoided.

There are radical defects in the "Prayer for a sick person," and the "Office for the visitation of the sick." Both are inapplicable to the case of sickness occurring among these colored objects of our love. Both assume that the patient, and not the proprietor of the patient, is the person chiefly interested in the patient's recovery. The Church's intercession is for the former alone. She turns coldly away from the sorrow and trial of the owner, without a single prayer that he be spared the loss or enabled to bear it with resignation — though it may reduce him from the estate of a gentleman, and compel him to labor for his own subsistence. Should this be so?

Fearing to weary you by pointing out specifically all the additions and changes which the Prayer Book requires, we pause here, only hinting at a few further questions too important to be overlooked.

Should not provision be made in cases where a parish church needs repair or enlargement, for raising the necessary funds by the sale of a sufficient number of colored communicants?

Should not the want (at present so deeply felt,) of Collects against Peace, for Dis-unity, and against the inroads of education and intelligence be at once supplied?

In view of the present distressing depreciation in the market-value of colored Christians, would it not be well to make the petition in the Litany, that the Almighty would be pleased "to raise up those who fall," less unequivocal and more intensely earnest?

Can the present mode of collecting alms at the Offertory be so improved as to enable charitable Christians, anxious to give abundant alms of their substance, but temporarily deficient in the circulating medium, to slip a colored person or persons into the alms-dish, without noise and confusion?

Is there not reason to believe that the verse of the *Te Deum* which is now commonly printed, "We therefore pray Thee, help Thy *servants*," has been corrupted by Northern abolitionists? It certainly seems offensive and wrong. We recommend that in our revised Liturgy the word "servants" be stricken out, and "masters" or "owners" substituted in its place.

Should not a Commination service, like that of the Anglican Church, or a form of Cursing and Excommunication, like the austere but beautiful composition attributed to Ernulphus, be introduced into the Prayer Book, for the warning and intimidation of black Christians who may be tempted by Satan to think of unlawful emigration towards the ungenial regions of the North?

In view of the vast distinction between ourselves and the class in question, from which we have abstracted all the attributes of humanity which can be affected by human legislation, is it not meet and right that a change be made in our Communion Service? The Roman Church administers that sacrament to the laity in one kind only. Would it not be more consistent with the true spirit of our branch of the Church Catholic to administer the same to colored communicants in *neither* kind only?

We submit these grave points for your deliberation, and ask for such prompt action upon them as may vindicate the rights of Southern gentlemen and Churchmen.

And your memorialists will ever pray, &c.

MONTGOMERY, Geo., Nov. 22, 1862.

Pamphlet 30

Clement Laird Vallandigham

The Great Civil War in America. (Speech in the House of Representatives, January 14, 1863)

New York, 1863

[The most conspicuous Peace Democrat or Copperhead attack upon the Lincoln administration was an address that Clement L. Vallandigham of Ohio delivered before the House of Representatives on January 14, 1863. The Chicago *Tribune* excoriated it as "the self-unmasking of the hissing minion of Jefferson Davis." The *Tribune* exaggerated. Vallandigham (1820–1871), long an exponent of states' rights and civil liberties, hoped peace would lead to reunion, but he had energetically opposed every measure for national defense coming before the House. Contrary to the impression he gave in the opening remarks of his speech, Vallandigham was defeated in the 1862 elections. During the "lame duck" session of Congress in the winter of 1862–1863 he aroused so much excitement through his speeches and peace resolutions that an apprehensive colonel in the Middle West wrote his superior, "If this Vallandigham counsels resistance or defiance to any U.S. Statute . . . I wish authority to arrest him." Upon his return to Ohio, Vallandigham continued his criticisms, culminating in an unexceptional speech at Mount Vernon, Ohio, on May 1, 1863. General Ambrose E. Burnside, commander of the Department of the Ohio, without consulting Washington, promptly arrested Vallandigham for violating a military order he had issued a few days earlier. The arrest led to one of the most bitter civil rights controversies of the war. From the "military bastile," in Cincinnati where Vallandigham was imprisoned, he proclaimed, "I am a Democrat — for the Constitution, for law, for the Union, for liberty — this is my only 'crime.'" [1]]

Mr. Vallandigham. — Mr. Speaker, Indorsed at the recent election within the same district for which I still hold a seat on this

[1] [Randall, *Constitutional Problems Under Lincoln*, 176–179; Randall and Donald, *Civil War and Reconstruction*, 302–304; Michael David Goodman, "Vallandigham and the Civil War" (unpub. diss., Harvard Univ., 1959).]

floor, by a majority four times greater than ever before, I speak to-day in the name and by the authority of the people who, for six years, have intrusted me with the office of a Representative. Loyal, in the true and highest sense of the word to the Constitution and the Union, they have proved themselves devotedly attached to and worthy of the liberties to secure which the Union and the Constitution were established. With candor and freedom, therefore, as their Representative, and much plainness of speech, but with the dignity and decency due to this presence, I propose to consider the STATE OF THE UNION to-day, and to inquire what the duty is of every public man and every citizen in this the very crisis of the Great Revolution.

It is now two years, sir, since Congress assembled soon after the Presidential election. A sectional anti-slavery party had then just succeeded through the forms of the Constitution. For the first time a President had been chosen upon a platform of avowed hostility to an institution peculiar to nearly one-half of the States of the Union, and who had himself proclaimed that there was an irrepressible conflict because of that institution between the States; and that the Union could not endure "part slave and part free." Congress met, therefore, in the midst of the profoundest agitation, not here only, but throughout the entire South. Revolution glared upon us. Repeated efforts for conciliation and compromise were attempted in Congress and out of it. All were rejected by the party just coming into power, except only the promise in the last hours of the session, and that, too, against the consent of a majority of that party, both in the Senate and House, that Congress — not the Executive — should never be authorized to abolish or interfere with slavery in the States where it existed. South Carolina seceded; Georgia, Alabama, Florida, Mississippi, Louisiana, and Texas speedily followed. The Confederate Government was established. The other slave States held back. Virginia demanded a Peace Congress. The Commissioners met, and, after some time, agreed upon terms of final adjustment. But neither in the Senate nor the House were they allowed even a respectful consideration. The President elect left his home in February, and journeyed toward this capital, jesting as he came; proclaiming that the crisis was only artificial, and that "nobody was hurt." He entered this city under cover of night and in disguise. On the 4th of March he was inaugurated, surrounded by soldiery;

and, swearing to support the Constitution of the United States, announced in the same breath that the platform of his party should be the law unto him. From that moment all hope of peaceable adjustment fled. But for a little while, either with unsteadfast sincerity, or in premeditated deceit, the policy of peace was proclaimed, even to the evacuation of Sumter, and the other Federal forts and arsenals in the seceded States. Why that policy was suddenly abandoned, time will fully disclose.

But just after the spring elections, and the secret meeting in this city of the Governors of several Northern and Western States, a fleet carrying a large number of men, was sent down ostensibly to provision Fort Sumter. The authorities of South Carolina eagerly accepted the challenge, and bombarded the fort into surrender, while the fleet fired not a gun, but, just so soon as the flag was struck, bore away and returned to the North. It was Sunday, the 14th of April, 1861; and that day the President, in fatal haste and without the advice or consent of Congress, issued his proclamation, dated the next day, calling out seventy-five thousand militia for three months, to re-possess the forts, places, and property seized from the United States, and commanding the insurgents to disperse in twenty days. Again the gage was taken up by the South, and thus the flames of a civil war, the grandest, bloodiest, and saddest in history, lighted up the whole heavens. Virginia forthwith seceded. North Carolina, Tennessee, and Arkansas followed. Delaware, Maryland, Kentucky and Missouri were in a blaze of agitation, and, within a week from the proclamation, the line of the Confederate States was transferred from the Cotton States to the Potomac, and almost to the Ohio and the Missouri, and their population and fighting men doubled.

In the North and West, too, the storm raged with the fury of a hurricane. Never in history was anything equal to it. Men, women, and children, native and foreign born, Church and State, clergy and laymen, were all swept along with the current. Distinction of age, sex, station, party, perished in an instant. Thousands bent before the tempest; and here and there only was one found bold enough, foolhardy enough it may have been, to bend not, and him it smote as a consuming fire. The spirit of persecution for opinion's sake, almost extinct in the Old World, now, by some mysterious transmigration, appeared incarnate in the New. Social relations were dissolved; friendships broken up; the ties of family and kindred snapped asunder. Stripes and hanging were everywhere threatened, sometimes executed. Assassination was invoked; slander sharpened his tooth; falsehood crushed truth to the earth; reason fled; madness reigned. Not justice only escaped to the skies, but peace returned to the bosom of God, whence she came. The gospel of love perished; hate sat enthroned, and the sacrifices of blood smoked upon every altar.

But the reign of the mob was inaugurated only to be supplanted by the iron domination or arbitrary powers. Constitutional limitation was broken down; *habeas corpus* fell; liberty of the press, of speech, of the person, of mails, of travel, of one's own house, and of religion; the right to bear arms, due process of law, judicial trial, trial by jury, trial at all; every badge and muniment of freedom in republican government or kingly government — all went down at a blow; and the chief law officer of the crown — I beg pardon, sir, but it is easy now to fall into this courtly language — the Attorney-General, first of all men, proclaimed in the United States the maxim of Roman servility: *Whatever pleases the President, that is law!* Prisoners of State were then first heard of here. Midnight and arbitrary arrests commenced; travel was interdicted; trade embargoed; passports demanded; Bastiles were introduced; strange oaths invented; a secret police organized; "piping" began; informers multiplied; spies now first appeared in America. The right to declare war, to raise and support armies, and to provide and maintain a navy, was usurped by the Executive; and in a little more than two months a land and naval force of over three hundred thousand men was in the field, or upon the sea. An army of public plunderers followed, and corruption struggled with power in friendly strife for the mastery at home.

On the 4th of July Congress met, not to seek peace; not to rebuke usurpation; nor to restrain power; not certainly to deliberate; not even to legislate, but to register and ratify the edicts and acts of the Executive; and in your language, sir, upon the first day of the session, to invoke an universal baptism of fire and blood amid the roar of cannon and the din of battle. Free speech was had only at the risk of a prison; possibly of life. Opposition was silenced by the fierce clamor of "disloyalty." All business not of war was voted out of order. Five hundred thousand men, an immense navy, and two hundred and fifty millions of money were speedily granted. In twenty, at most in sixty days, the rebellion was to be crushed out. To doubt it, was treason. Abject submission was demanded. Lay down your arms, sue for peace, surrender your leaders — forfeiture, death — this was the only language heard on this floor. The galleries responded; the corridors echoed; and contractors and placemen, and other venal patriots everywhere gnashed upon the friends of peace as they passed by. In five weeks, seventy-eight public and private acts and joint resolutions, with declaratory resolutions, in the Senate and House, quite as numerous, all full of slaughter, were hurried through without delay and almost without debate.

Thus was CIVIL WAR inaugurated in America. Can any man to-day see the end of it?

And now pardon me, sir, if I pause here a moment to define my own position at this time upon this great question.

Sir, I am one of that number who have opposed Abolitionism, or the political development of the anti-slavery sentiment of the North and West, from the beginning. In school, at college, at the bar, in public assemblies, in the Legislature, in Congress, boy and man, as a private citizen and in public life, in time of peace and in time of war, at all times and at every sacrifice, I have fought against it. It cost me ten years' exclusion from office and honor, at the period of life when honors are sweetest. No matter; I learned early to do right and to wait. Sir, it is but the development of the spirit of intermeddling, whose children are strife and murder. Cain troubled himself about the sacrifices of Abel, and slew him. Most of the wars, contentions and litigation and bloodshed, from the beginning of time, have been its fruits. The spirit of non-intervention is the very spirit of peace and concord. I do not believe that if slavery had never existed here we would have had no sectional controversies. This very civil war might have happened fifty, perhaps a hundred years later. Other and stronger causes of discontent and of disunion, it may be, have existed between other States and sections, and are now being developed every day into maturity. The spirit of intervention assumed the form of Abolitionism, because slavery was odious in name and by association to the Northern mind, and because it was that which most obviously marks the different civilizations of the two sections. The South herself, in her early and later efforts to rid herself of it, had exposed the weak and offensive parts of slavery to the

world. Abolition intermeddling taught her at last to search for and
defend the assumed social, economic, and political merit and values
of the institution.

But there never was an hour from the beginning when it did not
seem to me as clear as the sun at broad noon, that the agitation in
any form in the North and West of the slavery question must sooner
or later end in disunion and civil war. This was the opinion and
prediction for years, of Whig and Democratic statesmen alike; and
after the unfortunate dissolution of the Whig party in 1854, and the
organization of the present Republican party upon an exclusively
anti-slavery and sectional basis, the event was inevitable; because,
in the then existing temper of the public mind, and after the education through the press and by the pulpit, the lecture and the
political canvass, for twenty years, of a generation taught to hate
slavery and the South, the success of that party, possessed, as it was,
of every engine of political, business, social, and religious influence,
was certain. It was only a question of time, and short time. Such
was its strength, indeed, that I do not believe that the union of the
Democratic party in 1860 on any candidate, even though he had
been supported also by the entire so-called conservative anti-Lincoln vote of the country, would have availed to defeat it; and if it
had, the success of the Abolition party would only have been postponed four years longer. The disease had fastened too strongly upon
the system to be healed until it had run its course. The doctrine of
the "irrepressible conflict" had been taught too long and accepted
too widely and earnestly to die out, until it should culminate in
secession and disunion: and, if coercion were resorted to, then in
civil war. I believed from the first that it was the purpose of some
of the apostles of that doctrine to force a collision between the
North and the South, either to bring about a separation, or to find
a vain but bloody pretext for abolishing slavery in the States. In any
event, I knew, or thought I knew, that the end was certain collision,
and death to the Union.

Believing thus, I have for years past denounced those who taught
that doctrine with all the vehemence, the bitterness, if you choose
— I thought it a righteous, a patriotic bitterness — of an earnest and
impassioned nature. Thinking thus, I forewarned all who believed
the doctrine, or followed the party which taught it, with a sincerity
and a depth of conviction as profound as ever penetrated the heart

of man. And when, for eight years past, over and over again, I have proclaimed to the people that the success of a sectional anti-slavery party would be the beginning of disunion and civil war in America, I believed it. I did. I had read history, and studied human nature, and meditated for years upon the character of our institutions, and form of government, and of the people South as well as North: and I could not doubt the event. But the people did not believe me, nor those older and wiser and greater than I. They rejected the prophecy, and stoned the prophets. The candidate of the Republican party was chosen President. Secession began. Civil war was imminent. It was no petty insurrection, no temporary combination to obstruct the execution of the laws in certain States, but a REVOLUTION, systematic, deliberate, determined, and with the consent of a majority of the people of each State which seceded. Causeless it may have been; wicked it may have been; but there it was; not to be railed at, still less to be laughed at, but to be dealt with by statesmen as a fact. No display of vigor or force alone, however sudden or great, could have arrested it, even at the outset. It was disunion at last. The wolf had come. But civil war had not yet followed. In my deliberate and most solemn judgment, there was but one wise and masterly mode of dealing with it. Non-coercion would avert civil war, and compromise crush out both Abolitionism and Secession. The parent and the child would thus both perish. But a resort to force would at once precipitate war, hasten secession, extend disunion, and, while it lasted, utterly cut off all hope of compromise. I believed that war, if long enough continued, would be final, eternal disunion. I said it; I meant it; and according to the utmost of my ability and influence, I exerted myself in behalf of the policy of non-coercion. It was adopted by Mr. Buchanan's Administration, with the almost unanimous consent of the Democratic and constitutional Union parties in and out of Congress; and, in February, with the concurrence of a majority of the Republican party in the Senate and this House. But that party, most disastrously for the country, refused all compromise. How, indeed, could they accept any? That which the South demanded and the Democratic and conservative parties of the North and West were willing to grant, and which alone could avail to keep the peace and save the Union, implied a surrender of the sole vital element of the party and its platform — of the very principle, in fact, upon which it had just won the contest for the Presidency; not, indeed, by a majority of the popular vote — the majority was nearly a million against it — but under the forms of the Constitution. Sir, the crime, the "high crime" of the Republican party was not so much its refusal to compromise, as its original organization upon a basis and doctrine wholly inconsistent with the stability of the Constitution and the peace of the Union.

But to resume: the session of Congress expired. The President-elect was inaugurated; and now, if only the policy of non-coercion could be maintained, and war thus averted, time would do its work in the North and the South, and final, peaceable adjustment and re-union be secured. Some time in March it was announced that the President had resolved to continue the policy of his predecessor, and even go a step further, and evacuate Sumpter and the other Federal forts and arsenals in the seceded States. His own party acquiesced; the whole country rejoiced. The policy of non-coercion had triumphed, and for once, sir, in my life, I found myself in an immense majority. No man then pretended that a Union founded in consent could be cemented by force. Nay, more, the President and the Secretary of State went further. Said Mr. Seward, in an official diplomatic letter to Mr. Adams: "For these reasons he (the President) would not be disposed to reject a cardinal dogma of theirs, (the Secessionists,) namely, that the Federal Government could not reduce the seceding States to obedience by conquest, although he were disposed to question that proposition. But, in fact, the President willingly accepts it as true. Only an imperial or despotic Government could subjugate thoroughly-disaffected and insurrectionary members of the State."

Pardon me, sir, but I beg to know whether this conviction of the President and his Secretary is not the philosophy of the persistent and most vigorous efforts made by this Administration, and first of all through this same Secretary, the moment war broke out, and ever since till the late elections, to convert the United States into an imperial or despotic Government? But Mr. Seward adds, and I agree with him: "This Federal Republican system of ours is, of all forms of government, the very one which is most unfitted for such a labor."

This, sir, was on the 10th of April, and yet that very day the fleet was under sail for Charleston. The policy of peace had been abandoned. Collision followed: the militia were ordered out; civil war began.

Now, sir, on the 14th of April, I believed that coercion would bring on war, and war disunion. More than that, I believed, what you all in your hearts believe to-day, that the South could never be conquered — never. And not that only, but I was satisfied — and you of the Abolition party have now proved it to the world — that the secret but real purpose of the war was to abolish slavery in the States. In any event, I did not doubt that whatever might be the momentary impulses of those in power, and whatever pledges they might make in the midst of their fury for the Constitution, the Union, and the flag, yet the natural and inexorable logic of revolutions, would, sooner or later, drive them into that policy, and with it to its final but inevitable result, the change of our present democratical form of government into an imperial despotism.

These were my convictions on the 14th of April. Had I changed them on the 15th, when I read the President's proclamation, and become convinced that I had been wrong all my life, and that all history was a fable, and all human nature false in its development from the beginning of time, I would have changed my public conduct also. But my convictions did not change. I thought that if war was disunion on the 14th of April, it was equally disunion on the 15th, and at all times. Believing this, I could not, as an honest man, a Union man, and a patriot, lend an active support to the war; and I did not. I had rather my right arm were plucked from its socket and cast into eternal burnings, than, with my convictions, to have thus defiled my soul with the guilt of moral perjury. Sir, I was not taught in that school which proclaims that "all is fair in politics." I loathe, abhor, and detest the execrable maxim. I stamp upon it. No State can endure a single generation, whose public men practice it. Whoever teaches it is a corruptor of youth. What we most want in these times, and at all times, is honest and independent public men. That man who is dishonest in politics is not honest, at heart, in any thing; and sometimes moral cowardice is dishonesty. Do right; and trust to God, and truth, and the people. Perish office, perish honors, perish life itself, but do the thing that is right, and do it like a man. I did it. Certainly, sir, I could not doubt what he must suffer who dare defy the opinions and the passions, not to say the madness, of twenty millions of people. Had I not read history? Did

I not know human nature? But I appealed to Time, and right nobly hath the Avenger answered me.

I did not support the war; and to-day I bless God that not the smell of so much as one drop of its blood is upon my garments. Sir, I censure no brave man who rushed patriotically into this war; neither will I quarrel with any one here or elsewhere, who gave to it an honest support. Had their convictions been mine, I, too, would doubtless have done as they did. With my convictions I could not. But I was a Representative. War existed — by whose act no matter — not mine. The President, the Senate, the House, and the country, all said that there should be war — war for the Union; a union of consent and good-will. Our Southern brethren were to be whipped back into love and fellowship at the point of the bayonet. Oh, monstrous delusion! I can comprehend a war to compel a people to accept a master; to change a form of Government; to give up territory; to abolish a domestic institution; in short, a war of conquest and subjugation; but a war for Union! Was the Union thus made? Was it ever thus preserved? Sir, history will record that, after nearly six thousand years of folly and wickedness in every form and administration of Government — theocratic, democratic, monarchic, oligarchic, despotic, and mixed — it was reserved to American statesmanship, in the nineteenth century of the Christian era, to try the grand experiment, on a scale the most costly and gigantic in its proportions, of creating love by force, and developing fraternal affection by war; and history will record, too, on the same page, the utter, disastrous, and most bloody failure of the experiment.

But to return: the country was at war; and I belonged to that school of politics which teaches that when we are at war, the Government — I do not mean the Executive alone, but the Government — is entitled to demand and have, without resistance, such number of men, and such amount of money and supplies generally as may be necessary for the war, until an appeal can be had to the people. Before that tribunal alone, in the first instance, must the question of the continuance of the war be tried. This was Mr. Calhoun's opinion, and he laid it down very broadly and strongly in a speech on the Loan Bill, in 1841. Speaking of supplies, he said: "I hold that there is a distinction in this respect between a state of peace and war. In the latter, the right of withholding supplies ought ever to be held subordinate to the energetic and successful prosecution of the war. I go further, and regard the withholding supplies, with a view of forcing the country into a dishonorable peace, as not only to be what it has been called, moral treason, but very little short of actual treason itself."

Upon this principle, sir, he acted afterward in the Mexican war. Speaking of that war, in 1847, he said: "Every Senator knows that I was opposed to the war; but none knows but myself the depth of that opposition. With my conception of its character and consequences, it was impossible for me to vote for it."

And again, in 1848: "But, after the war was declared, by authority of the Government, I acquiesced in what I could not prevent, and which it was impossible for me to arrest; and I then felt it to be my duty to limit my efforts to give such direction to the war as would, as far as possible, prevent the evils and dangers with which it threatened the country and its institutions."

Sir, I adopt all this as my own position and my defense; though, perhaps, in a civil war I might fairly go further in opposition. I could not, with my convictions, vote men and money for this war, and I would not, as a Representative, vote against them. I meant that, without opposition, the President might take all the men and all the money he should demand, and then to hold him to a strict accountability before the people for the results. Not believing the soldiers responsible for the war, or its purposes, or its consequences, I have never withheld my vote where their separate interest were concerned. But I have denounced from the beginning the usurpations and the infractions, one and all, of law and Constitution, by the President and those under him; their repeated and persistent arbitrary arrests, the suspension of *habeas corpus,* the violation of freedom of the mails, of the private house, of the press and of speech, and all the other multiplied wrongs and outrages upon public liberty and private right, which have made this country one of the worst despotisms on earth for the past twenty months; and I will continue to rebuke and denounce them to the end; and the people, thank God, have at last heard and heeded, and rebuked them, too. To the record and to time I appeal again for my justification.

And now, sir, I recur to the state of the Union to-day. What is it? Sir, twenty months have elapsed, but the rebellion is not crushed out; its military power has not been broken; the insurgents have not dispersed. The Union is not restored; nor the Constitution maintained; nor the laws enforced. Twenty, sixty, ninety, three hundred, six hundred days have passed; a thousand millions been expended; and three hundred thousand lives lost or bodies mangled; and to-day the Confederate flag is still near the Potomac and the Ohio, and the Confederate Government stronger many times than at the beginning. Not a State has been restored, not any part of any State has voluntarily returned to the Union. And has any thing been wanting that Congress, or the States, or the people in their most generous enthusiasm, their most impassioned patriotism, could bestow? Was it power? And did not the party of the Executive control the entire Federal Government, every State Government, every county, every city, town, and village in the North and West? Was it patronage? All belonged to it. Was it influence? What more? Did not the school, the college, the church, the press, the secret orders, the municipality, the corporation, railroads, telegraphs, express companies, the voluntary associations, all, all yield it to the utmost! Was it unanimity? Never was an Administration so supported in England or America. Five men and a half a score of newspapers made up the opposition. Was it enthusiasm? The enthusiasm was fanatical. There has been nothing like it since the Crusades. Was it confidence? Sir, the faith of the people exceeded that of the patriarch. They gave up Constitution, law, right, liberty, all at your demand for arbitrary power, that the rebellion might, as you promised, be crushed out in three months, and the Union restored. Was credit needed? You took control of a country, young, vigorous, and inexhaustible in wealth and resources, and of a Government almost free from public debt, and whose good faith had never been tarnished. Your great national loan bubble failed miserably, as it deserved to fail; but the bankers and merchants of Philadelphia, New York, and Boston lent you more than their entire banking capital. And when that failed, too, you forced credit by declaring your paper promises-to-pay a legal tender for all debts. Was money wanted? You had all the revenues of the United States, diminished, indeed, but still in gold. The whole wealth of the country, to the last dollar, lay at your feet. Private individuals, municipal corporations, the State governments, all, in their frenzy, gave you money or means with reckless prodigality. The great eastern cities lent you $150,000,000. Congress voted, first, $250,000,000, and next $500,000,-

ooo more in loans; and then, first, $50,000,000, then $10,000,000, next $90,000,000, and, in July last, $150,000,000 in Treasury-notes; and the Secretary has issued also a "paper postage currency," in sums as low as five cents, limited in amount only by his discretion. Nay, more; already since the 4th of July, 1861, this House has appropriated $2,017,864,000, almost every dollar without debate, and without a recorded vote. A thousand millions have been expended since the 15th of April, 1861; and a public debt or liability of $1,500,000,000 already incurred. And to support all this stupendous outlay and indebtedness, a system of taxation, direct and indirect, has been inaugurated, the most onerous and unjust ever imposed upon any but a conquered people.

Money and credit, then, you have had in prodigal profusion. And were men wanted? More than a million rushed to arms. Seventy-five thousand first, (and the country stood aghast at the multitude,) then eighty-three thousand more were demanded; and three hundred and ten thousand responded to the call. The President next asked for four hundred thousand, and Congress, in its generous confidence, gave him five hundred thousand; and, not to be outdone, he took six hundred and thirty-seven thousand. Half of these melted away in their first campaign; and the President demanded three hundred thousand more for the war, and then drafted yet another three hundred thousand for nine months. The fabled hosts of Xerxes have been outnumbered. And yet victory strangely follows the standards of the foe. From Great Bethel to Vicksburg, the battle has not been to the strong. Yet every disaster, except the last, has been followed by a call for more troops, and every time so far they have been promptly furnished. From the beginning the war has been conducted like a political campaign, and it has been the folly of the party in power that they have assumed that numbers alone would win the field in a contest not with ballots but with musket and sword. But numbers you have had almost without number — the largest, best appointed, best armed, fed, and clad host of brave men, well organized and well disciplined, ever marshalled. A navy, too, not the most formidable, perhaps, but the most numerous and gallant, and the costliest in the world, and against a foe almost without a navy at all.

Thus, with twenty millions of people, and every element of strength and force at command — power, patronage, influence, unanimity, enthusiasm, confidence, credit, money, men, and army and a navy, the largest and the noblest ever set in the field or afloat upon the sea; with the support, almost servile, of every State, county, and municipality in the North and West; with a Congress swift to do the bidding of the Executive; without opposition anywhere at home, and with an arbitrary power which neither the Czar of Russia nor the Emperor of Austria dare exercise; yet after nearly two years of more vigorous prosecution of war than ever recorded in history; after more skirmishes, combats, and battles than Alexander, Cæsar, or the first Napoleon ever fought in any five years of their military career, you have utterly, signally, disastrously — I will not say ignominiously — failed to subdue ten millions of "rebels," whom you had taught the people of the North and West not only to hate but to despise. Rebels did I say? Yes, your fathers were rebels, or your grandfathers. He who now before me on canvas looks down so sadly upon us, the false, degenerate, and imbecile guardians of the great Republic which he founded, was a rebel. And yet we, cradled ourselves in rebellion, and who have fostered and fraternized with every insurrection in the nineteenth century everywhere throughout the globe, would now, forsooth, make the word "rebel" a reproach. Rebels certainly they are; but all the persistent and stupendous efforts of the most gigantic warfare of modern times have, through your incompetency and folly, availed nothing to crush them out, cut off though they have been by your blockade from all the world, and dependent only upon their own courage and resources. And yet they were to be utterly conquered and subdued in six weeks, or three months! Sir, my judgment was made up and expressed from the first. I learned it from Chatham: "My lords, you can not conquer America." And you have not conquered the South. You never will. It is not in the nature of things possible; much less under your auspices. But money you have expended without limit, and blood poured out like water. Defeat, debt, taxation, sepulchres, these are your trophies. In vain the people gave you treasure, and the soldier yielded up his life. "Fight, tax, emancipate, let these," said the gentleman from Maine, [Mr. Pike,] at the last session, "be the trinity of our salvation." Sir, they have become the trinity of your deep damnation. The war for the Union is, in your hands, a most bloody and costly failure. The President confessed it on the 22d of September, solemnly, officially, and under the broad seal of the United States. And he has now repeated the confession. The priests and rabbis of abolition taught him that God would not prosper such a cause. War for the Union was abandoned; war for the negro openly begun, and with stronger battalions than before. With what success? Let the dead at Fredericksburg and Vicksburg answer.

And now, sir, can this war continue? Whence the money to carry it on? Where the men? Can you borrow? From whom? Can you tax more? Will the people bear it? Wait till you have collected what is already levied. How many millions more of "legal tender" — to-day forty-seven per cent. below the par of gold — can you float? Will men enlist now at any price? Ah, sir, it is easier to die at home. I beg pardon; but I trust I am not "discouraging enlistments." If I am, then first arrest Lincoln, Stanton, and Halleck, and some of your other generals, and I will retract; yes, I will recant. But can you draft again? Ask New England — New York? Ask Massachusetts. Where are the nine hundred thousand? Ask not Ohio — the North-west. She thought you were in earnest, and gave you all, all — more than you demanded.

> The wife, whose babe first smiled that day,
>   The fair, fond bride of yester eve,
> And aged sire, and matron gray,
> Saw the loved warriors haste away,
>   And deemed it sin to grieve.

Sir, in blood she has atoned for her credulity; and now there is mourning in every house, and distress and sadness in every heart. Shall she give you any more?

But ought this war to continue? I answer, no — not a day, not an hour. What then? Shall we separate? Again I answer, no, no, no! What then? And now, sir, I come to the grandest and most solemn problem of statesmanship from the beginning of time; and to the God of Heaven, Illuminer of hearts and minds, I would humbly appeal for some measure, at least, of light, and wisdom, and strength, to explore and reveal the dark, but possible future of this land.

CAN THE UNION OF THESE STATES BE RESTORED? HOW SHALL IT BE DONE?

And why not? Is it historically impossible? Sir, the frequent civil wars and conflicts between the States of Greece did not prevent their cordial union to resist the Persian invasion; nor did even the thirty years Peloponnesian war, springing, in part, from the abduction of slaves, and embittered and disastrous as it was — let Thucidides speak — wholly destroy the fellowship of those States. The wise Romans ended the three years' social war after many bloody battles, and much atrocity, by admitting the States of Italy to all the rights and privileges of Roman citizenship — the very object to secure which these States had taken up arms. The border wars between Scotland and England, running through centuries, did not prevent the final union, in peace and by adjustment, of the two kingdoms under one monarch. Compromise did at last what ages of coercion and attempted conquest had failed to effect. England kept the crown, while Scotland gave the king to wear it; and the memories of Wallace, and the Bruce of Bannockburn, became part of the glories of British history. I pass by the union of Ireland with England — a union of force, which God and just men abhor; and yet precisely "the Union as it should be" of the abolitionists of America. Sir, the rivalries of the houses of York and Lancaster filled all England with cruelty and slaughter; yet compromise and intermarriage ended the strife at last, and the white rose and the red were blended in one. Who dreamed a month before the death of Cromwell that in two years the people of England, after twenty years of civil war and usurpation, would, with great unanimity, restore the house of Stuart, in the person of its most worthless prince, whose father but eleven years before they had beheaded? And who could have foretold in the beginning of 1812, that within some three years, Napoleon would be in exile upon a desert island, and the Bourbons restored? Armed foreign intervention did it; but it is a strange history. Or who then expected to see a nephew of Napoleon, thirty-five years later, with the consent of the people, supplant the Bourbon and reign Emperor of France? Sir, many States and people, once separate, have become united in the course of ages through natural causes and without conquest; but I remember a single instance only in history, of States or people once united, and speaking the same language, who have been forced permanently asunder by civil strife or war, unless they were separated by distance or vast natural boundaries. The secession of the Ten Tribes is the exception; these parted without actual war; and their subsequent history is not encouraging to secession. But when Moses, the greatest of all statesmen, would secure a distinct nationality and government to the Hebrews, he left Egypt and established his people in a distant country. In modern times, the Netherlands, three centuries ago, won their independence by the sword; but France and the English Channel separated them from Spain. So did our Thirteen Colonies; but the Atlantic ocean divorced us from England. So did Mexico, and other Spanish colonies in America; but the same ocean divided them from Spain. Cuba, and the Canadas still adhere to the parent Government. And who now, North or South, in Europe or America, looking into history, shall presumptuously say that because of civil war the re-union of these States is impossible? War, indeed, while it lasts, is disunion, and, if it lasts long enough, will be final, eternal separation first, and anarchy and despotism afterward. Hence I would hasten peace now, to-day, by every honorable appliance.

Are there physical causes which render reunion impracticable? None. Where other causes do not control, rivers unite; but mountains, deserts, and great bodies of water — *oceani dissociabiles* — separate a people. Vast forests originally, and the lakes now, also divide us — not very widely or wholly — from the Canadas, though we speak the same language, and are similar in manners, laws, and institutions. Our chief navigable rivers run from North to South. Most of our bays and arms of the sea take the same direction. So do our ranges of mountains. Natural causes all tend to Union, except as between the Pacific coast and the country east of the Rocky mountains to the Atlantic. It is "manifest destiny." Union is empire. Hence, hitherto we have continually extended our territory, and the Union with it, South and West. The Louisiana purchase, Florida, and Texas all attest it. We passed desert and forest, and scaled even the Rocky mountains to extend the Union to the Pacific. Sir, there is no natural boundary between the North and the South, and no line of latitude upon which to separate; and if ever a line of longitude shall be established, it will be east of the Mississippi valley. The Alleghanies are no longer a barrier. Highways ascend them everywhere, and the railroad now climbs their summits and spans their chasms, or penetrates their rockiest sides. The electric telegraph follows, and, stretching its connecting wires along the clouds, there mingles its vocal lightnings with the fires of heaven.

But if disunionists in the East will force a separation of any of these States, and a boundary purely conventional is at last to be marked out, it must and it will be either from Lake Erie upon the shortest line to the Ohio river, or from Manhattan to the Canadas.

And, now, sir, is there any difference of race here, so radical as to forbid reunion? I do not refer to the negro race, styled now, in unctuous official phrase by the President, "Americans of African descent." Certainly, sir, there are two white races in the United States, both from the same common stock, and yet so distinct — one of them so peculiar — that they develop different forms of civilization, and might belong, almost, to different types of mankind. But the boundary of these two races is not at all marked by the line which divides the slaveholding from the non-slaveholding States. If race is to be the geographical limit of disunion, then Mason and Dixon's can never be the line.

Next, sir, do not the causes which, in the beginning, impelled to Union, still exist in their utmost force and extent? What were they?

First, the common descent — and therefore consanguinity — of the great mass of the people from the Anglo-Saxon stock. Had the Canadas been settled originally by the English, they would doubtless have followed the fortunes of the Thirteen Colonies. Next, a common language, one of the strongest of the ligaments which bind a people. Had we been contiguous to Great Britain, either the causes which led to a separation would have never existed, or else been speedily removed; or, afterward we would long since have been reunited as equals, and with all the rights of Englishmen. And along with these were similar, at least not essentially dissimilar, manners, habits, laws, religion, and institutions of all kinds, except one. The common defense was another powerful incentive, and is named in the Constitution as one among the objects of the "more perfect Union" of 1787. Stronger yet than all these, perhaps, but made up of all of them, was a common interest. Variety of climate and soil, and therefore of production, implying also extent of country, is not an element of separation, but, added to contiguity, becomes a part of the ligament of interest, and is one of its toughest strands. Variety of production is the parent of the earliest commerce and trade; and these, in their full development, are, as between foreign nations, hostages for peace; and between States and people united, they are the firmest bonds of Union. But, after all, the strongest of the many original impelling causes to the Union, was the securing of domestic tranquillity. The statesmen of 1787 well knew that between thirteen independent but contiguous States without a natural boundary, and with nothing to separate them except the machinery of similar governments, there must be a perpetual, in fact an "irrepressible conflict" of jurisdiction and interest, which, there being no other common arbiter, could only be terminated by the conflict of the sword. And the statesmen of 1862 ought to know that two or more confederate governments, made up of similar States, having no natural boundary either, and separated only by different governments, can not endure long together in peace, unless one or more of them be either too pusillanimous for rivalry, or too insignificant to provoke it, or too weak to resist aggression.

These, sir, along with the establishment of justice, and the securing of the general welfare, and of the blessings of liberty to themselves and their posterity, made up the causes and motives which impelled our fathers to the Union at first.

And now, sir, what one of them is wanting? What one diminished? On the contrary, many of them are stronger to-day than in the beginning. Migration and intermarriage have strengthened the ties of consanguinity. Commerce, trade, and production have immensely multiplied. Cotton, almost unknown here in 1787, is now the chief product and export of the country. It has set in motion three-fourths of the spindles of New England, and given employment, directly or remotely, to full half the shipping, trade, and commerce of the United States. More than that: cotton has kept the peace between England and America for thirty years; and had the people of the North been as wise and practical as the statesmen of Great Britain, it would have maintained union and peace here. But we are being taught in our first century, and at our own cost, the lessons which England learned through the long and bloody experience of eight hundred years. We shall be wiser next time. Let not cotton be king, but peacemaker, and inherit the blessing.

A common interest, then, still remains to us. And union for the common defense at the end of this war, taxed, indebted, impoverished, exhausted, as both sections must be, and with foreign fleets and armies around us, will be fifty-fold more essential than ever before. And finally, sir, without union our domestic tranquillity must forever remain unsettled. If it can not be maintained within the Union, how then outside of it, without an exodus or colonization of the people of one section or the other to a distant country? Sir,

I repeat, that two governments, so interlinked and bound together every way by physical and social ligaments, can not exist in peace without a common arbiter. Will treaties bind us? What better treaty than the Constitution? What more solemn, more durable? Shall we settle our disputes, then, by arbitration and compromise? Sir, let us arbitrate and compromise now, inside of the Union. Certainly it will be quite as easy.

And now, sir, to all these original causes and motives which impelled to union at first, must be added certain artificial ligaments, which eighty years of association under a common Government have most fully developed. Chief among these are canals, steam navigation, railroads, express companies, the post office, the newspaper press, and that terrible agent of good and evil mixed — "spirit of health, and yet goblin damned" — if free, the gentlest minister of truth and liberty; when enslaved, the supplest instrument of falsehood and tyranny — the magnetic telegraph. All these have multiplied the speed or the quantity of trade, travel, communication, migration, and intercourse of all kinds between the different States and sections; and thus, so long as a healthy condition of the body-politic continued, they became powerful cementing agencies of union. The numerous voluntary associations, artistic, literary, charitable, social, and scientific, until corrupted and made fanatical; the various ecclesiastical organizations, until they divided; and the political parties, so long as they remained all national and not sectional, were also among the strong ties which bound us together. And yet all of these, perverted and abused for some years in the hands of bad or fanatical men, became still more powerful instrumentalities in the fatal work of disunion; just as the veins and arteries of the human body, designed to convey the vitalizing fluid through every part of it will carry also, and with increased rapidity it may be, the subtle poison which takes life away. Nor is this all. It was through their agency that the imprisoned winds of civil war were all let loose at first with such sudden and appalling fury; and, kept in motion by political power, they have ministered to that fury ever since. But, potent alike for good and evil, they may yet, under the control of the people, and in the hands of wise, good, and patriotic men, be made the most effective agencies, under Providence, in the reunion of these States.

Other ties also, less material in their nature, but hardly less persuasive in their influence, have grown up under the Union. Long association, a common history, national reputation, treaties and diplomatic intercourse abroad, admission of new States, a common jurisprudence, great men whose names and fame are the patrimony of the whole country, patriotic music and songs, common battle-fields, and glory won under the same flag. These make up the poetry of Union; and yet, as in the marriage relation, and the family with similar influences, they are stronger than hooks of steel. He was a wise statesman, though he may never have held an office, who said, "Let me write the songs of a people, and I care not who makes their laws." Why is the Marseillaise prohibited in France? Sir, Hail Columbia and the Star Spangled Banner — Pennsylvania gave us one, and Maryland the other — have done more for the Union than all the legislation, and all the debates in this Capitol for forty years; and they will do more yet again than all your armies, though you call out another million of men into the field. Sir, I would add "Yankee Doodle;" but first let me be assured that Yankee Doodle loves the Union more than he hates the slaveholder.[2]

And now sir, I propose to briefly consider the causes which led to disunion and the present civil war; and to inquire whether they are eternal and ineradicable in their nature, and at the same time powerful enough to overcome all the causes and considerations which impel to reunion.

Having two years ago discussed fully and elaborately the more abstruse and remote causes whence civil commotions in all governments, and those also which are peculiar to our complex and Federal system, such as the consolidating tendencies of the General Government, because of the executive power and patronage, and of the tariff, and taxation and disbursement generally, all unjust and burdensome to the West equally with the South, I pass them by now.

What, then, I ask, is the immediate, direct cause of disunion and this civil war? Slavery, it is answered. Sir, that is the philosophy of the rustic in the play — "that a great cause of the night, is lack of the sun." Certainly slavery was in one sense — very obscure indeed — the cause of the war. Had there been no slavery here, this particular war about slavery would never have been waged. In a like sense,

[2] In truth, the song was written in derision, by a British officer, and not by an American.

the Holy Sepulcher was the cause of the war of the Crusades; and
had Troy or Carthage never existed, there never would have been
Trojan or Carthaginian war, and no such personages as Hector and
Hannibal; and no Iliad or Æneid would ever have been written.
But far better say that the negro is the cause of the war; for had
there been no negro here, there would be no war just now. What
then? Exterminate him? Who demands it? Colonize him? How?
Where? When? At whose cost? Sir, let us have an end of this folly.

But slavery is the cause of the war. Why? Because the South
obstinately and wickedly refused to restrict or abolish it at the demand of the philosophers or fanatics and demagogues of the North
and West. Then, sir, it was abolition, the purpose to abolish or interfere with and hem in slavery, which caused disunion and war. Slavery is only the *subject,* but abolition the *cause,* of this civil war. It
was the persistent and determined agitation in the free States of the
question of abolishing slavery in the South, because of the alleged
"irrepressible conflict" between the forms of labor in the two sections, or in the false and mischievous cant of the day, between
freedom and slavery, that forced a collision of arms at last. Sir, that
conflict was not confined to the Territories. It was expressly proclaimed by its apostles, as between the States also, against the institution of domestic slavery everywhere. But, assuming the plat-
forms of the Republican party as the standard, and stating the case
most strongly in favor of that party, it was the refusal of the South
to consent that slavery should be excluded from the Territories,
that led to the continued agitation, North and South, of that question, and finally to disunion and civil war. Sir, I will not be answered
now by the old clamor about "the aggressions of the slave-power."
That miserable specter, that unreal mockery, has been exorcised and
expelled by debt and taxation and blood. If that power did govern
this country for the sixty years preceding this terrible revolution,
then the sooner this Administration and Government return to the
principles and policy of southern statesmanship, the better for the
country; and that, sir, is already, or soon will be, the judgment of
the people. But I deny that it was the "slave power" that governed
for so many years, and so wisely and well. It was the Democratic
party, and its principles and policy, molded and controlled, indeed,
largely by southern statesmen. Neither will I be stopped by that
other cry of mingled fanaticism and hypocrisy, about the sin and

barbarism of African slavery. Sir, I see more of barbarism and sin, a thousand times, in the continuance of this war, the dissolution of the Union, the breaking up of this Government, and the enslavement of the white race by debt and taxes and arbitrary power. The day of fanatics and sophists and enthusiasts, thank God, is gone at last; and though the age of chivalry may not, the age of practical statesmanship is about to return. Sir, I accept the language and intent of the Indiana resolution to the full — "that in considering terms of settlement we will look only to the welfare, peace, and safety of the white race, without reference to the effect that settlement may have upon the condition of the African." And when we have done this, my word for it, the safety, peace, and welfare of the African will have been best secured. Sir, there is fifty-fold less of anti-slavery sentiment to-day in the West than there was two years ago; and if this war be continued, there will be still less a year hence. The people there begin, at last, to comprehend that domestic slavery in the South is a question, not of morals, or religion, or humanity, but a form of labor, perfectly compatible with the dignity of free white labor in the same community, and with national vigor, power, and prosperity, and especially with military strength. They have learned, or begin to learn, that the evils of the system affect the master alone, or the community and State in which it exists; and that we of the free States partake of all the material benefits of the institution, unmixed with any part of its mischiefs. They believe also in the subordination of the negro race to the white where they both exist together, and that the condition of subordination, as established in the South, is far better every way for the negro than the hard servitude of poverty, degradation, and crime to which he is subjected in the free States. All this, sir, may be "proslaveryism," if there be such a word. Perhaps it is; but the people of the West begin now to think it wisdom and good sense. We will not establish slavery in our own midst; neither will we abolish or interfere with it outside of our own limits.

Sir, an anti-slavery paper in New York, (the Tribune,) the most influential, and, therefore, most dangerous of all of that class — it would exhibit more of dignity, and command more of influence, if it were always to discuss public questions and public men with a decent respect — laying aside now the epithets of "secessionist" and "traitor," has returned to its ancient political nomenclature, and calls certain members of this House "pro-slavery." Well, sir, in the old sense of the term as applied to the Democratic party, I will not object. I said years ago, and it is a fitting time now to repeat it:

If to love my country; to cherish the Union; to revere the Constitution; if to abhor the madness and hate the treason which would lift up a sacrilegious hand against either; if to read in the past, to behold it in the present, to foresee it in the future of this land, which is of more value to us and to the world for ages to come than all the multiplied millions who have inhabited Africa from the creation to this day! — If this it is to be pro-slavery, then in every nerve, fiber, vein, bone, tendon, joint, and ligament, from the topmost hair of the head to the last extremity of the foot, I am all over and altogether a pro-slavery man.

And now, sir, I come to the great and controlling question within which the whole issue of union or disunion is bound up: is there an "irrepressible conflict" between the slaveholding and non-holding States? Must the "cotton and rice fields of South Carolina and the sugar plantations of Louisiana," in the language of Mr. Seward, "be ultimately tilled by free labor, and Charleston and New Orleans become marts for legitimate merchandise alone, or else the rye fields and wheat fields of Massachusetts and New York again be surrendered by their farmers to slave culture and the production of slaves, and Boston and New York become once more markets for trade in the bodies and souls of men?" If so, then there is an end of all union and forever. You can not abolish slavery by the sword; still less by proclamations, though the President were to "proclaim" every month. Of what possible avail was his proclamation of September? Did the South submit? Was she even alarmed? And yet he has now fulmined another "bull against the comet" — *brutum fulmen* — and, threatening servile insurrection with all its horrors, has yet coolly appealed to the judgment of mankind, and invoked the blessing of the God of peace and love! But declaring it a military necessity, an essential measure of war to subdue the rebels, yet, with admirable wisdom, he expressly exempts from its operation the only States and parts of States in the South where he has the military power to execute it.

Neither, sir, can you abolish slavery by argument. As well attempt to abolish marriage or the relation of paternity. The South is resolved to maintain it at every hazard and by every sacrifice; and if "this Union can not endure part slave and part free," then it is already and finally dissolved. Talk not to me of "West Virginia." Tell me not of Missouri, trampled under the feet of your soldiery. As well talk to me of Ireland. Sir, the destiny of those States must abide the issue of the war. But Kentucky you may find tougher. And Maryland —

E'en in her ashes live their wonted fires.

Nor will Delaware be found wanting in the day of trial.

But I deny the doctrine. It is full of disunion and civil war. It is disunion itself. Whoever first taught it ought to be dealt with as not only hostile to the Union, but an enemy of the human race. Sir, the fundamental idea of the Constitution is the perfect and eternal compatibility of a union of States "part slave and part free;" else the Constitution never would have been framed, nor the Union founded; and seventy years of successful experiment have approved the wisdom of the plan. In my deliberate judgment, a confederacy made up of slaveholding and non-slaveholding States is, in the nature of things, the strongest of all popular governments. African slavery has been, and is, eminently conservative. It makes the absolute political equality of the white race everywhere practicable. It dispenses with the English order of nobility, and leaves every white man, North and South, owning slaves or owning none, the equal of every other white man. It has reconciled universal suffrage throughout the free States with the stability of government. I speak not now of its material benefits to the North and West, which are many and more obvious. But the South, too, has profited many ways by a union with the non-slaveholding States. Enterprise, industry, self-reliance, perseverance, and the other hardy virtues of a people living in a higher latitude and without hereditary servants, she has learned or received from the North. Sir, it is easy, I know, to denounce all this, and to revile him who utters it. Be it so. The English is, of all languages, the most copious in words of bitterness and reproach. "Pour on: I will endure."

Then, sir, there is not an "irrepressible conflict" between slave labor and free labor. There is no conflict at all. Both exist together in perfect harmony in the South. The master and the slave, the white laborer and the black, work together in the same field or the same shop, and without the slightest sense of degradation. They are not equals, either socially or politically. And why not, then, can not Ohio, having only free labor, live in harmony with Kentucky, which has both slave and free? Above all, why can not Massachusetts allow the same right of choice to South Carolina, separated as they are a thousand miles, by other States who would keep the peace and live in good will? Why this civil war? Whence disunion? Not from slavery — not because the South chooses to have two kinds of labor instead of one; but from *sectionalism,* always and everywhere a disintegrating principle. Sectional jealousy and hate — these, sir, are the only elements of conflict between these States, and though powerful, they are yet not at all irrepressible. They exist between families, communities, towns, cities, counties, and States; and if not repressed, would dissolve all society and government. They exist also between other sections than the North and South. Sectionalism East, many years ago, saw the South and West united by the ties of geographical position, migration, intermarriage, and interest, and thus strong enough to control the power and policy of the Union. It found us divided only by different forms of labor; and, with consummate but most guilty sagacity, it seized upon the question of slavery as the surest and most powerful instrumentality by which to separate the West from the South, and bind her wholly to the North. Encouraged every way from abroad by those who were jealous of our prosperity and greatness, and who knew the secret of our strength, it proclaimed the "irrepressible conflict" between slave labor and free labor. It taught the people of the North to forget both their duty and their interests; and aided by the artificial ligaments and influence which money and enterprise had created between the sea-board and the Northwest, it persuaded the people of that section, also, to yield up every tie which binds them to the great valley of the Mississippi, and to join their political fortunes especially, wholly, with the East. It resisted the fugitive slave law, and demanded the exclusion of slavery from all the Territories and from this District, and clamored against the admission of any more slave States into the Union. It organized a sectional anti-slavery party, and thus drew to its aid as well political ambition and interest as fanaticism; and after twenty-five years of incessant and vehement agitation, it obtained possession finally, and upon that issue of the Federal Government and of every State government North and West. And to-day, we are in the midst of the greatest, most cruel, most destructive civil war ever waged. But two years, sir, of blood and debt and taxation and incipient commercial ruin are teaching the people of the West, and I trust of the North also, the folly and madness of this crusade against African slavery, and the wisdom and necessity of a union of the States, as our fathers made it, "part slave and part free."

What, then, sir, with so many causes impelling to reunion, keeps us apart to-day? Hate, passion, antagonism, revenge, all heated seven times hotter by war. Sir, these, while they last, are the most powerful of all motives with a people, and with the individual man; but fortunately they are the least durable. They hold a divided sway in the same bosoms with the nobler qualities of love, justice, reason, placability; and, except when at their height, are weaker than the sense of interest, and always, in States at least, give way to it at last. No statesman who yields himself up to them can govern wisely or well; and no State whose policy is controlled by them can either prosper or endure. But war is both their offspring and their ailment, and while it lasts, all other motives are subordinate. The virtues of peace can not flourish, can not even find development in the midst of fighting; and this civil war keeps in motion the centrifugal forces of the Union, and gives to them increased strength and activity every day. But such, and so many and powerful, in my judgment, are the cementing or centripetal agencies impelling us together, that nothing but perpetual war and strife can keep us always divided.

Sir, I do not under-estimate the power of the prejudices of section, or what is much stronger, of race. Prejudice is colder, and, therefore, more durable than the passions of hate and revenge, or the spirit of antagonism. But, as I have already said, its boundary in the United States is not Mason and Dixon's line. The long-standing mutual jealousies of New England and the South do not primarily grow out of slavery. They are deeper, and will always be the chief obstacle in the way of full and absolute reunion. They are founded in difference of manners, habits, and social life, and different notions about politics, morals, and religion. Sir, after all, this whole war is not so much one of sections — least of all between the slaveholding and non-slaveholding sections — as of races, representing not difference in blood, but mind and its development, and different types of civilization. It is the old conflict of the Cavalier and the Roundhead, the Liberalist and the Puritan; or rather, it is a conflict upon new issues, of the ideas and elements represented by those names. It is a war of the Yankee and the Southron. Said a Boston writer the other day, eulogizing a New England officer who fell at Fredericksburg: "This is Massachusetts's war; Massachusetts and South Carolina made it." But in the beginning, the Roundhead outwitted the Cavalier, and by a skillful use of slavery and the negro, united all New England first, and afterward the entire North and West, and finally sent out to battle against him Celt and Saxon, German and Knickerbocker, Catholic and Episcopalian, and even a part of his own household and of the descendants of his own stock. Said Mr. Jefferson, when New England threatened secession some sixty years ago: "No, let us keep the Yankees to quarrel with." Ah, sir, he forgot that quarreling is always a hazardous experiment; and after some time the countrymen of Adams proved themselves too sharp at that work for the countrymen of Jefferson. But every day the contest now tends again to its natural and original elements. In many parts of the Northwest — I might add of Pennsylvania, New Jersey, and New York city — the prejudice against the "Yankee" has always been almost as bitter as in the South. Suppressed for a little while by the anti-slavery sentiment and the war, it threatens now to break forth in one of those great but unfortunate popular uprisings, in the midst of which reason and justice are for the time utterly silenced. I speak advisedly; and let New England heed, else she, and the whole East, too, in their struggle for power, may learn yet from the West the same lesson which civil war taught to Rome, that *evulgato imperii arcano, posse principem alibi, quam Romæ fieri.* The people of the West demand peace, and they begin to more than suspect that New England is in the way. The storm rages; and they believe that she, not slavery, is the cause. The ship is sore tried; and passengers and crew are now almost ready to propitiate the waves by throwing the ill-omened prophet overboard. In plain English — not very classic, but most expressive — they threaten to "set New England out in the cold."

And now, sir, I, who have not a drop of New England blood in my veins, but was born in Ohio, and am wholly of southern ancestry — with a slight cross of Pennsylvania Scotch-Irish — would speak a word to the men of the West and the South, in behalf of New England. Sir, some years ago, in the midst of high sectional controversies, and speaking as a western man, I said some things harsh of the North, which now, in a more catholic spirit as a United

States man, and for the sake of reunion, I would recall. My prejudices, indeed, upon this subject, are as strong as any man's; but in this, the day of great national humiliation and calamity, let the voice of prejudice be hushed.

Sir, they who would exclude New England in any reconstruction of the Union, assume that all New Englanders are "Yankees" and Puritans; and that the Puritan or pragmatical element, or type of civilization, has always held undisputed sway. Well, sir, Yankees certainly they are, in one sense; and so to old England we are all Yankees, North and South; and to the South just now, or a little while ago, we of the middle and western States, also, are, or were Yankees, too. But there is really a very large, and most liberal and conservative non-Puritan element in the population of New England, which, for many years, struggled for the mastery, and sometimes held it. It divided Maine, New Hampshire, and Connecticut, and once controlled Rhode Island wholly. It held the sway during the Revolution, and at the period when the Constitution was founded, and for some years afterward. Mr. Calhoun said very justly, in 1847, that to the wisdom and enlarged patriotism of Sherman and Ellsworth on the slavery question, we were indebted for this admirable Government; and that, along with Paterson, of New Jersey, "their names ought to be engraven on brass, and live forever." And Mr. Webster, in 1830, in one of those grand historic word-paintings, in which he was so great a master, said of Massachusetts and South Carolina: "Hand in hand they stood around the Administration of Washington, and felt his own great arm lean on them for support." Indeed, sir, it was not till some thirty years ago that the narrow, presumptuous, intermeddling, and fanatical spirit of the old Puritan element began to reappear in a form very much more aggressive and destructive than at first, and threatened to obtain absolute mastery in church, and school, and State. A little earlier it had struggled hard, but the conservative proved too strong for it; and so long as the great statesmen and jurists of the Whig and Democratic parties survived, it made small progress, though John Quincy Adams gave to it the strength of his great name. But after their death it broke in as a flood, and swept away the last vestige of the ancient, liberal, and tolerating conservatism. Then every form and development of fanaticism sprang up in rank and most luxuriant growth, till abolitionism, the chief fungus of all, overspread the whole of New England first, and then the middle States, and finally every State in the Northwest.

Certainly, sir, the more liberal or non-Puritan element was mainly, though not altogether, from the old Puritan stock, or largely crossed with it. But even within the first ten years after the landing of the Pilgrims, a more enlarged and tolerating civilization was introduced. Roger Williams, not of the Mayflower, though a Puritan himself, and thoroughly imbued with all its peculiarities of cant and creed and form of worship, seems yet to have had naturally a more liberal spirit; and, first perhaps of all men, some three or more years before the Ark and the Dove touched the shores of the St. Mary's, in Maryland, taught the sublime doctrine of freedom of opinion and practice in religion. Threatened first with banishment to England, so as to "remove as far as possible the infection of his principles;" and afterwards actually banished beyond the jurisdiction of Massachusetts, because, in the language of the sentence of the General Court, "he broached and divulged divers new and strange doctrines against the authority of magistrates" over the religious opinions of men, thereby disturbing the peace of the colony, he became the founder of Rhode Island, and, indeed, of a large part of New England society. And, whether from his teaching and example, and in the persons of his descendants and those of his associates, or from other causes and another stock, there has always been a large infusion throughout New England of what may be called the *Roger Williams element,* as distinguished from the extreme Puritan or *Mayflower and Plymouth Rock* type of the New Englander; and its influence, till late years, has always been powerful.

The SPEAKER. The gentleman's hour has expired.

Mr. VALLANDIGHAM. I ask for a short time longer.

Mr. POTTER. I hope there will be no objection from this side of the House.

The SPEAKER. If there be no objection the gentleman will be allowed further time.

There was no objection; and it was ordered accordingly.

Mr. VALLANDIGHAM. Sir, I would not deny or disparage the austere virtues of the old Puritans of England or America. But I do believe that, in the very nature of things, no community could exist long in peace, and no Government endure long alone, or become great, where that element in its earliest or its more recent form holds supreme control. And it is my solemn conviction that there can be no possible or durable reunion of these States until it shall have been again subordinated to other and more liberal and conservative elements, and, above all, until its worst and most mischievous development, abolitionism, has been utterly extinguished. Sir, the peace of the Union and of this continent demands it. But, fortunately, those very elements exist abundantly in New England herself; and to her I look with confidence to secure to them the mastery within her limits. In fact, sir, the true voice of New England has for some years past been but rarely heard here or elsewhere in public affairs. Men now control her politics and are in high places, State and Federal, who, twenty years ago, could not have been chosen selectmen in old Massachusetts. But let her remember at last her ancient renown; let her turn from vain-glorious admiration of the stone monuments of her heroes and patriots of a former age, to generous emulation of the noble and manly virtues which they were designed to commemorate. Let us hear less from her of the Pilgrim Fathers and the Mayflower and of Plymouth Rock, and more of Roger Williams and his compatriots and his toleration. Let her banish now and forever her dreamers and her sophists and her fanatics, and call back again into her State administration and into the national councils "her men of might, her grand in soul" — some of them still live — and she will yet escape the dangers which now threaten her with isolation.

Then, sir, while I am inexorably hostile to Puritan domination in religion or morals or literature or politics, I am not in favor of the proposed exclusion of New England. I would have the Union as it was; and first, New England as she was. But if New England will have no union with slaveholders; if she is not content with "the Union as it was," then upon her own head be the responsibility for secession. And there will be no more coercion now. I, at least, will be exactly consistent.

And now, sir, can the central States, New York, New Jersey, and Pennsylvania, consent to separation? Can New York city? Sir, the trade of the South made her largely what she is. She was the factor and banker of the South — cotton filled her harbor with shipping and her banks with gold. But in an evil hour the foolish, I will not say bad, "men of Gotham" persuaded her merchant princes — against their first lesson in business — that she could retain or force

back the southern trade by war. War, indeed, has given her, just
now, a new business and trade greater and more profitable than the
old. But with disunion that, too, must perish. And let not Wall
street, or any other great interest, mercantile, manufacturing, or
commercial, imagine that it shall have power enough or wealth
enough to stand in the way of reunion through peace. Let them
learn, one and all, that a public man who has the people as his
support, is stronger than they, though he may not be worth a million, nor even one dollar. A little while ago the banks said that they
were king, but President Jackson speedily taught them their mistake. Next, railroads assumed to be king; and cotton once vaunted
largely his kingship. Sir, these are only of the royal family — princes
of the blood. There is but one king on earth. Politics is king.

But to return: New Jersey, too, is bound closely to the South,
and the South to her; and more and longer than any other State,
she remembered both her duty to the Constitution, and her interest
in the Union. And Pennsylvania, a sort of middle ground, just between the North and the South, and extending, also, to the West,
is united by nearer, if not stronger ties, to every section, than any
other one State, unless it be Ohio. She was — she is yet — the keystone in the great, but now crumbling arch of the Union. She is a
border State; and, more than that, she has less within her of the
fanatical or disturbing element than any of the States. The people of
Pennsylvania are quiet, peaceable, practical, and enterprising, without being aggressive. They have more of the honest old English
and German thrift than any other. No people mind more diligently
their own business. They have but one idiosyncrasy or speciality
— the tariff; and even that is really far more a matter of tradition
than of substantial interest. The industry, enterprise, and thrift of
Pennsylvania are abundantly able to take care of themselves against
any competition. In any event, the Union is of more value, many
times, to her than any local interest.

But other ties also bind these States — Pennsylvania and New
Jersey, especially — to the South, and the South to them. Only an
imaginary line separates the former from Delaware and Maryland.
The Delaware river, common to both Pennsylvania and New Jersey,
flows into Delaware bay. The Susquehanna empties its waters,
through Pennsylvania and Maryland, into the Chesapeake. And

that great watershed itself, extending to Norfolk, and, therefore, almost to the North Carolina line, does belong, and must ever belong, in common to the central and southern States, under one Government; or else the line of separation will be the Potomac to its head waters. All of Delaware and Maryland, and the counties of Accomac and Northampton, in Virginia, would, in that event, follow the fortunes of the northern confederacy. In fact, sir, disagreeable as the idea may be to many within their limits on both sides, no man who looks at the map, and then reflects upon history and the force of natural causes, and considers the present actual and the future probable position of the hostile armies and navies at the end of this war, ought for a moment to doubt that either the States and the counties which I have named must go with the North, or Pennsylvania and New Jersey with the South. Military force on either side can not control the destiny of the States lying between the mouth of the Chesapeake and the Hudson. And if that bay itself were made the line, Delaware, and the Eastern Shore of Maryland and Virginia, would belong to the North; while Norfolk, the only capacious harbor on the south-eastern coast, must be commanded by the guns of some new fortress upon Cape Charles; and Baltimore, the now queenly city, seated then upon the very boundary of two rival, yes, hostile confederacies, would rapidly fall into decay.

And now, sir, I will not ask whether the Northwest can consent to separation from the South. Never. Nature forbids. We are only a part of the great valley of the Mississippi. There is no line of latitude upon which to separate. Neither party would desire the old line of 36° 30′ on both sides of the river; and there is no natural boundary east and west. The nearest to it are the Ohio and Missouri rivers. But that line would leave Cincinnati and St. Louis, as border cities, like Baltimore, to decay, and, extending fifteen hundred miles in length, would become the scene of an eternal border warfare without example even in the worst of times. Sir, we can not, ought not, will not, separate from the South. And if you of the East, who have found this war against the South, and for the negro, gratifying to your hate or profitable to your purse, will continue it till a separation be forced between the slaveholding and your non-slaveholding States, then, believe me, and accept it, as you did not the other solemn warnings of years past, *the day which divides the North from the South, that self-same day decrees eternal divorce between the West and the East.*

Sir, our destiny is fixed. There is not one drop of rain which, descending from the heavens, and fertilizing our soil, causes it to yield an abundant harvest, but flows into the Mississippi, and there, mingling with the waters of that mighty river, finds its way, at last, to the Gulf of Mexico. And we must and will follow it with travel and trade, not by treaty, but by right, freely, peaceably, and without restriction or tribute, under the same Government and flag, to its home in the bosom of that Gulf. Sir, we will not remain, after separation from the South, a province or appanage of the East, to bear her burdens and pay her taxes; nor hemmed in and isolated as we are, and without a sea-coast, could we long remain a distinct confederacy. But wherever we go, married to the South or the East, we bring with us three-fourths of the territories of that valley to the Rocky mountains, and it may be to the Pacific — the grandest and most magnificent dowry that bride ever had to bestow.

Then, sir, New England, freed at last from the domination of her sophisters, dreamers, and bigots, and restored to the control once more of her former liberal, tolerant, and conservative civilization, will not stand in the way of the re-union of these States upon terms of fair and honorable adjustment. And in this great work the central free and border slave States, too, will unite heart and hand. To the West, it is a necessity, and she demands it. And let not the States now called confederate insist upon separation and independence. What did they demand at first? Security against abolitionism within the Union. Protection from "the irrepressible conflict," and the domination of the absolute numerical majority. A change of public opinion, and consequently of political parties in the North and West, so that their local institutions and domestic peace should no longer be endangered. And now, sir, after two years of persistent and most gigantic effort on the part of this Administration to compel them to submit, but with utter and signal failure, the people of the free States are now or are fast becoming satisfied that the price of the Union is the utter suppression of abolitionism or anti-slavery as a political element, and the complete subordination of the spirit of fanaticism and intermeddling which gave it birth. In any event, they are ready now, if I have not greatly misread the signs of the times, to return to the old constitutional and actual basis of fifty years ago — three-fifths rule of representation, speedy return of fugitives from labor, equal rights in the Territories, no more slavery agitation anywhere, and transit and temporary sojourn with slaves, without molestation, in the free States. Without all these there could be neither peace nor permanence to a restored union of States "part slave and part free." With it, the South, in addition to all the other great and multiplied benefits of union, would be far more secure in her slave property, her domestic institutions, than under a separate government. Sir, let no man North or West, tell me that this would perpetuate African slavery. I know it. But so does the Constitution. I repeat, sir, it is the price of the Union. Whoever hates negro slavery more than he loves the Union, must demand separation at last. I think that you can never abolish slavery by fighting. Certainly you never can till you have first destroyed the South, and then, in the language, first of Mr. Douglas, and afterward of Mr. Seward, converted this Government into an imperial despotism. And, sir, whenever I am forced to a choice between the loss to my own country and race, of personal and political liberty with all its blessings, and the involuntary domestic servitude of the negro, I shall not hesitate one moment to choose the latter alternative. The sole question to-day is between the Union with slavery, or final disunion, and, I think, anarchy and despotism. I am for the Union. It was good enough for my fathers. It is good enough for us and our children after us.

And, sir, let no man in the South tell me that she has been invaded, and that all the horrors implied in those most terrible of words, civil war, have been visited upon her. I know that, too. But we, also, of the North and West, in every State and by thousands, who have dared so much as to question the principles and policy, or doubt the honesty, of this Administration and its party, have suffered everything that the worst despotism could inflict, except only loss of life itself upon the scaffold. Some even have died for the cause by the hand of the assassin. And can we forget? Never, never. Time will but burn the memory of these wrongs deeper into our hearts. But shall we break up the Union? Shall we destroy the Government because usurping tyrants have held possession and perverted it to the most cruel of oppressions? Was it ever so done in any other country? In Athens? Rome? England? Anywhere? No, sir; let us expel the usurper, and restore the Constitution and laws, the rights of the States, and the liberties of the people; and then, in the country of our fathers, under the Union of our fathers, and the old flag — the symbol once again of the free and the brave — let us fulfill the grand mission which Providence has appointed for us among the nations of the earth.

And now, sir, if it be the will of all sections to unite, then upon what terms? Sir, between the South and most of the States of the North, and all of the West, there is but one subject of controversy — slavery. It is the only question, said Mr. Calhoun, twenty-five years ago, of sufficient magnitude and potency to divide this Union; and divide it it will, he added, or drench the country in blood if not arrested. It has done both. But settle it on the original basis of the Constitution, and give to each section the power to protect itself within the Union, and now, after the terrible lessons of the past two years, the Union will be stronger than before, and, indeed, endure for ages. Woe to the man, North or South, who, to the third or fourth generation, should teach men disunion.

And now the way to reunion: what so easy? Behold to-day two separate governments in one country, and without a natural dividing line; with two Presidents and Cabinets, and a double Congress; and yet each under a Constitution so exactly similar, the one to the other, that a stranger could scarce discern the difference. Was ever folly and madness like this? Sir, it is not in the nature of things that it should so continue long.

But why speak of ways or terms of reunion now? The will is yet wanting in both sections. Union is consent and good-will and fraternal affection. War is force, hate, revenge. Is the country tired at last of war? Has the experiment been tried long enough? Has sufficient blood been shed, treasure expended, and misery inflicted in both the North and the South? What then? Stop fighting. Make an armistice — no formal treaty. Withdraw your army from the seceded States. Reduce both armies to a fair and sufficient peace establishment. Declare absolute free trade between the North and South. Buy and sell. Agree upon a zollverein. Recall your fleets. Break up your blockade. Reduce your navy. Restore travel. Open up railroads. Re-establish the telegraph. Reunite your express companies. No more Monitors and iron-clads, but set your friendly steamers and steamships again in motion. Visit the North and West. Visit the South. Exchange newspapers. Migrate. Intermarry. Let slavery alone. Hold elections at the appointed times. Let us choose a new President in sixty-four. And when the Gospel of peace shall have descended again from heaven into their hearts, and the gospel of abolition and of hate been expelled, let your clergy and the churches meet again in Christian intercourse, North and South. Let the secret orders and voluntary associations everywhere reunite as brethren once more. In short, give to all the natural and all the artificial causes which impel us together, their fullest sway. Let time do his office — drying tears, dispelling sorrows, mellowing passion, and making herb and grass and tree to grow again upon the hundred battle-fields of this terrible war.

"But this is recognition." It is not formal recognition, to which I will not consent. Recognition now, and attempted permanent treaties about boundary, travel, trade, and partition of Territories would end in a war fiercer and more disastrous than before. Recognition is absolute disunion; and not between the slave and the free States, but with Delaware and Maryland as part of the North, and Kentucky and Missouri part of the West. But whatever the actual line, every evil and mischief of disunion is implied in it. And for similar reasons, sir, I would not at this time press hastily a convention of the States. The men who now would hold seats in such a convention, would, upon both sides, if both agreed to attend, come together full of the hate and bitterness inseparable from a civil war. No, sir; let passion have time to cool, and reason to resume its sway. It cost thirty years of desperate and most wicked patience and industry to destroy or impair the magnificent temple of this Union. Let us be content if, within three years, we shall be able to restore it.

But certainly what I propose is informal, practical recognition. And that is precisely what exists to-day, and has existed, more or less defined, from the first. Flags of truce, exchange of prisoners, and all your other observances of the laws, forms, and courtesies of war are acts of recognition. Sir, does any man doubt to-day that there is a Confederate Government at Richmond, and that it is a "belligerent?" Even the Secretary of State has discovered it at last, though he has written ponderous folios of polished rhetoric to prove that it is not. Will continual war, then, without extended and substantial success, make the Confederate States any the less a government in fact?

"But it confesses disunion." Yes, just as the surgeon, who sets your fractured limb in splints, in order that it may be healed, admits that it is broken. But the Government will have failed to "crush out the rebellion." Sir, it has failed. You went to war to prove that we had a Government. With what result? To the people of the loyal States it has, in your hands, been the Government of King Stork, but to the Confederate States, of King Log. "But the rebellion will have triumphed." Better triumph to-day than ten years hence. But I deny it. The rebellion will at last be crushed out in the only way in which it ever was possible. "But no one will be hung at the end of the war." Neither will there be, though the war should last half a century, except by the mob or the hand of arbitrary power. But really, sir, if there is to be no hanging, let this Administration, and all who have done its bidding everywhere, rejoice and be exceeding glad.

And now, sir, allow me a word upon a subject of very great interest at this moment, and most important it may be in its influence upon the future — FOREIGN MEDIATION. I speak not of armed and hostile intervention, which I would resist as long as but one man was left to strike a blow at the invader. But friendly mediation — the kindly offer of an impartial Power to stand as a daysman between the contending parties in this most bloody and exhausting strife — ought to be met in a spirit as cordial and ready as that in which it is proffered. It would be churlish to refuse. Certainly, it is not consistent with the former dignity of this Government to ask for mediation; neither, sir, would it befit its ancient magnanimity to reject it. As proposed by the Emperor of France, I would accept it at once. Now is the auspicious moment. It is the speediest, easiest, most graceful mode of suspending hostilities. Let us hear no more of the mediation of cannon and the sword. The day for all that has gone by. Let us be statesmen at last. Sir, I give thanks that some, at least, among the Republican party seem ready now to lift themselves up to the height of this great argument, and to deal with it in the spirit of the patriots and great men of other countries and ages, and of the better days of the United States.

And now, sir, whatever may have been the motives of England, France, and the other great powers of Europe, in withholding recognition so long from the Confederate States, the South and the North are both indebted to them for an immense public service. The South has proved her ability to maintain herself by her own strength and resources, without foreign aid, moral or material. And the North and West — the whole country, indeed — these great Powers have served incalculably, by holding back a solemn proclamation to the world, that the Union of these States was finally and formally dissolved. They have left to us every motive and every chance for reunion; and if that has been the purpose of England especially — our rival so long; interested more than any other in disunion, and the consequent weakening of our great naval and commercial power, and suffering, too, as she has suffered, so long and severely because of this war — I do not hesitate to say that she has performed an act of unselfish, heroism without example in history. Was such, indeed, her purpose? Let her answer before the impartial tribunal of posterity. In any event, after the great reaction in public sentiment in the North and West, to be followed after some time by a like reaction in the South, foreign recognition now of the Confederate States could avail little to delay or prevent final reunion; if, as I firmly believe, reunion be not only possible but inevitable.

Sir, I have not spoken of foreign arbitration. That is quite another question. I think it impracticable, and fear it as dangerous. The very Powers — or any other Power — which have hesitated to aid disunion directly, or by force, might, as authorized arbiters, most readily pronounce for it at last. Very grand, indeed, would be the tribunal before which the great question of the Union of these States, and the final destiny of this continent for ages, should be heard, and historic through all time, the ambassadors who should argue it. And if both belligerents consent, let the subjects in controversy be referred to Switzerland, or Russia, or any other impartial and incorruptible Power or State in Europe. But at last, sir, the people of these several States here, at home, must be the final arbiter of this great quarrel in America; and the people and States of the Northwest, the mediators who shall stand like the prophet betwixt the living and the dead, that the plague of disunion may be flayed.

Sir, this war, horrible as it is, has taught us all some of the most important and salutary lessons which ever a people learned.

First, it has annihilated, in twenty months, all the false and pernicious theories and teachings of abolitionism for thirty years, and which a mere appeal to facts and argument could not have untaught in half a century. We have learned that the South is not weak, dependent, unenterprising or corrupted by slavery, luxury, and idleness; but powerful, earnest, warlike, enduring, self-supporting, full of energy, and inexhaustible in resources. We have been taught, and now confess it openly, that African slavery, instead of being a source of weakness to the South, is one of her main elements of strength; and hence the "military necessity," we are told, of abolishing slavery in order to suppress the rebellion. We have learned, also, that the non-slaveholding white men of the South, millions in number, are immovably attached to the institution and are its chief support; and abolitionists have found out, to their infinite surprise and disgust, that the slave is not "panting for freedom," nor pining in silent but revengeful grief over cruelty and oppression inflicted upon him; but happy, contented, attached deeply to his master, and unwilling — at least not eager — to accept the precious boon of freedom which they have proffered him. I appeal to the President for the proof. I appeal to the fact that fewer slaves have escaped, even from Virginia, in now nearly two years, than Arnold and Cornwallis carried away in six months of invasion in 1781. Finally, sir, we have learned, and the South, too, what the history of the world ages ago, and our own history might have taught us, that servile insurrection is the least of the dangers to which she is exposed. Hence, in my deliberate judgment, African slavery as an institution, will come out of this conflict fifty-fold stronger than when the war began.

The South, too, sir, has learned most important lessons; and among them, that personal courage is a quality common to all sections, and that in battle the men of the North, and especially of the West, are their equals. Hitherto there has been a mutual and most mischievous mistake upon both sides. The South overvalued its own personal courage, and undervalued ours, and we too readily consented; but at the same time she exaggerated our aggregate strength and resources, and underestimated her own; and we fell into the same error; and hence the original and fatal mistake or vice of the military policy of the North, and which has already broken down the war by its own weight the belief that we could bring overwhelming numbers and power into the field and upon the sea, and crush out the South at a blow. But twenty months of terrible warfare have corrected many errors, and taught us the wisdom of a century. And now, sir, every one of these lessons will profit us all for ages to come, and if we do but reunite, will bind us in a closer, firmer, more durable union than ever before.

I have now, Mr. Speaker, finished what I desired to say at this time, upon the great question of the reunion of these States. I have spoken freely and boldly — not wisely, it may be, for the present, or for myself personally, but most wisely for the future and for my country. Not courting censure, I yet do not shrink from it. My own immediate personal interests, and my chances just now for the more material rewards of ambition, I again surrender as hostages to that GREAT HEREAFTER, the echo of whose footsteps already I hear along the highway of time. Whoever, here or elsewhere, believes that war can restore the Union of these States; whoever would have a war for the abolition of slavery, or disunion; and he who demands Southern independence and final separation, let him speak, for him I have offended. Devoted to the Union from the beginning, I will not desert it now in this the hour of its sorest trial.

Sir, it was the day-dream of my boyhood, the cherished desire of my heart in youth, that I might live to see the hundredth anniversary of our national independence, and, as orator of the day, exult in the expanding glories and greatness of the still United States. That vision lingers yet before my eyes, obscured, indeed, by the clouds and thick darkness, and the blood of civil war. But, sir, if the men of this generation are wise enough to profit by the hard experience of the past two years, and will turn their hearts now from bloody intents to the words and arts of peace, that day will find us again the United States. And if not earlier, as I would desire and believe, at least, upon that day let the great work of reunion be consummated; that thenceforth, for ages, the States and the people who shall fill up this mighty continent, united under one Constitution, and in one Union, and the same destiny, shall celebrate it as the birthday both of Independence and of the Great Restoration.

Sir, I repeat it, we are in the midst of the very crisis of this revolution. If, to-day, we secure peace, and begin the work of reunion, we shall yet escape; if not, I see nothing before us but universal political and social revolution, anarchy, and bloodshed, compared with which the Reign of Terror in France was a merciful visitation.

Pamphlet 31

Abraham Lincoln

The Truth from an Honest Man. The Letter of the President. President Lincoln's Views. An Important Letter on the Principles Involved in the Vallandigham Case. Correspondence in Relation to the Democratic Meeting, at Albany, N.Y.
(*Union League No. 31*)
Philadelphia, 1863

[One of the most effective pamphleteers of the war was — indirectly — President Lincoln, numerous of whose speeches and statements were distributed in pamphlet form. A conspicuous example was his letter containing the rhetorical query, "Must I shoot a simple-minded soldier-boy who deserts, while I must not touch a hair of a wily agitator who induces him to desert?" The occasion for the letter was an upsurge of protests in the aftermath of the military confinement and trial of Clement L. Vallandigham, leader of the Ohio Peace Democrats or Copperheads. Vallandigham was convicted and sentenced to military prison, but Lincoln instead banished him to the Confederacy from which he escaped to Canada. Throughout the country Democrats denounced as unconstitutional the administration procedure: military arrest, denial of habeas corpus, and trial by military commission. Erastus Corning (1794–1872), one of the most prominent Democrats in the House of Representatives and President of the New York Central Railroad, sent Lincoln a set of indignant resolutions voted at a meeting in Albany. This occasioned Lincoln's eloquent reply, which the Union League of Philadelphia distributed in pamphlet form.[1]]

[1] [Randall, *Constitutional Problems Under Lincoln*, 184–185; Randall, *Lincoln the President*, III, 212–238.]

LETTER OF THE COMMITTEE.

ALBANY, *May* 19, 1863.

To His Excellency the

PRESIDENT OF THE UNITED STATES: —

The undersigned, officers of a public meeting held at the city of Albany on the 16th day of May, instant, herewith transmit to your Excellency a copy of the resolutions adopted at the said meeting, and respectfully request your earnest consideration of them. They deem it proper on their personal responsibility to state that the meeting was one of the most respectable as to numbers and character, and one of the most earnest in the support of the Union ever held in this city.

Yours with great regard,

ERASTUS CORNING, *President.*

Vice-Presidents.

ELI PERRY,	LEMUEL W. RODGERS,
PETER GANSEVOORT,	WILLIAM SEYMOUR,
PETER MONTEATH,	JEREMIAH OSBORN,
SAMUEL W. GIBBS,	WILLIAM S. PADOCK,
JOHN NIBLACK,	J. B. SANDERS,
H. W. McCLELLAN,	EDWARD MULCAHY,

D. V. N. RADCLIFFE.

Secretaries.

WILLIAM A. RICE,	M. A. NOLAN,
EDWARD NEWCOMB,	JOHN R. NESSEL,
R. W. PECKHAM, JR.,	C. W. WEEKS.

RESOLUTIONS

ADOPTED AT THE MEETING HELD IN ALBANY, N.Y., ON THE 16TH OF MAY, 1863.

Resolved, That the Democrats of New York point to their uniform course of action during the two years of civil war through which we have passed, to the alacrity which they have evinced in filling the ranks of the army, to their contributions and sacrifices, as to the evidence of their patriotism and devotion to the cause of our imperiled country. Never in the history of civil war has a government been sustained with such ample resources of means and men as the people have voluntarily placed in the hands of the Administration.

Resolved, That as Democrats we are determined to maintain this patriotic attitude, and, despite of adverse and disheartening circumstances, to devote all our energies to sustain the cause of the Union, to secure peace through victory, and to bring back the restoration of all the States under the safeguards of the Constitution.

Resolved, That while we will not consent to be misapprehended upon these points, we are determined not to be misunderstood in regard to others not less essential. We demand that the Administration shall be true to the Constitution; shall recognize and maintain the rights of the States and the liberties of the citizen; shall everywhere, outside of the lines of necessary military occupation and the scenes of insurrection, exert all its powers to maintain the supremacy of the civil over military law.

Resolved, That in view of these principles we denounce the recent assumption of a military commander to seize and try a citizen of Ohio, Clement L. Vallandigham, for no other reason than words addressed to a public meeting, in criticism of the course of the Administration, and in condemnation of the military orders of that general.

Resolved, That this assumption of power by a military tribunal, if successfully asserted, not only abrogates the right of the people to assemble and discuss the affairs of government, the liberty of speech and of the press, the right of trial by jury, the law of evidence, and the privilege of habeas corpus, but it strikes a fatal blow at the supremacy of law, and the authority of the State and Federal constitutions.

Resolved, That the Constitution of the United States — the supreme law of the land — has defined the crime of treason against the United States to consist "only in levying war against them, or adhering to their enemies, giving them aid and comfort;" and has provided that "no person shall be convicted of treason, unless on the testimony of two witnesses to the same overt act, or on confession in open court." And it further provides, that "no person shall be held to answer for a capital or otherwise infamous crime, unless on a presentment or indictment of a grand jury, except in cases arising in the land and naval forces, or in the militia, when in actual service in time of war or public danger;" and further, that "in all criminal prosecutions, the accused shall enjoy the right of a speedy and public trial by an impartial jury of the State and district wherein the crime was committed."

Resolved, That these safeguards of the rights of the citizen against the pretensions of arbitrary power were intended more especially for his protection in times of civil commotion. They were secured substantially to the English people, after years of protracted civil war, and were adopted into our Constitution at the close of the Revolution. They have stood the test of seventy-six years of trial under our republican system, under circumstances which show that, while they constitute the foundation of all free government, they are the elements of the enduring stability of the Republic.

Resolved, That in adopting the language of Daniel Webster, we declare "it is the ancient and undoubted prerogative of this people to canvass public measures and the merits of public men." It is a "home-bred right," a fireside privilege. It has been enjoyed in every house, cottage, and cabin in the nation. It is as undoubted as the right of breathing the air or walking on the earth. Belonging to private life as a right, it belongs to public life as a duty, and it is the last duty which those whose representatives we are shall find us to abandon. Aiming at all times to be courteous and temperate in its use, except when the right itself is questioned, we shall place ourselves on the extreme boundary of our own right, and bid defiance to any arm that would move us from our ground. "This high constitutional privilege we shall defend and exercise in all places — in time of peace, in time of war, and at all times. Living, we shall assert it; and should we leave no other inheritance to our children, by the blessing of God we will leave them the inheritance of free principles, and the example of a manly, independent, and constitutional defence of them."

Resolved, That in the election of Governor Seymour the people of this State by an emphatic majority, declared their condemnation of the system of arbitrary arrests, and their determination to stand by the Constitution. That the revival of this lawless system can have but one result: to divide and distract the North, and to destroy its confidence in the purposes of the Administration. That we deprecate it as an element of confusion at home, of weakness to our armies in the field, and as calculated to lower the estimate of American character and magnify the apparent peril of our cause abroad. And that, regarding the blow struck at a citizen of Ohio as aimed at the rights of every citizen of the North, we denounce it as against the spirit of our laws and Constitution, and most earnestly call upon the President of the United States to reverse the action of the military tribunal which has passed a "cruel and unusual punishment" upon the party arrested, prohibited in terms by the Constitution, and to restore him to the liberty of which he has been deprived.

Resolved, That the president, vice-presidents, and secretary of this meeting, be requested to transmit a copy of these resolutions to his Excellency the President of the United States, with the assurance of this meeting of their hearty and earnest desire to support the Government in every constitutional and lawful measure to suppress the existing rebellion.

MR. LINCOLN'S REPLY.

EXECUTIVE MANSION, WASHINGTON,
June 12, 1863.

HON. ERASTUS CORNING, and others:

GENTLEMEN: — Your letter of May 19, inclosing the resolutions of a public meeting held at Albany, N.Y., on the 16th of the same month, was received several days ago.

The resolutions, as I understand them, are resolvable into two propositions, first, the expression of a purpose to sustain the cause of the Union, to secure peace through victory, and to support the Administration in every constitutional and lawful measure to suppress the rebellion; and secondly, a declaration of censure upon the Administration for supposed unconstitutional action, such as the making of military arrests. And, from the two propositions, a third is deduced, which is, that the gentlemen composing the meeting are resolved on doing their part to maintain our common government and country, despite the folly or wickedness, as they may conceive, of any Administration. This position is eminently patriotic, and as such I thank the meeting and congratulate the nation for it. My own purpose is the same; so that the meeting and myself have a common object, and can have no difference except in the choice of means or measures for effecting that object.

And here I ought to close this paper, and would close it, if there were no apprehension that more injurious consequences than any merely personal to myself might follow the censures systematically cast upon me for doing what, in my view of duty, I could not forbear. The resolutions promise to support me in every constitutional and lawful measure to suppress the rebellion; and I have not knowingly employed, nor shall knowingly employ, any other. But the meeting, by their resolutions, assert and argue that certain military arrests, and proceedings following them, for which I am ultimately responsible, are unconstitutional. I think they are not. The resolutions quote from the Constitution the definition of treason, and also the limiting safeguards and guarantees therein provided for the citizen on trial for treason, and on his being held to answer for capital or otherwise infamous crimes, and, in criminal prosecutions, his rights to a speedy and public trial by an impartial jury. They proceed to resolve, "that these safeguards of the rights of the citizen against the pretensions of arbitrary power were intended more *especially* for his protection in times of civil commotion." And, apparently to demonstrate the proposition, the resolutions proceed: "They were secured substantially to the English people *after* years of protracted civil war, and were adopted into our Constitution at the *close* of the Revolution." Would not the demonstration have been better if it could have been truly said that these safeguards had been adopted and applied *during* the civil wars and *during* our Revolution, instead of *after* the one and at the *close* of the other? I, too, am devotedly for them *after* civil war, and *before* civil war, and at all times, "except when, in cases of rebellion or invasion, the public safety may require" their suspension. The resolutions proceed to tell us that these safeguards "have stood the test of seventy-six years of trial, under our republican system, under circumstances which show that, while they constitute the foundation of all free government, they are the elements of the enduring stability of the Republic." No one denies that they have so stood the test up to the beginning of the present rebellion, if we except a certain occurrence at New Orleans; nor does any one question that they will stand the same test much longer after the rebellion closes. But these provisions of the Constitution have no application to the case we have in hand, because the arrests complained of were not made for treason — that is not for *the* treason defined in the Constitution, and upon conviction of which the punishment is death — nor yet were they made to hold persons to answer for any capital or otherwise infamous crimes; nor were the proceedings following, in any constitutional or legal sense, "criminal prosecutions." The arrests were made on totally different grounds, and the proceedings following accorded with the grounds of the arrests. Let us consider the real case with which we are dealing, and apply to it the parts of the Constitution plainly made for such cases.

Prior to my installation here, it had been inculcated that any State had a lawful right to secede from the national Union, and that it would be expedient to exercise the right whenever the devotees of the doctrine should fail to elect a President to their own liking. I was elected contrary to their liking; and, accordingly, so far as it was legally possible, they had taken seven States out of the Union, had seized many of the United States forts, and had fired upon the United States flag, all before I was inaugurated, and, of course, before I had done any official act whatever. The rebellion thus began soon ran into the present civil war; and, in certain respects, it began on very unequal terms between the parties. The insurgents had been preparing for it more than thirty years, while the Government had taken no steps to resist them. The former had carefully considered all the means which could be turned to their account. It undoubtedly was a well-pondered reliance with them that, in their own unrestricted efforts to destroy Union, Constitution, and Law, all together, the Government would, in great degree, be restrained by the same Constitution and law from arresting their progress. Their sympathizers pervaded all departments of the Government and nearly all communities of the people. From this material, under cover of "liberty of speech," "liberty of the press," and "habeas corpus," they hoped to keep on foot among us a most efficient corps of spies, informers, suppliers, and aiders and abettors of their cause in a thousand ways. They knew that in times such as they were inaugurating, by the Constitution itself, the "habeas corpus" might be suspended; but they also knew they had friends who would make a question as to *who* was to suspend it; meanwhile, their spies and others might remain at large to help on their cause. Or, if, as has happened, the Executive should suspend the writ, without ruinous waste of time, instances of arresting innocent persons might occur, as are always likely to occur in such cases; and then a clamor could be raised in regard to this, which might be, at least, of some service to the insurgent cause. It needed no very keen perception to discover this part of the enemy's programme, so soon as, by open hostilities, their machinery was fairly put in motion. Yet, thoroughly imbued with a reverence for the guaranteed rights of individuals, I was slow to adopt the strong measures which by degrees I have been forced to regard as being within the exceptions of the Constitution, and as indispensable to the public safety. Nothing is better known to history than that courts of justice are utterly incompetent to such cases. Civil courts are organized chiefly for trials of individuals, or, at most, a few individuals acting in concert; and this in quiet times, and on charges of crimes well defined in the law. Even in times of peace, bands of horse-thieves and robbers frequently grow too numerous and powerful for the ordinary courts of justice. But what comparison, in numbers, have such bands ever borne to the insurgent sympathizers even in many of the loyal States? Again: a jury too frequently has at least one member more ready to hang the panel than to hang the traitor. And yet, again, he who dissuades one man from volunteering, or induces one soldier to desert, weakens the Union cause as much as he who kills a Union soldier in battle. Yet this dissuasion or inducement may be so conducted as to be no defined crime of which any civil court would take cognizance.

Ours is a case of rebellion — so called by the resolutions before me — in fact, a clear, flagrant, and gigantic case of rebellion; and the provision of the Constitution that "the privilege of the writ of habeas corpus shall not be suspended, unless when, in cases of rebellion or invasion, the public safety may require it," is *the* provision which specially applies to our present case. This provision plainly attests the understanding of those who made the Constitution, that ordinary courts of justice are inadequate to "cases of rebellion" — attests their purpose that, in such cases, men may be held in custody whom the courts, acting on ordinary rules, would discharge. Habeas corpus does not discharge men who are proved to be guilty of defined crime; and its suspension is allowed by the Constitution on purpose that men may be arrested and held who cannot be proved to be guilty of defined crime, "when, in cases of rebellion or invasion, the public safety may require it." This is precisely our present case — a case of rebellion, wherein the public safety *does* require the suspension. Indeed, arrests by process of courts, and arrests in cases of rebellion, do not proceed altogether upon the same basis. The former is directed at the small per-centage of ordinary and continuous perpetration of crime; while the latter is directed at sudden and extensive uprisings against the Government, which, at most, will succeed or fail in no great length of time. In the latter case, arrests are made, not so much for what has been done, as for what probably would be done. The latter is more for the preventive and less for the vindictive than the former. In such cases, the purposes of men are much more easily understood than in cases of ordinary crime. The man who stands by and says nothing when the peril of his Government is discussed, cannot be misunderstood. If not hindered, he is sure to help the enemy; much more, if he talks ambiguously — talks for his country with "buts" and "ifs" and "ands." Of how little value the constitutional provisions I have quoted will be rendered, if arrest shall never be made until defined crimes shall have been committed, may be illustrated by a few notable examples. Gen. John C. Breckinridge, Gen. Robert E. Lee, Gen. Joseph E. Johnson, Gen. John B. Magruder, Gen. William B. Preston, Gen. Simon B. Buckner, and Commodore Franklin Buchanan, now occupying the very highest places in the Rebel war service, were all within the power of the Government since the Rebellion began, and were nearly as well known to be traitors then as now. Unquestionably if we had seized and held them, the insurgent cause would be much weaker. But no one of them had then committed any crime defined in the law. Every one of them, if arrested, would have been discharged on habeas corpus were the writ allowed to operate. In view of these and similar cases, I think the time not unlikely to come when I shall be blamed for having made too few arrests rather than too many.

By the third resolution, the meeting indicate their opinion that military arrests may be constitutional in localities where rebellion actually exists, but that such arrests are unconstitutional in localities where rebellion or insurrection does *not* actually exist. They insist that such arrests shall not be made "outside of the lines of necessary military occupation, and the scenes of insurrection." Inasmuch, however, as the Constitution itself makes no such distinction, I am unable to believe that there *is* any such constitutional distinction. I concede that the class of arrests complained of can be constitutional only when, in cases of rebellion or invasion, the public safety may require them; and I insist that in such cases they are constitutional *wherever* the public safety may require them; as well in places to which they may prevent the rebellion extending as in those where it may be already prevailing; as well where they may restrain mischievous interference with the raising and supplying of armies to suppress the rebellion, as where the rebellion may actually be; as well where they may restrain the enticing men out of the army, as where they would prevent mutiny in the army; equally constitutional at all places where they will conduce to the public safety, as against the dangers of rebellion or invasion. Take the particular case mentioned by the meeting. It is asserted, in substance, that Mr. Vallandigham was, by a military commander, seized and tried "for no other reason than words addressed to a public meeting, in criticism of the course of the Administration, and in condemnation of the military orders of the General." Now, if there be no mistake about this; if this assertion is the truth and the whole truth; if there was no other reason for the arrest, then I concede that the arrest was wrong. But the arrest, as I understand, was made for a very different reason. Mr. Vallandigham avows his hostility to the war on the part of the Union; and his arrest was made because he was laboring, with some effect, to prevent the raising of troops; to encourage desertions from the army; and to leave the rebellion without an adequate military force to suppress it. He was not arrested because he was damaging the political prospects of the Administration, or the personal interests of the commanding general, but because he was damaging the army, upon the existence and vigor of which the life of the nation depends. He was warring upon the military, and this gave the military constitutional jurisdiction to lay hands upon him. If Mr. Vallandigham was not damaging the military power of the country, then his arrest was made on mistake of fact, which I would be glad to correct on reasonably satisfactory evidence.

I understand the meeting, whose resolutions I am considering, to be in favor of suppressing the rebellion by military force — by armies. Long experience has shown that armies cannot be maintained unless desertions shall be punished by the severe penalty of death. The case requires, and the law and the Constitution sanction, this punishment. Must I shoot a simple-minded soldier-boy who deserts, while I must not touch a hair of a wily agitator who induces him to desert? This is none the less injurious when effected by getting a father, or brother, or friend, into a public meeting, and there working upon his feelings till he is persuaded to write the soldier-boy that he is fighting in a bad cause, for a wicked Administration of a contemptible Government, too weak to arrest and punish him if he shall desert. I think that in such a case to silence the agitator and save the boy is not only constitutional, but withal a great mercy.

If I be wrong on this question of constitutional power, my error lies in believing that certain proceedings are constitutional when, in cases of rebellion or invasion, the public safety requires them, which would not be constitutional when, in the absence of rebellion or invasion, the public safety does *not* require them; in other words, that the Constitution is not, in its application, in all respects the same, in cases of rebellion or invasion involving the public safety, as it is in time of profound peace and public security. The Constitution itself makes the distinction; and I can no more be persuaded that the Government can constitutionally take no strong measures in time of rebellion, because it can be shown that the same could not be lawfully taken in time of peace, than I can be persuaded that a particular drug is not good medicine for a sick man, because it can be shown not to be good food for a well one. Nor am I able to appreciate the danger apprehended by the meeting, that the American people will, by means of military arrests during the rebellion, lose the right of public discussion, the liberty of speech and the press, the law of evidence, trial by jury, and habeas corpus, throughout the indefinite peaceful future which I trust lies before them, any more than I am able to believe that a man could contract so strong an appetite for emetics during temporary illness as to persist in feeding upon them during the remainder of his healthful life.

In giving the resolutions that earnest consideration which you request of me, I cannot overlook the fact that the meeting speak as "Democrats." Nor can I, with full respect for their known intelligence, and the fairly presumed deliberation with which they prepared their resolutions, be permitted to suppose that this occurred by accident, or in any way other than that they preferred to designate themselves as "Democrats" rather than "American citizens." In this time of national peril, I would have preferred to meet you upon a level one step higher than any party platform; because I am sure that, from such more elevated position, we could do better battle for the country we all love than we possibly can from those lower ones where, from the force of habit, the prejudices of the past, and selfish hopes of the future, we are sure to expend much of our ingenuity and strength in finding fault with, and aiming blows at each other. But, since you have denied me this, I will yet be thankful, for the country's sake, that not all Democrats have done so. He on whose discretionary judgment Mr. Vallandigham was arrested and tried is a Democrat, having no old party affinity with me; and the judge who rejected the constitutional view expressed in these resolutions, by refusing to discharge Mr. Vallandigham on habeas corpus, is a Democrat of better days than these, having received his judicial mantle at the hands of President Jackson. And still more, of all those Democrats who are nobly exposing their lives and shedding their blood on the battle-field, I have learned that many approve the course taken with Mr. Vallandigham, while I have not heard of a single one condemning it. I cannot assert that there are none such. And the name of President Jackson recalls an instance of pertinent history: After the battle of New Orleans, and while the fact that the treaty of peace had been concluded was well known in the city, but before official knowledge of it had arrived, Gen. Jackson still maintained martial or military law. Now that it could be said the war was over, the clamor against martial law, which had existed from the first, grew more furious. Among other things, a Mr. Louiallier published a denunciatory newspaper article. Gen. Jackson arrested him. A lawyer by the name of Morel procured the United States Judge Hall to issue a writ of habeas corpus to relieve Mr. Louiallier. Gen. Jackson arrested both the lawyer and the judge. A Mr. Hollander ventured to say of some part of the matter that "it was a dirty trick." Gen. Jackson arrested him. When the officer undertook to serve the writ of habeas corpus, Gen. Jackson took it from him, and sent him away with a copy. Holding the judge in custody a few days, the General sent him beyond the limits of his encampment, and set him at liberty, with an order to remain till the ratification of peace should be regularly announced, or until the British should have left the Southern coast. A day or two more elapsed, the ratification of a treaty of peace was regularly announced, and the judge and others were fully liberated. A few days more, and the judge called Gen. Jackson into court and fined him $1,000 for having arrested him and the others named. The General paid the fine and there the matter rested for nearly thirty years, when Congress refunded principal and interest. The late Senator Douglas, then in the

House of Representatives, took a leading part in the debates in which the constitutional question was much discussed. I am not prepared to say whom the journals would show to have voted for the measure.

It may be remarked: First that we had the same Constitution then as now; secondly, that we then had a case of invasion, and now we have a case of rebellion; and thirdly, that the permanent right of the people to public discussion, the liberty of speech and of the press, the trial by jury, the law of evidence, and the habeas corpus, suffered no detriment whatever by that conduct of Gen. Jackson, or its subsequent approval by the American Congress.

And yet, let me say that, in my own discretion, I do not know whether I would have ordered the arrest of Mr. Vallandigham. While I cannot shift the responsibility from myself, I hold that, as a general rule, the commander in the field is the better judge of the necessity in any particular case. Of course I must practice a general directory and revisory power in the matter.

One of the resolutions expresses the opinion of the meeting that arbitrary arrests will have the effect to divide and distract those who should be united in suppressing the rebellion, and I am specifically called on to discharge Mr. Vallandigham. I regard this as at least a fair appeal to me on the expediency of exercising a constitutional power which I think exists. In response to such appeal, I have to say it gave me pain when I learned that Mr. Vallandigham had been arrested; that is, I was pained that there should have seemed to be a necessity for arresting him, and that it will afford me great pleasure to discharge him so soon as I can, by any means, believe the public safety will not suffer by it. I further say that, as the war progresses, it appears to me, opinion and action, which were in great confusion at first, take shape, and fall into more regular channels, so that the necessity for strong dealing with them gradually decreases. I have every reason to desire that it should cease altogether; and far from the least is my regard for the opinions and wishes of those who, like the meeting at Albany, declare their purpose to sustain the Government in every constitutional and lawful measure to suppress the rebellion. Still, I must continue to do so much as may seem to be required by the public safety.

ABRAHAM LINCOLN.

Pamphlet 32

John V. L. Pruyn, *et al.*

Reply to President Lincoln's Letter of 12th June, 1863. (Papers from the Society for the Diffusion of Political Knowledge, No. 10)

New York, 1863

[The Albany committee which had prepared and reported the resolutions censuring President Lincoln for his arbitrary strictures upon civil liberties quickly framed a reply to his letter defending himself. It went even further than the original resolutions: "In the special case of Mr. Vallandigham, the injustice commenced by your subordinate was consummated by a sentence of exile from his home pronounced by you. That great wrong, more than any other which preceded it, asserts the principles of a supreme despotism."]

REPLY

TO

PRESIDENT LINCOLN'S LETTER

OF 12TH JUNE, 1863.

Henry Laurens was President of the Continental Congress in 1779. In 1780 he was sent as Minister to Holland. On his way he was captured, and imprisoned in the Tower of London for fourteen months. When Lord Shelburne became Premier, Laurens was brought up, on Habeas Corpus, and released. After his release, he was treated with great kindness and respect by the British authorities. He dined with Lord Shelburne. After dinner, the conversation turned on the separation of the two countries. Lord Shelburne remarked:

"I AM SORRY FOR YOUR PEOPLE." "WHY SO?" ASKED LAURENS. "THEY WILL LOSE THE HABEAS CORPUS," WAS THE REPLY. "LOSE THE HABEAS CORPUS!" SAID LAURENS. "YES," SAID LORD SHELBURNE. "WE PURCHASED IT WITH CENTURIES OF WRANGLING, MANY YEARS OF FIGHTING, AND HAD IT CONFIRMED BY AT LEAST

FIFTY ACTS OF PARLIAMENT. ALL THIS TAUGHT THE NATION ITS VALUE; AND IT IS SO INGRAINED INTO THEIR CREED, AS THE VERY FOUNDATION OF THEIR LIBERTY, THAT NO MAN OR PARTY WILL EVER DARE TRAMPLE ON IT. YOUR PEOPLE WILL PICK IT UP, AND ATTEMPT TO USE IT; BUT, HAVING COST THEM NOTHING, THEY WILL NOT KNOW HOW TO APPRECIATE IT. AT THE FIRST GREAT INTERNAL FEUD THAT YOU HAVE, THE MAJORITY WILL TRAMPLE UPON IT, AND THE PEOPLE WILL PERMIT IT TO BE DONE, AND SO WILL GO YOUR LIBERTY!"

Published Journal of Henry Laurens.

To His Excellency Abraham Lincoln, President of the United States:

Sir: Your answer, which has appeared in the public prints, to the resolutions adopted at a recent meeting in the city of Albany, affirming the personal rights and liberties of the citizens of this country, has been referred to the undersigned — the Committee who prepared and reported those resolutions. The subject will now receive from us some further attention, which your answer seems to justify, if not to invite. We hope not to appear wanting in the respect due to your high position, if we reply with a freedom and earnestness suggested by the infinite gravity and importance of the questions upon which you have thought proper to take issue at the bar of public opinion.

You seem to be aware that the Constitution of the United States, which you have sworn to protect and defend, contains the following guarantees to which we again ask your attention: (1) Congress shall make no law abridging the freedom of speech or of the press. (2) The right of the people to be secure in their persons against unreasonable seizures, shall not be violated, and no warrant shall issue but upon probable cause supported by oath. (3) No person except soldiers and mariners in the service of the Government shall be held to answer for a capital or infamous crime, unless on presentment or indictment of a grand jury, nor shall any person be deprived of life, liberty, or property without due process of law. (4) In all criminal prosecutions, the accused shall enjoy the right of a speedy and public trial by an impartial jury of the State or District in which the crime shall have been committed, and to be confronted with the witnesses against him.

You are also, no doubt, aware that on the adoption of the Constitution, these invaluable provisions were proposed by the jealous caution of the States, and were inserted as amendments for a perpetual assurance of liberty against the encroachments of power. From your earliest reading of history, you also know that the great principles of liberty and law which underlie these provisions were derived to us from the British Constitution. In that country they were secured by *Magna Charta* more than six hundred years ago, and they have been confirmed by many and repeated statutes of the realm. A single palpable violation of them in England would not only arouse the public indignation, but would endanger the throne itself. For a persistent disregard of them, Charles the First was dethroned and beheaded by his rebellious subjects.

The fact has already passed into history, that the sacred rights and immunities which were designed to be protected by these constitutional guarantees, have not been preserved to the people during your administration. In violation of the first of them, the freedom of the press has been denied. In repeated instances newspapers have been suppressed in the loyal States, because they criticised, as constitutionally they might, those fatal errors of policy which have characterized the conduct of public affairs since your advent to power. In violation of the second of them, hundreds and, we believe, thousands of men, have been seized and immured in prisons and bastiles, not only without warrant upon probable cause, but without any warrant, and for no other cause than a constitutional exercise of freedom of speech. In violation of all these guarantees, a distinguished citizen of a peaceful and loyal State has been torn from his home at midnight by a band of soldiers, acting under the order of one of your generals, tried before a military commission, without judge or jury, convicted and sentenced without even the suggestion of any offense known to the Constitution or laws of this country. For all these acts you avow yourself ultimately responsible. In the special case of Mr. Vallandigham, the injustice commenced by your subordinate was consummated by a sentence of exile from his home, pronounced by you. That great wrong, more than any other which preceded it, asserts the principles of a supreme despotism.

These repeated and continued invasions of constitutional liberty and private right, have occasioned profound anxiety in the public mind. The apprehension and alarm which they are calculated to produce have been greatly enhanced by your attempt to justify them, because in that attempt you assume to yourself a rightful authority possessed by no constitutional monarch on earth. We accept the declaration that you prefer to exercise this authority with a moderation not hitherto exhibited. But believing as we do, that your forbearance is not the tenure by which liberty is enjoyed in this country, we propose to challenge the grounds on which your claim of supreme power is based. While yielding to you as a constitutional magistrate the deference to which you are entitled, we can not accord to you the despotic power you claim, however indulgent and gracious you may promise to be in wielding it.

We have carefully considered the grounds on which your pretensions to more than regal authority are claimed to rest; and if we do not misinterpret the misty and clouded forms of expression in which those pretensions are set forth, your meaning is, that while the rights of the citizen are protected by the Constitution in time of peace, they are suspended or lost in time of war, when invasion or rebellion exist. You do not, like many others in whose minds reason and the love of regulated liberty seem to be overthrown by the excitements of the hour, attempt to base this conclusion upon a supposed military necessity existing outside of and transcending the Constitution, a military necessity behind which the Constitution itself disappears in a total eclipse. We do not find this gigantic and monstrous heresy put forth in your plea for absolute power, but we do find another equally subversive of liberty and law, and quite as certainly tending to the establishment of despotism. You claim to have found not outside, but within the Constitution, a principle or germ of arbitrary power, which in time of war expands at once into an absolute sovereignty, wielded by one man; so that liberty perishes, or is dependent on his will, his discretion, or his caprice. This extraordinary doctrine you claim to derive wholly from that clause of the Constitution which, in case of invasion or rebellion, permits the writ of *habeas corpus* to be suspended. Upon this ground your whole argument is based.

You must permit us to say to you, with all due respect, with the earnestness demanded by the occasion, that the American people will never acquiesce in this doctrine. In their opinion the guarantees of the Constitution which secure to them freedom of speech and of the press, immunity from arrest for offenses unknown to the laws

of the land, and the right of trial by jury before the tribunals provided by those laws, instead of military commissions and drum-
head courts-martial, are living and vital principles IN PEACE AND
IN WAR, at all times and under all circumstances. No sophistry or
argument can shake this conviction, nor will the people require its
confirmation by logical sequences and deductions. It is a conviction
deeply interwoven with the instincts, the habits, and the education
of our countrymen. The right to form opinions upon public measures
and men, and to declare those opinions by speech or writing, with
the utmost latitude of expression; the right of personal liberty,
unless forfeited according to established laws, and for offenses previously defined by law; the right, when accused of crime, to be tried
where law is administered, and punishment is pronounced only
when the crime is legally ascertained — all these are rights instantly
perceived without argument or proof. No refinement of logic can
unsettle them in the minds of freemen; no power can annihilate
them, and no force at the command of any chief magistrate can
compel their surrender.

So far as it is possible for us to understand, from your language,
the mental process which has led you to the alarming conclusions
indicated by your communication, it is this: the *habeas corpus* is a
remedial writ, issued by courts and magistrates, to inquire into the
cause of any imprisonment or restraint of liberty; on the return of
which and upon due examination, the person imprisoned is discharged, if the restraint is unlawful, or admitted to bail if he appears
to have been lawfully arrested, and is held to answer a criminal
accusation. Inasmuch as this process may be suspended in time of
war, you seem to think that every remedy for a false and unlawful
imprisonment is abrogated; and from this postulate you reach, at
a single bound, the conclusion that there is no liberty under the
Constitution which does not depend on the gracious indulgence of
the Executive only. This great heresy once established, and by this
mode of induction, there springs at once into existence a brood of
crimes or offenses undefined by any rule, and hitherto unknown to
the laws of this country; and this is followed by indiscriminate arrests, midnight seizures, military commissions, unheard-of modes of
trial and punishment, and all the machinery of terror and despotism.
Your language does not permit us to doubt as to your essential
meaning, for you tell us, that "arrests are made not so much for

what has been done, as for what probably would be done." And, again: "The man who stands by and says nothing when the peril of his government is discussed, can not be misunderstood. If not hindered, (of course by arrest,) he is sure to help the enemy, and much more if he talks ambiguously, talks for his country with 'buts' and 'ifs' and 'ands.'" You also tell us that the arrests complained of have not been made "for the treason defined in the Constitution," nor "for any capital or otherwise infamous crimes, nor were the proceedings following, in any constitutional or legal sense, criminal prosecutions." The very ground, then, of your justification is, that the victims of arbitrary arrest were obedient to every law, were guiltless of any known and defined offense, and therefore were without the protection of the Constitution. The suspension of the writ of *habeas corpus,* instead of being intended to prevent the enlargement of arrested criminals until a legal trial and conviction can be had, is designed according to your doctrine, to subject innocent men to your supreme will and pleasure. Silence itself is punishable according to this extraordinary theory, and still more so the expression of opinions, however loyal, if attended with criticism upon the policy of the Government. We must respectfully refuse our assent to this theory of constitutional law. We think that men may be rightfully silent if they so choose, while clamorous and needy patriots proclaim the praises of those who wield power; and as to the "buts," the "ifs," and the "ands," these are Saxon words, and belong to the vocabulary of freemen.

We have already said that the intuition of a free people instantly rejects these dangerous and unheard-of doctrines. It is not our purpose to enter upon an elaborate and extended refutation of them. We submit to you, however, one or two considerations, in the hope that you will review the subject with the earnest attention which its supreme importance demands. We say, then, we are not aware that the writ of *habeas corpus* is now suspended in any of the peaceful and loyal States of the Union. An act of Congress, approved by you on the third of March, 1863, authorized the President to suspend it during the present rebellion. That the suspension is a legislative, and not an executive act, has been held in every judicial decision ever made in this country, and we think it can not be delegated to any other branch of the Government. But passing over that consideration, you have not exercised the power which Congress attempted to confer upon you, and the writ is not suspended in any part of the country where the civil laws are in force. Now, inasmuch as your doctrine of the arbitrary arrest and imprisonment of innocent men, in admitted violation of express constitutional guarantees, is wholly derived from a suspension of the *habeas corpus,* the first step to be taken, in the ascent to absolute power, ought to be to make it known to the people that the writ is in fact suspended, to the end that they may know what is their condition. You have not yet exercised this power, and therefore, according to your own constitutional thesis, your conclusion falls to the ground. It is one of the provisions of the Constitution, and of the very highest value, that no *ex post facto* law shall be passed the meaning of which is, that no act which is not against the law when committed, can be made criminal by subsequent legislation. But your claim is, that when the writ of *habeas corpus* is suspended, you may lawfully imprison and punish for the crimes of silence, of speech, and opinion. But as these are not offenses against the known and established law of the land, the constitutional principle to which we now refer plainly requires that you should, before taking cognizance of such offenses, make known the rule of action, in order that the people may be advised in due season, so as not to become liable to its penalties. Let us turn your attention to the most glaring and indefensible of all the assaults upon constitutional liberty, which have marked the history of your administration. No one has ever pretended that the writ of *habeas corpus* was suspended in the State of Ohio, where the arrest of a citizen at midnight, already referred to, was made, and he placed before a military court-martial for trial and sentence, upon charges and specifications which admitted his innocence according to the existing laws of this country. Upon your own doctrine, then, can you hesitate to redress that monstrous wrong?

But, sir, we can not acquiesce in your dogmas that arrests and imprisonment, without warrant or criminal accusation, in their nature lawless and arbitrary, opposed to the very letter of constitutional guarantees, can become in any sense rightful, by reason of a suspension of the writ of *habeas corpus.* We deny that the suspension of a single and peculiar remedy for such wrongs brings into existence new and unknown classes of offenses, or new causes for depriving men of their liberty. It is one of the most material purposes of that writ, to enlarge upon bail persons who, upon probable cause, are duly and legally charged with some known crime; and a suspension of the writ was never asked for in England or in this country, except to prevent such enlargement when the supposed offense was against the safety of the government. In the year 1807, at the time of Burr's alleged conspiracy, a bill was passed in the Senate of the United States, suspending the writ of *habeas corpus* for a limited time *in all cases where persons were charged on oath with treason or other high crime or misdemeanor,* endangering the peace or safety of the government. But your doctrine undisguisedly is, that a suspension of this writ justifies arrests without warrant, without oath, and even without suspicion of treason or other crime. Your doctrine denies the freedom of speech and of the press; it invades the sacred domain of opinion and discussion; it denounces the "ifs" and the "buts" of the English language, and even the refuge of silence is insecure.

We repeat, a suspension of the writ of *habeas corpus* merely dispenses with a single and peculiar remedy against an unlawful imprisonment; but if that remedy had never existed, the right to liberty would be the same, and every invasion of that right, would be condemned not only by the Constitution, but by principles of far greater antiquity than the writ itself. Our common law is not at all indebted to this writ for its action of false imprisonment, and the action would remain to the citizen if the writ were abolished forever. Again, every man when his life or liberty is threatened, without the warrant of law, may lawfully resist, and if necessary, in self-defense, may take the life of the aggressor. Moreover, the people of this country may demand the impeachment of the President himself for the exercise of arbitrary power. And when all these remedies shall prove inadequate for the protection of free institutions, there remains, in the last resort, the supreme right of revolution. You once announced this right with a latitude of expression which may well be considered dangerous in the present crisis of our national history. You said: "Any people anywhere, being inclined and having the power, have the right to rise up and shake off the existing government, and form a new one that suits them better. Nor is this right confined to cases where the people of an existing government may choose to exercise it. Any portion of such people that can may revolutionize and make their own of so much of the territory as they inhabit. More than this, a majority of any portion

of such people may revolutionize, putting down a minority inter-
mingled with or near about them, who may oppose their movements." (Vol. XIX., *Congressional Globe*, p. 94.) Such were your
opinions, and you had a constitutional right to declare them. If a
citizen now should utter sentiments far less dangerous in their
tendency, your nearest military commander would consign him to
a dungeon, or to the tender mercies of a court-martial, and you
would approve the proceeding.

In our deliberate judgment, the Constitution is not open to the
new interpretation suggested by your communication now before
us. We think every part of that instrument is harmonious and consistent. The possible suspension of the writ of *habeas corpus* is consistent with freedom of speech and of the press. The suspension of
that remedial process may prevent the enlargement of the accused
traitor or conspirator, until he shall be legally tried and convicted
or acquitted, but in this we find no justification for arrest and imprisonment without warrant, without cause, without the accusation
or suspicion of crime. It seems to us, moreover, too plain for argument that the sacred right of trial by jury, and in courts where the
law of the land is the rule of decision, is a right which is never
dormant, never suspended, in peaceful and loyal communities and
States. Will you, Mr. President, maintain, that because the writ of
habeas corpus may be in suspense, you can substitute soldiers and
bayonets for the peaceful operation of the laws, military commissions and inquisitorial modes of trial for the courts and juries prescribed by the Constitution itself? And if you can not maintain this
then let us ask, where is the justification for the monstrous proceeding in the case of a citizen of Ohio, to which we have called your
attention? We know that a recreant judge, whose name has already
descended to merited contempt, found the apology on the *outside*
of the supreme and fundamental law of the Constitution. But this is
not the foundation on which your superstructure of power is built.

We have mentioned the act of the last Congress professing to
authorize a suspension of the writ of *habeas corpus*. This act now
demands your special attention, because, if we are not greatly in
error, its terms and plain intention are directly opposed to all the
arguments and conclusions of your communication. That act, besides
providing that the *habeas corpus* may be suspended, expressly com-

mands that the names of all persons theretofore or thereafter arrested by authority of the President, or his cabinet ministers, *being citizens of states in which the administration of the laws has continued unimpaired,* shall be returned to the courts of the United States for the districts in which such persons reside, or in which their supposed offenses were committed; and such return being made, if the next grand jury attending the courts does not indict the alleged offenders, then the judges are commanded to issue an order for their immediate discharge from imprisonment. Now, we can not help asking whether you have overlooked this law, which most assuredly you are bound to observe, or whether it be your intention to disregard it? Its meaning certainly can not be mistaken. By it the national Legislature has said that the President may suspend the accustomed writ of *habeas corpus,* but at the same time it has commanded that all arrests under his authority shall be promptly made known to the courts of justice, and that the accused parties shall be liberated, unless presented by a grand jury according to the Constitution, and tried by a jury in the ancient and accustomed mode. The President may possibly, so far as Congress can give the right, arrest without legal cause or warrant. We certainly deny that Congress can confer this right, because it is forbidden by the higher law of the Constitution. But, waiving that consideration, this statute, by its very terms, promptly removes the proceeding in every case into the courts where the safeguards of liberty are observed, and where the persons detained are to be discharged, unless indicted for *criminal offenses* against the established and ascertained laws of the country.

Upon what foundation, then, permit us to ask, do you rest the pretension that men who are not accused of crime may be seized and imprisoned or banished at the will and pleasure of the President or any of his subordinates in civil and military positions? Where is the warrant for invading the freedom of speech and of the press? Where the justification for placing the citizen on trial without the presentment of a grand jury and before military commissions? THERE IS NO POWER IN THIS COUNTRY WHICH CAN DISPENSE WITH ITS LAWS. The President is as much bound by them as the humblest individual. We pray you to bear in mind, in order that you may duly estimate the feeling of the people on this subject, that for the crime of dispensing with the laws and statutes of Great Britain, our ancestors brought one monarch to the scaffold, and expelled another from his throne.

This power which you have erected in theory is of vast and illimitable proportions. If we may trust you to exercise it mercifully and leniently, your successor, whether immediate or more remote, may wield it with the energy of a Cæsar or Napoleon, and with the will of a despot and a tyrant. It is a power without boundary or limit, because it proceeds upon a total suspension of all the constitutional and legal safeguards which protect the rights of the citizen. It is a power not inaptly described in the language of one of your Secretaries. Said Mr. Seward to the British Minister in Washington: "I can touch a bell on my right hand, and order the arrest of a citizen of Ohio. I can touch the bell again, and order the imprisonment of a citizen of New-York, and no power on earth but that of the President can release them. Can the Queen of England, in her dominions, do as much?" This is the very language of a perfect despotism, and we learn from you, with profound emotion, that this is no idle boast. It is a despotism unlimited in principle, because the same arbitrary and unrestrained will or discretion which can place men under illegal restraint or banish them, can apply the rack or the thumbscrew, can put to torture or to death. Not thus have the people of this country hitherto understood their Constitution. No argument can commend to their judgment such interpretations of the Great Charter of their liberties. Quick as the lightning's flash, the intuitive sense of freemen perceives the sophistry and rejects the conclusion.

Some other matters which your Excellency has presented demand our notice.

In justification of your course as to Mr. Vallandigham, you have referred to the arrest of Judge Hall, at New-Orleans, by order of General Jackson; but that case differs widely from the case of Mr. Vallandigham. New-Orleans was then, as you truly state, under "martial or military law." This was not so in Ohio, where Mr. Vallandigham was arrested. The administration of the civil law had not been disturbed in that Commonwealth. The courts were open and justice was dispensed with its accustomed promptitude. In the case of Judge Hall, General Jackson in a few days sent him outside of the line of his encampments and set him at liberty; but you have undertaken to banish Mr. Vallandigham from his home. You seem also to have forgotten that General Jackson submitted implicitly to the judgment of the court which imposed the fine upon him; that he promptly paid it; that he enjoined his friends to assent, "as he most freely did, to the decision which had just been pronounced against him."

More than this, you overlook the fact that the then administration (in the language of a well-known author) "mildly but decidedly rebuked the proceedings of General Jackson," and that the President viewed the subject with "surprise and solicitude." Unlike President Madison, you, in a case much more unwarranted, approve the proceedings of your subordinate officer, and in addition, justify your course by a carefully considered argument in its support.

It is true that after some thirty years, Congress, in consideration of the devoted and patriotic services of General Jackson, refunded the amount of the fine he had paid! But the long delay in doing this proved how reluctant the American people were to do any thing which could be considered as in any way approving the disregard shown to the majesty of the law, even by one who so eminently enjoyed their confidence and regard.

One subject more, and we shall conclude. You express your regret that our meeting spoke "as Democrats," and you say that "in this time of national peril you would have preferred to meet us upon a level, one step higher than any party platform." You thus compel us to allude to matters which we should have preferred to pass by. But we can not omit to notice your criticism, as it casts at least an implied reproach upon our motives and our proceedings. We beg to remind you that when the hour of our country's peril had come; when it was evident that a most gigantic effort was to be made to subvert our institutions and to overthrow the Government; when it was vitally important that party feelings should be laid aside, and that all should be called upon to unite most cordially and vigorously to maintain the Union; at the time you were sworn into office as President of the United States, when you should have urged your fellow-citizens in the most emphatic manner to overlook all past differences, and to rally in defense of their country and its institutions; when you should have enjoined respect for the laws and the Constitution, so clearly disregarded by the South — you chose, for the first time under the like circumstances in the history of our country, to set up a party platform, called "the Chicago platform" as your creed, to advance it beyond the Constitution, and to speak disparagingly of that great conservative tribunal of our country, so highly respected by all thinking men who have inquired into our institutions — THE SUPREME COURT OF THE UNITED STATES.

Your administration has been true to the principles you then laid down. Notwithstanding the fact that several hundred thousand Democrats in the loyal States cheerfully responded to the call of their country, filled the ranks of its armies, and by "their strong hands and willing arms" aided to maintain your Excellency and the officers of Government in the possession of our national capital — notwithstanding the fact that the great body of the Democrats of the country have, in the most patriotic spirit, given their best efforts, their treasure, their brothers and their sons to sustain the Government and to put down the rebellion, you, choosing to overlook all this, have made your appointments to civil office from your cabinet officers and foreign ministers, down to the persons of lowest official grade among the tens of thousands engaged in collecting the revenues of the country, exclusively from your political associates.

Under such circumstances, virtually proscribed by your administration, and while most of the leading journals which supported it approved the sentence pronounced against Mr. Vallandigham, it was our true course, our honest course, to meet as "Democrats," that neither your Excellency nor the country might mistake our antecedents or our position.

In closing this communication, we desire to reäffirm our determination, and, we doubt not, that of every one who attended the meeting which adopted the resolutions we have discussed, expressed in one of those resolutions, to devote "all our energies to sustain the cause of the Union."

Permit us, then, in this spirit, to ask your Excellency to reëxamine the grave subjects we have considered, to the end that, on your retirement from the high position you occupy, you may leave behind you no doctrines and no further precedents of despotic power to prevent you and your posterity from enjoying that constitutional liberty which is the inheritance of us all, and to the end, also, that history may speak of your administration with indulgence, if it can not with approval.

We are, sir, with great respect, yours very truly,

> JOHN V. L. PRUYN,
> *Chairman of Committee.*
> JAMES KIDD,
> GILBERT C. DAVIDSON,
> J. V. P. QUACKENBUSH,
> WM. A. FASSETT,
> O. M. HUNGERFORD,
> JOHN HOGAN,
> HENRY LANSING,
> S. HAND,
> M. K. COHEN,
> JOHN CUTLER,
> C. VAN BENTHUYSEN,
> GEORGE H. THACHER,
> C. W. ARMSTRONG,
> WILLIAM DOYLE,
> FRANKLIN TOWNSEND,
> WILLIAM APPLETON,
> B. R. SPELMAN,
> JAMES McKOWN,
> A. H. TREMAIN,
> DANIEL SHAW,
> W. SIMON,
> A. E. STIMSON,
> ISAAC LEDERER.

ALBANY, June 30, 1863.

Pamphlet 33

A Few Words in Behalf of the Loyal Women of the United States by One of Themselves. (*Loyal Publication Society No. 10*)

New York, 1863

[Many of the pamphlets relied less upon careful argument than upon an arousing of emotions. One such, apparently written by a woman who had credulously swallowed some of the crude atrocity stories then widely in circulation, contrasted fantastically the Northern women with their Southern sisters.]

It has lately become the fashion to say that, with regard to their interest in the present most unhappy war, the women of the North have not equalled those of the South in patriotic interest, labors, and sacrifices. The first utterer of this opinion probably aimed at nothing more than a sensational paragraph; for had there been any more serious or earnest intent, some specifications would have been given, that those accused might have had either the opportunity to defend themselves, or valuable hints for their future guidance and incitement to duty. One writer says — and this is as distinct a form of the accusation as any we remember to have met with: "But for the courage and energy of the women of the South, we believe the Rebellion would not have survived to this time. Had the women of the North with like zeal addressed themselves to the work of encouraging a loyal and devoted spirit among us, the copperhead conspiracy in behalf of the enemy would have been strangled at its birth, and the rebels would have learned, long ago, the futility of expecting aid and comfort from such a source." This is so vague a charge that we may be excused for doubting whether the writer himself knew exactly what he did mean. It looks very like an expression of the feeling we are apt to indulge when things do not go well — a desire to find somebody to throw the blame on. There has certainly been room for reproach, but it does not seem to *us* to lie among loyal *women*. A gentleman from whom we might have expected something nobler, lately did his part towards giving currency to a report too vague to be fair, in the course of a speech, whose loyal fervor, arising in an unexpected quarter, called the attention as it received the plaudits of all good citizens, throughout the land. And we find in the written expression of a lady writer in the *Atlantic Monthly* of March, 1863, one whose sharp dicta are winged with such vehemence that they must doubtless sink deep in every mind within their reach, such words as these: "The women of to-day have not come up to the level of to-day. They do not stand abreast with its issues. They do not rise to the height of its great argument. I have beheld, O Dorcasses! with admiration and gratitude, the coats and garments, the lint and bandages which you have made. Tender hearts, if you could have finished the war with your needles, it would have been finished long ago; but stitching does not crush rebellion, does not annihilate treason, or hew traitors in pieces before the Lord. * * * The war cannot be finished by sheets and pillow-cases. Sometimes I am tempted to believe that it cannot be finished till we have flung them all away." And so on, through a very animated address, which we should all read and ponder, for we have much to learn. But the image which rises spontaneously in the mind as we read the exhortations to loyal women, is that of "Jael, the wife of Heber the Kenite," a loyal woman of old, whose "soul of fire," "burning white and strong and steady," enabled her with her own hand to drive a nail through and through the temples of her sleeping enemy-guest, so as to pin him to the ground in her tent, to which she had tempted him by the offer of much-needed refreshment. "At her feet he bowed, he fell, he lay down; where he bowed, there he fell down dead. The mother of Sisera looked out at a window, and cried through the lattice, Why is his chariot so long in coming?"[1] This is a heroine quite after the Southern pattern, if we may believe reports, but not one whose ferocious patriotism could ever become attractive to the women of the North. There is undoubtedly a radical difference between the women of the two sections. We knew it before there was a thought of war (on our part), and we have become still more thoroughly aware of it since.

[1] Judges, Chap. V.

That bright and fierce and fickle is the South,
And dark and true and tender is the North.

The gist of all that has been said of our deficiency in the present crisis, so far as we understand it, is that we have not shown *passion* enough; that we have acted naturally, in short. Why should we simulate a "white heat" if we did not feel it, or see any occasion for it? The time may come when our patriotic fire will need no incitement; when the "sacred fury" will burn of itself, as alone it should burn. When it does, it will be no straw-blaze of excitement, calling the eyes of spectators and dying out easily, if not fed by new supplies of its vain fuel. Thus far we have seen only obvious duties and anxiously fulfilled them to the best of our ability. It is a solemn truth that notwithstanding all the outrages of our traitorous assailants, we have never yet been able to get personally angry with them. Not that we do not from our souls hate and despise traitors and treachery, but that the old habit of friendship with our Southern neighbors makes it so difficult for us to connect those feelings with them and make it personal.

It can hardly be expected that the great body of loyal women should quietly accept the derogatory comparison alluded to. They must be permitted indignantly to repel the charge of indifference, and to call upon those who originated and those who have echoed it, for some specifications. If it were only for the sake of our soldiers, far away and looking homeward, they must deny the impeachment. To leave their brave defenders, who have offered their lives a ransom for us at home, and who have a right to expect from us every service, every sympathy, every tender and devoted feeling that our souls are capable of, to leave *them* to believe that we tacitly confess a shameful delinquency, would be to forget what is due to ourselves and to them. Soldiers! you can speak for us. Have we been indifferent to your wants and sufferings; have we chilled your noble devotion by our faint-hearted words; have our letters to you breathed a spirit of discontent and repining, or failed to hail your enthusiasm and give the full measure of praise and joy to your heroic achievements? You who have lately, in a time of need, spoken so nobly for your country and its government, to the confusion of blatant traitors, lift your voices once more, in behalf of the loyal women who await you at home! Say whether the tenderness which is our glory is of that fatal kind which unnerves its object, or of that nobler sort which makes his arm irresistible through the courage it inspires in his heart! Speak the truth of us as you know it, and we will accept it even though it rebuke and humble us!

The form of the accusation which touches us so nearly is that of a comparison between the women of the two parts of our country, as now divided or sought to be divided by the present bitter contest. No other measure is proposed for our duty than what the Southern women are supposed to have done. It would certainly be difficult to find proper and sufficient material for the implied contrast. Whoever set the idea afloat did not claim to have access to any extraordinary sources of information on either side, and must therefore be considered as having drawn his conclusion from what he, like others, had seen in the public prints, — the accounts of "regular" and "special" correspondents; anecdotes reported by casual observers; intercepted letters; and the stories of refugees or returned prisoners, as to the spirit and behavior of Southern women; while as to Northern women a good deal of pains should have been taken, by one who desired to judge and speak fairly, to discover what they were thinking and doing, since they are especially careful *not* to get into the newspapers, whether for good or evil. Public notice they consider not a reward, but a misfortune, and are ready, when it happens to them, to ask, "What wrong or foolish thing have I done?" But there is no evidence of any pains having been taken in the case, and therefore, even allowing that from public sources there might be drawn anything like a fair general idea of the spirit of Southern women, there does not appear, nor can there have existed, any grounds for conclusions worthy of respect as to the sentiments or actions of those of the North. This statement will be acknowledged by those who know us, to be literally and exactly correct. We have made no public demonstrations. The Southern people are obviously more demonstrative than we, and it is natural for superficial observers to conclude that the side which makes the greatest display has felt most warmly and made the most effort and sacrifice. We could not imitate them, and should be contemptible if we tried. The feelings of Northern women are rather deep than violent; their sense of duty is a quiet and constant rather than a headlong or impetuous impulse. It would be impossible to persuade them that any parade of sentiment is not unbecoming or even ridiculous. Among us it is only the more shallow and evanescent feelings that seek the light.

We never say much about our patriotism; we should as soon think of entertaining the world by protestations of affection for our parents or our children. We are willing and glad to live and labor for their sakes, even, if need were, to die for them, God giving us grace. But we should scarcely think of publishing this feeling of devotion, far less of priding ourselves on what we should blush not to feel. This settled aversion to show in matters of the heart, no doubt subjects Northern women to the imputation of coldness, but it is better to accept than to transgress the inborn sense of propriety which demands self-restraint.

Perhaps this habitual reserve or self-control is sometimes carried too far, as it may occasionally circumscribe their influence by lessening the sphere of their example. Instinct, education, and habit, all prompt them to err rather on that side than on the other. Passionate utterance is no evidence of right feeling; it is too often the mere ebullition of that which has no support in reason or principle. Yet passion in a noble cause may be both natural and useful, and it certainly becomes us to think whether our too-carefully restrained manner may not bring reproach upon our noble cause. We might at least extract so much good from the bitter things put forth against us, as the ancient Britons are said to have compounded healing medicines from the gall of their slain enemies.

After all, Christian women must be no boasters. When they have "done all," they are bound to feel themselves "unprofitable servants," and to seek no reward from the applause of man. During this war, how many such silent heroines have suffered and died among us! Who can tell how many lovely women — not hirelings, but belonging to rich and prosperous families — have sunk under their labors in our hospitals, or died of disease contracted there! Who knows their number, or has recorded for the public eye their service and suffering? There will come a time when we can sit down and reckon up the fearful loss brought upon us by the wild and cruel indulgence of unhallowed passions in those to whom passion seems better than reason. When that time comes, it will be due to the loved and lost that it shall be known how they lived, and why they died; and in the revelations of the hour it will become evident that under a calm and self-restrained exterior may be hidden a holy patriotic fire which consumes its tenement that it may give light and life to the suffering. Then, perhaps, some who rashly judge of love of country by the noise it makes may see cause to repent their hasty conclusions.

At first, before we learned what was the temper of the South, we did not anticipate any occasion for private and personal sacrifices. We did not even believe the possibility of war upon such grounds as were alleged. We fancied that good sense, justice, patriotism; the recollection of oft-repeated and recent oaths of unswerving allegiance; a feeling of brotherhood which would fain try every method of accommodation before resorting to the dread arbitrament of the sword, — that these and a thousand other elements of peace would be found powerful in averting a contest so fatal to our reputation as a nation, so discouraging to the friends of Liberty all over the world. Calm and confident in the sure knowledge that the Government under which we were all prosperous and happy had done nothing hostile to the interests of the Southern part of the great Republic, but had, in fact, been for years ruled by them for the benefit of their supposed interests, and having too much respect for the good sense and right feeling of the South to believe that the expression of private sentiment or even of public opinion, — free in all free countries, — against the institution of slavery, would be considered a sufficient reason for the murder of our husbands and our sons, we were slow to conceive the idea of anything more than a mere political *fracas;* a little more virulent expression of one of those threats which we had long been in the habit of hearing, whenever the South had in any case failed in Congress to carry a point in favor of slavery.

There had been no thirty years preparation of treason on our side, and though men judged better of the stern necessity, women walked as in a dream, hoping against hope. When successive outrages had made the war first inevitable, then actual, present, and terrible; when the clang of arms and the blare of trumpets filled our streets, and parting with the head and life and support of our homes, left no further room for self-delusion, loyal women set about doing whatever was required to be done, without passion except of sorrow, without words or noise; calling upon nobody to notice or admire them; in no sense putting themselves forward, but waiting to be called upon by those immediately engaged in public affairs. Surrounded by Southern people and Northern sympathizers with the rebellion, daily hearing galling words and odious sentiments, which could not but be very trying to the true and loyal-hearted, and seeing actual rejoicing over the sorrows which unprovoked violence soon brought into Northern homes and hearts, there were no recriminations or attempts to foment the unhappy strife. The prevailing tone among women was that of grief; they had not the heart to attempt to increase the indignation of their husbands at unprovoked wrong, though they sustained them, as far as was in their power, in the determination to resist it. There was a frightful calm; a boding silence, more terrible, almost, than the thunders of war they presaged.

But the cannon of Sumter and the awful reverberation of Bull Run shook the land to its centre, and at once changed the calm into a tempest. It was then, and not till then, that loyal women understood perforce what was required of them. As one awakened from a deep sleep is slow to recognize in the light which fills his chamber, the baleful signal of ruin, conflagration, and death, yet being once fully roused, finds all his faculties called into instant activity by the emergency, so they, when the awful moment of full comprehension came, sought and discovered in themselves powers as yet unsuspected, and energy which in peace, happiness, and luxury, had never been aroused to action. New life came to many an enervated mind and body; the rust of long prosperity could not withstand the power of noble feeling; even the gay and thoughtless votary of fashion hailed the new pleasure, — that of being disinterestedly, generously useful, — and proved how terrible is the waste of power going on in ordinary times within that golden circle. But even now what was said and done was of that quiet and unobtrusive kind that carries with it no suspicion of a hankering after observation and praise. There was nothing theatrical, nothing flaunting. The Northern daughter of the Republic might have said with Cordelia —

> Unhappy that I am, I cannot heave
> My heart into my mouth.

There was no speech or boast or threat of any Northern women recorded, so far as we know. Those heavy brown linen aprons, which came into vogue just then, were not like the stage disguises put on for effect, and from which the wearer is but to emerge more splendid than ever. They meant *work*, — hard, unpleasant, unshrinking work.

Those who wore them went into great packing-rooms, to spend the long summer days and weeks in assorting and preparing for use the countless thousands of garments and delicacies which the women of every State and town and hamlet were busy in preparing for the soldiers, or into the streets gathering money from door to door by the most painful of all processes, or into the hospitals, already overflowing with patients, to tend all sufferers alike, without a question or a thought whether rebel gray or loyal blue had clad the pale victim while he wore the garb of health and strength, dressing loathsome wounds, watching at the bedsides of camp fevers, cheering the faint-hearted, lifting up the trembling soul just parting from all on earth, and agonized at the thought of dear ones far away; physicians of all souls, practising under the license of a great love and pity, feeling that every man who needs help is a brother, though his rash hand may have been lifted against his country and shed her dearest blood. These days and nights of untiring mercy, — which we should not speak of as past, for they are as full of love and service at this moment as ever, — have made no noise in the world. The good and noble deeds they have witnessed never reach the newspapers, unless as, ever and anon, some fair and lovely ministrant sinks into the early grave from which she had saved many a son of Southern as well as Northern mother, her name and fate may fill a line of print, to let her distant friends and lovers know why she so suddenly faded in her bloom, to pass away and be seen no more on earth forever. In this, "we speak that we do know and testify that we have seen," and to the eye of Memory, dear and precious and beautiful forms rise up unbidden witnesses of the truth of what has here been said.

As we observed at the outset, there is no satisfactory amount of material for the proposed comparison, and we can but use what we have, confessing its insufficiency. The task of collecting and exhibiting the manifestations of Southern female feeling, as it has come to us in the newspapers of both sections, in innumerable intercepted letters, and in the reports of returned prisoners, would not be a gracious one. To perform it thoroughly, giving facts and data, would require an amount of enmity towards our "wayward sisters" which it is to be hoped few of us entertain. It is difficult, even, to believe in the reality of such hatred as they profess. The excuse of "fiery blood," "tropical imaginations," and other peculiarities rather boasted of by natives of the "Sunny South," does not cover a violence and brutality of tone, which has not, so far as we know, its parallel in the history, even of the most terrible wars of modern times, unless the sayings and doings of the "Dames de la Halle," — those terrible Parisian fish-women — in the darkest days of the French Revolution, may furnish a precedent. But those wretched *poissardes* had at least the apology of horrible oppression, while the venom of their modern imitators is self-grown and causeless. In the old Scandinavian mythology, we read of mythic heroes, at their Valhalla banquets, drinking blood from the skulls of their enemies; but even there, no *woman* is found partaking of the horrid feast, or preparing the skulls required for these detestable orgies, or decorating her person with ornaments made from human bones. This species of patriotism would not, even in barbarous times, have been considered appropriate in our sex, for mankind have from the beginning, unanimously required in women the kind and loving ministrations which the warrior and the man of peace equally find precious and sustaining. Fierce and passionate women may claim a dreary splendor, but unless "the rage of the vulture" is tempered by the "love of the turtle," no man prays that their number may increase. Many a Southern woman, during this war, has written to husband, brother, or lover, to bring home with him "a dead Yankee, pickled," or "a hand, or an ear, or a thumb, at least," if he expected to be well received at his return. Letters of this tenor are extant, and have been not unfrequently exhibited among the spoils of Southern camps, and the various trophies of our victories on Southern soil. Melancholy victories! not only as being won in civil war, but as bringing to our knowledge traits of character, and evidence of malignant feeling, whose existence in our country and in female bosoms, we should otherwise never have suspected.

We must by no means ascribe these sad exhibitions altogether to a peculiar sectional ferocity. Human nature has a bad side, and no one nation or people can justly be considered worse at heart than all others. The practice of Slavery, with the unsexing and degrading scenes belonging to it, familiarity with the sound of the lash, and the sight of the blood it draws from human flesh, with cries of anguish and prayers for mercy, answered only by derision; the habit of living on the unrequited earnings of a crushed and despoiled people, too weak to plead their own cause before the world, and appealing to every generous, every human feeling, but in vain! These form, doubtless, the leading reasons for the wide difference observable between that character of low-bred women, North and South.

Then, too, the ignorance which is the misfortune of the inferior whites of the South, may properly be counted an apology for some lack of self-control and some passionate rudeness. An ignorance so gross as to despise instruction, must, when it is the heritage left by mother to daughter, for successive generations, leave the soul the unresisting prey of degrading passions; and when the weaker part of a scattered population, like that of the South, has been persuaded by designing rulers to glory in such ignorance, the climax of unreason is reached. There may be virtues left, but manners must touch the lowest point which leaves social intercourse possible.

It is conceded, and can need no proof, that the patriotic feelings of our Northern women have never betrayed them into any violence of action or expression, even in moments of the greatest excitement. They have never been nerved by a feeling of deadly hatred. They have not tried the force of hideous grins, or insulting gestures, or unspeakable outrages on the nerves of blushing soldiers. No man in arms against the United States, since the April of Sumter, can testify that he ever saw or heard in a loyal woman of these States, a look or word unbecoming her sex. No woman within our borders, however low in the social scale, unless belonging to the unhappy class which is not nor can be loyal to God or man, to sex or nation, has brought reproach upon her country, or furnished matter of triumph to the enemy, by mistaking ferocity or vulgarity for patriotism. It is not in the nature of the true American woman to make such mistakes. She would rather crush back into her heart even the noble passion which rises naturally at the sight of those who are doing us unprovoked and cruel wrong, than risk being for a moment confounded with a class of females to whom violence is natural and insolence spontaneous. According to our Northern creed, when a woman ceases to be a woman, she becomes nothing, or worse than nothing.

Far be it ever from us to cast, even by remotest implication, the reproach due to brazen brows upon the great body of Southern women now unhappily looking upon us, their Northern sisters, as enemies. Who does not know their worth, their domestic virtues, their lady-like delicacy, their feminine grace? Where shall we look for better wives and mothers, or more devoted Christians, tried, as they often are, in ways of which Northern women can form but little idea? No Northern woman would claim for herself a character purer or more dignified, more moderate in prosperity, more patient under affliction, than that which she freely accords to Southern women of her acquaintance. It is hardly probable that any of us here ever beheld the face of one of the hideous termagants who have done their best to bring disgrace upon all the women of the fair Southern land. In times of war and commotion, bad women, like bad men, find an opportunity of coming to the surface, and they eagerly seize the chance which thus presents itself. This is natural and unavoidable; the only strange thing about it is, that beings like these should have been by any one supposed to be fair specimens of the women of the South, and that atrocities, which were the fruit of unreasoning hate, should have been counted as virtues, and indirectly recommended to loyal women for imitation!

The devotion of many women of high character to the bad cause of Secession, we are bound to believe sincere and ardent. That there are many such who secretly mourn over the suicidal course in which their husbands and friends are involved, we *know;* but even where they disapprove most, we may be sure they find place for woman's work — the care of the sick and wounded, the relief of the poor, and all the ceaseless, nameless good deeds, in their power, all the love-taught expedients, of which the sex is capable, to ameliorate some of the evils consequent upon the great wrong. Besides these, there are many who, having been bred and matured in the "State sovereignty" heresy — the feeling and belief that to the citizen the State is and should be a higher power than the Nation — go hand in hand with husbands, sons, and brothers in rebellion, and devote their best efforts to what they have learned to believe a righteous cause. And this is the occasion of no unwomanly display on their part. They may talk as Southern women are apt to do somewhat floridly of Southern "Chivalry," and Northern meanness, judged after their standard, but they will not parade their unreasoning patriotism in the newspapers, or in their zeal forget their womanhood.

We can know little of the conduct of the women belonging to Union families at the South, or of their interest and part in the war, until they are once more restored to their rights. Up to the present moment, the armed heel of a cruel despotism is upon them; their husbands and friends live with the sword suspended over their heads by the single hair, not of justice but of arbitrary power, and seclusion and quiet are their only safety. Whether they have been able to accomplish any thing for their country beyond the present sacrifice of all earthly good to high and noble principles, we are not permitted to inquire, but we may humbly hope that their trials are noted, and their great sacrifice recorded in the Book of Life. Surely "their prayers and their alms are come up for a memorial before God," and He has sustained them under all their afflictions. May our suffering sisters look up and say, "In the shadow of thy wings will I make my refuge, until these calamities be overpast." There is good hope that the end of their trial is drawing nigh, and that their faithfulness will ere long be crowned with rejoicing.

Setting aside all rude and personally disgusting modes of exhibiting what is intended to pass as patriotism, and with them the loud and offensive boasting which used to meet the ears of all who travelled by public conveyance in the early part of the war, before such treasonous interruptions of the public peace were put down by authority, let us look a little closer into the claim set up for the Southern women to a high-toned love of country. Considering, as before, the common newspapers, North and South, as the only authority attainable in the case, what do we find? Persons in the garb of ladies, remaining at the seat of government to play a double part, professing loyalty, and shrinking from no extent of falsehood which would enable them to betray the dearest interests of the country to which they vowed allegiance; taking advantage of their sex and position to do what would justly have condemned men to the "short shrift and strong cord," which in all countries is the doom of the spy, yet on detection, so devoid of honor and dignity as to make loud or whining complaints, as they happened to be more coarse or more weak, of the mere imprisonment by which our mildest of governments marked its sense of their misbehavior! We may be allowed to hope that few of the women of the North have not more fortitude, even in evil.

And what shall we say of women claiming a respectable position in society, at our seat of government again, going into the hospitals there, after the battle of Bull Run, to offer their services to secessionist prisoners, making their way to the bedsides of our suffering and dying men, our Union soldiers, to look with malignant pleasure upon their sufferings, saying, "You deserve it all! You ought to have been killed!" This was zeal which we pray God may never be exhibited by loyal women, whatever the provocation of such conduct.

The poisoning of food and water for our soldiers, which must have been done by female connivance at least, is too black a crime to be attributed to any cause but the fiendish passions of a few individuals who would disgrace any country, though specimens of the class may, perhaps, be found in all. But we cannot help noticing that in no case which ever became known at the North was it reprehended by any Southern print, but passed by as a trifle — a thing of course, or something praiseworthy. If it be true, as moralists declare, that women in civilized countries powerfully influence the tone of public opinion, how did it happen that women who must have known, at least, of these atrocities, did not insist on their being disclaimed and branded with a public stigma?

And taking this influence for granted, what share of the inhuman cruelties practised at the South upon Union prisoners shall we ascribe to the women? If the Southern women have indeed "inspired" the men, what shall we think of such inspiration? It would be hard to convince us that if women had pleaded against the authorized cruelties at which common humanity shudders, those of our poor boys who escape alive from Southern bondage might have a different story to tell, and far less appalling marks of bodily suffering to show. The recital of what the people of Chicago, women as well as men, have done for the six thousand Southern prisoners at Camp Douglas — the food and medicines for the sick and convalescent, the clothing and comforts of every kind sent in by private benevolence, and gladly received and distributed by the officers in charge; the schools kept for those willing to learn; in short, the general desire that the poor creatures should be the better, not the worse, for having been thrown by the fortunes of war into our care — would be a tolerable answer to those who depreciate the good works of Northern women in this war, for none of this was done without the warm and efficient co-operation of women. The utter astonishment evinced by the recipients of such bounty confirms, if that were necessary, the stories of barbarous treatment reported by our returning soldiers, for it was contrast that brought simple benevolence into such strong relief.

Now, the patriotic feeling which prompts deception and falsehood, the poisoning of hungry men, the taunting of wounded and suffering ones, and the deliberate torture of prisoners of war, excite in us of Northern blood no envy, no emulation. We are willing the credit of it should remain with those to whom it belongs. It requires all our Christian charity to say, "Father, forgive them!"

A more agreeable topic would be the services performed by Southern women in behalf of their armies, and of all their poor who may be suffering on account of the war. Our data for this purpose are few and small. No doubt Southern women have nursed in hospitals, and made garments, and furnished many comforts for their soldiers, and this often when dearth of material rendered the service peculiarly difficult. But, adhering to the idea of a *comparison*, could any especial merit be claimed for such services as these? Have *only* Southern women been giving their time and thoughts, their means, strength, and ingenuity to the necessities of the hour? This will hardly be claimed. We may, perhaps, say, without boasting, that here we should be quite ready to be weighed in the balance with our Southern sisters. What they have done for the poor, we have not heard. We know that General Butler found the poor of New Orleans starving, surrounded by wealth and luxury, and that wherever the armies of the United States have occupied our Southern territory, their first care and duty have been to feed the perishing poor, abandoned to famine and nakedness by those for whom they had all their lives been toiling unpaid. What the women of the South could have done towards preventing this disgrace and cruelty, we do not know, but we *do* know that such things could never have happened among us, for our poor are a part of ourselves, and the care of them part of our religion.

There may have been large subscriptions raised in Southern cities, and working committees of ladies everywhere, as among us, who gave themselves up to the duty of seeking out and relieving the distresses of the suffering classes, especially of that most unhappy of all God's poor — the class who "possess no rights which white men are bound to respect," but who on that very account, besides the fact that they are so "fond of their masters," and so "devoted" to them, should be tenderly cared for by white women. We hope there may have been such institutions and such exertions, but the accounts of them have not reached us. On the other hand, our Northern poor have only to show that he who was the support of the family has gone to the war, or died there, or come home disabled — to become the object of efficient public and private beneficence, and this to such an extent, that many of them are better housed, fed, and clothed than they ever were before. This state of things is so well known, that the favorite plea of the impostor who seeks charity fraudulently, is the absence or loss of husband or father in the army.

As to the "sacrifices" said to have been made by the women of the South, and which are insisted upon by their Northern sympathizers as proofs of heroic resolution, their merit must depend upon circumstances. It is no virtue to wear a coarse dress if you can obtain no other, or to live poorly when good living is too costly for your means. It is very probable that the sacrifices of the women have been greater than those of the men, if we exclude from the calculation the hardships which all soldiers in all wars must necessarily endure. But we cannot class such sacrifices with those voluntarily borne by our revolutionary mothers, for they suffered gladly in the cause of LIBERTY, while the women of the South have no higher incentive than the determination to uphold their husbands in the attempt to perpetuate SLAVERY. The sacrifices required by a war which the South voluntarily commenced should have been counted beforehand. A rebellion against just and lawful, kind and beneficent authority; a war which pretends to no high or holy motive, and can allege in its justification no public wrong or injury, can claim no general sympathy for the sufferings and sacrifices it compels a consenting people to bear, nor can sacrifices in a bad cause take the rank which belongs to those endured for a principle sanctioned alike by God and man. We know that women usually adopt the political views of their husbands, and we profess no surprise that Southern women should have done so. We see it among ourselves, and have felt it in the refusal of women whose husbands sympathize with the South to do anything for the country or the army in this crisis, but we must regret that their sacrifices should not have been made in a more worthy cause, and hope for their own sakes that they will never glory in them. To suffer for liberty is glorious; to deprive ourselves of the comforts and necessaries of life in behalf of slavery, can never be anything but ignominious, though human sympathy views with pity the sufferings of those so desperately mistaken.

It is true that we of the North have seen as yet little occasion for these personal sacrifices which, doubtless, press heavily upon our belligerent neighbors. Our industry has known no interruption, and our prosperity has been ample, so far as material things are concerned. We weep for our losses by this cruel war, but not for any lack experienced in the ordinary comforts of our firesides. There is a vacant place at many a board, and the feast loses its savor when we think of the absent or the lost one; but if abundance, or even luxury, could content us, we should have little cause to lament the present state of things. If the time of dearth should come; if by some miraculous interference we should change positions with our Southern sisters, and be obliged to deny ourselves in order to help our country in the great struggle against oppression and threatened barbarism, let us hope we may be found equal to the time, and, of all things, preserved from boasting of any services it may be in our power to render. Now, and ever, what we give to the soldiers in field or hospital we give to our own souls, to our flesh and blood, to our beloved country; and if more be required, we are ready to give more, even to all that we possess. But we promise never to claim any merit for it.

We are told of Southern housewives cutting up their carpets to make blankets for their soldiers, and we can easily believe it; for many of our good country-women who never had a carpet in their lives, except of rags, have given the blankets off their own beds to *our* soldiers, and used pieces of rag-carpet in place of them. Beyond question, there is many a good Southern wife who has toiled day and night, and denied herself everything, that she might sustain and comfort her husband in the miserable business he has undertaken, and many a poor Union woman who has endured still severer sacrifices without the support of the remotest sympathy in the cause. But we see in the Southern papers glowing accounts of the luxurious indulgences of the ladies of Richmond, side by side with paragraphs describing the fearful scarcity of provisions, and the deprivations of the poor. A few weeks ago the Richmond papers declared, with some show of natural indignation, that the army horses were starving, while certain gay people in the capital were pampering their useless steeds that the ladies might not lose their drives by moonlight! More recently we are told that three thousand women, of the classes that do *not* have many "drives by moonlight," have been driven by desperation to attack the shops where provisions and clothing are sold, in search of the necessaries of life for themselves and their families. Similar outbreaks occurred in less considerable places.

In the attempt to consider impartially the comparison forced upon us by circumstances, we sincerely deprecate the impression that loyal women desire to magnify their own patriotism, or to claim praise for anything which they have been able to do for the soldiers or their families. In truth, if any thing could induce a feeling of humility, it would be the review of what little it has been in our power to accomplish at a time like the present, when our country is shedding her best blood in a contest which involves her very existence. There are moments when we feel ashamed, almost, of living comfortably; of reading fresh and pleasant books or enjoying social gatherings; of giving our children and young people the indulgences common to their age; of letting our thoughts wander to a happy future, unmindful of what sorrow and suffering may lie between us and that perhaps distant time. We are but too sensible that while we are thus surrounded with comforts, hundreds of thousands of men are undergoing toil and hardships, privation and danger, that we and our children to remote generations may enjoy the blessings of peace and unity, under a free government — the achievement of our honored forefathers. We know that some of these are perishing in camps and battle-fields, in sea-storms or in poisonous bayous, or stretched helpless on hospital cots, lonely, sad, but resolute and devoted; thinking of home, longing for letters, wondering whether we really feel any warm interest in our defenders, or whether in our wealth, our pleasure, our luxury, and the interchange of happy domestic affection that is worth all the rest, we forget those who have accepted the duty of dying for us if need be! Thoughts like these keep us humble enough, and we are sometimes forced, for mere consolation, to recall what we have done and are doing and mean to go on doing for these beloved ones, every one of whom, seen in the golden light shed around him by his patriotic devotion and the ever impending danger which so ennobles and separates him from common life, appears at once a hero and a brother. Self-complacency is not the fault we are just now most prone to, yet to put ourselves right in the estimation of the army, we would risk the appearance of it.

Besides, it is to be observed that we advance no claim to *superior-*

ity in zeal and devotedness, over the women of the South. It is to vindicate loyal women from a charge of *deficiency,* as compared with the other side, that we venture to speak. A charge lightly utterly and carelessly echoed may be keenly felt by those whose souls have been stirred to their inmost depths by the sublime impulses of the time. That American women — women whose mothers and grandmothers can remember Washington and the heroes and heroisms of the Revolution; women in whom love of country has always seemed so much a part of life, an impulse of nature, that they never thought of claiming it as a virtue; who have given their dearest blood to the war, followed their precious ones with anxious tendance and service, received them back maimed, broken, or coffined, yet never, even in their anguish, cried — "Submit to wrong, for why should we die!" — that *we* should be suspected of coldness, of selfish indifference, in this awful crisis; of a stupid want of interest in the great death-grapple of liberty with despotism; civilization with barbarism; of a love of ease and luxury powerful enough to unnerve our hands when they should be full of strength; of a willingness to renounce our birthright rather than our pleasures, and forfeit our great future sooner than relinquish the flowery path we have been treading — degenerate indeed must we be, unworthy alike of our sires and of our sons, if we deserved the insidious imputation. Our cheeks burn with shame and indignation at being obliged to repel it.

If we interpret aright the attempt to contrast us unfavorably with Southern women in devotion to the public service, the meaning is that *they* have sustained their men in fiery hate and contempt for their countrymen of the North, and done everything possible to incite and encourage them in the determination to found an empire, whose corner-stone should be human slavery. They, having seen slavery, felt it, known its horrors, suffered under its attendant evils, and learned, so far as they have learned Christianity, its incompatibility with God's benign law of love, have deliberately lent themselves and those dearer than life to them, to the perpetuation of so awful an evil, for the sake of an idea, however futile, of worldly prosperity! The separation of families, the lashing of women, brutal tortures of young girls from the most atrocious motives — all these and long list of crimes and outrages upon humanity, of which these are but specimens, excite no repugnance, it seems, in the minds of Southern women? They are willing to go on and on, and to uphold the whole abomination just as it is, and the reward for which they submit to this fearful self-degradation is the pleasure of a triumph over the hated "Yankees!" Great God! what ideas must have taken root in such minds, and what sympathy with such feelings can be recommended to Northern wives and mothers! What but blind and unreasoning passion can be urged as an excuse for complicity with a sin that cries to Heaven? That slavery is the cause of the war; that our Northern disapprobation of slavery is the source of all the bitter hatred expressed against us; that the "spirit" of the Southern women who are held up as examples for us has the same origin — these are truths which are seen and known and acknowledged by all. It is indeed mortifying to find Northern minds attempting to incite in us a corresponding passionate hatred.

The women of the South, the great body of the respectable portion, excluding on the one hand those who laboriously imitate, though at a greater distance than they imagine, the aristocracy of older countries, and who, though themselves generally the nurslings of a despised race, yet pride themselves on a supposed purity of blood; and on the other, those "poor whites" who, in intelligence and morality, compare not too favorably with that despised race — exclusive of these two extremes, the women of the South do not approve of slavery or desire its continuance. When they speak their honest sentiments, they tell their Northern friends that it is a greater curse to them and their children than even we suppose. Many a spontaneous and artless expression of this truth appears in their conversation and in their literature, scanty as it is. They have been instinctively and without design the exponents of that "morbid conscience of the South," which Mr. Mac Duffie, years ago, deprecated as threatening slavery most ominously. When they brought their sons and their daughters to the North to be educated, they often told us why! These women we do not hear from in these dark days. What has become of their abhorrence of slavery and its poisonous consequences? We are told of the sacrifices they have made in the cause of War — have they ever made a sacrifice in the cause of Truth? If all the women in the rebellious States who disapprove of slavery, and believe it to be an evil and a sin, had, as with one voice, remonstrated against this war for its extension and perpetuity, instead of weakly allowing passion to influence them, without regard to principle or conscience, there would have been no war. If every

Southern wife had done her whole duty by her husband, using the "still, small voice" to which God has given such power, in persuading him to listen to reason and duty, rather than to the trumpet-blare of a wicked and heartless ambition, what misery might have been saved! But not only failing to prevent, she has, so we are told, used all her power, and most successfully, to add fuel to the cruel flame, and to stifle, as far as possible, the whisper of conscience, which might at some happy moment have become audible.

Loyal sisters of the North, be not cast down by the hasty sentence which some, who thoughtlessly exalt passion above principle, have passed upon you. Listen to every good suggestion, but do not learn to be ashamed of having tried to do your whole duty instead of talking about it; and, above all, never be persuaded to regret that you have not stimulated the angry passions of your countrymen, whose high and holy cause is incitement enough for all brave and true hearts. If you have not been as vehement in expression as your Southern sisters, do not fancy it necessary or becoming to adopt their tone. You are at least able to "give a reason for the faith that is in you," and it is a reason which you will never be ashamed to bring before the world, since God sanctions it, and mankind everywhere, except in the rebel States, holds it noble and worthy. The saying which has stung you so keenly, may be only the spear-point of a heavenly messenger inciting you to a warmer devotion, a more thorough consecration of yourselves and all that you possess to the great service of your country. At least, accept it thankfully as such. Who can do enough for such a country? Perhaps greater dangers than any we have yet encountered await us, and we are about to need a new energy. Our opponents are Americans, and we know what that means. Look at the recent tremendous contest at Charleston. Human power and skill in the dread enginery of war, and human courage and bravery could go no further, and the whole civilized world looks on with breathless interest. We can but dimly guess what is before us. If we, as women, can devise new duties for ourselves, if we can find new channels of help, new inspiration for good, new modes of evincing our love of country without public demonstration, let us not shrink, but rejoice. The shades of our brave old grandmothers, who could run bullets and load guns for their husbands, and who marched in procession to bury their tea-cups, when principle forbade the use of them, will not frown upon us, be our efforts ever so humble. And it may be that some among us who, seeing no present distress, have never yet fairly awakened to the full perception of the requirements and privileges of the hour, will, for the honor of the sisterhood, now come forward, and, being fresh in the work, press on beyond the foremost. We are all needed, and we must not hold back, supposing the work to grow less pressing. The spring budding around us, reminds us that the time of comparative inaction in our armies is over, and that our boys will soon be in want of everything we can do for them. Let us abridge our luxuries for their sakes; let us give them of our leisure; let us consecrate a large portion of our thoughts to them; let us write them innumerable letters of hope, and love, and cheer, full of sweet home chat and bright visions of the future, when their toil shall be over and the victory won. Let us pledge ourselves to treat with a true disdain every insidious attempt at corrupting public feeling at the North; every man who is engaged in fomenting those miserable party divisions which form the last hope of our traitorous enemies. It is already the fashion among the brave, high-spirited Western girls, to scorn and reject the coward who eludes the draft; let the mode spread among all classes. It is better than any Paris fashion the spring ships may bring over the sea. When those *fainéants* return, who have skulked to Canada and Nova Scotia to cheat their country out of the only service they were ever likely to render — that of stopping a bullet which might otherwise have reached a better man — let them meet the reception they deserve. We need not make faces at them, or send them presents of female or infants' gear, for that would be imitating the Southern women. But we can let them severely alone, forever. Let us be on the alert, that nothing possible to be done for our soldiers, our over-tasked government, our politically-blinded friends, or our whole beloved country, shall be left undone.

Pamphlet 34

The Draft, or, Conscription Reviewed
by the People.

Providence, 1863

[Resentment against the Conscription Act of March, 1863, erupted that summer into rioting in many parts of the North. In New York City mobs burned the provost marshal's headquarters and for three days looted homes and stores and lynched Negroes. Basically the war was unpopular; above all it was the privations of the soldiers and their families and the shockingly long casualty lists against which the rioters were protesting. Inequities in the Act fed their feelings. A drafted man could be exempted from service if he furnished a substitute or, until a change was made in 1864, if he paid an indemnity of $300. This purchase of exemption, patterned after contemporary French law, together with the providing of substitutes, seemed an outrageous way to permit the well-to-do to shift the burden of military service to the poor. Conscription was used just to raise the unfilled portions of state quotas; only about six per cent of the Union forces were raised by this means. Throughout the war being drafted carried a stigma. Further, the draft established new, cumbersome Federal machinery and in a repugnant way extended Federal authority through the states. In a mild, dignified pamphlet, an anonymous Rhode Islander urged a return to the more democratic procedures of the Revolutionary War.[1]]

THE riotous demonstrations recently witnessed in New York and some other places, which have been occasioned by the *Draft*, are much to be deplored by all classes of citizens. No circumstances can justify such terrible proceedings, and their authors can offer no sufficient excuse for their conduct. But now, when the madness of the hour seems to have subsided, at least for the present, it may be wise for both people and rulers, to view the subject candidly and carefully. The public felt aggrieved by the proceedings under the conscription act; they felt that a great wrong had been done

[1] [Randall and Donald, *Civil War and Reconstruction*, 313–318; Freidel, *Lieber*, 348.]

them; they murmured in secret and in public, and the disturbances which we have witnessed were only the outcroppings of one universal indignation. That the people were not right in resorting to violent means to redress a wrong, is everywhere acknowledged; but whether they or the government most deserve censure is a question. It seems to us that well informed, far seeing men might have anticipated such results from such legislation. If men are wanted for the army, the government should endeavor to raise them by constitutional and legitimate means. A very brief examination of the question should be sufficient to convince any unbiassed enquirer that Congress had no constitutional right to pass the obnoxious conscription act. The constitution of the United States confers no such authority upon Congress. And the uniform conduct of the government, both in war and peace, before the passing of this conscription act, clearly shows that no such power was delegated or intended to be delegated to Congress. From its earliest beginning, each colonial government claimed and exercised entire control of its military, and the full exercise of this right was never abridged or interfered with by the government of Great Britain, during all the time that the colonies were subject to the crown. And during the revolutionary war, each state continued to exercise entire control over its military system. Each individual state decided when and how drafts should be made. It was wholly a state affair, and Congress never attempted to interfere. When the war was over, and the constitution was framed and adopted, this important article was annexed to it. "The powers not delegated to the United States by the constitution, nor prohibited by it to the states, are reserved to the states respectively or to the people." In the war of 1812, each state continued to exercise the same entire control over its militia matters. Drafting was done by state authority, and by state officers, and the requisitions of the general government upon the states for troops, were made through the chief magistrate of each state respectively. The general government confided in the intelligence and patriotism of the states. No insolent Marshals patrolled the state, disturbing the quiet of its peaceful citizens. State authorities had an eye to the rights and interests of their own people, and state rights had not yet been swallowed up by the powers at Washington.

It must be recollected, that during the war of 1812, the governors of several of the New England states refused to allow their state conscripts to be marched out of their respective states, declaring that the general government had no authority to use the militia of any state, out of its own limits. To the principle thus laid down, the general government made no formal opposition, and there the matter seemed to rest as an established principle pertaining to state rights. Now if this was sound constitutional doctrine then, it must be so now, and Mr. Lincoln's administration has no more right to override the reserved rights of the states, than that of Mr. Madison had. In accordance with this established principle of state rights, our own constitution declares, "That the militia shall be held in strict subordination to the civil authority." This provision would be a ridiculous nullity if the general government could at pleasure come in and snatch the militia from the civil authority, and use it for any purpose which Congress or the chief magistrate might choose. Such a power vested in the general government would nullify all the reserved rights of the states, and merge the whole in one central despotism. The time was when the Rhode Island people would have been among the first to sound the tocsin of alarm at any such encroachments upon their rights, either as a community or as individuals. And is it not the duty of state authorities now to protect their own people from any unconstitutional requirements of the general government? This right and duty of state governments was not long ago set up in open defiance of the general government, by the enactment of personal liberty bills in nearly every free state. And whether all those state acts were strictly constitutional or otherwise, they recognized a sound principle, and declared it the duty of state governments to protect their own citizens from the encroachments of arbitrary power.

But an attempt is made to justify the existing conscription act, on the ground that the war in which we are engaged at the present time, is not a foreign war, but only an insurrection, and therefore Congress has a right to use the militia to suppress it. In answer to this it may be said that this is no such insurrection or invasion as the constitution contemplates; 'tis no mob, nor riot, nor temporary insurrection to be suppressed by a hasty appeal to the militia. But it is open war of mammoth proportions, against an organized government, recognized by all Europe, and by our intercourse with its authorities, as a belligerent power, having in all respects the character of a foreign enemy, and however unwilling we may be to acknowledge the fact, we are compelled to treat this enemy, not as a band of insurgents, but precisely as we should an English or French army. The present conflict is either a war in the fullest sense of the term, or no war at all, but simply an insurrection. The president claims that it is a war, and therefore he is authorized to suspend the writ of *habeas corpus* and do many other things which he would not be authorized to do in case of an insurrection only. Now if he is right in this, the conscription act is unconstitutional, and the president has no authority to enforce it. Much more might be said to show that this act and all proceedings under it are unauthorized by the Constitution of the United States, and in a legal sense absolutely void, but we have no time to pursue the investigation further. Whenever an appeal is made to the proper tribunal, it will undoubtedly be declared unconstitutional.

But if there was no constitutional impediment to the act, it must nevertheless be considered both unjust and unwise. By lot it inflicts a grievous wrong upon all who have the misfortune to fall under its ban. It is the most odious of all methods of raising troops, and belongs exclusively to despotic governments. It is said that Great Britain never during her long wars, ever resorted to this opprobrious method for recruiting her armies. During the fiery reign of Napoleon Bonaparte, when a military frenzy had taken possession of all France, this odious method was resorted to, and much of the best blood of the nation was shed in obedience to its requirements. The system in its nature and history is exclusively despotic. In nations where the masses are profoundly ignorant, and accustomed to implicit obedience to superiors, this method obtains, and the conscript may go to the army with as little complaint as the ox to the slaughter. But our Congress, when they concocted and passed this law, greatly mistook the temper of the American people. Unlike the serfs of Russia or Austria, the great masses of our people are intelligent and high minded, and habituated to think and judge for themselves. They make and unmake their rulers, and approve or disapprove their acts as they think proper, and no administration can long continue to outrage their rights with impunity, as a day of reckoning is pretty sure to come sooner or later. Until the inauguration of the present scheme of conscription, the policy of our government has been to depend upon voluntary enlistments for the regular army, and to make use of the militia only for brief periods, as occasion might require. The present is the first attempt in this country to create a regular army by arbitrary conscription, and it is such an audacious onslaught upon state rights and personal liberty as was never before witnessed in any free government.

During the revolutionary war, some portions of the troops were raised by draft. The term of service required was never more than three months at any one time. One portion of the militia was called and served three months, and when their term of service expired, unless they chose to remain as volunteers or substitutes, they returned to their families and resumed their ordinary business, and another set of drafted men took their places in the battle field. By these means the hardships, sacrifices and dangers incident to the war were equalized, and shared by all without complaining; poor men and their more fortunate neighbors labored and fought side by side in the same battles, and mingled their blood on the same plains. All hearts beat in unison and glowed with fervor in the cause of their common country. The present conscription measure is extremely unjust, because from the length of the service required it must work entire ruin to a considerable portion of those who are caught in its meshes. Many of them are young married men, farmers, merchants and mechanics, with small families and small means, just starting in business and beginning to live, with a hopeful prospect before them. Take the case of a young mechanic just engaged in a prosperous business, with all the fond endearments of home clustering round him — the die is cast, and he is drafted. The unrelenting decree puts a sudden stop to all his business arrangements, snatches him from the bosom of his family, and requires him to exchange the comforts of home for the hardships, privations and dangers of the camp and field of battle. He is doomed for three years, and whether he will live to return at the end of that time is a question that no one can answer; there is not more than an even chance in his favor. Perhaps he leaves a family without any adequate means for support. The town to which he belongs may mete out to his wife and children a stinted support during the time which he serves in the army, but if he falls in battle or by disease, the same blow that strikes him down, at the same instant cuts off the provision made for his family, and perhaps leaves them, forlorn and destitute, to the cold charities of an unfeeling world. But in whatever circumstances as to property such a family may be placed, it is left without its proper counsellor and guide, to struggle with the world as best it may. As to the conscript himself, if he survives, three years of camp life will work untold changes in him. If he returns at all, it will probably be with a constitution broken down, and with some lasting infirmity upon him; his mind brutalized and debased. Three years spent in indolence, amid all the corrupting influences of army life, demoralizes the once circumspect and industrious mechanic; his thoughts, habits and inclinations become changed, and he is unfitted for the quiet duties of civil life, in which the conscription found him. He may return, but not to the home he left — if he finds his family, they are strangers to him and he to them.

This conscription law is extremely unjust in its requirements. The service that should be shared by all as equally as possible, is arbitrarily demanded of a selected portion of the people, whilst nothing is required of others. There was no necessity for this. As before stated, the drafts in the revolutionary war, and also in the war of 1812, were for short periods, so that the able bodied men took turns, and the service was shared very equally by all. The people of Rhode Island, always jealous of their equal rights and immunities, when they adopted their constitution, took care to insert in it a clause declaring that "the burdens of the state ought to be fairly distributed among its citizens." The conscription law violates this principle, and was evidently framed in utter disregard of all the rights, interests and wishes of the people. Its main features were borrowed from despotisms, and the whole act is little more than a transcript of the Russian system. If the service required had been for six, or even nine months, it would have been submitted to without any serious complaint, and all the riotous outbreaks and scenes of horror and bloodshed would have been prevented; a sufficient number of men would have been raised, and the nation would have been saved from the mortification of its failure. The act was certainly very unwise, and does little credit to the heads or the hearts of its authors. The disturbance and universal opposition which it everywhere meets with, is doing more to strengthen and encourage the rebels than any victory of theirs ever has done. Again, the act is unjust, because the price of exemption is the same for the poor and the rich. From the rich it exacts an inconsiderable trifle, whilst it often takes from the poor man all he has. Some sell their little homes, others mortgage them to raise the money; many give their last dollar, and others borrow of their friends. The poor man must go or part with all he has. The curse has fallen upon him — he is broken up and ruined if he goes, and made a beggar if he stays; whilst the rich man, whose interest at stake is a thousand fold more than that of the poor man, is in no way incommoded. If the call had been peremptory: included the rich as well as the poor, and allowed neither substitutes nor a money commutation, the poor man would readily have marched to the scenes of conflict, shoulder to shoulder with his wealthy neighbor, and cheerfully have shared with him every danger and hardship. Such a course would make the condition of a soldier respectable, promote a spirit of genuine patriotism, and give character and efficiency to the army. Such men would feel that they had something at stake besides their own persons. One such man would be worth more than a score of simple hirelings. The rebels have had much the advantage of us in this respect; their men of substance have fought in the ranks, and their presence has inspired others with courage and devotion to their cause.

If there is any one clause in that act that is more reprehensible than another, it is that which provides that if the conscript fails to appear at the time and place designated, he shall be considered a deserter and dealt with accordingly. Without having committed any crime, or being guilty of the least offence, the absentee is by the law condemned as a deserter, and the penalty is death. The annals of tyranny may be searched in vain for a parallel to this. We would not rashly censure the conduct of our national legislature, or willingly impugn the motives of its members, but we are bound to regard the act under consideration as a sad mistake, which must inevitably seriously injure our cause, and dishonor us at home and abroad. The sovereign people have already pronounced their disapprobation of it; and it is much to be hoped that the government will somehow modify or repeal it, and quiet the popular murmurs. Yet we are aware that governments are too prone to turn a deaf ear to the complaints and admonitions of the common people, until the surges of popular indignation sweep over them.

But after all that may be said of the palpable injustice of the act in question, and the obvious disquietude which attends the pro-

ceedings under it, let it everywhere be distinctly understood that
the proper remedy is not to be found in open and violent resistance.
Such demonstrations are painful evidences of public sentiment, but
cannot directly correct the wrong. Therefore we earnestly entreat
every one wholly to abstain from all unlawful proceedings, to be
patient and bide his time, until the wrong can be corrected in a
constitutional manner; and if the constituted authorities fail to set
the matter right, the sovereign people will most assuredly do it in
their own good time.

Pamphlet 35

Daniel O'Connell

Daniel O'Connell and the Committee of the Irish Repeal Association of Cincinnati.

Cincinnati, 1863

[Numerous of the rioters against the draft in the summer of 1863 were Irish laborers, hostile to the war and to the cause of the emancipation of slaves. As a device to enlist their support, the Cincinnati *Catholic Telegraph* reprinted the powerful admonition that Daniel O'Connell, the Irish patriot, had sent to the pro-slavery Cincinnati Irish Repeal Association twenty years earlier. O'Connell (1775–1847), "the Liberator," for a generation had been the commanding figure in the Irish nationalist movement, first in the successful struggle for Catholic emancipation, then as head of the Irish Party in Parliament. He was a firm liberal in his political views.[1]]

THE COMMITTEE, *to whom the Address from the Cincinnati Irish Repeal Association, on the subject of Negro Slavery in the United States of America, was referred, have agreed to the following Report:* —

To D. T. DISNEY, ESQ.,

Corresponding Secretary.

W. HUNTER, ESQ.,

Vice-President.

❋ ❋ ❋ ❋ ❋ ❋   ❋ ❋ ❋ ❋ ❋
❋ ❋ ❋   ❋ ❋ ❋ ❋   *Executive Committee*
❋ ❋ ❋ ❋ ❋   ❋ ❋ ❋ ❋   *of the Cincinnati*
❋ ❋ ❋   ❋ ❋ ❋ ❋   *Irish Repeal Association.*

[1] [Angus Macintyre, *The Liberator; Daniel O'Connell and the Irish Party, 1830–1847* (London, 1965). The Union League of Philadelphia also issued the pamphlet in October, 1863; under the title Daniel O'Connell, *The Irish Patriot. Daniel O'Connel's* [sic] *Legacy to Irish Americans* (Union League No. 60).]

CORN EXCHANGE ROOMS, DUBLIN, ⎱
11th October, 1843.   ⎰

Gentlemen: — We have read, with the deepest affliction, not unmixed with some surprise and much indignation, your detailed and
anxious vindication of the most hideous crime that has ever stained
humanity — the slavery of men of color in the United States of
America. We are lost in utter amazement at the perversion of mind
and depravity of heart which your Address evinces. How *can* the
generous, the charitable, the humane, the noble emotions of the Irish
heart, have become extinct amongst you? How *can* your nature be
so totally changed as that you should become the apologists and
advocates of that execrable system, which makes man the property
of his fellow-man — destroys the foundation of all moral and social
virtues — condemns to ignorance, immorality and irreligion, millions of our fellow-creatures — renders the slave hopeless of relief,
and perpetuates oppression by law; and, in the name of what you
call a Constitution!

It was not in Ireland you learned this cruelty. Your mothers were
gentle, kind and humane. Their bosoms overflowed with the honey
of human charity. Your sisters are, probably, many of them, still
amongst us, and participate in all that is good and benevolent in
sentiment and action. *How*, then, can you have become so depraved?
How can your souls have become stained with a darkness blacker
than the negro's skin? You say you have no pecuniary interest in
negro slavery. Would that you had! for it might be *some* palliation
of your crime! but, alas! you have inflicted upon us the horror of
beholding you the VOLUNTEER advocates of despotism, in its most
frightful state; of slavery, in its most loathsome and unrelenting
form.

We were, unhappily, prepared to expect some fearful exhibition
of this description. There has been a testimony borne against the
Irish, by birth or descent, in America, by a person fully informed
as to the facts, and incapable of the slightest misrepresentation; a
noble of nature more than a titled birth; a man gifted with the
highest order of talent and the most generous emotions of the heart
— the great, the good Lord Morpeth — he, who, in the House of
Commons, boldly asserted the superior social morality of the poorer
classes of the Irish over any other people — he, the best friend of

any of the Saxon race that Ireland or the Irish ever knew; he, amidst congregated thousands, at Exeter Hall in London, mournfully, but firmly, denounced the Irish in America as being amongst the worst enemies of the negro slaves and other men of color.

It is, therefore, our solemn and sacred duty to warn you, in words already used, and much misunderstood by you — "to come out of her" — not thereby meaning to ask you to come out of America, but out of the councils of the iniquitous and out of the congregation of the wicked, who consider man a chattel and a property, and liberty an inconvenience. Yes. We tell you to come out of such assemblages; but we did not and do not invite you to return to Ireland. The volunteer defenders of slavery, surrounded by one thousand crimes, would find neither sympathy nor support amongst native, uncontaminated Irishmen.

Your advocacy of slavery is founded upon a gross error. You *take for granted* that man can be the property of his fellow-man. You speak in terms of indignation of those who would deprive white men of their *"property,"* and thereby render them less capable of supporting their families in affluence. You forget the other side of the picture. You have neither sorrow nor sympathy for the sufferings of those who are iniquitously compelled to labor for the affluence of others; those who work without wages — who toil without recompense — who spend their lives in procuring for others the splendor and wealth in which they do not participate. You totally forget the sufferings of the wretched black men, who are deprived of their ALL without any compensation or redress. If you, yourselves, all of you — or if any one of you, were, without crime or offence committed by you, handed over into perpetual slavery; if you were compelled to work from sunrise to sunset without wages, supplied only with such coarse food and raiment as would keep you in working order; if, when your *"owner"* fell into debt, you were sold to pay *his* debts, not your own; if it were made a crime to teach you to read and to write; if you were liable to be separated, in the distribution of assets, from your wives and your children; if you (above all) were to fall into the hands of a brutal master — and you condescend to admit that there are *some* brutal masters in America — if, among all those circumstances, some friendly spirits of a more generous order were desirous to give liberty to you and your families — with what ineffable disgust would not you laugh to scorn those who should traduce the generous spirits who would relieve you, as *you* now, pseudo-Irishmen — shame upon you! have traduced and vilified the Abolitionists of North America!

But, you come forward with a justification, forsooth! You say that the Constitution of America prohibits the abolition of slavery. Paltry and miserable subterfuge! The Constitution in America is founded upon the Declaration of Independence. That Declaration published to the world its glorious principles; that Charter of your Freedom contained these emphatic words:

"We hold these Truths to be self-evident — that ALL MEN ARE CREATED EQUAL; that they are endowed by their Creator with certain inalienable Rights; that amongst these are Life, LIBERTY, and the pursuit of happiness;" — and the conclusion of that Address is in these words:

"For the support of this Declaration, with a firm reliance on the protection of Divine Providence, we mutually pledge to each other our Lives, our Fortunes, and OUR SACRED HONOR."

There is American *honor* for you! *There* is a profane allusion to the adorable Creator!

Recollect that the Declaration does not limit the quality of Man, or the Right to Life and Liberty, to the White, to the Brown, or to the Copper-colored Races. It includes all Races. It excludes none.

We do not deign to argue with you on the terms of the American Constitution; and yet we cannot help asserting that, in that Constitution the word "Slavery" or "Slave," is not to be found. There are, indeed, the words — "persons bound to labor;" but it is not said *how* bound. And a Constitutional Lawyer or Judge, construing the American Constitution with a reference to the Declaration of Independence, which is its basis, would not hesitate to decide that, "bound to labor" ought, in a Court of Justice, to mean "bound *by contract* to labor;" and should not be held to imply, "*forced* or *compelled* to labor," in the absence of all contract, and for the exclusive benefit of others.

However, we repeat that we do not deign to argue this point with you; as we proclaim to the world our conviction that no Constitutional Law can create or sanction slavery. Slavery is repugnant to the first principles of society; but, it is enough for us to say, as regards Americans, that it is utterly repugnant to that Declaration of the Equality of all Men, and to the inalienable Right of all Men to

Life and Liberty. To this Declaration the free citizens of the United States have, in the persons of their ancestors, solemnly pledged their "SACRED HONOR."

We shall, at once, shew you how that "*sacred honor*" is basely violated; and also demonstrate how totally devoid of candor your Address is, inasmuch as you rely on the Constitution of the American States as precluding the abolition of slavery; whilst you totally omit all mention of *one* District, which the Constitutional Law, alleged by you, does not reach. We mean the District of Columbia.

In the District of Columbia there is no Constitutional Law to prevent the Congress from totally abolishing slavery within that District. Your Capitol is there. The Temple of American Freedom is there — the Hall of your Republican Representatives — the Hall of your Republican Senators — the National Palace of your Republican President is there — and Slavery is there too, in its most revolting form! The Slave Trade is there — the most disgusting Traffic in human beings is there — human flesh is bought and sold, like swine in the pig-market — aye, in your Capital — your Washington! Yes. Let Americans be as proud as they please, this black spot is on their escutcheon. Even under the shade of the Temple of their Constitution the man of color crawls a slave, and the tawny American stalks a Tyrant.

The cruelty of the slave principle rests not there — it goes much farther. The wretched slaves are totally prohibited even from petitioning Congress. The poor and paltry privilege even of prayer is denied them; and you, even *you* — pseudo-Irishmen! are the advocates and vindicators of such a system. What! would not you, *at least*, insist that their Groans should be heard!

It is carried still farther. Even the free-born white Americans are not allowed to petition upon any subject including the question of slavery: or, at least, no such petition can be read aloud or printed. And, although the Congress is entitled to abolish slavery in Columbia, the door for petition, praying that abolition, is closed without the power of being opened.

We really think that men, who came from generous and warm-hearted Ireland, should shrink into nonentity rather than become the advocates and defenders of the system of slavery. But we trust that the voice of indignant Ireland will scatter them, and prevent them from repeating such a Crime.

In another point of view, your Address is, if possible, more culpable. You state that before the Abolitionists proclaimed their wish to have slavery abolished, several slave-holding States were preparing for the gradual emancipation of their negroes; and that humane individuals in other States were about to adopt similar measures.

We utterly deny your assertion, and we defy you to shew any single instance of preparatory steps taken by any State for the emancipation of the negroes before the abolition demand was raised. You violate Truth in that Assertion. There were no such preparations. It is a pure fiction, invented by slave-holders out of their unjust animosity to the Abolitionists. It is said that the fear of abolition has rendered the slave-holders more strict, harsh and cruel towards their wretched slaves — and that they would be more gentle and humane if they were not afraid of the Abolitionists. We repeat that this is not true, and is merely an attempt to cast blame on those who would coalesce to put an end to negro slavery.

It is in the same spirit that the criminal calumniates his prosecutor, and the felon reviles his accuser. It is, therefore, utterly untrue that the slave-holders have made the chains of the negro more heavy through *any fear of abolition.*

Yet if you tell the truth; if the fact *be,* that the negro is made to suffer for the zeal of the Abolitionists; if he is treated with increased cruelty by reason of the fault of the friends of abolition, *then,* indeed, the slave-holders must be a truly Satanic race. Their conduct, according to you, is diabolical. The Abolitionists commit an offence, and the unhappy negroes are punished. The Abolitionists violate the law of property, and the penalty of their crime is imposed upon the negro! Can any thing be more repugnant to every idea of justice? Yet this is your statement.

We, on the other hand, utterly deny the truth of your allegations; and where we find you calumniate the slave-holders we become their advocates against your calumny. You calumniate everybody — slaves — Abolitionists and slave-owners — framers of Constitutions — makers of laws — everybody! The slave-holders are not favorites of ours, but we will do them justice, and will not permit you to impute an impossible crime to them.

You tell us, with an air of triumph, that public opinion, in your country, is the great Law-giver. If it be so, how much does it enhance the Guilt of your conduct, that you seek to turn public opinion against the slave and in favor of the slave-holder! that you laud the master as generous and humane, and disparage, as much as you can, the unhappy slave; instead of influencing, as Irishmen ought to do, the public mind in favor of the oppressed. You carry your exaggerations to a ludicrous pitch, denoting your utter ignorance of the history of the human race. You say that "the negro is really inferior as a race; that slavery has stamped its debasing influence upon the Africans; that between him and the white almost a century would be required to elevate the character of the one, and to destroy the antipathies of the other." You add — we use your own words — "The very odor of the negro is almost insufferable to the white; and however much humanity may lament it, we make no rash declaration when we say the two races cannot exist together on equal terms under our 'Government and our Institutions.'"

We quote this paragraph at full length, because it is replete with your mischievous errors and guilty mode of thinking.

In the first place, as to the odor of the negroes, we are quite aware that they have not as yet come to use much of the otto of Roses or *Eau de Cologne*. But we implore of your fastidiousness to recollect that multitudes of the children of white men have negro women for their mothers; and that our British travelers complain in loud and bitter terms of the overpowering stench of stale tobacco-spittle, as the prevailing "odor" amongst the native free Americans. It would be, perhaps, better to check this nasal sensibility on both sides, on the part of the whites as well as of blacks. But it is, indeed, deplorable that you should use a ludicrous assertion of that description as one of the inducements to prevent the abolition of slavery. The negroes would certainly smell at least as sweet when free, as they now do being slaves.

Your important allegation is, that the negros are, naturally, an inferior race. That is a totally gratuitous assertion upon your part. In America you can have no opportunity of seeing the negro educated. On the contrary, in most of your States it is a crime — sacred Heaven! a *crime* to educate even a free negro! How, then, can you judge of the negro race, when you see them despised and contemned by the educated classes; reviled and looked down upon as inferior? The negro race has, naturally, some of the finest qualities. They are naturally gentle, generous, humane, and very grateful for kindness. They are as brave and as fearless as any other of the

races of human beings; but the blessings of education are kept from
them, and they are judged of, not as they would be with proper
cultivation, but as they are rendered by cruel and debasing oppression. It is as old as the days of Homer, who truly asserts that the
day which sees a man a slave takes away half his worth. Slavery
actually brutalizes human beings. It is about sixty years ago when
one of the Sheiks, not far South of Fez, in Morocco, who was in the
habit of accumulating white slaves — upon being strongly remonstrated with by an European power, gave for his reply, that, by his
own experience, he found it quite manifest that white men were of
an inferior race, intended by nature for slaves; and he produced his
own brutalized white slaves to illustrate the truth of his assertion.
And a case of an American, with a historic name — John Adams
— is quite familiar: Some twenty-five years ago — not more, John
Adams was the sole survivor of an American crew, wrecked on the
African Coast. He was taken into the interior as the slave of an
Arab Chief. He was only for three years a slave, and the English and
American Consuls having been informed of a white man's slavery,
claimed him and obtained his liberation. In the short space of three
years he had become completely brutalized; he had completely forgotten the English language, without having acquired the native
tongue. He spoke a kind of gabble, as unintellectual as the dialects
of most of your negro slaves; and many months elapsed before he
recovered his former habits and ideas.

It is, also, a curious fact, as connected with America, that the
children of the Anglo-Saxon race and of other Europeans born in
America, were, for many years, considered as a degraded and
inferior class. Indeed it was admitted, as if it were an axiom, that
the native-born American was in nothing equal to his European
progenitor; and so far from the fact being disputed, many philo-
sophic dissertations were published endeavoring to account for the
alleged debasement. The only doubt was about the *cause* of it.
"Nobody doubted," to use your own words, "that the native-born
Americans were really an inferior race." Nobody dares to say
so now; and nobody thinks it. Let it, then, be recollected that
you have never yet seen the negro educated. An English traveler
through Brazil, some few years ago, mentions having known a negro
who was a Priest, and who was a learned, pious and exemplary man
in his sacerdotal functions. We have been lately informed of two

negroes being educated at the Propaganda and ordained Priests —
both having distinguished themselves in their scientific and theo-
logical course. The French papers say that one of them celebrated
Mass and delivered a short but able sermon before Louis Philippe.
It is believed they have both gone out with the Right Rev. Dr.
Baron on the African Mission.

We repeat, therefore, that to judge properly of the negro, you
should see him educated and treated with the respect due to a
fellow-creature — uninsulted by the filthy aristocracy of the skin,
and untarnished to the eye of the white by any associations connected with his state of slavery.

We next refer to your declaration that the two races, viz., the
Black and the White, cannot exist, on equal terms, under your
Government and your Institutions. This is an extraordinary assertion
to be made at the present day. You allude, indeed, to Antigua and
the Bermudas. But we will take you to where the experiment has
been successfully made upon a large scale — namely, to Jamaica.

There the two races are on a perfect equality in point of law.
There is no master — there is no slave. The law does not recognize
the slightest distinction between the races. You have borrowed the
far greater part of your Address from the cant phraseology which
the West Indian slave-owners, and especially those of Jamaica,
made use of before emancipation. They used to assert, as you do
now, that abolition meant destruction; that to give freedom to the
negro would be to pronounce the assassination of the whites; that
the negro, as soon as free, would massacre their former owners and
destroy their wives and families. In short, your prophecies of the
destructive effects of emancipation are but faint and foolish echoes
of the prophetic apprehensions of the British slave-owners. They
might, perhaps, have believed their own assertions, because the
emancipation of the negroes was then an untried experiment. But
you — *you* are deprived of any excuse for the reassertion of a disproved calumny. The Emancipation has taken place — the compensation given by England was *not* given to the negroes, who were
the only persons that deserved compensation. It was given to the
so-called "owners." It was an additional wrong — an additional
cause of irritation to the negroes. But, gracious Heaven! how nobly
did that good and kindly race — the negroes — falsify the calum-
nious apprehensions of their task-masters! Was there one single

murder consequent on the emancipation? Was there one riot — one tumult — even one assault? Was there one single white person injured either in person or property? Was there any property spoiled or laid waste? The proportion of negroes in Jamaica to white men is as 300 to 60 or eighty per cent. Yet the most perfect tranquility has followed the Emancipation. The Criminal Courts are almost unemployed, nine-tenths of the jails are empty and open; universal tranquility reigns. Although the Landed proprietors have made use of the harshest landlord power to exact the hardest terms by way of rent from the negroes, and have also endeavored to extort from him the largest possible quantity of labor for the smallest wages, yet the kindly negro race have not retaliated by one single act of violence or of vengeance: the two races exist together, upon equal terms, under the British Government and under British Institutions.

Or shall you say that the British Government and British Institutions are preferable to yours? The vain and vaporing spirit of mistaken Republicanism will not permit you to avow the British superiority. You are bound, however reluctantly, to admit that superiority or else to admit the falsity of your own assertions. Nothing can, in truth, be more ludicrous than your declaration in favor of slavery. It, however, sometimes rises to the very border of Blasphemy. Your words are, "God forbid that we should advocate 'human bondage in any shape.'"

Oh! shame upon you! How can you take the name of the All-Good Creator thus in vain! What are you doing! Is not the entire of your Address an advocacy of human Bondage?

Another piece of silliness. You allege that it is the Abolitionists who make the slave restless with his condition, and that they scatter the seeds of discontent. How can you treat us with such contempt as to use assertions of that kind in your Address? How can you think we could be so devoid of intellect as to believe the negro would not know the miseries of slavery, which he feels every hour of the four-and-twenty, unless he were told by some Abolitionist that slavery was a miserable condition?

There is nothing that makes us think so badly of you as your strain of ribaldry in attacking the Abolitionists.

The desire to procure abolition is, in itself, a virtue and deserves our love for its charitable disposition, as it does respect and veneration for its courage under unfavorable circumstances. Instead of the ribaldry of your attack upon the Abolitionists, you ought to respect and countenance them. If they err by excessive zeal, they err in a righteous and a holy cause. You would do well to check their errors and mitigate their zeal within the bounds of strict propriety. But if you had the genuine feelings of Irishmen you never would confound their errors with their virtues. In truth, we much fear or rather we should candidly say, we readily believe that you attribute to them imaginary errors for no other reason than that they really possess one brilliant virtue — namely, the love of human freedom in intense perfection.

Again, we have to remark that you exaggerate exceedingly when you state that there are fifteen millions of the white population in America whose security and happiness are connected with the maintenance of the system of negro slavery. On the contrary, the system of slavery inflicts nothing but mischief upon the far greater part of the inhabitants of America. The only places in which individual interest is connected with slavery are the slave-holding States. Now, in those States, almost without an exception (if, indeed, there be any exception), the people of color greatly exceed the whites; and thus, even if an injury were to be inflicted on the whites by depriving them of their slaves, the advantages would be most abundantly counterbalanced and compensated for by the infinitely greater number of persons, who would thus be restored to that greatest of human blessings — personal Liberty. Thus the noble Benthamite maxim of "doing the greatest possible good to the greatest possible number," would be amply carried out into effect by the Emancipation of the negroes.

You charge the Abolitionists, as with a crime, that they encouraged a negro, flying from Kentucky, to steal a horse from an inhabitant of Ohio, in order to aid him, if necessary, in making his escape. We are not, upon full reflection, sufficiently versed in casuistry to decide whether, under such circumstances, the taking of the horse would be an excusable act or not. But, even conceding that it would be sinful, we are *of this* quite certain, that there is not one of you that address us who, if he were under similar circumstances, that is, having no other means of escaping perpetual slavery, would not make free with your neighbor's horse to effectuate your just and reasonable purpose. And we are also sure of this, that there is not one of you who, if he were compelled to spend the rest of his life as a personal slave, worked, and beaten, and sold, and transferred from hand to hand, and separated, at his master's caprice, from wife and family — consigned to ignorance — working without wages, toiling without reward — without any other stimulant to that toil and labor than the driver's cart-whip — we do say that there is not one of you who would not think that the name of pick-pocket, thief or felon, would not be too courteous a name for the being who kept you in such thraldom.

We cannot avoid repeating our astonishment that you, Irishmen, should be so devoid of every trace of humanity as to become the voluntary and pecuniarily-disinterested advocates of human slavery; and especially, that you should be so in America. But what excites our unconquerable loathing is to find that in your Address you speak of man being the property of man — of one human Being being the property of another, with as little doubt, hesitation or repugnance, as if you were speaking of the beasts of the field. It is this that fills us with utter astonishment. It is this that makes us disclaim you as countrymen. We cannot bring ourselves to believe that you breathed your natal air in Ireland — Ireland, the first of all the nations on the earth that abolished the dealing in slaves. The slave trade of that day was, curiously enough, a slave trade in British youths — Ireland, that never was stained with negro slave trading — Ireland, that never committed an offence against the men of color — Ireland, that never fitted out a single vessel for the traffic in blood on the African Coast.

It is, to be sure, afflicting and heart-rending to us to think that so many of the Irish in America should be so degenerate as to be amongst the worst enemies of the people of color. Alas! alas! we have that fact placed beyond doubt by the indisputable testimony of Lord Morpeth. This is a foul blot that we would fain wipe off the 'scutcheon of expatriated Irishmen.

Have you enough of the genuine Irishman left amongst you to ask what it is that we require you to do? It is this:

First — We call upon you, in the sacred name of humanity, never again to volunteer on behalf of the oppressor; nor even for any self-interest to vindicate the hideous crime of personal slavery.

Secondly — We ask you to assist in every way you can in promoting the education of the free men of color, and in discountenancing the foolish feeling of selfishness — of that criminal selfishness which makes the white man treat the man of color as a degraded or inferior being.

Thirdly — We ask you to assist in obtaining for the free men of color the full benefit of all the rights and franchises of a Freeman in whatever State he may inhabit.

Fourthly — We ask you to exert yourselves in endeavoring to procure for the man of color, in every case, the benefit of a Trial by Jury; and especially where a man insisting that he is a Freeman is claimed to be a slave.

Fifthly — We ask you to exert yourselves in every possible way to induce slave-owners to emancipate as many slaves as possible. The Quakers in America have several societies for this purpose. Why should not the Irish imitate them in that virtue?

Sixthly — We ask you to exert yourselves in all the ways you possibly can to put an end to the internal slave trade of the States. The breeding of slaves for sale is, probably, the most immoral and debasing practice ever known in the world. It is a crime of the most hideous kind; and if there were no other crime committed by the Americans, this alone would place the advocates, supporters and practisers of American slavery in the lowest grade of criminals.

Seventhly — We ask you to use every exertion in your power to procure the abolition of slavery by the Congress in the District of Columbia.

Eighthly — We ask you to use your best exertions to compel the Congress to receive and read the petitions of the wretched negroes; and, above all, the petitions of their white advocates.

Ninthly — We ask you never to cease your efforts until the crime of which Lord Morpeth has accused the Irish in America, of "being the worst enemies of the men of color," shall be atoned for, and blotted out and effaced forever.

You will ask how you can do all these things? You have already answered that question yourselves; for you have said that public opinion is the Law of America. Contribute, then, each of you in his sphere to make up that public opinion. Where you have the electoral franchise, give your vote to none but those who will assist you in so holy a struggle.

Under a popular Government, the man who has right, and reason, and justice, and charity, and Christianity itself at his side, has great instruments of legislation and legal power. He has the elements about him of the greatest utility; and even if he should not succeed he can have the heart-soothing consolation of having endeavored to do great and good actions. He can enjoy, even in defeat, the sweet comfort of having endeavored to promote benevolence and charity.

It is no excuse to allege that the Congress is restricted from emancipating the slaves by one General Law. Each particular slave State has that power within its own precincts; and there is every reason to be convinced that Maryland and Virginia would have followed the example of New York, and long ago abolished slavery but for the diabolical practice of "raising," as you call it, slaves for the Southern market of pestilence and death.

Irishmen and the sons of Irishmen have, many of them, risen to high distinction and power in America. Why should not Irishmen and the sons of Irishmen write their names in the brightest pages of the chapter of humanity and benevolence in American story?

Irishmen! our Chairman ventures to think, and we agree with him, that he has claims on the attention of Irishmen in every quarter of the globe. The Scotch and French philosophers have proved by many years of experiment that the Irishman stands first among the races of man in his physical and bodily powers. America and Europe bear testimony to the intellectual capacity of Irishmen. Lord Morpeth has demonstrated in the British Parliament the superior morality of the humbler classes of Irish in all social and family relations. The religious fidelity of the Irish nation is blazoned in glorious and proverbial certainty and splendor.

Irishmen! sons of Irishmen! descendants of the kind of heart and affectionate in disposition, think, oh think only with pity and compassion on your colored fellow-creatures in America. Offer them the hand of kindly help. Soothe their sorrows. Scathe their oppressor. Join with your countrymen at home in one cry of horror against the oppressor; in one cry of sympathy with the enslaved and oppressed,

> 'Till prone in the dust slav'ry shall be hurl'd,—
> Its name and nature blotted from the world.

We cannot close our observations upon the unseemly, as well as silly attacks you make upon the advocates of abolition, without reminding you that you have borrowed this turn of thought from the persons who opposed Catholic Emancipation in Ireland, or who were the pretended friends of the Catholics. Some of you must recollect that it was the custom of such persons to allege that but for the "violence" and "misconduct" of the agitators, and more particularly of our Chairman, the Protestants were about to emancipate the Catholics gradually. It was the constant theme of the newspaper press, and even of the speeches in the Houses of Parliament, that the violence and misconduct of agitators prevented Emancipation. It was the burthen of many pamphlets, and especially of *two*, which were both written, under the title of "Faction Unmasked," by Protestants of great ability. They asserted themselves to be friends of Emancipation in the abstract; but they alleged that it was impossible to grant Emancipation to persons whose Leaders misconducted themselves as the Agitators did. They gratified their hatred to the Catholics as you gratify your bad feeling towards the negroes, by abuse of the Catholic leaders as virulent as yours is against the Abolitionists. But they deceived nobody. Neither do you deceive anybody. Every humane being perceives the futility and folly of your attacks upon the Abolitionists, and understands that those are but the exhibition of rancor and malignity against the tried friends of humanity.

You say that the Abolitionists are fanatics and bigots, and especially entertain a virulent hatred and unchristian zeal against Catholicity and the Irish. We do not mean to deny, nor do we wish to conceal that there are amongst the Abolitionists many wicked and calumniating *enemies* of Catholicity and the Irish, especially in that most intolerant class — the Wesleyan Methodists; but the best way to disarm their malice is *not* by giving up to *them* the side of humanity, while you, yourselves, take the side of slavery. But, on the contrary, by taking a superior station of Christian virtue in the cause of benevolence and charity, and in zeal for the freedom of all mankind.

We wish we could burn into your souls the turpitude attached to the Irish in America by Lord Morpeth's charge. Recollect that it reflects dishonor not only upon you but upon the land of your birth. There is but one way of effacing such disgrace, and that is by becoming the most kindly towards the colored population, and the most energetic in working out in detail, as well as in general principle, the amelioration of the state of the miserable Bondsmen.

You tell us, indeed, that many Clergymen, and especially the

Catholic Clergy, are ranged on the side of the slave-holders. We do not believe your accusation.

The Catholic Clergy may endure, but they assuredly do not encourage the slave-owners. We have, indeed, heard it said that some Catholic Clergymen have slaves of their own; but, it is added, and we are assured positively, that no Irish Catholic Clergyman is a slave-owner. At all events, every Catholic knows how distinctly slave-holding, and especially slave-trading, is condemned by the Catholic Church. That most eminent man, His Holiness, the present Pope, has, by an Allocution published throughout the world, condemned all dealing and traffic in slaves. Nothing can be more distinct nor more powerful than the Pope's denunciation of that most abominable crime. Yet it subsists in a more abominable form than His Holiness could possibly describe, in the traffic which still exists in the sale of slaves from one State in America to another. What, then, are we to think of you, Irish Catholics, who send us an elaborate vindication of slavery without the slightest censure of that hateful crime? a crime which the Pope has so completely condemned — namely, the diabolical raising of slaves for sale, and selling them to other States.

If you be Catholics you should devote your time and best exertions to working out of pious intentions of His Holiness. Yet you prefer — oh, sorrow and shame! to volunteer your vindication of everything that belongs to the guilt of slavery.

If you be Christians at all, recollect that slavery is opposed to the first, the highest, and the greatest principles of Christianity, which teach us "to love the great and good God above all things whatsoever;" and the next "to love our fellow-man as ourselves;" which commands us "to do unto others as we would be done by." These sacred principles are inconsistent with the horrors and crimes of slavery; sacred principles which have already banished domestic bondage from civilized Europe, and which will also, in God's own good time, banish it from America, despite the advocacy of such puny declaimers as *you* are.

How bitterly have we been afflicted at perceiving by the American newspapers, that recently in the city which you inhabit an opportunity was given to the Irish to exhibit benevolence and humanity to a colored fellow-creature, and was given in vain! We allude to the case of the girl Lavinia, who was a slave in another

State, and brought by her owner into that of Ohio. She by that means became entitled to her freedom, if she had but one friend to assert it for her. She *did* find friends — may the great God of Heaven bless them! Were they Irish? Alas! alas! not one. You sneer at the sectaries. Behold how they here conquer you in goodness and charity. The owner's name, it seems, was Scanlan; unhappily a thorough Irish name. And *he*, it appears, has boasted that he took his revenge, by the most fiendish cruelty, *not* upon Lavinia or her protectors, for they were not in his power, but on her unoffending father, mother and family!

And *this* is the system which you, Irishmen, through many folio pages of wicked declamation, seek at least to palliate if not justify. Our cheeks burn with shame to think that such a monster as Scanlan could trace his pedigree to Ireland. And yet *you*, Irishmen, stand by in the attitude rather of friends and supporters, than of impugners of the monstrous cruelty. And you prefer to string together pages of cruel and heartless sophistry in defence of the source of his crimes, rather than take part against him.

Perhaps it would offend your fastidiousness if such a man were compared to a pick-pocket or a felon. We respect your prejudices and call him no reproachful *name*. It is, indeed, unnecessary.

We conclude by conjuring you, and all other Irishmen in America, in the name of your fatherland — in the name of humanity — in the name of the God of Mercy and Charity; we conjure you, Irishmen and descendants of Irishmen, to abandon for ever all defense of the hideous negro slavery system. Let it no more be said that your feelings are made so obtuse by the air of America that you cannot feel as Catholics and Christians ought to feel this truth — this plain truth, that ONE MAN CANNOT HAVE ANY PROPERTY IN ANOTHER MAN. There is not one of you who does not recognize that principle in his own person. Yet we perceive — and this agonizes us almost to madness — that *you*, boasting on Irish descent, should, without the instigation of any pecuniary or interested motive, but out of the sheer and single love of wickedness and crime, come forward as the volunteer defenders of the most degrading species of human slavery. Woe! Woe! Woe!

There is one consolation still amid the pulsations of our hearts. There are — there *must be* genuine Irishmen in America — men of sounds heads and Irish hearts, who will assist us to wipe off the foul stain that Lord Morpeth's proven charge has inflicted on the Irish character — who will hold out the hand of fellowship, with a heart in that hand, to every honest man of every caste and color — who will sustain the cause of humanity and honor, and scorn the paltry advocates of slavery — who will shew that the Irish heart is in America as benevolent and as replete with charitable emotions as in any other clime on the face of the earth.

We conclude. The spirit of democratic liberty is defiled by the continuance of negro slavery in the United States. The United States, themselves, are degraded below the most uncivilized nations, by the atrocious inconsistency of talking of liberty and practising tyranny in its worst shape. The Americans attempt to palliate their iniquity by the futile excuse of personal interest; but the Irish, who have not even that futile excuse, and yet justify slavery, are utterly indefensible.

Once again — and for the last time — we call upon you to come out of the councils of the slave-owners, and at all events to free yourselves from participating in their guilt.

Irishmen, I call on you to join in crushing slavery, and in giving Liberty to every man of every caste, creed and color.

Signed by order,

DANIEL O'CONNELL,
Chairman of the Committee.

Pamphlet 36

Rebel Conditions of Peace and the Mechanics of the South. (*Loyal Publication Society No. 30*)

New York, 1863

[While many of the pamphlets issued by the Union League of Philadelphia and the Loyal Publication Society in New York were complex and
careful in their argument, aimed at well-educated people, increasingly
others appeared that were simple in their appeal and propagandistic in
tone. From two numbers of Richmond newspapers, the materials for this
pamphlet were culled to try to convince readers that the Confederates
were ready to make extreme demands for peace and keep workingmen in
a state of subservience. "The mechanics of the North can plainly see
what their fate would be should the rebel hopes of success be fulfilled,"
the pamphlet proclaimed — a statement scarcely substantiated by the ex-
cerpt from the Richmond *Examiner*.]

THE spirit which animates the leaders of the southern rebellion,
and the abject condition to which the despotism they have established in the southern territory, which still remains subject to their
rule, has reduced the people of the South, are portrayed in the
following articles from the Richmond *Enquirer,* entitled "Peace,"
and the "Mechanics of the South." The free and intelligent people
of the Northern States will do well to read and ponder upon the
conditions which these haughty oligarchs propose to the free
Democracy of America.

"They have learned nothing, and forgotten nothing," and with
Maryland, Missouri, Tennessee, Kentucky, Louisiana, and Mississippi, wrested from their unholy grasp, and their Minister Mason,
retiring in disgust from the doorways of the British Minister, whose
ante-chambers have been steadily and constantly closed to his
entreaties, they still imagine themselves, if not the masters of the
world, at least the arbiters of American destinies.

The result of their schemes is shown in the miserable condition to which they have reduced their misguided, deluded and betrayed people, and the mechanics of the North can plainly see what their fate would be should the rebel hopes of success be fulfilled.

Fortunately the present position of their affairs gives neither warrant to their hopes, nor reason for their insolence.

REBEL CONDITIONS OF PEACE.

FROM THE RICHMOND *Enquirer* OF OCTOBER 16, 1863:

PEACE.

Save on our own terms, we can accept no peace whatever, and must fight till doomsday, rather than yield an iota of them, and our terms are:

Recognition by the enemy of the independence of the Confederate States.

Withdrawal of the Yankee forces from every foot of Confederate ground, including Kentucky and Missouri.

Withdrawal of the Yankee soldiers from Maryland, until that State shall decide, by a free vote, whether she shall remain in the old Union, or ask admission into the Confederacy.

Consent, on the part of the Federal Government, to give up to the Confederacy its proportion of the navy as it stood at the time of secession, or to pay for the same.

Yielding up of all pretension, on the part of the Federal Government, to that portion of the old Territories which lies west of the Confederate States.

An equitable settlement on the basis of our absolute independence and equal rights of all accounts of the public debt and public lands, and the advantages accruing from foreign treaties.

These provisions, we apprehend, comprise the minimum of what we must require before we lay down our arms. That is to say, the North must yield all, — we nothing. The whole pretension of that country to prevent, by force, the separation of the States must be abandoned, which will be equivalent to an avowal that our enemies were wrong from the first; and, of course, as they waged a causeless and wicked war upon us, they ought, in strict justice, to be required, according to usage in such cases, to reimburse to us the whole of our expenses and losses in the course of that war. Whether this last proviso is to be insisted upon or not, certain we are that we cannot have any peace at all, until we shall be in a position, not only to demand and exact, but also to enforce and collect treasure for our own reimbursement out of the wealthy cities in the enemy's country. In other words, unless we can destroy or scatter their armies, and break up their Government, we can have no peace; and if we can do that, then we ought not only to extort from them our own full terms and ample acknowledgment of their wrong, but also a handsome indemnity for the trouble and expense caused to us by their crime.

Now, we are not yet in position to dictate those terms to our enemies, with ROSECRANS' army still in the heart of our country, and MEADE still on Virginia soil, but though it is too soon to propose such conditions to them, yet it is important that we should keep them plainly before our own eyes as the only admissible basis of any conceivable peace. This well fixed in the Confederate mind, there will be no more fearful looking for news from Europe, as if that blessed peace were to come to us over the sea, and not to be conquered on our own ground. There will be no more gaping for hints of recognition and filling of the belly with the East wind; no more distraction or diversion from the single momentous business of bracing up every nerve and sinew of the country for battle.

It is especially now, at the moment when great and perhaps decisive battles are impending at two or three points, that we think it most essential to insist upon the grand and entire magnificence of the stake and cause.

Once more we say it is all or nothing. This Confederacy or the Yankee nation, one or other, goes down, down to perdition. That is to say, one or the other must forfeit its national existence and lie at the mercy of its mortal enemy.

We all know by this time the fate in store for us if we succumb. The other party has no smaller stake.

As surely as we completely ruin their armies — and without that is no peace nor truce at all — so surely shall we make them pay our war debt, though we wring it out of their hearts. And they know it well, and, therefore, they cannot make peace except through their utter exhaustion and absolute inability to strike another blow.

The stake they have to forfeit, then, if they lose this dreadful game, is as vital as ours. So is the stake to be won if they win anything. It is no less than the entire possession of our whole country, with us in it, and everything that is ours, from Ohio to the Rio Grande, to have and to hold, to them and their heirs forever.

But, on the other hand, what we mean to win is utter separation from them for all time. We do not want to govern their country, but after levying upon it what seemeth good to us by way of indemnity, we leave it to commence its political life again from the beginning, hoping that the lesson may have made them sadder and wiser Yankees.

We shut them out forever, with all their unclean and scoundrelly ways, intending to lead our lives here in our own Confederate way, within our own well-guarded bounds, and without, as St. John says, are dogs.

And let no Confederate feeble knees and tremulous backbone say to us, this complete triumph is impossible; say that we must be content with some kind of compromise, and give and take; on the contrary, we must gain all or lose all, and that the Confederates will indeed win the giant game, we take to be as certain as any future event in this uncertain world.

MEADE's army and ROSECRANS' once scattered, LINCOLN can get no more armies. The draft turns out manifestly fruitless. Both the German and Irish element are now for peace. The Yankees have to bear the brunt of the war themselves, but in the meantime their inevitable bankruptcy is advancing like an armed man. Hungry ruin has them in the wind. It cannot be long before the Cabinet of Washington will have, indeed, to consider seriously proposals for peace, under auspices and circumstances very different from the present. For the present the war rolls and thunders on, and may God defend the right.

THE MECHANICS OF THE SOUTH

ABJECT POSTURE OF LABOR AND LABORERS.

The Richmond *Examiner*, of the 12th inst., says: That on Saturday, the 10th inst., a very large and spontaneous meeting of the mechanics and working men of Richmond was held to consider their interests, and obtain a free expression of the sentiments of the people generally.

From the resolutions passed, we select the two following:

Resolved, That awakened to a sense of the abject posture to which labor and we who labor have been reduced, and to the privileges, which as citizens and people, the Institutions of our Country vest in us, *we will not sleep again until our grasp has firmly clenched the rights and immunities which are ours as Americans and men: until our just demands have been met by the concessions of all opposing elements.*

Resolved, That it is the duty of the Government to take care of the unfortunate, and not the rich.

The *Enquirer* is extremely indignant at this assemblage, and deals with the "working men" in the following fashion:

"The mechanics of Richmond enjoy all the 'rights and immunities' that any and every other man enjoys, *and they will not be permitted to 'grasp' or 'clench' any more.* We hope the Legislature of Virginia will not permit itself to be influenced by such minatory resolutions, to pass a law forbidden by the experience of all history, and opposed by the teachings of every public economist, and which is now opposed by some of the ablest and wisest men of their own body. The men who compose the armies of the Confederacy have, for the last two years, permitted all their 'rights and immunities' to be most materially circumscribed, their 'privileges' reduced to the one high and holy privilege of shooting and being shot for their country. These men, without shoes, blankets, provisions — in want, and suffering with wounds, and even unto death, have nobly and gallantly borne all these hardships, unmurmuring and uncomplaining. Upon what are these sleepless resolutionists to fix their 'grasps?' We leave the Governor and Mayor to answer these questions, and to interpret these resolutions, *and to decide what their respective duties may be when the 'grasping' and 'clenching' begins.*"

———◆◄◆►◆———

Pamphlet 37

Charles Sumner

Our Domestic Relations: or, How to Treat the Rebel States.

Boston, 1863

[The Confederate tide was slowly ebbing through the second half of 1863, even though the draft riots had given evidence of low morale in the North. The surrender of Vicksburg, opening the Mississippi, and the Battle of Gettysburg ending General Robert E. Lee's northern thrust, marked a decisive turn. Before the end of the year, the debate over Reconstruction was becoming of immediate concern. What should be the relationship of territory wrested from the retreating Confederate military power to the remainder of the Federal Union? Since the beginning of the war, President Lincoln had been following an experimental course, varying according to locale and circumstances, but one clearly intended to keep the process of Reconstruction under executive control. In October, 1863, Senator Charles Sumner of Massachusetts, one of the Radical Republican leaders, set forth in the *Atlantic Monthly* (which issued it immediately in pamphlet form) a detailed argument, bolstered by many citations to historic and legal precedents, for Congressional control of Reconstruction. His strictures against Reconstruction through military governors appointed by the President curiously paralleled some of the Democratic criticisms of Lincoln; his positive program would give them scant comfort. His was one of the opening statements in a controversy that stretched on for years. In December, 1863, President Lincoln announced a moderate plan of Reconstruction through which former Confederate states could obtain executive recognition. At the beginning of July, 1864, Sumner and his cohorts obtained passage of the much more drastic Wade-Davis bill, which would have established congressional jurisdiction over Reconstruction. President Lincoln let it die through exercising a pocket veto. Sumner (1811–1874), "the scholar in politics," in the 1850's had been one of the most forceful opponents of slavery in the Senate. In retaliation for alleged insults in his "Crime Against Kansas" speech, a South Carolina congressman had severely beaten him at his desk; thereafter he was a hero in Massachusetts. During the Civil War, he was not only one of the most powerful senators in determining domestic policy but also chairman of the Senate Committee on Foreign Relations. He conferred frequently with President Lincoln.[1]]

AT this moment our Domestic Relations all hinge upon one question: *How to treat the Rebel States?* No patriot citizen doubts the triumph of our arms in the suppression of the Rebellion. Early or late, this triumph is inevitable. It may be by a sudden collapse of the bloody imposture, or it may be by a slower and more gradual surrender. For ourselves, we are prepared for either alternative, and shall not be disappointed, if we are constrained to wait yet a little longer. But when the day of triumph comes, political duties will take the place of military. The victory won by our soldiers must be assured by wise counsels, so that its hard-earned fruits may not be lost.

The relations of the States to the National Government must be carefully considered, — not too boldly, not too timidly, — in order to see in what way, or by what process, *the transition from Rebel forms may be most surely accomplished.* If I do not greatly err, it will be found that the powers of Congress, which have thus far been so effective in raising armies and in supplying moneys, will be important, if not essential, in fixing the conditions of perpetual peace. But there is one point on which there can be no question. The dogma and delusion of State Rights, which did so much for the Rebellion, must not be allowed to neutralize all that our arms have gained.

Already, in a remarkable instance, the President has treated the pretension of State Rights with proper indifference. Quietly and without much discussion, he has constituted military governments in the Rebel States, with governors nominated by himself, — all of which testifies against the old pretension. Strange will it be, if this extraordinary power, amply conceded to the President, is denied to Congress. Practically the whole question with which I began is opened here. Therefore to this aspect of it I ask your first attention.

CONGRESSIONAL GOVERNMENT *VS.* MILITARY GOVERNMENT.

FOUR military governors have been already appointed: one for

---

[1] [David Donald, *Charles Sumner and the Coming of the Civil War* (New York, 1960); Donald, *Lincoln Reconsidered* (New York, 1956); William B. Hesseltine, *Lincoln's Plan of Reconstruction* (Tuscaloosa, Alabama, 1960).]

Tennessee, one for South Carolina, one for North Carolina, and the other for Louisiana. So far as is known, the appointment of each was by a simple letter from the Secretary of War. But if this can be done in four States, where is the limit? It may be done in every Rebel State, and if not in every other State of the Union, it will be simply because the existence of a valid State government excludes the exercise of this extraordinary power. But assuming, that, as our arms prevail, it will be done in every Rebel State, we shall then have *eleven* military governors, all deriving their authority from one source, ruling a population amounting to upwards of nine millions. And this imperatorial dominion, indefinite in extent, will also be indefinite in duration; for if, under the Constitution and laws, it be proper to constitute such governors, it is clear that they may be continued without regard to time, — for years, if you please, as well as for weeks, — and the whole region which they are called to sway will be a military empire, with all powers, executive, legislative, and even judicial, derived from one man in Washington. Talk of the "one-man power." Here it is with a vengeance. Talk of military rule. Here it is, in the name of a republic.

The bare statement of this case may put us on our guard. We may well hesitate to organize a single State under a military government, when we see where such a step will lead. If you approve one, you must approve all, and the National Government may crystallize into a military despotism.

In appointing military governors of States, we follow an approved example in certain cases beyond the jurisdiction of our Constitution, as in California and Mexico after their conquest and before peace. It is evident that in these cases there was no constraint from the Constitution, and we were perfectly free to act according to the assumed exigency. It may be proper to set up military governors for a conquered country beyond our civil jurisdiction, and yet it may be questionable if we should undertake to set up such governors in States which we all claim to be within our civil jurisdiction. At all events, the two cases are different, so that it is not easy to argue from one to the other.

In Jefferson's Inaugural Address, where he develops what he calls "the essential principles of our government, and consequently those which ought to shape its administration," he mentions *"the supremacy of the civil over the military authority"* as one of these "essential principles," and then says: —

"These should be the creed of our political faith, — the text of civil instruction, — the touchstone by which to try the services of those we trust; and should we wander from them in moments of error or alarm, let us hasten to retrace our steps, and to regain the road which alone leads to peace, liberty, and safety."

In undertaking to create military governors of States, we reverse the policy of the republic, as solemnly declared by Jefferson, and subject the civil to the military authority. If this has been done, in patriotic ardor, without due consideration, in a moment of error or alarm, it only remains, that, according to Jefferson, we should "hasten to retrace our steps, and to regain the road which alone leads to peace, liberty, and safety."

There is nothing new under the sun, and the military governors whom we are beginning to appoint find a prototype in the Protectorate of Oliver Cromwell. After the execution of the King and the establishment of the Commonwealth, the Protector conceived the idea of parcelling the kingdom into military districts, of which there were *eleven*, — being precisely the number which it is now proposed, under the favor of success, to establish among us. Of this system a great authority, Mr. Hallam, in his "Constitutional History of England," speaks thus: —

"To govern according to law may sometimes be an usurper's wish, but can seldom be in his power. The Protector abandoned all thought of it. Dividing the kingdom into districts, he placed at the head of each a major-general, as *a sort of military magistrate,* responsible for the subjection of his prefecture. These were *eleven in number,* men bitterly hostile to the Royalist party, and insolent towards all civil authority." [2]

Carlyle, in his "Life of Cromwell," gives the following glimpse of this military government: —

"The beginning of a universal scheme of major-generals: the Lord-Protector and his Council of State having well considered and found it the feasiblest, — 'if not *good,* yet best.' 'It is an arbitrary government,' murmur many. Yes, arbitrary, but beneficial. *These are powers unknown to the English Constitution, I believe; but they*

---

[2] *Constitutional History of England,* Vol. II. p. 310.

are very necessary for the Puritan English nation at this time." [3]

Perhaps no better words could be found in explanation of the Cromwellian policy adopted by our President.

A contemporary Royalist, Colonel Ludlow, whose "Memoirs" add to our authentic history of those interesting times, characterizes these military magistrates as so many "bashaws." Here are some of his words: —

"The major-generals carried things with unheard-of insolence in their several precincts, decimating to extremity whom they pleased, and interrupting the proceedings at law upon petitions of those who pretended themselves aggrieved, *threatening such as would not yield a manly submission to their orders with transportation to Jamaica or some other plantation in the West Indies.*" [4]

Again, says the same contemporary writer:—

"There were sometimes bitter reflections cast upon the proceedings of the major-generals by the lawyers and country-gentlemen, who accused them to have done many things oppressive to the people, in interrupting the course of the law, and *threatening such as would not submit to their arbitrary orders with transportation beyond the seas.*" [5]

At last, even Cromwell, at the height of his power, found it necessary to abandon the policy of military governors. He authorized his son-in-law, Mr. Claypole, to announce in Parliament, "that he had formerly thought it necessary, in respect to the condition in which the nation had been, that the major-generals should be intrusted with the authority which they had exercised; but in the present state of affairs he conceived it inconsistent with the laws of England and liberties of the people to continue their power any longer." [6]

The conduct of at least one of our military magistrates seems to have been a counterpart to that of these "bashaws" of Cromwell; and there is no argument against that early military despotism which may not be urged against any attempt to revive it in our day. Some of the acts of Governor Stanley in North Carolina are in themselves an argument against the whole system.

It is clear that these military magistrates are without any direct sanction in the Constitution or in existing laws. They are not even

[3] Carlyle's *Life of Cromwell*, Part IX. Vol. II. p. 168.
[4] Ludlow's *Memoirs*, p. 559.
[5] *Ibid.* p. 580.
[6] *Ibid.* p. 582.

"major-generals," or other military officers, charged with the duty of enforcing martial law; but they are special creations of the Secretary of War, acting under the President, and charged with universal powers. As governors within the limits of a State, they obviously assume the extinction of the old State governments for which they are substituted; and the President, in appointing them, assumes a power over these States kindred to his acknowledged power over Territories of the Union; but, in appointing governors for Territories, he acts in pursuance of the Constitution and laws, by and with the advice and consent of the Senate.

That the President should assume the vacation of the State governments is of itself no argument against the creation of military governors; for it is simply the assumption of an unquestionable fact. But if it be true that the State governments have ceased to exist, then the way is prepared for the establishment of provisional governments by Congress. In short, if a new government is to be supplied, it should be supplied by Congress rather than by the President, and it should be according to established law rather than according to the mere will of any functionary, to the end that ours may be a government of laws and not of men.

There is no argument for military governors which is not equally strong for Congressional governments, while the latter have in their favor two controlling considerations: first, that they proceed from the civil rather than the military power; and, secondly, that they are created by law. Therefore, in considering whether Congressional governments should be constituted, I begin the discussion by assuming everything in their favor which is already accorded to the other system. I should not do this, if the system of military dictators were not now recognized, so that the question is sharply presented, which of the two to choose. Even if provisional governments by Congress are not constitutional, it does not follow that military governments, without the sanction of Congress, can be constitutional. But, on the other hand, I cannot doubt, that, if military governments are constitutional, then, surely, the provisional governments by Congress must be so also. In truth, there can be no opening for military governments which is not also an opening for Congressional governments, with this great advantage for the latter, that they are in harmony with our institutions, which favor the civil rather than the military power.

In thus declaring an unhesitating preference for Congressional governments, I am obviously sustained by reason. But there is positive authority on this identical question. I refer to the recorded opinion of Chancellor Kent, as follows: —

"Though the Constitution vests the executive power in the President, and declares him Commander-in-Chief of the army and navy of the United States, *these powers must necessarily be subordinate to the legislative power in Congress.* It would appear to me to be the policy or true construction of this simple and general grant of power to the President, not to suffer it to interfere with those specific powers of Congress which are more safely deposited in the legislative department, and that *the powers thus assumed by the President do not belong to him, but to Congress.*" [7]

Such is the weighty testimony of this illustrious master with regard to the assumption of power by the President, in 1847, over the Mexican ports in our possession. It will be found in the latest edition of his "Commentaries" published during the author's life. Of course, it is equally applicable to the recent assumptions within our own territory. His judgment is clear in favor of Congressional governments.

Of course, in ordinary times, and under ordinary circumstances, neither system of government would be valid. A State, in the full enjoyment of its rights, would spurn a military governor or a Congressional governor. It would insist that its governor should be neither military nor Congressional, but such as its own people chose to elect; and nobody would question this right. The President does not think of sending a military governor to New York; nor does Congress think of establishing a provisional government in that State. It is only with regard to the Rebel States that this question arises. The occasion, then, for the exercise of this extraordinary power is found in the Rebellion. Without the Rebellion, there would be no talk of any governor, whether military or Congressional.

STATE RIGHTS.

AND here it becomes important to consider the operation of the Rebellion in opening the way to this question. To this end we must understand the relations between the States and the National Government, under the Constitution of the United States. As I approach

[7] Kent's *Commentaries*, Vol. I. p. 292, note *b.*

this question of singular delicacy, let me say on the threshold, that for all those rights of the States which are consistent with the peace, security, and permanence of the Union, according to the objects grandly announced in the Preamble of the Constitution, I am the strenuous advocate, at all times and places. Never through any word or act of mine shall those rights be impaired; nor shall any of those other rights be called in question by which the States are held in harmonious relations as well with each other as with the Union. But while thus strenuous for all that justly belongs to the States, I cannot concede to them immunities inconsistent with that Constitution which is the supreme law of the land; nor can I admit the impeccability of States.

From a period even anterior to the Federal Constitution there has been a perverse pretension of State Rights, which has perpetually interfered with the unity of our government. Throughout the Revolution this pretension was a check upon the powers of Congress, whether in respect to its armies or its finances; so that it was too often constrained to content itself with the language of advice or persuasion rather than of command. By the Declaration of Independence it was solemnly declared that "these United Colonies are, and of right ought to be, free and independent *States,* and that, as such, they have full powers to levy war, to contract alliances, to establish commerce, and to do all other acts which independent *States* may of right do." Thus by this original charter the early colonies were changed into independent States, under whose protection the liberties of the country were placed.

Early steps were taken to supply the deficiencies of this government, which was effective only through the generous patriotism of the people. In July, 1778, two years after the Declaration, Articles of Confederation were framed, but they were not completely ratified by all the States till March, 1781. The character of this new government, which assumed the style of "The United States of America," will appear in the title of these Articles, which was as follows: — "Articles of Confederation and Perpetual Union *between the States* of New Hampshire, Massachusetts Bay, Rhode Island and Providence Plantations, Connecticut, New York, New Jersey, Pennsylvania, Delaware, Maryland, Virginia, North Carolina, South Carolina, and Georgia." By the second article it was declared, that "*each State retains its sovereignty,* freedom, and independence, and every power, jurisdiction, and right which is not by this Confederation expressly delegated to the United States in Congress assembled." By the third article it was further declared, that "the said *States* hereby severally enter into a *firm league* of friendship with each other, for their common defence, the security of their liberties, and their mutual and general welfare." By another article, a "committee of the *States*, or any nine of them," was authorized in the recess to execute the powers of Congress. The government thus constituted was a compact between *sovereign States*, — or, according to its precise language, "a firm league of friendship" between *these States*, administered, in the recess of Congress, by a "committee of *the States*." Thus did State Rights triumph.

But its imbecility from this pretension soon became apparent. As early as December, 1782, a committee of Congress made an elaborate report on the refusal of Rhode Island, one of the States, to confer certain powers on Congress with regard to revenue and commerce. In April, 1783, an address of Congress to *the States* was put forth, appealing to their justice and plighted faith, and representing the consequence of a failure on their part to sustain the Government and provide for its wants. In April, 1784, a similar appeal was made to what were called "the several States," whose legislatures were recommended to vest "the United States in Congress assembled" with certain powers. In July, 1785, a committee of Congress made another elaborate report on the reason why the States should confer upon Congress powers therein enumerated, in the course of which it was urged, that, "unless *the States* act together, there is no plan of policy into which they can separately enter, which they will not be separately interested to defeat, and, of course, all their measures must prove vain and abortive." In February and March, 1786, there were two other reports of committees of Congress, exhibiting the failure of *the States* to comply with the requisitions of Congress, and the necessity for a complete accession of *all the States* to the revenue system. In October, 1786, there was still another report, most earnestly renewing the former appeals to *the States*. Nothing could be more urgent.

As early as July, 1782, even before the first report to Congress, resolutions were adopted by the State of New York, declaring "that the situation of *these States* is in a peculiar manner critical," and "that the radical source of most of our embarrassments is *the want of sufficient power in Congress* to effectuate that ready and perfect coöperation of *the different States* on which their immediate safety and future happiness depend." Finally, in September, 1786, at Annapolis, commissioners from several States, after declaring "the situation of the United States delicate and critical, calling for an exertion of the united virtue and wisdom of all the members of the Confederacy," recommended the meeting of a Convention "to devise such further provision as shall appear necessary to render the Constitution of the Federal Government adequate to the exigencies of the Union." In pursuance of this recommendation, the Congress of the Confederation proposed a Convention "for the purpose of revising the Articles of Confederation and Perpetual Union between the United States of America, and reporting such alterations and amendments of the said Articles of Confederation as the representatives met in such Convention shall judge proper and necessary to render them adequate to the preservation and support of the Union."

In pursuance of the call, delegates to the proposed Convention were duly appointed by the legislatures of the several States, and the Convention assembled at Philadelphia in May, 1787. The present Constitution was the well-ripened fruit of their deliberations. In transmitting it to Congress, General Washington, who was the President of the Convention, in a letter bearing date September 17, 1787, made use of this instructive language: —

"It is obviously impracticable in the Federal Government of *these States to secure all rights of independent sovereignty to each,* and yet provide for the interest and safety of all. Individuals entering into society must give up a share of liberty to preserve the rest. The magnitude of the sacrifice must depend as well on situation and circumstance as on the object to be obtained. It is at all times difficult to draw with precision the line between those rights which must be surrendered and those which may be reserved; and on the present occasion this difficulty will be increased by a difference *among the several States* as to their situation, extent, habits, and particular interests. In all our deliberations we kept steadily in view that which appears to us the greatest interest of every true American, — THE CONSOLIDATION OF OUR UNION, — in which is involved our prosperity, safety, perhaps our national existence.

"GEORGE WASHINGTON."

The Constitution was duly transmitted by Congress to the several legislatures, by which it was submitted to conventions of delegates "chosen in each State by the people thereof," who ratified the same. Afterwards, Congress, by resolution, dated September 13, 1788, setting forth that the Convention had reported "a Constitution *for the people of the United States*," which had been duly ratified, proceeded to authorize the necessary elections under the new government.

The Constitution, it will be seen, was framed in order to remove the difficulties arising from *State Rights*. So paramount was this purpose, that, according to the letter of Washington, it was kept steadily in view in all the deliberations of the Convention, which did not hesitate to declare *the consolidation of our Union* as essential to our prosperity, safety, and perhaps our national existence.

The unity of the government was expressed in the term "Constitution," instead of "Articles of Confederation between the States," and in the idea of "a more perfect union," instead of a "league of friendship." It was also announced emphatically in the Preamble: —

"*We, the people of the United States, in order to form a more perfect union;* establish justice, insure domestic tranquillity, provide for the common defence, promote the general welfare, and secure the blessings of liberty to ourselves and our posterity, do ordain and establish this Constitution for the United States of America."

Not "we, the States," but "we, the people of the United States." Such is the beginning and origin of our Constitution. Here is no compact or league between States, involving the recognition of State rights; but a government ordained and established by the people of the United States for themselves and their posterity. This government is not established *by the States*, nor is it established *for the States*; but it is established *by the people*, for themselves and their posterity. It is true, that, in the organization of the government, the existence of the States is recognized, and the original name of "United States" is preserved; but the sovereignty of the States is absorbed in that more perfect union which was then established. There is but one sovereignty recognized, and this is the sovereignty of the United States. To the several States is left that special local control which is essential to the convenience and business of life, while to the United States, as a *Plural Unit*, is allotted that commanding sovereignty which embraces and holds the whole country within its perpetual and irreversible jurisdiction.

This obvious character of the Constitution did not pass unobserved at the time of its adoption. Indeed, the Constitution was most strenuously opposed on the ground that the States were absorbed in the Nation. Patrick Henry protested against consolidated power. In the debates of the Virginia Convention he exclaimed: —

And here I would make this inquiry of those worthy characters who composed a part of the late Federal Convention. I am sure they were fully impressed with the necessity of forming a great consolidated government, instead of a confederation. *That this is a consolidated government is demonstrably clear;* and the danger of such a government is to my mind very striking. I have the highest veneration for those gentlemen; but, Sir, give me leave to demand, What right had they to say, "We, the people?" Who authorized them to speak the language of "We, the people," instead of "We, the States?" [8]

And again, at another stage of the debate, the same patriotic opponent of the Constitution declared succinctly: — "The question turns, Sir, on that poor little thing, the expression, 'We, *the people,*' instead of *the States* of America." [9]

In the same convention another patriotic opponent of the Constitution, George Mason, following Patrick Henry, said: — "Whether the Constitution is good or bad, the present clause clearly discovers that it is a National Government, and no longer a Confederation." [10]

But against all this opposition, and in the face of this exposure, the Constitution was adopted, in the name of the people of the United States. Much, indeed, was left to the States; but it was no longer in their name that the government was organized, while the miserable pretension of State "sovereignty" was discarded. Even in the discussions of the Federal Convention Mr. Madison spoke thus plainly: — "Some contend that States are *sovereign,* when, in fact, they are only political societies. The States never possessed the essential rights of sovereignty. These were always vested in Congress."

Grave words, especially when we consider the position of their author. They were substantially echoed by Elbridge Gerry of Massachusetts, afterwards Vice-President, who said: — "It appears

[8] Elliott's *Debates,* Vol. III. p. 22.
[9] Elliott's *Debates,* Vol. III. p. 44.
[10] *Ibid.* p. 29.

to me that the States never were independent. They had only corporate rights."

Better words still fell from Mr. Wilson of Pennsylvania, known afterwards as a learned judge of the Supreme Court, and also for his Lectures on Law: — "Will a regard to State rights justify the sacrifice of the rights of men? If we proceed on any other foundation than the last, our building will neither be solid or lasting."

The argument was unanswerable then. It is unanswerable now. Do not elevate the sovereignty of the States against the Constitution of the United States. It is hardly less odious than the early pretension of sovereign power against Magna Charta, according to the memorable words of Lord Coke, as recorded by Rushworth: — "Sovereign power is no Parliamentary word. In my opinion, it weakens Magna Charta and all our statutes; for they are absolute without any saving of sovereign power. And shall we now add it, we shall weaken the foundation of law, and then the building must needs fall. Take we heed what we yield unto. *Magna Charta is such a fellow that he will have no sovereign.*" [11]

But the Constitution is our Magna Charta, which can bear no sovereign but itself, as you will see at once, if you will consider its character. And this practical truth was recognized at its formation, as may be seen in the writings of our Rushworth, — I refer to Nathan Dane, who was a member of Congress under the Confederation. He tells us plainly, that the terms "sovereign States," "State sovereignty," "State rights," "rights of States," are not "constitutional expressions."

POWERS OF CONGRESS.

In the exercise of its sovereignty Congress is intrusted with large and peculiar powers. Take notice of them, and you will see how little of "sovereignty" is left to the States. Their simple enumeration is an argument against the pretension of State Rights. Congress may lay and collect taxes, duties, imposts, and excises, to pay the debts and *provide for the common defence and general welfare of the United States.* It may borrow money on the credit of the United States; regulate commerce with foreign nations, and *among the several States,* and with the Indian tribes; establish a uniform rule of naturalization, and uniform laws on the subject of bankruptcy,

[11] Rushworth's *Historical Collections,* Vol. I. p. 609.

throughout the United States; coin money, regulate the value
thereof, and fix the standard of weights and measures; establish
post-offices and post-roads; promote the progress of science and the
useful arts by securing for limited times to authors and inventors the
exclusive right to their respective writings and discoveries; define
and punish piracies and felonies committed on the high seas, and
offences against the law of nations; declare war; grant letters of
marque and reprisal; make rules concerning captures on land and
water; raise and support armies; provide and maintain a navy; make
rules for the government and regulation of the land and naval forces;
provide for calling forth the militia to execute *the laws of the
Union,* suppress insurrections, and repel invasions; provide for organizing, arming, and disciplining the militia, and for governing
such part of them as may be employed in the service of the United
States, reserving to the States respectively the appointment of officers and the authority of training the militia *according to the discipline prescribed by Congress;* and make all laws necessary and
proper for carrying into execution the foregoing powers and all
other powers vested in the Government of the United States.

Such are the ample and diversified powers of Congress, embracing all those powers which enter into sovereignty. With the
concession of these to the United States there seems to be little left
for the several States. In the power to "declare war" and to "raise
and support armies," Congress possesses an exclusive power, in itself
immense and infinite, over persons and property in the several
States, while by the power to "regulate commerce" it may put limits
round about the business of the several States. And even in the
case of the militia, which is the original military organization of
the people, nothing is left to the States except "the appointment of
the officers," and the authority to train it "according to the discipline *prescribed by Congress.*" It is thus that these great agencies
are all intrusted to the United States, while the several States are
subordinated to their exercise.

Constantly, and in everything, we behold the constitutional subordination of the States. But there are other provisions by which the
States are expressly deprived of important powers. For instance:
"No State shall enter into any treaty, alliance, or confederation; coin
money; emit bills of credit; make anything but gold and silver coin
a tender in payment of debts." Or, if the States may exercise cer-

tain powers, it is only with the consent of Congress. For instance: "No State shall, *without the consent of Congress,* lay any duty of tonnage, keep troops or ships of war in time of peace, enter into any agreement or compact with another State or with a foreign power." Here is a magistral power accorded to Congress, utterly inconsistent with the pretensions of State Rights. Then, again: "No State shall, *without the consent of the Congress,* lay any imposts or duties on imports or exports, except what may be absolutely necessary for executing its inspection laws; and the net produce of all duties and imposts laid by any State on imports or exports shall be for the use of the treasury of the United States; *and all such laws shall be subject to the revision and control of the Congress.*" Here, again, is a similar magistral power accorded to Congress, and, as if still further to deprive the States of their much vaunted sovereignty, the laws which they make with the consent of Congress are expressly declared to be subject "to the revision and control of the Congress." But there is another instance still. According to the Constitution, "Full faith and credit shall be given in each State to the public acts, records, and judicial proceedings of every other State:" but here mark the controlling power of Congress, which is authorized to "prescribe the manner in which such acts, records, and proceedings shall be proved, and the effect thereof."

SUPREMACY OF THE NATIONAL GOVERNMENT.

BUT there are five other provisions of the Constitution by which its supremacy is positively established. 1. "The citizens of each State shall be entitled to all privileges and immunities of citizens in the several States." As Congress has the exclusive power to establish "an uniform rule of naturalization," it may, under these words of the Constitution, secure for its newly entitled citizens "all privileges and immunities of citizens in the several States," in defiance of State Rights. 2. "New States may be admitted *by the Congress* into this Union." According to these words, the States cannot even determine their associates, but are dependent in this respect upon the will of Congress. 3. But not content with taking from the States these important powers of sovereignty, it is solemnly declared that the Constitution, and the laws of the United States made in pursuance thereof, and all treaties under the authority of the United States, "SHALL BE THE SUPREME LAW OF THE LAND, *anything in the Constitu-*

tion or laws of any State to the contrary notwithstanding." Thus are
State Rights again subordinated to the National Constitution, which
is erected into the paramount authority. 4. But this is done again
by another provision, which declares that "*the members of the several State legislatures,* and all executive and judicial officers of *the
several States,* shall be bound by oath or affirmation to support this
Constitution"; so that not only State laws are subordinated to the
National Constitution, but the makers of State laws, and all other
State officers, are constrained to declare their allegiance to this Constitution, thus placing the State, alike through its acts and its agents,
in complete subordination to the sovereignty of the United States.
5. But this sovereignty is further proclaimed in the solemn injunc-
tion, that "the United States shall guarantee to every State in this
Union a republican form of government, and shall protect each of
them against invasion." Here are duties of guaranty and protection
imposed upon the United States, by which their position is fixed as
the supreme power. There can be no such guaranty without the
implied right to examine and consider the governments of the several States; and there can be no such protection without a similar
right to examine and consider the condition of the several States:
thus subjecting them to the rightful supervision and superintendence of the National Government.

Thus, whether we regard the large powers vested in Congress,
the powers denied to the States absolutely, the powers denied to the
States without the consent of Congress, or those other provisions
which accord supremacy to the United States, we shall find the pretension of State sovereignty without foundation, except in the
imagination of its partisans. Before the Constitution such sovereignty may have existed; it was declared in the Articles of Confederation; but since then it has ceased to exist. It has disappeared and been lost in the supremacy of the National Government, so that it can no longer be recognized. Perverse men, insisting that it still existed, and weak men, mistaking the shadow
of former power for the reality, have made arrogant claims in
its behalf. When the Constitution was proclaimed, and George
Washington took his oath to support it as President, our career
as a Nation began, with all the unity of a nation. The States
remained as living parts of the body, important to the national
strength, and essential to those currents which maintain national

life, but plainly subordinate to the United States, which then and there stood forth a Nation, one and indivisible.

MISCHIEFS IN THE NAME OF STATE RIGHTS.

BUT the new government had hardly been inaugurated before it was disturbed by the pestilent pretension of State Rights, which, indeed, has never ceased to disturb it since. Discontent with the treaty between the United States and Great Britain, negotiated by that purest patriot, John Jay, under instructions from Washington, in 1794, aroused Virginia, even at that early day, to commence an opposition to its ratification, *in the name of State Rights.* Shortly afterwards appeared the famous resolutions of Virginia and those of Kentucky, usually known as the "Resolutions of '98," declaring that the National Government was founded on a compact between the States, and claiming for the States the right to sit in judgment on the National Government, and to interpose, if they thought fit; all this, as you will see, *in the name of State Rights.* This pretension on the part of the States increased, till, at last, on the mild proposition to attach a prospective prohibition of Slavery as a condition to the admission of Missouri into the Union as a new State, the opposition raged furiously, even to the extent of menacing the existence of the Union; and this, too, was done *in the name of State Rights.* Ten years later, the pretension took the familiar form of Nullification, insisting that our government was only a compact of States, any one of which was free to annul an act of Congress at its own pleasure; and all this *in the name of State Rights.* For a succession of years afterwards, at the presentation of petitions against Slavery, — petitions for the recognition of Hayti, — at the question of Texas, — at the Wilmot Proviso, — at the admission of California as a Free State, — at the discussion of the Compromises of 1850, — at the Kansas Question, — the Union was menaced; and always *in the name of State Rights.* The menace was constant, and it sometimes showed itself on small as well as great occasions, but always *in the name of State Rights.* When it was supposed that Fremont was about to be chosen President, the menace became louder, and mingling with it was the hoarse mutter of war; and all this audacity was *in the name of State Rights.*

But in the autumn of 1860, on the election of Mr. Lincoln, the case became much worse. Scarcely was the result of this election known by telegraph before the country was startled by other intelligence, to the effect that certain States at the South were about to put in execution the long-pending threat of Secession, of course *in the name of State Rights*. First came South Carolina, which, by an ordinance adopted in a State convention, undertook to repeal the original act by which the Constitution was adopted in this State, and to declare that the State had ceased to be one of the States of the Union. At the same time a Declaration of Independence was put forth by this State, which proceeded to organize itself as an independent community. This example was followed successively by other States, which, by formal acts of Secession, undertook to dissolve their relations with the Union, always, be it understood, *in the name of State Rights*. A new Confederation was formed by these States, with a new Constitution, and Jefferson Davis at its head; and the same oaths of loyalty by which the local functionaries of all these States had been bound to the Union were now transferred to this new Confederation, — of course, in utter violation of the Constitution of the United States, but always *in the name of State Rights*. The ordinances of Secession were next maintained by war, which, beginning with the assault upon Fort Sumter, convulsed the whole country, till, at last, all the States of the new Confederation are in open rebellion, which the Government of the United States is now exerting its energies, mustering its forces, and taxing its people to suppress. The original claim, *in the name of State Rights*, has swollen to all the proportions of an unparalleled war, which, *in the name of State Rights*, now menaces the national life.

But the pretensions in the name of State Rights are not all told. While the ordinances of Secession were maturing, and before they were yet consummated, Mr. Buchanan, who was then President, declined to interfere, on the ground that what had been done was done by States, and that it was contrary to the theory of our government "to coerce a State." Thus was the pretension of State Rights made the apology for imbecility. Had this President then interfered promptly and loyally, it cannot be doubted that this whole intolerable crime might have been trampled out forever. And now, when it is proposed that Congress shall organize governments in these States, which are absolutely without loyal governments, we are met by the objection founded on State Rights. The same disastrous voice which from the beginning of our history has sounded in our ears still makes itself heard; but, alas! it is now on the lips of our friends. Of course, just in proportion as it prevails will it be impossible to establish the Constitution again throughout the Rebel States. State Rights are madly triumphant, if, first, in their name Rebel governments can be organized, and then, again, in their name Congressional governments to displace the Rebel governments can be resisted. If they can be employed, first to sever the States from the Union, and then to prevent the Union from extending its power over them, State Rights are at once a sword and buckler to the Rebellion. It was through the imbecility of Mr. Buchanan that the States were allowed to use the sword. God forbid that now, through any similar imbecility of Congress, they shall be allowed to use the buckler!

SHALL CONGRESS ASSUME JURISDICTION OF THE REBEL STATES?

AND now, in this discussion, we are brought to the practical question which is destined to occupy so much of public attention. It is proposed to bring the action of Congress to bear directly upon the Rebel States. This may be by the establishment of provisional governments under the authority of Congress, or simply by making the admission or recognition of the States depend upon the action of Congress. The essential feature of this proposition is, *that Congress shall assume jurisdiction of the Rebel States.* A bill authorizing provisional governments in these States was introduced into the Senate by Mr. Harris of the State of New York, and was afterwards reported from the Judiciary Committee of that body; but it was left with the unfinished business, when the late Congress expired on the fourth of March. The opposition to this proposition, so far as I understand it, assumes two forms: first, that these States are always to be regarded as States, with State rights, and therefore cannot be governed by Congress; and, secondly, that, if any government is to be established over them, it must be simply a military government, with a military governor, appointed by the President, as is the case with Tennessee and North Carolina. But State rights are as much disturbed by a military government as by a Congressional government. The local government is as much set aside in one case as in the other. If the President, within State limits, can proceed to organize a military government to exercise all the powers of the State, surely Congress can proceed to organize a civil government within the same limits for the same purpose; nor can any pretension of State Rights be effective against Congress more than against the President. Indeed, the power belongs to Congress by a higher title than it belongs to the President: first, because a civil government is more in harmony with our institutions, and, wherever possible, is required; and, secondly, because there are provisions of the Constitution under which this power is clearly derived.

Assuming, then, that the pretension of State Rights is as valid against one form of government as against the other, and still further assuming, that, in the case of military governments, this pretension is practically overruled by the President at least, we are brought again to consider the efficacy of this pretension when advanced against Congressional governments.

It is argued that the Acts of Secession are all inoperative and void, and that therefore the States continue precisely as before, with their local constitutions, laws, and institutions in the hands of traitors, but totally unchanged, and ready to be quickened into life by returning loyalty. Such, I believe, is a candid statement of the pretension for State Rights against Congressional governments, which, it is argued, cannot be substituted for the State governments.

In order to prove that the Rebel States continue precisely as before, we are reminded that Andrew Johnson continued to occupy his seat in the Senate after Tennessee had adopted its Act of Secession and embarked in rebellion, and that his presence testified to the fact that Rebel Tennessee was still a State of the Union. No such conclusion is authorized by the incident in question. There are two principles of Parliamentary law long ago fixed: first, that the power once conferred by an election to Parliament is *irrevocable,* so that it is not affected by any subsequent change in the constituency; and, secondly, that a member, when once chosen, is *a member for the whole kingdom,* becoming thereby, according to the words of an early author, not merely knight or burgess of the county or borough which elected him, but knight or burgess of England.[12] If these two principles are not entirely inapplicable to our political system, then the seat of Andrew Johnson was not in any respect affected by the subsequent madness of his State, nor can the legality of his seat be any argument for his State.

[12] See Cushing, *Parliamentary Law,* p. 284.

We are also reminded that during the last session of Congress two Senators from Virginia represented that State in the Senate; and the argument is pressed, that no such representation would be valid, if the State government of Virginia was vacated. This is a mistake. Two things are established by the presence of these Senators in the National Senate: first, that the old State government of Virginia is extinct, and, secondly, that a new government has been set up in its place. It was my fortune to listen to one of these Senators while he earnestly denounced the idea that a State government might disappear. I could not but think that he strangely forgot the principle to which he owed his seat in the Senate, — as men sometimes forget a benefactor.

It is true, beyond question, that the Acts of Secession are all inoperative and void against the Constitution of the United States. Through matured in successive conventions, sanctioned in various forms, and maintained ever since by bloody war, these acts — no matter by what name they may be called — are all equally impotent to withdraw an acre of territory or a single inhabitant from the rightful jurisdiction of the United States. But while thus impotent against the United States, it does not follow that they were equally impotent in the work of self-destruction. Clearly, the Rebels, by utmost efforts, could not impair the National jurisdiction; but it remains to be seen if their enmity did not act back with fatal rebound upon those very State Rights in behalf of which they commenced their treason.

STATE SUICIDE.

It is sometimes said that the States themselves committed *suicide*, so that as States they ceased to exist, leaving their whole jurisdiction open to the occupation of the United States under the Constitution. This assumption is founded on the fact, that, whatever may be the existing governments in these states, they are in no respect constitutional, and since the State itself is known by the government, with which its life is intertwined, it must cease to exist constitutionally when its government no longer exists constitutionally. Perhaps, however, it would be better to avoid the whole question of the life or death of the State, and to content ourselves with an inquiry into the condition of its government. It is not easy to say what constitutes that entity which we call a State; nor is the discussion much advanced by any theory with regard to it. To my mind it seems a topic fit for the old schoolmen or a modern debating society; and yet, considering the part it has already played in this discussion, I shall be pardoned for a brief allusion to it.

There are well-known words which ask and answer the question, "What constitutes *a State?*" But the scholarly poet was not thinking of a "State" of the American Union. Indeed, this term is various in its use. Sometimes it stands for civil society itself. Sometimes it is the general name for a political community, not unlike "nation" or "country," — as where our fathers, in the Resolution of Independence, which preceded the Declaration, spoke of "the *State* of Great Britain." Sometimes it stands for the government, — as when Louis XIV., at the height of his power, exclaimed, "The *State*, it is I"; or when Sir Christopher Hatton, in the famous farce of "The Critic," ejaculates, —

> Oh pardon me, if my conjecture 's rash,
> But I surmise ———— *the State* ————
> Some danger apprehends.

Among us the term is most known as the technical name for one of the political societies which compose our Union. Of course, when used in the latter restricted sense, it must not be confounded with the same term when used in a different and broader sense. But it is obvious that some persons attribute to the one something of the qualities which can belong only to the other. Nobody has suggested, I presume, that any "State" of our Union has, through rebellion, ceased to exist as a *civil society*, or even as a *political community*. It is only as a *State of the Union*, armed with State rights, or at least as a *local government*, which annually renews itself, as the snake its skin, that it can be called in question. But it is vain to challenge for the technical "State," or for the annual government, that immortality which belongs to civil society. The one is an artificial body, the other is a natural body; and while the first, overwhelmed by insurrection or war, may change or die, the latter can change or die only with the extinction of the community itself, whatever may be its name or its form.

It is because of confusion in the use of this term that there has been so much confusion in the political controversies where it has been employed. But nowhere has this confusion led to greater absurdity than in the pretension which has been recently made in the name of State Rights, — as if it were reasonable to attribute to a technical "State" of the Union that immortality which belongs to civil society.

From approved authorities it appears that a "State," even in a broader signification, may lose its life. Mr. Phillimore, in his recent work on International Law, says: — "A State, like an individual, may die," and among the various ways, he says, "by its submission and the donation of itself to another country." [13] But in the case of our Rebel States there has been a plain submission and donation of themselves, — *effective, at least, to break the continuity of government,* if not to destroy that immortality which has been claimed. Nor can it make any difference, in breaking this continuity, that the submission and donation, constituting a species of attornment, were to enemies at home rather than to enemies abroad, — to Jefferson Davis rather than to Louis Napoleon. The thread is snapped in one case as much as in the other.

But a *change of form* in the actual government may be equally effective. Cicero speaks of a change so complete as "to leave no image of a State behind." But this is precisely what has been done throughout the whole Rebel region: there is no image of a *constitutional* State left behind. Another authority, Aristotle, whose words are always weighty, says, that, *the form of the State being changed, the State is no longer the same,* as the harmony is not the same when we modulate out of the Dorian mood into the Phrygian. But if ever an unlucky people modulated out of one mood into another, it was our Rebels, when they undertook to modulate out of the harmonies of the Constitution into their bloody discords.

Without stopping further for these diversions, I content myself with the testimony of Edmund Burke, who, in a striking passage, which seems to have been written for us, portrays the extinction of a political community; but I quote his eloquent words rather for suggestion than for authority: —

"In a state of *rude* Nature there is no such thing as a people. A number of men in themselves have no collective capacity. The idea of people is the idea of a corporation. It is wholly artificial, and made, like all other legal fictions, by common agreement. What the particular nature of that agreement was is collected from the form

[13] Phillimore's *International Law,* Vol. I. p. 147.

into which the particular society has been cast. Any other is not *their* covenant. *When men, therefore, break up the original compact or agreement which gives its corporate form and capacity to a State, they are no longer a people; they have no longer a corporate existence;* they have no longer a legal coactive force to bind within, nor a claim to be recognized abroad. They are a number of vague, loose individuals, and nothing more. With them all is to begin again. Alas! they little know how many a weary step is to be taken before they can form themselves into a mass which has a true politic personality." [14]

If that great master of eloquence could be heard, who can doubt that he would blast our Rebel States, as senseless communities who have sacrificed that corporate existence which makes them living, component members of our Union of States?

STATE FORFEITURE.

BUT again it is sometimes said, that the States, by their flagrant treason, have *forfeited* their rights as States, so as to be civilly dead. It is a patent and indisputable fact, that this gigantic treason was inaugurated with all the forms of law known to the States; that it was carried forward not only by individuals, but also by States, so far as States can perpetrate treason; that the States pretended to withdraw bodily in their corporate capacities; — that the Rebellion, as it showed itself, was *by* States as well as *in* States; that it was by the governments of States as well as by the people of States; and that, to the common observer, the crime was consummated by the several corporations as well as by the individuals of whom they were composed. From this fact, obvious to all, it is argued, that, since, according to Blackstone, "a traitor hath abandoned his connection with society, and hath no longer any right to the advantages which before belonged to him purely as a member of the community," by the same principle the traitor State is no longer to be regarded as a member of the Union. But it is not necessary, on the present occasion, to insist on the application of any such principle to States.

STATE ABDICATION.

AGAIN it is said, that the States by their treason and rebellion, levying war upon the National Government, have *abdicated* their

[14] Burke's *Appeal from the New to the Old Whigs.*

places in the Union; and here the argument is upheld by the historic example of England, at the Revolution of 1688, when, on the flight of James II., and the abandonment of his kingly duties, the two Houses of Parliament voted, that the monarch, "having violated the fundamental laws, and having withdrawn himself out of the kingdom, *had abdicated the government,* and that the throne had thereby become vacant." [15] But it is not necessary for us to rely on any allegation of abdication, applicable as it may be.

RIGHTFUL GOVERNMENT IN THE REBEL STATES VACATED.

IT only remains that we should see things as they are, and not seek to substitute theory for fact. On this important question I discard all theory, whether it be of State suicide or State forfeiture or State abdication, on the one side, or of State rights, immortal and unimpeachable, on the other side. Such discussions are only endless mazes in which a whole senate may be lost. And in discarding all theory, I discard also the question of *de jure,* — whether, for instance, the Rebel States, while the Rebellion is flagrant, are *de jure* States of the Union, with all the rights of States. It is enough, that, for the time being, and *in the absence of a loyal government,* they can take no part and perform no function in the Union, *so that they cannot be recognized by the National Government.* The reason is plain. There are in these States no local functionaries bound by constitutional oaths, so that, in fact, there are no constitutional functionaries; and since the State government is necessarily composed of such functionaries, there can be no State government. Thus, for instance, in South Carolina, Pickens and his associates may call themselves the governor and legislature, and in Virginia, Letcher and his associates may call themselves governor and legislature; but we cannot recognize them as such. Therefore to all pretensions in behalf of State governments in the Rebel States I oppose the simple FACT, that for the time being no such governments exist. The broad spaces once occupied by those governments are now abandoned and vacated.

That patriot Senator, Andrew Johnson, — faithful among the faithless, the Abdiel of the South, — began his attempt to reorganize Tennessee by an Address, as early as the 18th of March, 1862, in which he made use of these words: —

[15] Macaulay's *History of England,* Vol. II. p. 623.

"I find most, if not all, of the offices, both State and Federal, *vacated, either by actual abandonment, or by the action of the incumbents in attempting to subordinate their functions* to a power in hostility to the fundamental law of the State and subversive of her national allegiance."

In employing the word "vacated," Mr. Johnson hit upon the very term which, in the famous resolution of 1688, was held to be most effective in dethroning King James. After declaring that he had abdicated the government, it was added, "that the throne had thereby become *vacant*," on which Macaulay happily remarks: —

"The word *abdication* conciliated politicians of a more timid school. To the real statesman the simple important clause was that *which declared the throne vacant;* and if that clause could be carried, he cared little by what preamble it might be introduced." [16]

And the same simple principle is now in issue. It is enough that the Rebel States be declared *vacated*, as *in fact* they are, by all local government which we are bound to recognize, so that the way is open to the exercise of a rightful jurisdiction.

TRANSITION TO RIGHTFUL GOVERNMENT.

AND here the question occurs, How shall this rightful jurisdiction be established in the vacated States? Some there are, so impassioned for State rights, and so anxious for forms even at the expense of substance, that they insist upon the instant restoration of the old State governments in all their parts, through the agency of loyal citizens, who meanwhile must be protected in this work of restoration. But, assuming that all this is practicable, as it clearly is not, it attributes to the loyal citizens of a Rebel State, however few in numbers, — it may be an insignificant minority, — a power clearly inconsistent with the received principle of popular government, that the majority must rule. The seven voters of Old Sarum were allowed to return two members of Parliament, because this place, — once a Roman fort, and afterwards a sheepwalk, — many generations before, at the early casting of the House of Commons, had been entitled to this representation; but the argument for State Rights assumes that all these rights may be lodged in voters as few in number as ever controlled a rotten borough of England.

Pray, admitting that an insignificant minority is to organize the

[16] Macaulay's *History of England*, Vol. II. p. 624.

new government, how shall it be done? and by whom shall it be set in motion? In putting these questions I open the difficulties. As the original government has ceased to exist, and there are none who can be its legal successors, so as to administer the requisite oaths, it is not easy to see how the new government can be set in motion without a resort to some revolutionary proceeding, instituted either by the citizens or by the military power, — unless Congress, in the exercise of its plenary powers, should undertake to organize the new jurisdiction.

But every revolutionary proceeding is to be avoided. It will be within the recollection of all familiar with our history, that our fathers, while regulating the separation of the Colonies from the parent country, were careful that all should be done according to the forms of law, so that the thread of *legality* should continue unbroken. To this end the Continental Congress interfered by a supervising direction. But the Tory argument in that day denied the power of Congress as earnestly as it denies this power now. Mr. Duane, of the Continental Congress, made himself the mouthpiece of this denial: —

"*Congress ought not to determine a point of this sort about instituting government.* What is it to Congress how justice is administered? You have no right to pass the resolution, any more than Parliament has. How does it appear that no favorable answer is likely to be given to our petitions?" [17]

In spite of this argument, the Congress of that day undertook, by formal resolutions, to indicate the process by which the new governments should be constituted.[18]

If we seek, for our guidance, the principle which entered into this proceeding of the Continental Congress, we shall find it in the idea, that nothing must be left to illegal or informal action, but that all must be done according to rules of constitution and law previously ordained. Perhaps this principle has never been more distinctly or powerfully enunciated than by Mr. Webster, in his speech against the Door Constitution in Rhode Island. According to him, this principle is a fundamental part of what he calls our American system, requiring that the right of suffrage shall be prescribed by *previous law,* including its qualifications, the time and place of its

[17] John Adams's *Works*, Vol. II. p. 490.
[18] *Ibid.* Vol. III. pp. 17, 19, 45, 46.

exercise, and the manner of its exercise; and then again, that the results are to be certified to the central power by some certain rule, *by some known public officers,* in some clear and definite form, to the end that two things may be done: first, that every man entitled to vote may vote; secondly, that his vote may be sent forward and counted, and so he may exercise his part of sovereignty, in common with his fellow-citizens. Such, according to Mr. Webster, are the minute forms which must be followed, if we would impart to the result the crowning character of law. And here are other positive words from him on this important point: —

"We are not to take the will of the people from public meetings, nor from tumultuous assemblies, by which the timid are terrified, the prudent are alarmed, and by which society is disturbed. These are not American modes of signifying the will of the people, and they never were. . . .

"Is it not obvious enough, that men cannot get together and count themselves, and say they are so many hundreds and so many thousands, and judge of their own qualifications, and call themselves the people, and set up a government? Why, another set of men, forty miles off, on the same day, with the same propriety, with as good qualifications, and in as large numbers, may meet and set up another government. . . .

"When, in the course of human events, it becomes necessary to ascertain the will of the people on a new exigency, or a new state of things, or of opinion, *the legislative power provides for that ascertainment by an ordinary act of legislation.*

"What do I contend for? I say that the will of the people must prevail, when it is ascertained; but there must be *some legal and authentic mode of ascertaining that will;* and then the people may make what government they please. . . .

"All that is necessary here is, that the will of the people should be ascertained by some regular rule of proceeding, *prescribed by previous law.* . . .

"But the law and the Constitution, the whole system of American institutions, do not contemplate a case in which a resort will be necessary to proceedings *aliunde,* or *outside of the law and the Constitution,* for the purpose of amending the frame of government." [19]

[19] Webster's *Works,* Vol. VI. pp. 225, 226, 227, 228, 231.

CONGRESS THE TRUE AGENT.

BUT, happily, we are not constrained to any such revolutionary proceeding. The new governments can all be organized by Congress, which is the natural guardian of people without any immediate government, and within the jurisdiction of the Constitution of the United States. Indeed, with the State governments already *vacated* by rebellion, the Constitution becomes, for the time, the supreme and only law, binding alike on President and Congress, so that neither can establish any law or institution incompatible with it. And the whole Rebel region, deprived of all local government, lapses under the exclusive jurisdiction of Congress, precisely as any other territory; or, in other words, the lifting of the local governments leaves the whole vast region without any other government than Congress, unless the President should undertake to govern it by military power. Startling as this proposition may seem, especially to all who believe that "there is a divinity that doth hedge" a State, hardly less than a king, it will appear, on careful consideration, to be as well founded in the Constitution as it is simple and natural, while it affords an easy and constitutional solution to our present embarrassments.

I have no theory to maintain, but only the truth; and in presenting this argument for Congressional government, I simply follow teachings which I cannot control. The wisdom of Socrates, in the words of Plato, has aptly described these teachings, when he says: —

"These things are secured and bound, even if the expression be somewhat too rude, with iron and adamant; and unless you or some one more vigorous than you can break them, it is impossible for any one speaking otherwise than I now speak to speak well; since, for my part, I have always the same thing to say, that I know not how these things are, but that out of all with whom I have ever discoursed, as now, not one is able to say otherwise and to maintain himself." [20]

Show me that I am wrong, — that this conclusion is not founded in the Constitution, and is not sustained by reason, — and I shall at once renounce it; for, in the present condition of affairs, there can be no pride of opinion which must not fall at once before the sacred demands of country. Not as a partisan, not as an advocate, do I

---

[20] The *Gorgias* of Plato.

make this appeal; but simply as a citizen, who seeks, in all sincerity, to offer his contribution to the establishment of that policy by which Union and Peace may be restored.

THREE SOURCES OF CONGRESSIONAL POWER.

IF we look at the origin of this power in Congress, we shall find that it comes from three distinct fountains, any one of which is ample to supply it. Three fountains, generous and hospitable, will be found in the Constitution ready for this occasion.

First. From the necessity of the case, *ex necessitate rei,* Congress must have jurisdiction over every portion of the United States *where there is no other government;* and since in the present case there is no other government, the whole region falls within the jurisdiction of Congress. This jurisdiction is incident, if you please, to that guardianship and eminent domain which belong to the United States with regard to all its territory and the people thereof, and it comes into activity when the local government ceases to exist. It can be questioned only in the name of the local government; but since this government has disappeared in the Rebel States, the jurisdiction of Congress is uninterrupted there. The whole broad Rebel region is *tabula rasa,* or "a clean slate," where Congress, under the Constitution of the United States, may write the laws. In adopting this principle, I follow the authority of the Supreme Court of the United States in determining the jurisdiction of Congress over the Territories. Here are the words of Chief-Justice Marshall: —

"Perhaps the power of governing a territory belonging to the United States, which has not, by becoming a State, acquired the means of self-government, *may result necessarily from the facts that it is not within the jurisdiction of any particular State* and is within the power and jurisdiction of the United States. The right to govern may be the natural consequence of the right to acquire territory." [21]

If the right to govern may be the natural consequence of the right to acquire territory, surely, and by much stronger reason, this right must be the natural consequence of the sovereignty of the United States wherever there is no local government.

Secondly. This jurisdiction may also be derived from the *Rights of War,* which surely are not less abundant for Congress than for

[21] *American Insurance Company v. Carter,* 1 Peters, p. 542.

the President. If the President, disregarding the pretension of State Rights, can appoint military governors within the Rebel States, to serve a temporary purpose, who can doubt that Congress can exercise a similar jurisdiction? That of the President is derived from the war-powers; but these are not sealed to Congress. If it be asked where in the Constitution such powers are bestowed upon Congress, I reply, that they will be found precisely where the President now finds his powers. But it is clear that the powers to "declare war," to "suppress insurrections," and to "support armies," are all ample for this purpose. It is Congress that conquers; and the same authority that conquers must govern. Nor is this authority derived from any strained construction; but it springs from the very heart of the Constitution. It is among those powers, latent in peace, which war and insurrection call into being, but which are as intrinsically constitutional as any other power.

Even if not conceded to the President these powers must be conceded to Congress. Would you know their extent? They will be found in the authoritative texts of Public Law, — in the works of Grotius, Vattel, and Wheaton. They are the powers conceded by civilized society to nations at war, known as the Rights of War, at once multitudinous and minute, vast and various. It would be strange, if Congress could organize armies and navies to conquer, and could not also organize governments to protect.

De Tocqueville, who saw our institutions with so keen an eye, remarked, that, since, in spite of all political fictions, the preponderating power resided in the State governments, and not in the National Government, a civil war here "would be nothing but a foreign war in disguise." [22] Of course the natural consequence would be to give the National Government in such a civil war all the rights which it would have in a foreign war. And this conclusion from the observation of the ingenious publicist has been practically adopted by the Supreme Court of the United States in those recent cases where this tribunal, after the most learned argument, followed by the most careful consideration, adjudged, that, since the Act of Congress of July 13th, 1861, the National Government has been waging "a *territorial* civil war," in which all property afloat belonging to a resident of the *belligerent territory* is liable to capture and condemnation as lawful prize. But surely, if the National Govern-

[22] *Democracy in America,* Vol. II. ch. 25, p. 343.

ment may stamp upon all residents in this *belligerent territory* the character of foreign enemies, so as to subject their ships and cargoes to the penalties of confiscation, it may perform the milder service of making all needful rules and regulations for the government of this territory under the Constitution, so long as may be requisite for the sake of peace and order; and since the object of war is "indemnity for the past and security for the future," it may do everything necessary to make these effectual. But it will not be enough to crush the Rebellion. Its terrible root must be exterminated, so that it may no more flaunt in blood.

Thirdly. But there is another source for this jurisdiction which is common alike to Congress and the President. It will be found in the constitutional provision, that "the United States shall guarantee to every State in this Union a republican form of government, and shall protect each of them against invasion." Here, be it observed, are words of guaranty and an obligation of protection. In the original concession to the United States of this twofold power there was an open recognition of the ultimate responsibility and duty of the National Government, *conferring jurisdiction above all pretended State rights;* and now the occasion has come for the exercise of this twofold power thus solemnly conceded. The words of twofold power and corresponding obligation are plain and beyond question. If there be any ambiguity, it is only as to what constitutes a republican form of government. But for the present this question does not arise. It is enough that a wicked rebellion has undertaken to detach certain States from the Union, and to take them beyond the protection and sovereignty of the United States, with the menace of seeking foreign alliance and support, even at the cost of every distinctive institution. It is well known that *Mr. Madison anticipated this precise danger from Slavery, and upheld this precise grant of power in order to counteract this danger.* His words, which will be found in a yet unpublished document, produced by Mr. Collamer in the Senate, seem prophetic.

Among the defects which he remarked in the old Confederation was what he called "want of guaranty" to the States of their constitutions and laws *against internal violence.*" In showing why this guaranty was needed, he says, that, "according to republican theory, right and power, being both vested in the majority, are held to be synonymous; according to fact and experience, a minority may, in an appeal to force, be an overmatch for the majority"; and he then adds, in words of wonderful prescience, *"where Slavery exists the republican theory becomes still more fallacious."* This was written in April, 1787, before the meeting of the Convention that formed the National Constitution. But here we have the origin of the very clause in question. The danger which this statesman foresaw is now upon us. When a State fails to maintain a republican government *with officers sworn according to the requirements of the Constitution,* it ceases to be a constitutional State. The very case contemplated by the Constitution has arrived, and the National Government is invested with plenary powers, whether of peace or war. There is nothing in the storehouse of peace, and there is nothing in the arsenal of war, which it may not employ in the maintenance of this solemn guaranty, and in the extension of that protection against invasion to which it is pledged. But this extraordinary power carries with it a corresponding duty. Whatever shows itself dangerous to a republican form of government must be removed without delay or hesitation; and if the evil be Slavery, our action will be bolder when it is known that the danger was foreseen.

In reviewing these three sources of power, I know not which is most complete. Either would be ample alone; but the three together are three times ample. Thus, out of this triple fountain, or, if you please, by this triple cord, do I vindicate the power of Congress over the vacated Rebel States.

But there are yet other words of the Constitution which cannot be forgotten: "New States may be admitted by the Congress into this Union." Assuming that the Rebel States are no longer *de facto* States of this Union, but that the territory occupied by them is within the jurisdiction of Congress, then these words become completely applicable. It will be for Congress, in such way as it shall think best, to regulate the return of these States to the Union, whether in time or manner. No special form is prescribed. But the vital act must proceed from Congress. And here again is another testimony to that Congressional power which, under the Constitution, will restore the Republic.

UNANSWERABLE REASONS FOR CONGRESSIONAL GOVERNMENTS.

AGAINST this power I have heard no argument which can be called an argument. There are objections founded chiefly in the baneful pretension of State Rights; but these objections are animated by prejudice rather than reason. Assuming the impeccability of the States, and openly declaring that States, like kings, can do no wrong, while, like kings, they wear the "round and top of sovereignty," politicians treat them with most mistaken forbearance and tenderness, as if these Rebel corporations could be dandled into loyalty. At every suggestion of rigor State Rights are invoked, and we are vehemently told not to destroy the States, when all that Congress proposes is simply to recognize the actual condition of the States and to undertake their temporary government, by providing for the condition of political syncope into which they have fallen, and, during this interval, to substitute its own constitutional powers for the unconstitutional powers of the Rebellion. Of course, therefore, Congress will blot no star from the flag, nor will it obliterate any State liabilities. But it will seek, according to its duty, in the best way, to maintain the great and real sovereignty of the Union, by upholding the flag unsullied, and by enforcing everywhere within its jurisdiction the supreme law of the Constitution.

At the close of an argument already too long drawn out, I shall not stop to array the considerations of reason and expediency in behalf of this jurisdiction; nor shall I dwell on the inevitable influence that it must exercise over Slavery, which is the motive of the Rebellion. To my mind nothing can be clearer, as a proposition of constitutional law, than that everywhere within the exclusive jurisdiction of the National Government Slavery is impossible. The argument is as brief as it is unanswerable. Slavery is so odious that it can exist only by virtue of positive law, plain and unequivocal; but no such words can be found in the Constitution. Therefore Slavery is impossible within the exclusive jurisdiction of the National Government. For many years I have had this conviction, and have constantly maintained it. I am glad to believe that it is implied, if not expressed, in the Chicago Platform. Mr. Chase, among our public men, is known to accept it sincerely. Thus Slavery in the Territories is unconstitutional; but if the Rebel territory falls under the exclusive jurisdiction of the National Government, then Slavery will be impossible there. In a legal and constitutional sense, it will die at once. The air will be too pure for a slave. I cannot doubt that this great triumph has been already won. The moment that the States fell, Slavery fell also; so that, even without any

Proclamation of the President, Slavery had ceased to have a legal and constitutional existence in every Rebel State.

But even if we hesitate to accept this important conclusion, which treats Slavery within the Rebel States as already dead in law and Constitution, it cannot be doubted, that, by the extension of the Congressional jurisdiction over the Rebel States, many difficulties will be removed. Holding every acre of soil and every inhabitant of these States within its jurisdiction, Congress can easily do, by proper legislation, whatever may be needful within Rebel limits in order to assure freedom and to save society. The soil may be divided among patriot soldiers, poor-whites, and freedmen. But above all things, the inhabitants may be saved from harm. Those citizens in the Rebel States, who, throughout the darkness of the Rebellion, have kept their faith, will be protected, and the freedmen will be rescued from hands that threaten to cast them back into Slavery.

But this jurisdiction, which is so completely practical, is grandly conservative also. Had it been early recognized that Slavery depends exclusively upon the local government, and that it falls with that government, who can doubt that every Rebel movement would have been checked? Tennessee and Virginia would never have stirred; Maryland and Kentucky would never have thought of stirring. There would have been no talk of neutrality between the Constitution and the Rebellion, and every Border State would have been fixed in its loyalty. Let it be established in advance, as an inseparable incident to every Act of Secession, that it is not only impotent against the Constitution of the United States, but that, on its occurrence, both soil and inhabitants will lapse beneath the jurisdiction of Congress, and no State will ever again pretend to secede. The word "territory," according to an old and quaint etymology, is said to come from *terreo*, to terrify, because it was a bulwark against the enemy. A scholiast tells us, *"Territorium est quicquid hostis terrendi causa constitutum,"* "A territory is something constituted in order to terrify the enemy." But I know of no way in which our Rebel enemy would have been more terrified than by being told that his course would inevitably precipitate him into a territorial condition. Let this principle be adopted now, and it will contribute essentially to that consolidation of the Union which was so near the heart of Washington.

The necessity of this principle is apparent as a restraint upon the lawless vindictiveness and inhumanity of the Rebel States, whether against Union men or against freedmen. Union men in Virginia already tremble at the thought of being delivered over to a State government wielded by original Rebels pretending to be patriots. But the freedmen, who have only recently gained their birthright, are justified in a keener anxiety, lest it should be lost as soon as won. Mr. Saulsbury, a Senator from Delaware, with most instructive frankness, has announced, in public debate, what the restored State governments will do. Assuming that the local governments will be preserved, he predicts that in 1870 there will be more slaves in the United States than there were in 1860, and then unfolds the reason as follows, — all of which will be found in the "Congressional Globe" [23]: —

"By your acts you attempt to free the slaves. You will not have them among you. You leave them where they are. Then what is to be the result? — I presume that local State governments will be preserved. If they are, if the people have a right to make their own laws, and to govern themselves, they will not only reenslave every person that you attempt to set free, but they will reenslave the whole race."

Nor has the horrid menace of reenslavement proceeded from the Senator from Delaware alone. It has been uttered even by Mr. Willey, the mild Senator from Virginia, speaking in the name of State Rights. Newspapers have taken up and repeated the revolting strain. That is to say, no matter what may be done for Emancipation, whether by Proclamation of the President, or by Congress even, the State, on resuming its place in the Union, will, in the exercise of its sovereign power, reenslave every colored person within its jurisdiction; and this is the menace from Delaware, and even from regenerated Western Virginia! I am obliged to Senators for their frankness. If I needed any additional motive for the urgency with which I assert the power of Congress, I should find it in the pretensions thus savagely proclaimed. In the name of Heaven, let us spare no effort to save the country from this shame, and an oppressed people from this additional outrage!

"Once free, always free." This is a rule of law, and an instinct of

[23] Thirty-Seventh Congress, Second Session, 21 May, 1862, Part III. p. 1923.

humanity. It is a self-evident axiom, which only tyrants and slave-traders have denied. The brutal pretension thus flamingly advanced, to reenslave those who have been set free, puts us all on our guard. There must be no chance or loop-hole for such an intolerable, Heaven-defying iniquity. Alas! there have been crimes in human history; but I know of none blacker than this. There have been acts of baseness; but I know of none more utterly vile. Against the possibility of such a sacrifice we must take a bond which cannot be set aside, — and this can be found only in the powers of Congress.

Congress has already done much. Besides its noble Act of Emancipation, it has provided that every person guilty of treason, or of inciting or assisting the Rebellion, "shall be disqualified to hold any office under the United States." And by another act, it has provided that every person elected or appointed to any office of honor or profit under the Government of the United States shall, before entering upon its duties, *take an oath* "that he has not voluntarily borne arms against the United States, or given aid, countenance, counsel, or encouragement to persons engaged in armed hostility thereto, or sought or accepted or attempted to exercise the functions of any office whatever under any authority, or pretended authority, in hostility to the United States." [24] This oath will be a bar against the return to *National office* of any who have taken part with the Rebels. It shuts out in advance the whole criminal gang. But these same persons, rejected by the National Government, are left free to hold office in the States. And here is another motive to further action by Congress. The oath is well as far as it goes; more must be done in the same spirit.

But enough. The case is clear. Behold the Rebel States in arms against that paternal government to which, as the supreme condition of their constitutional existence, they owe duty and love; and behold all legitimate powers, executive, legislative, and judicial, in these States, abandoned and vacated. *It only remains that Congress should enter and assume the proper jurisdiction.* If we are not ready to exclaim with Burke, speaking of Revolutionary France, "It is but an empty space on the political map," we may at least adopt the response hurled back by Mirabeau, that this empty space is a volcano red with flames and overflowing with lava-floods. But

[24] Act of Congress, July 2, 1862, ch. 123.

whether we deal with it as "empty space" or as "volcano," the jurisdiction, civil and military, centres in Congress, to be employed for the happiness, welfare, and renown of the American people, — changing Slavery into Freedom, and present chaos into a Cosmos of perpetual beauty and power.

Charles Godfrey Leland and Henry P. Leland

Ye Book of Copperheads

Philadelphia, 1863

["A very eccentric pamphlet," Charles Godfrey Leland later called the collection of cartoons and limericks that he and his brother Henry P. Leland published anonymously in 1863. It appeared in Philadelphia in German as well as English, and was reprinted in Indianapolis during the campaign of 1864. Among the persons identifiable in the verses are the Union naval hero, Admiral David Dixon Porter, and a wide array of administration opponents: Benjamin and Fernando Wood of New York, Clement L. Vallandigham of Ohio, Governor Horatio Seymour of New York, William Bradford Reed of Pennsylvania, Ezekiel Forman Chambers of Maryland, James Brooks of the New York *Express*, Manton Marble of the New York *World*, S. F. B. Morse and George Ticknor Curtis, both of New York, and George Stillman Hillard of Boston. Charles Leland (1824–1903), an erudite linguist, the translator of Heine and master of several gypsy tongues, and a promoter of industrial arts education, was best known for his German dialect ballads and their hero, Hans Breitmann. Leland noted in his memoirs, "When Abraham Lincoln died two books were found in his desk. One was the 'Letters of Petroleum V. Nasby,' . . . [and the other] my 'Book of Copperheads.'"[1]]

[1] [Charles Godfrey Leland, *Memoirs* (New York, 1893), I, 250–251.]

The original edition of *Ye Book of Copperheads* carried each cartoon on a separate page, each approximately the size of a full page here.

PHILADELPHIA:
FREDERICK LEYPOLDT.
1863.

"Continue this united LEAGUE."—Richard the Third, III. 1.

There once was a Copperhead snake   tried to bite Uncle Sam by mistake;
But the Seven LEAGUE Boot   on old Uncle Sam's foot
Soon crushed this pestiferous snake.

1

A soldier came back from the war,   with many an honorable scar;
But the Copperheads cried,   "Served you right if you'd died
In this curst *Abolitionist* war!"
2

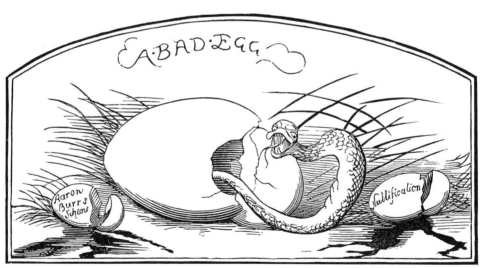

The old Tory dragon is dead,   but she left us some eggs in her stead;
Two were smashed in the yolk,   but the third hatched and broke,
And out came a vile Copperhead.
3

There was once a young giant asleep,   and round him two serpents did creep;
But he stopped their vile breath,   and squeezed them to death,
This giant aroused from his sleep.
4

There once was a Copperhead vile,   who attempted to damage a file,
So he tried it in truth,   but soon broke every tooth
On that rusty and crusty Old File.
5

"Nor doth this Wood lack *Worlds*."—*Midsummer Night's Dream*, II. 2.

There was an old Snake in New York   said for peace all the people should work;
"But if war *must* come,   let us fight here *at home ! !*"
Quoth sanguiloquent Ben of New York.
6

"One of those who worship dirty gods."—*Cymbeline*, III. 6.

There once was a chap named Vallandigham,   whom the Copperheads chose for commanding 'em;
But a trip to the South   soon silenced his mouth,
And the world as a *Tory* is branding him.
7

Yᵉ Mower mows on though the Adder may writhe,
And the Copperhead coil round the blade of his Scythe.

With War Democrats Seymour's for war;   with Peace cowards for peace he'll hurrah;
Let him get in the way   of the mower some day,
And he'll find there's no quibbling with war.

8

The Copperhead lotterie   hath a curious policie;
For a man of low rank   can draw naught save a blank,
Unless an accomplice he be.

9

There once was a twistified Reed, who took for his pattern Snake-*Weed*;
  Till the Copperheads all, great, middling, and small,
   Seemed *straight* by the side of this Reed.
10

(*The Pipe of Peace.*)

There's a character very well known, Who bubbles for ages has blown;
  But the best he has made since at *bubbling* he played,
   From a Copperhead pipe have been thrown.
11

"And what Stock he springs of!!!"—*Coriolanus*, II. 3.

Copper stocks are uncertain to buy,   though this Copperhead's stock's very high;
   But we still might improve   this stock of his love,
      By adding the *right* sort of tie.
12

"Ascend, my CHAMBERS!"—*Merry Wives of Windsor*, III. 3.

There was an old War Horse, a clerical,   who thought our Republic chimerical;
   "For the Union," he said,   "he never had prayed,"
      This mordacious old War Horse cholerical.
13

"There is no goodness in the worm."—*Antony and Cleopatra*, V. 2.

The abominable Copperhead worms! With their wriggles, and twists, and their squirms!
But the gardener, they say, will soon find out a way
To kill the vile Copperhead worms.
14

"There are many complaints, Davy, about that."—*King Henry IV.*, V. 1.

There was a Stern Statesman astute, who so often went in to *recruit*,
That a Rattlesnake fat revolved in his hat,
While a Copperhead squirmed in his boot.
15

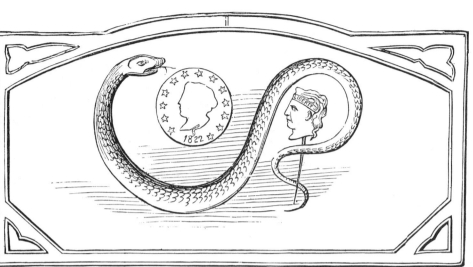

"So much dishonor my fair stars."—*King Richard III.*, IV. 1.

The traitor our Common Cents mars,   And on Liberty plainly he wars,
Taking Freedom away   from the Union, I say,
When he cuts out her head from the stars.
16

"And so the *lion* vanished."—*Midsummer Night's Dream*, V. 1.

While it did us great harm, Abolition   was the height of the Lion's ambition;
Now with Copperhead *tale*   he stings himself pale,
And furaciously scorns Abolition.
17

"Will this Wood take fire?"—*Merry Wives of Windsor*, V. 5.

To show *Union*, a fagot we take;   But 'twould be a tremendous mistake,
To use rotten old WOOD   which never was good,
And then bind it up with a Snake.
18

"*Black*, forsooth!"—*King Henry VI.*, II. 1.

There once was a Patriot whose rigor   reached such a remarkable figure,
That he'd rather go down   in the water and drown
Than be saved by the help of a nigger.
19

"*Reading* them ill-favoredly."—*As You Like It*, III. 2.

There once were some rascals near Reading   thought fighting was easy as wedding;
But being well kicked,   and most terribly licked,
They mournfully mizzled from Reading.

20

"O wicked WALL!"—*Midsummer Night's Dream*, V. 1.

There once was an old *party*-WALL,   quite *cracked* and just ready to fall;
The Copperheads came   and completed its shame
By sticking their Bills on this Wall.

21

There once was a bottle of PORTER,   which the Copperheads thought was all water;
But when the cork popped,   the Copperheads dropped,
And were stunned by the *vim* of the Porter!
22

There once was a Snake who said " Hey !   There's an Eagle I'll take for my prey !"
But the bird with his bill   did the Copperhead kill,
And bore him in triumph away.
23

"*Exit* shall be strangling a snake."—*Love's Labor's Lost*, V. 1.

The Copperhead traitors all, our army "base hirelings" call!
But some fine summer day The "boys," just for play,
Will settle the Copperheads all.
AMEN!
24

Finis or ye End of ye Tale

He wired in and he wired out—Leaving the people still in doubt—Whether the Snake upon the track was going South or coming back"

REED And REFLECT

Pamphlet 39

George Franklin Comstock

"Let Us Reason Together." (Papers from the Society for the Diffusion of Political Knowledge, No. 18)

New York, 1864

[There were those who would accept neither the views of Reconstruction being advanced by Senator Charles Sumner, Representative Thaddeus Stevens, and the Radical Republicans, nor the plan President Lincoln announced in December, 1863. The Society for the Diffusion of Political Knowledge published a pamphlet taking a rigid, mechanistic, constitutional view. Its author, George F. Comstock (1811–1892), a distinguished equity lawyer and prime mover in establishing Syracuse University, had been justice of the New York Court of Appeals from 1855 to 1861. Comstock argued that the Constitution had so firmly and permanently fixed the relationship between the states and the Federal government that not only had secession been illegal on the part of the states but also, since they could not leave the Union, their powers within it remained unimpaired. The Federal government could not redefine the status of the states; especially it could not tamper with slavery: "Under the Constitution of the United States there is no shadow of right, in peace or war, by its laws or its military power, to spread or to propagate the opinions or sentiments of any class or section, upon social and moral questions." Apparently as the Confederate armies were pushed back, Reconstruction should automatically take place as the Southern states resumed their previous functions in the Federal Union, as though the war had not taken place.]

THE writer of the following pages will only venture to say of himself that he brings to the subjects of discussion a mind somewhat accustomed to the examination of questions of constitutional and public law, and an anxious wish to be right in the views which he presents. To him it is a source of unspeakable amazement, that the simplest and most obvious principles underlying the fabric of society and government, in this country, have become so unsettled in the public mind as to be in danger of absolute overthrow. He will endeavor to reassert some of those principles with all the simplicity and plainness of argument at his command, and to show how fearfully and fatally we are departing from them. If he feels obliged to speak with the utmost freedom of political parties and their action, this must be pardoned, because it is a necessity of the occasion. The awful crisis in which we stand compels a choice between the great parties which divide the suffrages of the people, and that choice must be soberly and intelligently made. In times of smooth and peaceful administration the ascendancy of this or that political party does not involve the safety of the government or people; but now, in the hour of *supreme peril,* when the differences between those who have the conduct of national affairs and their opponents are so broad and so fundamental that whichever party is right the other is fatally wrong, there is no longer a middle ground, upon which the man of hesitation and doubt can permit himself to linger or stand.

What, then, is our situation? By what processes have we reached it? and to what results are we tending? Let us reason together on these momentous subjects. It certainly ought not to be assumed that a majority of the people of this country do not prefer to stand by a Constitution and Government under which they have been prosperous and happy beyond any example afforded in history. Yet it is true — alas! too true — that at the present moment this Constitution, and the beneficent Government which springs from it, are passing away in the roar and whirlwind of revolution. The danger is extreme that we shall lose both the principles and forms of our institutions, and that society itself will receive incalculable injury, while we are engaged in a great and passionate struggle of arms — a struggle not merely to preserve the territorial unity of the republic, but to extend over it a government not derived from a written constitution, and unknown to any law which has the sanction of civilized men. It may not yet be too late to arrest the downward course of events, by calm appeals to the intelligence, the reason, and the conscience of the people.

One of the delusions of the hour is, that the Union must be maintained at the expense of the Constitution, and even after the Constitution is overthrown. This is a sentiment which demands unity of territory and people *without a Constitution!* Such is the Union of bleeding and prostrate Poland with despotic Russia, and such is the Union which it is now proposed shall be forced by the power of arms upon millions of unwilling people. The sentiment may be paraphrased thus: Perish the Union under the Constitution; perish the Constitution itself, which made the Union and is the Union; perish the independence and sovereignty of the States; perish the States themselves, with their constitutions and laws; perish all things else, so that the *National unity* be maintained. A fitting adjunct to this novel theory of our nationality is the dogma that in the different parts of our empire there must be uniformity of social systems and institutions; and to compel this very uniformity has now become the primary object of the terrible struggle which is desolating the country. This precise statement of fact admits of no candid denial, because the National Administration to-day stands pledged before the world, by the repeated and solemn proclamations of its chief, to accept no peace — no submission from the rebellious States — without the immediate surrender and destruction of the institution of slavery.

But a National Union outside of the written compact of the Constitution! who can define such a form of government? Who can say what are the limitations of its power, and what the rights of the people, and of the States subject to its dominion? If the Union has outgrown and can outlive the Constitution, what shall we call it? What are its characteristics? Do the States remain, or are they to be extinguished and blotted out? If they remain are they to be provinces, merely, of a central authority, or will the people who inhabit them retain the power of self government, through local laws and local administrations? What and where is to be the dividing line between the sovereignty which the people exercise, through their State Legislatures, Governors and Judiciary, and the sovereignty and power of a National Union, which of necessity is to exist without restraint, when we have rejected the restraints of the Constitution? Will there be any such dividing line? Most assuredly there cannot be, because the partition of powers cannot exist at all, any more than a partition of land or territory can exist without some deed, compact or constitution, in which the boundary is defined. Conflict and change, therefore, are the necessary conditions of such a Union, until the States yield their attributes and become mere departments of a consolidated empire.

In France and in Russia national unity is a perfectly simple and intelligible conception, because the whole mass of sovereignty is possessed and wielded by a single government. In those magnificent empires there are no republics with the attributes of States, possessing political and sovereign power. But such is not the unity of the American people and States. We have a Union or central government, and we have local and State governments. One of these conclusions must, therefore, be the basis of all government in this country: either — 1. The Union must have all power and the States must perish; or — 2. The States must have all power and the Union must perish; or — 3. The powers of sovereignty must be divided by an inflexible organic law, assigning to each its due proportion, and erecting an impassable barrier against invasion or transgression by either. That organic law is the Constitution. Under it the Union and the States both exist, and may exist forever. But the very idea of National Union, without the Constitution as its basis and life, is absurd and impossible. Infinitely more than this, it is a revolutionary and chaotic idea, engendering discord and strife, and sapping the foundations of government and society. The direct consequence of this vague and shadowy conception of a Union with attributes and functions not derived from a written constitution, has been to mingle social theories and moral questions with national politics, producing hatred and strife between the great sections of the country, and culminating in the civil war which now desolates the whole land.

Our safety then must be found in a faithful adherence to the Constitution, because we thereby preserve from annihilation or disturbance the just sovereignty of the States, and the local laws and institutions which have immediate relation to the happiness and wants of every individual. Our highest duty lies in the same direction. The Federal Government has no more right to invade one section of the Union for a purpose outside of the Constitution, no more right to propagate by force of arms in one State the theories, sentiments and opinions of other States, than it has to invade the Kingdom of Brazil to abolish slavery, or the Turkish Empire to abolish poligamy. And if such is become the fixed and determined character of the war, as now waged by the National Government, we are enacting a stupendous crime, unsurpassed in atrocity by any recorded in the history of nations. The laws of the civilized world denounce such a crime, and it is equally condemned by the dictates of unchangeable and eternal justice.

It is an elementary and fundamental truth of our political system, that the Constitution and the Union are essentially the same. If a difference of phraseology can be employed in describing them, it is this: the Constitution is the compact or instrument from which the Union sprung, and Union is the condition of the States and of the people under the Constitution. So from the marriage contract springs the relation or condition of matrimony, and it is quite as intelligible to speak of the relation of husband and wife, without any agreement of the parties, as to speak of the Union of the States without the written Constitution which brought them together. It is true, that men and women may find their affinities, but the American States do not live together by affinity. They are united only by the legal bond of the Constitution.

And what is this Constitution in its grand and fundamental characteristics? After nearly eighty years of National existence under it, this is a question which springs suddenly into a living and vital significance. So smooth and peaceful have been the events of our history — so few and so light have been the shocks felt by the political and social fabric — that we forget how we became, and why we are a Nation. We have looked at the grandeur of results, and minds which do not or cannot discriminate have contemplated our nationality and our Union as they do the nationality and unity of other empires or republics of the past or present. We seem to have outlived the Constitution, and to have grown into a national unity resting on ideas, habits and emotions; and from this illusion have sprung theories and convictions fatally hostile to the Union established by the Constitution and to the peace of the country. The suppositious sins and errors of local communities have troubled the consciences of other communities as sins and errors of the whole nation. The opinions and sentiments of the North opposed to those of the South, aroused angry and dangerous discussion. Ambitious statesmen seized upon the subject of strife, and converted it into a political issue. A thousand pens and ten thousand tongues united in the chorus of invective and denunciation; and the invasion prompted by the blinded patriotism and burning conscience of John Brown, became the true and appropriate illustration of the ideal and emotional Union which seemed to have taken the place of the legal and constitutional Union established by our fathers.

Standing, as we do, in the presence of a great revolution which is rocking society to its base, we look around us for some safe standard of political duty and conduct, for some prop to steady and support the tottering fabric; and where shall we find it but in the Constitution? If we appeal to those moral and social impressions which prevail in one State or class of States, we are met by directly opposite convictions in other States and communities, and we thus invoke the very issue involved in the terrible struggle which has caused a shudder in every truly Christian and benevolent heart throughout the civilized world. In demanding uniformity of institutions, habits and thoughts, we demand no less than a surrender by those who differ from us of their own institutions, habits and modes of thought; and when we seek to enforce this demand by the power of arms, we appeal to the spirit of intolerance and conquest which in all ages has been so fatal to the peace of the world. Holland and the Netherlands were once dependencies of the Spanish monarchy, but they rejected the Roman Catholic religion with its adjuncts of the Inquisition and torture. An intolerant monarch, fanatically devoted to his religion, invaded those provinces, and ravaged them with fire and sword to "preserve the life of his nation," to maintain the unity of his empire, and to enforce uniformity of religious faith and observance. From the Spanish point of view, Protestantism was the cause of a war which, after a struggle of eighty years' duration — marked by every circumstance of atrocity and horror — resulted in separation and disunion; and Protestantism must, therefore, be abolished. In a sense altogether and exactly similar, slavery in the Southern States is the cause of the war, shocking to the humanity and civilization of the age, which now rages between the sections of this country. Philip II was a fanatic, a propagandist, and consequently a tyrant. He merited and has received the execrations of mankind. Let the casuist — let the ministers of religion answer how much better we shall stand before the Throne of Eternal Justice, if, overleaping constitutional barriers in pursuit of our own theories of national unity and social organization, we carry fire and sword and desolation into sister communities, having equal dignity and rights with us. The wail of anguish from the whole land, the shrieks of the wounded and dying, the smoke of burning cities and towns, have ascended to heaven, and as certainly as there is a Judge of all the Earth, so certainly must all men answer for the part they take in this terrible drama.

If the revolution which is shaking the pillars of society cannot be arrested, it is because it has proceeded too far for the utterance, the comprehension, and the acceptance of the plainest and simplest constitutional truths. But let us never despair while there is ground for hope. We say, then, it is a fundamental truth, to be accepted or rejected by men, as they wish to save or destroy the political institutions of their country, *that under the Constitution of the United States there is no shadow of right, in peace or war, by its laws or its military power, to spread or to propagate the opinions or sentiments of any class or section, upon social and moral questions.* Let this great truth sink into the minds of the people; let it be carried at once into their political action, and, while on the one hand it leaves all the material power of the nation free to be exercised in the enforcement of law, on the other it puts aside issues and purposes which are revolutionary and aggressive, and which impart to the pending contests its bitterness of sentiment and a despairing energy of resistance.

How then did we become a nation, and what is our mode of national existence? The colonies were separate appendages of the crown of Great Britain. By their declaration of independence they announced themselves to the world as "Free and independent States, with full power to levy war, conclude peace, contract alliances, establish commerce, and to do all other acts and things which independent States may of right do." By the Treaty of Peace with Great Britain they were acknowledged to be "Free and independent States." By the Articles of Confederation, adopted during the revolutionary struggle, they styled themselves "The United States of America," but declared thus: "Each State retains its sovereignty, freedom and independence, and every power, jurisdiction and right which is not by this Confederation expressly delegated to the United States, in Congress assembled." Those articles then set forth the terms of "a firm league of friendship between the States, for their common defence, the security of their liberties, and their mutual and general welfare." Less than ten years later they were superseded by the CONSTITUTION OF THE UNITED STATES, which, like the Confederation, was a compact between the same States, separately accepted and ratified by each; a compact which delegated certain named powers and functions to the United States, but reserved all other powers, in the following exact and comprehensive language:

"The powers not delegated to the United States by the Constitution, nor prohibited by it to the States, are reserved to the States respectively, or to the people." The grand distinction between the Confederation and the Constitution was, that the former established no government to execute the specified powers which were granted, while the latter did establish one in the three departments — Legislative, Judicial, and Executive. The Confederation was more a treaty than a government. The Constitution is more a government than a treaty. If we have to-day any rightful National Government it is this Constitution. No other has ever been ordained. It is not a Government of ideas, emotions, or traditions. Its powers are derivative, and they are defined by a written instrument. They are ample for the national purposes intended, and they are, according to Northern opinion, incapable of revocation by the States which granted them.

There are many good and intelligent people, who will be astonished to know the smallness, not in dignity and importance, but in number and specification, of the powers of sovereignty which the States, by their constitutions, granted to the Union. In these enumerated powers, legislative and executive, and in a judiciary department to interpret the Constitution, treaties and the laws of Congress, is comprehended the whole sovereignty of the Union, while all the other attributes of sovereign and independent communities are reserved to the States. The Government of the Union is certainly of great dignity and importance. It regulates commercial and diplomatic intercourse with other nations. It holds in its hands the destinies of peace and war. It coins the currency of the country. It establishes postal communications, and it has certain other relations to the general happiness and welfare. But with all its dignity and power it cannot pass a law for the observance of the Sabbath; it cannot enact a single regulation of internal trade; it cannot prescribe the requisites of a deed or will; it cannot regulate the protest of a note; it has nothing to do with the marriage relation, with parental or filial duties; it cannot punish adultery, polygamy, or petit larceny; it cannot suppress immorality of any description; it has no general jurisdiction over crime or the civil rights of the citizens of the States; it cannot dissolve the indenture of an apprentice, and it cannot MAKE OR EMANCIPATE A SLAVE. Of course we are speaking only of powers to be exercised within the States.

There are few minds which consider, and none which can grasp the infinite number and variety of the relations which, in a civilized and commercial country, exist between political sovereignty or government on the one hand and the citizen on the other. They are indeed without number, and wholly incapable of specification; and we arrive at some just conception of our political duties and situation when we reflect that in all these relations, except the few enumerated and specified in the constitutional grant of power to the National Union, it is State sovereignty and State law which impose their restraints upon us and throw around us their protection. All government is organized human society, and the range of subjects over which it extends its visible and invisible influence is therefore boundless and infinite. If, then, we take the number one thousand to represent conventionally the total mass of political sovereignty, we cannot hesitate to affirm that nine hundred and ninety-nine parts belong to the government of each State, while only one is held by the common agent of all the States, the Government of the Union.

Not merely the Declaration of Independence, the Articles of Confederation, and the Constitution of the United States, but the fundamental laws and constitutions of the States themselves, announce their sovereignty in the most unmistakable language. The Constitution of Massachusetts declares as follows: — "The People of this Commonwealth have the sole and exclusive right of governing themselves as a free and independent State." And again: "The People inhabiting the territory of Massachusetts Bay do hereby solemnly and mutually agree with each other to form themselves into a sovereign and independent body politic or State, by the name of the Commonwealth of Massachusetts." The organic law of New Hampshire is cast in the same language. The Constitution of Maine declares that, "We, the people of Maine, do agree to form ourselves into a free and independent State, by the name and style of the State of Maine." In the first Constitution of New York it is ordained and declared "that no authority shall, on any pretence whatever, be exercised over the people or members of this State, but such as shall be derived from and granted by them." Similar declarations of sovereignty may be found in the fundamental ordinances of all the States. In Louisiana, where the President is now engaged in regulating the elective franchise, and in establishing a government to be based on military force and the consent of *one tenth of the people,* the State Constitution declares: — "We, the people of Louisiana, do form ourselves into a free and independent State;" and further, "no power of suspending the laws of this State shall be exercised unless by the Legislature or its authority." The President has not merely suspended but annulled those laws, and proposes to force upon nine tenths of the people, whether loyal or disloyal, another constitution and different laws!

There is a further and most conclusive illustration of this subject. Nothing so distinctly marks political sovereignty as the right of succession to the land or soil of a country, when there is no individual owner — in other words, when the private owner dies without a will and without heirs entitled to the inheritance. It is a fundamental principle of the Constitution of Great Britain that the Crown is the original proprietor of all lands within the realm, that all private titles are derived from the Crown, and that the King succeeds by escheat when the title becomes vacant by intestacy and the want of heirs. When the American Revolution separated the colonies from that Empire, each colony succeeded as a State to this prerogative of the Crown. The State governments, as political sovereignties, became the original and ultimate proprietors of all lands within their boundaries, and no other power on earth exercised the slightest dominion over their soil. This principle of sovereignty, which prevails incontestably in every State in the Union, is expressed with entire accuracy in an original statute of New York: "The people of this State, in their right of sovereignty, are deemed to possess the original and ultimate property in and to all lands within the jurisdiction of the State; and all lands the title to which shall fail from a defect of heirs, shall revert on escheat to the people." And again says another statute: "The sovereignty and jurisdiction of this State extend to all places within the boundaries thereof, but the extent of such jurisdiction over places that have been or may be ceded to the United States, shall be qualified by the terms of such cession." Probably, in all the States, locations have been granted or ceded to the Union for forts, arsenals, hospitals, military or naval schools, etc., and in those localities the Union exercises such a degree of political sovereignty as the States have thought proper to yield, and no other.

Now it would seem to be a doctrine to be accepted by every person of common intelligence, that the sovereignty of a country is that authority, whether wielded by king or people, under and from which the land within its boundaries is held by subjects or citizens, and to which the land returns when private ownership ceases. The principle has been received for ages, and if we try the question by this standard, there can be no hesitation in affirming that in this country original and primary sovereignty belongs to the States, as organized political societies.

This sovereignty, as we have seen, comprehends the innumerable mass of political powers which are wielded to meet the ever varying and extending wants and wishes of human society. It nevertheless lacks something of completeness and perfection, because each State, on entering into the Union, agreed by the compact of the Constitution to surrender certain particular powers, exceedingly few in number, although conceded to be of great importance to the general welfare and defence. The powers surrendered, as we have also seen, are enumerated with great precision of language, while all others are reserved.

Our political system is, therefore, a compound one, because with us sovereignty, in its complete and perfect sense, is compounded by that which belongs to the Union and that which belongs to the States. If to the latter we add the limited and special powers granted to the Union, the result is government in the fullness of all its attributes. As the powers of government are thus wielded by two agencies, with a line of distinction or separation between them which is marked by the Constitution, so the allegiance of the citizen must correspond exactly with that division. To the Federal Government he owes allegiance in respect to the powers which the States in the Constitution have granted to it, and he owes to it no other allegiance, deference or duty. To the State of which he is a citizen, and whose laws protect him in the great mass of his interests and social relations, he owes all other allegiance. Allegiance to the Federal Government is special, because its powers and functions are special. Allegiance to the State is general, because its powers and sovereignty are general, and exist without enumeration or specification, or grant from any other power.

Now, those who advocate the doctrine of secession as a Constitutional right, simply maintain that as the government of the Union is incontestably a grant of certain powers by the States, so the States can revoke the grant, and thus dissolve the allegiance of the citizen to that government. This pretension is met by the antagonistic

proposition that the grant is irrevocable and perpetual. So we think
—so we maintain. And this is the true question between the Union
and the rebellious States. It can only be in a mind and conscience
darkened by error or passion that the soldiers and bayonets of the
Federal Government have any other mission upon the soil of those
States than to enforce the powers granted to the Union by the Constitution. It is a mission of force whenever resistance exists. When
resistance ceases the mission is accomplished; the Union remains,
the States remain; and government, no longer obstructed in its functions, resumes its peaceful sway. This is the doctrine of all true and
enlightened loyalists, of all men who have a sincere and intelligent
wish for peace, with the restoration of order and law; of all men
who have a rational hope of saving from the fathomless gulf of
anarchy the political and social institutions of this country. Whoever has purposes of a different character, whoever invokes the
terrible agencies of war and desolation for the dissemination of his
own theories and wishes, upon social and moral questions, is a
propagandist and revolutionist, whether he be the busy Politician
of a Ward, a Preacher of the Gospel, a Senator in Congress, or the
President of the United States.

Rejecting, as we do, the heresy of secession, the States cannot
absolve the citizen from the obedience which he owes to the constitutional powers of the Union. But as he owes to the State all other
obedience, it is a conclusion of common sense and public law equally
plain, that there is no power in any branch of the Federal Government which can dissolve the allegiance due from the citizen to the
State. This divided yet harmonious allegiance, resulting from the
partition of powers between two sovereignties, is the grand and
chief characteristic of our institutions. Each of these sovereignties
acts directly upon the citizen and demands equally his obedience.
The sovereignty of the Union is not over the States or the laws and
constitutions of the States. On the contrary, it is wholly derived by a
grant from the States as the original and primary sovereigns. It is a
sovereignty over the citizen precisely commensurate with that grant.
Every attempt to exercise over him a power not conferred by the
Constitution, is simply an attempt to interfere with his allegiance
to the State, which is a duty not less solemn and sacred than his allegiance to the Union. In the sum total of allegiance due from the
citizen, the whole belongs to the State, except the portion sub-

stracted by the terms of the written Constitution and transferred by the States to the Union. The exertion of armed power by one sovereign to subvert the allegiance of the citizen or subject of another, by assuming to itself the sovereign power, is identical with an effort to overthrow such other sovereignty. Invasion and conquest are the principles involved in such an effort, and this is condemned by the laws of the civilized world. The invaded sovereign and people have not only the right, but it is their duty to repel such invasion.

This very doctrine that the Federal Government acts only upon individuals in the exercise of its enumerated powers, is exactly the opposite of secession by States. In it lies the strength and majesty of the Union. It exhibits the Union as supreme in the exercise of its granted powers over all the citizens of this country, while it admits the supremacy of the States in the exercise of all other powers. It is a doctrine which alone gives to the judicial arm of the government the power and right to arraign, to try, and to punish the individual for treason to its sovereignty, while it clothes the government with the thunders and panoply of war, to put down armed resistance to its just authority.

The Constitution of the United States recognizes and defines the crime of treason against its sovereignty, and primarily it consists in *"levying war against them."* Nothing can more distinctly proclaim the sovereignty of the Union to be over individuals, and not over States, or the laws and constitutions of States. Confining our attention to domestic war against the United States, the traitor is the party who levies the war, and the party who levies the war is the traitor. But treason, like other crimes, is an individual offence, to be charged by indictment, tried by jury, and punished according to the laws of the land. To impute treason to a State involves an utter absurdity. A State cannot be indicted and tried for treason, any more than it can for a larceny or a burglary. A State cannot be imprisoned or put to death. It cannot be subjected to forfeiture or punishment of any description, because it is incapable of the commission of crime. It cannot forfeit its sovereignty, its constitution and laws. A State no more owes allegiance to the Union than the Union does to a State, and neither owes such allegiance. But the citizens of each State owe part of their allegiance to the Union and all the residue to the States. Citizens in greater or in smaller numbers may be rebels and traitors, by "levying war," but the States, as political societies, cannot. If such, at the present moment, is not the true relation between the Union and the rebellious people of the South, then Jefferson Davis is not a traitor to the government of the United States. We repeat, States cannot rebel. Nor can they secede. They are fixed in the Union forever, and can no more forsake it than a planet can forsake its orbit around the sun. The citizens of a State combining in sufficient numbers may gain possession of the powers of administration in a State government and wield those powers against the Union; but sovereignty is not lost or destroyed, although its powers are misdirected. A sovereignty may be subjugated by force, but it cannot be a rebel.

But, say the advocates of war overleaping the bounds of the Constitution, of desolating and exterminating war, "*Slavery, by rebellion, has sinned away its day of grace.*" We answer neither virtue nor vice, nor social institutions, whether good or bad, can be guilty of the crime of rebellion. They cannot be indicted and tried. They are incapable of personification except in the rhapsodies of transcendental politicians and preachers who seek to pervert a war to enforce obedience to a fixed Constitution and established laws, into a war of aggression and conquest; a war upon ideas, habits and institutions. Such are the wars which in all ages have desolated the earth. Certainly the owner of slaves may be a rebel, and so may a Roman Catholic or a Presbyterian. So may the sinless Puritan of Massachusetts. The defence of a principle or an institution may prompt the action of the individual. But Government, in the maintenance of its just authority, deals with the individual and not with the principle, opinion or institution which animates his conduct. Undoubtedly, Governments whose sovereignty is unlimited may enact laws which bear upon social relations and moral questions. But the sovereignty of the United States has no such attribute or function to be exercised within the States. How stupendous the crime; then, of attempting to accomplish by the terrible agencies of force, of fire and sword, that which the national sovereignty is utterly powerless to ordain by law!

The relation between the Union and the States is that of co-ordinate sovereignties, the former having the right to execute its enumerated powers within the territory of the latter. To execute those powers the Union has a Judiciary, an Army and a Navy. Whosoever resists their execution is guilty of the offence of treason. If resistance assumes the form of organized war, all engaged in it are guilty of that offence. War may be made upon them, they may be wounded or slain in battle, even as an armed band of smugglers may who forcibly defy the law. Such a war may even assume vast proportions, according to the strength and numbers of those engaged in resistance; and questions may spring up during its continuance to be determined by the rules which regulate the conduct of belligerent nations. Prisoners may be exchanged, and captures on the sea may be condemned as prizes of war. But the moment that armed rebellion is suppressed, and the war ended, all such questions pass away; constitutions and laws resume their peaceful sway, and disturbance no longer exists in the fixed relations between the Government and the citizen.

Standing on the principles herein enunciated, on the one hand we hold the sovereignty of the Union strictly to its circumscribed powers, while on the other we maintain the allegiance of every citizen of this land to the Constitution and laws. On the same principles we also maintain that the Union is a perpetual and unchangeable relation of the States to each other and to the national Government. If we are right, the Union is not dissolved, but is now composed of thirty-four States, fixed in their positions by a perpetual Constitution as the planets are fixed in their orbits by an irreversible law of nature. If to-morrow every rebel should lay down his arms and return to allegiance, the Union would remain not only perfect in theory, perfect in all its parts, but undisturbed in the exercise of its constitutional and accustomed functions and powers. But as the Union cannot be perfect with less than all the States, the States would also remain in all their perfection as local sovereignties with their constitutions and laws unimpaired. And there is no power on earth except armed and lawless power, to change the Constitution and laws of a single one of these thirty-four States. We say the Union is perpetual because the States with their just sovereignty and rights are perpetually its members, and there is no Union without the parts of which it is composed. The assurance of perpetuity is in the unchangeable law of the Constitution, made by the States themselves, in the benefits of Union, in the love which it ought to inspire, and in the power of coercion to compel individuals everywhere to submit to its authority. When all the citizens who compose the sovereignty of a State are obedient also to the sovereignty of the Union, when their allegiance is rendered to each sovereignty according to the constitutional partition of powers, the State, by a logical and constitutional necessity, is in the Union, and all parts of our noble political system work harmoniously together.

In opposition to those principles which alone can save the government and preserve society from the shocks of revolution, we find the leaders and guides of a great political party disseminating over the land crude and monstrous theories which admit and proclaim the Union already dissolved, and the Constitution already overthrown. Animated by one ruling and all pervading wish, that of overthrowing the institutions and sovereignty of the Southern States, they find the doctrine of a fixed and perpetual Union under the limitations of the Constitution, a Union such as the fathers of the republic ordained, standing directly in their way, and this must therefore be disposed by some new conception of the crisis into which they have plunged the country. We purpose to notice these deformed and misbegotten theories. But first let us recall what but recently seemed to be the opinion of the whole country concerning the rebellion and the duties of the situation.

On the 4th of March, 1861, Abraham Lincoln was inaugurated President of the United States. The people of six states had then passed ordinances of secession, and had organized the Southern Confederacy. On that imposing occasion Mr. Lincoln, after taking a solemn oath "to protect and defend the Constitution," in the course of his inaugural address said "If the destruction of the Union by all or a part only of the States be lawfully possible, the Union is less perfect than before the Constitution, having lost its vital element of perpetuity. It follows from these views that no State, upon its own mere motion can lawfully get out of the Union; that laws and ordinances to that effect are equally void, and that acts of violence within any State against the authority of the United States are insurrectionary or revolutionary according to circumstances. *I therefore consider that, in view of the Constitution and laws, the Union is unbroken.*" As Mr. Lincoln then said, so the country believed. Widely as men differed as to the policy which had brought the crisis upon us, and as to the mode of treating it, the sentiment that the Union was indestructible and the Constitution in force, with all its anthority and all its limitations, met with a universal response. As Mr. Lincoln then said, so we have now said, and maintained with all the power of argument and illustration at our command.

Again, less than two months later, on the 22d of April, 1861, after the flame of actual war had been kindled, Mr. Seward, the President's Prime Minister, thus expressed himself in a diplomatic paper: "The condition of slavery in the States will remain just the same whether it (the rebellion) shall succeed or fail. There is not even a pretext for the complaint that the disaffected States are to be conquered by the United States if the revolution fail, for the rights of the States and the condition of every human being in them will remain subject to exactly the same laws and forms of administration whether the rebellion shall succeed or shall fail. Their constitution, laws, customs, habits and institutions, in either case, will remain the same. It is hardly necessary to add to this incontestable statement the further fact, that the new President, as well as the citizens through whose suffrage he has come into the administration, has always repudiated all designs, whatever and wherever imputed to him, of disturbing the system of slavery as it is existing under the constitution and laws. The case would, however, not be fully presented if I were to omit to say that any such efforts on his part would be unconstitutional."

Such were the sentiments of the President, as enunciated in his name and by his authority, and such we are told were the views of "the citizens" by whose suffrage he had been elevated to power. Since then how fearful and how rapid has been the descent into the abyss of revolution and crime.

And again, two months later, on the 22d of July, 1861, when eleven States had seceded from the Union, when we stood in the midst of the terrible realities of war, the Congress of the United States, in order to arouse and confirm the loyalty of the people in all sections of the country, and to repel all charges that the war was to be prosecuted for any unconstitutional and revolutionary purpose, unanimously resolved, "That this war is not waged in any spirit of aggression, or for any purpose of conquest or subjugation, or purpose of overthrowing or interfering in the rights of established institutions of the States, but to defend and maintain the supremacy of the Constitution, and to preserve the Union with all the dignity, equality and rights of the several States unimpaired, and that as soon as those are objects accomplished the war ought to cease."

Such then were the issues and purposes of the war as proclaimed by the President and the Congress of the United States. It was to be a war to maintain a Union unbroken by ordinances of secession, unbroken even by the actual presence of rebellion and war, a war to maintain an existing and perpetual Union of equal States by the suppression of armed resistance to its authority. Let us mark the shameful contrast. Now, in the same Representative hall from which the foregoing resolution was sent forth to arouse the patriotism of the people, an unsexed woman proclaims a new purpose of war, to wit, the overthrow of States and Constitutions by conquest — proclaims a new Union founded on the emotions of passion and hate, of love for the negro and hatred for the whites — a Union unknown to the political system of this country; and this is done with the President of the United States sitting on her right hand, Vice-President on her left, and the Speaker in the chair! A responsive echo to this passionate female voice is found in the public declaration of Mr. Chase, a cabinet minister, and perhaps the greatest of the leaders of Republican opinion, who tells us *the Nation is to be born again.* This is the very language of the Dantons, the Marats and the Robespierres of the French Revolution. It is the language of revolution and anarchy in all ages and countries.

That the sudden and violent enfranchisement of the four millions of slaves in the Southern States has now become the leading principle and animating purpose of the war as carried on by the National Administration, we suppose, is no longer a disputed proposition. When the President, in September, 1862, launched his preliminary, and on the 1st January, 1863, his final thunderbolt of emancipation, a great body of his supporters failed to see the vast and revolutionary scope of that edict. Many were unconscious themselves of a purpose to overthrow the constitutions and laws of eleven States of the Union. The meaning of the edict was sufficiently plain because, by its very terms, it declared the slaves to be "forever free," and pledged the armies and navies of the Union to "maintain that freedom." But as this political decree could not have its literal effect without overthrowing the constitution and subverting the fundamental principles on which the Union is based, timid and halting

Republicans interpreted it as a mere order of a military commander inviting slaves to join the invading forces, but totally powerless to change the constitution and laws of States; and therefore powerless to affect the *legal status* or condition of any human being. This was in substance denying to it any effect whatever, except as an illusive and deceptive invitation to slaves to abandon their masters. But with this false and erroneous interpretation of the Presidential manifesto, it received the plaudits of a united party. The hesitating Seward, who had denied even the possibility of such an invasion of the sovereignty and constitutional rights of States, approved it as a "war measure," while the exultant Chase grasped its literal, its terrible import.

The false interpretation of this imperial decree has been removed by its author. The President in his message and "amnesty" proclamation of December, 1863, has plainly announced to the world his purpose of continuing this devastating and exhausting war, not merely until resistance to the laws of the Union has ceased, but until the laws and constitutions of the States maintaining the institution of slavery shall be changed by the compulsion of arms. And those who approved the proclamation of emancipation under a frivolous interpretation which deprived it of all legal significance are now understood to have surrendered their transient scruples, and to yield to it their support without that or any other reservation. We state what we suppose to be now an admitted fact when we say, that nowhere in all the councils of the republican party is there a single voice raised in favor of the Union of the States without emancipation, and with the equality and rights to which the Constitution entitles them. We know that the words "Union and the Constitution" have not wholly passed from use. But they mean simply unity and consolidation under the pressure of power to be enforced by a desolating and exterminating war, and not the union of co-equal sovereignties ordained by the Constitution.

It is, however, a conclusion plain even to passionate fanatics and heated partisans that the Constitution does not justify the proposed invasion of equal States and the intended destruction of their institutions. Every mind must assent to the doctrine that if we proceed according to the Constitution, it must not be transcended, and that simple obedience to its authority is the object and the limit of war. But the purpose to use the military power of the nation, in order to overthrow all the laws and constitutions of States by which slavery is maintained, has diffused itself throughout a great political party, and this purpose must find some doctrinal justification or be abandoned. Out of this necessity various theories have arisen to justify a war of invasion and conquest *outside of the Constitution.*

The first of these theories is the illogical and illshapen conception of Mr. Sumner. According to his view of the political situation, an abolition war is justified upon the doctrine that State sovereignty was lost, and the Southern States themselves extinguished by their ordinances of secession and their resistance to constitutional authority. This being assumed, it is then asserted that the States, in a sense both geographical and political, have become mere provinces or territories of the Union, and as such may be governed absolutely. From the right to govern absolutely, necessarily flows the right to annul all local laws and overturn all local institutions.

To these conclusions, we oppose the self-evident proposition that a State or sovereignty cannot commit suicide. A political State is composed of its people, their laws and constitution of government, and perpetual succession and sovereignty are its necessary attributes. It may be invaded and conquered by lawless power, but it cannot cease to exist by the force of a legal or logical proposition. The very conception of forfeiture implies that the whole of sovereignty with its infinite mass of power is held of some superior sovereign, and this is a contradiction in terms. That which has a superior cannot be a sovereign. The separate sovereignties of the Union and of the States have been elucidated in those pages. As we have shown each is exercised upon different questions or subjects with a constitutional aim of partition between them, and each is perpetual, if the Constitution is perpetual. But from the very nature of the system, if all the States should withdraw from the compact the sovereignty of the Union would be lost. But the Union cannot withdraw the sovereignty of the States or of any of them. It can enforce obedience to its constitutional authority, but there its rightful powers end.

Equally false and illogical is the Sumner theory in another aspect. The States which formed the Union were certainly never territories of the Union. The Union sprung from the States and not the States from the Union. As pre-existing sovereignties their soil never belonged to the Union. By inevitable logic, if the separation of States is possible, they return to their original situation, with all the attributes of perfect and separate sovereignty. The separation of a State, if possible, is simply a revocation of the enumerated powers granted to the Union. So far it impairs the sovereignty of the latter and reannexes to the State the portion which had been granted away. Jefferson Davis says this separation is possible, and so says Mr. Sumner. We hold them both to be wrong, and that ordinances of secession are void and inoperative to all intents and purposes whatever. If they are not void, then Mr. Davis is right as to all the consequences and results which flow from the separation. Then the seceded States are in the rightful possession of a perfect sovereignty, and Mr. Sumner proposes a war of invasion and conquest, for which there is not only no warrant in the Constitution, but which is condemned by the rules of Christianity and the law of the civilized world.

Opposed to the Sumner theory of State suicide, but equally false, is another, probably of still wider influence. One of its most prominent advocates is Mr. Stevens, "The Chancellor of the Exchequer" in the House of Representatives, whose speech is before us as we write. Like Mr. Sumner, he declares the seceding States to be out of the Union, but with infinitely better logic, instead of remanding them to a territorial and provincial condition, he holds them to be foreign powers, and that the war against the "Confederate States" is a war against a foreign nation. He, too, like Sumner, is an Abolitionist; and, upon this doctrine, he relieves himself from the restraints of the Constitution. He says: "'The Union as it was and the Constitution as it is,' is an atrocious idea;" and thus throwing off all constitutional restraints, those who darken their intelligence and delude their consciences by this doctrine, write "emancipation" on their banners, and march their invading hosts against the sovereignty, institutions, and laws of a foreign power. By a singular incongruity of logic and of thought, these theorists, after conquering and subduing the Southern States as a foreign power, propose to punish the citizens of those States as domestic traitors. Confiscation, widespread and universal, desolation and destruction, are the concomitants of this humane and enlightened policy!

Now, the transparent vice of this theory is, that it accepts the secession of States not only as a fact, but as a fixed conclusion of public law. To this conclusion, also, we oppose the doctrine of the perpetuity of the Union and the irrevocable compact of the Constitution. As Mr. Lincoln said, in 1861, as all loyal men then said so we say now: the Union is legally and constitutionally unbroken, and the only mission of our army is to vindicate its just authority, and that mission, we say here, should be attended by the mightier agencies of conciliation and kindness.

Words need not be wasted on a doctrine which proclaims the Union already dissolved. If Mr. Thaddeus Stevens is right, so, we repeat, Jefferson Davis is right; for they both agree in the essential proposition that the seceding States are a foreign power. But, in imputing to them that character, it is necessarily implied that they are rightfully independent of all other powers on the earth. What can be more absurd in logic or atrocious in morals than a doctrine which assigns to the Southern States a place outside of the Union for the purpose of carrying on a war against them outside of the Constitution, yet instantly returns them to the Union for the purpose of confiscation and punishment for treason to its authority? Such an absurdity needs no refutation. If the doctrine is right in its first and fundamental proposition, that the seceding States are a foreign power, then this war is without cause and cannot be rightfully prosecuted a moment longer. We have no cause of war with the South as a foreign nation; and, in the name of outraged humanity and Christian civilization, let it come to an end. If there be a settled maxim in the law of the modern world, it is, that the independence of nations ought to be respected, and that no social or moral theories can justify an invasion of their sovereignty or soil. Christian Europe has for ages not only tolerated but maintained the polygamous Empire of Turkey. This great principle lies at the very foundation of the peace of the world. More than any thing else, it distinguishes modern civilization from the intolerance and barbarism of other times. "Death or the Koran" was the battle-cry of the Mohammedan hosts, as they swept over the nations to disseminate the religion of their prophet. "Death or Abolition" is now the motto of a great political party and the Oriflamme borne at the head of our invading armies.

But the President of the United States has also a doctrine and a policy of his own, which are exhibited in his latest message to Congress, and in the contemporaneous so-called "Amnesty Proclamation." Unable to withdraw himself from the fearful and revolutionary pledge contained in his Proclamation of Emancipation, and rejecting the interpretation which falsified its meaning, he has invented a grotesque and novel theory to relieve himself from the inconvenience of the Constitution which he swore to maintain in peace and in war. Accordingly he has found in the pardoning function of his office a power to overthrow the constitutions of eleven States of the Union. By an inversion of logic of thought and sentiment which would be astonishing were it not so common, the attribute of pardoning mercy which the Constitution has bestowed on the chief magistrate of the Union is converted into a power which the whole government of the United States does not possess, and into a terrible engine of oppression and wrong.

Stripped of all useless and circumlocutory forms of expression, this latest manifestation of the President's views and policy may be stated in the following sequence: 1st. All persons who have been engaged in the present Rebellion are guilty of treason. 2d. The President has, under the Constitution, the pardoning power. 3. He will graciously pardon the greater number of those persons provided they will support his Proclamation of Emancipation and all other proclamations, past or future, relating to slavery, and will take an oath to that effect. 4th. He will recognize new State governments without the institution of slavery, which governments are to be created and organized by the suffrages of one-tenth of the voters in the States who take such oath. Necessarily the *existing* constitutions, laws, and sovereignty of the States are annulled and destroyed. 5. The other nine-tenths of the people refusing to take the oath are outlawed, even if they were never rebels, or if, having been rebels, they are willing to lay down their arms and submit to the Constitution and laws of the United States. We beg to be understood as stating in this sequence, with entire and absolute accuracy, the policy of Mr. Lincoln as announced to the country in his last message and proclamation.

Now if this policy, like that of Thaddeus Stevens, regards the seceded States as foreign powers; or if, like that of Mr. Sumner, it considers them extinguished and degraded to mere Territories, then besides the fatal objections already considered, it is liable to the further and equally fatal one, that the President has no shadow of authority to recognize or admit new States into the Union. If he can do this, then by the power of arms and a presidential edict Cuba can be annexed. If he can do this, then he may admit the Territory of Nevada as a State with such a constitution as he chooses to dictate. These assumptions need no further refutation.

But the President probably regards the Union as unbroken, as stated in his inaugural address, and all the States as held in Territories by the perpetual bond of the Constitution. Such is our doctrine. But by inexorable logic it follows that acts of secession and war are the treasonable acts of the individuals engaged in them; and the States being in the Union are necessarily there with their sovereignty, their constitutions, and laws. How, then, can the President overthrow that sovereignty and expunge those constitutions and laws by the punishment or the pardon of individuals, or by any power known to the Constitution? The very conception of punishment or pardon implies that the persons who are subjects of either of these dispensations owe allegiance to the Union. But that is impossible, unless they are citizens of a State which is a member of the Union.

But again, the President's amnesty is conditioned on the emancipation of slaves, and an oath to observe and obey all his proclamations on that subject. Now, a conditional pardon or amnesty *is a punishment for the supposed crime.* A remission of a sentence of death, on a condition of perpetual imprisonment, is simply a punishment for the offense by a perpetual imprisonment. But neither the President nor Congress has any power to punish. They can only make war against armed insurrection or treason. The power to punish, by a sacred provision of the Constitution, belongs to the judiciary alone, which must proceed by indictment and trial. But without indictment, trial, or sentence, the President proposes, by his conditional pardon or amnesty, to punish by a universal confiscation of property. The alternatives are outlawry and exile, or death. Submission to the laws simply and purely he refuses to accept. Submission to the laws is submission to all the chances of indictment and trial according to law. The President demands, not this submission, but without trial he exacts a punishment which can be inflicted only after a trial and conviction in the courts. We repeat, a conditional pardon is a punishment precisely commensurate with the condition imposed.

This punishment, we add, is universal. Millions of people rebel, and millions are to be punished. Such an atrocious and vindictive assertion of sovereignty was never before heard of, or even conceived, in the history of the whole world. A large number of the people of England engaged in the rebellion of Monmouth against the throne and sovereignty of James the Second. Some three hundred of them were punished, not by the king, but tried and condemned according to law. "The bloody assizes," and the name of Judge Jeffries, have received the execrations of mankind. Mr. Lincoln, without the attributes of a judge, hurls the penalty of confiscation against a million of offenders. But infinitely worse, he punishes the innocent with the guilty. The impressed soldier and voluntary rebel fall equally under his condemnation. Women and minors, noncombatants and Unionists, equally with the open traitor, are assumed to need a pardon which mercifully spares their lives on condition of submitting to a different form of punishment.

But the crowning feature of this extraordinary policy is its assertion of authority, not merely to overthrow State governments, but to re-create them by the vote of one-tenth of the people who by the pressure of arms may be willing to accept the proffered amnesty. These new governments are to be "recognized," and necessarily the power of the Union is pledged to sustain them against the other nine-tenths of the people who may adhere to their existing constitutions and laws. Of this nine-tenths, all who have been rebels may be willing to lay down their arms and submit to the authority of the Union, claiming only the rights to which they are entitled under the laws of their States. Yet unless they are willing also to accept the pardon of the President with its punitive conditions, they are excluded from citizenship and subjected to the political domination of the remaining one-tenth, and this relation between the majority and the minority is to be maintained by the military power of the nation. In the result the pardoned traitors in all the rebellious States amounting to one-tenth of the voting population may wield all the powers of sovereignty over more than equal numbers of subject and enslaved people who, having never been disloyal, decline to accept a vindictive pardon for their loyalty. In this manner Mr. Lincoln and his Generals are now proceeding to organize new civil governments in the Southern States. If the powers thus assumed by him were known to the Constitution, their execution would nevertheless be a monstrous and gigantic wrong. But in the consummation of such a scheme the Constitution itself must be trampled under foot. The

President has no power to admit or "recognize" States, or to organize or reorganize civil governments in them. He is commander-in-chief of the Army and Navy, and he may execute the laws of the Union. But he is not the sovereign of this country, nor can he establish such a tyranny in any portion of it until constitutional liberty is crushed beneath the iron heel of military power.

This one-tenth of the voting population composed of repentant and pardoned rebels, of camp followers and parasites of power, sustained by the soldiers and bayonets of the United States, is not only to wield the sovereignties of eleven States, but the same minorities will bring these sovereignties into the Government of the Union. Each spurious State will be entitled to two senators in Congress, and the number of its representatives in the other house will be undiminished by the exclusion from civil rights of the proscribed nine-tenths of the people.

Now, one-tenth of the white population of the seceded States amounts to but little over half a million of souls. Their representation in the Senate of the United States will equal that of eleven loyal States having a population of more than sixteen millions; and in the other branch of the National Legislature it will equal that of States which number over eight millions. Such is to be the Government of this Union under the administration of Abraham Lincoln. Let us conceive a President of the United States chosen by electoral votes counted in the Capitol at Washington on the appointed day and based on eleven State sovereignties thus "recognized" and created. The Union would be shaken from center to circumference. It needs no prophetic eye to foresee that the days of such a Government must be speedily numbered.

We have done with the policy of Mr. Lincoln. We have done also with the other wild and fantastic theories which have been invented to drug the intellect and appease the consciences of men whose overmastering wish is to escape plain constitutional restraints and duties so that the spirit of intolerance and the lust of conquest may have free scope to accomplish their unholy purposes. We have, as we persuade ourselves, presented the undeniable truths of our political system — truths which impose upon every citizen in every station not only the restraints of the fundamental law, but the very highest corresponding moral obligations; and we have dissected and examined all the false conceptions and ideas of the situation, which having assumed a tangible form, and having responsible authors, seemed to challenge discussion.

There are still other illusions floating in minds incapable of rational deduction or consecutive thought. One of these takes the form of a postulate like the following: "The rebels having rejected and repudiated the Constitution, are not entitled to demand its protection." This exceedingly shallow sophistry, perhaps, has done more to unsettle minds and plunge the country into the vortex of revolution, than even the mischievous dogmas which we have examined. Shallow as the sophistry is, it deserves to be refuted for the evil it has done.

The rebellious people of the South most certainly have rejected the Constitution and laws, and have resisted them by force. What, then, is their offence? Every mind must answer, it is simply *treason*. It is no more and no less. They are in the eye of the law criminals, and that is all. Their offence is defined by the Constitution, and the laws have provided the mode of punishment. Now the greatest criminal, equally with the most exalted saint, is entitled to the protection of law. He is entitled to be tried by his peers, and, if convicted, to be punished only *according to the law*. When law is broken, Government must keep within it, and may inflict the punishment which it prescribes. Government goes one step further, it becomes itself the offender, and resistance to its usurpation is an undoubted right. When citizens defy the laws, the business of Government is to compel them to submit to the laws. The feeblest mind can comprehend and apply the principle. The rebels resist the authority of the Constitution, and force may be used to compel their obedience to it. But as their obedience is only due to the Constitution and the laws, the use of force by the Government to overthrow the Constitution, and to set up in its place some other authority, instantly reverses the relations of the parties and changes the principles of the contest. And thus a lawless rebellion may be converted at once into a necessary self-defence, justified by the laws of nature and of all nations. If such has now become the relative situation of the Government and the present rebellion, it is an unspeakable misfortune, into which the country has been plunged by the blind infatuation of party, which embraces every wretched delusion and inverts all principle and truth.

But the rebellious people of the Southern States *do not demand the protection of the Constitution.* On the contrary, they say they are *outside* of the Constitution; and so says the miserable sophism we are refuting. And this postulate being agreed on, the rebels demand not the protection of the Constitution, but peace and repose. Accepting the formula, "you are outside of the Constitution," they press these terrible questions upon us, "Why then do you invade us? Why then do you march your armed hosts to desolate our land? Why do you wrap a continent in the all devouring and devastating flame of war? If not for the sake of your Constitution, why is humanity compelled to shudder at the scenes you are enacting?" How shall we escape the inexorable logic of these all searching enquiries? Let those whom constitutions and laws cannot bind, come forward and answer.

In the meantime, a powerful political organization is sweeping on in its work of destruction. One class of revolutionists adopts the theory of State suicide and the degradation of States to territorial and provincial subjection. Another maintains that the States, bound to the Union by a perpetual constitution, have passed into the condition of foreign powers, and are to be conquered and subdued as such in opposition to the laws of the civilized and Christian world. Others, like the President, find in the pardoning power, mercifully bestowed on the national executive, an authority to inflict universal punishment without trial, to overturn States and re-create them by the terrible instrumentalities of war and desolation. Thousands seem to be profoundly ignorant of all political institutions and restraints, while numbers equally great are reckless of every social and constitutional obligation. To all these add the numberless throng of official dependents and expectants, of mercenaries and parasites, and we have a great political party whose brief but disastrous domination has brought and is bringing upon the country greater calamities than would the visitations of God in the forms of pestilence and famine.

Let us not despair. The time for the great yet peaceful uprising of the people is approaching. There are millions of loyal and Christian hearts which are not in a war of aggression, conquest and revolution, which are not in a war whose duration is interminable, because it necessarily awakens the fiercest passions of human nature, and arouses a resistance to be maintained by the tremendous energies of despair. There are millions of hearts which sigh for the peace and repose of a constitutional government; and there is an all-pervading intelligence which is able to comprehend the crisis and the obligations it imposes. Reason will resume her throne, and conscience will assert her imperial sway over the wills and the conduct of men.

FINIS.

EXTRACT.

What you need, as it seems to me, is to be fully impressed with a belief in your mission, and in your capacity to fulfil it. That mission is to save the Constitution of the United States. By saving it I mean, of course, that you are to save it for the whole Union — for the South and the North, for the East and the West — with every right which it protects completely reëstablished. I can see no other mode of saving it; for it is to my mind apparent that a war prosecuted against the South, for the acquisition of power over their domestic institutions, which the Constitution expressly withholds from the Federal Government, can result in nothing but the establishment of a system under which there can be no local rights of self-government left for any section or any State. This it is your mission to prevent. You cannot prevent it by uniting with those who proffer support of the war without the slightest protest against the unconstitutional policy with which it is prosecuted. In all the late popular proceedings looking to the establishment of what are styled "Loyal Leagues," I have not seen one word of indignant remonstrance against the unconstitutional measures of the Administration. You cannot expect, and need not look for such remonstrance from assemblies largely composed of those who are the peculiar political supporters of the Administration, and who are more or less responsible for its measures. Public opinion, if it is to make itself *heard* and *felt* against all violations of the Constitution, must make its utterances through the action and the voice of those who have never failed to protest against the policy that has created for us so much peril. If that public opinion fails to recognize this necessary channel of expression — if it yields itself to a fatal apathy, or *will not* see how it can at once save a Government and change an Administration — then all will be lost, and there will remain to us only the consolation that we have individually done our duty.

You are then (permit me to add) to seek, by every constitutional and upright method, to obtain the control of all the organisms of government. If, in the meantime, you cannot induce the present Executive of the United States to change his policy, then, remembering his position, possess your souls in patience until you can give him a constitutional successor. Let everything be prepared with one fixed and unselfish purpose — namely, to make every successive election reverse the doctrines, and dogmas, and usurpations which you know you should condemn. By this course of action instead of weakening you will strengthen your government, for you will make it apparent to the whole world that the present arbitrary rule is to be succeeded by a period when the CONSTITUTION is once more, in all its beneficence and all its power, to be "THE SUPREME LAW OF THE LAND." Fail to do this, and the Nation, losing heart and hope, will lose sight of the methods by which a constitutional succession can be preserved to a better day, and will yield itself to the despair which welcomes despotism, or to the rage which welcomes monarchy.

Pamphlet 40

Abraham Lincoln. (*Union League No. 69*)

Philadelphia, 1864

[From the beginning of 1864 the forthcoming presidential election cast its long shadow. Victory would not be easy for the Republicans; they had done badly in the congressional elections of 1862. Nor were they very enthusiastic about President Lincoln. Nevertheless some of them began to endorse him for a second term; he seemed stronger then in the gloomy summer ahead. Early in January the New Hampshire Republican convention acted, followed by the Republicans in the Pennsylvania legislature. In New York City, Francis Lieber noted privately, "The mind of the people is rapidly settling, or is already settled on Lincoln's re-election." A Philadelphian commented, "The masses have an abiding faith in his honesty and ability." On January 11, the Union League of Philadelphia passed resolutions presenting Lincoln as "the People's candidate for the Presidency." In March they published the resolutions as the preface to a thoughtful anonymous essay on Lincoln.[1]]

AT a special meeting of the UNION LEAGUE, OF PHILADELPHIA, held at the League House, on the 11th day of January, 1864, on motion of Mr. MORTON MCMICHAEL, seconded by Mr. WM. D. LEWIS, the following preamble and resolutions were unanimously adopted:

"*Whereas,* The skill, courage, fidelity, and integrity with which, in a period of unparalleled trial, ABRAHAM LINCOLN has conducted the administration of the National Government, have won for him the highest esteem and the most affectionate regard of his grateful countrymen:

"*And Whereas,* The confidence which all loyal men repose in his honesty, his wisdom, and his patriotism, should be proclaimed on every suitable occasion, in order that his hands may be strengthened for the important work he has yet to perform:

"*And Whereas,* The Union League of Philadelphia, composed, as it is, of those who, having formerly belonged to various parties, in this juncture recognize no party but their country; and repre-

[1] [J. G. Randall and R. N. Current, *Lincoln the President; Last Full Measure* (New York, 1955), 120–121.]

senting, as it does, all the industrial, mechanical, manufacturing, commercial, financial, and professional interests of the city, is especially qualified to give, in this behalf, an unbiassed and authentic utterance to the public sentiment. Therefore,

"*Resolved,* That to the prudence, sagacity, comprehension, and perseverance of Mr. Lincoln, under the guidance of a benign Providence, the nation is more indebted for the grand results of the war, which southern rebels have wickedly waged against Liberty and the Union, than to any other single instrumentality, and that he is justly entitled to whatever regard it is in the power of the nation to bestow.

"*Resolved,* That we cordially approve of the policy which Mr. Lincoln has adopted and pursued, as well the principles he has announced as the acts he had performed; and that we shall continue to give an earnest and energetic support to the doctrines and measures by which his administration has thus far been directed and illustrated.

"*Resolved,* That as Mr. Lincoln has had to endure the largest share of the labor required to suppress the rebellion, now rapidly verging to its close, he should also enjoy the largest share of the honors which await those who have contended for the right; and as, in all respects, he has shown pre-eminent ability in fulfilling the requirements of his great office, we recognize with pleasure the unmistakable indications of the popular will in all the loyal States, and heartily join with our fellow citizens, without any distinction of party, here and elsewhere, in presenting him as the People's candidate for the Presidency at the approaching election.

"*Resolved,* That a Committee of seventy-six be appointed, whose duty it shall be to promote the object now proposed, by correspondence with other loyal organizations, by stimulating the expression of public opinion, and by whatever additional modes shall, in their judgment, seem best adapted to the end; and that this committee have power to supply vacancies in their own body, and to increase their number at their own discretion.

"*Resolved,* That a copy of these proceedings, properly engrossed and attested, be forwarded to President Lincoln; and that they also be published in the loyal newspapers."

GEORGE H. BOKER.
Secretary.

ABRAHAM LINCOLN.

WHAT will be the place assigned by history to Abraham Lincoln? Will he be recorded in the future as the "gorilla" of the Richmond rhetorician, the "baboon" of the Northern Pro-slavery Democrat, or will he be blazoned in the Annals of the Great Republic as the honest, sagacious, steadfast man who conducted the country through the most fearful perils that ever threatened the life of a nation?

Few of us can forget the feelings of doubt and distrust with which we regarded his advent to the Presidential chair. The system of delegate elections and packed conventions had so long ruled the politics of the country, that nominations to office had become the sport of party hacks and managers, and no man widely known, or of national reputation, could hope to be selected as a presidential candidate. The mass of the people, immersed in their individual cares, and blindly trusting in the proverbial good fortune of the United States, considered the choice of a President as a matter comparatively unimportant, and surrendered their political duties to the professional wire-pullers, whose livelihood lay in the pursuit and occupation of office. That the choice of the Chicago Convention, therefore, should fall upon a man of whom little was known, was not a subject of surprise. As the representative of a principle, he received the support of his party, and that support, owing to the dissensions of the democracy, was sufficient to elect him.

As events came thickly crowding upon us, in the interval between the election and the inauguration, men inquired more curiously as to the man who was called upon to confront dangers so unexpected and so unprecedented. That his native energy had elevated him from a youth of poverty and labor was reassuring, and yet the narrow sphere in which his life had mostly been passed seemed to deprive him of the opportunities of familiarity with the great principles and details of statesmanship requisite for the perilous contingencies of the future. That he was universally admitted to be an honest man was satisfactory, yet the training of the Illinois bar did not pre-suppose the ability to grapple with the sternest and the largest questions which, since the great French Revolution, have tasked the intellect of a leader of men.

The January and February of 1861 wore drearily on. Mr. Buchanan's imbecility and pusillanimity depressed the popular heart, until at length we began to ask ourselves whether we really had a country and a nationality; whether "coercion" might not truly be the "heresy" which secessionists proclaimed it; whether the Constitution had provided for its own perpetuation; and whether there was any inherent force in the Federal Union to prevent its dissolution at the first shock of a discontented number. We felt that nothing could be worse or weaker than the existing administration, and yet we knew not whether the incoming one would be better or stronger; while the people, humiliated by the unavenged outrage and unrepressed bravado of rebels, looked vainly around for some rallying point, and, in the sickness of despair at their own impotence, were almost ready to abandon institutions which had proved so powerless to resist the assaults of defiant treason.

At this moment of supreme agony, Abraham Lincoln, new and untried, assumed the Chief Magistracy of the distracted country. Even in the North, a powerful party longed to strike hands with rebellion, and his first foretaste of office was the plot to assassinate him in Baltimore, which forced him to enter the capital by stealth. An empty Treasury, to which timid capitalists offered money at thirty-six per cent. per annum; a navy scattered to the four quarters of the globe; an army cunningly stationed where its most effective strength was at the mercy of traitors; arsenals despoiled and the arms in the hands of rebels; eight States in open revolt; six more trembling on the verge and only awaiting a decent excuse; furious partisans throughout the North openly threatening armed resistance if "coercion" were attempted; such was the condition of affairs which greeted his accession to office. Nor was this all, for our least dangerous enemies were those who openly threw up their commissions and joined the rebellion. The democracy had left us a legacy of traitors in office, civil and military, who remained in the enjoyment of place and pay for the purpose of serving the enemies of the country. The new President was surrounded with spies and could trust the fidelity of scarce any one connected with the machinery of government.

Thus with doubt, confusion and demoralization around him, with no landmarks in the past to serve as a guide for the present or as a precedent for the future, did Mr. Lincoln undertake the awful responsibilities of his high position. A less resolute man would have shrunk from the fearful trial, or would have fatally compromised the people, who from want of faith in their rulers had begun to lose faith in their institutions and in themselves. Fortunately he had no such misgivings. A man of the people, he had seen deep into the popular heart, and he knew that under the chaotic surface there lay an all pervading love of country which could be moulded into as stern and self-sacrificing a patriotism as ever illustrated the annals of Greece or Rome. Thus relying on himself and on the people, he boldly set to work to restore the Republic.

Men breathed freer as they read his inaugural address. Conciliatory to the South, it closed no door by which erring States could return to their duty, but yet it declared in unmistakable tones that the Union was perpetual, and that the Constitution and the laws should be enforced at every cost. More than all, it breathed an honesty of purpose and an integrity of soul that satisfied even his opponents that the times of chicanery and double dealing were past, and that at last we had a ruler who said what he meant, and who meant only what he felt to be honest and true.

It was a great point gained when the people thus could feel confidence in their chief. It remained to be seen whether they were worthy of the confidence which he reposed in them. The glorious uprising in April proved this, but it also proved more. The bombardment of Sumter was not a more belligerent or rebellious act in principle than the firing on the "Star of the West" in January, nor so dangerous as the ordinances of secession which eight States had previously adopted. Our forts had been seized by force or fraud, our arsenals had been plundered, our soldiers had been captured, our flag had been insulted and desecrated with every circumstance of ignominy, and yet the North had borne all this like a whipped child, for it had lost faith and was fast losing self-respect. Under Buchanan, the fall of Sumter would but have added another to the long category of wrongs tamely submitted to. Five weeks under Lincoln found the people in a different mood. Faith in him had restored faith in themselves. They again felt that they had institutions to be perpetuated and a destiny to be worked out, and with that feeling came confidence in their right and in their might. The country was saved so soon as the people recognized in their President a man who believed that he could save it, and who honestly intended to do so.

Had Abraham Lincoln done no more than this, he would have

merited a place between Washington and Jackson. It is a great thing to lift a nation to the highest level of its duties and responsibilities, and few men to whom, in the world's history, the opportunity has been vouchsafed, have accomplished the task so thoroughly.

This one great fact rendered possible all that followed. While Europe unanimously declared that the Union was hopelessly destroyed, and that any attempt to restore it by force could only lead to universal anarchy, the national credit was restored and our finances were redeemed, notwithstanding the necessity for unexampled expenditure. Great armies were organized with unprecedented rapidity. Arms and munitions of war were accumulated with a promptitude hitherto unknown. A navy was extemporized, which enforced a blockade, pronounced impossible by wondering nations. A diplomacy of mingled firmness and moderation has kept in check, amid bewildering complications, the jealous powers which eagerly sought occasion to complete our ruin. And now, the third year of gigantic war, in drawing to its close, finds the nation stronger and more confident than ever. The rebellion is split in two, and the dissevered parts are each hemmed in on every side by our victorious forces. It is gathering up its remaining energies for one last despairing effort. If that fails, and if its military strength is broken, it has no reserve to fall back upon, and must yield perforce. Our task will then be to reconstruct the shattered edifice of Southern society, to bind together again in harmonious union the lately warring sections, and to efface by the arts of peace the havoc and desolation inseparable from civil war.

And now the momentous question arises before the American people — to whose hands shall be confided the delicate trust of restoring the Union of our fathers? Not the Union of Calhoun and Polk and Pierce and Buchanan, which mutual distrust rendered a Union but in name. With a lavish expenditure of blood and treasure we have bought the right to demand that in future our country shall be one in feeling and in interest; that no jarring sections shall disturb the general harmony, but that a homogeneous and united people shall enjoy in peace and mutual good-will the priceless blessings which, under God, nature and our institutions rendered possible in our land. Who is there that can secure for us these results for which we have paid so heavy a price?

As Abraham Lincoln, on ascending the Presidential chair, paved the way to a restoration of the Union by establishing a long-forgotten confidence between the Government and the people, so he confirmed that confidence by showing himself the leader of the people and not of a party. If, in this, he has aroused the opposition of extremists who assisted to elect him, it but gives him an additional claim on reasonable men of all parties.

The great duty to which Mr. Lincoln has dedicated himself with rare singleness of purpose is the one thought which engrosses every true American heart — the re-establishment of the Union on a permanent basis. To this, all else for the moment is secondary, and every obstacle in its way must be removed. Few among us, at the outbreak, recognized that slavery was such an obstacle. We all imagined that a moderate display of force, accompanied by evidences that we wished no evil, save to those who had misled our brethren, would soon cause the South to confess its error and to return to those who were ready to welcome its repentance. Our generals were ordered to disturb as lightly as might be the framework of Southern society, and to protect the interests of individuals as no invading army ever guarded them before. Offers of assistance were made to suppress anticipated slave insurrections, and when Fremont in Missouri, and Hunter in South Carolina, undertook to interfere with the relations of master and slave, their acts were promptly disavowed, and they were recalled. Even in July, 1862, a threatened veto was interposed to soften the rigor of a confiscation act, which had a clear majority in the national councils.

The progress of the war dispelled many illusions, not the least of which was, that we could fight with gloves. We recognised that the tyranny of the Southern oligarchy was too strong and all pervading for us to expect aid from Southern Unionists, crushed to the earth and unable to take a step in defence of their rights. We found that slavery was not only the cause of the rebellion, but that, in place of being, as we had supposed, an inherent weakness, it was really a source of strength. Its destruction became, therefore, necessary to the overthrow of the rebel chiefs, and also to the permanency of the triumph of the national cause.

This last consideration, however, was slowly reached, and the Emancipation Proclamation was issued solely as a military measure. In September, 1862, Mr. Lincoln wrote to those who urged him to convert the war for the Union into a war against slavery —

"If there be those who would not save the Union unless they could, at the same time, save slavery, I do not agree with them.

"If there be those who would not save the Union, unless they could at the same time destroy slavery, I do not agree with them.

"My paramount object is to save the Union, and not either to save or destroy slavery."

In these terse sentences are embodied the sentiment which animates the great mass of the American people, and to this sentiment has Mr. Lincoln thoroughly proved his fidelity.

That the Emancipation Proclamation was a war measure, designed solely to destroy the power of rebellious resistance, and not to divert the war from its original design, is easily shown. A hundred days were given before it should take effect, in hopes that the rebels might avert it by laying down their arms. The door was held wide open for their return, for during those hundred days of grace, and before the repulse of Fredericksburg, in his letter to Fernando Wood, Mr. Lincoln promised "a full and general amnesty," if they would return to the Union and send representatives to the National Congress. Most men will think that this betrays over-eagerness for peace, when they reflect that for more than a year we might have had Davis and Benjamin, Lee and Slidell domineering in Congress, and that the approaching election would have been secured to the slave power by the customary alliance between the South and the Northern Democracy.

The rebels fortunately declined to avail themselves of this error. The hundred days elapsed, and the Proclamation took effect. As an exercise of the war power, it was undoubtedly justifiable. If the slave were regarded as property, aiding by his labor in the support of hostile armies, he could be seized and converted to our own use, like any other article of property. If he were a man, bound to us by community of interests, though inhabiting the enemy's territory, no law of war could prevent our accepting the assistance which he was so eager to tender. Circumstances had forced us to extend to rebels in arms the rights of belligerents, and with those rights they had also to accept the concurrent responsibilities.

The results of the war during the last twelve-month have not shown that the Proclamation was a mistake in military policy.

When Mr. Lincoln recommended the plan of compensated emancipation which was adopted by Congress, he showed that he recognised fully how great an element of future strife lay in the institution of slavery, and how beneficial to the whole country, its abolition would be. Yet he hesitated long to act upon his convictions, and he waited until the people should be prepared to support and endorse his views. Moderate in all his opinions, he wanted a gradual, not a violent change, and long after his Emancipation Proclamation was issued, he provoked the wrath of the radical emancipationists in Missouri, by lending what aid he constitutionally could, to the "conservatives" in that State, who desired that the extinction of slavery should be brought about gradually. Possibly in this Mr. Lincoln was mistaken, yet if so, the error arose from the desire which he has constantly manifested, to harmonize the conflicting interests of the country, even at the expense of temporary popularity.

The wisest statesman does not disdain to profit by experience, nor can the head of a popular government adopt measures of fundamental change before the people are ripe for them. It is probable that Mr. Lincoln learned much as the war wore on; at all events, the people did, and the conviction became steadily stronger as the forces of rebellion ebbed, that no peace could be lasting which should leave the slaveholders in possession of power to control the States of the South, and to weld them as of old, into one compact body, all powerful for offence or defence. Whole States had been wrested from the enemy, and were in an anomalous condition under military rule. Their position had to be defined, and this definition involved the permanent settlement of the slavery question and the mode by which the war would probably be terminated. These issues had to be promptly met, and upon their sagacious solution depended the destinies of the nation.

Theorists and enthusiasts eagerly contended that the territory won by our arms should be held as conquered provinces; fanatics demanded that the ancient proprietors of the soil should be expatriated, and that their lands should be given to the freedmen; Southern sympathizers urged that no rights had been forfeited by rebellion, and that each State should resume its position untrammelled, that our councils might again be ruled by the chivalry for whom the cohesive power of public plunder could in the future, as in the past, purchase abundance of Northern allies. Moderate men of all parties trembled before the mighty problem, so seemingly insoluble, until the AMNESTY PROCLAMATION came suddenly to relieve their doubts and fears, and to provoke the objurgations of enthusiasts, fanatics and sympathizers.

It is on this great measure that the reputation of Mr. Lincoln as a practical statesman, will chiefly rest. It dissociates the rebel leaders from those who have been entrapped or forced into treason; it modifies the harshness of confiscation laws by maintaining the rights of property of those who return to their allegiance; it points out the way by which the mass of the people can resume their civil and political privileges; it preserves the States from external interference, and commits their reform to the hands of their own citizens; it assures us against any resumption of the quarrel, by making the triumph of the national arms complete the suicide of slavery; and its exceptions from full amnesty draw the line about as well as it can be done in gross, subject of course to the innumerable exceptions which will be made in favor of those who may hereafter prove themselves worthy of grace. There is no danger, indeed, that a magnanimous people will be disposed to press its victory too sorely. Indemnity for the past will never be required. Security for the future is all that will be asked for, and this will be attained by a few examples, leaving the mass of the leaders to the punishment of their own consciences and the indignation of their outraged and deluded followers.

In the events which have crowded his presidential term, Mr. Lincoln has thus, by adhering with unwavering fidelity to the one great object of restoring the Union, succeeded in impressing upon friends and enemies the conviction of his caution, rectitude, firmness, and honesty of purpose. There are many who have richly earned the gratitude of the people for eminent services rendered to the Republic in the hour of her trials. There is no one who has so signally centered upon himself the confidence of all. There have been mistakes of detail in military, naval, and financial matters — mistakes inseparable from the sudden transition from profound and prolonged peace to civil war upon the largest scale. Yet in the general policy of the administration, in its principles of statesmanship, there have been few errors save those arising from a too generous disbelief in the sincerity of Southern madness. This disbelief the people shared with their rulers, and the policy now admitted to be indispensable would have been impossible at the earlier stage of the war, on account of the popular repugnance which it would have excited.

Had Mr. Lincoln moved faster than he has done, he would have left the people behind him, and lost the support without which no popular government can conduct an exhausting war. Had he moved more slowly, our resources would have been more reduced than they now are, while the rebellion would have been incomparably stronger, and the end would have been more distant than ever. As a MAN OF THE PEOPLE, understanding them and trusted by them, he has proved himself the man for the time. There is no one whose name so spontaneously evokes an instinct of kindly confidence; no one who so thoroughly understands the complicated details of our civil and military difficulties, and no one whose sagacity has shown itself so rarely at fault. If we are to have four or five years more of desperate war, it is barely possible that some military man may be found whose peculiar training may fit him better for the Commandership which is attached to our Chief Magistracy. If, however, the fighting shall be virtually ended by the fourth of March, 1865, and if the next Presidential term is to be occupied in removing the traces of civil war, in binding the nation together in indestructible bonds, in starting it anew on its high career of prosperity, and in forgetting all of the past save the lessons which it teaches — if such are to be the duties of the next four years, then no one can be named who unites, like Abraham Lincoln, the kindliness and firmness, the skill and experience, the native sagacity and honesty to bring about an harmonious settlement, and to extort from repentant rebels the implicit confidence which those high qualities have won from all loyal men.

Pamphlet 41

James Russell Lowell

The President's Policy. (Union League No. 71)

Philadelphia, 1864

[James Russell Lowell, not only an outstanding literary figure but also one of the most respected political commentators of his era, wrote a shrewd, balanced appraisal of the Lincoln administration for the January, 1864, *North American Review*. It was an effective presentation of the moderate Republican view. The Philadelphia Union League reprinted it in pamphlet form in March, 1864, to appear just after its own manifesto endorsing Lincoln. Lowell (1819–1891), a poet, professor, editor, literary critic, and some years later ambassador to the Court of St. James, had become famous during the Mexican War for his rhymed political satire, *The Biglow Papers*, sharply critical of the war. By the time of the secession crisis in 1861 his youthful radicalism had disappeared, and he wrote, "The matter at hand is the reestablishment of order, the reaffirmation of national unity, and the settling once for all whether there can be such a thing as government without the right to use its power in self-defense." During the Civil War he returned to the device of the *Biglow Papers;* moderation ran through this second series. It was logical in 1864 for Lowell to see merit in Lincoln's practical, middle course.[1]]

THERE have been many painful crisises since the impatient vanity of South Carolina hurried ten prosperous Commonwealths into a crime whose assured retribution was to leave them either at the mercy of the nation they had wronged, or of the anarchy they had summoned but could not control, when no thoughtful American opened his morning paper without dreading to find that he had no longer a country to love and honor. Whatever the result of the convulsion whose first shocks were beginning to be felt, there would still be enough square miles of earth for elbow-room; but that ineffable sentiment made up of memory and hope, of instinct and tra-

[1] Frederickson, *The Inner Civil War*, 59–60, 120–121. See also Wilson, *Patriotic Gore*, 474–479.]

dition, which swells every man's heart and shapes his thought, though perhaps never present to his consciousness, would be gone from it, leaving common earth and nothing more. Men might gather rich crops from it, but that ideal harvest of priceless associations would be reaped no longer; that fine virtue which sent up messages of courage and security from every sod of it would have evaporated beyond recall. We should be irrevocably cut off from our past, and be forced to splice the ragged ends of our lives upon whatever new conditions chance might twist for us.

We confess that we had our doubts at first, whether the patriotism of our people were not too narrowly provincial to embrace the proportions of national peril. We had an only too natural distrust of immense public meetings and enthusiastic cheers, and we knew that the plotters of rebellion had aroused a fanaticism of caste in the Southern States sure to hold out longer than that fanaticism of the flag which was preached in the North, for hatred has deeper roots than sentiment, though we knew also that frenzy would pass through its natural stages, to end in dejection, as surely in Carolina as in New York.

That a re-action should follow the holiday enthusiasm with which the war was entered on, that it should follow soon, and that the slackening of public spirit should be proportionate to the previous over-tension, might well be foreseen by all who had studied human nature or history. Men acting gregariously are always in extremes; as they are one moment capable of higher courage, so they are liable, the next, to baser depression, and it is often a matter of chance whether numbers shall multiply confidence or discouragement. Nor does deception lead more surely to distrust of men, than self-deception to suspicion of principles. The only faith that wears well and holds its color in all weathers, is that which is woven of conviction and set with the sharp mordant of experience. Enthusiasm is good material for the orator, but the statesman needs something more durable to work in, — must be able to rely on the deliberate reason and consequent firmness of the people, without which that presence of mind, no less essential in times of moral than of material peril, will be wanting at the critical moment. Would this fervor of the Free States hold out? Was it kindled by a just feeling of the value of constitutional liberty? Had it body enough to withstand the inevitable dampening of checks, reverses, delays? Had our population intelligence enough to comprehend that the choice was between order and anarchy, between the equilibrium of a government by law and the tussle of misrule by *pronunciamiento?* Could a war be maintained without the ordinary stimulus of hatred and plunder, and with the impersonal loyalty of principle? These were serious questions, and with no precedent to aid in answering them.

At the beginning of the war there was, indeed, occasion for the most anxious apprehension. A President known to be infected with the political heresies, and suspected of sympathy with the treason of the Southern conspirators, had just surrendered the reins, we will not say of power, but of chaos, to a successor known only as the representative of a party whose leaders, with long training in opposition, had none in the conduct of affairs; an empty treasury was called on to supply resources beyond precedent in the history of finance; the trees were yet growing and the iron unmined with which a navy was to be built and armored; officers without discipline were to make a mob into an army; and, above all, the public opinion of Europe, echoed and re-inforced with every vague hint and every specious argument of despondency by a powerful faction at home, was either contemptuously skeptical or actively hostile. It would be hard to over-estimate the force of this latter element of disintegration and discouragement among a people where every citizen at home, and every soldier in the field, is a reader of newspapers. The pedlers of rumor in the North were the most effective allies of the rebellion. A nation can be liable to no more insidious treachery than that of the telegraph, sending hourly its electric thrill of panic along the remotest nerves of the community, till the excited imagination makes every real danger loom heightened with its unreal double. The armies of Jefferson Davis have been more effectually strengthened by the phantom regiments of Northern newspapers, than by the merciless dragoonery of his conscription.

And even if we look only at more palpable difficulties, the problem to be solved by our civil war was so vast, both in its immediate relations and its future consequences; the conditions of its solution were so intricate and so greatly dependent on incalculable and uncontrollable contingencies; so many of the data, whether for hope or fear, were, from their novelty, incapable of arrangement under any of the categories of historical precedent, — that there were moments of crisis when the firmest believer in the strength and sufficiency of the democratic theory of government might well hold his breath in vague apprehension of disaster. Our teachers of political philosophy, solemnly arguing from the precedent of some petty Grecian, Italian, or Flemish city, whose long periods of aristocracy were broken now and then by awkward parentheses of mob, had always taught us that democracies were incapable of the sentiment of loyalty, of concentrated and prolonged effort, of far-reaching conceptions; were absorbed in material interests; impatient of regular, and much more of exceptional restraint; had no natural nucleus of gravitation, nor any forces but centrifugal; were always on the verge of civil war, and slunk at last into the natural almshouse of bankrupt popular government, a military despotism. Here was indeed a dreary outlook for persons who knew democracy, not by rubbing shoulders with it lifelong, but merely from books, and America only by the report of some fellow-Briton, who, having eaten a bad dinner or lost a carpet-bag here, had written to the Times demanding redress, and drawing a mournful inference of democratic instability. Nor were men wanting among ourselves who had so steeped their brains in London literature as to mistake Cockneyism for European culture, and contempt of their country for cosmopolitan breadth of view, and who, owing all they had and all they were to democracy, thought it had an air of high-breeding to join in the shallow epicedium that our bubble had burst. Others took up the Tory gabble, that all the political and military genius was on the side of the Rebels, and even yet are not weary of repeating it, when there is not one of Jefferson Davis' prophecies as to the course of events, whether at home or abroad, but has been utterly falsified by the event, when his finance has literally gone to rags, and when even the journals of his own capital are beginning to inquire how it is, that, while their armies are always victorious, the territory of the Confedracy is steadily diminishing.

But beside any disheartening influences which might affect the timid or the despondent, there were reasons enough of settled gravity against any over-confidence of hope. A war — which, whether we consider the expanse of the territory at stake, the hosts brought into the field, or the reach of the principles involved, may fairly be reckoned the most momentous of modern times — was to be waged by a people divided at home, unnerved by fifty years of peace, under a chief magistrate without experience and without reputation, whose every measure was sure to be cunningly hampered by a jealous and unscrupulous minority, and who, while dealing with unheard-of complications at home, must soothe a hostile neutrality abroad, waiting only a pretext to become war. All this was to be done without warning and without preparation, while at the same time a social revolution was to be accomplished in the political condition of four millions of people, by softening the prejudices, allaying the fears, and gradually obtaining the co-operation of their unwilling liberators. Surely, if ever there were an occasion when the heightened imagination of the historian might see Destiny visibly intervening in human affairs, here was a knot worthy of her shears. Never, perhaps, was any system of government tried by so continuous and searching a strain as ours during the last three years; never has any shown itself stronger; and never could that strength be so directly traced to the virtue and intelligence of the people, — to that general enlightenment and prompt efficiency of public opinion possible only under the influence of a political framework like our own. We find it hard to understand how even a foreigner should be blind to the grandeur of the combat of ideas that has been going on here, — to the heroic energy, persistency, and self-reliance of a nation proving that it knows how much dearer greatness is than mere power; and we own that it is impossible for us to conceive the mental and moral condition of the American who does not feel his spirit braced and heightened by being even a spectator of such qualities and achievements. That a steady purpose and a definite aim have been given to the jarring forces which, at the beginning of the war, spent themselves in the discussion of schemes which could only become operative, if at all, after the war was over; that a popular excitement has been slowly intensified into an earnest national will; that a somewhat impracticable moral sentiment has been made the unconscious instrument of a practical moral end; that the treason of covert enemies, the jealousy of rivals, the unwise zeal of friends, have been made not only useless for mischief, but even useful for good; that the conscientious sensitiveness of England to the horrors of civil conflict has been prevented from complicating a domestic with a foreign war; — all these results, any one of which might suffice to prove greatness in a ruler, have been mainly due to the good sense, the good humor, the sagacity, the large-mindedness, and the unselfish honesty of the unknown man whom a blind fortune, as it seemed,

had lifted from the crowd to the most dangerous and difficult eminence of modern times. It is by presence of mind in untried emer-
gencies that the native metal of a man is tested; it is by the sagacity
to see, and the fearless honesty to admit, whatever of truth there may
be in an adverse opinion, in order more convincingly to expose the
fallacy that lurks behind it, that a reasoner at length gains for his
mere statement of a fact the force of argument; it is by a wise forecast which allows hostile combinations to go so far as by the inevitable re-action to become elements of his own power, that a
politician proves his genius for state-craft; and especially it is by so
gently guiding public sentiment that he seems to follow it, by so
yielding doubtful points that he can be firm without seeming obsti-
nate in essential ones, and thus gain the advantages of compromise
without the weakness of concession, by so instinctively comprehending the temper and prejudices of a people as to make them gradually conscious of the superior wisdom of his freedom from temper
and prejudice, — it is by qualities such as these that a magistrate
shows himself worthy to be chief in a commonwealth of freemen.
And it is for qualities such as these that we firmly believe History
will rank Mr. Lincoln among the most prudent of statesmen and the
most successful of rulers. If we wish to appreciate him, we have only
to conceive the inevitable chaos in which we should now be welter-
ing, had a weak man or an unwise one, been chosen in his stead.

"Bare is back," says the Norse proverb, "without brother behind
it;" and this is, by analogy, true of an elective magistracy. The
hereditary ruler in any critical emergency may reckon on the inexhaustible resources of *prestige,* of sentiment, of superstition, of
dependent interest, while the new man must slowly and painfully
create all these out of the unwilling material around him, by superiority of character, by patient singleness of purpose, by sagacious
presentiment of popular tendencies and instinctive sympathy with
the national character. Mr. Lincoln's task was one of peculiar and
exceptional difficulty. Long habit had accustomed the American
people to the notion of a party in power, and of a President as its
creature and organ, while the more vital fact, that the executive for
the time being represents the abstract idea of government as a permanent principle superior to all party and all private interest, had
gradually become unfamiliar. They had so long seen the public
policy more or less directed by views of party, and often even of

personal advantage, as to be ready to suspect the motives of a chief magistrate compelled, for the first time in our history, to feel himself the head and hand of a great nation, and to act upon the fundamental maxim laid down by all publicists, that the first duty of a government is to defend and maintain its own existence. Accordingly, a powerful weapon seemed to be put into the hands of the opposition by the necessity under which the administration found itself of applying this old truth to new relations. They were not slow in turning it to use, but the patriotism and common sense of the people were more than a match for any sophistry of mere party. The radical mistake of the leaders of the opposition was in forgetting that they had a country, and expecting a similar obliviousness on the part of the people. In the undisturbed possession of office for so many years, they had come to consider the government as a kind of public Gift Enterprise conducted by themselves, and whose profits were nominally to be shared among the holders of their tickets, though all the prizes had a trick of falling to the lot of the managers. Amid the tumult of war, when the life of the nation was at stake, when the principles of despotism and freedom were grappling in deadly conflict, they had no higher conception of the crisis than such as would serve the purpose of a contested election; no thought but of advertising the tickets for the next drawing of that private speculation which they miscalled the Democratic party. But they were too little in sympathy with the American people to understand them, or the motives by which they were governed. It became more and more clear that, in embarrassing the administration, their design was to cripple the country; that, by a strict construction of the Constitution, they meant nothing more than the locking up of the only arsenal whence effective arms could be drawn to defend the nation. Fortunately, insincerity by its very nature, by its necessary want of conviction, must erelong betray itself by its inconsistencies. It was hard to believe that men had any real horror of sectional war, who were busy in fomenting jealousies between East and West; that they could be in favor of a war for the Union as it was, who were for accepting the violent amendments of Rebellion; that they could be heartily opposed to insurrection in the South who threatened government with forcible resistance in the North; or that they were humanely anxious to stay the effusion of blood, who did not scruple to stir up the mob of our chief city to murder and arson, and to compliment the patriotism of assassins with arms in their hands. Believers, if they believed anything, in the divine right of Sham, they brought the petty engineering of the caucus to cope with the resistless march of events, and hoped to stay the steady drift of the nation's purpose, always setting deeper and stronger in one direction, with the scoop-nets that had served their turn so well in dipping fish from the turbid eddies of politics. They have given an example of the shortest and easiest way of reducing a great party to an inconsiderable faction.

The change which three years have brought about is too remarkable to be passed over without comment, too weighty in its lesson not to be laid to heart. Never did a President enter upon office with less means at his command, outside his own strength of heart and steadiness of understanding, for inspiring confidence in the people, and so winning it for himself, than Mr. Lincoln. All that was known of him was that he was a good stump-speaker, nominated for his *availability,* — that is, because he had no history, — and chosen by a party with whose more extreme opinions he was not in sympathy. It might well be feared that a man past fifty, against whom the ingenuity of hostile partisans could rake up no accusation, must be lacking in manliness of character, in decision of principle, in strength of will, — that a man who was at best only the representative of a party, and who yet did not fairly represent even that, — would fail of political, much more of popular, support. And certainly no one ever entered upon office with so few resources of power in the past, and so many materials of weakness in the present, as Mr. Lincoln. Even in that half of the Union which acknowledged him as President, there was a large, and at that time dangerous minority, that hardly admitted his claim to the office, and even in the party that elected him, there was also a large minority that suspected him of being secretly a communicant with the Church of Laodicea. All that he did was sure to be virulently attacked as ultra by one side; all that he left undone, to be stigmatized as proof of lukewarmness and backsliding by the other. Meanwhile he was to carry on a truly colossal war by means of both; he was to disengage the country from diplomatic entanglements of unprecedented peril undisturbed by the help or the hindrance of either, and to win from the crowning dangers of his administration, in the confidence of the people, the means of his safety and their own. He has contrived to do it, and perhaps none of our Presidents since Washington has stood so firm in the confidence of the people as he does after three years of stormy administration.

Mr. Lincoln's policy was a tentative one, and rightly so. He laid down no programme which must compel him to be either inconsistent or unwise, no cast-iron theorem to which circumstances must be fitted as they rose, or else be useless to his ends. He seemed to have chosen Mazarin's motto, *Le temps et moi*. The *moi*, to be sure, was not very prominent at first; but it has grown more and more so, till the world is beginning to be persuaded that it stands for a character of marked individuality and capacity for affairs. Time was his prime-minister, and, we began to think at one period, his general-in-chief also. At first he was so slow that he tired out all those who see no evidence of progress but in blowing up the engine; then he was so fast, that he took the breath away from those who think there is no getting on safely while there is a spark of fire under the boilers. God is the only being who has time enough; but a prudent man, who knows how to seize occasion, can commonly make a shift to find as much as he needs. Mr. Lincoln, as it seems to us in reviewing his career, though we have sometimes in our impatience thought otherwise, has always waited, as a wise man should, till the right moment brought up all his reserves. *Semper nocuit differre paratis,* is a sound axiom, but the really efficacious man will also be sure to know when he is *not* ready, and be firm against all persuasion and reproach till he is.

One would be apt to think, from some of the criticisms made on Mr. Lincoln's course by those who mainly agree with him in principle, that the chief object of a statesman should be rather to proclaim his adhesion to certain doctrines, than to achieve their triumph by quietly accomplishing his ends. In our opinion, there is no more unsafe politician than a conscientiously rigid *doctrinaire,* nothing more sure to end in disaster than a theoretic scheme of policy that admits of no pliability for contingencies. True, there is a popular image of an impossible He, in whose plastic hands the submissive destinies of mankind become as wax, and to whose commanding necessity the toughest facts yield with the graceful pliancy of fiction; but in real life we commonly find that the men who control circumstances, as it is called, are those who have learned to allow for the influence of their eddies, and have the nerve to turn them to account at the happy instant. Mr. Lincoln's perilous task has been to cast a rather shackly raft through the rapids, making fast the unrulier logs as he could snatch opportunity, and the country is to be congratulated that he did not think it his duty to run straight at all hazards, but cautiously to assure himself with his setting-pole where the main current was, and keep steadily to that. He is still in wild water, but we have faith that his skill and sureness of eye will bring him out right at last.

A curious, and as we think, not inapt parallel, might be drawn between Mr. Lincoln and one of the most striking figures in modern history, — Henry IV. of France. The career of the latter may be more picturesque, as that of a daring captain always is; but in all its vicissitudes there is nothing more romantic than that sudden change, as by a rub of Aladdin's lamp, from the attorney's office in a country town of illinois, to the helm of a great nation in times like these. The analogy between the characters and circumstances of the two men is in many respects singularly close. Succeeding to a rebellion rather than a crown, Henry's chief material dependence was the Huguenot party, whose doctrines sat upon him with a looseness distasteful certainly, if not suspicious, to the more fanatical among them. King only in name over the greater part of France, and with his capital barred against him, it yet gradually became clear to the more far-seeing even of the Catholic party, that he was the only centre of order and legitimate authority round which France could re-organize itself. While preachers who held the divine right of kings made the churches of Paris ring with declamations in favor of democracy rather than submit to the heretic dog of a Béarnois, — much as our *soi-disant* Democrats have lately been preaching the divine right of slavery, and denouncing the heresies of the Declaration of Independence, — Henry bore both parties in hand till he was convinced that only one course of action could possibly combine his own interests and those of France. Meanwhile, the Protestants believed somewhat doubtfully that he was theirs, the Catholics hoped somewhat doubtfully that he would be theirs, and Henry himself turned aside remonstrance, advice, and curiosity alike with a jest or a proverb, (if a little *high*, he liked them none the worse,) joking continually as his manner was. We have seen Mr. Lincoln contemptuously compared to Sancho Panza by persons incapable of appreciating one of the deepest pieces of wisdom in the profoundest romance ever written; namely, that, while Don Quixote was incomparable in theoretic and ideal statesmanship, Sancho, with his stock of proverbs, the ready money of human experience, made the best possible practical governor. Henry IV. was as full of wise saws and modern instances as Mr. Lincoln, but beneath all this was the thoughtful, practical, humane, and thoroughly earnest man, around whom the fragments of France were to gather themselves till she took her place again as a planet of the first magnitude in the European system. In one respect Mr. Lincoln was more fortunate than Henry. However some may think him wanting in zeal, the most fanatical can find no taint of apostasy in any measure of his, nor can the most bitter charge him with being influenced by motives of personal interest. The leading distinction between the policies of the two is one of circumstances. Henry went over to the nation; Mr. Lincoln has steadily drawn the nation over to him. One left a united France; the other, we hope and believe, will leave a re-united America. We leave our readers to trace the further points of difference and resemblance for themselves, merely suggesting a general similarity which has often occurred to us. One only point of melancholy interest we will allow ourselves to touch upon. That Mr. Lincoln is not handsome nor elegant, we learn from certain English tourists who would consider similar revelations in regard to Queen Victoria as thoroughly American in their want of *bienséance*. It is no concern of ours, nor does it affect his fitness for the high place he so worthily occupies; but he is certainly as fortunate as Henry in the matter of good looks, if we may trust contemporary evidence. Mr. Lincoln has also been reproached with Americanism by some not unfriendly British critics; but, with all deference, we cannot say that we like him any the worse for it, or see in it any reason why he should govern Americans the less wisely.

The most perplexing complications that Mr. Lincoln's government has had to deal with have been the danger of rupture with the two leading commercial countries of Europe, and the treatment of the slavery question. In regard to the former, the peril may be considered as nearly past, and the latter has been withdrawing steadily, ever since the war began, from the noisy debating-ground of faction to the quieter region of practical solution by convincingness of facts and consequent advance of opinion which we are content to call Fate.

As respects our foreign relations, the most serious, or at least the most obvious, cause of anxiety has all along been the irritation and ill-will that have been growing up between us and England. The sore points on both sides have been skilfully exasperated by interested and unscrupulous persons, who saw in a war between the two countries the only hope of profitable return for their investment in Confederate stock, whether political or financial. The always supercilious, often insulting, and sometimes even brutal tone of British journals and public men, has certainly not tended to soothe whatever resentment might exist in America.

> Perhaps it was right to dissemble your love,
> But why did you kick me down stairs?

We have no reason to complain that England, as a necessary consequence of her clubs, has become a great society for the minding of other people's business, and we can smile good-naturedly when she lectures other nations on the sins of arrogance and conceit; but we may justly consider it a breach of the political *convenances* which are expected to regulate the intercourse of one well-bred government with another, when men holding places in the ministry allow themselves to dictate our domestic policy, to instruct us in our duty, and to stigmatize as unholy a war for the rescue of whatever a high-minded people should hold most vital and most sacred. Was it in good taste, that we may use the mildest term, for Earl Russell to expound our own Constitution to President Lincoln, or to make a new and fallacious application of an old phrase for our benefit, and tell us that the Rebels were fighting for independence and we for empire? As if all wars for independence were by nature just and deserving of sympathy, and all wars for empire ignoble and worthy only of reprobation, or as if these easy phrases in any way characterized this terrible struggle, — terrible not so truly in any superficial sense, as from the essential and deadly enmity of the principles that underlie it. His Lordship's bit of borrowed rhetoric would justify Smith O'Brien, Nana Sahib, and the Maori chieftains, while it would condemn nearly every war in which England has ever been engaged. Was it so very presumptuous in us to think that it would be decorous in English statesmen if they spared time enough to acquire some kind of knowledge, though of the most elementary kind, in regard to this country and the questions at issue here, before they pronounced so off-hand a judgment? Or is political information expected to come Dogberry-fashion in England, like reading and writing, by nature?

And now all respectable England is wondering at our irritability, and sees a quite satisfactory explanation of it in our national vanity. *Suave mari magno,* it is pleasant, sitting in the easy-chairs of Downing Street, to sprinkle pepper on the raw wounds of a kindred people struggling for life, and philosophical to find in self-conceit the cause of our instinctive resentment. Surely we were of all nations the least liable to any temptation of vanity at a time when the gravest anxiety and the keenest sorrow were never absent from our hearts. Nor is conceit the exclusive attribute of any one nation. The earliest of English travellers, Sir John Mandeville, took a less provincial view of the matter when he said, "that in whatever part of the earth men dwell, whether above or beneath, it seemeth always to them that dwell there that they go more right than any other folk."

It is time for Englishmen to consider whether there was nothing in the spirit of their press and of their leading public men calculated to rouse a just indignation, and to cause a permanent estrangement on the part of any nation capable of self-respect, and sensitively jealous, as ours then was, of foreign interference. Was there nothing in the indecent haste with which belligerent rights were conceded to the Rebels, nothing in the abrupt tone assumed in the Trent case, nothing in the fitting out of Confederate privateers, that might stir the blood of a people already overcharged with doubt, suspicion, and terrible responsibility? The laity in any country do not stop to consider points of law, but they have an instinctive appreciation of the *animus* that actuates the policy of a foreign nation; and in our own case they remembered that the British authorities in Canada did not wait till diplomacy could send home to England for her slow official tinder-box to fire the "Caroline." Add to this, what every sensible American knew, that the moral support of England was equal to an army of two hundred thousand men to the Rebels, while it insured us another year or two of exhausting war. Even if we must come to grief, the openly expressed satisfaction of a disinterested acquaintance, and his triumphant "I told you so's," are not soothing to the best-regulated nerves; but in regard to the bearing of England toward ourselves, it was not so much the spite of her words (though the time might have been more tastefully chosen) as the actual power for evil in them that we felt as a deadly wrong. Perhaps the most immediate and efficient cause of mere irritation was the sudden and unaccountable change of manner on the other side of the water. Only six months before, the Prince of Wales had come over to call us cousins; and everywhere it was nothing but "our American brethren," that great offshoot of British institutions in the New World, so almost identical with them in laws, language, and literature, — this last of the alliterative compliments being so bitterly true, that perhaps it will not be retracted even now. To this outburst of long-repressed affection we responded with genuine warmth, if with a little of the awkwardness of a poor relation bewildered with the sudden tightening of the ties of consanguinity when it is rumored that he has come into a large estate. Then came the rebellion, and, *presto!* a flaw in our titles was discovered, the plate we were promised at the family table is flung at our head, and we were again the scum of creation, intolerably vulgar, at once cowardly and over-bearing, — no relations of theirs, after all, but a dreggy hybrid of the basest bloods of Europe. Panurge was not quicker to call Friar John his *former* friend. We could not help thinking of Walter Mapes's jingling paraphrase of Petronius, —

> Dummodo sim splendidis vestibus ornatus,
> Et multa familia sim circumvallatus,
> Prudens sum et sapiens et morigeratus,
> Et tuus nepos sum et tu meus cognatus, —

which we may freely render thus:

> So long as I was prosperous, I'd dinners by the dozen,
> Was well-bred, witty, virtuous, and everybody's cousin:
> If luck should turn, as well she may, her fancy is so flexile,
> Will virtue, cousinship, and all return with her from exile?

There was nothing in all this to exasperate a philosopher, much to make him smile rather; but the earth's surface is not chiefly inhabited by philosophers, and we revive the recollection of it now in perfect good humor, merely by way of suggesting to our *ci-devant* British cousins, that it would have been easier for them to hold their tongues than for us to keep our tempers under the circumstances.

The English Cabinet made a blunder, unquestionably, in taking it so hastily for granted that the United States had fallen forever from their position as a first-rate power, and it was natural that they should vent a little of their vexation on the people whose inexplicable obstinacy in maintaining freedom and order, and in resisting degradation, was likely to convict them of their mistake. But if bearing a grudge be the sure mark of a small mind in the individual, can it be a proof of high spirit in a nation? If the result of the present estrangement between the two countries shall be to make us more independent of British criticism, so much the better; but if it is to make us insensible to the value of British opinion, in matters where it gives us the judgment of an impartial and cultivated outsider, if we are to shut ourselves out from the advantages of English culture, the loss will be ours and not theirs. Because the door of the old homestead has been once slammed in our faces, shall we in a huff reject all future advances of conciliation, and cut ourselves foolishly off from any share in the humanizing influences of the place, with its ineffable riches of association, its heirlooms of immemorial culture, its historic monuments, ours no less than theirs, its noble gallery of ancestral portraits? We have only to succeed, and England will not only respect, but, for the first time, begin to understand us. And let us not, in our justifiable indignation at wanton insult, forget that England is not the England only of the snobs who dread the democracy they do not comprehend, but the England of history, of heroes, statesmen, and poets, whose names are dear, and their influence as salutary to us as to her.

Undoubtedly slavery was the most delicate and embarrassing question with which Mr. Lincoln was called on to deal, and it was one which no man in his position, whatever his opinions, could evade; for, though he might withstand the clamor of partisans, he must sooner or later yield to the persistent importunacy of circumstances, which thrust the problem upon him at every turn and in every shape. He must solve the riddle of this new Sphinx, or be devoured. Though Mr. Lincoln's policy in this critical affair has not been such as to satisfy those who demand an heroic treatment for even the most trifling occasion, and who will not cut their coat according to their cloth unless they can borrow the scissors of Atropos, it has been at least not unworthy of the long-headed king of Ithaca. Mr. Lincoln had the choice of Antonio offered him. Which of the three caskets held the prize which was to redeem the fortunes of the country? There was the golden one whose showy speciousness might have tempted a vain man; the silver of compromise, which might have decided the choice of a merely acute one; and the leaden, — dull and homely-looking, as prudence always is, — yet with something about it sure to attract the eye of practical wisdom. Mr. Lincoln dallied with his decision perhaps longer than seemed needful to those on whom its awful responsibility was not to rest, but when he made it, it was worthy of his cautious but sure-footed understanding. The moral of the Sphinx-riddle, and it is a deep one, lies in the childish simplicity of the solution. Those who fail in guessing it, fail because they are over-ingenious, and cast about for an answer that shall suit their own notion of the gravity of the occasion and of their own dignity, rather than the occasion itself.

In a matter which must be finally settled by public opinion, and in regard to which the ferment of prejudice and passion on both sides has not yet subsided to that equilibrium of compromise from which alone a sound public opinion can result, it is proper enough for the private citizen to press his own convictions with all possible force of argument and persuasion; but the popular magistrate, whose judgment must become action, and whose action involves the whole country, is bound to wait till the sentiment of the people is so far advanced toward his own point of view, that what he does shall find support in it, instead of merely confusing it with new elements of division. It was not unnatural that men earnestly devoted to the saving of their country, and profoundly convinced that slavery was its only real enemy, should demand a decided policy round which all patriots might rally, — and this might have been the wisest course for an absolute ruler. But in the then unsettled state of the public mind, with a large party decrying even resistance to the slaveholders's rebellion as not only unwise, but even unlawful; with a majority, perhaps, even of the would-be loyal so long accustomed to regard the Constitution as a deed of gift conveying to the South their own judgment as to policy and instinct as to right, that they were in doubt at first whether their loyalty were due to the country or to slavery; and with a respectable body of honest and influential men who still believed in the possibility of conciliation, — Mr. Lincoln judged wisely, that, in laying down a policy in deference to one party, he should be giving to the other the very fulcrum for which their disloyalty had been waiting.

It behooved a clear-headed man in his position not to yield so far to an honest indignation against the brokers of treason in the

North, as to lose sight of materials for misleading which were their stock in trade, and to forget that it is not the falsehood of sophistry which is to be feared, but the grain of truth mingled with it to make it specious, — that is not the knavery of the leaders so much as the honesty of the followers they may seduce, that gives them power for evil. It was especially his duty to do nothing which might help the people to forget the true cause of the war in fruitless disputes about its inevitable consequences.

The doctrine of State rights can be so handled by an adroit demagogue as easily to confound the distinction between liberty and lawlessness in the minds of ignorant persons, accustomed always to be influenced by the sound of certain words, rather than to reflect upon the principles which gave them meaning. For, though Secession involves the manifest absurdity of denying to a State the right of making war against any foreign power while permitting it against the United States; though it supposes a compact of mutual concessions and guarantees among States without any arbiter in case of dissention; though it contradicts common sense in assuming that the men who framed our government did not know what they meant when they substituted Union for Confederation; though it falsifies history, which shows that the main opposition to the adoption of the Constitution was based on the argument that it did not allow that independence in the several States which alone would justify them in seceding; — yet, as slavery was universally admitted to be a reserved right, an inference could be drawn from any direct attack upon it (though only in self-defence) to a natural right of resistance, logical enough to satisfy minds untrained to detect fallacy, as the majority of men always are, and now too much disturbed by the disorder of the times, to consider that the order of events had any legitimate bearing on the argument. Though Mr. Lincoln was too sagacious to give the Northern allies of the rebels the occasion they desired and even strove to provoke, yet from the beginning of the war the most persistent efforts have been made to confuse the public mind as to its origin and motives, and to drag the people of the loyal States down from the national position they had instinctively taken to the old level of party squabbles and antipathies. The wholly unprovoked rebellion of an oligarchy proclaiming negro slavery the cornerstone of free institutions, and in the first flush of over-hasty confidence venturing to parade the logical sequence of their leading dogma, "that slavery is right in principle, and has nothing to do with difference of complexion," has been represented as a legitimate and gallant attempt to maintain the true principles of democracy. The rightful endeavor of an established government, the least onerous that ever existed, to defend itself against a treacherous attack on its very existence, has been cunningly made to seem the wicked effort of a fanatical clique to force its doctrines on an oppressed population.

Even so long ago as when Mr. Lincoln, not yet convinced of the danger and magnitude of the crisis, was endeavoring to persuade himself of Union majorities at the South, and to carry on a war that was half peace in the hope of a peace that would have been all war, — while he was still enforcing the Fugitive Slave Law, under some theory that Secession, however it might absolve States from their obligations,[2] could not escheat them of their claims under the Constitution, and that slaveholders in rebellion had alone among mortals the privilege of having their cake and eating it at the same time, — the enemies of free government were striving to persuade the people that the war was an Abolition crusade. To rebel without reason, was proclaimed as one of the rights of man, while it was carefully kept out of sight that to suppress rebellion is the first duty of government. All the evils that have come upon the country, have been attributed to the Abolitionists, though it is hard to see how any party can become permanently powerful except in one of two ways, — either by the greater truth of its principles, or the extravagance of the party opposed to it. To fancy the ship of state, riding safe at her constitutional moorings, suddenly engulfed by a huge kraken of Abolitionism, rising from unknown depths and grasping it with slimy tentacles, is to look at the natural history of the matter with the eyes of Pontoppidan. To believe that the leaders in the Southern treason feared any danger from Abolitionism, would be to deny them ordinary intelligence, though there can be little doubt that they made use of it to stir the passions and excite the fears of their deluded accomplices. They rebelled, not because they thought slavery weak, but because they believed it strong enough, not to overthrow the government,

[2] This is a misconception, as the President never had a theory that Secession might absolve States from their obligations. — *Ed.*

but to get possession of it; for it becomes daily clearer that they used rebellion only as a means of revolution, and if they got revolution, though not in the shape they looked for, is the American people to save them from its consequences at the cost of its own existence? The election of Mr. Lincoln, which it was clearly in their power to prevent had they wished, was the occasion merely, and not the cause of their revolt. Abolitionism, till within a year or two, was the despised heresy of a few earnest persons, without political weight enough to carry the election of a parish constable; and their cardinal principle was disunion, because they were convinced that within the Union the position of slavery was impregnable. In spite of the proverb, great effects do not follow from small causes, — that is, disproportionately small, — but from adequate causes acting under certain required conditions. To contrast the size of the oak with that of the parent acorn, as if the poor seed had paid all costs from its slender strong-box, may serve for a child's wonder; but the real miracle lies in that divine league which bound all the forces of nature to the service of the tiny germ in fulfilling its destiny. Everything has been at work for the past ten years in the cause of anti-slavery, but Garrison and Phillips have been far less successful propagandists than the slaveholders themselves, with the constantly-growing arrogance of their pretensions and encroachments. They have forced the question upon the attention of every voter in the Free States, by defiantly putting freedom and democracy on the defensive. But, even after the Kansas outrages, there was no wide spread desire on the part of the North to commit aggressions, though there was a growing determination to resist them. The popular unanimity in favor of the war three years ago, was but in small measure the result of anti-slavery sentiment, far less of any zeal for abolition. But every month of the war, every movement of the allies of slavery in the Free States, has been making abolitionists by the thousand. The masses of any people, however intelligent, are very little moved by abstract principles of humanity and justice, until those principles are interpreted for them by the stinging commentary of some infringement upon their own rights, and then their instincts and passions, once aroused, do indeed derive an incalculable reinforcement of impulse and intensity from those higher ideas, those sublime traditions, which have no motive political force till they are allied with a sense of immediate personal wrong or imminent peril. Then at last the stars in their courses begin to fight against Sisera. Had any one doubted before that the rights of human nature are unitary, that oppression is of one hue the world over, no matter what the color of the oppressed; — had any one failed to see what the real essence of the contest was, — the efforts of the advocates of slavery among ourselves to throw discredit upon the fundamental axioms of the Declaration of Independence and the radical doctrines of Christianity, could not fail to sharpen his eyes. This quarrel, it is plain, is not between Northern fanaticism and Southern institutions, but between downright slavery and upright freedom, between despotism and democracy, between the Old World and the New.

The progress of three years has outstripped the expectation of the most sanguine, and that of our arms, great as it undoubtedly is, is trifling in comparison with the advance of opinion. The great strength of slavery was a superstition, which is fast losing its hold on the public mind. When it was first proposed to raise negro regiments, there were many even patriotic men who felt as the West Saxons did at seeing their high-priest hurl his lance against the temple of their idol. They were sure something terrible, they knew not what, would follow. But the earth stood firm, the heavens gave no sign, and presently they joined in making a bonfire of their bugbear. That we should employ the material of the rebellion for its own destruction, seems now the merest truism. In the same way men's minds are growing wonted to the thought of emancipation; and great as are the difficulties which must necessarily accompany and follow so vast a measure, we have no doubt that they will be successfully overcome. The point of interest and importance is, that the feeling of the country in regard to slavery is no whim of sentiment, but a settled conviction, and that the tendency of opinion is unmistakably and irrevocably in one direction, no less in the Border Slave States than in the Free. The chances of the war, which at one time seemed against us, are now greatly in our favor. The nation is more thoroughly united against any shameful or illusory peace than it ever was on any other question, and the very extent of the territory to be subdued, which was the most serious cause of misgiving, is no longer an element of strength, but of disintegration, to the conspiracy. The Rebel leaders can make no concessions;

the country is unanimously resolved that the war shall be prosecuted, at whatever cost; and if the war go on, will it leave slavery
with any formidable strength in the South? and without that, need
there be any fear of effective opposition in the North?

While every day was bringing the people nearer to the conclusion
which all thinking men saw to be inevitable from the beginning, it
was wise in Mr. Lincoln to leave the shaping of his policy to
events. In this country, where the rough and ready understanding
of the people is sure at last to be the controlling power, a profound
common-sense is the best genius for statesmanship. Hitherto the
wisdom of the President's measures have been justified by the fact
that they have always resulted in more firmly uniting public opinion. It is a curious comment on the sincerity of political professions, that the party calling itself Democratic should have been
the last to recognise the real movement and tendency of the popular
mind. The same gentlemen who two years ago were introducing
resolutions in Congress against coercion, are introducing them now
in favor of the war, but against subjugation. Next year they may
be in favor of emancipation, but against abolition. It does not seem
to have occurred to them that the one point of difference between
a civil and a foreign war is, that in the former, one of the parties
must by the very nature of the case be put down, and the other left
in possession of the government. Unless the country is to be divided,
no compromise is possible, and if one side must yield, shall it be
the nation or the conspirators? A government may make, and any
wise government would make, concessions to men who have risen
against real grievances; but to make them in favor of a rebellion
that had no juster cause than the personal ambition of a few bad
men, would be to abdicate. Southern politicians, however, have
always been so dexterous in drawing nice distinctions, that they
may find some consolation inappreciable by obtuser minds in being
coerced instead of subjugated.

If Mr. Lincoln continues to act with the firmness and prudence
which have hitherto distinguished him, we think he has little to fear
from the efforts of the opposition. Men without sincere convictions are hardly likely to have a well-defined and settled policy,
and the blunders they have hitherto committed must make them
cautious. If their personal hostility to the President be unabated,
we may safely count on their leniency to the opinion of majorities,

and the drift of public sentiment is too strong to be mistaken. They have at last discovered that there is such a thing as Country, which has a meaning for men's minds and a hold upon their hearts; they may make the further discovery, that this is a revolution that has been forced on us, and not merely a civil war. In any event, an opposition is a wholesome thing; and we are only sorry that this is not a more wholesome opposition.

We believe it is the general judgment of the country on the acts of the present administration, that they have been, in the main, judicious and well-timed. The only doubt about some of them seems to be as to their constitutionality. It has been sometimes objected to our form of government, that it was faulty in having a written constitution which could not adapt itself to the needs of the time as they arose. But we think it rather a theoretic than a practical objection; for in point of fact there has been hardly a leading measure of any administration, that has not been attacked as unconstitutional, and which was not carried nevertheless. Purchase of Louisianna, Embargo, Removal of the Deposits, Annexation of Texas, not to speak of others less important, — on the unconstitutionality of all these, powerful parties have appealed to the country, and invariably the decision has been against them. The will of the people for the time being has always carried it. In the present instance, we purposely refrain from any allusion to the moral aspects of the question. We prefer to leave the issue to experience and common sense. Has any sane man ever doubted on which side the chances were in this contest? Can any sane man who has watched the steady advances of opinion, forced onward slowly by the immitigable logic of facts, doubt what the decision of the people will be in this matter? The Southern conspirators have played a desperate stake, and, if they had won, would have bent the whole policy of the country to the interests of slavery. Filibustering would have been nationalized, and the slave-trade reestablished as the most beneficent form of missionary enterprise. But if they lose? They have, of their own choice, put the chance into our hands of making this continent the empire of a great homogeneous population, substantially one in race, language, and religion, — the most prosperous and powerful of nations. Is there a doubt what the decision of a victorious people will be? If we were base enough to decline the great commission which Destiny lays on us, should we not deserve to be ranked with those dastards whom the stern Florentine condemns as hateful alike to God and God's enemies?

We would not be understood as speaking lightly of the respect due to constitutional forms, all the more essential under a government like ours and in times like these. But where undue respect for the form will lose us the substance, and where the substance, as in this case, is nothing less than the country itself, to be over-scrupulous would be unwise. Who are most tender in their solicitude that we keep sacred the letter of the law, in order that its spirit may not keep us alive? Mr. Jefferson Davis and those who, in the Free States, would have been his associates, but must content themselves with being his political *guerilleros*. If Davis had succeeded, would he have had any scruples of constitutional delicacy? And if he has not succeeded, is it not mainly owing to measures which his disappointed partisans denounce as unconstitutional?

We cannot bring ourselves to think that Mr. Lincoln has done anything that would furnish a precedent dangerous to our liberties, or in any way overstepped the just limits of his constitutional discretion. If his course has been unusual, it was because the danger was equally so. It cannot be so truly said that he has strained his prerogative, as that the imperious necessity has exercised its own. Surely the framers of the Constitution never dreamed that they were making a strait waistcoat, in which the nation was to lie helpless while traitors were left free to do their will. In times like these, men seldom settle precisely the principles on which they *shall* act, but rather adjust those on which they *have* acted to the lines of precedent as well as they can after the event. This is what the English Parliament did in the Act of Settlement. Congress, after all, will only be called on for the official draft of an enactment, the terms of which have been already decided by agencies beyond their control. Even while they are debating, the current is sweeping them on toward new relations of policy. At worst, a new precedent is pretty sure of pardon, if it successfully meet a new occasion. It is a harmless pleasantry to call Mr. Lincoln "Abraham the First," — we remember when a similar title was applied to President Jackson; and it will not be easy, we suspect, to persuade a people who have more liberty than they know what to do with, that they are the victims of despotic tyranny.

Mr. Lincoln probably thought it more convenient, to say the least, to have a country left without a constitution, than a constitution without a country. We have no doubt we shall save both; for if we take care of the one, the other will take care of itself. Sensible men, and it is the sensible men in any country who at last shape its policy, will be apt to doubt whether it is true conservatism, after the fire is got under, to insist on keeping up the flaw in the chimney by which it made its way into the house. Radicalism may be a very dangerous thing, and so is calomel, but not when it is the only means of saving the life of the patient. Names are of great influence in ordinary times, when they are backed by the *vis inertiæ* of life-long prejudice, but they have little power in comparison with a sense of interest; and though, in peaceful times, it may be highly respectable to be conservative merely for the sake of being so, though without very clear notions of anything in particular to be conserved, what we want now is the prompt decision that will not hesitate between the bale of silk and the ship when a leak is to be stopped. If we succeed in saving the great landmarks of freedom, there will be no difficulty in settling our constitutional boundaries again. We have no sympathy to spare for the pretended anxieties of men who, only two years gone, were willing that Jefferson Davis should break all the ten commandments together, and would now impeach Mr. Lincoln for a scratch on the surface of the tables where they are engraved.

We cannot well understand the theory which seems to allow the Rebels some special claim to protection by the very Constitution which they rose in arms to destroy. Still less can we understand the apprehensions of many persons lest the institution of slavery should receive some detriment, as if it were the balance-wheel of our system, instead of its single element of disturbance. We admit that we always have thought, and think still, that the great object of the war should be the restoration of the Union at all hazards, and at any sacrifice short of honor. And however many honest men may scruple as to law, there can be no doubt that we are put under bonds of honor by the President's proclamation. If the destruction of slavery is to be a consequence of the war, shall we regret it? If it be needful to the successful prosecution of the war, shall any one oppose it? Is it out of the question to be constitutional, without putting the slaveholders back precisely where they were before they began the rebellion? This seems to be the ground taken by the opposition, but it becomes more and more certain that the people, instructed by the experience of the past three years, will never consent to any plan of adjustment that does not include emancipation. If Congress need any other precedent than *salus populi suprema lex* for giving the form and force of law to the public will, they may find one in the act of Parliament which abolished the feudal privileges of the Highland chiefs in 1747. A great occasion is not to be quibbled with, but to be met with that clear-sighted courage which deprives all objections of their force, if it does not silence them. To stop short of the only measure that can by any possibility be final and decisive, would be to pronounce rebellion a harmless eccentricity. To interpret the Constitution has hitherto been the exclusive prerogative of Slavery: it will be strange if Freedom cannot find a clause in it that will serve her purpose. To scruple at disarming our deadliest foe, would be mere infatuation. We can conceive of nothing parallel, except to have had it decided that the arrest of Guy Fawkes and the confiscation of his materials were a violation of Magna Charta; that he should be put back in the cellar of Westminster palace, his gunpowder, his matches, his dark-lantern, restored to him, with handsome damages for his trouble, and Parliament assembled overhead to give him another chance for the free exercise of his constitutional rights.

We believe, and our belief is warranted by experience, that all measures will be found to have been constitutional at last on which the people are overwhelmingly united. We must not lose sight of the fact, that whatever is *extra*-constitutional is not necessarily *un*-constitutional. The recent proclamation of amnesty will, we have no doubt, in due time bring a vast accession of strength to the emancipationists from the slaveholding States themselves. The danger of slavery has always been in the poor whites of the South; and wherever freedom of the press penetrates, — and it always accompanies our armies, — the evil thing is doomed. Let no one who remembers what has taken place in Maryland and Missouri think such anticipations visionary. The people of the South have been also put to school during these three years, under a sharper schoolmistress, too, than even ours has been, and the deadliest enemies of slavery will be found among those who have suffered most from its indirect evils. It is only by its extinction — for with-

out it no secure union would be possible — that the sufferings
and losses of the war can be repaid. That extinction accomplished,
our wounds will not be long in healing. Apart from the slaveholding class, which is numerically small, and would be socially insignificant without its privileges, there are no such mutual antipathies between the two sections as the conspirators, to suit their
own purposes, have asserted, and even done their best to excite.
We do not like the Southerners less for the gallantry and devotion
they have shown even in a bad cause, and they have learned to
respect the same qualities in us. There is no longer the nonsen-
sical talk about Cavaliers and Puritans, nor does the one gallant
Southerner any longer pine for ten Yankees as the victims of his
avenging steel. As for subjugation, when people are beaten they
are beaten, and every nation has had its turn. No sensible man
in the North would insist on any terms except such as are essential
to assure the stability of peace. To talk of the South as our future
Poland is to talk without book; for no region rich, prosperous, and
free could ever become so. It is a geographical as well as a moral
absurdity. With peace restored, slavery rooted out, and harmony
sure to follow, we shall realize a power and prosperity beyond
even the visions of the Fourth of July orator, and we shall see Freedom, while she proudly repairs the ruins of war, as the Italian poet
saw her, —

> Girar la Libertà mirai
> E baciar lieta ogni ruina e dire
> Ruin sí, ma servitù non mai.

Pamphlet 42

David Ames Wells

Our Burden and Our Strength, or, A Comprehensive and Popular Examination of the Debt and Resources of Our Country, Present and Prospective.

(*Loyal Publication Society No. 54*)

New York, 1864

[There was gloom and despondency in the North throughout the summer of 1864. Lee's army was inflicting punishing losses on Grant's forces, which seemed as far away from Richmond as ever. The war was costing a million dollars a day, a frightening sum, and the national debt was up to two and a half billion dollars. Greenback currency was depreciating, and prices seemed to be rising almost as fast as the number of casualties. There was serious question both at home and in Europe whether the Federal Union could remain solvent. Confederate propagandists were effectively contrasting the wavering greenback with the steady high price of cotton. George Palmer Putnam, a New York publisher and one of the active members of the Loyal Publication Society, was disturbed by a Confederate pamphlet his son sent him from Germany. He urged a friend and former publishing associate, David A. Wells, up to this time a scientific writer, to analyze the capability of the United States to pay its present and potential debt. Wells prepared a lengthy paper which he delivered early in 1864 in Troy, New York. Admirers published it in Troy in an abridged form. Putnam easily persuaded the Loyal Publication Society to issue it in a large edition — ultimately a hundred thousand copies. Altogether a quarter million copies circulated. Many were sent to banking representatives and consuls in Europe, and the pamphlet was translated into a number of other languages. Quite possibly it helped bolster the credit of the United States; it launched Wells upon a long career as an economic writer. Wells (1828–1898) became chairman of the National Revenue Commission in 1865, and then spent five years as special commissioner of the Revenue. An orthodox exponent of *laissez-faire*, he was a tax reformer and an opponent of the income tax, depreciated money, and protective tariffs.][1]

[1] [Herbert R. Ferleger, *David A. Wells and the American Revenue System, 1865–1870* (New York, 1942); Fred B. Joyner, *David Ames Wells, Champion of Free Trade*

CAN we pay our present and prospective National Debt, or even the interest upon it? Can we bear without impoverishment as a people, the burden of our present or future necessary taxation? These are questions which the continuance of the war and the exigencies of the times continually call up in the hearts, if they do not prompt to utterance upon the lips, of multitudes of our citizens.

All are more or less familiar with the general facts respecting the increase of the population of our country and its wondrous development in wealth and resources; but few have been enabled to bring the subject so definitely and clearly before them as to draw from it that trust and encouragement for the future, which it is certainly capable of affording. Recognizing this fact, it has occurred to the writer that good and timely service might now be rendered to the country, by instituting a large and accurate inquiry concerning our national ability — present and prospective — to pay our maximum future debt, *interest* and *principal;* and rising from this study, with the highest degree of encouragement, he begs leave to call the attention of his fellow-citizens to the statistics which he has been enabled to collect; hoping thereby, that the faith they feel in our ultimate and triumphant success, may be made the stronger; that anxiety and fear may be, in a degree, banished from their hearts; and by means of a courage justly entertained, and duties consequently well performed, they may aid in reducing the fluctuations of the currency; may sustain the laborer and the capitalist in their right relations; may help to give the dollar its just value; to labor its full reward; and by seeing that the production of national wealth is still advancing with giant strides, and that the war does not and cannot retard its progress, they may be further assured that the credit and honor of the country are to be amply and perfectly sustained.

The discussion of the topics involved in such an inquiry, must, of necessity, be mainly statistical, and therefore will undoubtedly be judged by some, *à priori,* as dry and uninteresting; for un-

(Cedar Rapids, Iowa, 1939). There were other pamphlets emphasizing the solvency of the North. Among the more significant were: William Elder, *Debt and Resources of the United States: and the Effect of Secession upon the Trade and Industry of the Loyal States* (Union League No. 37, Philadelphia, 1863); Samuel B. Ruggles, *Resources of the United States. Report to the International Statistical Congress at Berlin* (Loyal Publication Society No. 48, New York, 1864); and William E. Dodge, *Influence of the War on Our National Prosperity. A Lecture, Delivered in Baltimore, Md. on Monday Evening, March 13th, 1865* (New York, 1865).]

fortunately there are many disciples, in all countries, of the old Pasha, described by an English traveller, who, when asked to lend his authority to aid in the collection of statistical information, exclaimed, "Oh, joy of my liver, I have been sixty years in this province, and twenty years governor of this town, but never yet have I inquired as to the number of tiles on the houses, nor what kind of dirt the people take away in their carts. Mashallah! life is short, let us enjoy its blessings and ask no questions." If there are any such, perchance, among our readers, to them we shall offer no apology, but enter at once upon our subject.

Previous to 1861, the United States stood before the world in the anomalous position of a great nation, with substantially no national debt. Having since conformed in this respect to the usages of all other civilized people, it is desirable, in the outset of this inquiry, to compare our debt and its distribution *per capita* with the national debt of the leading nations of Europe. For this comparison we assume that the debt of the Federal Government, which at the close of the fiscal year in June, 1864, was about $1,750,000,000, will, at the close of the war, amount to $3,000,000,000 (three thousand millions), an amount which, with proper annual taxation, certainly ought not to be exceeded. The various figures tabulated, will then afford us the following exhibit: [See table on p. 943.]

It would thus appear from the [given] table (the figures and estimates of which are, it is believed, entirely reliable) that assuming the actual national debt at the close of the federal fiscal year, June, 1864, to be $1,750,000,000, the apportionment of debt to each individual of the loyal States would be $72.92, and of the annual interest $3.01. If we assume further, that the war terminates at or before the close of 1865, and that the national debt has reached at that period the sum of $3,000,000,000, then the debt for the population of the restored Union, will average $82.35 for each individual, and the annual interest $5.35. Supposing the debt to remain the same, (*i. e.*, $3,000,000,000) and the population to increase in the ratio of only 30 per cent. for each decennial period, the table shows the rapid decrease of individual liability for debt and interest during the remaining years of the present century.

The average increase of the population of the United States prior to 1860, has been generally assumed by statisticians, to have been at the rate of three per cent. per annum. That the actual increase

TABLE

Showing the present and prospective debt, interest and population of the United States, with the present debt, interest and population of Great Britain, France, Austria, Italy, and Holland.

	Public Debt.	Population.	Annual Interest.	Debt to each person.	Av. Interest to each person.
United Loyal States, July, 1864..........	$1,750,000,000	24,900,000	$ 75,000,000[2]	$72,92	$3.01
At the close of the war, assumed to take place in 1865..............	3,000,000,000	34,000,000	180,000,000	82.35	5.35
In 1870, assuming 30 per cent. as the average decennial increase of population[3]..........	3,000,000,000	40,950,000	180,000,000	73.26	4.38[4]
In 1880, do.	3,000,000,000	53,235,000	180,000,000	56.34	3.38
In 1890, do.	3,000,000,000	69,205,500	180,000,000	43.35	2.60
In 1900, do.	3,000,000,000	89,964,150	180,000,000	33.34	2.00
Great Britain, March, 1863..............	3,915,000,000	30,000,000	127,564,000	130.46	4.25
France, 1862..........	2,206,000,000	37,000,000	110,000,000	59.65	3.00
Austria, 1862..........	1,263,000,000	35,000,000		36.10	
Italy, 1863.............	764,000,000	22,000,000		34.73	
Holland, 1863..........	424,500,000	3,600,000	12,244,000	117.00	3.40

has, however, been always in excess of this ratio will be seen by the table [p. 944], in which the increase of the population of the United States is given for each decennial period since the establishment of the Constitution, and also the increase of the population of Great Britain during the same period; of France since the year 1801; and of Prussia since 1816.

Having thus presented an exhibit of our present and prospective national liabilities (in comparison with those of the leading

[2] Of the debt of the Loyal States, July 1st, 1864, as above given, an amount at least equal to $500,000,000 (existing in the form of currency) is not chargeable with interest.

[3] See table of population from 1790 to 1860, which follows.

[4] It must be borne in mind, in comparing the interest account of the debt of the United States with that of Great Britain and the other European states, that the rate per cent. varies greatly. In Great Britain the average rate of interest paid on the National debt does not exceed 3½ per cent. In France the highest rate paid is 4½ per cent. while much of the French debt pays a rate as low as 3 per cent.

TABLE

Showing the actual and percentage increase of the population of the United States by decades, from 1790 to 1860; of Great Britain, from 1793 to 1861; of France, from 1801 to 1861; and of Prussia, from 1816 to 1861.

	Year.	Population.	Increase per cent. by Decades.
United States.............	1790	3,929,827	
Great Britain.............	1793	14,500,000	
United States.............	1800	5,305,937	Increase 35.02 per cent.
Great Britain.............	1800	16,000,000	" 10.34 " "
France..................	1801	27,349,000	
United States.............	1810	7,239,814	Increase 36.43 per cent.
Great Britain.............	1812	18,000,000	" 12.50 " "
Prussia..................	1816	10,319,000	
United States.............	1820	9,638,191	Increase 33.13 per cent.
Great Britain.............	1823	21,193,438	" 17.42 " "
France..................	1821	30,461,000	
Prussia..................	1822	11,664,000	
United States.............	1830	12,866,020	Increase 33.49 per cent.
Great Britain.............	1833	24,304,799	" 14.60 " "
France..................	1831	32,569,000	
Prussia..................	1834	13,038,000	
United States.............	1840	17,069,453	Increase 32.67 per cent.
Great Britain.............	1841	27,041,031	" 11.35 " "
France..................	1841	34,230,000	
Prussia..................	1840	14,051,000	
United States.............	1850	23,191,876	Increase 35.87 per cent.
Great Britain.............	1850	27,300,000	" .97 " "
France..................	1851	35,283,000	
Prussia..................	1849	16,296,000	
United States.............	1860	31,445,080	Increase 35.59 per cent.
Great Britain.............	1861	29,334,788	" .70 " "
France..................	1861	37,400,000	
Prussia..................	1861	18,491,000	

SUMMARY.

United States, increase in 70 years............................ 700.41 per cent.
Great Britain,   "   " 68   "   .... 102.30   "
France,   "   " 60   "   .... 37.00   "
Prussia,   "   " 45   "   .... 79.00   "

nations of Europe), it is proper next to consider the subject of our national assets, and to inquire as to what are the resources on which, as a nation, we can *at present* rely to meet our pecuniary indebtedness.

The officially assessed value of *all* the real and personal property of the United States in 1860, was $16,159,000,000. Of this amount there was credited to the loyal States and territories the sum of $10,957,448,956; and to the disloyal, $5,202,167,500. Large as this valuation seems, it was, nevertheless, in the opinion of the best statisticians, considerably below a true estimate; inasmuch as real property, in actual practice, is rarely valued, for census returns and for purposes of assessment, at more than *two thirds* of its real value, while large amounts of personal property, from the facility with which it is concealed, escape valuation and assessment altogether. The increase in the value of real and personal property of the whole United States for the decennial period of 1850–60, was in the ratio of 126.45 per cent., and of the loyal States about 129 per cent. Supposing, for the sake of caution, that the general ratio of decennial increase has been reduced since 1860 from 126 to 100 per cent. (the reverse, however, being probably more in accordance with the truth), then the value of all the real and personal property of the loyal States, on the 1st of July, 1864, would be about $15,300,000,000.

Supposing the whole of the property to be distributed equally *per capita* among the existing population of 24,900,000, then the apportionment to each individual would be $614.95.

Supposing the rebellion to terminate at or before the close of 1865, the population of the restored Union (which was 31,500,000 in 1860) to be 34,000,000, the debt $3,000,000,000, and the value of the real and personal property of the seceding States to be somewhat less than that prior to 1860 (*i. e.*, $5,000,000,000), then the value of the real and personal property of the whole Union would be about $21,579,000,000, the average wealth *per capita* $634.52; the average debt *per capita* $82, and the average annual interest *per capita* $5.35. Large though these proportions may seem, yet applying them, practically, we should not consider the case of an individual as particularly one for commiseration, whose debts and liabilities were less than *one seventh* of his available assets, and if not the individual, then certainly not the country, restored, renewed, reinvigorated, as it must be with the termination of the rebellion and extinguishment of Slavery.

But as the payment of our national debt is not a necessity of the present, but of the future, it is pertinent next to inquire as to what are the resources which the future will be able to command for the purpose of meeting the financial burden to be laid upon it. In prosecuting this inquiry, we have to deal with facts and figures of an entirely anomalous character. European history furnishes us with no precedents which can be quoted as either examples or parallels. In fact, there is nothing in all human history, to which the regular increase of the national wealth of this country, since the establishment of the Constitution, can be likened. It is the most wonderful fact of our wonderful national history, and like most other things peculiarly American, must be judged of by our own standard and forecasted entirely from our own precedents. Previous to the year 1840, no attempt was made by the government to obtain, by actual investigation, accurate data for the estimation of the value of the real and personal property of the United States, or of the value of the annual product of the agricultural, manufacturing and commercial operations of the nation. Estimates, however, have been made by several statisticians, from various available data, of the national valuation of the five decennial periods anterior to 1840, which are believed to be approximately accurate; and since 1840 we have had official valuations of the property of the Union at the end of each census decade. All of these valuations are known to be defective in various particulars, and especially prominent among these, is that of under valuation. This, although a matter to be regretted, has, however, the advantage that it frees an exhibit like the one we are presenting, from all suspicion of undue overstatement. The following table shows the population of the country and its decennial percentage increase; the estimated or the official valuation of the wealth of the country for each decennial period since 1791; the increased decennial percentage value; the average property to each person, and the average value of the yearly national product.

It thus appears from the statistics [table on p. 944] that while the population of the United States increased from 1850 to 1860 in the large ratio of 35.5 per cent. the wealth of the nation increased during the same period in the much more remarkable ratio of 126.45 per cent.; or from $7,125,780,000 in 1850 to $16,159,616,-000 in 1860; or at the rate of more than nine hundred millions ($902,383,584) per annum. During the same period, Great Britain experienced an increase of less than *one* per cent. in population, and an estimated increase of national wealth amounting to about *thirty-three per cent*. But startling and unprecedented as has been this extraordinary increase of our national wealth, one needs but a

TABLE

*Showing the population and wealth of the United States by decades from 1790 to 1860;
population of the loyal States in 1864; decennial percentage increase of population;
decennial percentage increase of national wealth; average property to each person; average
annual value of the national product.*

Year.	Population.	Value of real and personal property.	Decennial percentage increase of populat'n.	Decennial percentage increase of wealth.	Average property to each person.	Average annual value of the national product.
1790	3,929,827	(estimated) $750,000,000			$187,00	$187,500,000
1800	5,305,937	(estimated) 1,072,000,000	35.02 per cent.	43 per cent.	202.13	300,000,000
1810	7,239,814	(estimated) 1,500,000,000	36.43 per cent.	39 per cent.	207.20	420,000,000
1820	9,638,191	(estimated) 1,882,000,000	33.13 per cent.	25.4 per cent.	195.00	526,960,000
1830	12,866,020	(estimated) 2,653,000,000	33.49 per cent.	41 per cent.	206.00	742,840,000
1840	17,069,453	(official) 3,764,000,000	32.67 per cent.	41.7 per cent.	220.00	1,063,135,000
1850	23,191,876	(official) ⁵7,135,780,000	35.87 per cent.	89.6 per cent.	307.67	2,004,000,000
1860	31,500,000	(official) ⁵16,159,000,000	35.59 per cent.	126.42 per cent.	510.00	3,804,000,000
1864	Loyal States 24,900,000	(estimated) 15,300,000,000	{four years 12 per cent.	{four years 40 per cent.	614.95	4,018,000,000
1865	Rest'd Union assumed 34,000,000	(estimated) 21,574,000,000			634.52	[5,713,500,000

⁵ A question has been raised in some quarters, as to the correctness of these valuations of 1850 and 1860, in embracing in the valuation of 1850 $961,000,000, and in the valuation of 1860 $1,936,000,000, as the assessed values of slaves, insisting that black men are persons and not property, and should be regarded, like other men, only as producers and consumers. If this view of the subject should be admitted, the valuation of 1850 would be reduced to $6,174,780,000, and that of 1860 to $14,223,618,-068, leaving the increase in the decade $8,048,825,840.

The advance, even if reduced to $8,048,825,840 is an increase of property over the valuation of 1859 of 130 per cent. while the increase of population in the same decade was but 35.59. As the value of slaves to the country as laborers is obviously not affected by transferring them from the schedule of property to that of persons, we have adopted the census estimates of 1850 and 1860 as officially given. In the future the cursory glance at the details to feel satisfied that the exhibit is every way reliable and correct.

Thus, for example, the wealth of the State of Iowa increased from $23,714,000 in 1850, to $247,338,000 in 1860, or in the decennial ratio of nearly 943 per cent. California, the second State in respect to the rapidity of growth in wealth during the same decade, increased from $22,161,000 in 1850, to $207,874,000 in 1860, or nearly 838 per cent.; while Wisconsin increased her valuation 550 per cent.; Illinois 467 per cent.; and Michigan 330 per cent. Nor was the rapid increase of wealth confined to the new States of the West solely, although the augmentation there during the last census decade, was by far the most remarkable. Thus, Connecticut increased her wealth from $155,707,000 in 1850, to $444,274,000 in 1860, or in the ratio of 185 per cent.; while Ohio added to her wealth the value of $689,-000,000, or 138 per cent.; and Pennsylvania $694,000,000, or about 96 per cent. New York, though adding not quite 71 per cent. to her wealth of 1850, yet absolutely augmented it by $763,000,000; a sum more than $20,000,000 in excess of three times the value of the wealth of Iowa; $200,000,000 more than has been acquired by South Carolina since her existence as a State; and exceeding in amount the entire wealth of any other State in 1860, with the exception of Massachusetts, Ohio, Pennsylvania, Illinois, and Virginia.

The two States which increased their valuation the least during the decade in question, were Vermont and Massachusetts, yet the former added to her wealth 33 per cent., and the latter 42 per cent.; the absolute increase in Vermont being more than $30,000,000; and the absolute increase in Massachusetts $242,000,000. We have, therefore, in these detailed statements, elements which show precisely how and where this enormous increase of 126.45 per cent. in the wealth of the nation from 1850 to 1860, was effected.

Supposing now the war to close at or before the end of 1865, with a restoration of the dominion of the old Union; supposing also the wealth of the loyal States to have increased since 1860 at the decennial ratio of 100 per cent. (an under rather than an over estimate); and the valuation of the disloyal States at that period to be one thousand millions less than in 1860; then the re-united nation

---

country will undoubtedly be greatly the gainer in wealth by the change in the condition of the Southern laborers from a state of servitude to one of freedom. This point will be considered hereafter.

will start anew on its era of peace, with a capital of twenty thousand millions, and an annual increase of wealth which certainly cannot be estimated at less than $2,000,000,000.[6] This sum, it should be borne in mind, is not the *income* of the nation, out of which the population are to pay for their subsistence and their luxuries, but the profit over and above our expenses as a nation; or in other words, it is an actual increase of capital — the product of labor, machinery and commerce — which is to be annually applied to the permanent improvement of the country, and to be made the instrument of earning more wealth. So much, then, for the resources of the country at the close of the war, or at the close of the year 1865.

Let us now cautiously prospect the resources of the future, basing our estimates on the teachings of the present and the past. For this purpose we assume the decennial increase of the population of the country for the remainder of the present century (commencing back with the year 1860) to be 30 per cent., and the decennial increase of our national wealth to be 100 per cent.; and from these data as the basis of our calculations, we deduce the figures of the following table:

Years.	Population.	National Wealth.	Average property to each person.	Average debt (assumed at $3,000,000,000) for each person.	Annual interest per capita.	Percentage of debt to property.	Average annual value of the national product; the annual ratio of increase assumed being 10 p. c.
1860	31,500,000	$16,159,000,000	$510.00				$3,804,000,000
1865	34,000,000	21,574,000,000	634.52	$82.35	$5.35		5,713,500,000
1870	40,950,000	32,318,000,000	789.00	73.26	4.38	9.28	7,608,000,000
1880	53,235,000	64,636,000,000	1214.00	56.35	3.38	4.64	15,216,000,000
1890	69,205,500	129,272,000,000	1878.00	43.43	2.60	2.32	30,632,000,000
1900	89,964,150	258,514,000,000	2873.00	33.34	2.00	1.16	61,264,000,000

In the above table, one of the points brought out, which is most worthy of interest after the statement of the enormous prospective increase of our national wealth, is the exhibit of the manner in which, in a growing, flourishing state, the burden of a national debt

[6] Adopting the ratio of increase at 100 per cent. for every ten years, instead of 126.45 per cent., the ratio of increase from 1850 to 1860.

decreases relatively to the burden of the property which must pay it. This, which we show prospectively in the estimates above given for the future, is also strikingly illustrated by actual facts derived from the financial history of Great Britain. Thus in forty-two years, from 1816 to 1858, the percentage of national debt to national wealth fell from 40 to 13 per cent., while the capital of the debt itself was reduced less than three hundred millions on $4,200,000,-000; or the burden fell as from 40 to 13, while the debt fell only as from 40 to 37; or to put the case in a still stronger light, the debt of 1858, which would have been a charge of 37½ per cent. on the whole private wealth of Great Britain in 1816, was only 13.4 per cent. on the property of 1858.[7]

But objections will naturally arise in the minds of many persons. Surprised at the apparently incredible results deduced from our statistics respecting the future, they will urge that there must be some mistake in the ratios and estimates we have assumed or calculated upon; or if not this, then that we have no reasonable grounds for believing the future of our country is to develop itself, as respects wealth and population, in anything like the ratios of the past. It is therefore proper before proceeding further in our inquiry, to review in a degree the ground we have gone over, and if possible detect and make allowance for all real or probable errors.

And first, as regards population. The ratio of decennial increase from 1860 to 1900, the conclusion of the present century, we have assumed at 30 per cent. Now the actual increase has not fallen to so low a ratio as this, during any one of the seven decades that have elapsed since the establishment of the Constitution to 1860. During the three most unpromising periods of our national history, viz.: the decade embracing the first federal administration, when order was being restored from the previous revolutionary chaos; the decade of the last war with Great Britain, when the Capitol of the nation was taken and burnt; and the decade which includes the disastrous financial years of 1837–38 — the ratios of increase were respectively 35, 33, and 32.67 per cent. It must, therefore, be evident, that so far as all inferences from the past are concerned, we should be justified in fixing the ratio of the prospective increase of population in the United States at considerably above 30 per cent. In the official report of the *eighth census,* published during the present

[7] Dr. William Elder. National Almanac, 1864.

year (1864), the following are the calculated estimates of the population of the country for the remaining four decades of the present century, viz: 1870, 42,300,000; 1880, 56,450,000; 1890, 77,266,000; 1900, 100,355,000. The figures we have assumed in our calculations are considerably less than these official estimates, viz.: 1870, 40,950,-000; 1880, 53,235,000; 1890, 69,205,500; 1900, 89,964,150.

Some light on this subject, so far as the present decade is concerned, may also be obtained from an examination of the recent statistics of emigration. The following table exhibits the amount of foreign emigration into the United States for the forty years included in the *four* last census periods, or from 1820 to 1860:

From 1820 to 1830	244,490
" 1830 to 1840	552,000
" 1840 to 1850	1,558,300
" 1850 to 1860	2,707,624
Total	5,062,414

Being a yearly average of 126,560 for the last forty years, and 270,-762 for the last ten years. Immigration reached its maximum in the year 1854, when the number of aliens arriving in this country was reported for that year at 427,833. Subsequent to this year, foreign immigration rapidly diminished, viz.: to 200,000 in 1855; 200,000 in 1856; 251,000 in 1857; 123,000 in 1858; and 121,000 in 1859. Since then, notwithstanding the breaking out and continuance of our domestic troubles, immigration has commenced to flow upon us in rapidly increasing proportion, viz.: 153,640 in 1860; 120,000 (estimated) in 1862; 182,000 in 1863; while, for the present year, the number will probably reach, if not exceed, 300,000; the average arrivals for May and June being reported at about a thousand per day. With the return of peace, and the opening up of opportunities for profitable mining upon the Pacific, of cotton cultivation in the South, and of employment at large wages in the various manufacturing establishments that are sure to originate or increase under a permanent protective tariff, immigration will undoubtedly continue to flow upon us in a rapidly augmenting ratio. So far, then, as our increase of population is dependent upon this agency, we think we are fully justified in believing that the decennial increase will not be less than the figures assumed, viz.: 30 per cent.

We come next to consider the subject of the prospective increase of our national wealth. The great facts developed by the statistics of the census of 1840–50, and of 1850–60, are the very remarkable ratios, according to which the increase of our national wealth progresses. These ratios constitute, in a great degree, the basis on which our estimates of the future augmentation of national values are founded; and the direct point of inquiry next before us is, are we justified in assuming them as standards of comparison? or, in other words, have we reasonable grounds for believing that the future of the country, as respects the development of its resources and the increase of its wealth, is to be, even approximately, like the experience of the past?

Large as was the official valuation of the national wealth, and the decennial ratio of increase, as returned by the census of 1860, there is, as has been already intimated, abundant and conclusive evidence in proof, that the estimates were considerably lower than the actual. In illustration of this assertion, we submit a few statements, easily capable of verification, relative to the estimated and the actual wealth of portions of the State of New York. We have selected this State simply because the documents embodying the facts in question were readily accessible to us; and not because we have any reason for inferring that the valuation of New York was more exceptionable than that of any other State.

Thus: It appears from the report of the State Assessors, presented to the Assembly of New York, January 12th, 1863, that the amount of *personal property* belonging to *citizens of New York*, insured December 12th, 1860, in the various insurance companies belonging to, or doing business in the State, was $1,471,000,000, a sum considerably greater than the valuation of all the *real and personal* property assessed by the State during the year 1861; and one thousand one hundred millions ($1,138,000,000) in excess of the official valuation of all the personal property of the State for the year 1863.

Again: The value of all the real and personal property of the city of Troy, in the State of New York, as returned to and adopted by the State and county authorities for the purpose of assessment in the year 1863, was a little less than $14,000,000. In May, 1862, a fire occurred in this city, which was estimated to have destroyed from one fifteenth to one twentieth of the property of the entire city. The money value of the property *actually* destroyed was officially estimated by the Fire Commissioners at $2,724,000 (an amount exceeding one half of the assessed valuation of *all the personal* property of the city); on this an insurance was paid of $1,396,000, an amount equivalent to one tenth of the assessed value of *all* the property of the city. If we now assume, as we have every reason to do, that the valuation by the Fire Commissioners of the property destroyed was correct, and that this amount represented as much as one tenth, instead of one fifteenth, of all municipal values, then the correct valuation of the entire city in 1863 — making due allowance for the losses over and above the insurance — would be, instead of $14,000,000, $25,912,000. To this must further be added the valuation of the land within the city limits, as the value of this within the burnt district was not impaired by the fire, and consequently was not included in the estimate of the losses returned by the Commissioners. It is thus evident, that the official valuation of the property of one of the large cities of the State and country did not, at its maximum, approximate within fifty per cent. of the true and actual valuation.

But this excessive under-valuation of property in official estimates is not, however, limited to large cities; it extends equally to the small, country, agricultural towns and districts. As an illustration of this, we have selected, at random, for examination, from the latest available official document of the State of New York, the returns of the town of Hoosic, a thriving agricultural, and to some extent, manufacturing town, in the northeast part of Rensselaer County, in the State of New York. The population of this town, by the census of 1860, was 4,446. The value of all the *personal* property of the town, as returned by the county assessors for 1863, was $188,412. For the purpose of testing the correctness of these figures, we propose now to institute an independent inquiry respecting the valuation of the personal property of this town, deriving our data for this purpose from official documents and other sources of information equally open to the public, and, at the same time, premising that the writer has never visited the town in question, and does not enjoy a personal acquaintance with any of its inhabitants.

We find, first, by referring to the tables of the last New York State census, that the number of sheep returned as belonging to the town of Hoosic, was 22,394, of fleeces 25,800, and a yearly product of wool amounting to 85,519 lbs. Estimating the wool at 50 cents per pound, and the sheep after shearing at $2.50 per head, we have then of personal property in the items of sheep and wool alone, a valuation of $98,729, or more than one half of the officially-returned value of all the personal property of the town. But in addition to the sheep and wool, there was also returned as belonging to the town for the census year, the following other items, which are regarded in valuations as personal property, to wit: 863 horses; 2,600 swine; 1,700 head of cattle; agricultural tools and implements to the value of $46,600; and of farm produce, 69,000 lbs. of butter; 36,000 lbs. of cheese; 6,500 tons of hay; 63,000 bushels of oats; 5,000 bushels of wheat; 13,000 bushels of rye; 6,900 bushels of barley; 4,300 bushels of buckwheat; 52,000 bushels of corn; 33,000 bushels of potatoes; 266,000 lbs. lint of flax; 8,300 bushels of flaxseed; 5,600 bushels of apples; 3,000 lbs. of honey; while the annual value of poultry and eggs sold was returned as upwards of $6,000. The town also contains one of the largest manufactories of agricultural implements in the country; an extensive cotton-mill, a woollen-mill, paper-mill, iron-foundry, saw-mill, grist-mill, &c., &c.; in all, representing personal property to the amount of at least $200,000. In addition to the above, we have also obtained from gentlemen, whose opportunities for forming a judgment have been good, an estimate, that the value of stocks (Government, State, manufacturing and bank), and other interest-bearing securities, held by the inhabitants of this town, could not, at any time within the last five years, have less than a valuation of from two hundred and fifty to three hundred thousand dollars. If now to the items thus enumerated we allow a fair amount for certain non-enumerated articles, whose valuation is always a matter of difficulty, — such as household furniture, wearing apparel, small stocks of merchandise, jewelry, watches, carriages and the like — we think we are fully warranted in assuming that, at the time the personal property of the town of Hoosic was estimated by the State officials of $188,412, its actual and real value could not have been less than $800,000, and, in all probability, was in excess of a million.

Now whether we are justified in inferring, from the above facts and statistics, that a discrepancy between the real and appraised value of property, equal to that which, we think, we have shown to exist in the State of New York, applies to the whole country, may be a matter of doubt, and we therefore leave it to the judgment of our readers. But this much, we affirm, can most unquestionably be asserted, viz.: that wherever the judgment of competent appraisers can be obtained, respecting the valuation of the real or personal property of any town, city, or district, in any State, such estimate will be found to exceed by at *least* 30 per cent., any coincident valuation officially made, for census or assessment purposes.

The conclusions to which our investigations therefore lead us are, that the national valuation of sixteen thousand millions in 1860, and the decennial increase of 126 per cent. (remarkable as these results truly are), must have been really much less than the actual and true values and their augmenting ratio. And we think, further-more, that the facts warrant us in believing, that the total wealth of the country was, in 1860, upward of twenty thousand millions, and the decennial ratio of increase nearer 150 than 126 per cent.

The results of the past, then, as we have stated them in our tables and estimates, do not therefore admit of a doubt, and we come next to the task of examining the nature of the increase of our wealth and population from 1860 to the present time.

The decennial ratio of increase in the wealth of the loyal States, we assumed to have diminished since 1860, in consequence of the war, from 129 per cent. (the census estimate) to 100 per cent., and we have also adopted these latter figures as the prospective ratio of the increase of the wealth of the whole country for the remaining decades of the present century. As no official valuations (National or State) have been made since 1860, the store of facts from which we can draw, to fortify our assumptions respecting the progress of the last four years and of the future, must be necessarily limited. The few that we have at our command, are, however, interesting and highly significant.

The returns of the various "joint-stock Fire Insurance Companies" of the State of New York, as made to the State Insurance Bureau, show an increase in the property insured against fire during the year 1862, of $173,000,000 over the amount insured in the same companies in 1861; and an increase of 360,000,000 for the year 1863, over the amount insured in 1862. The returns of the Fire Insurance Companies in Massachusetts also show an increase of $29,800,000 in the amount of risks taken in 1862, over those taken in 1861. We are well aware that any deductions which can be drawn from these statistics must be very indefinite; yet they nevertheless truly indicate a great progressive increase of wealth in the country during a most extensive and expensive war.

The returns of Savings Banks, in the few States where annual and accurate reports are officially published, furnish us, however, with more definite information respecting the recent increase of public wealth; and especially of the material condition of the laboring classes. Thus, in the State of New York, the deposits in the Savings Banks increased from 1858 to 1861 (inclusive) as follows:

1858	$41,472,000	1860	$58,178,000
1859	48,194,000	1861	67,440,000

In 1857, the total deposits in all the Savings Banks of Great Britain and Ireland (the United Kingdom) amounted to £37,000,-000 ($185,000,000). In 1857, the population of the United Kingdom was estimated to have been about 29,000,000, while that of the State of New York in 1861, was probably about 4,000,000. The latter, therefore, with a population in 1861 a little less than one seventh of that of Great Britain, in 1857 had more than a third as large deposits in her Savings Banks; a most striking commentary on the relative prosperity of the laboring classes of the two countries.

The returns of the Savings Banks of Massachusetts are more complete than those of New York, and are consequently more interesting. Thus, taking the ten years from 1850 to 1860, the deposits in that State increased 231 per cent. In the same period the population of the State increased about 24 per cent.; the total valuation, about 50 per cent.; and the bank capital (the means required to carry on the business of the State), about 75 per cent. The accumulation of industrial savings, therefore, exceeded all the other ratios of State development in the above-mentioned period.[8] The deposits from 1860 to 1863 (inclusive) have been as follows:

1860	$45,054,000	1862	$50,403,000
1861	44,785,000	1863	56,883,000

Returns from Maine, New Hampshire, Vermont, Rhode Island, and Connecticut, also show a similar progressive increase of deposits during the last few years in their respective Savings Banks;

---

[8] Complete returns of the Savings Banks in the State of New York, prior to 1858, are not obtainable; but for the four years next subsequent to 1857, the yearly increase of deposits was more rapid than in Massachusetts.

and the same is also probably true of the Savings Banks of most of the other loyal States, although, from the lack of official reports, this cannot be positively asserted.

Now these facts and statistics, like others previously referred to, have no parallels to the history of the Savings Banks of Great Britain or of Europe. There, on the breaking out of war; the interruption of great branches of industry; the failure of crops; or during seasons of great financial embarrassment, the deposits are not merely suspended, but they are rapidly withdrawn. Thus, in Great Britain, in nine out of the seventeen years which elapsed from 1841 to 1857 inclusive, the withdrawals exceeded the deposits; and in the years 1847 and 1848, which were periods of great commercial distress in England, the excess of withdrawals over deposits was more than twenty-five millions of dollars. On the other hand, in 1861, when the loyal portion of the United States was entering upon a struggle, growing out of an attempt to destroy the whole future of their Government — thereby involving in a common ruin all public and private credit; when Southern indebtedness to the North, to the estimated amount of $200,000,000, was deliberately repudiated; and when, as a legitimate consequence of this state of things, the trade, industry, and commerce of the country were everywhere extremely depressed; then, in this disastrous year, the withdrawal of deposits from the American savings banks were so small as to be hardly worthy of notice; the decline in the aggregate deposits in Massachusetts being only $269,000 out of a capital of $45,500,000; while in New York, there was an actual excess of deposits over withdrawals of more than six and a half millions, and an aggregate gain in capital of more than nine millions. It should also be borne in mind in this connection, that, since the commencement of the war, large sums have been continually diverted from savings banks to government securities; and it is the opinion of those well qualified to judge, that the decline in the savings bank deposits of Massachusetts for 1861, was due almost entirely to the diversion of investments into this and other channels, and not to the impairment of the popular resources.[9]

[9] For the above statistics relative to Savings Banks, we are mainly indebted to the report of the Bank Commissioners of Massachusetts for 1861 (issued in 1862); a report which, through its exhibit of the condition of the savings banks of Massachusetts

The statistics respecting the production of the great agricultural staples of the loyal States since the year 1859, as published in the reports of the National Bureau of Agriculture, also indicate a continued and large increase in these important elements of our country's wealth and strength. Thus, the product of wheat, which in 1859 was 138,000,000 bushels, was, in 1862, 189,000,000; and in 1863, 191,000,000. This great increase of 1862 and 1863 over 1859 cannot, however, be altogether considered as a regular increase, inasmuch as the crop of 1859, on which the last census returns were based, was somewhat below an average, while the crop of 1862 was one of the best ever harvested. In 1863, the crop of wheat gathered in the summer was good; but the fall crops of corn, barley, potatoes, &c., were badly injured; first, by long-continued droughts; and secondly, by remarkably early and destructive frosts. These facts must also be borne in mind in considering the following agricultural statistics of the loyal States for 1859, 1862, and 1863, which, for convenience, we have arranged with those of wheat given above, in the form of a table:

Productions.	1859.	1862.	1863.
Wheat	138,000,000 bushels.	189,000,000 bushels.	191,000,000 bushels.
Oats	152,168,000 "	172,520,000 "	174,858,000 "
Rye	18,792,000 "	21,254,000 "	20,798,000 "
Barley	15,433,000 "	17,781,000 "	16,760,000 "
Corn	547,029,000 "	586,704,000 "	452,446,000 "
Potatoes	107,337,000 "	114,533,000 "	101,457,000 "
Tobacco	230,343,000 pounds.	208,807,000 pounds.	267,302,000 pounds.
Hay	19,073,000 tons.	21,500,000 tons.	20,000,000 tons.
Wool	50,183,000 pounds.	60,744,000 pounds.	79,405,000 pounds.

It will thus be seen that there was a very large increase in the product of all the crops enumerated in the year 1862 over 1859, notwithstanding the existence of the war; and that there was also a very marked increase in the articles of wheat, oats, tobacco, and wool, produced in 1863 (the third year of the war) over 1862; which increase would doubtless have also extended to all the other

and New York for the first year of our civil war, is said to have made so great an impression upon a leading European banker, as to induce him to keep a copy of it constantly by him, as a most unanswerable argument in favor of the ample ability of the loyal States to prosecute their war and carry any consequent debt without the slightest aid from European capitalists.

crops, but for the occurrence of unusual drought and frosts. The State of Iowa, which, out of a population in 1860, of 675,000, furnished to the federal army, from May, 1861, to the end of 1863, 52,240 men, nevertheless increased her number of acres of improved land from 3,445,000 in 1859, to 4,700,000 in 1862, and 4,900,000 in 1863; and her product of wheat, from 8,795,000 bushels in 1862, to 14,592,000 in 1863. In 1859, the amount of wheat raised in the State of Indiana was 15,219,000 bushels; while in 1863, notwithstanding the State, out of its population, in 1860, of 1,350,000, had furnished to the army more than 124,000 fighting men, the annual product of wheat exceeded 20,000,000 of bushels. Nor are these facts concerning Iowa and Indiana, remarkable as they most certainly are, exceptionable; for although exact statistics on this subject are not readily available, yet enough is known to render it certain that the products of industry have greatly increased in all the loyal States during the war, notwithstanding the constant draughts that have from time to time been made upon the numbers of their producing classes.

A few statistics illustrative of the rapid increase of wealth in California, derived from other sources than that of mining, are also interesting in this connection. In 1855, all the vines in the State did not number 1,000,000; but in 1862 the number had increased to 10,592,762; while the product of wine for 1862 was estimated by a committee of the Legislature at 700,000 gallons. The value of the exports of the products of the vine from California for the last three years is returned as follows: 1861, $8,000; 1862, $25,000; 1863, $81,456. The value of wool exported from California, which in 1860 was about $1,000,000, rose in 1862 to $6,000,000, and in 1863 to $8,000,000.

The number of immigrants arriving in this country during the three years of war has also been greater than the number which arrived during the three years immediately preceding the war, as will be seen from the following figures; 1858, number of immigrants arriving, 123,000; 1859, 121,000; 1860, 153,000. Total, 397,000. Since the war; number arriving in 1861, 150,000; 1862, 120,000; 1863, 182,000. Total, 452,000; and if we add the probable number of the present year, 300,000, we shall have an aggregate of immigration during four years of war, of 752,000. Thirty years ago, a writer in Blackwood, in commenting on the fact that the population of England, Scotland, and Wales had increased specifically about a million from 1801 to 1821, in consequence of the influx of Irish laborers seeking employment, observed that "there was no similar instance (to the one referred to) on record, of so great an inundation of inhabitants breaking into any country, barbarous or civilized, not even when the Goths and Vandals overwhelmed the Roman Empire." What would this writer have said, could he have foreseen, that in the twenty years that were to elapse between 1840 and 1860, an inundation of 4,265,000 people would journey 3,000 miles, instead of a brief hundred, to seek a home and a livelihood within the limits of the United States!

An examination of the tables of our exports and imports for the five years next preceding 1863, furnishes also some very significant facts illustrative of the vast aggregate wealth of the whole country, and particularly of the loyal States, during the first two years of the war. Thus, the total amount of exports for the three years, from 1858 to 1861 inclusive, when cotton and other Southern staples constituted a large portion of their value, was $1,167,768,000; and of imports, $1,051,704,000; leaving a balance to our credit as the result of three years trade, of $116,063,000. This was then considered, and most justly, as a gratifying proof of the prosperity and strength of the country; and yet in the next two years, or from 1861 to 1863, with war on a gigantic scale prevailing, and with a total loss of what were our former chief exports, the credits arising from trade with foreign nations were $102,878,000;[10] or in other words, the loyal part of our divided country realized in two years from its foreign trade, a sum nearly as large as had accrued to the whole country in the preceding three years of peace, with all our staples available for export.

We come now more particularly to the consideration of the future; and our task in this respect, can be little else than the pointing out of the national resources available for development.

We have already dwelt at some length on the subject of immigration; but there are features of great interest connected with it that we have not alluded to. The total number of immigrants who have

---

[10] The following are the figures in detail:

	Exports.	Imports.	Balances.
1858–59	$356,789,462	$338,765,130	$18,024,338
1859–60	400,122,296	362,163,941	37,958,355
1860–61	410,856,818	350,775,835	60,080,983
1861–62	229,790,280	205,819,823	23,970,457
1862–63	331,844,247	252,935,872	78,908,375

arrived in this country since the commencement of 1861, has already been given as about 452,000; and the probable number, up to the close of the present year, as 752,000. The general agent in charge of the immigrant landing depot in New York City, estimates the average amount of coin in the possession of each immigrant landing, from the 1st of January to the 1st of May, 1864, in New York, at $80. Assuming this amount *per capita* to remain constant, and that the total immigration for 1864 reaches the number of 300,000, then the specie brought into the country for this year only, will amount to $24,000,000 — a sum exceeding two thirds of all the specie held by the banks of New York, Boston, and Philadelphia, on the 1st of July of the present year.

Supposing $80 to represent the amount of coin belonging to each immigrant arriving from January 1, 1861, to December 31, 1864, then the total aggregate of specie thus brought into the country would be $67,160,000; or if we reduce the individual average from $80 to $50, $37,600,000.[11]

But the value of an immigrant to the country is not to be estimated merely by the amount of personal property he possesses, or brings with him. As a laborer and a producer, or if you please, as a consumer of products, yielding a revenue to the state, he has a value which belongs to the country, as much so as the value of a slave is arrogated to belong to him who calls himself his master. This value, counting Caucasian blood at the North to be worth as much as Ethiopian was at the South before the war, and reducing it according to the Southern tariff for uneducated labor to a money basis, we may fairly estimate to average $500 per head for each immigrant man, woman, and child, arriving in this country. Adopting this standard, then, we have, as the aggregate cash value to the country of the immigration of 1864, the sum of $150,000,000; and of the immigration from 1861 to the close of 1864 inclusive, the sum of $376,-000,000. If we assume further, that for the remaining five years of the present decade, *i. e.* from January 1, 1855, to December 31, 1869, the annual immigration averages only 250,000; then, we have, as the cash value to the country for the present decade of this constant

[11] Mr. John A. Kennedy, formerly Superintendent of the New York Castle Garden Immigration Depot, stated some years since, in a letter addressed to the American Geographical Society, that "a careful, systematic inquiry, extending over a period of seventeen months, gave an average of $100 (almost entirely in coin) as the money property of each immigrant man, woman, and child," landing at New York.

influx of population, the enormous sum of one thousand millions of dollars.

If any are inclined to the opinion, that our estimate of $500 as the cash value to the country of each immigrant arriving is too high, we would call his attention to the following circumstances: 1st, that the number of slaves, of all ages and conditions returned by the census of 1860, was, 3,950,000; and that their assessed value was $1,936,000,000; or nearly $490 per head; 2d, that the price of an able-bodied field laborer — man or woman — at the South, has not been less than a thousand dollars per head for many years; and 3d, that a great majority of the immigrants arriving in this country are in the prime of life; in full health; are possessed of some little property, in money or tools, and are very often highly skilled in some department of mechanical industry. We leave it, therefore, to our readers to say, whether our estimate of $500 could not with fairness be rather placed at $1,000 *per capita*.

It should also be borne in mind, that all the strength and wealth derived by a country from such an addition to the population, as the United States have been receiving, and the loyal States do still receive, constitute an advantage absolutely unknown to England and the other European states. In the case of Great Britain, it has been estimated, that the number of foreigners who arrive upon her shores, with the expectation of making that country their permanent home, does not exceed one thousand souls per annum. Therefore, in respect to immigration, as has been heretofore remarked, in respect to our decennial increase of wealth, the position of the country, is entirely anomalous, and without precedent in history; and our ability to sustain and pay off an immense debt cannot be rightfully judged of by any foreign precedents.

The amount of arable, fertile land in the possession of a state or country, is always regarded as one of its great, if not its chief element of wealth; inasmuch as all wealth comes originally from the soil, and all commerce is but the interchange of the raw or manufactured products of the soil. Now it is well known, that the Federal Government has yet in its possession one of the largest domains of unoccupied fertile soil, upon the face of the globe, all of which is open to the actual settler, without money and without price. It is well, however, in calculating upon our ability to pay debts and taxes, to know more than generally; what our national assets are in this particular, and we therefore invite the attention of our readers to the following statement of facts:

On the 30th of September, 1863, the quantity of public lands remaining in the possession of the Federal Government, was (1,044,-628,000) one thousand and forty-four millions of acres, embracing an area of over 2,000,000 square miles. This domain is about two thirds of our geographical extent, and is nearly three times the area of the territory of the United States at the commencement of their existence as a nation. It is an extent of territory sufficient to make thirty-two additional States, each as large as the great central State of Ohio. It includes the extensive and rich mining districts of California, Nevada, Colorado, Oregon, Washington Territory, Arizona, and New Mexico. "It embraces soils capable of abundant yield of the rich productions of the tropics, of sugar, cotton, rice, tobacco, and the grape (now a staple of California), and of the great cereals of the more temperate zones — wheat and corn. Instead of a dreary waste as this land was formerly supposed to be, the millions of buffalo, elk, deer, and mountain sheep, the primitive inhabitants of the soil, fed by the hand of nature, attest its capacity for the abundant support of a dense population through the skilful toil of the agriculturist. Furthermore, not only is the yield of food for man in this region abundant, but it holds in its bosom the richest known deposits of gold, silver, and mercury; and of the so-called useful metals, lead, copper, and iron." The value of this vast national property, if estimated at the former government price of land, viz.: one dollar and a quarter per acre, would be $1,305,785,000.

Previous to the war, cotton was regarded as one of the chief elements of our national wealth and prosperity. Owing to favoring circumstances of climate and soil, American cotton was superior in quality and inferior in price to all raised elsewhere; and it had come to form so large a part of the commerce and manufacturing industry of the world, as to acquire the appellation of "King." Nor was the title inappropriate. Cotton was indeed "King," and his throne in 1860 was 5,000,000 of bales, raised by the labor and watered by the tears of four millions of the most miserable of slaves. Though now dethroned, cotton will be King again, but his dominion henceforth, will be infinitely wider, and his tenure of authority infinitely stronger, inasmuch as it will be based on free labor, and the skilful appliances which economical and skilled agriculture knows how to prepare and use. Are we speaking boastfully or metaphorically? Let us see.

It is now generally admitted by all authorities, that while a full supply of cotton may, in course of time, and under the stimulus of high prices, be procured elsewhere; yet, whenever its cultivation is resumed, under favorable circumstances, in the United States, this country will again become the main dependence of the world;[12] as much so as in 1860, when 89½ per cent. of all the cotton consumed in Great Britain was the product of the Southern States.

Some idea of the increased product of cotton required yearly, to meet the demands of the world's consumption, may be formed from the fact, that the average increased consumption of England alone, from 1850 to 1860, was at the rate of 87,880 bales (of 450 pounds each) per annum, or 39,546,000 pounds. Some idea of the capacity of this country to supply this annually increasing demand, may also be formed from the fact, that, of the land available and suitable for the cultivation of cotton, in the so-called cotton States, *the maximum amount ever cultivated did not exceed one and seven tenths* ($1^{634}/_{1000}$) *per cent.*

That the supply of cotton from the South, under its system of slave labor, has not been for many years equal to the demand made upon it, is clearly shown by the fact, that, notwithstanding the annual crop increased from 2,394,000 bales, in 1844, to 4,675,000, in 1859, the price advanced in Liverpool, during the same time from 8¾ to 11 cents per pound, or $9.67½ cents per bale.

The time, therefore, had fully come, when some change in the system of labor was absolutely needed at the South, in order to

---

[12] The only region which has yet been discovered outside of the United States, where all the conditions for the successful cultivation of cotton are met with (for it appears to be essential that it shall not be a tropical region) is in Queensland, Australia. Here, however, the great distance from market, the scarcity and high price of labor, and the proximity to rich gold fields, must prevent any very rapid development in the cultivation. — *Report by Edward Atkinson, to the Boston Board of Trade,* 1863.

In a more recent publication upon the future supply of cotton, Mr. Atkinson modifies the above statement, and gives the details of the unexpected increase in the cotton crop of Egypt, and the successful attempt to introduce the cultivation of cotton in Turkey and Asia Minor; and he also states that the cultivation of the staple in these countries will probably be maintained even at ordinary prices, as the best English and French skill and machinery are being applied, but that no crop can be raised in many years which shall more than meet the increased demand which will prevail when low prices are restored, or which can interfere with the demand on this country for larger crops than were ever before raised.

enable it to meet the demands of the world for its great staple; and that this change was, to a certain extent, in progress before the war, is demonstrated by the fact that, of the cotton crop of 1850, one ninth part was the product of free labor. How rapidly the change will take place after the war, and how rapidly the supremacy of our country in the cotton markets of the world will be again attained to, is thus shown by Edward Atkinson, Esq., in an able and exhaustive report, "On the manufacture and supply of cotton," made to the Boston Board of Trade in 1863, and to whom we are mainly indebted for our statistics on this subject. He says: "The principal cotton region of the South is not upon the unhealthy coast line where malarious fevers prevail, but is mostly a healthy, interior upland country, the largest portion being far more healthy than many of the Western States. An able-bodied man can easily raise, and, with the assistance of his children, can pick, 5,000 pounds of cotton per annum; at the same time raising an ample supply of food for his family. This can be done with less hard work than is required of farm laborers in New England. It is not probable that large crops of cotton will be raised for the next five years, or that cotton will in that time rule below an average of 25 cents per pound. How rapid a settlement of the cotton region will be induced by the ability of a common laborer to raise in each year an ample supply of food, and a crop of cotton which will bring $1,250 in gold on demand, let each one judge."

. We come next to consider the probable future augmentation of our national wealth and national revenues from the development of the mineral deposits of the country, especially the deposits of the precious metals, which are known to exist throughout the Western portion of the continent, and extend, according to the Report of the Commissioner of the General Land Office (December, 1862), over an area of more than a million square miles of our territory.

The gold product of California, from 1848 to 1862, inclusive, is variously estimated at from $734,000,000 (Hittel), to $1,049,000,000 (*Bankers' Magazine*). The annual gold product of California, at the present time, is believed to be about $44,000,000; while the product of all the mining industry of the State (gold, quicksilver, &c.), for the past three years is returned as follows: 1861, $42,100,000; 1862,

$44,105,000; 1863, $47,982,000. The amount of treasure shipped from San Francisco during 1863, was $46,071,000.[13]

Reliable data for accurately estimating the *present* gold and silver production of the loyal States and Territories are not now obtainable; but there are reasonable grounds for believing that the value of the product for the year 1864 will not fall short of $125,-000,000. With a view of assisting our readers to form a judgment on this topic, we submit the following statements: The amount of gold derived from the mines of Washington Territory, for 1862, was estimated at $5,000,000; from the mines of Colorado for the same year, $12,000,000; the receipts of silver at San Francisco, from the Washoe and Esmeralda mines of Nevada, were $12,430,000 in 1863, against $6,000,000 in 1862; while the total produce of these mines for 1863 was estimated to exceed $15,000,000. The product of the Oregon mines in 1862 was estimated, from carefully collected data, to exceed $12,000,000; and, according to Mr. S. B. Ruggles, their product for 1863 was estimated at $20,000,000. The Commissioner of the General Land Office, in his official report, made December 29th, 1862, in speaking of the "great auriferous region of the United States" in the Western portion of the continent, says:

"The yield of the precious metals alone of this region will not fall below one hundred millions of dollars the present year, and it will augment with the increase of population for centuries to come." "Within ten years the annual produce of these mines will reach two hundred millions of dollars in the precious metals, and in coal, iron, tin, lead, quicksilver, and copper, half that sum." He adds that, "with an amount of labor relatively equal to that expended in California applied to the gold fields already known to exist outside of that State, the production of this year, including that of California, would exceed four hundred millions." And yet no fact is more unquestionable than that this great territory is in its infancy of mining.

---

[13] The Custom-House exhibit of the export of gold from San Francisco is an uncertain test by which to determine the total gold product of California. Messrs. Hussey, Bond & Hale of San Francisco, in a recent circular regarding the gold product of California, state that the amount carried home by returning passengers, the exports to Europe, China, the Pacific ports of South America, the amount carried overland to Mexico, and the amount retained in California for purposes of currency, is equal to seventy-five per cent upon the amount of exports as exhibited by the manifests of the American steamers to Panama. One returning passenger is known to have carried $80,000 as baggage, to save freight. A single passenger on board the ill-fated Central America is known to have carried twenty thousand dollars in his valise.

But these magnificent results of mining upon the Pacific slope, and their still more magnificent promise for the future, should not cause us to overlook the steady development of mining industry in other portions of our country. The production of coal, iron, copper, lead, and salt, in the loyal States east of the Mississippi has everywhere greatly increased since the commencement of the war, and in no locality diminished. Take for example the statistics of the mineral region of Lake Superior. In 1862, the quantity of iron shipped from Marquette was 115,721 tons; in 1863, the quantity exceeded 200,000 tons. The product of copper from the mines of this region has also increased since 1858, as follows: Product in 1858, 3,500 tons; 1859, 4,200 tons; 1860, 6,000 tons; 1861, 7,400 tons; 1863, 8,548 tons. This last amount exceeds one half of all the copper annually obtained from all the well-known mines of Great Britain. In 1858, there was also added to our mineral wealth and industry an article whose production, in a measure peculiar to our country, has increased since the commencement of the war in a manner unparalleled in the history of the world's trade and commerce. We allude to the article *petroleum*, or *"coal oil."* In 1859, petroleum held no place in the list of our country's exports. In 1861, however, 1,112,000 gallons were exported; in 1862, the quantity increased to 10,800,000 gallons; while for 1863, the exports exceeded 28,000,000 gallons; which would have required for its conveyance the services of 252 ships of the average burden capacity of 1,000 tons each. The whole national product of petroleum for the year 1863 undoubtedly exceeded 60,000,000 gallons, which, at its average price of thirty cents per gallon, added to the annual product of the country a value of eighteen millions of dollars.

In the census returns of 1860, Michigan was not even mentioned as one of the States in which the manufacture of salt constituted a notable branch of industry; yet in 1863, the amount of salt manufactured in this State exceeded two millions of bushels; a growth in two years equal to that attained by the celebrated Onondaga salt-works of New York, thirty-eight years after these salt-springs had passed under the superintendence of the State.

Thus rapidly has the mineral wealth of the loyal States developed since the commencement of the war.

One great and acknowledged source of wealth to Great Britain has been the product of her mines; the officially returned value of which for 1862 was $170,000,000 (£34,000,000). Large as this amount is, and much as it undoubtedly contributed to the resources of the kingdom, the mineral product of the loyal States for 1863 undoubtedly exceeded it in value; our estimate for the year being as follows

Precious Metals (Gold and Silver)	$100,000,000
Coal (valuation in 1860 by Census report, $19,365,000)	36,000,000
Petroleum	18,000,000
Quicksilver	2,000,000
Pig Iron (valuation by Census of 1860, $19,487,000)	30,000,000
Copper	2,500,000
Lead (valuation of 1860, $977,281)	1,000,000
Salt (valuation of 1860, $2,265,000)	2,500,000
Other products, zinc, nickel, chrome, &c	200,000
Total	$182,200,000

And this in the mere inception of our mining industry, when we may be said to have done little more than "scratch the ground."

No estimate of future resources of the country, furthermore, can be considered complete, which fails to take into account the great augmentation of values which is sure to accrue in time to the South from the substitution of free for slave labor. This matter is set in a clear light by the following statement, which any one who doubts can verify for himself by referring to the official statistics of the census of 1860:

If the product per head of the population in the Slave States had been the same in 1859 that it was in the Free States, there would have been added to the aggregate national wealth returned at that time, the additional value of $1,531,631,000; a sum nearly equal to the entire national debt, June, 1864.

The advantage of a system of free labor over slave labor, in increasing the aggregate national wealth, is also clearly shown by comparing Maryland in 1860, one of the most prosperous of the slave States, with Massachusetts, one of the most prosperous of the free States. Maryland has 11,124 square miles; Massachusetts 7,000 square miles. Maryland has a shore line — sea and river — of 1,336 miles; Massachusetts, 764 miles. Maryland has double the area of good land that Massachusetts has. With these natural advantages on the side of the former, let us now contrast the industrial and other advantages which have been obtained by the latter. Rate of mortality in Massachusetts, 1 in 92; in Maryland, 1 in 57. Value of the products of Massachusetts in 1860, $287,000,000; in Maryland, $66,-009,000. Value of products per head in Massachusetts, $235; in Maryland, $96. That is to say, the average annual value of the labor of each person in Massachusetts was greatly more than double that of Maryland. The value of all property, real and personal, in Massachusetts, in 1860, was $815,000,000; in Maryland, $376,000,000. Comparing this with the value of products before mentioned, the profit on capital was in Massachusetts 35 per cent.; in Maryland, 17 per cent., or less than one half; and it is a noticeable fact, that only in two slave States, Delaware and Missouri, was the rate of profit larger than in Maryland, and in both of these were comparatively fewer slaves. Another remarkable fact, recently brought out by Hon. R. J. Walker (to whom we are indebted for these slave and free State statistics), is, that as Maryland is to Massachusetts, so is South Carolina to Maryland; the product per head in 1860 being in Massachusetts, $235; in Maryland, $96; in South Carolina, $56; or in free Massachusetts the reward of labor is more than double that in Maryland, and four times that in South Carolina.

Now, the way to make the Southern States as rich and productive as the Northern, and even more so, as Mr. James Brooks, editor of the N. Y. Express, justly observed more than thirty years ago, during a journey in the South, is to abolish slavery. "Substitute skilful, intelligent, interested free labor for unskilled, ignorant, and uninterested slave labor," and, as he remarked, "South Carolina would be the wealthiest State in the Union."

Now, we are going to have the assistance of this added and hitherto undeveloped wealth, to pay, not only the interest, but the principal of our national debt. With "small farms and divided free labor taking the place of the feudal system," as Mr. Brooks says, all the immense, undeveloped natural resources of the Southern States will vastly increase our national wealth and prosperity. This increase, Mr. R. J. Walker (whose advantages and capability for forming a judgment are not surpassed by any other person) estimates will amount in *ten* years to the great sum of over *seventeen thousand millions of dollars.*

Thus the mere addition we shall make in ten years to our national wealth, by abolishing the "institution" which has been so long a curse and a source of dissension to us, would many times over pay our national debt.

Moreover, the abolition of slavery cannot fail to add immensely and directly to our national revenue. A slave paid no taxes, directly; and indirectly but little more than a horse or a cow. His two annual suits of linsey-woolsey, and his weekly peck of corn meal and a few pounds of bacon, contributed little to national revenue, and he had no wages to spend; but as freed men, they become at once consumers of taxed articles. This is strikingly shown in the last year's (1863) history of the colonies of freed blacks upon the sea islands of South Carolina. In these colonies, nearly every woman has provided herself with a silk dress and a pair of gold ear rings out of the product of their earnings — a thing remarkable in itself, inasmuch as many of the purchasers, as slaves, had never, in the whole course of their lives, been the possessors of a single dollar; while upon one of the smaller islands, a colony of a few hundred emancipated slaves are reported to have bought and paid for domestic goods, in a twelve-month, to the value of over $20,000. "Our Southern trade" — though so valuable in former years — will, therefore, when peace is restored, by the recognition of federal authority, be undoubtedly a hundred times more extensive and profitable than it has ever been. Four millions of consumers, not only of necessaries, but of luxuries, will be at once added to the tax-paying population. "Also by freeing the slaves, white labor will be relieved of a ruinous competition, and will reap a large reward in that vast territory from which it has been for years almost entirely shut out. This will add still more largely to the consumption, as well as to the internal commerce and revenue of the country." [14]

[14] "The Philadelphia" (Freedmen's Aid) "Society has a store on St. Helena Island. In this store alone — and there are others on the island carried on by private enterprise — two thousand dollars' worth of goods are sold monthly. There is a great demand for plates, knives, forks, tinware, and better clothing, including even hooped skirts. Negro cloth, as it is called, osnaburgs, russet-colored shoes, in short, the distinctive apparel formerly dealt out to them, are very generally rejected. But there is no article of household furniture or wearing apparel used by persons of moderate means which they will not purchase, when they are allowed the opportunity of labor and earning wages. What a market the South would open under the new system! It would set all the mills and workshops astir. Four millions of people would become purchasers of all the various articles of manufacture and commerce, in place of the few coarse, simple necessaries laid in for them in gross by the planters. When these people can be no longer used as slaves, men will try to see how they can make the

Finally, in estimating the future resources of the country, and its capacity to carry a large burden of debt and taxation, it should not be overlooked that the opportunity for a civilized nation to increase its aggregate wealth was never before, in the history of the world, so great as at present, and therefore no former precedents respecting the actual burden of a great debt upon a nation can be fairly quoted as applicable to the present. This is due mainly to two circumstances: 1st, *The accumulation of national capital: and 2d, to the introduction of labor-saving machinery.*

In relation to the *first*, it is simply necessary to direct the attention of the reader to the fact that *wealth makes wealth:* or, in other words, that resources and capital accumulated, and properly used, invariably bring large additional resources and capital. The man that had ten talents could produce more easily ten additional talents, than he who had one could produce a single additional one; and so in regard to this country, or the loyal part of it. With a capital in 1860 more than double what it possessed in 1850, its capacity and power to increase its wealth in 1860 was of necessity more than double what it could have been in 1850.

2d. The opportunity or power of a country to increase its national wealth or capital is greatly augmented by the introduction of labor-saving machinery. A single statistical fact illustrates this proposition better than volumes of assertion. It was shown by official statistics in Great Britain, some years since, that if the stage-coach system, which was the main reliance of that country in 1830 for the transportation of travellers, had continued in use up to 1854, and had then been required to do the work of passenger transportation alone, which the railway system of that year effected, the increased cost of the business would have been £40,000,000 ($200,000,000) per annum more than the whole cost of the railway passenger and freight

---

most of them as freemen. Your Irishman honestly thinks he hates the negro; but, when the war is over, he will have no objection to going South and selling him groceries and household implements at fifty per cent. advance on New York prices.— *Atlantic Monthly, September, 1863.*

Let us also, in this connection, glance at the effects of emancipation on the trade and industry of the British West India Islands. Emancipation took place in British Guiana, Barbadoes, Trinidad, and Antigua, in 1830. The average value of the annual export of sugar from these islands, for 1827 to 1830, was $8,840,000. The average annual value, from 1851 to 1860, was $14,600,000. Land in Barbadoes has doubled in value since emancipation. Under slavery, the value of American imports to Barbadoes did not average more than £60,000 per annum; at present it is from £300,000 to £400,000 annually.

conveyancé of the same year; or, in other words, the introduction and use of railways in Great Britain added to the productive capital of the country for the year 1854 the sum of $200,000,000, "an amount," as Robert Stevenson expressed it, "exceeding by 50 per cent. the yearly interest of the (British) national debt."

With such a return from a single department of improved industry, who can estimate the yearly addition to the wealth and capital of a country like ours, where the invention and introduction of labor-saving machinery is universally regarded as a leading and peculiar feature of its civilization and history?

The census of 1860 returned the population of Massachusetts as 1,230,000; yet how inadequately the mere enumeration of the number of individuals composing a State like this expresses its power and resources is evident, when we remember that, in 1860, the machinery of Massachusetts was returned as capable of doing the work of *more than a hundred millions of men*. Now, such an addition to the productive capacity of a State fifty years ago, was not possible, inasmuch as a great part of the machinery and appliances by which it had been evoked were not then in existence; and if we are not warranted in predicating of the next fifty years an equal progress in improvement, we think we are justified in believing that a nearly equal gain in resources will accrue to the whole country from the more extensive introduction and use of the labor-saving inventions and processes already in existence. We would also call the attention of our readers, in this connection, to the very interesting circumstance, that war and the embarrassed condition of our finances, so far from restricting the inventive genius of the country and retarding the introduction of improvements, has acted rather as a stimulant. This is proved by the increased number of patents issued during the last three years (*i. e.*, 1861, 2,581; 1862, 3,522; 1863, 4,170); and also by the fact that, notwithstanding the great draft of men from the agricultural States to the ranks of the army, the harvests, through the more extensive use of machinery, have rather increased than diminished.[15]

---

[15] An interesting illustration of the manner in which American industry is enabled, through the machinery it invents, to compete with and outdistance the cheapest known labor of the world, is to be found in the machine recently invented for splitting cane (rattan) used for the manufacture of "cane-seat" chairs. The strips of cane used for this purpose are derived from the outer and "glassy" layer of the "East India rattan;" and in order to take advantage of the low price of Chinese labor (some few cents per

We have thus endeavored to present an accurate and popular, but by no means complete, exhibit of the growth and development of our country during the past; and its present financial and industrial strength; and, guided by the experience of former years, have sought to forecast and estimate, in a degree, its increase in the future. Fear, however, of extending this essay to an inordinate length, has induced us to refrain from the mention of various topics of nearly equal interest to those presented — such as the wonderful increase of our tonnage (temporarily interrupted in its growth by the existence of war and legalized piracy); of the increased value given to land by the extension of our railway system; of the addition to our agricultural resources of new staples for culture, as the sorghum,[16] and the like. But enough, we think, has been said; enough of statistics (which no partisan zeal can wrest from their true meaning) have been given, to satisfy our readers that the country cannot be destroyed, or even crippled, by any *probable* future debt; and to induce every loyal man, as he reflects upon our resources as a nation, to *"Thank God and take courage."*

But some may say, after reading this essay, "Admitting all that has been stated respecting the history of the past; admitting, also, that all the conditions for a future enormous increase and development of national wealth actually exist; yet, will not the necessity for the imposition of a future heavy taxation effectually cripple and check the industry and progress of the nation?" To this we reply, that the history of Great Britain furnishes us with a sufficient answer and refutation.

---

day), they have usually been split or peeled from the rattan before exportation. Within a comparatively recent period, however, a machine has been invented in this country, and successfully used, which, at one operation, takes off the whole outer portion of the rattan in strips, so much more rapidly, cheaply, and perfectly, as to forbid all competition from the Chinaman; and, in addition to this, leaves the interior of the rattan so well adapted for conversion into "artificial whalebone" for the manufacture of umbrella-frames, that the latter possesses a value, and sells in the market for as much as the first cost of the original cane as imported. We might also refer, as an example of recent American inventions, which have swept away, as it were, at one stroke, entire and ancient crafts of hand-labor, to the American cork-cutting machine, which cuts in one hour more and more perfect corks than ten expert workmen can cut in a day; and of inventions more particularly induced by the exigencies of the times, to that of "paper string" or "twine," so much cheaper and stronger than ordinary "cotton twine," that the use of this latter will undoubtedly be hereafter, in a great degree, discontinued.

[16] Of sorghum molasses, which was not known to this country in 1850, there was manufactured, in 1860, *over seven millions of gallons.*

Thus, in 1816, Great Britain, with a population of 19,275,000, without one mile of railway, or a single ocean steamer, with comparatively few labor-saving machines, and with onerous (and now obsolete) restrictions upon her industry, carried and sustained the maximum debt of her history, viz.: $4,205,000,000; and not only has Great Britain carried and sustained this enormous debt for the last forty-eight years (during which time she has almost constantly been engaged in war in some quarter of the globe) but she has so greatly thriven and prospered under it, that she now ranks *first* in wealth, and *first* in industrial power of all the nations that at present exist, or have ever existed. Shall the loyal States in 1864 (to say nothing of the whole country), with a present advantage of 30 per cent. in population, 33 per cent. in property, and more than 100 per cent. in the value of annual production — with a virgin soil, enormous emigration, a system of land tenure which conduces to the highest prosperity of the greatest number, and a condition of society in which individual enterprise is encouraged and fostered — shall the loyal States, we ask, with all these advantages, sink under a burden of debt less than two thirds that which Great Britain sustained in 1816?

Pamphlet 43

Timothy Shay Arthur

Growler's Income Tax.
(Loyal Publication Society, No. 57)

New York, 1864

[Many middle-class people objected to a new Federal intrusion, the income tax, which first went into effect in 1863. It was not an overwhelming burden. The income tax act of 1861 provided for an exemption of eight hundred dollars — as much as the best paid skilled worker earned. On income over that amount the tax was three per cent. In 1864 the exemption was lowered to six hundred dollars (the annual pay of a drug clerk), and a rate of five per cent was levied on incomes up to five thousand dollars, increasing to seven-and-one-half per cent from five thousand dollars to ten thousand dollars, and ten per cent on income over ten thousand dollars. The total amount raised by the tax during the remaining years of the war, from 1863 through 1865, was a trifling fifty-five million dollars. It was a minor source of income and a considerable irritation. Timothy Shay Arthur (1809–1885), writer of innumerable moral stories whose greatest success came in 1854 when he published the temperance novel *Ten Nights in a Barroom,* tried in the same vein to shame his compatriots into enthusiasm for the income tax.[1]]

My neighbor Growler, an excitable man by the way, is particularly excited over his Income Tax, or, as he called it, his "War Tax." He had never liked the war — thought it unnecessary and wicked; the work of politicians. The fighting of brother against brother was a terrible thing in his eyes. If you asked him who begun the war? — who struck at the nation's life? — if self defence were not a duty? — he would reply with vague generalities, made up of partisan tricky sentences, which he had learned without comprehending their just significance.

[1] [Randall and Donald, *Civil War and Reconstruction,* 344–345, 484–485; Timothy Shay Arthur, *Ten Nights in a Bar-Room,* ed. Donald A. Koch (Cambridge, 1964), v–xliii.]

Growler came in upon me the other day flourishing a square piece of blue writing paper, quite moved from his equanimity.

"There it is! Just so much robbery! Stand and deliver, is the word. Pistols and bayonets! Your money or your life!"

I took the piece of paper from his hand and read:

"Philadelphia, Sept., 1863.

"RICHARD GROWLER, ESQ.,

"*To* JOHN M. RILEY.   *Dr.*
"*Collector Internal Revenue for the 4th District of Pennsylvania. Office 427 Chestnut St.*

"For Tax on Income, for the year 1862 as per return made to the Assessor of the District, $43,21.

"Rec'd payment,
"JOHN M. RILEY, Collector."

"You're all right," I said smiling.

"I'd like to know what you mean, by all right!" Growler was just a little offended at my way of treating this serious matter — serious in his eyes, I mean. "I've been robbed of forty-three dollars and twenty-one cents," he continued.

"Do you say it is all right! A minion of the Government has put his hands into my pocket and taken just so much of my property. Is that all right?"

"The same thing may be set forth in very different language," I replied, "Let me state the case."

"Very well — state it!" said Growler, dumping himself into a chair, and looking as ill-humored as possible.

"Instead of being robbed," said I, "you have been protected in your property and person, and guaranteed all the high privileges of citizenship, for the paltry sum of forty-three dollars and twenty-one cents, as your share of the protection."

"O, that's only your way of putting the case," retorted Growler, dropping a little from his high tone of indignation.

"Let me be more particular in my way of putting the case. Your income is from the rent of property?"

"Yes."

"What would it have cost you to defend that property from the army of Gen. Lee, recently driven from our State by the nation's soldiers?"

"Cost me?" Growler looked at me in a kind of maze, as if he thought me half in jest.

"Exactly! What would it have cost you? Lee, if unopposed, would certainly have reached this city and held it; and if your property had been of use to him or to any of his officers or soldiers it would have been appropriated without so much as saying — 'By your leave, sir'? Would forty-three dollars and twenty-one cents have covered the damage? Perhaps not. Possibly, you might have lost one half or two thirds of all you are worth."

Growler was a trifle bewildered at this way of putting the case. He looked puzzled.

"You have a store on South wharves?" said I.

"Yes."

"What has kept the Alabama or the Florida from running up the Delaware and burning the whole city front? Do you have forts and ships of war for the protection of your property? If not who provides them? They are provided, and you are safe. What is your share of the expenses for a whole year! Just forty-three dollars and twenty-one cents! It sounds like a jest!"

Growler did not answer. So I kept on.

"But for our immense armies in the field, and navy on the water, this rebellion would have succeeded. What then? Have you ever pondered the future of this country in such an event? Have you thought of your own position? of the loss or gain to yourself? How long do you think we would be at peace with England or France, if the nation were dismembered, and a hostile Confederation established on our Southern border? Would our war taxes be less than now? Would life and property be more secure? Have you not an interest in our great army and navy, as I and every other member of the Union. Does not your safety as well as mine lie in their existence? Are they not, at this time, the conservators of everything we hold dear as men and citizens? Who equips and pays this army? Who builds and furnishes these ships? Where does the enormous sums of money required come from? It is the nation's work — the people aggregate in power and munificence, and so irresistible in might — unconquerable. Have you no heart swelling of pride in this magnificent exhibition of will and strength? No part in the nation's glory? No eager hand helping to stretch forth?"

Growler was silent still.

"There was no power in you or me to check the wave of destruction that was launched by parricidal hands against us. If unresisted, by the nation as an aggregate power, it would have swept in desolation over the whole land. Traitors in our midst and traitors moving in arms against us would have united to destroy our beautiful fabric of civil liberty. The Government, which dealt with all good citizens so kindly and gentle, not that one in a thousand felt its touch beyond the weight of a feather, would have been subverted; and who can tell under what iron rule we might have fallen for a time, or how many years of strife would have elapsed before that civil liberty which ensures the greatest good to numbers would have been again established? But the wave of destruction was met — nay, hurled back upon the enemies who sought our ruin. We yet dwell in safety. Your property is secure. You still gather your annual income, protected in all your rights by the strong national arm. And what does the nation assess to you as your share in the cost of this security? Half your property? No, not a farthing of that property! only a small per centage of your income from that property! *Just forty-three dollars and twenty-one cents!* Pardon me for saying it, friend G., but I am more than half ashamed of you."

"And seeing the way you put the case I am more than half ashamed of myself," he answered frankly. "Why, taking your view this is about the cheapest investment I ever made."

"You certainly get more money than in any other line of expenditure. Yesterday I had a letter from an old friend living in the neighborhood of Carlisle. The rebels took from him six fine horses, worth two hundred dollars apiece; six cows and oxen; and over two hundred bushels of grain. And not content with plundering him, they burnt down a barn which cost him nearly two thousand dollars. But for the men raised and equipped by the nation, in support of which you and I are taxed so lightly, we might have suffered as severely. How much do you think it cost in money for the protection we have received in this particular instance!"

"A million dollars perhaps?"

"Nearer ten millions of dollars. From the time our army left the

Rappahannock, until the battle of Gettysburg, its cost to the Government could scarcely have been less than we have mentioned. Of this sum your proportion can scarcely have been more than three or four dollars; and for that trifle your property and perhaps your life was held secure."

"No more of that, if you please," said Growler, showing some annoyance. "You are running the thing into the ground. I own up square. I was quarreling with my best friend. I was striking at the hand that gave protection. If my war tax next year should be a hundred dollars instead of forty-three, I will pay it without a murmur."

"Don't say without a murmur friend Growler."

"What then?"

"Say gladly, as a means of safety."

"Put it as you will," he answered folding up Collector Riley's receipt which he still held in his hand and bowing himself out.

Not many days afterwards I happened to hear some grumbling in my neighbor's presence about some income tax. Growler hardly waited to hear him through. My lesson was improved in his hands. In significant phrase he pitched into the offender and read him a lesson so much stronger than mine, that I felt myself thrown into the shade.

"You have been assessed fifty-eight dollars," he said in his excited way, "fifty-eight dollars, one would think from the noise you make about it, that you have been robbed of half your property. Fifty-eight dollars for security at home and abroad! Fifty-eight dollars as your share of the expenses of defence against an enemy that, if unopposed, will desolate our home and destroy our government! Already it has cost the nation for your safety and mine over a thousand million dollars; and you are angry because it asks for your little part of the expense. Sir you not worthy the name of an American citizen!"

"That is hard talk Growler, and I won't hear it!" said the other.

"It is true talk and you will have to bear it!" was retorted. "Fretting over the mean little sum of fifty-eight dollars! Why sir, I know a man who has given his right arm in the cause; and another who has given his right leg. Do they grumble? No sir! I never heard a word of complaint from their lips. Thousands and tens of thousands have given their sons, and wives have given their husbands

— sons and husbands who will never more return! They are with the dead. Sir you are dishonoring yourself in the eyes of men. A grumbler over this paltry war tax, for shame!"

I turned away saying in my thoughts:

"So much good done! My reclaimed sinner has become a preacher of righteousness."

Pamphlet 44

The Lincoln Catechism, Wherein the Eccentricities & Beauties of Despotism Are Fully Set Forth. A Guide to the Presidential Election of 1864.

New York, 1864

[Throughout the war, President Lincoln was frequently an object of ridicule to his political opponents. The scurrility of some of the attacks during the campaign of 1864 must have been an embarrassment to the Democratic party and of political benefit to the Republicans. The *Lincoln Catechism* is interesting as an illustration of how far these attacks could go in print. It was a lexicon of anti-Lincoln and anti-administration sloganeering, gossip, and libel; occasionally, as concerning civil liberties, it was clever and painfully close to the mark, but more often it reached beyond the bounds of truth or decency. J. F. Feeks, the publisher, also produced the *Trial of Abraham Lincoln, By the Great Statesmen of the Republic,* and *Abraham Africanus I, Mysteries of the White House.* One of the government charges against the Sons of Liberty was that they were circulating these pamphlets among themselves. Some Republican and Democratic pamphlets were almost as farfetched. Campaign Document No. 11 of the Society for the Diffusion of Political Knowledge was *Miscegenation Indorsed by the Republican Party.*]

LESSON THE FIRST.

I.

What is the Constitution?
A compact with hell — now obsolete.

II.

By whom hath the Constitution been made obsolete?
By Abraham Africanus the First.

III.

To what end?
That his days may be long in office — and that he may make himself and his people the equal of the negroes.

IV.

What is a President?
A general agent for negroes.

V.

What is Congress?
A body organized for the purpose of taxing the people to buy negroes, and to make laws to protect the President from being punished for his crimes.

VI.

What is an army?
A provost guard, to arrest white men, and set negroes free.

VII.

Who are members of Congress supposed to represent?
The President and his Cabinet.

VIII.

What is the meaning of *coining money?*
Printing green paper.

IX.

What did the Constitution mean by freedom of the Press?
Throwing Democratic newspapers out of the mails.

X.

What is the meaning of the word Liberty?
Incarceration in a vermin-infested bastile.

XI.

What is the duty of a Secretary of War?
To arrest freemen by telegraph.

XII.

What are the duties of a Secretary of the Navy?
To build and sink gunboats.

XIII.

What is the business of a Secretary of the Treasury?
To destroy State Banks and fill the pockets of the people full of worthless, irredeemable U. S. shinplasters.

XIV.

What is the chief business of a Secretary of State?
To print five volumes a year of Foreign Correspondence with himself, to drink whisky, and prophesy about war.

XV.

What is the meaning of the word "patriot?"
A man who loves his country less, and the negro more.

XVI.

What is the meaning of the word "traitor?"
One who is a stickler for the Constitution and the laws.

XVII.

What is the meaning of the word "Copperhead?"
A man who believes in the Union as it was, the Constitution as it is, and who cannot be bribed with greenbacks, nor frightened by a bastile.

XVIII.

What is a "loyal league?"
A body of men banded together, with secret signs and pass words, for the purpose of making a negro of a white man, and of controlling elections by force or fraud.

XIX.

What is the meaning of the word "law?"
The will of the President.

XX.

How were the States formed?
By the United States.

XXI.

Is the United States Government older than the States which made it?

It is.

XXII.

Have the States any rights?

None whatever, except when the President allows.

XXIII.

Have the people any rights?

None but such as the President gives.

XXIV.

Who is the greatest martyr of history?

John Brown.

XXV.

Who is the wisest man?

Abraham Lincoln.

XXVI.

Who is Jeff. Davis?

The devil.

LESSON THE SECOND.

I.

What is the *"habeas corpus?"*

The power of the President to imprison whom he pleases, as long as he pleases.

II.

What is Trial by Jury?

Trial by military commission.

III.

What is "security from unreasonable searches and seizures?"

The liability of a man's house to be entered by any Provost Marshal who pleases.

IV.

What is the meaning of the promise that, "no person shall be held to answer for any crime unless on a presentment or indictment of a Grand Jury?"

That any person may be arrested whenever the President or any of his officers please.

V.

What is the meaning of the promise that, "no person shall be deprived of life, liberty or property, without due process of law?"

That any person may be deprived of life, liberty and property, whom the President orders to be so stripped.

VI.

What is the meaning of "the right to a speedy and public trial by an impartial jury?"

A remote secret inquisition conducted by a man's enemies.

VII.

What is the meaning of the promise that the accused shall be tried "in the State and district wherein the crime shall have been committed?"

That he shall be sent away from the State and beyond the jurisdiction of the district where the offence is said to be committed.

VIII.

What is the meaning of the declaration that the accused shall "have the assistance of counsel for his defense?"

That, in the language of Seward to the prisoners in Fort Warren, "the employment of counsel will be deemed new cause for imprisonment."

IX.

What is the meaning of the declaration that, "the right of the people to keep and bear arms shall not be infringed?"

That a man's house may be searched, and he be stripped of his arms, whenever and wherever a provost marshal dare attempt it.

X.

What is the meaning of the declaration that "the accused shall be informed of the nature and cause of the accusation," against him?

That he shall not be informed of the nature of his offence.

XI.

What is the meaning of the promise that an accused man may "be confronted with the witnesses against him?"

That he shall not be allowed to confront them.

XII.

What is the meaning of the declaration that the accused "shall have compulsory process for obtaining witnesses in his favor?"

That he shall not be allowed any witnesses.

XIII.

What is the meaning of the declaration that "the judicial Power of the United States shall be vested in the Supreme Court," etc.?

That it shall be vested in the President and his provost marshals.

XIV.

What is the meaning of the declaration that "No bill of Attainder, or *ex post facto* law shall be passed?"

That such a law may be passed whenever Congress pleases.

XV.

What is the meaning of the President's oath that he, "will to the best of his ability, Preserve, protect and defend the Constitution of the United States?"

That he will do all in his power to subvert and destroy it.

XVI.

What is the meaning of that part of his oath in which he swears to "take care that the laws be faithfully executed?"

That he will appoint provost marshals to override and disobey the laws.

XVII.

What is the meaning of the declaration that "The United States shall guarantee to every state a Republican form of government?"

That Congress shall assist the President in destroying the Republican form of government in the States, and substituting a military government whenever he pleases — witness Missouri, Kentucky, Maryland, and Delaware.

XVIII.

What is the meaning of the declaration that "No attainder of Treason shall work corruption of blood, or forfeiture, except during the life of the person attainted?"

That a person accused of Treason may have his property confiscated not only during his life, but for all time, so that his children and heirs shall be punished for the crimes alleged against him.

XIX.

What is the meaning of the declaration, that "No person shall be convicted of treason unless on the testimony of two witnesses to some overt act, or on confession in open court?"

That a man may be convicted of treason without any witness, and without judge or jury, and without having committed any overt act.

XX.

What is the meaning of the declaration that "No money shall be drawn from the Treasury but in consequence of appropriations made by law?"

That the President may draw money from the Treasury whenever he pleases, for such things as sending missionaries and teachers to teach contrabands to read and write, or to build sheds and houses for stolen or run-away negroes.

XXI.

What is the meaning of the government?
The President.

XXII.

What is the meaning of an oath?
To swear not to do the thing you promise.

XXIII.

What is truth?
A lie.

LESSON THE THIRD.

I.

Do loyal leaguers believe in the Ten Commandments?

They do.

II.

What are the Ten Commandments?

Thou shalt have no other God but the negro.

Thou shalt make an image of a negro, and place it on the Capitol as the type of the new American man.

Thou shalt swear that the negro shall be the equal of the white man.

Thou shalt fight thy battles on the Sabbath day, and thy generals, and thy captains, and thy privates, and thy servants, shall do all manner of murders, and thefts as on the other six days.

Thou shalt not honor nor obey thy father nor thy mother if they are Copperheads; but thou shalt serve, honor and obey Abraham Lincoln.

Thou shalt commit murder — of slaveholders.

Thou mayest commit adultery — with the contrabands.

Thou shalt steal — everything that belongeth to a slaveholder.

Thou shalt bear false witness — against all slaveholders.

Thou shalt covet the slave-holder's man-servant and his maid-servant, and shalt steal his ox and his ass, and everything that belongeth to him.

For on these commandments hang all the law and the honor of loyal leaguers.

III.

Do loyal leaguers believe the teachings of the gospel?

They do.

IV.

What does the gospel teach?

That we shall hate those who believe not with us, and persecute those who never wronged us.

V.

What else does the gospel teach?
That we shall resist evil, and that we shall overcome evil with evil.

VI.

What does the gospel say of peace-makers?
That they shall be accursed.

VII.

Whose children are the peace-makers?
The children of the devil.

VIII.

Do Loyal Leagues believe in the Sermon on the Mount?
They do.

IX.

Repeat the Sermon on the Mount.
Blessed are the proud and the contractors, for theirs is the kingdom of greenbacks.
Blessed are they that do not mourn for them that are murdered in the abolition war, for they shall be comforted with office.
Blessed are the haughty, for they shall inherit shinplasters.
Blessed are they that do hunger and thirst after the blood of slaveholders, for they shall be filled.
Blessed are the unmerciful, for they shall obtain command.
Blessed are the vile in heart, for they shall be appointed judges.
Whosoever does not smite thee on one cheek, smite him on both.
And if he turn away from thee, turn and hit him again.
If thou findest a chance to steal a slaveholder's coat, steal his cloak also.
Give to a negro that asketh not, but from the poor white man turn thou away.
Be ye therefore unkind, spiteful, and revengeful, even as your father the devil is the same.
Take heed that ye give alms in public to the negroes, otherwise ye have no reward of your father Abraham, who is in Washington.

Therefore when thou givest thine alms to a negro, do thou sound a trumpet before thee, as the ministers and hypocrites do in the churches and in the streets, that they may have glory of the contrabands.

And when thou doest alms let each hand know what the other hand doeth.

That thine alms may not be secret; and thy father the devil, who established the leagues, shall reward thee openly.

And when thou prayest, go to the Academy of Music, or to Cooper's Institute, that thou mayest be seen of men, after the manner of Cora Hatch and Henry Ward Beecher.

Do not forgive men their trespasses, for if you do God will not forgive your trespasses.

Moreover, when you pretend to fast, fast not at all, but eat turkies, ducks, and especially roosters, that ye may crow over the Copperheads, and stuff yourselves with whatsoever a shinplaster buyeth.

Lay up for yourselves treasures in greenbacks and five-twenties, and whatever else ye may steal from the Custom House and the Treasury.

Every man can serve two masters, the devil and the Abolitionists.

Take no thought to get raiment by honest toil, but go down South and steal it. Consider the vultures and the hawks, how they toil not neither do they sow, and yet no creature was ever stuffed out with so much fatness, except a contraband that feedeth at the public crib.

Judge another without judge or jury, but destroy the laws, so that your own measure shall not be measured unto you again.

If thou hast a beam in thine own eye, shut thine eye so that it cannot be seen, and go to picking out the mote that is in the Copperhead's eye.

If a poor white man ask bread, give him a stone, if he ask a fish, give him an alligator.

Therefore, whatsoever ye would that the slaveholder should not do unto you, do it even unto him: for this is the law of the loyal leagues.

X.

Have the loyal leagues a prayer?
They have.

XI.

Repeat it.

Father Abram, who art in Washington, of glorious memory —
since the date of thy proclamation to free negroes.

Thy kingdom come, and overthrow the republic; thy will be done,
and the laws perish.

Give us this day our daily supply of greenbacks.

Forgive us our plunders, but destroy the Copperheads.

Lead us into fat pastures; but deliver us from the eye of detectives; and make us the equal of the negro; for such shall be our
kingdom, and the glory of thy administration.

LESSON THE FOURTH.

I.

What is the motto of loyal leagues?
"Liberty to the slave, or death to the Union."

II.

Does this place the negro above the Union?
It does.

III.

What do loyal leagues call the masses of the people?
"A herd of cattle" — *vide* Secretary Stanton.

IV.

How many of this "Herd of cattle" have the abolitionists caused
to be maimed or slain in this war?
One million.

V.

How many widows have they made?
Five hundred thousand.

VI.

How many orphans?
Ten hundred thousand.

VII.

What will Lincoln's administration cost the country?
Four thousand millions of dollars.

VIII.

What is the annual interest on this debt?
Two hundred and eighty millions of dollars.

IX.

How much will this interest amount to in ten years?
Two thousand and eight hundred million of dollars.

X.

How much will that be in twenty years?
Five thousand and six hundred million of dollars.

XI.

Would the entire surplus export production of the North pay the interest on its debt?
It would not.

XII.

How will this affect the people?
It will humble their pride, and make them feel that they have a government.

XIII.

What effect will this debt have on the farmer?
It will mortgage his farm to the Government for nearly the amount of the interest on its cash value.

XIV.

What effect will it have on the workingman?
It will mortgage his muscle and the sweat of his brow to the Government as long as he lives.

XV.

Is there any way for the people to get rid of this debt?
None whatever, but by repudiation.

XVI.

In case of repudiation, will "five twenties" go with the rest?
Yes — all government paper will sink together.

XVII.

How do the Republicans propose to prevent repudiation?
By a standing army of *negroes*, to force the people to pay at the point of the bayonet.

XVIII.

Who must pay the expense of the standing army?
The people; which will add three hundred millions annually to their debt.

XIX.

What will be the great advantage of this debt?
It will enslave the people, and bring them into the same wholesome subjection that they are in the Old World.

XX.

Is there any other benefit?
Yes — It will enable the children of the rich to live, without industry, upon the earnings of the poor from generation to generation.

XXI.

Should Mr. Lincoln be re-elected, what debt will he leave upon the country at the end of his second term?
Eight billions, or *eight thousand millions* of dollars!

XXII.

What will be the interest annually on this debt?
Five hundred and sixty millions of dollars.

XXIII.

What will be the annual expense for interest, and the standing army?
Eight hundred and sixty millions of dollars!

XXIV.

Will it be possible for the people to stand such a pressure of taxes?
They will have to stand it, or stand the prick of the bayonet.

XXV.

Suppose the people should take it into their heads to abandon their property and quit the country?

They will not be allowed — but will be compelled to remain and work for the support of the Government.

XXVI.

Will this be just?
Yes — "the government must be supported."

LESSON THE FIFTH.

I.

What was Abraham Lincoln by trade?
A rail-splitter.

II.

What is he now?
Union-splitter.

III.

Who is Sumner?
A free American of African descent, who would swear to support the Constitution "only as he understood it."

IV.

Who is Phillips?
One of the founders of the Republican party who "labored nineteen years to take fifteen states out of the Union."

V.

Who is Garrison?
A friend of the President, who went to hell, and found the original copy of the Constitution of the United States there.

VI.

Who is Seward?
A Prophet in the Temple of black dragons, and a taster in the government whiskey distillery.

VII.

Who is Chase?
The foreman of a green paper printing office.

VIII.

Who is Banks?
A dancing master, who wanted to slide down hill with the Union.

IX.

Who is Wade?
An amiable Christian gentleman who wanted to *"wade* up to his knees in the blood of slaveholders."

X.

Who is Francis S. Spinner?
A *spinner* of black yarn, who swore he would "abolish slavery, dissolve the Union, or have civil war," now Register of the Treasury.

XI.

Who is James S. Pike?
A stale fish which Mr. Lincoln presented as a Minister to the Netherlands, because, he said, "The Union is not worth supporting in connection with the South."

XII.

Who is Judge Spaulding?
A bad pot of *glue*, which would not hold the Union together, but declared in the Fremont Convention, "I am for dissolution, and I care not how soon it comes."

XIII.

Who is Jack Hale?
A hail fellow-well-met with the negroes, who introduced a petition to dissolve the Union in 1850.

XIV.

Who is Thomas F. Meagher?

An absconding prisoner from Botany Bay, who came to New York to "squelch the Copperheads."

XV.

Who is Simeon Draper?

A political *draper* by trade, who tried to *dress out* poor *Barney* of the Custom House, that he might make a *nice suit* for himself.

XVI.

Who is Horace Greeley?

A celebrated poet, who wrote a poem on the American Flag, beginning thus:

> Tear down the flaunting lie!
> Half-mast the starry flag!
> Insult no sunny sky,
> With hate's polluted rag.

XVII.

Who is Owen Lovejoy?

A fat and spongy Albino from Illinois. When it was supposed that his soul had floated off to Tartarus on the waves of his own fat, a brother member of Congress kindly wrote his epitaph:

> Beneath this stone good Owen Lovejoy lies,
> Little in everything except in size;
> What though his burly body fills this hole,
> Still through hell's key-hole crept his little soul.

And when good Owen returned to this mundane sphere, his arrival was celebrated by the following complimentary additional verse:

> The Devil finding Owen there,
> Began to flout and rave — and sware
> That hell should ne'er endure the stain,
> And kicked him back to earth again.

XVIII.

Who is Andrew Curtin?

A highly colored *screen,* to cover the whiskey in the Excutive Chamber of Pennsylvania.

XIX.

Who is John A. Dix?
A brave and invincible General, who never having had a chance to show prowess in battle, seized the Park Barracks containing seventy-five sick and wronged soldiers, and twenty-seven bushels of vermin.

XX.

Who is Park Godwin?
A celebrated Lexicographer, in the pay of Mr. Lincoln, who defines theft — "annoyance" and "botheration."

XXI.

Who is Henry J. Raymond?
A giant from the blood-stained plains of Solferino, enjoying a pension as Liar Extraordinary to the Administration.

XXII.

Who is the Rev. Henry Bellows?
A *windy instrument* of the abolitionists, who is trying very hard to make himself the equal of a negro.

XXIII.

Who is General Schenck?
A creature of very mixed *black and white* principles, which made an awful stink in Maryland.

XXIV.

Who is Thad Stephens?
An amalgamationist from Pennsylvania, who honestly practices what he preaches.

XXV.

Who is General Burnside?
A *fiery* commander who has had wonderful success in seizing peaceable and unarmed civilians, when they were asleep in their own beds at midnight; and who was once caught in a trap by a famous old trapper of the name of Lee.

XXVI.

Who is James T. Brady?

A gentleman of great political versatility, now affiliated with the amalgamationists, who believes that "A rose by any other name would smell as sweet."

XXVII.

Who is Anna Dickinson?

Ask Ben. Butler and William D. Kelly.

XXVIII.

Who is Ben. Butler?

A Satyr, who has the face of a devil and the heart of a beast, who laughed when Banks supplanted him in New Orleans, saying, "he will find it a squeezed lemon."

XXIX.

Who is William D. Kelly?

A member of Congress, and a wagon contractor, who plays a bass viol in the orchestra of the female loyal leagues.

XXX.

Who is Henry P. Stanton?

A white man, whose negro principles, are undergoing a bleaching process, in consequence of his having been made a scape-goat for all of Chase's forty thieves in the Custom House.

LESSON THE SIXTH.

I.

What is the chief end of the loyal leagues?

The end of the Union.

II.

What are States?

Colonies of the Federal Government.

III.

What is a Judge?
A provost marshal.

IV.

What is a court of law?
A body of soldiers, appointed by a General to try civilians without law.

V.

What is a Bastile?
A Republican meeting-house, for the involuntary assembling of men who believe in the Union as it was, and the Constitution as it is.

VI.

What is the meaning of the word "demagogue?"
Ask those members of Congress, who believe the war is for the negro, and for the destruction of the Union, and yet vote it supplies of men and money.

VII.

What is a Governor?
A general agent for the President.

VIII.

What is a negro?
A white man with a black skin.

IX.

What is a white man?
A negro with a white skin.

X.

What will be the effect of amalgamation?
It is the doctrine of the Leagues that a superior race will spring from amalgamation.

XI.

Is this according to science?
No, — science teaches that the progeny of amalgamation would run out, and become extinct after the fourth or fifth generation.

XII.

Is science true?

No — it must be a lie; or the Leaguers are the greatest fools or knaves that ever lived.

XIII.

Is amalgamation now practiced to a greater extent than formerly?

It is, to a much greater extent.

XIV.

Where?

Everywhere where Leagues prevail.

XV.

Is it prosperous in Washington?

It is — so much so that more than five thousand of the fruits of amalgamation have been born in that city since the election of Mr. Lincoln.

XVI.

Is it spreading elsewhere?

Yes — wherever the officers of our army go in the South, it is doing well.

XVII.

How is it in New Orleans?

Well; — but there are a great many squint-eyed yellow babies there, supposed to have been occasioned by fright at the presence of Ben. Butler.

XVIII.

Did the same thing occur at Fortress Monroe, after Ben. Butler was in command there?

It did.

XIX.

The effects of fright are very wonderful in such cases, are they not?

They are wonderful indeed.

XX.

Do such remarkable imitations ever spring from any other cause than fright?

Yes — as in cases where such imitations follow good looking men, like Senators Wilson and Sumner.

XXI.

Is the science of amalgamation now in its infancy?

Comparatively — but, under the patronage of the loyal leagues, a great number of practical and experimental works will soon be *issued.*

XXII.

Who are engaged on these works?

The learned abolition clergy, Members of Congress, and all *competent* loyal leaguers.

XXIII.

Are the loyal leagues intended to be *"nurseries"* of the new science of amalgamation?

They are.

XXIV.

Is amalgamation considered the true doctrine of *negro equality* as taught by Mr. Lincoln in his debates with Mr. Douglas?

It is.

XXV.

Is this what Anna Dickinson really means by "the lesson of the hour?"

It is.

XXVI.

Is this what the President means by "Rising with the occasion?"

It is.

LESSON THE SEVENTH.

I.

Were the framers of the Constitution shortsighted and foolish men?

They were.

II.

Are their pernicious sentiments condemnatory of our most righteous abolition war?

They are.

III.

What did Jefferson, the father of the Declaration of Independence, teach?

That, "the several states which framed the Constitution have the unquestionable right to judge of infractions."

IV.

What did James Madison, the father of the Constitution, say?

That, "in case of a deliberate, palpable and dangerous exercise of powers not granted in the Compact, the States have a right to interfere, for maintaining within their respective limits the authorities, rights and liberties appertaining to them."

V.

What did John Quincy Adams say?

That, "if the day shall come — may Heaven avert it! — when the affections of the people of these States shall be alienated from each other, when this fraternal spirit shall give way to cold indifference, or collisions of interest shall fester into hatred — then the bands of political association will not hold together parties no longer attracted by the magnetism of conciliated interests and kindly sympathies, and far better will it be for the people of the disunited States to part in friendship from each other than to be held together by restraint."

VI.

Have still later statesmen and politicians been affected with the same damnable idea?

They have.

VII.

What did Daniel Webster say?

"A bargain broken on one side is a bargain broken on all sides."

VIII.

What did Andrew Jackson say in his farewell address?

That, "If such a struggle is once begun, and the citizens of one section of the country are arrayed in arms against those of the other, in doubtful conflict, let the battle result as it may, there will be an end of the Union, and with it an end of the hope of freedom. The victory of the injured would not secure to them the blessings of liberty; it would avenge their wrongs, but they would themselves share in the common ruin. The Constitution cannot be maintained nor the Union preserved, in opposition to public feeling, by the mere exertion of the coercive powers confided to the government."

IX.

What did Abraham Lincoln say in Congress in 1848?

That, "Any people anywhere, being inclined, and having the power, have the RIGHT to rise up and shake off the existing government, and form a new one that suits them better. This is a most valuable, a most sacred right — a right which we hope and believe, is to liberate the world. Nor is the right confined to the cause in which the whole people of an existing government may choose to exercise it. ANY PORTION of such people that CAN, MAY revolutionize and make their OWN of so much of the Territory as they inhabit."

X.

What did Henry Clay say?

That, "When my State is right — when it has cause for resistance — when tyranny and wrong and oppression insufferable arise, I will share her fortunes."

XI.

What did U. S. Senator Levi Woodbury of New Hampshire say?

That, "If the bonds of a common language, a common government and all the common glories of the last century, cannot make us conciliatory and kind — cannot make all sides forgive and forget something, — cannot persuade to some sacrifice even, if necessary, to hold us together, FORCE IS AS UNPROFITABLE TO ACCOMPLISH IT AS FRATRICIDE IS TO PERPETUATE PEACE IN A COMMON FAMILY."

XII.

What did Horace Greeley say in the *Tribune*, Nov. 26, 1860?

That, "If the Cotton States unitedly and earnestly wish to withdraw peacefully from the Union, we think they should be allowed to do so. Any attempt to compel them by force to remain, would be contrary to the principles enunciated in the immortal Declaration of Independence."

XIII.

What did Mr. Greeley say in the *Tribune*, Dec. 17, 1860?

That, "We have repeatedly asked those who dissent from our view of this matter, to tell us frankly whether they do or do not assent to Mr. Jefferson's statement in the Declaration of Independence, that governments 'derive their just powers from THE CONSENT OF THE GOVERNED; and that, whenever any form of government becomes destructive of these ends, *it is the right of the people to alter or abolish it,* and to institute a new government, &c., &c.' We do heartily accept this doctrine, believing it intrinsically *sound, beneficent,* and one that, universally accepted, is calculated to *prevent the shedding of seas of human blood.* AND, IF IT JUSTIFIED THE SECESSION FROM THE BRITISH EMPIRE OF THREE MILLIONS OF COLONISTS IN 1776, WE DO NOT SEE WHY IT WOULD NOT JUSTIFY THE SECESSION OF FIVE MILLIONS OF SOUTHERNERS FROM THE FEDERAL UNION in 1861. If we are mistaken on this point why does not some one attempt to show wherein and why? For our own part, while we deny the right of slaveholders to hold slaves against the will of the latter, we cannot see how Twenty Millions of people can rightfully hold Ten or even Five Millions in a detested Union with them BY MILITARY FORCE.

"If even 'seven or eight States' send agents to Washington to say,

'We want to get out of the Union,' we shall feel constrained by our devotion to Human Liberty to say, *Let them go!* And we do not see how we could take the other side WITHOUT COMING IN DIRECT CONTACT WITH THOSE RIGHTS OF MAN WHICH WE HOLD PARAMOUNT TO ALL PO-LITICAL ARRANGEMENTS, however convenient and advantageous."

XIV.

What did Chancellor Walworth say March 1st 1861?

That, "It would be as brutal to send men to butcher their brothers of the Southern States, as it would be to massacre them in Northern States."

XV.

What did David S. Dickenson say in 1860?

That, "The Union is not to be maintained by force."

XVI.

What did Judge Amasa J. Parker say?

That, "our people shrink back aghast at the idea of repeating, in this enlightened age, that first great crime of man, the staining of their hands with a brother's blood."

XVII.

What did Senator Stephen A. Douglas say:

That, "I don't understand how a man can claim to be a friend of the Union, and yet be in favor of war upon ten millions of people in the Union. You cannot cover this up much longer under the pre-text of love for the Union."

XVIII.

What did the address of the Democratic State Convention of New York say in 1861?

That "the worst and most ineffective argument that can be ad-dressed by the Federal Government, or its adhering members, to the seceding States, is civil war. Civil war will not restore the Union, but will defeat forever its reconstruction."

XIX.

What did the Tammany Hall resolutions of March 1st, 1861, say?

That, "No State shall be coerced into remaining in this Union, when, in the judgment of her people, her safety requires that she should secede in order to protect the lives and property of her citizens.

"We will oppose any attempt on the part of the Republicans in power to make any armed aggression under the plea of 'enforcing the laws,' or 'preserving the Union,' upon the Southern States."

XX.

Are not the sentiments expressed by all the above named statesmen and politicians, the same as now held by such infamous traitors as Clement Vallandigham and C. Chauncey Burr?

They are.

XXI.

What ought to be done with such men as Vallandigham and Burr, who "cling to these dogmas of the dead past?"

They ought to be hanged.

XXII.

Were Gen. Jackson and John Quincy Adams to come on earth again and teach the same as they once did, would they deserve to be hanged?

They would.

XXIII.

What should be done to Tammany Hall if it held the same doctrine now that it did three years ago?

It should be hanged, individually and collectively.

XXIV.

What should be done to Abraham Lincoln if he believed now as he did in 1848?

The king can do no wrong.

XXV.

Are all who believe as our fathers taught, "traitors" and "sympathizers?"

They are.

XXVI.

What will become of all who believe in the Union as it was, and the Constitution as it is?

They shall be damned.

XXVII.

What shall be the reward of all such as believe the Union was a covenant with death, and the Constitution a compact with hell?

They shall be received into a negro Paradise.

LESSON THE NINTH.

I.

Is the United States a consolidated government?

It is.

II.

Who consolidated it?

Abraham Lincoln.

III.

Does consolidation mean to annihilate the States?

Yes — to a great extent.

IV.

Had he a right to do this?

Yes — under the war power.

V.

Who invented the war power?

Abraham Lincoln.

VI.

For what purpose did he invent the war power?

That he might not have to return to the business of splitting rails.

VII.

Was Mr. Lincoln ever distinguished as a military officer?

He was — In the Black Hawk war.

VIII.

What high military position did he hold in that war?
He was a cook.

IX.

Was he distinguished for anything except for his genius as a cook?
Yes — he often pretended to see Indians in the woods, where it was afterwards proved that none existed.

X.

Was he ever in any battle?
No — he prudently skedaddled, and went home at the approach of the first engagement.

XI.

Is there proof of this?
Yes — there are several men still living in Sangamon County, Illinois, who were present in the brigade at the time.

XII.

Does the Republican party intend to change the name of the United States?
It does.

XIII.

What do they intend to call it?
New Africa.

XIV.

How will New Africa be bordered?
On the North by the North Star, on the East by Boston, on the West by Sunset, and on the South by Salt-river.

XV.

Are the people of the United States happy?
They are, very.

XVI.

What do they live upon?
Chiefly on blood.

XVII.

What do the Republicans understand by the word people?
Abolitionists, mesmerisers, spiritual mediums, free-lovers and negroes.

XVIII.

What is to be the established religion of New Africa?
Infidelity.

XIX.

How are the people to be divided?
Into the rich, the poor, the wise and the foolish.

XX.

Who are the rich?
The Generals, the office-holders, and the thieves.

XXI.

Who are the poor?
The soldiers, and all the people who are neither office-holders or thieves.

XXII.

Who are the wise?
The Copperheads, because they are "serpents."

XXIII.

Who are the foolish?
The black-snakes, because they are fast wriggling into a spot where they will run against the fangs of the Copperheads.

XXIV.

Is the black-snake afraid of the Copperheads?
Yes — as he is of the devil.

XXV.

What is the uniform of a chaplain of the leagues?
A shirt, a revolver, and a dirk.

XXVI.

How was this found out?

By the discovery of a Reverend loyal leaguer in full uniform in a lady's chamber, in Massachusetts.

XXVII.

When caught did he confess that every loyal leaguer is pledged to be always armed with these implements?

He did.

XXVIII.

Did he make a clean breast of the secrets of the order?

Yes, he made a good deal cleaner *breast* than *shirt*.

XXIX.

What did the lady leaguer say when this loyal chaplain was found in her room?

She said her husband was a brute to come home when he wasn't wanted.

XXX.

Are all husbands brutes who go home when the loyal league brethren are visiting their wives?

They are, great brutes.

LESSON THE TENTH.

I.

Are the loyal leaguers taught to hate any man?

They are.

II.

Who is he?

George B. McClellan.

III.

Why are they taught to hate McClellan?

Because he wished to restore the Union as it was, and preserve the Constitution as our fathers made it.

IV.

Why do the loyal leagues wish the Union as it was, and the Constitution as it is, destroyed?

Because in no other way can they destroy the property of the South, and make the negro the equal of the white man.

V.

Is this the object of the war?
It is.

VI.

For what other reason are the leagues taught to hate McClellan?

Because he refused to let the army under his command steal or destroy the private property of the Southern people.

VII.

Are these the reasons why he was removed from command?

They are — because his great popularity with the soldiers might render him a stumbling-block in the Presidential campaign for 1864.

VIII.

Has Mr. Lincoln any other stumbling-blocks?
He has.

IX.

Can you name them?
General Fremont is one, and Lincoln fears, a very dangerous one.

X.

Is this the reason Mr. Lincoln has not given him a command?
It is.

XI.

Did Mr. Lincoln approve of the principles of Fremont's campaign in the West?

He did, approve of every thing except his aspirations for the presidency, and his popularity among the Germans.

XII.

What other stumbling-block has Mr. Lincoln?

Chase, who is trying to buy his own nomination, by putting extra steam on his high-pressure greenback printing machines.

XIII.

What is Mr. Seward in this contest?

A broken bubble.

XIV.

When does Seward think the war will end?

In sixty days.

XV.

When does Lincoln expect it will end?

When Afric's woods are moved to Washington.

XVI.

Who is Mrs. Lincoln?

The wife of the government.

XVII.

Who is Mr. Lincoln?

A successful contractor to supply the government with mules.

XVIII.

Who is Master Bob Lincoln?

A lucky boy, yet in his teens, who has been so happy as to obtain shares in Government Contracts by which he has realized $300,000.

LESSON THE ELEVENTH.

I.

What is the meaning of the word swamp?

It is a place in Florida where Mr. Lincoln proposes to hide a small number of Yankees, to act as presidential electors for him next fall.

II.

What is a lagoon?
A place in Louisiana to be used for the same purpose.

III.

What is the meaning of the phrase to count chickens before they are hatched?
Mr. Lincoln's reckoning upon the quiet submission of all the states to his scheme of electoral frauds.

IV.

What does he fear?
That, when the pinch comes at last, the people will fly to arms and make an end of his rotten borough system and of himself together.

V.

What is a bank-director?
A silly coon, caught in one of Chase's traps.

VI.

What is a government bank?
A new engine turned loose on the track to run over all the State banks.

VII.

What will be the result?
That all banks, State and National, will be smashed up together.

VIII.

What are Five-Twenties?
Lincoln *I. O. U's.* — made redeemable in government slips of paper, in five or twenty years.

IX.

What else are they?
Baits to catch *flat* fish.

X.

Are loyal leaguers allowed to refer to the Constitution?
Only in terms of reproach.

XI.

Is it a disloyal practice to refer to the exploded right of trial by jury?
It is very disloyal.

XII.

Is it disloyal to refer to the size of Old Abe's feet?
It is.

XIII.

Is it disloyal to speak of white men as a superior race?
It is, very.

XIV.

Is it disloyal for a husband to object to his house being visited by strange men whose acquaintance his wife forms at the meetings of the loyal leagues?
It is, shockingly disloyal.

XV.

Is it disloyal to believe in the Union as it was?
It is.

XVI.

Is it a disloyal practice to say that the abolitionists ought to do the fighting in their war for the negroes?
It is, dangerously disloyal.

XVII.

Is it disloyal to allude to the rate at which the Republicans are plundering the Treasury and the people?
It is.

XVIII.

Is it disloyal to allude to the difference between an old fashioned

Democratic gold dollar and the Republican green paper dollars?
   It is.

XIX.

   Is it disloyal to allude to the opinions and practices of our fathers on civil liberty or the rights of the States?
   It is.

XX.

   Is it disloyal for a man to sympathize with the family of a murdered friend or relative in the South?
   It is, wickedly disloyal.

XXI.

   Is it disloyal to honestly believe in one's heart that if Lincoln is not a fool he is a knave, and that if he is not a knave he is a fool?
   It is, horribly disloyal.

Pamphlet 45

The Great Surrender to the Rebels in Arms. The Armistice. (Union Executive Congressional Committee, No. 4)

Washington, 1864

[The Republicans, styling themselves the Union party, tried to affix upon the Democrats the name Copperhead during the campaign of 1864, and more important, to label them the party of treason. The Democrats who were, in the overwhelming majority, loyal to the Union cause, and whose quarrels with the Lincoln administration were over civil liberties, emancipation, and the conduct of the war, rather than over preservation of the Federal Union, nevertheless played into the Republicans' hands. They allowed Clement L. Vallandigham, who had slipped back into the United States from his Canadian exile, to dominate the platform committee at the Democratic convention, and write into it a "peace plank." This plank proclaimed the war a failure, but did not concede that the Confederacy should be granted its independence. Rather it called for "a cessation of hostilities with a view to an ultimate convention of the States or other peaceable means to the end that at the earliest practicable moment peace may be restored upon the basis of the Federal Union of the States." Republicans wrested out of this context the words "Immediate efforts be made for a cessation of hostilities," and used them repeatedly with effect. Just after the convention came the capture of Atlanta and other striking Union victories; it was easy for the Republicans to ridicule the Democratic assumption that the war was a failure, and, more than that, to make Democratic victory appear to be the one remaining Southern hope.

This pamphlet also included one of the standard ingredients of numerous Northern propaganda productions during the war years, the spurious "great Union speech" of Alexander H. Stephens, the Vice-President of the Confederacy. Stephens had indeed opposed secession, but not in the rabid tones which time and again were ascribed to him in broadsides and pamphlets. While milder, genuine speeches of Stephens were also published, they attracted far less attention than the spectacular fraud. The Loyal Publication Society in 1864 alone printed nearly one hundred thousand copies of it. The Union League of Philadelphia far eclipsed this figure, issuing it as part of the content of pamphlets, and also as a broadside in both English and German. James G. Randall has shown that this, the supposed

Georgia State Convention speech of January, 1861, was manifestly fraudulent. In part it was manufactured from Hinton R. Helper's *Impending
Crisis* (1857) which Republicans had circulated in the campaign of 1860.[1]]

"Immediate efforts be made for a cessation of hostilities." — *Peace
and Disunion Platform of the Chicago Copperhead Convention.*

FOR more than three years our beloved country has been engaged in a bloody and desolating war to restore the Union and
uphold and maintain our Constitution. This war, the most causeless
and wanton that history has ever recorded, was commenced by bold,
bad, and ambitious men to throw off the salutary restraints of a
good Government, and establish a republic which should have for
its corner-stone the institution of human bondage. A few base and
infamous men in the North have sometimes undertaken the ignoble
task of excusing the traitors who have taken up arms against the
Government by attempting to show that the rights of the slaveholding States had been invaded. There can be no better answer
to these men who have been so swift to apologize for rebels, than
that made by the Hon. ALEXANDER H. STEPHENS, of Georgia, (now
the Vice President of the bogus Confederacy,) in the Convention in
Georgia, in 1861, which passed the secession ordinance. The candid
reader is requested to carefully peruse what Mr. Stephens says, and
see how completely he answers the miserable lickspittles and Southern sympathizers in the North, who palliate and excuse the great
crime of secession. Mr. Stephens said:

> This step (Secession) once taken, can never be recalled; and all the baneful
> consequences that must follow must rest on the convention for all coming time.
> When we and our posterity shall see our lovely South desolated by the demon
> of war, which this act of yours will inevitably invite and call forth; when our
> green fields of waving harvests shall be trodden down by the murderous
> soldiery and the fiery car of war sweeping over our land, our temples of justice
> laid in ashes, all the horrors and desolations of war upon us, who but this con-

---

[1] [James G. Randall, *Civil War and Reconstruction* (Boston, 1937), 638. *Cf.*, A. H.
Stephens and E. W. Gantt, *Prophecy and Fulfillment. Speech of A. H. Stephens . . .
Address of E. W. Gantt of Arkansas . . .* (Loyal Publication Society No. 36, New
York, 1863); *Two Ways of Treason; or, The Open Traitor of the South Face to Face
with His Skulking Abettor at the North* (Loyal Publication Society No. 33, New York,
1863); Stephens, *The Great Union Speech of Hon. Alexander H. Stephens . . .* (Union League Broadside No. 1, Philadelphia, 1863); [John Austin Stevens, Jr.], *Proceedings at the Second Anniversary Meeting . . .* (Loyal Publication Society No. 78,
New York, 1865), 18.]

vention will be held responsible for it, and who but he that shall give his vote for this unwise and ill-timed measure shall be held to strict account for this suicidal act by the present generation, and probably cursed and execrated by posterity in all coming time, for the wide and desolating ruin that will inevitably follow this act you now propose to perpetrate?

Pause, I entreat you, and consider for a moment what reasons you can give that will even satisfy yourselves in calmer moments, what reasons you can give to your fellow sufferers in the calamity that it will bring. What reasons can you give to the nations of the earth to justify it? They will be the calm and deliberate judges in the case; and to what cause, or one overt act, can you point on which to rest the plea of justification? What right has the North assailed? What interest of the South as been invaded? What justice has been denied, or what claim founded in justice and right has been withheld? Can any of you to-day name one governmental act of wrong deliberately and purposely done by the Government at Washington, of which the South has a right to complain? I challenge the answer.

On the other hand, let me show the facts of which I wish you to judge; I will only state facts which are clear and undeniable, and which now stand as records authentic in the history of our country. When we of the South demanded the slave trade, or the importation of Africans for the cultivation of our lands, did they not yield the right for twenty years? When we asked for a three-fifths representation in Congress for our slaves, was it not granted? When we demanded the return of any fugitive from justice, or the recovery of those persons owing labor or allegiance, was it not incorporated in the Constitution, and again ratified and strengthened in the fugitive slave law of 1850? When we asked that more territory should be added that we might spread the institution of slavery, have they not yielded to our demands, in giving Louisiana, Florida, and Texas, out of which four States might have been carved, and ample territory for four more to be added in due time, if you, by this unwise and impolitic act, do not destroy this hope, and by it lose all, and have your last slave wrenched from you by stern military rule, as South America and Mexico were, or by the vindictive decree of universal emancipation, which may reasonably be expected to follow?

But what have we to gain by this proposed change of our relation to the General Government? We have always had the control of it, and can yet if we remain in it, and are united as we have been. We have had a majority of the Presidents chosen from the South, as well as the control and management of most of those chosen from the North. We have had sixty years of Southern Presidents to their twenty-four, thus controlling the Executive department. So of the judges of the Supreme Court, we have had eighteen from the South, and but eleven from the North. Although nearly four-fifths of the judicial business has arisen in the free States, yet a majority of the court has always been from the South. This we have required, so as to guard against any interpretation of the Constitution unfavorable to us. In like manner, we have been equally watchful to guard our interests in the legislative branch of government. In choosing the presiding Presidents (pro tem.) of the Senate, we have had twenty-four to their eleven. Speakers of the House, we have had twenty-three and they twelve. While the majority of Representatives, from their greater population, have always been from the North, yet we have so generally secured the Speaker, because he, to a great extent, shapes and controls the legislation of the country.

Nor have we had less control in every other department of the General Government. Of Attorney Generals we have had fourteen, while the North has had but five. Of foreign Ministers we have had eighty-six, and they had but fifty-four. While three-fourths of the business which demands diplomatic agents abroad is clearly from the free States, from their greater commercial interest, yet we have had the principal embassies, so as to secure the world's markets for our cotton, tobacco, and sugar, on the best possible terms. We have had a vast majority of the higher officers of both army and navy, while a large proportion of the soldiers and sailors were drawn from the North. Equally so of clerks, auditors, and comptrollers filling the Executive departments. The record shows for the last fifty years, that of the three thousand thus employed, we have had more than two-thirds of the same, while we have but one-third of the white population of the Republic. Again, look at another item, in which we have a great and vital interest, that of revenue, or means of supporting Government. From official documents we learn that a fraction over three-fourths of the revenue collected for the support of Government, has uniformly been raised from the North.

Pause now, while you can, and contemplate carefully and candidly these important items. Leaving out of view for the present of countless millions of dollars you must expend in war with the North, with tens of thousands of your sons and brothers slain in battle and offered up as sacrifices upon the alter of your ambition — and for what? Is it for the overthrow of the American Government, established by our common ancestry, cemented and built up by their sweat and blood, and founded on the broad principles of right, justice, and humanity? And as such, I must declare here, as I have often done before, and which has been repeated by the greatest and wisest of statesmen and patriots in this and other lands, that it is the best and freest government, the most equal in its rights, the most just in its decisions, the most lenient in its measures, and the most inspiring in its principles to elevate the race of men, that the sun of heaven ever shone upon. Now, for you to attempt to overthrow such a Government as this, unassailed, is the heighth of madness, folly, and wickedness.

No language can measure the awful consequences that have followed, since the rebels made war upon our Government, by firing on our flag at Fort Sumter. It will be left for the weeping voice of history to record how much blood has been shed, how many precious lives have been sacrificed, how great have been the mourning and anguish throughout all the land, what oceans of treasure have been expended to put down this rebellion, and restore the Union and

Constitution of our fathers. But this same history will record on its brightest page, and in letters of living light, the achievements and the glories of our countrymen in arms. Posterity to the latest ages, will read with gratitude and pride of the "battles fought and victories won" by the noble men who have gone out from among us, to sustain our Government and vindicate the honor of our insulted flag. The magnificent fighting that has been done by our troops, illustrating on so many fields their heroism and their valor, the splendid record of what they have accomplished in their great work, shall stand out as the marvel of all coming time. *To-day*, the power of the rebellion reels and totters to its final and complete overthrow. The old sea-dog, FARRAGUT, whose naval achievements are without parallel in the history of naval warfare, has, by unheard of skill and gallantry, captured all the approaches to Mobile harbor, taking Forts Gaines and Morgan (the two strongest forts on this continent) with their garrison and armament; and sealing up that port against British blockade runners. The invincible and heroic SHERMAN, advancing over half an empire, fighting a succession of victorious battles and challenging the admiration and gratitude of his countrymen, with his battle-scarred and war-worn veterans, has pierced the very heart of rebeldom in the Southwest. Atlanta, the very keystone of the rebel arch of the best half of their bogus Confederacy, falls before his marvellous skill and the unrelenting energy of his unconquerable legions. GRANT, the "Hero of the Mississippi," whose unequaled achievement in the capture of Vicksburg, opened the "Father of Waters" so that the commerce of the northwest now floats "unvexed to the sea." He fought a battle above the clouds at Chattanooga, snatching victory from the jaws of defeat, and opened the gateway to Georgia. Taking command of the Army of the Potomac, with unparalleled audacity and courage, he attacks Lee with his chosen army in his works on the Rapid Ann, and by a series of the most bloody battles ever fought, drives the rebel chieftain through sixty miles of his intrenchments to the defences of Richmond. There, by a masterly maneuver, he plants himself on the south side of James river, obtains and holds possession of the Weldon railroad, the great artery into the capital of the rebel government. He has fixed his bull-dog grasp on the very throat of the rebellion, and that grasp will never be relaxed until the success of a disloyal party shall demand it, or until the American flag shall float in triumph and glory from the dome of the rebel capitol.

Who cannot see that the rebellion is at its last gasp. A great part of the rebellious territory has been recovered. The "Star Spangled Banner" now floats *in every State of the Union*. There are now only two or three States where the rebel power pretends to maintain itself even partially intact.

Lieutenant General GRANT, in the following letter written to a friend, gives his ideas of the present military and political situation. Such words coming from that great chieftain, who knows and judges so well, should sink deep into every loyal heart:

WASHINGTON, September 8, 1864.
HEADQUARTERS OF THE ARMIES OF THE UNITED STATES,
CITY POINT, Virginia, August 16, 1864.

Hon. E. B. WASHBURNE:

DEAR SIR: I state to all citizens who visit me that all we want now to insure an early restoration of the Union is *a determined unity of sentiment in the North*. The rebels have now in their ranks their last man. The little boys and old men are guarding prisoners, guarding railroads and bridges, and forming a good part of their garrisons for intrenched positions. A man lost by them cannot be replaced. *They have robbed the cradle and the grave equally to get their present force.* Besides what they lose in frequent skirmishes and battles, they are now losing from desertion and other causes at least one regiment per day. With this drain upon them the end is not far distant, *if we will only be true to ourselves*. Their only hope now is in a divided North. This might give them reinforcements from Tennessee, Kentucky, Maryland and Missouri, while it would weaken us. With the draft quietly enforced, the enemy would become despondent, and would make but little resistance. I have no doubt but the enemy are exceedingly anxious to hold out until after the Presidential election. They have many hopes from its effects. They hope a counter revolution. They hope the election of the peace candidate; in fact, like Micawber, they hope for "something to turn up." *Our peace friends, if they expect peace from separation are much mistaken. It would be but the beginning of war*, with thousands of Northern men joining the South, because of our disgrace in allowing separation. To have peace on any terms, the South would demand the restoration of their slaves already freed. They would demand indemnity for losses sustained, *and they would demand a treaty which would make the North slave hunters for the South*. They would demand pay, or the restoration of every slave escaping to the North.

Yours, truly,   U. S. GRANT.

The view expressed by Gen. Grant in his letter in relation to what the rebels expect from the Presidential election is sustained by the best rebel authority. Senator Semmes, of Mississippi, delivered a speech at Jackson, Miss., on the 15th ult., in which he said:

Our hopes for an early peace were dependant entirely on the success of the Democratic party at the North in the approaching Presidential election. The whole population of the North, the rich as well as the poor, were now called to face the war with all its horrors; and he believed that they would not submit to the draft ordered for the 5th of September next; that they would resist by force of arms first; that the Peace party would continue to grow and be successful in the approaching canvass.

The honorable rebel gentleman gave his views of military affairs as follows:

He said he did not desire to excite any undue expectations or alarm, that everything depended upon Sherman being routed from Atlanta. That Richmond was safe, and Atlanta would be the great battle-field of this war. Everything indicated that the enemy were concentrating all their available forces there; our Government was doing the same. Mississippi would have to take care of herself for the present, for the fall of Atlanta would establish a trans-Chattahoochee department, cut us off from Richmond, and entail upon us the same difficulties which now existed with regard to the trans-Mississippi department; it would enable Lincoln to enforce his draft upon the 5th of September next, secure the re-election of that black-hearted monster, and prolong the war to an indefinite period of time.

Such is the condition of things. After the most terrific military struggle the world has ever seen, the war approaches its triumphant termination with a restored Union, with the Constitution vindicated, and with a strength and a power and a glory that makes us the first nation on the globe. But we now have to contemplate an appalling fact. A great party in the North, prostituting the name of "Democracy" to its base and disloyal purposes, and acting in sympathy and in concert with traitors in arms, have recently held a Convention at Chicago, which was in open sympathy with the rebels. The New York *Herald*, a paper that is independent of all parties, in speaking of this Convention, utters the following important truths:

We have not the slightest doubt that there is a mutual understanding between the Seymours, the Woods, Vallandigham, and the rebels. This understanding is shown in the secession platform adopted by the Chicago Convention, and in the nomination of Mr. Pendleton, of Ohio — who is a practical secessionist — for Vice-President. We have now driven the rebels completely to the wall. General Grant has the best of them at Richmond, and General Sherman has succeeded in capturing Atlanta. This is not the time, then, that any reasonable man would be talking about "an immediate cessation of hostilities." We are in favor of an armistice, like that between Prussia and Denmark, where both sides hold their ground, and are ready to begin the conflict at any moment. But there is a vast deal of difference between such an armistice and the "immediate cessation of hostilities" which the Chicago platform requires. Nothing can explain such a platform, except the hypothesis that it was dictated by Jeff. Davis to the Peace Democrats, and that these peace men foisted it upon the Chicago Convention, as the price of their endorsement of General McClellan's nomination.

This Convention made a declaration of the principles which should govern the party in case of its advent to power. Such a declaration of principles is more familiarly called a "platform." The architect of that platform was Clement L. Vallandigham, of Ohio, who, a little more than one year ago, was arrested, tried, convicted, and sentenced to transportation beyond our lines, for his notorious and admitted disloyalty to our Government. This platform was adopted by the Convention with only four dissenting votes. It is a platform of PEACE AND DISUNION, and must forever remain a monument of infamy to the party that adopted it. It is not only an unpardonable insult to the country, and a foul libel upon our soldiers and sailors, in declaring that we have failed in the experiment of war, but in its atrocious demand for a "cessation of hostilities," it virtually demands that our armies shall ground their arms — that the veterans who have borne the victorious eagles of Grant and Sherman in a hundred battles, shall surrender as prisoners of war. It means the recognition of the rebel Confederacy. It means that Farragut shall withdraw his fleet from Mobile harbor, and Dahlgren his iron-clads from Charleston, that our blockading squadrons shall everywhere abandon the blockade, and let the rebels send out all their cotton to replenish their exhausted treasury. It means that our navy shall be left to rot at our wharves, and that rebel pirates may roam unmolested over the ocean destroying our commerce, which so lately dotted over all the seas with whiteness.

THE ARMISTICE.

"A cessation of hostilities" in the language of the Copperhead platform of peace and disunion, is what is technically called by all military authorities, "an armistice," and it is well to consider what an armistice is. *It is a complete suspension of all military and naval power as between belligerents.* Before the first step could be taken for this "cessation of hostilities" demanded by the Copperhead platform, it would be necessary to acknowledge the rebel government, and that would be but a preparatory step towards treating with it as if enjoying all the powers of an independent sovereignty. With such a step once taken, it would be the merest infatuation to suppose that the government thus recognized would *deny itself,* either in a preliminary convention, or a subsequent treaty. "An armistice," such as the Copperheads demand, must be between two nations, because it is the mutual acknowledgment of two independent powers. It points to nothing less than an abandonment of the war by the Government of the United States, with a corresponding acknowledgment of the complete success of the rebellion. It is thus shown beyond all cavil what the Copperhead convention meant when it demanded this "cessation of hostilities." It meant the recognition of the so-called "Confederate States of America," as an independent sovereign power; and it therefore meant DISUNION, to be followed by consequences so terrible as to appal the stoutest heart in contemplating them. This view as to what the Copperhead convention meant by this demand for an armistice, is made clear by their nomination of an open disunionist as their candidate for Vice President, George H. Pendleton. This man boldly stood up in the House of Representatives on the 18th day of January, 1861, and proclaimed as follows:

My voice to-day is for conciliation; my voice is for compromise, and it is but the echo of the voice of my constituents. I beg you, gentlemen, who with me represent the Northwest; you who, with me, represent the State of Ohio; you who, with me, represent the city of Cincinnati, I beg you, gentlemen, to hear that voice. If you will not; *if you find conciliation impossible; if your differences are so great that you cannot or will not reconcile them, then,* GENTLEMEN, LET THE SECEDING STATES DEPART IN PEACE; LET THEM ESTABLISH THEIR GOVERNMENT AND EMPIRE, AND WORK OUT THEIR DESTINY ACCORDING TO THE WISDOM WHICH GOD HAS GIVEN THEM.

Further along in the same speech he says:

If these Southern States cannot be reconciled, and if you, gentlemen, cannot find it in your hearts to grant their demands; if they must leave the family mansion, *I would signalize their departure by tokens of love; I would bid them farewell so tenderly that they would forever be touched by the recollection of it; and if in the vicissitudes of their separate existence, they should desire to come together again in our common Government, there should be no pride to be humiliated, there should be no wound inflicted from any hand to be healed. They should come and be welcome to the place they now occupy.*

Further extracts from Pendleton's speeches of a like character might be adduced, but it is unnecessary, for his whole record in Congress proves his intense hostility to our Government and his sympathy with the traitors in arms.

The Chicago Copperhead Convention which nominated McClellan and the above-named Pendleton upon their platform of peace and disunion, was controlled by the most notoriously disloyal men in the country; men who have never failed to express their sympathy for the rebels and their hatred for the good old constitutional Government of our fathers. The following extracts from speeches made there prove the base purposes of the Copperhead leaders to betray the country into the hands of the blood-stained and barbarous foe.

Hon. W. A Richardson, the Copperhead United States Senator from Illinois, spoke as follows, as reported in the Chicago rebel organ, the *Times:*

> To re-elect Mr. Lincoln is to accept four years more of war, four years more of trouble, of disaster, of woe, of lamentations, of ruin to the country. [Applause.] To defeat Mr. Lincoln, to accept the nominee of the Chicago Convention, [cheers,] is to bring peace and harmony and concord and union to these States. [Loud applause.]
>
> But these Republicans say they would be very much disgraced if they were to propose terms of settlement with rebels with arms in their hands. *These people with arms in their hands are the very people I want to settle with. I am not afraid of a man if he has no arms.*

Mr. Stambaugh, a delegate from Ohio, said:

> That if he was called upon to elect between the freedom of the nigger and disunion and separation, *he should choose the latter.* [Cheers.] Bayonets and cannon, and above all, negro emancipation, cannot conquer a permanent peace. His plan for the solution of these difficulties, was an armistice, and an arrangement for a joint Convention, in which to talk over and arrange all family grievances. He was certain that in Ohio the entire community were in favor of peace.

The notorious Captain Rynders, of New York city, spoke as follows:

> After three years of despotism he stood before them a free man — before

a free people. With reference to the remark which he had referred to, he would now speak after the digression he had just made. It was a remark he did not approve of. He had heard one of the speakers state that the people of the South were traitors, which were harsh words, as the people of the South were as brave and chivalrous a people as were ever put on this earth. [Cheers.] He had regretted that they took the step they did for the settlement of their grievances, for they had great grievances. He was sorry they took these steps, and his advice was to stay in the Democratic party, and they would right their grievances. They, however, seemed to think differently, and he was sorry for it. Never had one word come from his lips against them, and he hoped his lips would be sealed when he did injustice to a brave, noble, and chivalrous people. [Applause.]

Hon. Mr. Curtis, of New York, said:

I trust the day will never come when the scenes witnessed in the Commonwealth of Kentucky — a State rendered glorious by the associations of the past — will be enacted on this soil; when the Administration will endeavor by force of arms to interfere with the free sentiment and free will of the people. But, if that day should come, before God and in sight of Heaven, I would invoke the aid of counter revolution. [Loud cheering.] A people who would submit to that degree of outrage and tyranny which destroys the charter of their liberties — (to wit, to be required to swear allegiance to the United States before voting in a State claimed to belong to the confederacy) — are not fitted to live and stand up as men, but should lie down and die as slaves. [Cheers, and cries of 'good'] I warn the Government now in power not to trample too far upon the liberties which are left to us; for if they do, they will be swept before a storm as a ship is swept from the sea in a storm. [Cheers.]

John Fuller, of Michigan, characterized the war for the Union as —

This unholy, cruel, and abominable struggle. [Loud cheers.] Gentlemen, are you willing longer to submit to this state of things? [Cries of "No."] Our land is already wet with fraternal blood. Our press has been shackled, the liberty of speech has been suppressed, the writ of *habeas corpus* has been suspended, and he who dared to raise his voice against these arbitrary and unconstitutional acts has been arrested by the minions of the Government, and incarcerated in dungeons or banished from his native land. [Cheers.] Are you willing, I again ask, to bear these hardships and to submit to this tyranny and oppression? [Renewed cries of "No, no!"] Are you willing to follow in the footsteps of Abraham Lincoln, the perjured wretch who has violated the oath he took before high Heaven to support the Constitution and preserve the liberties of the people? [Cheers.]

Mr. G. C. Sanderson said the Union must not be restored by war.

Fellow-citizens, what say you? Is it not time that this infernal war should stop? [Voices "Yes."] Has not there been blood enough shed? Has there not been property enough destroyed? Have we not all been bound, hand and foot, to the abolition car that is rolling over our necks like the wheels of another Juggernaut? We all love our country. There is nothing would rejoice us more than to see the stars and stripes, the glorious emblem of our Union, re-established all over this country, but it ought to be done by concession and compromise. [Applause. A voice, "That is the doctrine."] It must not be by a further shedding of blood. It cannot be. [A voice, "It will never be done by blood."] We must have peace. Peace is our motive; nothing but peace. If the Southern Confederacy, by any possibility, be subjugated by this abolition Administration, the next thing they would turn their bayonets on the free men of the North and trample you in the dust.

In the face of this record here presented to the consideration of the honest and loyal people of this country, it is demanded, if the proof is not overwhelming, that the Copperheads of the country, speaking through their Chicago Convention and elsewhere, have virtually proposed to surrender the country to the rebels in arms against it, and at the very moment that the rebellion is about to be finally crushed out by our brave soldiers in the field, and the Union restored and the Constitution vindicated.

> Oh! for a tongue to curse the slave,
> Whose treason, like a deadly blight,
> Comes o'er the counsel of the brave,
> And blasts them in the hour of might.

Pamphlet 46

A Few Plain Words with the Rank and File
of the Union Armies. (Union Executive
Congressional Committee, No. 6)

Washington, 1864

[Republicans devoted a considerable amount of their pamphleteering to soliciting the soldier vote. *A Few Plain Words with the Rank and File of the Union Armies* epitomizes the approach and the arguments of these pamphlets: the intelligence, patriotism, and democracy of the Union soldiers; the soundness and patriotism of the Union (that is, Republican) platform; the defeatism and cowardice of the Copperhead (that is, Democratic) platform; the weakness of McClellan, the Democratic candidate; and the gloriousness of the Union victories in the field, that could be thwarted only by a Democratic election victory. In those states where soldiers could not vote by absentee ballot, the Republicans pressured the administration to furlough large numbers of soldiers home to the polls. Apparently this concentration upon the Union soldiers was worthwhile; they seem to have voted three- or four-to-one for the Republican ticket. William B. Hesseltine has estimated that the soldiers' vote in six crucial states furnished Lincoln with the margin of victory.[1]]

I.

NAPOLEON wittily warned governments to "beware when bayonets should learn *to think;*" but with us far from being a subject of fear, it is our glory and pride that the war for the Union has been upheld by a million of "thinking bayonets." Despots may tremble when the bayonets that sustain their thrones learn *to think;* but when free men rise in arms to defend free institutions, what "thinking" can be more true, more wise, more patriotic than theirs?

It is thinking bayonets that compose our army. It is "thinking" that inspired those bayonets; and it is because they are in the grasp of thinking men that they are clothed with all their majesty and

[1] [Hesseltine, *Lincoln and the War Governors,* 380–384.]

power. When dark days have come upon our land, when the sibilant tongue of the copperhead has been heard to hiss his base whispers of surrender, when the wisest could not see their way clear, and the hearts of the most patriotic sunk within them, hope and fight and courage have flashed forth from the gleam of those same thinking bayonets.

It is you, Oh million of thinking bayonets, that have led the way, that have shamed our pusillanimity, that have taught the nation what *patriotism* is. If Peace now begins to dawn on our land, it is because through four years of dread war, in bright and dark days, you have carried the Union in your hearts and *on your bayonets*. When peace comes it will be honorable and lasting because your bayonets have *made* it so; and yours will be the glory and the honor. "When the war closes," says the great captain who has led the army of the West from Chattanooga to Atlanta, in a letter lately written to a humble private soldier in his army: "When the war closes I will, if I survive it, make it my study to give full honor and credit to the soldiers in the ranks, who, though in humble capacity, *have been the working hands by which the nation's honor and manhood have been vindicated.*"

The voice of the nation re-affirms this declaration of General Sherman. History will celebrate as the true heroes of the grand War for the Union not those who have held the high places of command, but those hundreds of thousands of what Kossuth called "nameless heroes" — the rank and file of our armies, who, *shoulder to shoulder and touching elbows,* have carried the war through to results which ensure its glorious consummation.

II.

If ever there was a time when Union bayonets were called on to *think,* it is now. The crisis of the war, when our armies have the rebellion in their grasp and are preparing to deal its death-blow, finds the country precipitated into the turmoil of a Presidential election. This election touches you, because in becoming *soldiers* you did not cease to be *citizens;* but it touches you even more closely than it does those of us who are merely citizens and *not* soldiers: for the issue is presented whether this war for the Union in which you are battling is a delusion and a mockery — whether the priceless blood shed shall go for no more than water spilt on the ground — whether you shall lay down your arms and sue rebels to make on *their* terms the peace you thought your valor had nearly won. That you may see this and no other is the real issue which will be tried on the 8th day of November next — read with all the care you can command the creed of the two candidates claiming your suffrages:

The *Union* platform resolves:

That it is the highest duty of every American citizen *to maintain against all their enemies the integrity of Union,* and the paramount authority of the Constitution and laws of the United States, and that laying aside all differences and political opinions, we pledge ourselves as Union men, animated by a common sentiment, and aiming at a common object, to do everything in our power to aid the Government in quelling by force of arms the rebellion now raging against its authority, and in bringing to the punishment due to their crimes the rebels and traitors arrayed against it.

That we approve the determination of the Government of the United States not to compromise with rebels or to offer any terms of peace except such as may be based upon an "UNCONDITIONAL SURRENDER" of their hostility and a return to their just allegiance to the Constitution and the laws of the United States; and that we call upon the Government to maintain this position and to prosecute the war with the utmost possible vigor to the most complete suppression of the rebellion, in full reliance upon the self-sacrifice, the patriotism, the heroic valor and the undying devotion of the American people to their country and its free institutions.

That the thanks of the American people are due to the soldiers and sailors of the army and navy, who have periled their lives in defense of their country and in vindication of the honor of the flag; that the nation owes to them some permanent recognition of their patriotism and their valor, and ample and permanent provision for those of their survivors who have received disabling and honorable wounds in the service of the country: and that the memories of those who have fallen in its defense shall be held in grateful and everlasting remembrance.

The *Copperhead* platform resolves:

That this convention does explicitly declare as the sense of the American people that after FOUR YEARS OF FAILURE TO RESTORE THE UNION BY THE EXPERIMENT OF WAR, during which, under the pretence of a military necessity, or war power higher than the Constitution, the Constitution itself has been disregarded in every part, and public liberty and private right alike trodden down, and the material prosperity of the country essentially impaired, justice, humanity, liberty, and the public welfare demand that IMMEDIATE EFFORT BE MADE FOR A CESSATION OF HOSTILITIES, with a view to an ultimate convention of all the States, or other peaceable means, to the end that at the earliest practicable moment peace may be restored on the basis of the Federal Union of the States.

There are other declarations made in each; but they do not touch essentials. The vital principle in each case is contained in these utterances.

The former, it need not be said, is the platform on which it is proposed Abraham Lincoln shall continue for another term the administration of the government. The latter is the platform on which George B. McClellan comes forward to claim your suffrages and those of the nation.

The issue here drawn in such clear and palpable lines that no man — far less any *soldier* can mistake it. It is not a personal issue. It is not a question whether Abraham Lincoln or George B. McClellan shall be President. It is a question whether or not we shall have a Constitution and a country left us.

The prime points in the Chicago copperhead platform — those which give its distinctive character — are these:

1. The assertion of our *"failure to restore the Union by the experiment of war."*

2. The demand that *"immediate efforts be made for a cessation of hostilities."*

The copperhead creed very properly joins these assertions in the relation of logical sequence: that is, "immediate efforts should be made for a cessation of hostilities" *because* "the experiment of war" has been a "failure." The premises granted, the conclusion naturally follows.

But suppose you do *not* grant it — suppose a voice, which is already audible in the air, mingling the fierce protests of indignant men with the dread clamor of triumphant artillery and vollied thunders along the line, rolls up from Petersburg to Atlanta and from Atlanta to Mobile Bay, to hurl back the slander that dares thus belittle your matchless achievements. We tell you, soldiers, that voice is echoed back by a nation that thinks with you that a war which in three years has reclaimed from the rebels three-fourths of a territory as large as all Europe, has driven their armies from point to point, beaten them in scores of the greatest battles on record, reduced their whole fighting material from more than three-quarters of a million to between a hundred and a hundred and fifty thousand, captured their chief cities, destroyed their great lines of communication and now holds their whole coast in strictest blockade, will need some other word than "failure" to sum up its swelling content and result. "Failure in the *experiment* of war," forsooth! It is an insult to your glorious deeds and your glorious dead, and could only have been used by men with whom the *wish* of "failure" was father to the *thought.*

In what magnificent contrast with the slanderous falsehoods of these miserable men stand the declarations lately made by the Lieutenant General commanding the armies of the United States! Standing on an eminence whence he surveys the whole continental field of battle, whence his eyes take in all the elements that enter into the dread problem of war, he affirms that the rebellion is doomed, that the rebel armies are all but used up, and that *the one thing needed to "secure an early restoration of the union is a determined unity of sentiment at the North."* "The rebels," says he, "have now in their ranks their last man. The little boys and old men are guarding prisoners, guarding railroad bridges, and forming a good part of their garrisons or intrenched positions. A man lost by them cannot be replaced. They have robbed the cradle and the grave equally to get their present force. Besides what they lose in frequent skirmishes and battles, they are now losing from desertions and other causes at least one regiment per day. With this drain upon them, *the end is not far distant, if we will only be true to ourselves. Their only hope now is a divided North."* It is in this state of facts, when the life-blood of the rebellion is ebbing away, when our victorious columns are marching on from victory to victory, when the soul of the nation is stirred and vivified with a breath of the old-time patriotic fire, when the Government finds the revival of the volunteer spirit such (reaching from five to ten thousand recruits per day) that it can afford to dispense with the operations of the draft as a slower recruiting agent than the spontaneous patriotism of the people presents, — it is amid this inspiring presentment of material and moral elements that the resolutions of a great convention propose that *"immediate* efforts be made for a cessation of hostilities"! Is this the sober utterance of men claiming to control the destinies of a great nation, or is it only a piece of hideous and untimely irony? You are to turn back, you victorious columns that have pushed the lines of imperial conquest from Chattanooga to Atlanta and driven the army of the rebellion in rout and demoralization to the borders of the Gulf; you are to loose your hold on the vital communications of the enemy, you, veterans of Virginia, that have fought your way to where you stand in a campaign that makes historic wars a plaything and marks your path from the Rapidan to the James in characters of blood and flame, — all, all are to retire and allow copperheads and conspirators to settle, over the graves of Union soldiers fallen in a useless war, the terms of surrender to Jeff Davis and his crew. *Such* are copperhead principles, such is the copperhead platform.

III.

In the sad total of "failure in the experiment of war," which you will first learn from the creed of Chicago sums up the history of four years, you are invited by its framers to accept their — *"sympathy."* You have, according to the doctrines and declarations of these men, not only *failed,* but you have been *fooled.* Your love of the old flag, your determination to defend it, your hatred of treason, your deathless patriotism are mere fancy and fustian, the great army of martyrs that have offered up their lives a willing sacrifice on the altar of the Union were poor simpletons, the tens of thousands of your comrades who pine in rebel prisons, and the hundreds of thousands who bear about in their bodies the insignia of glorious wounds are deluded victims — and in this unhappy predicament you are offered their profound "sympathy." Sympathy — it is a precious quality; but there are times when it is the most stinging of insults. We can fancy the feelings with which the war-worn veterans of Grant and Sherman will receive this gushing tender of copperhead "sympathy." From the enemy in your front you have won something more than *sympathy:* you have extorted *his respect,* and you rightly regard this as much more valuable than the hollow commisseration of copperheads. For *their* sympathy, the Chicago resolutions sufficiently show where *that* goes. Men who have nothing but contumely for the government you are defending, and whose declaration of principles contains not a word against treason and rebellion, not a syllable about the infernal treatment of our prisoners by the rebels, not a whisper of reproof for the crime of those southern politicians which has desolated half a continent, show their hands too plainly to blind you as to the real drift of their "sympathy." You will indignantly tell them to take it where it will be better appreciated and not awaken that disgust which it must stir in the breast of every patriotic soldier.

IV.

The Copperheads know your sentiments. They know that the army is sound and incorruptible. They know that there has been no time during the past three years that you would not as lief fight them as fight rebels — no time that you would not willingly leave the enemy in your front to attend to the equally base, but far less brave, enemy in your rear.

It is for this reason that they will court you, and try to wheedle you. They know that their doctrines are a stench in your nostrils. They will try to hide this by pretence and palaver. They are huckstering for the army vote. The Copperheads at Chicago carried the platform, nominated Pendleton, one of their rankest members (who has opposed the army and the war in every vote of his in Congress,) as Vice President, and, to blind you, put up McClellan as President. This is a *ruse de guerre*. They care nothing for McClellan — he is with them only "a name to conjure by," a tub thrown to the whale. They calculate that there are many men in our armies who will vote for McClellan *anyhow*. It does not occur to them that you look beneath the surface, that you penetrate the real issue, that this issue is the country's salvation and that you prefer your country's salvation before the fortunes of any man. American soldiers are not the material out of which to make Pretorian guard on whose bayonets any man can be hoisted into power.

The armies outside of the Army of the Potomac *never* were affected by the McClellan mania. The men who have fought with Grant, campaigned with Rosecrans and marched with Sherman, are not the men to fall in love with McClellan's feeble and fruitless style of warfare. A nation that has shared in the glories of Vicksburg and Stone River and Chattanooga and Atlanta has got a long ways beyond the point of being deluded by bombastic "changes of base" and "masterly inactivity."

But of the old soldiers of the Potomac army, there are still doubtless many left who retain those traditions that time and events have long since effaced from the memories of men. Around the bivouac, in the loll of long summer days, or in the close contact of the winter's tent, you hear these men tell of the "Young Napoleon" and his career. Prejudices and predilections, natural to them but nothing to you, gradually, by force of repetition, steal their way into your minds. Falsehoods, innocently believed by the old men, but of which you have no means of knowing the falsity, are told you — perhaps believed by you. You are told how the Administration thwarted McClellan's plans, withheld promised troops, threw obstacles in his path, and ensured defeat where he had organized victory.

Under another issue than that to-day presented to the country and to the army, these questions might be in place. It might be in place to inquire whether General McClellan was a great military genius, as some believe, or an incompetent and blunderer, as others believe; whether the men and material needed to make his campaigns successful were withheld from him, or whether he had lavished upon him the generous resources of the nation; whether the Administration is blameable for removing him when it did, or whether it is blameable for not sooner discovering his incompetence. These are interesting questions no doubt, and they will long be discussed with the warmth of partisan affection and the bitterness of partisan hate. But they are not in issue just now. For our individual part, we believe the record of the Administration to be singularly clear on all these points. We believe McClellan to be neither a great general nor an aggrieved man. We see nothing in his career, either of talent, character, or success that fits him to be President of the United States. But let that pass. It is not a question of his merits or his demerits. It is a question of the principles which he represents. McClellan might have the purity of a Washington, the statesmanship of a Pitt, and the generalship of a Napoleon, yet did he not plant himself fair and square on the issue of the life or death of this nation, he and his claims would pass for nothing.

V.

McClellan, after a delay, the length of which showed the extreme unpopularity of the platform on which he was nominated, accepted the nomination of the Chicago Convention. His declaration of principles had been anxiously looked for, because he had put himself on record in letters to his army friends, that he could only consent to run on a war platform. Would he renounce the platform and thereby renounce the candidacy, or would he accept the platform and ruin himself? The solution of this perplexing problem, given by McClellan in his letter of acceptance, only serves to show the insuperable difficulties that attend his position, and the impossibility of securing votes enough to elect him without making dupes of the one or the other faction of the party to which he looks for support.

The issue made by the Chicago platform is clear and unmistakeable, and demanded to be met with downright assent or dissent. On this McClellan palters in a double sense, keeping the promise of patriotism to the ear and breaking it to the heart. Whether he thinks "the experiment of war a failure" or not, is impossible to determine. He expresses the opinion that the war should have been carried on in a different way from what it has been. There is no end of people who think the same way. For a year and a half we tried *his* way of carrying on war, and we submit how much of the "failure in the experiment" is due to himself. We have since carried on war in a quite *other* way; and so far from seeing "failure," we find all around the horizon of the war the signs and symbols of magnificent and accumulating success. We think your valor will, ere long, carry this success through to its final consummation in the complete crushing of the rebellion, and the restoration of Union and peace. The Chicago platform declares this impossible. McClellan declares neither the one thing nor the other.

Neither does McClellan pronounce on this question whether "this failure in the experiment of war," as declared by the Chicago platform, should be pushed to the logical result that platform draws, namely the "demand that immediate efforts be made for a cessation of hostilities." His sole utterance on this point is in these words: "So soon as it is clear, or even probable, that our present adversaries are ready for peace, upon the basis of the Union, we should ex-

haust all the resources of statesmanship practiced by civilized nations, and taught by the traditions of the American people, consistent with the honor and interests of the country, to secure such
peace, re-establish the Union, and guarantee for the future the
Constitutional rights of every State." The platform says *"immediate,"*
which we understand. The nominee says: *"so soon as it is clear or
probable,"* which is just saying nothing at all. Who doubts that
so soon as it is clear or probable that the rebels are ready for peace
upon the basis of the Union, we are ready to make such a peace?
The expression is an evasive platitude, which McClellan never could
have used *had he had in his heart the honest determination to carry
through the war to the only point when it will be either "clear or
probable" that the rebels will ask for peace.*

How thoroughly are these tortuous windings characteristic of a
man who, never instructed by the maxim of the great master of
war, that "half measures always fail," gave throughout his military
career a lamentable example of its truth, and is destined to add
conspicuous confirmation of its verity by his career as a politician.

VI.

From these unintelligible utterances and evasive subtleties, those
who seek the rule of action of the party that has set up George B.
McClellan as its Presidential candidate are thrown back on the
declarations of this party as embodied in its platform. Here we find
something we can understand at least. The proposition for a cessation of hostilities on account of the failure of the war, if a lie in its
antecedent and an insult in its consequent, is at least intelligible,
and leaves plain people in no maze of doubt as to its meaning. And
let McClellan refine, and evade, and spout "Union," without any
hint of the means that are to secure Union, *the principles of the
platform are the principles by which he would be governed if the
disaster of his election should befall this nation.* If he were ten times
the patriot he is, he would be drawn by the irresistible gravitation
of his associations, his necessities, and the creed of his party, into
the *policy* of his party. What that policy is, soldiers of the Union,
you know. Is there anything in it but what you, holding a Union
musket in your hands, must spit out of your mouth with scorn?
Surely there is not, unless you are willing that the heroes shall
have died in vain, unless you are willing that the trials and the

triumphs of the grandest of wars shall pass for nothing, unless you are willing to break your weapons of war and retire to the ignominy which must come upon men who, fighting the battles of humanity till victory was won, had not the courage to snatch its fruits!

The Copperheads have put up McClellan because they hope your suffrages will enable them to carry through their cherished project of a surrender to Jeff. Davis. *They forget the terrible rebuke that came up from your ranks, like a great Atlantic swell, when their nominee, a year ago in his Woodward letter hinted, in a far feebler way than he now does by running on the Chicago platform, his affiliation with the peace party.* It would indeed be time to despair of the Republic if American soldiers could be the dupes of so base a plot as the Copperheads have laid. But the country is destined to no such humiliation. The voice of the Army will on the 8th of November, proclaim in thunder-tones that the war must be prosecuted till the rebellion is quelled and the Union restored. And as the rebels chose to *secede* from the administration of Abraham Lincoln, you are going to see to it that they swallow that particular pill by *succumbing* to the administration of Abraham Lincoln.

Pamphlet 47

[U.S. Bureau of Military Justice], Report of the Judge Advocate General, on the "Order of American Knights," or "Sons of Liberty." A Western Conspiracy in Aid of the Southern Rebellion.

Washington, 1864

[In their efforts to equate the Democratic party with treason, the Republicans made effective use of the bumbling secret societies in the Middle West, the Sons of Liberty, successors to the Knights of the Golden Circle. It was easily infiltrated by government agents, and easily could have been shattered at almost any time. Governor Oliver P. Morton of Indiana chose, however, to wait until election time in 1864 before instigating the army to bring a group of so-called conspirators to military trial. They were convicted, sentenced to death, and at one point came within hours of being executed before, in 1866, the Supreme Court in the notable *Ex parte* Milligan decision held that military trial of civilians was illegal, causing their release. Meanwhile, in October, 1864, Joseph Holt, the judge advocate general of the army, who seemed to believe every wild story emanating in the Middle West, wrote a perfervid official report to the secretary of war declaring, "Judea produced but one Judas Iscariot and Rome from the sinks of her demoralization produced but one Catiline; and yet, as events proved, there has arisen in our land an entire brood of such traitors all animated by the same parricidal spirit and all struggling with the same relentless malignity for the dismemberment of our Union." The Republican New York *Tribune*, printing the report, proclaimed it a startling revelation. The Democratic New York *World* dismissed it as a campaign document. And so literally it was. Francis Lieber obtained quantities of copies of the government-printed report and distributed them bearing the rubber-stamped insignia of the Loyal Publication Society. Holt (1807–1894), a Kentuckian, had been President Buchanan's postmaster-general and, at the time of the secession crisis, secretary of war. As judge advocate general during and after the Civil War, he was popular for his prosecution of Copperheads, but later notorious for having suppressed evidence favorable to Mrs. Mary Surratt, executed as a fellow conspirator in the assassination of Lincoln.[1]]

[1] [On the Peace Democrats, see Richard O. Curry, "The Union As It Was: A Critique of Recent Interpretations of the 'Copperheads,'" *Civil War History*, XIII

War Department, Bureau of Military Justice,
Washington, D. C., October 8, 1864.

Hon. E. M. Stanton, Secretary of War:

Sir: Having been instructed by you to prepare a detailed report upon the mass of testimony furnished me from different sources in regard to the *Secret Associations and Conspiracies against the Government,* formed, principally in the Western States, by traitors and disloyal persons, I have now the honor to submit as follows:

During more than a year past it has been generally known to our military authorities that a secret treasonable organization, affiliated with the Southern rebellion, and chiefly military in its character, has been rapidly extending itself throughout the West. A variety of agencies, which will be specified herein, have been employed, and successfully, to ascertain its nature and extent, as well as its aims and its results; and, as this investigation has led to the arrest in several States of a number of its prominent members as dangerous public enemies, it has been deemed proper to set forth in full the acts and purposes of this organization, and thus to make known to the country at large its intensely treasonable and revolutionary spirit.

The subject will be presented under the following heads:

I. The origin, history, names, &c. of the Order.
II. Its organization and officers.
III. Its extent and numbers.
IV. Its armed force.
V. Its ritual, oaths, and interior forms.

VI. Its written principles.
VII. Its specific purposes and operations.
VIII. The witnesses and their testimony.

I. — THE ORIGIN, HISTORY, NAMES, ETC., OF THE ORDER.

This secret association first developed itself in the West in the year 1862, about the period of the first conscription of troops, which it aimed to obstruct and resist. Originally known in certain localities as the "Mutual Protection Society," the "Circle of Honor," or the

(March, 1967), 25–39; Wood Gray, *The Hidden Civil War: The Story of the Copperheads* (New York, 1942); and Frank L. Klement, *The Copperheads in the Middle West* (Chicago, 1960). Concerning the Indiana conspiracy and trials, see Stampp, *Indiana Politics during the Civil War,* 239–249. Cf. *The Great Northern Conspiracy of the O. S. L.* (Union League No. 95, Philadelphia, 1864).]

"Circle," or "Knights of the Mighty Host," but more widely as the "Knights of the Golden Circle," it was simply an inspiration of the rebellion, being little other than an extension among the disloyal and disaffected at the North of the association of the latter name, which had existed for some years at the South, and from which it derived all the chief features of its organization.

During the summer and fall of 1863 the Order, both of the North and South, underwent some modifications as well as a change of name. In consequence, of a partial exposure which had been made of the signs and ritual of the "Knights of the Golden Circle," Sterling Price had instituted as its successor in Missouri a secret political association, which he called the "Corps de Belgique," or "Southern League;" his principal coadjutor being Charles L. Hunt, of St. Louis, then Belgian Consul at that city, but whose *exequatur* was subsequently revoked by the President on account of his disloyal practices. The special object of the Corps de Belgique appears to have been to unite the rebel sympathizers of Missouri, with a view to their taking up arms and joining Price upon his proposed grand invasion of that State, and to their recruiting for his army in the interim.

Meanwhile, also, there had been instituted at the North, in the autumn of 1863, by sundry disloyal persons — prominent among whom were Vallandigham and P. C. Wright, of New York — a secret Order, intended to be general throughout the country, and aiming at an extended influence and power, and at more positive results than its predecessor, and which was termed, and has since been widely known as the O. A. K., or *"Order of American Knights."*

The opinion is expressed by Colonel Sanderson, Provost Marshal General of the Department of Missouri, in his official report upon the progress of this Order, that it was founded by Vallandigham during his banishment, and upon consultation at Richmond with Davis and other prominent traitors. It is, indeed, the boast of the order in Indiana and elsewhere, that its "ritual" came direct from Davis himself; and Mary Ann Pitman, formerly attached to the command of the rebel Forrest, and a most intelligent witness — whose testimony will be hereafter referred to — states positively that Davis is a member of the Order.

Upon the institution of the principal organization, it is represented that the "Corps de Belgique" was modified by Price, and became a

Southern section of the O. A. K., and that the new name was generally adopted for the Order, both at the North and South.

The secret signs and character of the Order having become known
to our military authorities, further modifications in the ritual and
forms were introduced, and its name was finally changed to that
of the O. S. L., or "Order of the *Sons of Liberty*," or the "Knights of
the Order of the Sons of Liberty." These later changes are represented to have been first instituted, and the new ritual compiled, in
the State of Indiana, in May last, but the new name was at once
generally adopted throughout the West, though in some localities
the association is still better known as the "Order of American
Knights."

Meanwhile, also, the Order has received certain local designations.
In parts of Illinois it has been called at times the "Peace Organization," in Kentucky the "Star Organization," and in Missouri the
"American Organization;" these, however, being apparently names
used outside the lodges of the order. Its members have also been
familiarly designated as "Butternuts" by the country people of Illinois, Indiana, and Ohio, and its separate lodges have also frequently
received titles intended for the public ear; that in Chicago, for instance, being termed by its members the "Democratic Invincible
Club," that in Louisville the "Democratic Reading Room," &c.

It is to be added that in the State of New York, and other parts of
the North, the secret political association known as the "*McClellan
Minute Guard*" would seem to be a branch of the O. A. K., having
substantially the same objects, to be accomplished, however, by
means expressly suited to the localities in which it is established. For,
as the Chief Secretary of this association, Dr. R. F. Stevens, stated
in June last to a reliable witness whose testimony has been furnished,
"those who represent the McClellan interest are compelled to preach
a vigorous prosecution of the war, in order to secure the popular
sentiment and allure voters."

II. — ITS ORGANIZATION AND OFFICERS.

From printed copies, heretofore seized by the government, of the
Constitutions of the Supreme Council, Grand Council, and County
Parent Temples, respectively, of the Order of Sons of Liberty, in
connexion with other and abundant testimony, the organization of
the Order, in its latest form, is ascertained to be as follows:

1. The government of the Order throughout the United States is vested in a Supreme Council, of which the officers are a Supreme Commander, Secretary of State, and Treasurer. These officers are elected for one year, at the annual meeting of the Supreme Council, which is made up of the Grand Commanders of the several States *ex officio,* and two delegates elected from each State in which the order is established.

2. The government of the Order in a State is vested in a Grand Council, the officers of which are a Grand Commander, Deputy Grand Commander, Grand Secretary, Grand Treasurer, and a certain number of Major Generals, or one for each Military District. These officers also are elected annually by "representatives" from the County Temples, each Temple being entitled to two representatives, and one additional for each thousand members. This body of representatives is also invested with certain legislative functions.

3. The Parent Temple is the organization of the Order for a county, each Temple being formally instituted by authority of the Supreme Council, or of the Grand Council or Grand Commander of the State. By the same authority, or by that of the officers of the Parent Temple, branch or subordinate Temples may be established for townships in the county.

But the strength and significance of this organization lie in its *military* character. The secret constitution of the Supreme Council provides that the Supreme Commander *"shall be commander-in-chief of all military forces belonging to the Order in the various States when called into actual service;"* and further, that the Grand Commanders *"shall be commanders-in-chief of the military forces of their respective States."* Subordinate to the Grand Commander in the State are the *"Major Generals,"* each of whom commands his separate district and army. In Indiana the Major Generals are four in number. In Illinois, where the organization of the order is considered most perfect, the members in each Congressional District compose a *"brigade,"* which is commanded by a *"Brigadier General."* The members of each county constitute a *"regiment,"* with a *"colonel,"* in command, and those of each township form a *"company."* A somewhat similar system prevails in Indiana, where also each company is divided into *"squads,"* each with its chief — an arrangement intended to facilitate the *guerilla* mode of warfare in case of a general outbreak or local disorder.

The "McClellan Minute Guard," as appears from a circular issued by the Chief Secretary in New York in March last, is organized upon a military basis similar to that of the Order proper. It is composed of companies, one for each election district, ten of which constitute a "brigade," with a "brigadier general" at its head. The whole is placed under the authority of a "Commander-in-chief." A strict obedience on the part of members to the orders of their superiors is enjoined.

The first "Supreme Commander" of the Order was P. C. Wright, of New York, editor of the New York *News,* who was in May last placed in arrest and confined in Fort Lafayette. His successor in office was Vallandigham, who was elected at the annual meeting of the Supreme Council in February last. Robert Holloway, of Illinois, is represented to have acted as Lieutenant General, or Deputy Supreme Commander, during the absence of Vallandigham from the country. The Secretary of State chosen at the last election was Dr. Massey, of Ohio.

In Missouri, the principal officers were Chas. L. Hunt, Grand Commander, Charles E. Dunn, Deputy Grand Commander, and Green B. Smith, Grand Secretary. Since the arrest of these three persons (all of whom have made confessions which will be presently alluded to) James A. Barrett has, as it is understood, officiated as Grand Commander. He is stated to occupy also the position of chief of staff to the Supreme Commander.

The Grand Commander in Indiana, H. H. Dodd, is now on trial at Indianapolis by a military commission for "conspiracy against the Government," "violation of the laws of war," and other charges. The Deputy Grand Commander in that State is Horace Heffren, and the Grand Secretary, W. M. Harrison. The Major Generals are W. A. Bowles, John C. Walker, L. P. Milligan, and Andrew Humphreys. Among the other leading members of the Order in that State are Dr. Athon, State Secretary, and Joseph Ristine, State Auditor.

The Grand Commander in Illinois is — Judd, of Lewistown; and B. B. Piper, of Springfield, who is entitled "Grand Missionary" of the State, and designated also as a member of Vallandigham's staff, is one of the most active members, having been busily engaged throughout the summer in establishing Temples and initiating members.

In Kentucky, Judge Bullit, of the Court of Appeals, is Grand Commander, and, with Dr. U. F. Kalfus and W. R. Thomas, jailor in Louisville, two other of the most prominent members, has been arrested and confined by the military authorities. In New York, Dr. R. F. Stevens, the chief secretary of the McClellan Minute Guard, is the most active ostensible representative of the Order.

The greater part of the chief and subordinate officers of the Order and its branches, as well as the principal members thereof, are known to the Government, and, where not already arrested, may regard themselves as under a constant military surveillance. So complete has been the exposure of this secret league, that however frequently the conspirators may change its names, forms, passwords, and signals, its true purposes and operations cannot longer be concealed from the military authorities.

It is to be remarked that the Supreme Council of the Order, which annually meets on February 22, convened this year at New York city, and a special meeting was then appointed to be held at Chicago on July 1, or just prior to the day then fixed for the convention of the Democratic party. This convention having been postponed to August 29, the special meeting of the Supreme Council was also postponed to August 27, at the same place, and was duly convened accordingly. It will be remembered that a leading member of the convention, in the course of a speech made before that body, alluded approvingly to the session of the Sons of Liberty at Chicago at the same time, as that of an organization in harmony with the sentiment and projects of the convention.

It may be observed, in conclusion, that one not fully acquainted with the true character and intentions of the Order might well suppose that, in designating its officers by high military titles, and in imitating in its organization that established in our armies, it was designed merely to render itself more popular and attractive with the masses, and to invest its chiefs with a certain sham dignity; but when it is understood that the order comprises within itself a large army of well-armed men, constantly drilled and exercised as soldiers, and that this army is held ready at any time for such forcible resistance to our military authorities, and such active co-operation with the public enemy, as it may be called upon to engage in by its commanders, it will be perceived that the titles of the latter are not assumed for a mere purpose of display, but that they are the chiefs of an actual and formidable force of conspirators against the life of the Government, and that their military system is, as it has been re-marked by Colonel Sanderson, "the grand lever used by the rebel Government for its army operations."

III. — ITS EXTENT AND NUMBERS.

The "Temples" or "Lodges" of the Order are numerously scattered through the States of Indiana, Illinois, Ohio, Missouri, and Kentucky. They are also officially reported as established, to a less extent, in Michigan and the other Western States, as well as in New York, Pennsylvania, New Hampshire, Rhode Island, Connecticut, New Jersey, Maryland, Delaware, and Tennessee. Dodd, the Grand Commander of Indiana, in an address to the members in that State of February last, claims that at the next annual meeting of the Supreme Council (in February, 1865) every state in the Union will be represented, and adds, "this is the first and only true national organization the Democratic and Conservative men of the country have ever attempted." A provision made in the constitution of the Council for a representation from the *Territories* shows, indeed, that the widest extension of the Order is contemplated.

In the States first mentioned the Order is most strongly centred at the following places, where are situated its principal "Temples." In Indiana, at Indianapolis and Vincennes; in Illinois, at Chicago, Springfield, and Quincy, (a large proportion of the lodges in and about the latter place having been founded by the notorious guerilla chief, Jackman;) in Ohio, at Cincinnati, Dayton, and in Hamilton county (which is proudly termed by members "the South Carolina of the North;") in Missouri, at St. Louis; in Kentucky, at Louisville; and in Michigan, at Detroit, (whence communication was freely had by the leaders of the order with Vallandigham during his banishment, either by letters addressed to him through two prominent citizens and members of the Order, or by personal interviews at Windsor, C. W.) It is to be added that the regular places of meeting, as also the principal rendezvous and haunts of the members in these and less important places, are generally well known to the Government.

The actual *numbers* of the Order have, it is believed, never been officially reported, and cannot, therefore, be accurately ascertained. Various estimates have been made by leading members, some of which are no doubt considerably exaggerated. It has been asserted by delegates to the Supreme Council of February last, that the number was there represented to be from 800,000 to 1,000,000; but Vallandigham, in his speech last summer at Dayton, Ohio, placed it at 500,000, which is probably much nearer the true total. The number of its members in the several States has been differently estimated in the reports and statements of its officers. Thus, the force of the Order in Indiana is stated to be from 75,000 to 125,000; in Illinois, from 100,000 to 140,000; in Ohio, from 80,000 to 108,000; in Kentucky, from 40,000 to 70,000; in Missouri, from 20,000 to 40,000; and in Michigan and New York, about 20,000 each. Its representation in the other States above mentioned does not specifically appear from the testimony; but, allowing for every exaggeration in the figures reported, they may be deemed to present a tolerably faithful view of what, at least, is regarded by the Order as its true force in the States designated.

It is to be noted that the Order, or its counterpart, is probably much more widely extended at the South even than at the North, and that a large proportion of the officers of the rebel army are represented by credible witnesses to be members. In Kentucky and Missouri the Order has not hesitated to admit as members, not only officers of that army, but also a considerable number of guerillas, a class who might be supposed to appreciate most readily its spirit and purposes. It is fully shown that as lately as in July last several of these ruffians were initiated into the first degree by Dr. Kalfus, in Kentucky.

IV. — ITS ARMED FORCE.

A review of the testimony in regard to the *armed* force of the Order will materially aid in determining its real strength and numbers.

Although the Order has from the outset partaken of the military character, it was not till the summer or fall of 1863 that it began to be generally organized as an armed body. Since that date its officers and leaders have been busily engaged in placing it upon a military basis, and in preparing it for a revolutionary movement. A general system of drilling has been instituted and secretly carried out. Members have been instructed to be constantly provided with weapons, and in some localities it has been absolutely required that each member should keep at his residence, at all times, certain arms and a specified quantity of ammunition.

In March last the entire armed force of the Order, capable of being mobilized for effective service, was represented to be 340,000 men. As the details, upon which this statement was based are imperfectly set forth in the testimony, it is not known how far this number may be exaggerated. It is abundantly shown, however, that the Order, by means of a tax levied upon its members, has accumulated considerable funds for the purchase of arms and ammunition, and that these have been procured in large quantities for its use. The witness Clayton, on the trial of Dodd, estimated that *two-thirds* of the Order are furnished with arms.

Green B. Smith, grand secretary of the Order in Missouri, states in his confession of July last: "I know that arms, mostly revolvers, and ammunition have been purchased by members in St. Louis to send to members in the country where they could not be had;" and he subsequently adds that he himself alone clandestinely purchased and forwarded, between April 15th and 19th last, about 200 revolvers, with 5,000 percussion caps and other ammunition. A muster-roll of one of the country lodges of that State is exhibited, in which, opposite the name of each member, are noted certain numbers, under the heads of "Missouri Republican" "St. Louis Union," "Anzeiger," "Miscellaneous Periodicals," "Books," "Speeches," and "Reports;" titles which, when interpreted, severally signify *single-barrelled guns, double-barrelled guns, revolvers, private ammunition, private lead, company powder, company lead* — the roll thus actually setting forth the amount of arms and ammunition in the possession of the lodge and its members.

In the States of Ohio and Illinois the Order is claimed by its members to be unusually well armed with revolvers, carbines, &c.; but it is in regard to the arming of the Order in Indiana that the principal statistics have been presented, and these may serve to illustrate the system which has probably been pursued in most of the States. One intelligent witness, who has been a member, estimates that in March last there were in possession of the Order in that State 6,000 muskets and 60,000 revolvers, besides private arms. Another member testifies that at a single lodge meeting of two hundred and fifty-two persons, which he attended early in the present year, the sum of $4,000 was subscribed for arms. Other members present statements in reference to the number of arms in their respective counties, and all agree in representing that these have been constantly forwarded from Indianapolis into the interior. Beck & Brothers are designated as the firm in that city to which most of the arms were consigned. These were shipped principally from the East; some packages, however, were sent from Cincinnati, and some from Kentucky, and the boxes were generally marked "pick-axes," "hardware," "nails," "household goods," &c.

General Carrington estimates that in February and March last nearly 30,000 guns and revolvers entered the State, and this estimate is based upon an actual inspection of invoices. The true number introduced was therefore probably considerably greater. That officer adds that on the day in which the sale of arms was stopped by his order, in Indianapolis, nearly 1,000 additional revolvers had been contracted for, and that the trade could not supply the demand. He further reports that after the introduction of arms into the Department of the North had been prohibited in General Orders of March last, a seizure was made by the Government of a large quantity of revolvers and 135,000 rounds of ammunition, which had been shipped to the firm in Indianapolis, of which H. H. Dodd, Grand Commander, was a member; that other arms about to be shipped to the same destination were seized in New York city; and that all these were claimed as the private property of John C. Walker, one of the Major Generals of the Order in Indiana, and were represented to have been *"purchased for a few friends."* It should also be stated that at the office of Hon. D. W. Voorhees, M. C., at Terre Haute, were discovered letters which disclosed a correspondence between him and ex-Senator Wall, of New Jersey, in regard to the purchase of 20,000 Garibaldi rifles, to be forwarded to the West.

It appears in the course of the testimony that a considerable quantity of arms and ammunition were brought into the State of Illinois from Burlington, Iowa, and that ammunition was sent from New Albany, Indiana, into Kentucky; it is also represented that, had Vallandigham been arrested on his return to Ohio, it was contemplated furnishing the Order with arms from a point in Canada, near Windsor, where they were stored and ready for use.

There remains further to be noticed, in this connexion, the testimony of Clayton upon the trial of Dodd, to the effect that arms were to be furnished the Order from Nassau, N. P., by way of Canada; that, to defray the expense of these arms or their transportation, a formal assessment was levied upon the lodges, but that the transportation into Canada was actually to be furnished by the Confederate authorities.

A statement was made by Hunt, Grand Commander of Missouri, before his arrest, to a fellow member, that shells and all kinds of munitions of war, as well as infernal machines, were manufactured for the Order at Indianapolis: and the late discovery in Cincinnati of samples of hand-grenades, conical shells, and rockets, of which one thousand were about to be manufactured, under a special contract, for the O. S. L., goes directly to verify such a statement.

These details will convey some idea of the attempts which have been made to place the Order upon a war footing and prepare it for aggressive movements. But, notwithstanding all the efforts that have been put forth, and with considerable success, to arm and equip its members as fighting men, the leaders have felt themselves still very deficient in their armament, and numerous schemes for increasing their armed strength have been devised. Thus, at the time of the issuing of the general order in Missouri requiring the enrolment of all citizens, it was proposed in the lodges of the O. A. K., at St. Louis, that certain members should raise companies in the militia, in their respective wards, and thus get command of as many Government arms and equipments as possible, for the future use of the Order. Again it was proposed that *all* the members should enrol themselves in the militia, instead of paying commutation, in this way obtaining possession of United States arms, and having the advantage of the drill and military instruction. In the councils of the Order in Kentucky, in June last, a scheme was devised for disarming all the negro troops, which it was thought could be done without much difficulty, and appropriating their arms for military purposes.

The despicable treachery of these proposed plans, as evincing the *animus* of the conspiracy, need not be commented upon.

It is to be observed that the Order in the State of Missouri has counted greatly upon support from the enrolled militia, in case of an invasion by Price, as containing many members and friends of the O. A. K.; and that the "Paw-Paw militia," a military organization of Buchanan county, as well as the militia of Platte and Clay counties, known as "Flat Foots," have been relied upon, almost to a man, to join the revolutionary movement.

V. — ITS RITUAL, OATHS, AND INTERIOR FORMS.

The ritual of the Order, as well as its secret signs, passwords, &c., has been fully made known to the military authorities. In August last one hundred and twelve copies of the ritual of the O. A. K. were seized in the office of Hon. D. W. Voorhees, M. C., at Terre Haute, and a large number of rituals of the O. S. L., together with copies of the constitutions of the councils, &c., already referred to, were found in the building at Indianapolis, occupied by Dodd, the Grand Commander of Indiana, as had been indicated by the Government witness and detective, Stidger. Copies were likewise discovered at Louisville, at the residence of Dr. Kalfus, concealed within the mattress of his bed, where Stidger had ascertained that they were kept.

The ritual of the O. A. K. has also been furnished by the authorities at St. Louis. From the ritual, that of the O. S. L. does not materially differ. Both are termed "progressive," in that they provide for *five* separate *degrees* of membership, and contemplate the admission of a member of a lower degree into a higher one only upon certain vouchers and proofs of fitness, which, with each ascending degree, are required to be stronger and more imposing.

Each degree has its commander or head, the Fourth or "Grand" is the highest in a State; the Fifth or "Supreme" the highest in the United States; but to the first or lower degree only do the great majority of members attain. A large proportion of these enter the Order, supposing it to be a "Democratic" and political association merely; and the history of the Order furnishes a most striking illustration of the gross and criminal deception which may be practised upon the ignorant masses by unscrupulous and unprincipled leaders. The members of the lower degree are often for a considerable period kept quite unaware of the true purposes of their chiefs. But to the latter they are bound, in the language of their obligation, "*to yield prompt and implicit obedience to the utmost of their ability, without remonstrance, hesitation, or delay,*" and meanwhile their minds, under the discipline and teachings to which they are subjected, become educated and accustomed to contemplate with comparative unconcern the treason for which they are preparing.

The oaths, "invocations," "charges," &c., of the ritual, expressed as they are in bombastic and extravagant phraseology, would excite in the mind of an educated person only ridicule or contempt, but upon the illiterate they are calculated to make a deep impression, the effect and importance of which were doubtless fully studies by the framers of the instrument.

The *oath* which is administered upon the introduction of a member into any degree is especially imposing in its language; it prescribes as a penalty for a violation of the obligation assumed "a shameful death," and further, that the body of the person guilty of such violation shall be divided in four parts and cast out at the four "gates" of the Temple. Not only, as has been said, does it enjoin a blind obedience to the commands of the superiors of the Order, but it is required to be held of *paramount obligation* to any oath which may be administered to a member in a court of justice or elsewhere. Thus, in cases where members have been sworn by officers empowered to administer oaths to speak the whole truth in answer to questions that may be put to them, and have then been examined in reference to the Order, and their connexion therewith, they have not only refused to give any information in regard to its character, but have denied that they were members, or even that they knew of its existence. A conspicuous instance of this is presented in the cases of Hunt, Dunn, and Smith, the chief officers of the Order in Missouri, who, upon their first examination under oath, after their arrest, denied all connexion with the Order, but confessed, also under oath, at a subsequent period, that this denial was wholly false, although in accordance with their obligations as members. Indeed, a deliberate system of deception in regard to the details of the conspiracy is inculcated upon the members, and studiously pursued; and it may be mentioned, as a similarly despicable feature of the organization, that it is held bound to injure the Administration and officers of the Government, in every possible manner, by misrepresentation and falsehood.

Members are also instructed that their oath of membership is to be held paramount to an oath of allegiance, or any other oath which may impose obligations inconsistent with those which are assumed upon entering the Order. Thus, if a member, when in danger, or for the purpose of facilitating some traitorous design, has taken the oath of allegiance to the United States, he is held at liberty to violate it on the first occasion, his obligation to the Order being deemed superior to any consideration of duty or loyalty prompted by such oath.

It is to be added that where members are threatened with the penalties of perjury, in case of their answering falsely to questions propounded to them in regard to the Order before a court or grand jury, they are instructed to refuse to answer such questions, alleging, as a ground for their refusal, that their answers may *criminate* themselves. The testimony shows that this course has habitually been pursued by members, especially in Indiana, when placed in such a situation.

Besides the oaths and other forms and ceremonies which have been alluded to, the ritual contains what are termed "Declarations of Principles." These declarations, which are most important as exhibiting the creed and character of the Order, as inspired by the principles of the rebellion, will be fully presented under the next branch of the subject.

The *signs, signals, passwords,* &c., of the Order are set forth at length in the testimony, but need only be briefly alluded to. It is a significant fact, as showing the intimate relations between the Northern and Southern sections of the secret conspiracy, that a member from a Northern State is enabled to pass without risk through the South by the use of the signs of recognition which have been established throughout the Order, and by means of which members from distant points, though meeting as strangers, are at once made known to each other as "brothers." Mary Ann Pitman expressly states in her testimony that whenever important despatches are required to be sent by rebel generals beyond their lines, members of the Order are always selected to convey them. Certain passwords are also used in common in both sections, and of these, none appears to be more familiar then the word "Nu-oh-lac," or the name "Calhoun" spelt backward, and which is employed upon entering a Temple of the first degree of the O. A. K. — certainly a fitting password to such dens of treason.

Besides the signs of recognition, there are *signs of warning and danger,* for use at night as well as by day; as, for instance, signs to warn members of the approach of United States officials seeking to make arrests. The Order has also established what are called *battle-*

signals, by means of which, as it is asserted, a member serving in the army may communicate with the enemy in the field, and thus escape personal harm in case of attack or capture. The most recent of these signals represented to have been adopted is a five-pointed copper star, worn under the coat, which is to be disclosed upon meeting an enemy, who will thus recognize in the wearer a sympathizer and an ally. A similar star of German silver, hung in a frame, is said to be numerously displayed by members or their families in private *houses* in Indiana, for the purpose of insuring protection to their property in case of a raid or other attack; and it is stated that in many dwellings in that State a portrait of John Morgan is exhibited for a similar purpose.

Other signs are used by members, and especially the officers of the Order in their *correspondence.* Their letters, when of an official character, are generally conveyed by special messengers, but when transmitted through the mail are usually in cipher. When written in the ordinary manner, a character at the foot of the letter, consisting of a circle with a line drawn across the centre, signifies to the member who receives it that the statements as written are to be understood in a sense directly the opposite to that which would ordinarily be conveyed.

It is to be added that the meetings of the Order, especially in the country, are generally held at night and in secluded places, and that the approach to them is carefully guarded by a line of sentinels, who are passed only by means of a special *countersign,* which is termed the "picket."

VI. — ITS WRITTEN PRINCIPLES.

The *"Declaration of Principles,"* which is set forth in the ritual of the Order, has already been alluded to. This declaration, which is specially framed for the instruction of the great mass of members, commences with the following proposition:

"All men are endowed by the Creator with certain rights, equal as far as there is equality in the capacity for the appreciation, enjoyment, and exercise of those rights." And subsequently there is added: "In the Divine economy no individual of the human race must be permitted to encumber the earth, to mar its aspects of transcendent beauty, nor to impede the progress of the physical or intellectual man, neither in himself nor in the race to which he belongs. Hence, a people, upon whatever plane they may be found in the ascending scale of humanity, whom neither the divinity within them nor the inspirations of divine and beautiful nature around them can impel to virtuous action and progress onward and upward, should be subjected to a just and humane servitude and tutelage to the superior race until they shall be able to appreciate the benefits and advantages of civilization."

Here, expressed in studied terms of hypocrisy, is the whole theory of human bondage — the right of the strong, because they are strong, to despoil and enslave the weak, because they are weak! The languages of earth can add nothing to the cowardly and loathsome baseness of the doctrine, as thus announced. It is the robber's creed, sought to be nationalized, and would push back the hand on the dial plate of our civilization to the darkest periods of human history. It must be admitted, however, that it furnishes a fitting "cornerstone" for the government of a rebellion, every fibre of whose body and every throb of whose soul is born of the traitorous ambition and slave-pen inspirations of the South.

To these detestable tenets is added that other pernicious political theory of State sovereignty, with its necessary fruit, the monstrous doctrine of secession — a doctrine which, in asserting that in our federative system a part is greater than the whole, would compel the general government, like a Japanese slave, to commit hari-kari whenever a faithless or insolent State should command it to do so.

Thus, the ritual, after reciting that the States of the Union are "free, independent, and sovereign," proceeds as follows:

"The government designated 'The United States of America' has no *sovereignty*, because that is an attribute with which the people, in their several and distinct political organizations, are endowed and is inalienable. It was constituted by the terms of the *compact*, by all the States, through the express will of the people thereof, respectively — a common agent, to use and exercise certain named, specified, defined, and limited powers which are inherent of the sovereignties within those States. It is permitted, so far as regards its status and relations, as common agent in the exercise of the powers carefully and jealously delegated to it, to call itself 'supreme,' but not 'sovereign.' In accordance with the principles upon which is founded the *American theory*, government can exercise only delegated power; hence, if those who shall have been chosen to administer the government shall assume to exercise powers not delegated, they should be regarded and treated as *usurpers*. The reference to 'inherent power,' 'war power,' or 'military necessity,' on the part of the functionary for the sanction of an arbitrary exercise of power by him, we will not accept in palliation or excuse."

To this is added, as a corollary, "it is incompatible with the history and nature of our system of government that Federal authority should coerce by arms a sovereign State."

The declaration of principles, however, does not stop here, but proceeds one step further, as follows:

"Whenever the chosen officers or delegates shall fail or refuse to administer the Government in strict accordance with the letter of the accepted Constitution, it is the inherent right and the solemn and imperative duty of the people to *resist* the functionaries, and, if need be, to *expel them by force of arms!* Such resistance is not revolution, but is solely the assertion of right — the exercise of all the noble attributes which impart honor and dignity to manhood."

To the same effect, though in a milder tone, is the platform of the order in Indiana, put forth by the Grand Council at their meeting in February last, which declares that "the right to alter or *abolish* their government, whenever it fails to secure the blessings of liberty, is one of the inalienable rights of the people that can never be surrendered."

Such, then, are the principles which the new member swears to observe and abide by in his obligation, set forth in the ritual, where he says: "I do solemnly promise that I will ever cherish in my heart of hearts the sublime creed of the E. K., (Excellent Knights,) and will, so far as in me lies, illustrate the same in my intercourse with men, and will defend the principles thereof, if need be, with my life, whensoever assailed, in my own country first of all. I do further solemnly declare that I will never take up arms in behalf of any government which does not acknowledge the sole authority or power to be the will of the governed."

The following extracts from the ritual, may also be quoted as illustrating the principle of the right of revolution and resistance to constituted authority insisted upon by the Order:

"Our swords shall be unsheathed whenever the great principles which we aim to inculcate and have sworn to maintain and defend are assailed."

Again: "I do solemnly promise, that whensoever the principles which our Order inculcates shall be assailed in my own State or country, I will defend these principles with my sword and my life, in whatsoever capacity may be assigned me by the competent authority of our Order."

And further: "I do promise that I will, at all times, if need be, take up arms in the cause of the oppressed — in my own country first of all — against any power or government usurped, which may be found in arms and waging war against a people or peoples who are endeavoring to establish, or have inaugurated, a government for themselves of their own free choice."

Moreover, it is to be noted that all the addresses and speeches of its leaders breathe the same principle, of the right of forcible resistance to the Government, as one of the tenets of the Order.

Thus P. C. Wright, Supreme Commander, in his general address of December, 1863, after urging that "the spirit of the fathers may animate the free minds, the brave hearts, and still unshackled limbs of the *true democracy*," (meaning the members of the Order,) adds as follows: "To be prepared for the crisis now approaching, we must catch from afar the earliest and faintest breathings of the spirit of the storm; to be successful when the storm comes, we must be watchful, patient, brave, confident, organized, *armed*."

Thus, too, Dodd, Grand Commander of the Order in Indiana, quoting, in his address of February last, the views of his chief, Vallandigham, and adopting them as his own, says:

"He (Vallandigham) judges that the Washington power will not yield up its power until it is taken from them by an indignant people *by force of arms*."

Such, then, are the written principles of the Order in which the neophyte is instructed, and which he is sworn to cherish and observe as his rule of action, when, with arms placed in his hands, he is called upon to engage in the overthrow of his Government. This declaration — first, of the absolute right of slavery; second, of State sovereignty and the right of secession; third, of the right of armed resistance to constituted authority on the part of the disaffected and the disloyal, whenever their ambition may prompt them to revolution — is but an assertion of that abominable theory which, from its first enunciation, served as a pretext for conspiracy after conspiracy against the Government on the part of Southern traitors, until their detestable plotting culminated in open rebellion and bloody civil war. What more appropriate password, therefore, to be communicated to the new member upon his first admission to the secrets of the order could have been conceived, than that which was actually adopted — "Calhoun!" — a man who, baffled in his lust for power, with gnashing teeth turned upon the Government that had lifted him to its highest honors, and upon the country that had borne him, and down to the very close of his fevered life labored incessantly to scatter far and wide the seeds of that poison of death now upon our lips. The thorns which now pierce and tear us are of the tree he planted.

VII. — ITS SPECIFIC PURPOSES AND OPERATIONS.

From the principles of the Order, as thus set forth, its general purpose of co-operating with the rebellion may readily be inferred, and, in fact, those principles could logically lead to no other result. This general purpose, indeed, is distinctly set forth in the personal statements and confessions of its members, and particularly of its prominent officers, who have been induced to make disclosures to the Government. Among the most significant of these confessions are those already alluded to, of Hunt, Dunn, and Smith, the heads of the Order in Missouri. The latter, whose statement is full and explicit, says: "At the time I joined the Order I understood that its object was to aid and assist the Confederate Government, and endeavor to restore the Union as it was prior to this rebellion." He adds: "The Order is hostile in every respect to the General Government, and friendly to the so-called Confederate Government. It is exclusively made up of disloyal persons — of all Democrats who are desirous of securing the independence of the Confederate States with a view of restoring the Union as it was."

It would be idle to comment on such gibberish as the statement that "the independence of the Confederate States" was to be used as the means of restoring "the Union as it was;" and yet, under the manipulations of these traitorous jugglers, doubtless the brains of many have been so far muddled as to accept this shameless declaration as true.

But proceeding to the *specific* purposes of the Order, which its leaders have had in view from the beginning, and which, as will be seen, it has been able, in many cases, to carry out with very considerable success, the following are found to be most pointedly presented by the testimony.

1. *Aiding Soldiers to Desert and Harboring and Protecting Deserters.* — Early in its history the Order essayed to undermine such portions of the army as were exposed to its insidious approaches. Agents were sent by the K. G. C. into the camps to introduce the Order among the soldiers, and those who became members were instructed to induce as many of their companions as possible to desert, and for this purpose the latter were furnished by the Order with money and citizens' clothing. Soldiers who hesitated at desertion, but desired to leave the army, were introduced to lawyers who engaged to furnish them some *quasi* legal pretext for so doing, and a certain attorney of Indianapolis, named Walpole, who was particularly conspicuous in furnishing facilities of this character to soldiers who applied to him, has boasted that he has thus aided five hundred enlisted men to escape from their contracts. Through the schemes of the Order in Indiana whole companies were broken up — a large detachment of a battery company, for instance, deserting on one occasion to the enemy with two of its guns — and the camps were imbued with a spirit of discontent and dissatisfaction with the service. Some estimate of the success of these efforts may be derived from a report of the Adjutant General of Indiana, of January, in 1863, setting forth that the number of deserters and absentees returned to the army through the post of Indianapolis alone, during the month of December, 1862, was nearly two thousand six hundred.

As soon as arrests of these deserters began to be generally made, writs of *habeas corpus* were issued in their cases by disloyal judges, and a considerable number were discharged thereon. In one instance in Indiana, where an officer in charge of a deserter properly refused to obey the writ, after it had been suspended in such cases by the President, his attachment for contempt was ordered by the chief justice of the State, who declared that "the streets of Indianapolis might run with blood, but that he would enforce his authority against the President's order." On another occasion certain United States officers who had made the arrest of deserters in Illinois were themselves arrested for kidnapping, and held to trial by a disloyal judge, who at the same time discharged the deserters, though acknowledging them to be such.

Soldiers, upon deserting, were assured of immunity from punishment and protection on the part of the Order, and were instructed to bring away with them their arms, and, if mounted, their horses. Details sent to arrest them by the military authorities were in several cases forcibly resisted, and, where not unusually strong in numbers, were driven back by large bodies of men, subsequently generally ascertained to be members of the Order. Where arrests were effected, our troops were openly attacked and fired upon on their return. Instances of such attacks occurring in Morgan and Rush counties, Indiana, are especially noticed by General Carrington. In the case of the outbreak in Morgan county, J. S. Bingham, editor of the Indianapolis *Sentinel,* a member or friend of the order, sought to forward to the disloyal newspapers of the West false and inflammatory telegraphic despatches in regard to the affair, to the effect that cavalry had been sent to arrest all the Democrats in the country, that they had committed gross outrages, and that several citizens had been shot; and adding "ten thousand soldiers cannot hold the men arrested this night. Civil war and bloodshed are inevitable." The assertions in this despatch were entirely false, and may serve to illustrate the fact heretofore noted, that a studious misrepresentation of the acts of the Government and its officers is a part of the prescribed duty of members of the Order. It is proper to mention that seven of the party in Morgan county who made the attack upon our troops were convicted of their offence by a State court. Upon their trial it was proved that the party was composed of members of the K. G. C.

One of the most pointed instances of protection afforded to deserters occurred in a case in Indiana, where seventeen deserters intrenched themselves in a log cabin with a ditch and palisade, and were furnished with provisions and sustained in their defence against our military authorities for a considerable period by the Order or its friends.

2. *Discouraging Enlistments and Resisting the Draft.* — It is especially inculcated by the Order to oppose the re-enforcement of our armies, either by volunteers or drafted men. In 1862 the Knights of the Golden Circle organized generally to resist the draft in the Western States, and were strong enough in certain localities to greatly embarrass the Government. In this year and early in 1863 a number of enrolling officers were shot in Indiana and Illinois. In Blackford county, Indiana, an attack was made upon the court-

house, and the books connected with the draft were destroyed. In several counties of the State a considerable military force was required for the protection of the United States officials, and a large number of arrests were made, including that of one Reynolds, an ex-Senator of the Legislature, for publicly urging upon the populace to resist the conscription — an offence of the same character, in fact, as that upon which Vallandigham was apprehended in Ohio. These outbreaks were no doubt, in most cases, incited by the Order and engaged in by its members. In Indiana nearly 200 persons were indicted for conspiracy against the Government, resisting the draft, &c., and about sixty of these were convicted.

Where members of the Order were forced into the army by the draft, they were instructed, in case they were prevented from presently escaping, and were obliged to go to the field, to use their arms against their fellow-soldiers rather than the enemy, or, if possible, to desert to the enemy, by whom, through the signs of the Order, they would be recognized and received as friends. Whenever a member volunteered in the army he was at once expelled from the Order.

3. *Circulation of Disloyal and Treasonable Publications.* — The Order, especially in Missouri, has secretly circulated throughout the country a great quantity of treasonable publications, as a means of extending its own power and influence, as well as of giving encouragement to the disloyal and inciting them to treason. Of these, some of the principal are the following: "Pollard's Southern History of the War," "Official Reports of the Confederate Government," "Life of Stonewall Jackson," Pamphlets containing articles from the "Metropolitan Record," "Abraham Africanus, or Mysteries of the White House," "The Lincoln Catechism, or a Guide to the Presidential Election of 1864," "Indestructible Organics," by Tirga. These publications have generally been procured by formal requisitions drawn upon the grand commander by leading members in the interior of a State. One of these requisitions, dated June 10th last, and drawn by a local secretary of the Order at Gentryville, Missouri, is exhibited in the testimony. It contains a column of the initials of subscribers, opposite whose names are entered the number of disloyal publications to be furnished, the particular book or books, &c., required being indicated by fictitious titles.

4. *Communicating with, and Giving Intelligence to the Enemy.* —

Smith, Grand Secretary of the order in Missouri, says, in his confession: "Rebel spies, mail-carriers, and emissaries have been carefully protected by this Order ever since I have been a member." It is shown in the testimony to be customary in the rebel service to employ members of the Order as spies, under the guise of soldiers furnished with furloughs to visit their homes within our lines. On coming within the territory occupied by our forces, they are harbored and supplied with information by the Order. Another class of spies claim to be deserters from the enemy, and at once seek an opportunity to take the oath of allegiance, which, however, though voluntarily taken, they claim to be administered while they are under a species of duress, and, therefore, not to be binding. Upon swearing allegiance to the Government, the pretended deserter engages, with the assistance of the Order, in collecting contraband goods or procuring intelligence to be conveyed to the enemy, or in some other treasonable enterprise. In his official report of June 12th last, Colonel Sanderson remarks: "This department is filled with rebel spies, all of whom belong to the Order."

In Missouri regular mail communication was for a long period maintained through the agency of the Order from St. Louis to Price's army, by means of which private letters, as well as official despatches between him and the Grand Commander of Missouri were regularly transmitted. The mail-carriers started from a point on the Pacific railroad, near Kirkwood Station, about fourteen miles from St. Louis, and, travelling only by night, proceeded (to quote from Colonel Sanderson's report) to "Mattox Mills, on the Maramee river, thence past Mineral Point to Webster, thence to a point fifteen miles below Van Buren, where they crossed the Black river, and thence to the rebel lines." It is, probably, also by this route that the secret correspondence, stated by the witness Pitman to have been constantly kept up between Price and Vallandigham, the heads of the order at the North and South, respectively, was successfully maintained.

A similar communication has been continuously held with the enemy from Louisville, Kentucky. A considerable number of women in that State, many of them of high position in rebel society, and some of them outwardly professing to be loyal, were discovered to have been actively engaged in receiving and forwarding mails, with the assistance of the Order and as its instruments. Two of the most notorious and successful of these, Mrs. Woods and Miss Cassell, have been apprehended and imprisoned.

By means of this correspondence with the enemy the members of the Order were promptly apprised of all raids to be made by the forces of the former, and were able to hold themselves prepared to render aid and comfort to the raiders. To show how efficient for this purpose was the system thus established, it is to be added that our military authorities have, in a number of cases, been informed, through members of the Order employed in the interest of the Government, of impending raids and important army movements of the rebels, not only days, but sometimes weeks, sooner than the same intelligence could have reached them through the ordinary channels.

On the other hand, the system of *espionage* kept up by the Order, for the purpose of obtaining information of the movements of our own forces, &c., to be imparted to the enemy, seems to have been as perfect as it was secret. The Grand Secretary of the Order in Missouri states, in his confession: "One of the especial objects of this Order was to place members in steamboats, terry-boats, telegraph offices, express offices, department headquarters, provost marshal's office, and, in fact, in every position where they could do valuable service;" and he proceeds to specify certain members who, at the date of his confession, (August 2d last,) were employed at the express and telegraph offices in St. Louis.

5. *Aiding the Enemy, by recruiting for them or Assisting them to Recruit, within our lines.* — This has also been extensively carried on by members of the Order, particularly in Kentucky and Missouri. It is estimated that 2,000 men were sent south from Louisville alone during a few weeks in April and May, 1864. The Order and its friends at that city have a permanent fund, to which there are many subscribers, for the purpose of fitting out with pistols, clothing, money, &c., men desiring to join the southern service; and, in the lodges of the Order in St. Louis and Northern Missouri, money has often been raised to purchase horses, arms, and equipments for soldiers about to be forwarded to the Southern army. In the latter State, parties empowered by Price, or by Grand Commander Hunt as his representative, to recruit for the rebel service, were nominally authorized to "*locate lands*," as it was expressed, and in their reports, which were formally made, the number of acres, &c., located

represented the number of men recruited. At Louisville, those desiring to join the Southern forces were kept hidden, and supplied with food and lodging until a convenient occasion was presented for their transportation South. They were then collected, and conducted at night to a safe rendezvous of the Order, whence they were forwarded to their destination, in some cases stealing horses from the United States corrals on their way. While awaiting an occasion to be sent South, the men, to avoid the suspicion which might be excited by their being seen together in any considerable number, were often employed on farms in the vicinity of Louisville and the farm of one Moore, in that neighborhood, (at whose house, also, meetings of the Order were held,) is indicated in the testimony as one of the localities where such recruits were rendezvoused and employed.

The same facilities which were afforded to recruits for the Southern army were also furnished by the Order to persons desiring to proceed beyond our lines for any illegal purpose. By these Louisville was generally preferred as a point of departure, and, on the Mississippi river, a particular steamer, the Graham, was selected as the safest conveyance.

6. *Furnishing the Rebels with Arms, Ammunition, &c.* — In this, too, the Order, and especially its female members and allies, has been sedulously engaged. The rebel women of Louisville and Kentucky are represented as having rendered the most valuable aid to the Southern army, by transporting large quantities of percussion caps, powder, &c., concealed upon their persons, to some convenient locality near the lines, whence they could be readily conveyed to those for whom they were intended. It is estimated that at Louisville, up to May 1 last, the sum of $17,000 had been invested by the Order in ammunition and arms, to be forwarded principally in this manner to the rebels. In St. Louis several firms, who are well known to the Government, the principal of which is Beauvais & Co., have been engaged in supplying arms and ammunition to members of the Order, to be conveyed to their Southern allies. Mary Ann Pitman, a reliable witness, and a member of the O. A. K., who will hereafter be specially alluded to, states in her testimony that she visited Beauvais & Co. three times, and procured from them on each occasion about $80 worth of caps, besides a number of pistols and cartridges, which she carried in person to Forrest's command,

as well as a much larger quantity of similar articles which she caused to be forwarded by other agents. The guerillas in Missouri also received arms from St. Louis, and one Douglas, one of the most active conspirators of the O. A. K. in Missouri, and a special emissary of Price, was arrested while in the act of transporting a box of forty revolvers by railroad to a guerilla camp in the interior of the State. Medical stores in large quantities were likewise, by the aid of the Order, furnished to the enemy, and a "young doctor" named Moore, said to be now a medical inspector in the rebel army, is mentioned as having "made $75,000 by smuggling medicines" — principally from Louisville — through the lines of our army. Supplies were, in some cases, conveyed to the enemy through the medium of professed loyalists, who, having received permits for that purpose from the United States military authorities, would forward their goods as if for ordinary purposes of trade, to a certain point near the rebel lines, where, by the connivance of the owners, the enemy would be enabled to seize them.

7. *Co-operating with the Enemy in Raids and Invasions.* — While it is clear that the Order has given aid, both directly and indirectly, to the forces of the rebels, and to guerilla bands when engaged in making incursions into the border States, yet because, on the one hand, of the constant restraint upon its action exercised by our military authorities, and, on the other, of the general success of our armies in the field over those of the enemy, their allies at the North have never thus far been able to carry out their grand plan of a general armed rising of the Order, and its co-operation on an extended scale with the Southern forces. This plan has been two-fold, and consisted, first, of a rising of the Order in Missouri, aided by a strong detachment from Illinois, and a co-operation with a rebel army under Price; second, of a similar rising in Indiana, Ohio, and Kentucky, and a co-operation with a force under Breckinridge, Buckner, Morgan, or some other rebel commander, who was to invade the latter State. In *this* case the Order was first to cut the railroads and telegraph wires, so that intelligence of the movement might not be sent abroad and the transportation of Federal troops might be delayed, and then to seize upon the arsenals at Indianapolis, Columbus, Springfield, Louisville, and Frankfort, and, furnishing such of their number as were without arms, to kill or make prisoners of department, district, and post commanders, release the

rebel prisoners at Rock Island, and at Camps Morton, Douglas, and Chase, and thereupon join the Southern army at Louisville or some other point in Kentucky, which State was to be permanently occupied by the combined force. At the period of the movement it was also proposed that an attack should be made upon Chicago by means of steam-tugs mounted with cannon. A similar course was to be taken in Missouri, and was to result in the permanent occupation of that State.

This scheme has long occupied the minds of members of the Order, and has been continually discussed by them in their lodges. A rising somewhat of the character described was intended to have taken place in the spring of this year, simultaneously with an expected advance of the army of Lee upon Washington; but the plans of the enemy having been anticipated by the movements of our own generals, the rising of the conspirators was necessarily postponed. Again, a general movement of the Southern forces was expected to take place about July 4, and with this the Order was to co-operate. A speech to be made by Vallandigham at the Chicago Convention was, it is said, to be the signal for the rising; but the postponement of the convention, as well as the failure of the rebel armies to engage in the anticipated movement, again operated to disturb the programme of the Order. During the summer, however, the grand plan of action above set forth has been more than ever discussed throughout the Order, and its success most confidently predicted, while at the same time an extensive organization and preparation for carrying the conspiracy into effect have been actively going on. But up to this time, notwithstanding the late raids of the enemy in Kentucky, and the invasion of Missouri by Price, no such general action on the part of the Order as was contemplated has taken place — a result, in great part, owing to the activity of our military authorities in strengthening the detachments at the prisons, arsenals, &c., and in causing the arrest of the leading conspirators in the several States, and especially in the seizure of large quantities of arms which had been shipped for the use of the Order in their intended outbreak. It was doubtless on account of these precautions that the day last appointed for the rising of the order in Indiana and Kentucky (August 16) passed by with but slight disorder.

It is, however, the inability of the public enemy, in the now declining days of the rebellion, to initiate the desired movements which has prevented the Order from engaging in open warfare; and it has lately been seriously considered in their councils whether they should not proceed with their revolt, relying alone upon the guerilla bands of Syphert, Jesse, and others, for support and assistance.

With these guerillas the Order has always most readily acted along the border, and in cases of capture by the Union forces of Northern members of the Order engaged in co-operating with them, the guerillas have frequently retaliated by seizing prominent Union citizens and holding them as hostages for the release of their allies. At other times our Government has been officially notified by the rebel authorities that if the members of the order captured were not treated by us as ordinary prisoners of war, retaliation would be resorted to.

An atrocious plan of concert between members of the Order in Indiana and certain guerilla bands of Kentucky, agreed upon last spring, may be here remarked upon. Some 2,500 or 3,000 guerillas were to be thrown into the border counties, and were to assume the character of refugees seeking employment. Being armed, they were secretly to destroy Government property wherever practicable, and subsequently to control the elections by force, prevent enlistments, aid deserters, and stir up strife between the civil and military authorities.

A singular feature of the raids of the enemy remains only to be adverted to, viz: that the officers conducting these raids are furnished by the rebel Government with quantities of United States Treasury notes for use within our lines, and that these are probably most frequently procured through the agency of members of the Order.

Mary Ann Pitman states that Forrest, of the rebel army, at one time exhibited to her a letter to himself from a prominent rebel sympathizer and member of the Order in Washington, D. C., in which it was set forth that the sum of $20,000 in "greenbacks" had actually been forwarded by him to the rebel Government at Richmond.

8. *Destruction of Government Property.* — There is no doubt that large quantities of Government property have been burned or otherwise destroyed by the agency of the Order in different localities. At Louisville, in the case of the steamer Taylor, and on the Mississippi river, steamers belonging to the United States have been

burned at the wharves, and generally when loaded with Government stores. Shortly before the arrest of Bowles, the senior of the major generals of the Order in Indiana, he had been engaged in the preparation of "Greek Fire," which it was supposed would be found serviceable in the destruction of public property. It was generally understood in the councils of the Order in the State of Kentucky that they were to be compensated for such destruction by the rebel Government, by receiving a commission of ten per cent. of the value of the property so destroyed, and that this value was to be derived from the estimate of the loss made in each case by Northern newspapers.

9. *Destruction of Private Property and Persecution of Loyal Men.* — It is reported by General Carrington that the full development of the order in Indiana was followed by "a state of terrorism" among the Union residents of "portions of Brown, Morgan, Johnson, Rush, Clay, Sullivan, Bartholomew, Hendricks, and other counties" in that State; that from some localities individuals were driven away altogether; that in others their barns, hay, and wheat-ricks, were burned; and that many persons, under the general insecurity of life and property, sold their effects at a sacrifice and removed to other places. At one time in Brown county, the members of the Order openly threatened the lives of all "Abolitionists" who refused to sign a peace memorial which they had prepared and addressed to Congress. In Missouri, also, similar outrages committed upon the property of loyal citizens are attributable in a great degree to the secret Order.

Here the outbreak of the miners in the coal districts of eastern Pennsylvania, in the autumn of last year, may be appropriately referred to. It was fully shown in the testimony adduced, upon the trials of these insurgents, who were guilty of the destruction of property and numerous acts of violence, as well as murder, that they were generally members of a secret treasonable association, similar in all respects to the K. G. C., at the meetings of which they had been incited to the commission of the crimes for which they were tried and convicted.

10. *Assassination and Murder.* — After what has been disclosed in regard to this infamous league of traitors and ruffians, it will not be a matter of surprise to learn that the cold-blooded assassination of Union citizens and soldiers has been included in their devilish scheme of operations. Green B. Smith states in his confession that

"the secret assassination of United States officers, soldiers, and Government employes has been discussed in the councils of the Order and recommended." It is also shown in the course of the testimony that at a large meeting of the Order in St. Louis, in May or June last, it was proposed to form a secret police of members for the purpose of patrolling the streets of that city at night and killing every detective and soldier that could be readily disposed of; that this proposition was coolly considered, and finally rejected, not because of its fiendish character — no voice being raised against its criminality — but because only it was deemed premature. At Louisville, in June last, a similar scheme was discussed among the Order for the waylaying and butchering of negro soldiers in the streets at night; and in the same month a party of its members in that city was actually organized for the purpose of throwing off the track of the Nashville railroad a train of colored troops and seizing the opportunity to take the lives of as many as possible. Again, in July, the assassination of an obnoxious provost marshal, by betraying him into the hands of guerillas, was designed by members in the interior of Kentucky. Further, at a meeting of the Grand Council of Indiana at Indianapolis on June 14 last, the murder of one Coffin, a Government detective, who, as it was supposed, had betrayed the Order, was deliberately discussed and unanimously determined upon. This fact is stated by Stidger in his report to General Carrington of June 17 last, and is more fully set forth in his testimony upon the trial of Dodd. He deposes that at the meeting in question, Dodd himself volunteered to go to Hamilton, Ohio, where Coffin was expected to be found, and there "dispose of the latter." He adds that prior to the meeting, he himself conveyed from Judge Bullit, at Louisville, to Bowles and Dodd, at Indianapolis, special instructions to have Coffin "put out of the way" — "murdered" — "at all hazards."

The opinion is expressed by Colonel Sanderson, under date of June 12 last, that "the recent numerous cold-blooded assassinations of military officers and unconditional Union men throughout the military district of North Missouri, especially along the western border," is to be ascribed to the agency of the Order. The witness Pitman represents that it is "a part of the obligation or understanding of the Order" to kill officers and soldiers *whenever it can be done by stealth,*" as well as loyal citizens when considered important or influential persons; and she adds, that while at Memphis, during the past summer, she *knew* that men on picket were secretly killed by members of the Order approaching them in disguise.

In this connexion may be recalled the wholesale assassination of Union soldiers by members of the Order and their confederates at Charleston, Illinois, in March last, in regard to which, as a startling episode of the rebellion, a full report was addressed from this office to the President, under date of July 26 last. This concerted murderous assault upon a scattered body of men, mostly unarmed — apparently designed for the mere purpose of destroying as many lives of Union soldiers as possible — is a forcible illustration of the utter malignity and depravity which characterize the members of this Order in their zeal to commend themselves as allies to their fellow-conspirators at the South.

11. *Establishment of a Northwestern Confederacy.* — In concluding this review of some of the principal specific purposes of the Order, it remains only to remark upon a further design of many of its leading members, the accomplishment of which they are represented as having deeply at heart. Hating New England, and jealous of her influence and resources, and claiming that the interests of the West and South, naturally connected as they are through the Mississippi valley, are identical, and actuated further by an intensely revolutionary spirit as well as an unbridled and unprincipled ambition, these men have made the establishment of a Western or Northwestern Confederacy, in alliance with the South, the grand aim and end of all their plotting and conspiring. It is with this steadily in prospect that they are constantly seeking to produce discontent, disorganization, and civil disorder at the North. With this in view, they gloat over every reverse of the armies of the Union, and desire that the rebellion shall be protracted until the resources of the Government shall be exhausted, its strength paralyzed, its currency hopelessly depreciated, and confidence everywhere destroyed. Then, from the anarchy which, under their scheme, is to ensue, the new Confederacy is to arise, which is either to unite itself with that of the South, or to form therewith a close and permanent alliance. Futile and extravagant as this scheme may appear, it is yet the settled purpose of many leading spirits of the secret conspiracy, and is their favorite subject of thought and discussion. Not only is this scheme deliberated upon in the lodges of the order, but it is openly proclaimed. Members of the Indiana Legislature, even have

publicly announced it, and avowed that they will take their own State out of the Union, and recognize the independence of the South. A citizen captured by a guerilla band in Kentucky last summer, records the fact that the establishment of a new confederacy as the deliberate purpose of the Western people was boastfully asserted by these outlaws, who also assured their prisoner that in the event of such establishment there would be "a greater rebellion than ever!"

Lastly, it is claimed that the new confederacy is already organized; that it has a "provisional government," officers, departments, bureaus, &c., in secret operation. No comment is necessary to be made upon this treason, not now contemplated for the first time in our history. Suggested by the present rebellion, it is the logical consequence of the ardent and utter sympathy therewith which is the life and inspiration of the secret Order.

VIII. — THE WITNESSES, AND THEIR TESTIMONY.

The facts detailed in the present report have been derived from a great variety of dissimilar sources, but all the witnesses, however different their situations, concur so pointedly in their testimony, that the evidence which has thus been furnished must be accepted as of an entirely satisfactory character.

The principal witnesses may be classified as follows:

1. Shrewd, intelligent men, employed as detectives, and with a peculiar talent for their calling, who have gradually gained the confidence of leading members of the Order, and in some cases have been admitted to its temples and been initiated into one or more of the degrees. The most remarkable of these is Stidger, formerly a private soldier in our army, who, by the use of an uncommon address, though at great personal risk, succeeded in establishing such intimate relations with Bowles, Bullit, Dodd, and other leaders of the Order in Indiana and Kentucky, as to be appointed grand secretary for the latter State, a position the most favorable for obtaining information of the plans of these traitors and warning the Government of their intentions. It is to the rare fidelity of this man, who has also been the principal witness upon the trial of Dodd, that the Government has been chiefly indebted for the exposure of the designs of the conspirators in the two States named.

2. Rebel officers and soldiers voluntarily or involuntarily making disclosures to our military authorities. The most valuable witnesses

of this class are prisoners of war, who, actuated by laudable motives, have of their own accord furnished a large amount of information in regard to the Order, especially as it exists in the South, and of the relations of its members with those of the Northern section. Among these, also, are soldiers at our prison camps, who, without designing it, have made known to our officials, by the use of the signs, &c., of the Order, that they were members.

3. Scouts employed to travel through the interior of the border States, and also within or in the neighborhood of the enemy's lines. The fact that some of these were left entirely ignorant of the existence of the Order, upon being so employed, attaches an increased value to their discoveries in regard to its operations.

4. Citizen prisoners, to whom, while in confinement, disclosures were made relative to the existence, extent, and character of the Order by fellow-prisoners who were leading members, and who, in some instances, upon becoming intimate with the witness, initiated him into one of the degrees.

5. Members of the Order, who, upon a full acquaintance with its principles, have been appalled by its infamous designs, and have voluntarily abandoned it, freely making known their experience to our military authorities. In this class may be placed the female witness, Mary Ann Pitman, who, though in arrest at the period of her disclosures, was yet induced to make them for the reason that, as she says, "at the last meeting which I attended they passed an order which I consider as utterly atrocious and barbarous; so I told them I would have nothing more to do with them." This woman was attached to the command of the rebel Forrest, as an officer under the name of "Lieutenant Rawley;" but, because her sex afforded her unusual facilities for crossing our lines, she was often employed in the execution of important commissions within our territory, and, as a member of the Order, was made extensively acquainted with other members, both of the Northern and Southern sections. Her testimony is thus peculiarly valuable, and, being a person of unusual intelligence and force of character, her statements are succinct, pointed, and emphatic. They are also especially useful as fully corroborating those of other witnesses regarded as most trustworthy.

6. Officers of the Order of high rank, who have been prompted to present confessions, more or less detailed, in regard to the Order and their connexion with it. The principals of these are Hunt,

Dunn, and Smith, grand commander, deputy grand commander, and grand secretary of the Order in Missouri, to whose statements frequent reference has been made. These confessions, though in some degree guarded and disingenuous, have furnished to the Government much important information as to the operations of the Order, especially in Missouri, the affiliation of its leaders with Price, &c. It is to be noted that Dunn makes the statement in common with other witnesses that, in entering the Order, he was quite ignorant of its ultimate purposes. He says: "I did not become a member understandingly; the initiatory step was taken in the dark, without reflection and without knowledge."

7. Deserters from our army, who, upon being apprehended, confessed that they had been induced and assisted to desert by members of the Order. It was, indeed, principally from these confessions that the existence of the secret treasonable organization of the K. G. C. was first discovered in Indiana, in the year 1862.

8. Writers of anonymous communications, addressed to heads of departments or provost marshals, disclosing facts corroborative of other more important statements.

9. The witnesses before the grand jury at Indianapolis, in 1863, when the Order was formally presented as a treasonable organization, and those whose testimony has been recently introduced upon the trial of Dodd.

It need only be added that a most satisfactory test of the credibility and weight of much of the evidence which has been furnished is afforded by the printed testimony in regard to the character and intention of the Order, which is found in its national and State constitutions and its ritual. Indeed, the statements of the various witnesses are but presentations of the logical and inevitable consequences and results of the principles therein set forth.

In concluding this review, it remains only to state that a constant reference has been made to the elaborate official reports, in regard to the Order of Brigadier General Carrington, commanding District of Indiana, and of Colonel Sanderson, Provost Marshal General of the Department of Missouri. The great mass of the testimony upon the subject of this conspiracy has been furnished by these officers; the latter acting under the orders of Major General Rosecrans, and the former co-operating, under the instructions of the

Secretary of War, with Major General Burbridge, commanding District of Kentucky, as well as with Governor Morton, of Indiana, who, though at one time greatly embarrassed, by a Legislature strongly tainted with disloyalty, in his efforts to repress this domestic enemy, has at last seen his State relieved from the danger of a civil war.

But, although the treason of the Order has been thoroughly exposed, and although its capacity for fatal mischief has, by means of the arrest of its leaders, the seizure of its arms, and the other vigorous means which have been pursued, been seriously impaired, it is still busied with its plottings against the Government, and with its perfidious designs in aid of the Southern rebellion. It is reported to have recently adopted new signs and passwords, and its members assert that foul means will be used to prevent the success of the Administration at the coming election, and threaten an extended revolt in the event of the re-election of President Lincoln.

In the presence of the rebellion and of this secret Order — which is but its echo and faithful ally — we cannot but be amazed at the utter and widespread profligacy, personal and political, which these movements against the Government disclose. The guilty men engaged in them, after casting aside their allegiance, seem to have trodden under foot every sentiment of honor and every restraint of law, human and divine. Judea produced but one Judas Iscariot, and Rome, from the sinks of her demoralization, produced but one Catiline; and yet, as events prove, there has arisen together in our land an entire brood of such traitors, all animated by the same parricidal spirit, and all struggling with the same relentless malignity for the dismemberment of our Union. Of this extraordinary phenomenon — not paralleled, it is believed, in the world's history — there can be but one explanation, and all these blackened and fetid streams of crime may well be traced to the same common fountain. So fiercely intolerant and imperious was the temper engendered by Slavery, that when the Southern people, after having controlled the national councils for half a century, were beaten at an election, their leaders turned upon the Government with the insolent fury with which they would have drawn their revolvers on a rebellious slave in one of their negro quarters; and they have continued since to prosecute their warfare, amid all the barbarisms and atrocities naturally and necessarily inspired by the infernal institution in whose interests they are sacrificing alike themselves and their country.

Many of these conspirators, as is well known, were fed, clothed, and educated at the expense of the nation, and were loaded with its honors at the very moment they struck at its life with the horrible criminality of a son stabbing the bosom of its own mother while impressing kisses on his cheeks. The leaders of the traitors in the loyal States, who so completely fraternize with these conspirators, and whose machinations are now unmasked, it is as clearly the duty of the Administration to prosecute and punish as it is its duty to subjugate the rebels who are openly in arms against the Government. In the performance of this duty, it is entitled to expect, and will doubtless receive, the zealous co-operation of true men everywhere, who, in crushing the truculent foe ambushed in the haunts of this secret Order, should rival in courage and faithfulness the soldiers who are so nobly sustaining our flag on the battle-fields of the South.

Respectfully submitted.

J. HOLT, *Judge Advocate General.*

Pamphlet 48

Robert Charles Winthrop

Great Speech of Hon. Robert C. Winthrop,
at New London, Conn., October 18. The Principles
and Interests of the Republican Party Against the
Union. The Election of McClellan the Only Hope
for Union and Peace. (Campaign Document
No. 23)
New York, 1864

[The best reasoned advocacy of General George B. McClellan, the Democratic candidate for President in 1864, was that of an avowed conservative, Robert C. Winthrop of Boston. The New York Democrats (presumably those who had constituted the Society for the Diffusion of Political Knowledge), appended to the speech McClellan's persuasive letter of acceptance together with several odds and ends, and issued the whole as their Campaign Document No. 23. It was their most powerful statement; they issued it in an edition of two hundred thousand. Winthrop (1809–1894), as a protégé of Daniel Webster had risen spectacularly in politics. He was speaker of the House of Representatives at 38, and a Whig Senator from Massachusetts at 41 — only to be eclipsed in 1851 by the militant opponent of slavery, Charles Sumner, who won his seat in the Senate. Winthrop never again held public office. In 1861 he supported the Bell-Everett Constitutional Union ticket, but during the Civil War was friendly toward Lincoln. Although he would not support the President in the election of 1864, after Lincoln's assassination the following April he eulogized him as "the man, who, of all other men, could be least spared to the administration of our government." Winthrop reasoned privately that Lincoln had pursued a far different and more satisfactory course in the six months following his re-election. Although Winthrop had been a stern opponent of abolition, he devoted many years after the war to service as the chairman of the board of the Peabody Education Fund which fostered Negro education in the South.[1]]

[1] [Robert C. Winthrop, Jr., A *Memoir of Robert C. Winthrop* (Boston, 1897).]

New London, Conn., Oct. 18.

Hon. Robert C. Winthrop addressed the citizens of New London, on Tuesday evening, at Lawrence Hall. The meeting could not have been larger with out an extension of the walls of the building. The front seats and galleries were occupied by many ladies, and the audience was composed of the eminently solid and respectable people of the community.

Mr. Waller, the President of the McClellan Club, called the meeting to order, and nominated for chairman, Hon. Abiel Converse.

Mr. Winthrop now came upon the platform and was received with the greatest enthusiasm. He was introduced by the chairman, as follows:

Fellow-citizens: We are to-night honored with the presence of a distinguished gentleman, who fondly turns to New London as the birthplace of his father and the home of a long line of illustrious ancestors; a gentleman whose elegant culture and enlightened statesmanship have made him a national — nay, a worldwide reputation; a gentleman who in the better days of the republic was a leading spirit in the national Whig party, but who to-night stands with us shoulder to shoulder in the ranks of the only Constitutional Union party of the country — the party which proposes to place in the Presidential chair George B. McClellan. (Loud cheers.) Fellow-citizens, allow me to present to you the Honorable Robert C. Winthrop.

After the cheering with which he was greeted had subsided, Mr. Winthrop spoke as follows:

MR. WINTHROP'S SPEECH

Fellow Citizens: I am deeply sensible to the kindness and the compliment of this reception. I thank you for this inspiring welcome to your city. I have come at your request to address you on the great subject which is uppermost in all our minds and in all our hearts. I am here for no purpose of declamation or display. I am here to appeal to no prejudices or passions. No arts of rhetoric can meet the exigencies of this hour. If I were ever capable of them, I abandon and discard them all to-night. I am here only from a deep sense of the duty which rests upon each one of us to contribute what we can by word or by deed, for a suffering, bleeding country.

Compelled by engagements or by my health, to refuse a hundred other invitations, I could not resist the appeal which was made to me from New London. (Applause.) And if any word of mine may be thought worthy of being listened to or regarded, in Connecticut or elsewhere, there is no place from which it may more fitly go forth than from this old and honored home of my fathers. (Applause.) It is a time, I am aware, my friends, when the best and wisest, and most patriotic men may differ, and do differ, widely from each other. I would cast no reproaches upon my opponents. I do not forget the reproaches which have been cast upon myself in some quarters; but I have no heart for bandying personalities at a period like this. I pass by all such matters as unworthy of a moment's consideration. Or rather, let me say, they pass by me like the idle wind. The air, indeed, is full of them. Arbitrary and arrogant assumptions of superior patriotism and loyalty — coarse and malicious representations and imputations — opprobrious and insulting names and epithets, often applied by men who might well be conscious that nobody deserves them so much as themselves — the air is full of them. They come swarming up from stump and rostrum, and press and platform. We meet them at every turn. Let us not retort them. Let us not resent them. Let no one by any means be tempted or provoked by them into acts of vengeance or violence. Let us simply overwhelm them with contempt, and pass on, unawed and unintimidated, to the declaration of our own honest opinions, and to the assertion and exercise of our rights as freemen. (Applause.) Let us imitate the example of our own noble candidate, whose quiet endurance of injustice and calumny has been one of the most beautiful illustrations of his character, and has won for him a respect which will outlive the ephemeral notoriety of his revilers. Our country calls at this moment for the best thoughts, the bravest counsels, the freest utterances, the most unhesitating devotion of every one of her sons. Let us compare our opinions with each other honestly, independently, fearlessly: and let no man shrink from following his own conscientious convictions, wherever they may lead him. It may be a misfortune, fellow-citizens, that a new election of our national rulers should have come upon us precisely at this moment. We would all gladly keep our eyes steadily fixed upon our country's flag, as it waves and wavers upon yonder battlefields. We would willingly follow its gallant supporters, in the conflicts in which they are engaged, with undivided and uninterrupted sympathies. But it is not in our power to postpone the time appointed for our great political struggle. The Constitution of the United States has fixed that time unalterably, and nothing remains for us but to discharge our duties as intelligent and responsible citizens. A great, a tremendous responsibility, certainly, is upon us. When the votes of the people of the United States — your votes, Men of New London, and mine among them shall have once decided the question — by what party and upon what principles and policy the national government shall be administered for the next four years — they will have determined, under God, the destinies of our country for unborn generations. No one in his senses can doubt that the results of the administration of the next four years will be decisive of the fate of this republic. Within that period the Union is to be saved or lost. Within that period the Constitution is to be vindicated or overthrown. Within that period the old flag of our fathers is to be re-advanced in triumph over all the States of which it has ever been, or ever borne, the emblem; or, rent in twain and shorn of half its lustre, it is to droop over a divided land. If the stake of the impending contest, my friends, were anything less than this, if anything less or anything other than the rescue of the Union and the salvation of the republic, were to be the result of this election, we might well hesitate about entering into a political struggle and arraying ourselves against an existing administration in a time of civil war. But with such an issue of national life, or national death, before us, there ought to be, there can be, no hesitation on the part of any patriotic citizen. Every one of us, young and old, is called upon by considerations from which there can be no appeal, by obligations from which there can be no escape, to form a careful, dispassionate, conscientious opinion as to his own individual duty, and then to perform that duty without flinching or faltering. We may be pardoned for an honest mistake. We may be excused for an error of judgment. But we can never be excused, before men or before God, for standing neutral and doing nothing. There is no exemption from this warfare. Not only should it be written on every man's forehead what he thinks of the republic; but no man should give sleep to his eyes or slumber to his eyelids without asking himself: What can I do for my country? How can I exercise that most previous of all privileges, that greatest of all rights, the elective franchise, in a way to rescue her from the dangers by which she is encompassed? (Applause.)

GRATITUDE FOR VICTORIES.

And now, my friends, the first emotion which belongs to these occasions of assembling ourselves together, and the one to which we are all and always most eager to give expression, is that of joy and gladness and gratitude for the signal successes which have been recently vouchsafed to our arms. (Cheers.) Most signal they certainly have been. It cannot be denied that, since the nomination of Gen. McClellan was promulgated at Chicago (loud cheers), the military aspect of our affairs has been greatly improved. The gallant Sherman at Atlanta (cheers), and the daring and dashing Sheridan, in the Shenandoah valley (cheers), have achieved victories of vital importance to the cause of the Union; and most heartily would we unite with our fellow-citizens of all parties in paying a well-earned tribute of respect and admiration to the commanders, and to the soldiers, who have been instrumental in accomplishing these glorious results. (Applause.) We are told, indeed, that all these victories are impairing the prospects of our own political success, and diminishing the chances of General McClellan's election to the Presidency. (Laughter.) But we rejoice in them all, notwithstanding, and thank God for them with undivided hearts. ("Yes, yes.") The more of them the better, whatever may be their influence on the election before us. We are content to be so defeated — if that be their legitimate, or even their illegitimate, result — we are more than content. I venture to say, that our noble candidate would rejoice as heartily as President Lincoln himself at every success of our arms, even should the consequences be to leave him without a single electoral vote. He had rather see his country saved, and the Union restored, and the Constitution rescued, than to secure the highest honor for himself which it is in the power of man to bestow. Let us congratulate each other — for we have a right so to do — that his nomination has roused the administration to new efforts. Let us rejoice that the army has been spurred on to redeem the failures of the civil policy of the administration. (Cheers.) The supporters of General McClellan may well be satisfied — even should they accomplish nothing more — with having given an impulse to the prosecution of the war, which not only affords the best promise of military success in the future, but which has already given so glorious and earnest of the fulfillment of that promise.

But why, why, my friends, should success on the battlefield diminish the chances of General McClellan's election? What possible reason is there for such a result? Nobody imagines, I presume, that the hero of Antietam would be a less prudent or a less skillful superintendent of our military affairs than Abraham Lincoln or Secretary Stanton. Nobody dreams that he would be likely to interfere disadvantageously with the conduct of the war. The President, certainly, could not have thought so, when he so obviously connived a few weeks ago at offering him a high command if he would only decline to be a candidate for the Presidency. (Laughter and applause.) The Republican party will hardly be ready to accuse the President of being willing to buy off a dangerous competitor at the expense of putting a doubtful general into the field.

VICTORIES ALONE CANNOT RESTORE PEACE.

No, it is the civil policy of the government which General McClellan is relied upon to change. It is the civil policy of the administration which imperatively demands to be changed. We believe that this civil policy of the administration has prevented all our military successes in the past, and will, if continued, prevent all our military successes in the future from effecting the great end for which we are contending — the only end for which we could constitutionally take up arms. We believe that this civil policy — if anything the administration has recently done can fairly be called civil (laughter) — has been calculated to extinguish every spark of Union sentiment in the Southern States; that it has been calculated to drive those States finally out of the Union, instead of being adapted to draw them back to their old allegiance. ("That's so." Cheers.) We believe that this civil policy has tended to breathe a spirit of defiance and desperation into the breasts of every southern man and woman and child, that it has rendered the work of our own brave soldiers a thousand fold harder to be achieved, and has thus far given them only a barren and fruitless victory, whenever they have succeeded. Who is there wild enough to imagine that mere military triumphs can accomplish that great consummation of Union and peace, which is the devout wish and prayer of every patriotic heart? (Applause.) Why, my friends, we may go on conquering and to conquer month after month, and year after year; we may overcome armies, we may take possession of cities, we may strip and devastate whole territories and regions of country, we may make a solitude and call it peace; but the restoration of the old Union of our fathers, with all the States in their constitutional relations to the General Government, and all the stars upon the folds of our country's flag will require something more than any mere force of arms can effect. (Applause.) Nobody saw this more clearly, or admitted it more frankly than President Lincoln himself, when he declared so emphatically in his inaugural address: "Suppose you go to war, you cannot fight always; and when, after much loss on both sides and no gain on either, you cease fighting, the identical questions as to terms of intercourse are again upon you." The great advantage of victories, my friends, is in opening the way for a wise, conciliatory, healing policy to come in and settle the questions at issue; and it is thus at the very moment when those victories are achieved, that we most need men at the head of the Government who can turn the triumphs of our armies to the only account for which they are worth a straw. It is this — this application of a wise, conciliatory, healing policy — which must follow close upon the track of military triumph in order to render it fruitful, — it is for which the present administration, as we think, is wholly incapacitated, and for which we believe a new administration is the great and paramount necessity of the hour. It is in this view that victories, instead of impairing the prospects of General McClellan's election, ought to plead trumpet-tongued in his behalf. The question prompted by every victory shou'd be, "Where, where are the men who can turn all this conflict and carnage to account, and render a repetition of it needless? Where are the men who can save us from the reproach of having shed all this precious blood in vain, and can originate and pursue a policy which shall make that blood effective for the healing of the nation? Where are the men, where is the man, who can extricate his country from impending ruin, by first extricating himself from all mere sectional and partisan pledges and entanglements, and by planting himself on the simple platform of the Constitution?" (Loud cheers.) These are the questions which each succeeding victory should call upon us to put to ourselves, and these are the questions which, in my judgment, can only be satisfactorily answered by the resolution to change the administration.

If any man would vote for General McClellan in case our military successes had not occurred, a hundred fold more should vote for him now. (Cheers.) Without those successes it would have mattered little who was President. We could have accomplished nothing. But with them a way is opened for a new President to restore Union and peace to our land. Shall we not have a new President to take advantage of that opening? ("Yes, yes.")

A CHANGE OF CIVIL POLICY DEMANDED.

But let us look at the issue before us a little more closely, and more deliberately. You will not expect me, my friends, to go back to the origin of the great struggle in which we are involved. I can tell you nothing about the history of the past which is not abundantly familiar to you. You all know that a wanton and unjustifiable rebellion against our national government was inaugurated in South Carolina nearly four years ago; that it soon expanded to the proportions of the most gigantic civil war the world has ever witnessed, and that it is raging madly and wildly still. You all know the story of its rise and progress. You all know how much treasure and how much blood it has already cost. And you all know what has been accomplished. You have followed our brave soldiers and sailors in all their toils and perils, in all their reverses and in all their triumphs, on the land and on the sea, from that first most impressive scene at Fort Sumter, when the stars and stripes were lifted by the gallant Anderson on the breath of solemn prayer, down to the latest achievements of Sherman, and Farragut, and Sheridan, at Atlanta, and in Mobile Bay, and in the Valley of the Shenandoah. (Cheers.) You have watched, too, the course of our civil rulers at Washington. Their shifting and drifting policy — as it has been strangely developed in resolutions and proclamations, and manifestoes, "To whom it may concern," is familiar to you all. You know what they have promised, and you know what they have performed in the past; and you know what they propose for the future. And now it is for you, and for each one of you to say, whether you are satisfied to recommit the final destinies of this republic to the same hands; whether you are satisfied that the men now in power are in the way of bringing this fearful struggle to a safe and successful termination; whether, in a word, you are ready to take your share of the responsibility of continuing their domination through that presidential term of all others, which is to decide whether there shall ever again be a President over the whole United States of America? (Applause.) For myself, as I have said elsewhere, I have reflected deliberately and deeply on this question, and I have in vain attempted to resist the conclusion, that the best interests of our country, and the best hopes of restoring the Union of our country, demand a change of our national rulers. I have not been able to resist the conclusion, that almost any other party would be more able than the Republican party, and almost any other President would be more likely than Abraham Lincoln, to accomplish that great consummation which every Christian patriot ought to have, and must have, at heart — the earliest practicable restoration of Union, and peace, and constitutional liberty to our afflicted land. I have not been able to resist the conviction that there would be a better chance under any other administration than the present for speedily effecting a termination of the rebellion, upon that basis of "the Union as it was, and the Constitution as it is," which is the only legitimate aim of loyal men. (Cheers.)

CONCERNING THE SWAPPING OF HORSES.

And let me say, in the first place, my friends, that I should have come to this conclusion, as I think, without any regard to the peculiar policy which the Administration has adopted during the last two years. I should have come to this conclusion upon the same plain, common sense views which President Lincoln himself seems to have expressed upon a somewhat similar state of facts. Some of you may remember, perhaps, to have seen an account of an interview which certain very earnest anti-slavery gentlemen, of Massachusetts, held with the President not a great while ago, on the subject of substituting Gen. Fremont for my old and valued friend Edward Stanley, now of California, as the Provisional Governor of North Carolina. The account is given in a letter written by the Rev. Mr. Conway, dated London, July 20, 1864, and published in the Boston *Commonwealth*. In that letter President Lincoln is represented as saying, in his most characteristic style, "Gentlemen, it is generally the case that a man who begins a work is not the best man to carry it on to a successful termination. (Laughter.) I believe it was so in the case of Moses. Wasn't it? He got the children of Israel out of Egypt, but the Lord selected somebody else to bring them to their journey's end. A pioneer (continued President Lincoln) has hard work to do, and generally gets so battered and spattered that people prefer another, even though they may accept the principle. (Continued laughter.) Now, the letter of Mr. Conway gives us the application of these remarks in a manner that could hardly be mended. It quietly suggests that "Mr. Lincoln is averse to seeing the application of whatever truth there is in his theory to the one to whom it particularly applies — *himself;*" and Mr. Conway most pertinently adds: "Under him the war was begun; he had to deal with the disaffected; is it not possible that he has become so *battered and spattered* as to make it well for him to give up the leadership to some Joshua?" (Loud laughter and cheering.) It would seem, my friends, that nothing was said at this interview about "the danger of swapping horses in crossing a stream." (Laughter.) On the contrary, the President emphatically appealed to that memorable precedent in Holy Writ when the children of Israel, being themselves about to cross a stream, were compelled to follow a new leader, in order to get safely over. "I believe it was so (said he) in the case of Moses, wasn't it?" We all know it was so. We all know that the children of Israel could never have crossed the Jordan and entered into the promised land, had they refused to accept Joshua as their leader. And some of us are not a little afraid that the same fatality which attended the ancient Moses, is about to find a fresh illustration in the case of our modern Abraham. (Laughter and cheers.)

THE PRESENT ADMINISTRATION A STUMBLING BLOCK IN THE WAY OF
THE RESTORATION OF THE UNION.

Why, my friends, no one of us can have forgotten how much there was of mere personal prejudice and personal antipathy at the outset of that outrageous assault upon the national government by the Southern States. No one of us can fail to remember how deeply political and party antagonism entered into the origin of this rebellion. It has been said a thousand times, and everybody admits it to be true, that the first treasonable and fatal step could never have been taken but for the election of Abraham Lincoln as President. It has been said a thousand times, and no man denies it, that the Southern secession leaders — long as they may have contemplated their conspiracy against the Union, and earnestly as they may have desired to accomplish a separation of the States — could never have mustered followers enough to embolden them to attempt it, but for the success of the Republican party. We all know that the secession leaders aided and abetted the election of President Lincoln for that very purpose. (Applause.) He was their favorite candidate then, as I think he is their favorite candidate now. It was the triumph of that great sectional organization — the Republican party — which was originally relied upon for firing the heart of the Southern people. We cannot forget that the war cry of the South, at the time of their original revolt, was not so much — "We will not submit to the Constitution." "We will not abide by the Union," as "we will not have these men to rule over us." "We will not come under the dominion of the Black Republicans." Fellow-citizens, I need not say that this conduct on the part of the Southern States was utterly unwarrantable and worthy of all condemnation. The Republican party, to which I shall myself apply no opprobrious epithets, had prevailed fairly at the polls. The Southern States had enjoyed their full proportionate share in the national vote, and they were bound in honor as well as in law, to abide by the result. Nothing but the most direct and palpable violation of their rights would have furnished any shadow of justification for the course which they pursued. Abraham Lincoln was duly elected President of the United States for four years. I rejoice that he was elected for no more than four. (Laughter.) And though some of us at the North, as well as so many at the South, were earnestly opposed to him and to his party, and though not a few of us predicted the very results which have ensued, it was the bounden duty and sacred obligation of us all alike to acquiesce in the result, and to support him as long as he supported the Constitution. And I thank Heaven that the loyal States have supported him so unanimously. I thank Heaven that the whole people of the Northern States have sustained the government so ardently, and fought the battles of the Union so bravely under whatever leaders they have found in rightful authority over them. (Cheers.) No government on earth in any age has ever been sustained with a nobler disregard of all party prejudices and all personal opinions than our own government for the last four years. Men and money have been supplied without measure and without a murmur. Few and far between have been the voices of dissent or the notes of discord,

Where men could not approve the policy of the administration, they have generally been content to be silent, or at most to enter a passing protest in respectful terms. The exceptional cases, to which so much attention has been pointed, by the needless and unjustifiable severity with which they have been treated, have only served to illustrate more strikingly the general acquiescence of the people. And as it has been in the past, so it still is. We are all of us, I need not say ready and eager to sustain the administration in carrying on the government, and vindicating its constitutional authority, to the end of their term. We are ready to raise the men, we are ready to contribute the means, for a vigorous prosecution of the war. We will help them even to another draft, if another draft be necessary. We will pay our taxes and encourage their loans. We will rejoice in all their victories by sea and by land. They are no party triumphs. They are our victories as well as theirs. Sherman has taken Atlanta, and Sheridan has almost cleared the Shenandoah. We all hope and trust and pray that Grant and Meade may soon take Richmond (loud cheers), and that the brave work of our soldiers and sailors may go on unimpeded till nothing remains to be effected by force of arms. They shall have the best wishes of all our hearts, and the best help of all our hands to this end. But all this, my friends, is a different part of speech from supporting the claims of the Administration to a new term of the Presidency and a new lease of the White House. ("That's so," and laughter.) And now that after four years of civil war, waged at such an expenditure of life and treasure as the history of the world never before witnessed — now that a new election of rulers has come regularly round, is it not fit, is it not wise, is it not loyal and patriotic, for those who do not and cannot approve the policy of the Administration, and who have no faith in their capacity to accomplish the restoration of the Union, to call upon them to withdraw from the high places of the land, and to make way for men, against whom the Southern heart is not so hopelessly inflamed and embittered? Is it not the solemn duty of the people of the United States to ask themselves the question, whether, as things now stand, and in view of all the prospects before us, it is quite expedient, or quite just, to continue in place a President and a party, whose original election, justly or unjustly, was the immediate occasion of so deplorable a rebellion? Have not the people a right to ask — is it not their duty to ask — whether a simple change of administration might not do something, might not do much towards removing a stumbling-block in the way of the restoration of the Union; toward destroying the unanimity and mitigating the ferocity of our southern foes; toward conciliating the feelings of our southern friends if there are any still left; and thus toward opening the way for an easier progress of our arms and an earlier triumph of the great cause for which we are contending? (Applause.)

WHAT A PATRIOT IN LINCOLN'S PLACE WOULD HAVE SAID SIX MONTHS AGO.

Fellow citizens, I am not here to indulge in any personal imputations upon President Lincoln. Though I have never been one of his partisan supporters, I have never been one of his revilers. And let me say, in passing, that he has received harder blows from some of his own household — from Senator Wade and Representative Winter Davis and General Fremont, and from others who have been less brave and less open, but not less violent in their denunciations of him, than he has from any of his opponents. But I cannot help remarking, that in my humble judgment, he would have adopted a course worthy of all commendation if, instead of talking about swapping horses in crossing a stream, he could have been induced to say, six months ago, to the people of the United States, something of this sort:

"Fellow Citizens, you elected me fairly your President, and the President of the whole Union, four years ago. I have done my best to vindicate my title to the trust you conferred upon me, and I shall continue to do so to the end of my term. You of the loyal States have nobly supported me. You have given me all the men and all the money I have asked for. You have borne and forborne with me in many changes of policy, and in all the assertions of arbitrary power to which I have thought it necessary to resort. I shall go on to the best of my ability to the end of my allotted term. But I am ready then to return to the ranks. No pride of place, no love of patronage or power, shall induce me to stand in your way for a moment in your great struggle to restore the Union of our fathers. I do not forget how much of personal prejudice and party jealousy were arrayed against me at the outset. I do not forget how deeply political and sectional antagonisms entered into the causes of this rebellion. I am not insensible that the policy which I have recently felt constrained to adopt has increased and aggravated those prejudices and those antagonisms. Select a new candidate. Choose a new President, against whom, and against whose friends, there will be less of preconceived hostility and hate; and may God give him wisdom and courage to save the country and restore the Union." Ah, my friends, what a glorious example of patriotic self-denial and magnanimity this would have been! Who would not have envied President Lincoln the opportunity of exhibiting it? I am by no means sure it would not have re-elected him President in spite of himself. But it would certainly have gone far, very far, towards securing unanimity in favor of some worthy successor; and it was the way, and the only way to prevent that division of the Northern sentiment which is in some quarters so earnestly deplored as unfavorable to the success of our arms. (Applause.)

HOW MR. LINCOLN ABIDES BY HIS "NO-SWAP" POLICY.

But President Lincoln has thought fit to adopt the very reverse of this magnanimous and self-denying policy. He has quite forgotten that *one term* principle to which he and I were committed as members of the old Whig party. We see him clinging eagerly and desperately to patronage and place. We see him demanding to be re-nominated — demanding to be re-elected and claiming it almost as a test of patriotism and loyalty that we should all with one accord support him for four years more. We hear his Secretary of State comparing a vote against Abraham Lincoln to giving aid and comfort to the rebels, and even indulging in what is well called a portentous threat, that if the people shall dare to choose a new President, the government will be abdicated, and left to fall to pieces of itself, between the election and the inauguration. An absurd assumption, that a support of the government must necessarily involve a support of the policy of an existing administration — this absurd and preposterous assumption, which has been put forward so arrogantly during the last year or two, is now pushed on to the monstrous length of maintaining that, patriotism demands the re-election of an existing President in time of war, even though a majority of the people may have no confidence in the capacity of the incumbent, either for conducting the war or for negotiating a peace. (Cheers.) No changing Presidents in the hour of danger or struggle is the cry. No swapping horses in crossing a stream. Everything else may be changed or swapped. You may change commanders-in-chief in the very face of the enemy; you may remove a gallant leader, as you did General McClellan, (tremendous cheering,) when he had just achieved one glorious victory, and was on his way to the almost certain achievement of another, (continued cheering;) you may swap Secretaries of War, as you did Cameron for Stanton (laughter;) you may swap Secretaries of the Treasury, as you did Chase for Fessenden; you may swap Postmaster-Generals, as you have just done, Blair for Dennison, (continued laughter;) you may change your candidates for the Vice-Presidency, "handy-dandy," and leave Mr. Hannibal Hamlin to shoulder his musket in a Bangor militia company, (laughter.) Thus far you may go, but no further. You must not touch me. (Laughter.) You must not change Presidents. Patriotism requires that Abraham Lincoln should be exempt from all such casualties. And so we are all to be drummed into voting for him under a threat of the pains and penalties of treason. Indeed, my friends, this extraordinary doctrine is getting to be a little contagious about these times; and from some recent manifestations in my own part of the country at least — however it may be here or elsewhere — I should suppose it was fast becoming a cherished dogma among officeholders of all grades, both national and State, that the only true patriotism consisted in keeping them all snugly in place, and that a failure to vote for any or all of them was little better than disloyalty to the government! It is certainly very accommodating in our Presidents and governors, and senators, and representatives, thus to save the people the trouble of an election. (Laughter.) If the war only lasts four years more, we shall, perhaps, be spared the trouble of elections altogether. ("That's true.") My friends, if the people are wise, they will give some of their public servants a lesson on this subject before it is too late, and teach them that the freedom of elections is too precious a privilege to be abandoned at the dictation of those who have already enjoyed a greater length of service, as some of us think than is altogether consistent with the public welfare and the public safety. The progress of this terrible war is leaving its mark on not a few of our most cherished privileges as freemen. An overshadowing doctrine of necessity has obliterated not a few of the old constitutional limitations and landmarks of authority. An armed prerogative has gradually lifted itself to an appalling height throughout the land. But, thank heaven, it is still in the power of the people to assert their right to a fair and free election of their rulers. (Loud cheers.) And if they shall do so successfully — whatever may be the result — no nobler spectacle will have been witnessed in this land since it first asserted its title to be called a land of liberty. (Cheers.) Let it be seen that the American people can go through a Presidential election freely and fairly, even during the raging storm of civil war, and our institutions will have had a glorious triumph, whatever party, or whatever candidate may suffer a defeat. But, on the other hand, let the approaching election be overawed, or overruled by force or by fraud, and our institutions will have sustained a disastrous defeat, whatever may be the result to parties or to candidates. (Applause.)

THE UNION INIMICAL TO THE INTERESTS OF THE REPUBLICAN PARTY.

And here, fellow-citizens, let me say, that in this eager and desperate determination of the President and his party to prolong their official supremacy at all hazards, and even by the most unblushing exercise of all the patronage and power, and influence of the government, in their own behalf, I find renewed reason for fearing that they cannot safely be trusted for an early restoration of "the Union as it was, under the Constitution as it is." No one can help seeing that it is by no means for their interest, as a party, to accomplish that result. No one can help seeing that such a restoration, under present circumstances, would give the finishing stroke to that political supremacy which they so eagerly seek to perpetuate. They themselves, certainly, are not blind, nor indifferent to the fact that when the South shall return to its allegiance, their own party domination is at an end. Why, we all know how it was, even when the Republican party achieved its first and only great success by the election of President Lincoln. We all remember that even then their sceptre would have proved a powerless and barren sceptre, if there had been no secession and no rebellion. We all remember that if the Senators and Representatives of the Southern States had not withdrawn so rashly and wantonly from their seats, the Republican party would soon have been in a helpless minority in one, if not

in both branches of Congress. They could not have carried a measure, they could not have confirmed a nomination without the co-
operation or consent of their opponents. And does anybody imagine
that if the South were to lay down their arms to-morrow, and come
back again into the old family fold, they would send any Senators
or Representatives to Washington, whoever they might be, to sustain the measures or the men of the Republican party? No, my
friends, that party itself sees plainly that no such thing is within the
prospect of belief. That party sees that the restoration of union
and peace under the old Constitution of our fathers is thus the end
and upshot of their own dynasty. How, then, can we help fearing
that they will willingly, if not systematically, postpone a result
which is so sure to cut them off from any further enjoyment of
power — of that power to which they are clinging with so phrenzied
and frantic a grasp? The truth is, that the Republican party have
so thriven and fattened on this rebellion, and it has brought them
such an overflowing harvest of power-patronage, offices, contracts
and spoils, and they have become so enamored of the vast and
overshadowing influence which belongs to an existing administration at such an hour, that they are in danger of forgetting that their
country is bleeding and dying on their hands. ("That's so." Applause.) And this suggests to me, my friends, an idea to which I
cannot refrain from giving a brief expression. You have not forgotten, I am sure, that most memorable period which immediately
preceded the inauguration of President Lincoln, when the minds
and hearts of so many good men throughout the country were
earnestly intent on devising some mode of arresting and averting
that terrible struggle in which we were so soon afterward involved.
You all remember that Peace Convention, as it was called, which
assembled at Washington in February, 1861. You all remember the
high and sanguine hopes which greeted its assembly; and you have
not forgotten — no patriot can ever forget — how sadly those hopes
were disappointed. For one, I have never for a moment doubted that
if the incoming President and his friends in Congress had given
countenance and encouragement to that convention, and to the
measures it proposed, the secession would have ended with South
Carolina and the Gulf States, and we should have had Union and
peace before six months had expired. The rebellion would have

been nipped in the bud. It would have been crushed in the egg, and the wounds it had occasioned would have healed up, as the surgeons say, *by first intention*. I could furnish the opinions of some of the best men in our country, living and dead, to the effect. And why, why was that convention so repelled and repudiated by the ultra wing of the Republican party? Why did they stand idly by mocking at every effort to prevent and avert this great and terrible struggle, and rejoicing at what they called the glorious future before them? How can any one doubt that it was because the secession of the South, and the withdrawal of the Southern representation, would secure that party predominance which was essential to the carrying out of their cherished policy, as well as to the distribution of the spoils of victory. I was at Washington myself, during a portion of that period, in company with friends whom I esteem and honor to day, as I esteemed and honored them, though I find myself differing from more than one of them. We went on as the bearers of a petition of fifteen thousand citizens of Boston for the adoption of measures of conciliation and peace. It is not for me to say, even if I knew, what views were brought back by others of that little embassy; but I cannot forget the painful impression which was left upon my own mind, that there were men there, and in high places, too, who, instead of lifting a finger to arrest the dreadful catastrophe which was so obviously impending, were gloating and glorying over the departure of the successive southern delegations as furnishing a clearer field for the more successful prosecution of their own fanatical views, and for the more undisputed establishment of their own party supremacy. And can it be imagined that such men will be ready or willing to co-operate in bringing back the Southern States to their old allegiance to the Union? In bringing them back too, be it remembered, not merely with their old quota of representation, but with a much larger delegation in the House of Representatives than they have ever before enjoyed? For, my friends, if the President's proclamation is to have the full interpretation and sweeping efficacy which some of his friends claim for it, the representation of the Southern States, — after the next apportionment, certainly — is to be not merely on the old three-fifth principle, but on the whole black race, man for man, as well as on the whole white race. It will hardly lie in the mouth of the

Republican party, most assuredly, to refuse to the South a full representation on its whole black population. If the proclamation accomplished anything, it abolished the three-fifth principle of the Constitution — not, indeed, the way in which John Quincy Adams once tried to abolish it many years ago, by striking out all representation of those to whom it related; but by giving a full, complete five-fifths representation on the whole black population of the Southern States. I repeat, then fellow-citizens, that it is too much the interest of the Republican party, as a party, to defer and postpone the return of the Southern States to the Union, for that party to be safely trusted with the work of restoration. (Applause.) Or, indeed, does any one imagine that those States are to be brought back without any representation? Is any one proposing to bring them back only as so many desolated and subjugated provinces, to be held for generations in a state of subjection and vassalage by enormous standing armies, and at an immeasurable cost of treasure and blood? Are we deliberately bent on having an American Hungary, or an American Poland, or an American Venice, on our continent? Do we desire to see even an American Ireland? Are all our efforts for the abolition of black slavery to end in establishing a quasi-condition of white slavery? (Cheers.) Is that what we are fighting for, under the old Liberty Flag of our fathers? ("No, no.") No, no, my friends, we must have the Old Constitutional Union again, if we have anything — with all the States and with all the rights reserved to the States or to the people, as well as with all the powers secured to the general government. (Applause.) We are not fighting for a mere territorial Union. We are not fighting for a mere geographical area. We want, indeed, all the valleys and all the mountains and all the rivers, and all the lakes, which were ever included within the rightful limits of our once happy and prosperous land. But we want the men and women and children — white, certainly, not less than black — who have dwelt within those limits. And we want them in the old political organizations, which the Constitution has recognized, under their own State Governments, and with all the rights which belong to those governments. We want the Constitution of Washington, and Franklin, and Hamilton, and Madison, and Jay, without addition and without diminution. We want the glorious Union which that Constitution has secured to us in the past, and which, by the blessing of God overruling the madness of men, we trust, it is still destined to secure to us for the future. And Heaven forbid, that the temporary interests of any party should be suffered to interfere with the earliest practicable accomplishment of this great restoration! Heaven forbid, that this fratricidal war should be prolonged for a day or an hour, or an instant, in order to perpetuate or continue any mere party ascendancy! Heaven forbid, that so horrible a struggle should be suffered to degenerate into a great game of *Rouge et Noir* — blood and negroes — with nothing better than the spoils of office for its stake! (Cheers.) It is sometimes suggested, my friends, that the Democratic party have been too good friends with the South to be trusted in arranging this difficulty. Why, that is the very reason why they should be trusted. I have often had reason to find fault with the Southern proclivities of some of the Northern Democrats; but if those proclivities can now be turned to the account of saving the Union, they may well be forgiven for more than all the mischief they have ever done in the past. And now, bear with me once more, fellow-citizens, while I urge upon you, finally, that the principles or the policy of the Republican party, as well as their interest as a party, seem to me utterly incompatible with any early restoration of Union and peace. I refer, I need hardly say, to their policy or principles in regard to domestic slavery, as developed in the speeches of some of their leading members, and in the acts and express declarations of the President himself. We all know that the Administration have solemnly adopted the policy of complete emancipation as a necessary result of the rebellion and the war. We all know that after having rallied the country for two years on the plain, direct, constitutional issue of enforcing the laws, and restoring the Union, the President suddenly changed his hand, and, in the teeth of all his own declarations and arguments, put forth a solemn proclamation of universal emancipation. We all know that, at this moment, no man in the rebel States is allowed to return to his allegiance and resume his place as a loyal citizen, without swearing to support this proclamation, as well as to support the Constitution of the United States. And we all remember that recently, on the first authentic or unauthentic overtures of peace and submission, the President issued a formal manifesto — "To Whom it May Concern"

— making an abandonment of slavery a condition precedent for even the reception of any such proposals.

THE POLICY OF "NO UNION WITH SLAVEHOLDERS."

Meantime Mr. Secretary Seward, for whom I have nothing but the kindest feelings, and who I honestly believe regrets such extravagances as much as any of us, has expressly admitted in his recent and most extraordinary speech at Auburn, in New York, that there are those of the Republican party, "who want guarantees for swift, and universal, and complete emancipation, or they do not want the nation saved." Ah, my friends, is there not too much reason for apprehending that this class of men is more numerous than even Mr. Seward imagines, and that in the next four years they will have acquired — even if they have not already acquired — a prevailing and paramount influence over the Administration? (Applause.) Mark the words: "Men who want guarantees for swift, and universal, and complete emancipation, or they do not want the nation saved." And this, I suppose, is what these men would call unconditional Unionism! (Laughter.) But it is what you and I, fellow-citizens, should call conditional dis-unionism, and it can hardly fail to be so stigmatized wherever it is openly encountered. Why, what have we heard of late from gentlemen holding the highest official positions under the Republican regime in my own Commonwealth of Massachusetts? What have been the most recent utterances of the most distinguished Republicans in Faneuil Hall? I will not name names, for I have no taste for personality, but I will give the precise language. From one we have the declaration that "the appeal from sire to son should go on forever and forever until the last acre of southern land, baptised by Massachusetts' blood, should be rescued from the infidels to liberty." This, certainly, would seem very like preaching an eternal crusade against southern slavery, without regard either to Union, peace, or the Constitution. From another equally distinguished Republican, we have even more distinct declaration, that "the Baltimore Convention and Abraham Lincoln *ask something more than the Union* as the condition of peace;" and that "he has announced in his letter 'to all whom it may concern,' that all terms of peace must begin with the abandonment of slavery." While from the same eminent source we are assured, that a vote for Abraham Lincoln is to usher in the glorious day, when the eloquence of Wendell Phillips may be enjoyed at Richmond and Charleston, as it is now enjoyed at New York and Boston." (Laughter.) I may be told, indeed, that all this is only the rant and rhapsody of fanatical rhetoricians; but I cannot so regard it. What said the resolutions adopted at this same meeting? One of them concluded by the unequivocal announcement, that "the war must go on until the pride of the (southern) leaders is humbled, their power broken, and the civil and social structure of the South reorganized on the basis of free labor, free speech, and equal rights for all before the law."

HOW LONG MUST WAR CONTINUE TO ACCOMPLISH COMPLETE EMANCIPATION?

Well, now, my friends, there can be no misunderstanding the import of this language. It is clear, explicit, unequivocal. It does not pretend that the war is to be prosecuted for the restoration of the Union, but for something more than the restoration of the Union; and it expressly defines that something more to be "the total abandonment of slavery," and "reorganization of the social structure of the South on the basis of free labor, free speech, and equal rights for all before the law." These are the ends for which the war is to be prosecuted; and it is not to be permitted to cease until these ends are accomplished. From these declarations we may form, I think, a pretty distinct idea of the prospect before us if the Republican party remains in power, and make some approximate estimate of the chances of an early peace. Why, in what millenial period are all these results to be accomplished? By what process are they to be brought about? How is this total abandonment of slavery to be enforced? Are we to wait till each individual master has filed his separate bill of release? Are we to go on fighting till each individual State has adopted amendments to those constitutions which now prohibit any such proceeding? Or shall we recognize the power of the confederate government, and wait for that to initiate and enforce this reorganization of the social structure of the South? Within what period, I say, this side of the Greek kalends, can all this be accomplished? (Cheers.) Fellow-citizens, there is not a man in the loyal States who would not rejoice with all his heart and soul, if African slavery could be safely and legitimately brought to an end on this whole continent. The Republican party have no monopoly of the philanthropy or of the patriotism of the land, though some of them would seem to claim it. But, for one, I have never had a particle of faith that a sudden, sweeping, forcible emancipation could result in anything but mischief and misery for the black race, as well as the white. The proclamation, however, has been issued long ago, and its efficacy and its authority are to be the subjects of future experience and future adjudication. To those I willingly leave it. It was undoubtedly one of the greatest stretches of the doctrine of necessity — it was unquestionably one of the most startling exercises of the one man power, which the history of human government, free or despotic, ever witnessed. I have no disposition to question its wisdom or its authority, as a measure adopted for securing greater success to our arms, and an earlier termination of the war — though I cannot help entertaining grave doubts on both points. But the idea that it is now to be made the pretext for prolonging that war, after the original and only legitimate end for which it was undertaken shall have been accomplished; the idea that we are to go on fighting and fighting for "something more" than the Union; the idea that the war is not to be permitted to cease until the whole social structure of the South has been reorganized, is one abhorrent to every instinct of my soul, to every dictate of my judgment, to every principle which I cherish as a statesman or as a Christian. It is a policy, too, in my opinion, utterly unconstitutional; and as much in the spirit of rebellion as almost anything which has been attempted by the Southern States. Why, does any one doubt for an instant, that if the Southern States were to lay down their arms to-morrow, and throw themselves unreservedly on their rights under the Constitution, that it would be the bounden duty of the government to receive their submission, and recognize their rights, subject only to such pains and penalties as might be legally enforced upon individuals duly convicted of treason? I have often hoped that this question might be brought to a practical test. I have often hoped, and still hope, that some one State, like the old State of North Carolina, or the great State of Georgia, might be induced to try the experiment of simply coming back under the old flag, without asking any questions, or seeking to exact in advance any conditions whatever. (Cheers.) What President, what administration, what party shall dare to stand in the way, and tell either of those States that we have ceased to fight for the Union — that we are fighting for *something more* than the Union, and that she must stay out until she has reorganized her whole social structure? What President, what administration, what party, shall dare to repel and repulse such a returning sister, and tell her that she cannot be readmitted to the old family household until she has prepared herself for relishing the eloquence of Wendell Phillips, justly celebrated as that eloquence may be? Why, my friends, the proclamation of the President, as an instrument for achieving success and securing submission is one thing, but a demand for the total abandonment of slavery, and the reorganization of the whole social structure of the South, as conditions precedent for receiving and accepting submission whenever it shall be tendered, and after it has been secured, is a wholly different thing. The one may, perhaps, be justified on a constructive plea of necessity. But there can be no plea of necessity after the submission is accomplished. If the States in rebellion, one or all, were simply to lay down their arms to-morrow, and throw themselves unconditionally on the old Constitution, and range themselves once more under the old flag, what else could we do, what else should we do, but receive them with open arms to the old Union of our fathers? Pains and penalties might be enforced on individual offenders. The law and the officers of the law would have all that matter to look after. But pains and penalties would soon be almost forgotten in the joy which would pervade the country. The return of the prodigal son would be nothing to it. We should get a nearer and clearer impression than almost ever before of that exquisite idea of the good Book — that there is more joy over one sinner that repenteth, than over ninety and nine just men that need no repentance.

WHAT SHERMAN THINKS ABOUT IT.

Whatever the administration or the President might say, the great majority of the people of the United States, as I believe, would adopt the tone of that notable letter of the hero of Atlanta, when he said to the mayor of that captured city: "We don't want your negroes, or your horses, or your houses, or your land, or anything you have; but we do want, and will have, a just obedience to the laws of the United States." (Cheers.) "I want peace, and believe it can only be reached through Union and war, and I will ever conduct war purely with a view to early and perfect success. But, my dear sir, when that peace does come you may call on me for anything. Then will I share with you the last cracker, and watch with you to shield your homes and families against danger from every quarter. (Tremendous cheering.) Yes, not only would the gallant Sherman "watch with them to shield their homes and families against danger from every quarter," but that whole noble army, which has done such glorious service in the West, would watch with him, and we should witness such a fraternization, and such a jubilee, as would send a thrill of joy to the heart of every real friend of Union and peace and constitutional liberty in our land. (Cheers.) We should not stop to ask whether we had obtained anything more than Union and peace. We should leave the judicial tribunals to ascertain that. We should remit that question to the constables and the court-houses. We should feel that in vindicating the authority of the Constitution and laws, and in restoring the Union of our fathers, we had prepared the way for a glorious future for our country, and had accomplished the great end for which so many noble young men had shed their blood and laid down their lives. And so we should all thank God and be joyful. (Cheers.) Undoubtedly, my friends, it is the hope of us all, that, in some way or other, sooner or later, out of this abhorrent rebellion will have come the ultimate extinction of domestic slavery. Many of us believe that, if the war were to cease to-morrow, and the Southern States were to come back without any condition or terms whatever, slavery would be found to have received a wound from which it could never recover. Mr. Seward himself, in that same extraordinary speech from which I have already quoted, has expressly told us that, practically, slavery is no longer in question. "I told you here, (he says,) a year ago, that, practically, slavery was no longer in question — that it was perishing under the operation of the war." "That assertion," he adds, "has been confirmed. Jefferson Davis tells you in effect the same thing." And Jefferson Davis does indeed tell us very much the same thing, if the report is to be credited of his conversation with certain quasi-peace commissioners who went to Richmond under a pass furnished by General Grant at the request of President Lincoln. Jefferson Davis is stated in that report to have admitted that two millions of slaves — one half of the whole number in the Southern States — had been practically freed already.

THE UNION THE ONE CONDITION OF PEACE.

But whatever may be our opinions of this point, it will be enough for us all — enough, certainly, for General McClellan and his supporters, if we shall have succeeded in restoring the Union; and I believe the people of the loyal States will agree with him and agree with us, that the war ought not to be prosecuted another day, another hour, another instant, for any purpose under the sun, except the simple restoration of the Union. "The Union — the Union — the one condition of peace. We ask no more." (Cheers.) That is the platform of our candidate, and that is our platform. We are not for propagating philanthropy at the point of the bayonet. We are not for wading through seas of blood in order to reorganize the whole social structure of the South. Christianity forbids us; for it tells us not to do evil even that good may come. The Constitution forbids us; for, the moment the rebellion is suppressed, the war becomes unconstitutional, whatever may be its pretext. The condition of our country, which has already sent forth more than two millions of soldiers into the field, and which is already groaning beneath a debt of three or four thousand millions of dollars; the condition of our beloved country forbids us from sending another soldier, or spending another dollar, after the Union is saved. Fellow-citizens, a solemn oath to support "the Constitution of the United States as it is," is still upon all our rulers, and a solemn obligation to do so still rests upon the whole people. No rebellion elsewhere can justify rebellion on our part. We must pursue constitutional ends, and we must pursue them by constitutional means. Then we shall succeed, and then our success will be substantial and permanent. Oh, what a triumph it would be if the Constitution of our fathers should come out, after all, unscathed from this fiery trial; if it should be seen to have prevailed, by its own innate original force and vigor, over all the machinations and assaults of its enemies! How proudly, then might we hold it up before all mankind, in all time to come, as we have in all time past, as indeed the masterpiece of political and civil wisdom! How confidently could we then challenge all the world to show, us a system of government of equal stability and endurance. (Cheers.) It has already stood the strain of prosperity and of adversity. Foreign wars and domestic dissensions have hitherto assailed it in vain. The rains have descended, and the winds have blown, and the floods have come and beaten upon it, but it has not been shaken. The great final text is now upon it; rebellion, revolution, civil war, in their most formidable and appalling shape. Oh, if we can but carry it through this last trial unharmed! we never again need fear for its security. Let us then hold it up — Constitution, the whole Constitution, and nothing but the Constitution — as at once the end and the instrument of all our efforts. Let us demand a faithful adherence to all its forms and to all its principles. Let us watch jealously for the observance and fulfillment of all its provisions. And let us resolve that if it does fail and fall at last, it shall be by the madness of its enemies, and not by the supineness or willing surrender of its friends. (Applause.)

MR. LINCOLN MAKING FUN OF HIMSELF — A REMINISCENCE.

Fellow-citizens, with such issues before us, I need say but little about candidates. You know already, I am sure, all that you care to know about President Lincoln. Yet, perhaps, I can recall a little passage in his public life which may at least amuse you. His only term of Congressional service was during the period when I had the honor to preside over the House of which he was a member. He helped me to the Speaker's chair by his own vote, and I really wish I could find it in my conscience to return the compliment at this moment. (Laughter.) But I cannot forget a certain speech which he made, in the month of July, 1848, in reference to the nomination for the Presidency of a distinguished Democrat who still lives (I rejoice to remember), to enjoy the esteem and respect of all who knew him.

"By the way, Mr. Speaker, (said he,) did you know that I am a military hero? Yes sir, (continued he,) in the days of the Black Hawk war, I fought, bled, and came away. Speaking of General Cass's career, reminds me of my own. I was not at Stillman's defeat, but I was about as near it as Cass was to Hull's surrender; and like him, I saw the place soon afterward. It is quite certain that I did not break my sword, for I had none to break; but I bent a musket pretty badly on one occasion. If Cass broke his sword, the idea is, he broke it in desperation; I bent the musket by accident. If General Cass went in advance of me in picking whortleberries, I guess I surpassed him in charging upon the wild onions. (Laughter.) If he saw any live fighting Indians it was more than I did, but I had a good many bloody struggles with the mosquitoes; and, although I never fainted from loss of blood, I can truly say I was often very hungry. Mr. Speaker, if I should ever conclude to doff whatever our Democratic friends may suppose there is of black cockade federalism about me, *and thereupon they shall take me up as their candidate for the Presidency, I protest they shall not make fun of me, as they have of General Cass, by attempting to write me into a military hero.*" (Great laughter.)

Ah, my friends, what a blessed thing for the country it would have been if President Lincoln had only "recked his own rede;" if, after he became President, he had not made fun of himself by attempting to play the part of a military hero? Why, it is hardly too much to say that if he had never undertaken to direct and control the course of our armies, if he had not so rashly interfered with the movements of at least one of our generals, Richmond might have been taken, and the war triumphantly terminated, long before this time. You all know the General to whom I refer, and the circumstances of that interference. (Cheers.)

GENERAL M'CLELLAN'S CAREER AND MERITS.

Indeed the whole career of our noble candidate, is fresh in the minds and hearts of the whole American people. You have followed the story, I doubt not, as admirably narrated by my accomplished and excellent friend, Mr. Hilliard. You have traced him through that memorable campaign in Mexico, and have not forgotten his gallantry at Contreras, where like Washington at Braddock's defeat, he had two horses shot under him, but came off substantially unharmed. (Cheers.) You have accompanied him on his visit to the scene of the Crimean war, and have not forgotten his masterly report on the armies of Europe. (Applause.) You have followed him in that glorious little pioneer campaign in Western Virginia, at the outbreak of the rebellion, and have not forgotten the brilliant victories by which that campaign was crowned. (Applause.) You have seen him assume the command of the whole forces of the Union, and have not forgotten with what devotion, and with what consumate skill, he organized the grand Army of the Potomac. (Applause.) You have followed him through that terrible Peninsular campaign. (Cheers.) You have accompanied him through these fearful seven days of agony and glory. (Cheers.) You have seen how cruelly he was thwarted and stripped of his troops on the right hand and on the left, and you have not forgotten how bravely he bore up under all the grievous disappointments to which he was subjected. You have seen him assuming command again at the solicitation of the President, at an hour of the greatest peril to our capital and our country — reorganizing as by magic the brave but broken battallions of the Army of the Potomac, and achieving the glorious victory of Antietam on the very birthday of the Constitution. (Immense cheering.) And you have not failed to read his admirable dispatch from Harrison's Landing, his brilliant oration at West Point, and his noble letter accepting the nomination for the presidency. (Cheers.) No words of mine, no words of anybody could add anything to such a record. No words of his enemies can take away one jot or tittle from that record. I have no disposition to exaggerate his services or his merits, much less to disparage those of others. We all know that other commanders have done nobly, and have achieved victories which have entitled them to the honor and gratitude of the whole country. It has been their fortune, however, to be let alone. Many of them, too, are still in the field, privileged still to lead the armies and fight the battles of their country, instead of being unjustly deprived of their command and inexorably doomed to inaction. There will be an opportunity for doing full justice to their deserts hereafter. But what can be more fit, than for the people of the United States now to take up this young and gallant leader whom the rulers have so wantonly rejected, and to place him where his experience and abilities may be turned to account for the rescue of his country? In the full vigor of manhood, without a stain or a shade upon his character, a man of virtuous life and Christian principle, brave, prudent, patriotic, a stranger to all mere party politics a perfect stranger to anything like political management or political intrigue, one who has known how to command a great army and has never forgotten how to command himself, with no pledges on his lips or in his heart, except to the enforcement of the laws, the vindication of the Constitution, and the restoration of the Union; — what is there wanting in him to attract the confidence and support of all loyal men, and to secure the respect and admiration even of his enemies? (Loud and continued cheering.) Let me not forget, however, to remind you, my friends, that he has in his veins, in common with so many of you, and in common, as I am glad to remember, with myself, too, a little good old Connecticut blood, coming down from an ancestor who settled here a century ago. I am sure you will not think any the worse of him for that. (Cheers.)

A BIT OF TESTIMONY FROM THE SOUTH.

I fear, my friends, that I have already detained you too long. My own strength, certainly will hardly hold out longer, even if your indulgence and your patience be not already exhausted. But I must not take my leave of you without giving you a little piece of testimony of the highest interest and importance. Among the refugees from Atlanta, immediately after its capture, there came within our lines not many days ago a person of the most estimable and excellent character, who had enjoyed the best opportunities of understanding the southern heart. And what said he, do you think, on being interrogated as to the prospects of the future? I can give you his remarks from the most authentic source. They were communicated to me by a good friend of the Union in one of the border states. "If Mr. Lincoln is re-elected," said he, "the people of the South will fight for thirty years, for they feel that they can do nothing better, but if McClellan is elected, such an overwhelming Union party will be formed in the South, that peace will be the almost immediate result." ("That's so." Loud cheers.) "I speak," said he, "the sentiments of the people, not the officials. The leaders of the rebellion are anxious for the re-election of Mr. Lincoln, as giving most hope of the ultimate success of the rebel cause. But the people," he added, "respect McClellan, and believe in his honesty, capacity, and patriotism; and, being heartily tired of the war, they will be willing to trust him." (Cheers.) Such is the latest and most authentic testimony from the very heart of the Southern Confederacy. It was communicated to me from a source entitled to the highest confidence, and it concurs, I need hardly say, with every opinion which I have been able to form for myself. I do firmly and honestly believe that, if by the aid of this good old State of Connecticut, George Brinton McClellan shall be proclaimed President of the United States of America on the 4th day of March next, as I hope and trust he may be (cheers), another year will not have expired without witnessing the final termination of the rebellion;

and that the succeeding 4th of July will find us celebrating such a jubilee as has not been seen since that day was first hailed as the birthday of American independence. (Continued cheering.) I do not forget the danger of indulging in these ninety-days, or even twelve-months prophecies. ("That's so, too," and laughter.) I do not forget how many memorable warnings we have had of their fallacy. I can only say, that in that hope, in that trust, in that firm and unswerving confidence, I shall give my vote to the candidate of the Democratic party; and whether that vote shall prove to have been cast with the many or with the few, with majorities or with minorities, I shall feel that I have followed the dictates of my own best judgment, of my own conscientious convictions of duty, and of my own unalterable attachment and devotion to the Constitution and the Union of my country. (Loud cheering.)

DO NOT DESPAIR OF THE REPUBLIC.

I will not undertake to calculate the chances of success. The results of the late elections seem to decide nothing, except that the great battle is still to be fought, and that a victory is still within our reach. But whatever may be the results of the election, let us resolve never to despair of the republic. We are on the eve of one of the most memorable anniversaries in our history as a nation. Eighty-three years ago to morrow, on the 19th of October, 1781, the soil of Virginia was the scene of a far different spectacle from that which it unhappily witnesses at this hour. The soldiers of the North and of the South, instead of confronting each other in deadly strife, were then standing triumphantly side by side, under the glorious lead of Washington, to receive the final surrender of the forces which had been so long arrayed against our national independence. Would to Heaven that the precious memories of that event might be once more revived in every American heart! Would to Heaven that even now the associations of that day might overpower and disarm the unnatural hostility of our adversaries, and that the soldiers of the North and South might be seen like the soldiers in the old Roman story, rushing into each other's embrace under the old flag of our fathers! But even if such a result is to be longer, and still longer, and still longer postponed, let us never despair that such a day of final surrender will come; a day when rebellion will be everywhere suppressed and extinguished;

a day when a policy of Christian statesmanship, breathing something better than threatenings and slaughter, and based upon a juster idea than that the whole southern people are barbarians and outlaws, shall accomplish its legitimate work of restoring Union and peace to our afflicted land — a day when, by the blessing of God, that glorious vision of Daniel Webster may again be verified for us and for our children, from Lake Superior to the Gulf of Mexico, and from ocean to ocean: "One country, one Constitution, one destiny." (Enthusiastic cheers.) And when that day shall come, I can desire for myself no other distinction than to be thought not unworthy of some humble share in that inscription which was engraved on the old tomb of my ancestors two centuries and a half ago — before New London, before even Boston, had a name or a local habitation on the American continent — *"Beati Sunt Pacifici"* — blessed are the peace-makers. I can desire no other distinction for myself, than to be remembered among those who, in the words of our noble candidate, "would hail with unbounded joy the permanent restoration of peace on the basis of the Union under the Constitution, without the effusion of another drop of blood." (Loud and continued applause.)

The chairman said: My friends, I know you are anxious to testify your approbation of the eloquent and statesman like speech to which you have just listened, I therefore call upon you as the best method of doing so to give three cheers for the speaker.

They were given enthusiastically. After three hearty cheers for McClellan, the meeting adjourned.

GENERAL McCLELLAN'S LETTER OF ACCEPTANCE.

ORANGE, NEW JERSEY,
September 8, 1864. $\}$

GENTLEMEN: I have the honor to acknowledge the receipt of your letter informing me of my nomination by the Democratic National Convention, recently assembled at Chicago, as their candidate at the next election for President of the United States.

It is unnecessary for me to say to you that this nomination comes to me unsought.

I am happy to know that when the nomination was made the record of my public life was kept in view.

The effect of long and varied service in the army during war and peace, has been to strengthen and make indelible in my mind and heart the love and reverence for the Union, Constitution, laws, and flag of our country, impressed upon me in early youth.

These feelings have thus far guided the course of my life, and must continue to do so to its end.

The existence of more than one government over the region which once owned our flag is incompatible with the peace, the power, and the happiness of the people.

The preservation of our Union was the sole avowed object for which the war was commenced. It should have been conducted for that object only, and in accordance with those principles which I took occasion to declare when in active service.

Thus conducted, the work of reconciliation would have been easy, and we might have reaped the benefits of our many victories on land and sea.

The Union was originally formed by the exercise of a spirit of conciliation and compromise. To restore and preserve it, the same spirit must prevail in our councils, and in the hearts of the people.

The reëstablishment of the Union in all its integrity is, and must continue to be, the indispensable condition in any settlement. So soon as it is clear, or even probable, that our present adversaries are ready for peace, upon the basis of the Union, we should exhaust all the resources of statesmanship practised by civilized nations, and taught by the traditions of the American people, consistent with the honor and interests of the country, to secure such peace, reëstablish the Union, and guarantee for the future the constitutional rights of every State. The Union is the one condition of peace — we ask no more.

Let me add, what I doubt not was, although unexpressed, the sentiment of the Convention, as it is of the people they represent, that when any one State is willing to return to the Union, it should be received at once, with a full guarantee of all its constitutional rights.

If a frank, earnest, and persistent effort to obtain those objects should fail, the responsibility for ulterior consequences will fall upon those who remain in arms against the Union. But the Union must be preserved at all hazards.

I could not look in the face of my gallant comrades of the army and navy, who have survived so many bloody battles, and tell them that their labors and the sacrifice of so many of our slain and wounded brethren had been in vain; that we had abandoned that Union for which we have so often periled our lives.

A vast majority of our people, whether in the army and navy or at home, would, as I would, hail with unbounded joy the permanent restoration of peace, on the basis of the Union under the Constitution, without the effusion of another drop of blood. But no peace can be permanent without Union.

As to the other subjects presented in the resolutions of the Convention, I need only say that I should seek, in the Constitution of the United States and the laws framed in accordance therewith, the rule of my duty, and the limitations of executive power; endeavor to restore economy in public expenditure, reëstablish the supremacy of law, and, by the operation of a more vigorous nationality, resume our commanding position among the nations of the earth.

The condition of our finances, the depreciation of the paper money, and the burdens thereby imposed on labor and capital, show the necessity of a return to a sound financial system; while the rights of citizens, and the rights of States, and the binding authority of law over President, army, and people, are subjects of not less vital importance in war than in peace.

Believing that the views here expressed are those of the Convention and the people you represent, I accept the nomination.

I realize the weight of the responsibility to be borne should the people ratify your choice.

Conscious of my own weakness, I can only seek fervently the guidance of the Ruler of the universe, and, relying on His all-powerful aid, do my best to restore union and peace to a suffering people, and to establish and guard their liberties and rights.

I am, gentlemen,
very respectfully,
your obedient servant,
Geo. B. McClellan.

Hon. Horatio Seymour,
  and others, Committee.

GENERAL McCLELLAN'S VIEWS OF THE WAR AND THE COUNTRY.

THE HARRISON'S BAR LETTER.

Head-quarters, Army of the Potomac,
Camp near Harrison's Landing, Va., July 7, 1862.

Mr. President: You have been fully informed that the rebel army is in our front, with the purpose of overwhelming us by attacking our positions, or reducing us by blockading our river communications. I cannot but regard our condition as critical; and I earnestly desire in view of possible contingencies, to lay before your Excellency, for your private consideration, my general views concerning the existing state of the rebellion, although they do not strictly relate to the situation of this army, or strictly come within scope of my official duties. These views amount to convictions; and are deeply impressed upon my mind and heart. Our cause must never be abandoned; it is the cause of free institutions and self-government. The Constitution and the Union must be preserved, whatever may be the cost in time, treasure or blood. If secession is successful, other dissolutions are clearly to be seen in the future. Let neither military disaster, political faction, or foreign war, shake your settled purpose to enforce the equal operation of the laws of the United States upon the people of every State.

The time has come when the Government must determine upon a civil and military policy covering the whole ground of our national trouble. The responsibility of determining, declaring, and supporting such civil and military policy, and of directing the whole course of national affairs in regard to the rebellion must now be assumed and exercised by you, or our cause will be lost. The Constitution gives you power sufficient even for the present terrible exigency.

This rebellion has assumed the character of war; as such it should be regarded; and it should be conducted upon the highest principles known to Christian civilization. It should not be a war looking to the subjugation of the people of any State, in any event. It should not be at all a war upon population, but against armed forces and political organizations. Neither confiscation of property, political executions of persons, territorial organizations of States, or forcible abolition of slavery, should be contemplated for a moment. In prosecuting the war, all private property and unarmed persons should be strictly protected, subject only to the necessity of military operations. All private property, taken for military use, should be paid or receipted for; pillage and waste should be treated as high crimes; all unnecessary trespass sternly prohibited, and offensive demeanor by the military towards citizens promptly rebuked. Military arrests should not be tolerated, except in places where active hostilities exist; and oaths not required by enactments constitutionally made, should be neither demanded nor received. Military government should be confined to the preservation of public order, and the protection of political rights. Military power should not be allowed to interfere with the relations of servitude, either by supporting or impairing the authority of the master, except for suppressing disorder, as in other cases. Slaves contraband under the act of Congress, seeking military protection, should receive it. The right of the Government to appropriate permanently to its own service claims to slave labor, should be asserted; and the right of the owner to compensation therefor should be recognized.

This principle might be extended, upon grounds of military necessity and security, to all the slaves within a particular State; thus working manumission in such State; and in Missouri, perhaps in Western Virginia also, and possibly even in Maryland, the expediency of such a measure is only a question of time.

A system of policy thus constitutional and conservative, and pervaded by the influences of Christianity and freedom, would receive the support of almost all truly loyal men; would deeply impress the rebel masses and all foreign nations, and it might be humbly hoped that it would commend itself to the favor of the Almighty.

Unless the principles governing the future conduct of our struggle shall be made known and approved, the effort to obtain requisite forces will be almost hopeless. A declaration of radical views, especially upon slavery, will rapidly disintegrate our present armies.

The policy of the Government must be supported by concentration of military power. The national forces should not be dispersed in expeditions, posts of occupation and numerous armies; but should be mainly collected into masses, and brought to bear upon the armies of the Confederate States. Those armies thoroughly defeated, the political structure which they support will soon cease to exist.

In carrying out any system of policy which you may form, you will require a commander-in-chief of the army: one who possesses your confidence, understands your views, and who is competent to execute your orders by directing the military forces of the nation to the accomplishment of the objects by you proposed. I do not ask that place for myself. I am willing to serve you in such position as you may assign me, and I will do so as faithfully as ever subordinate served superior.

I may be on the brink of eternity; and as I hope for forgiveness from my Maker, I have written this letter with sincerity towards you and from love of my country.

Very respectfully,
Your obedient servant,
G. B. McClellan,
Major-General Commanding.

HENRY CLAY.

EXTRACT FROM A SPEECH OF THE HON. HENRY CLAY, IN THE SENATE OF THE UNITED STATES, ON THE SUBJECT OF ABOLITION PETITIONS, FEBRUARY 7, 1839.

"SIR, — I am not in the habit of speaking lightly of the possibility of dissolving this happy Union. The Senate knows that I have deprecated allusions, on ordinary occasions, to that direful event. The country will testify, that, if there be anything in the history of my public career worthy of recollection, it is the truth and sincerity of my ardent devotion to its lasting preservation. But we should be false in our allegiance to it if we did not discriminate between the imaginary and the real dangers by which it may be assisted. Abolition should no longer be regarded as an imaginary danger. The Abolitionists, let me suppose, succeed in their present aims of uniting the inhabitants of the Free States as one man, against the inhabitants of the Slave States. Union on the one side will beget union on the other. And this process of reciprocal consolidation will be attended with all the violent prejudices, imbittered passions, and implacable animosities which ever degraded or deformed human nature. A virtual dissolution of the Union will have already taken place, whilst the form of its existence remains. The most valuable element of union, mutual kindness, the feelings of sympathy, the fraternal bonds, which now happily unite us, will have been extinguished forever. One section will stand in menacing and hostile array against the other. The collision of opinion will be quickly followed by the clash of arms. I will not attempt to describe scenes which now lie happily concealed from our view. Abolitionists themselves would shrink back in dismay and horror at the contemplation of desolated fields, conflagrated cities, murdered inhabitants, and the overthrow of the fairest fabric of human government that ever rose to animate the hopes of civilized man. Nor should these Abolitionists flatter themselves, that, if they can succeed in their object of uniting the Free States, they will enter the contest with a numerical superiority that must insure victory. All history and experience proves the hazard and uncertainty of war; and we are admonished by Holy Writ, "that the race is not to the swift, nor the battle to the strong." But if they were to conquer, whom would they conquer? A foreign foe? one that had invaded our shores, insulted our flag, and laid our country waste? No, sir; no, sir. It would be a contest without laurels, without glory, — a self, a suicidal conquest, — a conquest of brothers over brothers, — achieved by one over another portion of the descendants of common ancestors, who, nobly pledging their lives, their fortunes, and their sacred honor, had fought and bled, side by side, in many a hard battle on land and ocean, severed our country from the British crown, and established our national independence.

The inhabitants of the Slave States are sometimes accused by their Northern brethren with displaying too much rashness and sensibility to the operations and proceedings of Abolitionists. But, before they can be rightly judged, there should be a reversal of conditions. Let me suppose that the people of the Slave States were to form societies, subsidize presses, make large pecuniary contributions, send forth numerous missionaries throughout all their own borders, and enter into machinations to burn the beautiful capitals, destroy the productive manufactories, and sink into the ocean the gallant ships of the Northern States. Would these incendiary proceedings be regarded as neighborly, and friendly, and consistent with the fraternal sentiments which should ever be cherished by one portion of the Union towards another? Would they excite no emotion, occasion no manifestations of dissatisfaction, nor lead to any acts of retaliatory violence? But the supposed case falls far short of the actual one, in a most essential circumstance. In no contingency could these capitals, manufactories, and ships rise in rebellion and massacre inhabitants of the Northern States.

"I am, Mr. President, no friend of slavery. The Searcher of all hearts knows that every pulsation of mine beats high and strong in the cause of civil liberty. Whenever it is safe and practicable I desire to see every portion of the human family in the enjoyment of it. But I prefer the liberty of my own country to that of any other people; and the liberty of my own race to that of any other race. The liberty of the descendants of Africa in the United States is incompatible with the safety and liberty of the European descendants. Their slavery forms an exception — an exception resulting from a stern and inexorable necessity — to the general liberty in the United States. We did not originate, nor are we responsible for, this necessity. Their liberty, if it were possible, could only be established by violating the incontestable powers of the States and subverting the Union. And beneath the ruins of the Union would be buried sooner or later, the liberty of both races."

THE MEANEST MAN IN CREATION.

We ask the attention of readers to the following extract from Judge Abbott's late speech at Boston: —

Let me ask for a moment who these men are who denounce those who appeal to the better part of man's nature? For twenty years past they have endeavored to destroy the Union; year in and year out they have denounced the glorious Constitution — the ark of our safety, as "a covenant with death and an agreement with hell;" who have scouted at and denounced the Union as it was and the Constitution as it is, and these are the men who denounce you and me. They don't want the Union. They are the men who have talked about war, war that is to last always, but who never have and never will risk a hair of their own miserable heads. When they talk of war they mean to risk the lives of your children and mine, while they remain at home. They belong to the class you have heard of before, who are willing to sacrifice all their wives' relations, and even consent to sacrifice their first cousins in the war, but not a mother's son of them will even get within the sound of a bullet.

They are the men who get your children and mine under false pretences — not for the Constitution, but for the negro. When they have got of us all they can get, — thank God they can get no more of mine, — their patriotism expends itself in buying negroes, and in sending to Germany for recruits to fight in a war they don't care anything about. Do you — I mean to be plain — do you want to know who is the meanest, most despicable creature, animal — I'll not call him man — who crawls? I'll tell you.

Voices — Wilson! Sumner!

Abbott — Gentlemen, don't call names. I'll describe a class. It is the man who constantly appeals to the worst passions of our nature; who is constantly urging us to battle, and who has not courage, ability, or capacity to risk a hair of his own head. You think of that, and when you have found such a man, you have found one of the most miserable wretches who crawls. That is one class. There is another. They who are constantly denouncing us if we say a word for peace and Union. If you ask these men to turn their pockets inside out, you will find them stuffed with "greenbacks," the spoils of your industry and mine. They want war because it means power and spoils. Of course these patent patriots don't want to end the war. These are the men who find fault with us because we want to restore the Union.

WATCHWORDS FOR PATRIOTS.

MOTTOES FOR THE CAMPAIGN, SELECTED FROM GENERAL MCCLELLAN'S WRITINGS.

Our cause must never be abandoned; it is the cause of free institutions and self-government. — *Harrison's Landing Letter.*

We are fighting solely for the integrity of the Union, to uphold the power of our national government, and to restore to the nation the blessings of peace and good order. — *Instructions to General Halleck, November* 11, 1861.

You will please constantly to bear in mind the precise issue for which we are fighting; that issue is the preservation of the Union and the restoration of the full authority of the general government over all portions of our territory. — *Instructions to General Buell, November 7, 1861.*

We shall most readily suppress this rebellion and restore the authority of the government by religiously respecting the constitutional rights of all. — *Instructions to General Buell, November 7, 1861.*

Be careful so to treat the unarmed inhabitants as to contract, not widen, the breach existing between us and the rebels. — *Instructions to General Buell, November 12, 1861.*

I have always found that it is the tendency of subordinates to make vexatious arrests on mere suspicion. — *Instructions to General Buell, November 12, 1861.*

Say as little as possible about politics or the negro. — *Instructions to General Burnside, January 7, 1862.*

The unity of this nation, the preservation of our institutions, are so dear to me that I have willingly sacrificed my private happiness with the single object of doing my duty to my country. — *Letter to Secretary Cameron, October, 1861.*

The Constitution and the Union must be preserved, whatever may be the cost in time, treasure, or blood. — *Harrison's Bar Letter.*

Neither confiscation of property, political executions of persons, territorial organization of States, nor forcible abolition of slavery should be contemplated for a moment. — *Letter to President Lincoln, July 7, 1862.*

In prosecuting this war, all private property and unarmed persons should be strictly protected, subject to the necessity of military operations. — *Letter to the President, July 7, 1862.*

Military arrests should not be tolerated, except in places where active hostilities exist; and oaths, not required by enactments constitutionally made, should be neither demanded nor received. — *Letter to the President, July 7, 1862.*

It should not be a war looking to the subjugation of the people of any State in any event. It should not be at all a war upon populations, but against armed forces and political organizations. — *Harrison's Bar Letter.*

If it is not deemed best to entrust me with the command even of my own army, I simply ask to be permitted to share their fate on the field of battle. — *Despatch to General Halleck, August 30, 1862.*

In the arrangement and conduct of campaigns the direction should be left to professional soldiers. — *General McClellan's Report.*

By pursuing the political course I have always advised, it is possible to bring about a permanent restoration of the Union — a re-union by which the rights of both sections shall be preserved, and by which both parties shall preserve their self-respect, while they respect each other. — *General McClellan's Report.*

I am devoutly grateful to God that my last campaign was crowned with a victory which saved the nation from the greatest peril it had then undergone. — *General McClellan's Report.*

At such a time as this, and in such a struggle, political partisanship should be merged in a true and brave patriotism, which thinks only of the good of the whole country. — *General McClellan's West Point Oration.*

A system of policy thus constitutional and conservative, and pervaded by the influences of Christianity and freedom, would receive the support of almost all truly loyal men, would deeply impress the rebel masses and all foreign nations, and it might be humbly hoped that it would commend itself to the favor of the Almighty. — *Harrison's Bar Letter.*

MARK THE CONTRAST.

DEMOCRATIC PRICES.		ABOLITION PRICES.	
Groceries.			
Teas	45a50c per lb.	Teas	$1 00a$2 50
Sugars	8 9c "	Sugars	20 30
Coffees	14 16c "	Coffees	65
Nutmegs	50 55c "	Nutmegs	$2 00
Pepper	8 9c "	Pepper	65
Allspice	6 8c "	Allspice	50
Cinnamon	20 22c "	Cinnamon	$1 00
Dry Goods — Domestic.			
Brown Sheetings	8½c per yd.	Brown Sheetings	65c per yd.
Prints, Calicoes, etc.	5½c "	Prints, Calicoes, etc.	40c "
Bleached Muslins	5½c "	Bleached Muslins	75c "
Canton Flannels	10c "	Canton Flannels	90c "
Foreign.			
Delaines	15½c per yd.	Delaines	75c per yd.
Dress Goods	25c "	Dress Goods	80c "
Velvets	$2 50c "	Velvets	$12 00c "

Raw Cotton, Etc.

Cotton Laps...............	18c per lb.	Cotton Laps..............	$1 75 per lb.
Wadding....................	40c "	Wadding.................	2 20 "
Carpet Chain..............	20c "	Carpet Chain............	1 10 "
Lamp Wick...............	20c "	Lamp Wick..............	1 50 "

Metals, Etc.

Lead......................	6c per lb.	Lead.....................	32c per lb.
Antimony..................	13c "	Antimony..................	75c "
Block Tin..................	31c "	Block Tin..................	90c "

Coal.

Of which the poor man's fire consumes as much as that which blazes in the rich man's fire — in former days could be had for *four or five dollars;* it now costs *fourteen and fifteen dollars.*

Cloths.

Satinets.. 45a50c per yd. $1 76 per yd.

Broadcloths, Cassimeres, etc., have increased from 106 to 150 per cent.

DRUGS have increased in price on an average of 200 per cent.

TOBACCO — Manufactured Cavendish Tobacco has risen from 35 cents to $1 25 per pound.

CIGARS have advanced from $20 to $60 and $200 per thousand.

FOREIGN STATIONERY, since the scarcity of specie, has risen 50 per cent.

Pamphlet 49

Hear Hon. Geo. H. Pendleton.

New York?, 1864

[The Peace Democrat, George H. Pendleton, the candidate for Vice-President in 1864, was the target of much Republican abuse. In his own defense he emphasized that he had voted for defense appropriations in Congress, and that he was opposed to independence for the Confederacy. He favored reestablishing the Federal Union as it had been before the war. The Democrats attached to expositions of Pendleton's views two extracts from Richmond newspapers to back their claim that the Confederates hoped for the re-election of Lincoln. (The Republicans were using quantities of Confederate quotations to back their opposite claim that the South wished McClellan elected.) Pendleton (1825–1889) was indeed a distinguished Ohio Democrat. He had served in Congress since 1857. After the Civil War his name was associated with the "Ohio idea" to pay United States bonds issued during the war with greenbacks. In the Senate he fought successfully for the Pendleton Act of 1883, the first Federal civil service legislation.]

LETTER TO HON. JOHN B. HASKIN.

CINCINNATI, October 17.

MY DEAR SIR: I have received your friendly letter. Malignant misrepresentations and falsehoods are so frequent in our political struggles, that I have rarely undertaken to correct or refute them.

I make no professions of a new faith, only repeat my reïterated professions of an old one, when I say that there is no one who cherishes a greater regard for the Union, who has a higher sense of its inestimable benefits, who would more earnestly labor for its restoration by all means which will effect that end, than myself. The Union is the guarantee of the peace, the power, the prosperity of this people; and no man would deprecate more heartily, or oppose more persistently, the establishment of another government over any portion of the territory ever within its limits.

I am in favor of exacting no conditions, insisting upon no terms,

not prescribed in the Constitution, and I am opposed to any course
of policy which will defeat the reëstablishment of the Government
upon its old foundations, and in its territorial integrity.

I am, very truly yours, etc.,

GEORGE H. PENDLETON.

Hon. JOHN B. HASKIN, N. Y.

LETTER TO HON. C. L. WARD.

CINCINNATI, October 18.

MY DEAR SIR: I have received your letter. In the very beginning
of this war — in the first days of the extra session of 1861 — I said
in my place in Congress, that I would vote for all measures necessary to enable the Government to maintain its honor and dignity
and prevent disaster to its flag. I have done so.

I thought, by the adoption of such measures, the faith of the
Government was pledged to the troops in the field, and must not
be forfeited by inadequate supplies. I never gave a vote which was
incompatible with this sentiment.

All appropriations, pure and simple, for the support and efficiency
of the army and navy, had my cordial concurrence. It was only
when they were connected with other, and improper, appropriations; when by reason of their popularity they were loaded down
with fraudulent items for the benefit of contractors and speculators,
and every attempt to separate them failed; when they were made
a stalking-horse for some abolition scheme, that I was constrained
reluctantly to vote against the whole bill.

But I repeat that I voted against no bill which was confined
simply to the object of supplies for the army and the navy.

I am, very truly yours,

GEORGE H. PENDLETON.

Hon. C. L. WARD, Philadelphia, Pa.

SPEECH AT NEW-YORK HOTEL,
OCTOBER 24th, 1864.

I THANK you for this manifestation of your kind feeling toward
myself. I am the more grateful for it as it comes from men who
have stood in the fore-front of danger, and periled their lives for
their country. (Loud cheers.) I accept it as an evidence of your

confidence in and of your sympathy with my devotion to the Union and the Constitution. (Three cheers for Geo. H. Pendleton.)

I have rarely found it necessary to reply to any personal attack. A friend has just handed me a pamphlet, which he tells me has extensive circulation both here and in the army. It professes to be a record of my speeches and votes in Congress, and to prove from them my hostility to the Republic. It professes to be published by the "Union Congressional Committee," and to be compiled from the *Congressional Globe,* to which it appeals for its entire accuracy. On the seventh page of that pamphlet, I am charged with having voted against certain resolutions on the seventh of July, 1864. Now, if any of you gentlemen will examine the *Globe,* or the file of any daily newspaper of your city, or will even tax his recollection, he will find that Congress adjourned on the fourth day of July, 1864. (Great laughter.) From this specimen of fraud and forgery, I leave you to judge of the credibility of the whole fabrication. (Laughter and applause.)

I was born in Ohio. I have lived all my life in the North-West. I know the sentiment of the people. I sympathize entirely with it. They are attached by every tie of affection and interest to this Union. (Loud cheering.)

Unlike New-York, they have never known another Government; they never existed as a political community before this Government was formed, and their hearts cling to this Government with indescribable tenacity. (Great applause.) Unlike you, they are an inland people chiefly devoted to agriculture. As an integral and controlling portion of the Union, they have prestige and power; they fear from disunion, isolation from the world, and the loss of that prestige and power. (Cheers.) Their interest requires that they should have speedy and easy communication with the ocean, and this they intend to have, both by the Gulf of Mexico and the city of New-York, by conciliation and peace if they can, by all the force and power which a teeming population and a fruitful soil give them if they must. (Loud cheers.) They believe that the first step toward maintaining the Union is the election of General McClellan. (Great cheering.) They believe that the restoration of the Democratic party to power will produce Union. (Cheers.) They believe the policy of this Administration toward both the Southern and Northern States is fatal to the Union. ("That's so.") General McClellan, in his Harrison Landing letter, said: "*Neither confiscation of property, nor political executions of persons, nor territorial organization of States, nor forcible abolition of slavery, should be for one moment thought of.*"

In his letter of acceptance he said: "*The Union was originally formed by the exercise of a spirit of conciliation and compromise. To restore and preserve it, a like spirit must prevail in the councils of the country and in the hearts of the people.*" (Cheers.)

The Democratic party is pledged to an unswerving fidelity to the Union under the Constitution. (Cheers.) It is pledged to "the restoration of peace on the basis of the Federal Union of the States." (Loud applause.)

We believe, nay, we know, that if this party shall be restored to power, if this policy shall prevail, the Union shall be restored; State after State will return to us, and the echoes of our rejoicing will come down to us from the vaults of heaven itself, in token that Deity approves that statesmanship which tempers all its policy with moderation, and justice, and conciliation. (Cheers.)

When next I meet you, I hope we may have already entered on that work. Again, gentlemen, I thank you for your attention, and wish you good-night. (Loud and long cheers followed the speech.)

LINCOLN THE REBEL CANDIDATE.

From the Richmond *Enquirer*, Sept. 5.

The Democratic nominees in the United States are McClellan for President and Pendleton for Vice-President. What concern have the people of the confederate States in the fate of these candidates at the approaching election? In our opinion, the interest and hope of peace is not greatly advanced by these nominations. From General McClellan our people can have but little hope of peace, other than a reconstruction peace. . . . What hope do his antecedents hold out that should encourage our people to believe that he would yield our nationality any sooner than Mr. Lincoln? *He is by far the more dangerous man for us; had his policy been persistently followed, and the war conducted on the principles of civilized warfare, he might have divided our people and perhaps conquered our liberties.* With consummate abilities, he clearly foresaw that emancipation might possibly free the negroes, but could not unite the sections;

that confiscation might enrich his soldiers, but could not reconcile our people; hence, with an earnest and honest love for the Union, he avoided these fatal acts, and conducted the war for the restoration of the Union, rather than the destruction of the South. His policy was the olive-branch in one hand and the sword in the other, to conquer by power and conciliate by kindness. *It was a most dangerous policy for us; for if the ameliorating hand of Federal kindness had softened the rigors of war, our people would not have been subjected to those terrible fires of suffering by which Mr. Lincoln has hardened every heart and steeled every sentiment* against our merciless foes. As a sincere secessionist, preferring war and nationality to peace and the Union, we looked upon the fact of a difference between Mr. Lincoln and General McClellan as to the proper policy of conducting the war, as peculiarly fortunate for our cause. We hailed the proclamations of emancipation and confiscation, and the policy of plunder and devastation, as sure pledges of our ultimate triumph; they were terrible ordeals, but they most effectually eradicated every sentiment of Union, and arousing the pride as well as the interest of our people, inflamed the patriotism of the whole, until they would have accepted death as preferable to ultimate defeat.

Now, between McClellan and Lincoln there are many points of difference; the former is a man of talent, of information, of firmness, and great military experience and ability; the latter is a supple, pliant, easy fool, a good but vulgar joker. While McClellan has the interest of the Union only at heart, Mr. Lincoln has the fanatical object of freeing negroes for his inspiration. Between "my plan," as General Grant has conducted it, and one by General McClellan, there could not have been the same success that has already attended our arms; *for we lost more men fighting the science of McClellan on the Peninsula, than we have in repelling the furious but ill-conducted assaults of General Grant. Thus, whether we look at this nomination in the light of peace or of war, we prefer Lincoln to McClellan. We can make better terms of peace with anti-slavery fanatics than with an earnest Unionist.* We can gain more military success in a war conducted on "my plan" than one of a real soldier like McClellan, and sooner destroy the resources and strength of our enemy where they are managed and manipulated by the light-fingered gentry of Messrs. Chase and Fessenden, than when husbanded and skilfully controlled by such a man as Guthrie. *Our best hope is from the honest fanatics of the United States,* men who believe in their hearts that slavery is the "sum of all villainies," and who really and sincerely believe it to be their duty to separate their country from this "relic of barbarism." *Such men, when they find that their people are tired of the war, will end it by a peace that sacrifices territory to freedom, and will let the South "go," provided she carries slavery with her.* These men believe no less that the just powers of government are derived from the consent of the governed, than "that all men are created free and equal." The two postulates are of like importance to an abolitionist.

Both the abolitionist and the Democrat is our enemy — the one, because we have slaves, the other, because we are disunionists. Nor does their enmity differ in degree; they both hate us most intensely. The Chicago platform is that "peace may be restored on the basis of the Federal Union of the States" — that is, reconstruction of the Union as it was, with slavery protected by the nominal laws, but warred upon by a real sentiment, aggravated and embittered by the war. The reconstructed Union of the Chicago platform would be the certain destruction — first, of slavery, and next of slaveholders. With Lincoln and the Baltimore platform, we of the confederate States know where we are — outside of the pale of mercy, devoted to ruin and destruction, with no hope save in the justice and protection of God, and the courage and manliness of our soldiers. *With swords and muskets and cannon we fight Lincoln, and the past affords no reason of apprehension of the future. But in the reconstructed Union of the Chicago platform we would be deprived of our weapons without being reconciled to our foes.*

The disruption of old political associations is always a hazardous experiment. The great majority of minds in a wealthy and prosperous community are averse to change and revolution, preferring to endure great evils rather than resort to sanguinary measures for redress. No men ever felt the weight of this truth more forcibly than those who inaugurated the movement for secession. The whole danger and risk of the experiment consisted in that conservative aversion to change and convulsion which possesses the popular masses. On this rock the secession cause might have split, if it *had not been safely piloted past it by the pains of Abraham Lincoln.* The cause was saved in 1862 by the conscription; and Lincoln — not the

Examiner newspaper — may be said to have been the author of the conscription; because, except for the ferocious policy which he pursued, it could never have been enforced. He has rendered resistance an absolute duty and necessity, and brought that duty and necessity home to every man's door, insomuch, that no man in the South having any self-respect or regard for the opinions of his neighbors, dares to disobey the call of his country to arms.

But for the incentives supplied by Mr. Lincoln, the South, by want of union and energy, might have failed to deserve the respect of mankind; might have been unable to levy great armies; and the forces in the field might have fought with little energy or resolution. The popular majority might have been disposed, at the first soft words from the enemy, to renounce the Southern cause, and return to the enjoyment of repose, prosperity, and dishonor. Mr. Lincoln has prevented such a contingency, and relieved the South of all these dangers by a course of policy which rendered reconciliation impossible. *By driving us to extremity, he has combined every element of our strength, and insured our success.* If the South could be conquered at all, there is but one mode by which it could be done. If the armies of the North were entirely withdrawn, and an invitation proposed for a convention of all the States, for the purpose of devising terms of conciliation, then our independence might be seriously endangered. Such would have been the policy of Pierce or Vallandigham; such, possibly, though not probably, might become the policy of McClellan. But Mr. Lincoln relieves us of this only possible danger by a policy which drives every man to arms, and renders reconstruction an opprobrium throughout the land.

While the South has much for which to thank Mr. Lincoln, the North has still more for which to curse him. His administration has cost the United States half a million of men, eleven States with ten millions of population, embracing many thousands of millions of wealth, and has entailed three thousand millions of public debt. He is the very genius of ruin and destruction to his country, and seems to have endeared himself in its affections by the very loss and woe he has inflicted upon it.

If the people of the United States choose to reëlect him, *they thereby pronounce a decree establishing the independence of the South.* We can bring larger armies into the field to fight Lincoln than any other Northern President, and his continuation in office will inspire every Southern breast with the resolve to win independence as the only alternative to extermination.

There is no question that between the two men General McClellan enjoys far more of the respect of the people of these States than Lincoln, and the Democratic party far more of our confidence than the Republican, and that *if reconstruction were possible, it would be more probable under General McClellan and the Democracy than under Lincoln and the Republicans.* The North-West inspires one, and New-England the other; but as long as New-England imposes the dogmas of her civilization and the tenets of her fanaticism upon the mind and people of the North-West, there may be peace and separation, but there can never be Union and harmony. If the North-West desires the restoration of the Union, let its people shake off the bondage of New-England, and *show to the world that a new era of toleration and fraternal kindness has risen in the place of fanatical Puritanism and selfish ostracism.*

From the Richmond *Examiner*, October 17.

Some doubt remains as to the political complexion of Pennsylvania. The press of the United States has become so radically mendacious, that it is impossible to put trust in the first accounts even of an event so public and plain as the result of an election. Some days may yet elapse before certitude is attained. But we entertain strong hopes that the Republicans have done what they seemed at first to have done, and confess a deep desire that the present result may foreshadow the reelection of Abraham Lincoln. *For Abraham Lincoln is the South's best ally.* This Confederacy had a million and a quarter men capable of bearing arms at the outset of the contest: a force sufficient to meet any invading power and defy the possibility of subjugation. The only danger lay in the difficulty of bringing this force into the field. *Abraham Lincoln removed that difficulty by the character which he imparted to the war.* He made Goths and Vandals of his troops, and proclaimed devastation, confiscation, and extermination as his purpose. It was thus that he invoked into the field those powerful Southern armies which have so successfully resisted his assaults. It is scarcely possible to conceive how a conflict could have been rendered more envenomed that the present one has become through that truculent policy of Mr. Lincoln. Yet this man found a means of intensifying its ferocity. He proclaimed insurrection to the slaves, and armed all the blacks which he could seduce into his service, against the whites who had been their masters. By this policy he effectually succeeded in calling out and combining every element of resistance in the South — a strong element of that resistance is yet to come, as will appear soon after the meeting of the confederate Congress. The enemy talk of the despotism which drags conscripts into the Southern armies, and forces old men and children into the ditches, but the despotism which coerces the South is seated at Washington, and not at Richmond. The Confederacy has proved that it had nerve and resolution to achieve an independent destiny; but it is indebted to Lincoln for forcing these qualities into action.

Pamphlet 50

Francis Lieber

*Lincoln or McClellan. Appeal to the Germans
in America. Translated from the German by T.C.
(Loyal Publication Society No. 67)*

New York, 1864

[In simple, brief fashion, Francis Lieber, who was ordinarily lengthy and involved in what he wrote, dashed off a manifesto to the Germans in America emphasizing point by point why it was to their best interest to vote for President Lincoln. The Loyal Publication Society published it in German, Dutch, and English; the Union League of Philadelphia reprinted it and the New York *Tribune* gave it wide circulation. Lieber was not entirely elated to learn that the *Tribune* was having to reprint the pamphlet to keep up with a heavy demand, and that throughout each day clusters of Germans stood reading a copy affixed to the *Tribune* bulletin board. He would have preferred to have received such acclaim for his lengthy treatises on political institutions. Lieber (1798–1872), a German liberal who had emigrated to the United States in 1827, had been for many years a professor at South Carolina College before moving to Columbia University in 1857. His sympathies were ardently with the Lincoln administration, for which he performed various services during the war.[1]]

Countrymen and Fellow-Citizens:[2]

[1] [Freidel, *Lieber*, 352–353. Cf., Lieber, *Lincoln oder McClellan? Aufruf an die Deutschen in Amerika* (Loyal Publication Society No. 59, New York, 1864); Lieber, *Lincoln or McClellan? Oproep aan die Hollanders in Amerika* (Loyal Publication Society No. 71, New York, 1864).]

[2] This appeal was written several weeks before the letter of Alexander H. Stephens to some friends in Georgia, and the report of Judge Advocate Holt, on the conspiracy in this country, for the subversion of its government in favor of the rebels, were published. These two documents, the first speaking of "the ultimate and absolute sovereignty of the states," the other showing many prominent men of the Chicago Convention loaded with crimes of the deepest dye — these documents would have furnished the writer of the appeal with many sad illustrations. — *Translator.*

The presidential election is rapidly approaching, and it is time for every citizen to reflect and decide conscientiously for whom he shall give his ballot. At an election of such importance, when everything dear to us, as citizens, is staked on the issue, it is unworthy — it is cowardly — to throw away the right of voting. No patriot will choose political impotency at this crisis. The entire political existence of this country, of which we became citizens by the choice of our mature years, and not by the accident of birth, rests upon the free ballot; and he who has the right, has also the duty to vote. If sensible and honest voters stay away from the polls, they may be sure that those whose votes have been bought, and those who have no right to vote at all, will be ready there to appear in their stead.

The great majority of those who come from Germany to America are Democrats in the true sense, and when they find in this country a large party, which for years has been called the Democratic party, many allow themselves to be deceived by the mere name. The assemblage which gathered at Chicago, and nominated General McClellan for the Presidency, also calls itself the Democratic party — and of what sort of people was this mixed-up convention composed? In the first place, a great proportion consisted of old "Know-nothings." They openly proclaimed themselves such. Can you, Germans, vote on the same side with these men, whose only principle has been to shut in your faces the gates of this wide continent, to which their own fathers came from Europe, or else, as you are here already, to take from you the right of citizenship? Will you vote with those who, like their friends, the rebels, would load you with infamy, and who speak of you as the offscouring of the earth? The Know-nothings plot in secret. They have their lodges, and form a secret society. Is that, in a free country, democratic? Freedom, above all, rests on publicity.

Another portion of the Chicago convention consisted of those who set State-Rights, as they call it, above everything else; who openly say that Americans have not a country! and that the sovereignty of the single state stands high above everything else — is absolute; that each state has the right to tear itself away, and be a separate dominion; that there is therefore no right anywhere to compel such a state to remain in the Union. They utter untruths, and they know it! What would these same people have done if Ohio or Massachusetts had suddenly broken away and declared itself a monarchy?

What do the rulers in Richmond at this very instant say of those men in North Carolina, who desire to withdraw their own state from the so-called confederacy? They call them rebels. How comes it that, up to this very day, there are men sitting in the congress at Richmond, as delegates from Missouri and Kentucky? Have these states seceded? Why have the rebels all along claimed Maryland as belonging to them? The delegates from Kentucky and Missouri sit in their congress; Maryland troops fight in their ranks, because Kentucky, Missouri, and Maryland are, or were, slaveholding states. With these enemies of the Union, therefore, slavery is the principle of cohesion of a new country, and state-sovereignty is not the basis of the right of secession. Why did these gentlemen all support General Jackson, when the old hero told South Carolina she should be compelled, by force of arms, to stay in the Union? And is the doctrine of state-sovereignty democratic? I feel almost ashamed to ask such a question of a German. The Democracy has always, and everywhere, been for the unity of the country; it will have but one country, worthy of a great nation. All Pumpernickel sovereignties, all the "Algerine states," as in Germany they are now called, have always been objects of loathing and execration to the Democracy.

Unquestionably each state in the United States has its rights, and ought to have them. But so, too, each man has his rights, and the rights of the individual which belong to every person in a free country are far more valuable, and are more important, taken on the whole, than the rights of states are. But the individual man is not for this reason a sovereign. Do you know that the word "sovereignty" does not once occur in that great instrument, the Constitution of the United States? The word "sovereignty" was smuggled into our political dictionary when this Constitution had already been adopted. Who then is sovereign in America if the states are not? Nobody! No man, no corporation, no congress, no president, no officer, no body of men, is sovereign in a free country. The United States are sovereign in respect to all other sovereign nations. We are sovereign when we treat with France and England, or when we engage in war; but within the country itself no one is sovereign.

This is no new theory, nor is it any theory at all. It is a fact. Two hundred years ago, when the famous Bill of Rights was under consideration in the English Parliament, the greatest lawyer in England declared that the word "sovereign" was not known to English law.

He said this because the dynasty which had just then been expelled had constantly talked of the king's sovereign power.

But can it be necessary to argue with Germans against a hankering after petty state domination and provincial pomposity. State sovereignty, indeed! Have we not had enough of that sort of thing in the land from which we came? If a German wants to have a stew of states, he never need come for it to America. Has he not got enough of sovereign states, big, little, and minute, at home?

What are the ideas which most animate the German in Germany? They are the unity of Germany and civil freedom. And shall he here give his vote for those who would see the country torn asunder in fragments while the cause of human slavery should triumph?

German working men! why did you leave home, family, the friends of your youth, and seek this distant America? It was because you had heard that in the United States you would find a country wherein you and your children would enjoy all the rights of the free citizen; where skill and industry would surely find their reward, and where your children would never find themselves debarred from any merited attainment by the privileges of others. If then you would not have, in place of this Union, a land where the working man should be delivered over to a grinding tyranny far worse than any endured in the oppressed countries of Europe, do not lend your aid to the party which would give up the Union to the dominion of the Southern landholders.

For do you know what this slave-owning, would-be oligarchy pretends to aim at? Perhaps you suppose they struggle only to retain possession of their negro slaves. The Southern slaveholders are fighting for that which was for so long a time the prerogative of the owners of the soil, the privilege of using the working man, whether white or black, as the instrument of their power, their pleasure, and their arrogance. The working man is to bear all the burdens of the state, but he is to have no rights in it. It is for him to obey, and for the rich man alone to rule. Hear what the secession leaders have said:

"No state can endure in which the laboring class has political rights. Those alone who own the soil and the capital must govern and be the masters of those who labor."

And they say this, remember it well: "Capital has an inherent right to own labor."

If you would have masters set up over you, on this principle, vote for McClellan. Would you retain your equal rights as the citizens of a free country, vote for Lincoln, who has been an honest working man like yourselves.

Another part of the Chicago Convention consisted of those who seem to believe that all can be made right if people will only keep on shouting "the Constitution, the Constitution," as loud as they can.

We think we understand the Constitution quite as well as these gentlemen, and respect it more. For it should be noticed that the so-called Democratic party has of late years always set the Constitution aside whenever it seemed to be for their advantage. Was Nullification constitutional? Was it constitutional when Mr. Douglas, shortly before the last Presidential election, promised the South to advocate a law subjecting to heavy punishment the mere discussion of the slavery question? Was it constitutional, when, for twenty years, and probably longer, the letterbags in the South were opened to see whether they contained abolition documents? Was it constitutional to deny the right of petition? Is Secession constitutional? Is it consistent with the Constitution to say with those Chicago people that it is the President's right and duty to release any State that may desire to leave the Union? Is it constitutional to speak of secession as "one of the reserved rights of the State"? Is it constitutional to declare that our whole political State-structure exists only to benefit a single class of men — a class known by the complexion of the skin? Even the ancient heathen had a higher view of the State and of the objects of civil government. Is it constitutional to represent one whole government as a mere Confederation or League — that poorest of all governments for a modern and free people? Was it in the spirit of the Constitution when Mr. Calhoun and all his followers proclaimed that the Senate should always be equally divided between slave states and free states, thus making for the first time in our history slavery an immutable institution? Was the precious Ostend proclamation conceived in a constitutional spirit?

We too honor the Constitution, but the Constitution is not a deity. We love our country, the nation, freedom; and these things are superior even to the Constitution; and it should never be forgotten that by this Southern Rebellion a state of things is brought upon us for which the Constitution never was, and never could be calculated. Shall we fold our hands, as did Mr. Buchanan, and declare that nothing can be done on our part to save the country because the Constitution does not prescribe what we are to do in such a case? Such was the opinion which his Attorney-General of the United States gave to Mr. Buchanan. God forbid! We are one nation; we mean to remain one people, and our country must not be suffered to perish. The life of the patient must be saved whether the case is mentioned in the recipe book or not. The Constitution did not make the people for the people made the Constitution. But has the Constitution been violated at all? We have not space for an examination of the question. But, my countrymen, admitting that some things may have occurred which could not be justified by existing laws, I am, as I think I may safely say, as well acquainted with the history of the past as any of these Chicago gentlemen, and I can advisedly affirm that never yet has there been any civil war, nor even any ordinary war in which the government has tolerated the thousandth part of that liberty which the enemies of the Government and the friends of those enemies enjoy among us — infinitely more, than the latter would allow us in a reversed case.

It is the so-called Democratic party which has brought this civil war upon us, and now they say that they only can end it. Why so? Does a man in America acquire some mysterious power or wisdom as soon as he calls himself a Democrat? They want to make up a peace, to give still greater guarantees to the South — everything to the rebels; in short, they belong to those in the North who have always been the obsequious servants of the South, and who seem to think themselves honored by fulfilling the behests of an arrogant slaveholder. Is that Democracy?

My friends, let us vote for Lincoln. Many of you doubtless say that he has done some things which you do not like, or that sometimes he has not acted with sufficient promptitude. But the simple question before the people now is, shall Lincoln or McClellan be the next President? No other man can be elected; and now is there a German who can hesitate, or one who can be so indifferent as not to vote for either. The one candidate is *national*, the other is not. The one is for freedom and for the removal of that which is the disgrace of this century — he is opposed to slavery, which has brought upon us the demon of civil war. The other would preserve slavery. The one is out-spoken and candid; is the other so? The one is for all the citizens of this great country, whether they were born here or not; the other owes his nomination in a great degree to the Know-Nothings. The one is truly a Democrat — he is a man of the people; the other is no real Democrat — at least those who have set him up before the people are anything but democratic in feeling. The one, though surrounded by unparalleled difficulties, has at least so guided the ship of state that we are now in sight of the desired haven; the other, when he was at the head of one of the grandest armies that had been seen in a century, did little more than hesitate, when he might, as the enemy now admits, have put an end to the war.

It is easy to understand why some very rich and some very poor Germans, who want to get into office, exert themselves for McClellan. But of every German who has no such views, who simply gives his vote for the honor, the unity, and the freedom of his adopted country, and who does not allow himself to be deluded by the mere name of "Democrat," we may naturally expect that when he has calmly reflected on the vast importance of the occasion, and the character of the candidates, he will vote for Lincoln.

Every citizen ought to exert himself to the utmost in this remarkable election, when a great nation is called upon at the very crisis of a gigantic civil war, to elect a ruler by the popular and untrammelled ballot. It is not sufficient to carry the election of Mr. Lincoln by a bare overplus of numbers. A sweeping national majority is required to prove to Europe, to the South, and to its friends here in the midst of us, that this people is resolved to maintain this country in its integrity, a great and unimpaired commonwealth. The result of this election should be like a great national harvest, garnering its full sheaves from every portion of the land.

Pamphlet 51

Charles Astor Bristed
The Cowards' Convention. (Loyal Publication Society, No. 68)

New York, 1864

[One of the more carefully reasoned attacks upon the Democrats was a series of letters Charles Astor Bristed wrote to the New York *Times*. It purported to analyze the work of the Democratic convention, which had met in Chicago on August 29, 1864. The convention had been fairly equally divided in power between two factions, the War Democrats and the Peace Democrats. While the War Democrats had succeeded in nominating General McClellan for President, the Peace Democrats had obtained the nomination of George Pendleton for Vice-President, and had dominated the platform committee. Thus it was possible for the Republicans to ignore the War Democrats and campaign against the Peace faction through grossly exaggerating its views. Bristed (1820–1874), a great-grandson of John Jacob Astor, wrote studies in philology and sharp essays on the American scene and was one of the active members of the Loyal Publication Society.]

NO. 1.

To the Editor of the New York Times:

> An open foe may prove a curse,
> But a pretended friend is worse. — GAY.

In this most portentous crisis of our political history, the first thing necessary for all loyal men is to know the full extent of our danger. It is no use mincing or dodging the matter. We have to do with enemies who, if successful, will complete the work of their fellow-traitors at the South. The secessionists tore the country in two; the framers of the Chicago platform would scatter it in fragments.

When thus speaking of the so-called Democratic party, I have no wish to say much against or about their nominal standard-bearer. He was a good, though slow business man; is a good driller, good engineer, and altogether a very fair *defensive* commander. And there is certainly this much propriety in his nomination, that if his party succeeds, we shall speedily have occasion to try our commander-in-chief's capacity in that species of warfare for which he is best adapted.

Nor is it intimated that the War Democrats, whom party organization and a misplaced fidelity to names will dragoon into the support of a peace platform, have any intention or desire of destroying the nation and dividing the country indefinitely. They will vote in ignorance of the real issues, as hundreds of thousands voted for Pierce in '52, as thousands voted for Seymour in '62. Though certainly not blameless, since there is an ignorance so blind and wilful that it is almost as wicked and quiet as harmful as wickedness itself, they may well be acquitted of voluntarily compassing the national destruction.

But neither the nominal leader nor the deluded War Democrats will have any hand in shaping the policy of the party. Its real managers are the framers of that precious confession of faith, the Chicago platform. Horatio Seymour, the Prince of Jesuits; Fernando Wood, a man capable of any enormity; Vallandigham, a Southerner by birth and a traitor by profession, as deadly an enemy of the Union as Jefferson Davis himself — these are the men who rule the Opposition, who direct it now, and will direct it if, for our sins, it is permitted to become the government.

The necessary results of their success are generally understood, but it is evident the loyal and patriotic public does not appreciate the extent of the danger. Thus we hear it constantly said, "If the Chicago candidate is elected, the restoration of the Union at once becomes impossible. We are humiliated by the recognition of a Southern confederacy; our democratic principles will be violated, and the contiguous existence of two rival nations will bring about a chronic state of war and all the inconveniences to which Continental Europe is subject," &c., &c. All which is true enough so far as it goes; but it goes a very little way into the matter. After enumerating these obvious results which the popular mind so strongly and so justly deprecates, we are only on the top layer of our Pandora's box. *If we could demonstrate with mathematical certainty that a Southern Confederacy might be acknowledged on terms neither dishonor-*

able nor destructive to ourselves, and that our democratic form of government might undergo various innovations with impunity, we should not have gone the first step toward proving that such terms could be procured and such innovations would be made by a "peace-at-any-price" President. On the contrary, the impossibility of the latter proposition would only become clearer by the proof of the former.

Let us, for the sake of argument, admit —

1. That a peace, acknowledging the independence of a Southern Confederacy, may be made without any disgrace to us.

2. That modifications in our democratic theory and practice of government may be made, without ruin, or even with benefit, to the country.

3. That two rival nations may co-exist on the territory of the old Union.

There is nothing in these admissions to interfere with the following conclusions:

1. That the peace made by the so-called Democratic party would be a most dishonorable one.

2. That the modifications of Democratic principles made or permitted by them would be highly injurious and destructive.

3. That the North could not exist as an independent nation under the rule and on the principles of the Peace Democrats.

(The first and third of these propositions are intimately connected, but as the third must come last, since all national evils are summed up in destruction, and the question of reconstruction or separation is the most pressing, and has, therefore, a right to the first place, I arrange them as above, though the division is somewhat awkward.)

First, then, we will admit, for the sake of argument, that a peace may be made recognizing a Southern Confederacy (note the indefinite articles), on terms not disgraceful to us.

(Observe that nothing is said about the safety of such a proceeding. Honor, and honor alone, is the subject of our story.)

Such an assumption may be made. It has been made by a whole class of persons — the English writers favorable to the North, who, disagreeing with the Pro-Slavery Britons on all other points, agreed, for some time at least, with them in this, that the war would be one "for boundary." However much a man like Professor Cairnes, for instance, may have mistaken the spirit or the wants of the American people, we cannot suspect him of wishing our disgrace.

But what sort of peace must this be in order not to be disgraceful? Clearly one of which we, rather than the Confederates, should fix the conditions, they making great sacrifice to obtain the acknowledgment of their "independence." It would naturally proceed, as far as possible, on the *uti possidetis* principle. It would give us all the Border States except East Virginia, whatever view be taken of their condition — whether, as we say, they are States which have remained faithful to the Union, or, as the Confederates and philo-Confederate Europeans say, they are "conquered provinces." We could not expect to keep New Orleans, but we should be obliged to retain one fortified position on the Mississippi, that our navigation of that river might not be at the mercy of paper agreement with repudiators. If we could suppose that phenomenon, a well-informed and impartial European, to act as umpire, the most he could ask of us would be to "rectify the frontier" by ceding Tennessee in exchange for Eastern Virginia. It is hardly necessary to add that we must have nothing to do with paying any of the Confederate expenses, directly or indirectly, or altering any of our institutions to suit them, or even acknowledge the right of secession, the Confederate independence being admitted merely as an accomplished fact, without regard to its merits.

In short, the supposed honorable peace must be such a one as would be honorable to us, had the North and the Gulf States originally been two distinct sovereignties, fighting for the border territory and the navigation of the Mississippi. Now, what chances are there that such terms of separation, or any like them, would be obtained by the Chicago policy of "immediate armistice and ultimate convention?"

None, whatever.

The claims of the Confederates are well known. They demand *every foot of territory* south of Mason and Dixon's line, including the national capital, the surrender of which involves the surrender of our national existence. (About this there will be somewhat to say hereafter; for the present, we are only speaking of national humiliation.) The sole doubtful point is whether they do or do not include

Kansas in this claim. Some time ago there were grounds for suspecting that they had relinquished their pretensions to Maryland and Delaware; but Davis has just disposed of that ambiguity in his answer to Col. Jaques. *He asks of us a territorial cession far more humiliating than that which the whole force of Germany has recently extorted from Denmark:* and this is *the only* condition on which *he* will agree to the "immediate armistice." And recollect that "Jefferson Davis says," is a much more comprehensive formula than "Abraham Lincoln says." The latter is not the people of the United States, though as the executive of their Government, and the representative of their majority, his words have great weight; but Davis *is the State,* in Secession, as much as Louis Napoleon is in France, despite his hypocritical pretence of being unable to interfere with the individual "sovereignties."

But this is not all. Far from it. The prominent rebel organs have repeatedly announced as *essential* conditions of peace, that we should acknowledge the right of secession, return to Slavery all the negroes whom the progress of the war has set free, or pay their value, repudiate our own debt, to punish the loyal men who hold it, and — last humiliation of a conquered people — do what they would never do for themselves, pay theirs!

Will it be said, "It is easy to claim anything, but would the North accede to these preposterous demands?" I answer, not only is it probable, from their uniform subserviency to their Southern masters, that the Peace Democrats would do it, *but it is certain that they must, if they mean to carry out their own principles consistently.* The right of secession they already acknowledge, and the rest follows, from their professed doctrines, by easy inference.

If, as the O'Conors, Brookses, and other Peace Democrats, are never weary of telling us, the negro is an inferior animal, without civil rights, then the disposition of a few hundred thousand blacks is a matter of no more consequence than the disposal of the same number of cattle, and becomes an insignificant detail in face of the great question of peace. If the war is "unconstitutional," as Horatio Seymour pronounces it to be, all the measures employed in carrying it on must be tainted with the same unconstitutionality; and, of these, the war-loans are not the least potent or prominent. If it is "unholy," as that Apostle of the New Gospel of Peace, F. Wood, declares — if we were impious and unchristian in taking up the gauntlet which the conspirators threw down to us at Sumter — then we, as repentant Christians, under the guidance of that eminent disciple, Saint Fernando, should make what restitution we can to our aggrieved and invaded secesh brethren.

Such is the immediate prospect of degradation presented to us by the sages and patriots of Chicago, a degradation so deep and damnable, that it would make us a scorn and a hissing throughout the world, and any man with a soul above a flea's would be ashamed to look his own wife and children in the face.

Let me conclude this part of our subject with a little anecdote, after the manner of our worthy Executive.

Mlle. Luther, a young and pretty Parisian actress, accepted the protection of a well-known restaurateur. A lady named Doche, of more experience in the profession, expostulated with her on the lowness of her choice — "My dear, you astonish me! An eating-house proprietor at your time of life? One keeps that sort of thing for the last."

So I say about submission to the enemy. *One should keep that sort of thing for the last.* When we are in the very ultimate ditch, with Washington besieged, Philadelphia taken, and Boston blockaded, with Gov. Seymour's friends pillaging and murdering in New York worse than they did last year, and no troops at hand to shoot them down, with gold at 2,000, and every boy of fifteen conscripted, *then* it will be time to talk of throwing away our arms and begging for peace. Submission on the part of those who cannot help themselves, if not honorable, is at least excusable. But what words can depict the infamy and degradation of those who surrender everything while they have the best of the fight, and run away from the battle when victory is hovering in their grasp?

NO. 2.

To the Editor of the New York Times:

Having shown that even were an honorable separation possible, it could not be obtained on the principles of the Chicago Convention, I proceed to the second proposition.

Let it be admitted, for the sake of argument, that innovations might be made in our Democratic theory and practice without injury.

Such a hypothesis may be framed without doing violence to our intelligence or even to probability. We (by *we* I mean all of us who are not demagogues and place-hunters, and do not get a living by lies and flattery) know that nothing of man's institution is perfect, that Democracy is no exception to this rule, and our Democracy no exception in this respect to other Democracies. Those of us who have looked deeper into the matter know that any government, as it goes on, has a tendency to intensify its own faults, and that the predominant element of it is constantly absorbing all checks. Thus, as what we may call the centripetal element is constantly gaining ground in an autocracy, and accumulating more and more power about the one source of it, so what we may call the centrifugal element, is as constantly gaining ground in a Democracy. This has been exemplified in our own history; for though the Federal Constitution has remained unaltered, thanks to the guards with which its wise framers surrounded it, the constitutions of nearly all the older states have been largely modified in a democratic sense.[1] In view of all which a change theoretically anomalous, might be practically beneficial.

Our assumption, then, is not unreasonable in its very nature. It is not like those impossible figments of the brain put forth by the leading spirits at Chicago, so dreamy and baseless that the very rebels for whose benefit they were devised, cannot help laughing at them — proposing, for instance, that we should give up five and a half states, of which we now hold possession, for the *chance* of getting them back *some time or other* by a convention — a piece of absurdity in comparison with which the fable of the dog and the shadow becomes a solid reality.

Among our hypothetical changes might be a prolongation of the Presidential term to eight or ten years; a return in all the states to a permanent judiciary; a limitation of universal suffrage in the great cities where its results have been so unsatisfactory; and generally, without multiplying examples, we may admit that a number of alterations, theoretically anti-democratic, might be made without overthrowing the government or ruining the country.

[1] This took place at the South less than at the North, owing to the continued preponderance of an oligarchic element in the former.

Note always, that these changes are not recommended. Their practicability is merely assumed for the sake of argument. And after this assumption, it is still true that the innovations brought about by the success of the Chicago platform, would be utterly subversive.

For, in the first place, yielding to the rebels would involve a self-condemnation of democratic government by confessing its impotence for self-protection; and in confessing this, we really give up everything. If such government were in all other respects perfect, without this element it would be worthless. It would resemble the horse who had but one fault — that he was dead. Once allow that a Government based on the voice of the majority may be resisted by a minority, and the whole theory of democracy is as practically disproved as the divine right of Kings was in England when William of Orange walked in and kicked out James II. and his court of French pensioners, the Woods and Vallandighams of that day. Its existence is at once rendered precarious, and put at the mercy of any minority bold and cunning enough to conspire against it. This is what the foreign enemies of our Union were continually predicting — that it was not able to resist internal pressure; and the Chicago leaders are intent on verifying their most sombre predictions. After this confession of weakness, our Government might not perish to-morrow or next month, but it would assuredly collapse as soon as another great strain was put upon it; and we shall see hereafter to what sort of strains it would speedily be subjected.

The utterly subversive character of this confession will become still clearer, if we consider the class in whose favor it is made.

If there is any principle which more than all others may be called fundamental in the theory and practice of our Constitution, it is that of political equality — equal rights and no class privileges. And as it is the chief distinction, so is it the chief virtue of our Government. Nobody doubts that a man of wealth and refinement, who is willing to live selfishly — that is for himself and his class — may live more comfortably in several European countries. He can get more for his money, and find more agreeable companions. Our institutions were of and for the people, expressly designed to promote the welfare and happiness of the greatest number. Consequently and naturally the people have always been jealous of anything that looked like a tendency toward the establishment of class prerogative.

At one time they had a great fear of moneyed corporations, and though some of its phases at the time were extravagant, the subsequent encroachments of railroad and other companies on public and private rights have proved that this fear was well founded. Hence too the "Native" movement, however provoked or even justified by the misconduct of some of our foreign citizens, could never take root in the country. In the case of the negro, one unfortunate exception was made to the rule of equal rights — an exception that has proved the rule with a vengeance!

But now this corner-stone of our Constitution is to be rejected, and at whose bidding? That of a sectional oligarchic class, amounting, according to the very largest estimate that has been made of them, to a million of persons — something less than one thirtieth of the whole population, and fewer, comparatively, than the aristocratic class of England.

And this is the upshot of so many years' teaching and practice of the once great Democratic party! A party which, spasmodically faithful to its name, every now and then rode its hobby at the most erratic pace; which hunted down banks and tariffs because it suspected in them the germ of a possible aristocracy; which, in pursuit of the largest liberty, assigned, both by executive appointment and popular votes, the most notorious violators of law to be its special administrators and guardians; which decried learning and good manners as unrepublican, and claimed to be the special servant, agent and friend of the working classes. The moment it finds itself face to face with an oligarchy of any courage and skill, it can suggest nothing except to surrender "body and boots."

The French Emperor and his flatterers boast that he has reconciled the strong points of an autocratic and a democratic government. On this subject the world is not quite agreed; many think the task too difficult even for a Napoleon. But, so much easier is evil than good, it is quite possible to combine some of the worst features of an oligarchy and ochlocracy; and this is what the Chicago schemers are endeavoring to give us. I want none of their patent mixture. To borrow the indignant words of Mr. John Jay, "it is hard to say whether the sham aristocracy of the Southern slave masters, or the sham Democracy of their Northern serfs, is the more despicable."

NO. 3.

To the Editor of the New York Times:

Having proved that the Chicago platform involves utter disgrace to the country, and a total abandonment of the fundamental principles of democracy, we shall now show how it will lead, and that not remotely, to a destruction of our national existence and an unlimited subdivision of the country.

Let us suppose, for the sake of argument, that the North and South might, under certain circumstances, co-exist as independent nations on the territory of the Union.

Of course they would not co-exist comfortably. There would be wars and a state of disturbance approaching to chronic. All we suppose is, that they might exist, as the nations of Continental Europe, though they live uncomfortable and expensively enough together, still live.

But to make this state of things even hypothetically possible, the North must be supposed to start fair with the South.

How the South would start we may pretty accurately foresee. It would be a strong military oligarchy, composed of three classes — a ruling aristocracy, white plebeians and black slaves. *Nominally,* it would be founded on a principle of mutual dissolution, the "State Sovereignty" theory; but it is obvious that this fiction was merely used as a means of getting certain States out of the Union, and that having served its purpose, it is now practically disregarded, as Davis' invasion of Kentucky and the recent language of his organs about North Carolina must clearly show. To resist the encroachments of such a power, the North would have to be *firmly united* under a real, live national government (not a league or a confederacy dissoluble at pleasure); also, she must come out of the war *unhumiliated* and unweakened by any cession of border territory. She could not afford to begin her separate existence as a conquered country.

Now, how can the Chicago policy satisfy either of these conditions?

In the first place, the "immediate armistice" demanded by it will only be granted by Davis, on condition of our surrendering all the territory south of Mason and Dixon's line, including the capital. The first essential preliminary therefore to the cessation of hostilities, is *our national destruction*, for there is no case in history of a nation surviving the alienation of its capital. When the seat of government becomes permanently attached to another country, the nation is annihilated. Let us, however, in order to give ourselves every chance, suppose either that we shall inaugurate the exceptions to this hitherto universal rule, or that Jefferson Davis shall be graciously pleased to leave us "My Maryland." Alas! this goes but a little way to save us, for the next moment we stumble on something which prevents us from ever having an efficient government — the doctrine of "State Sovereignty."

Doubtless the supporters of this disorganizing invention would like to use it as their master at Richmond has done, merely as a stepping-stone to power, which they might afterward cast aside. But they would find it impossible to lay the spirit of ruin they had evoked. The circumstances are not the same. We have no aristocratic and scarcely any plebeian class, no universal interest like Slavery to bind the States; their "sovereignty" would be for us a fearful reality, and that reality — anarchy.

The principle has been established that one or more states may lawfully and peaceably secede from the general government. As soon as the West is dissatisfied with a high tariff, or New-England with a new one; as soon as Pennsylvania wants a Fugitive Slave Law, or Ohio objects to one — quick, raise the standard of secession! The central government could only expect to maintain its integrity so long as it commanded a majority in every state.

Nay, how can we even hope that this disintegrating process would be confined to the separation of the states from one another? We shall have to descend to much smaller fractions of government before we reach the ultimate atoms. Every one of the larger states contains a variety of conflicting interests. So far from a state possessing any peculiar indivisibility, as the disunionists claim, it is much easier to divide a state than the Union. That states *can* be divided is proved by the fact that they *have* been. Maine was made out of Massachusetts, Vermont out of New York and New Hampshire, and recently West Virginia out of Virginia.

In estimating the destructive forces at work, we must not omit the outside influence of the Southern oligarchy, and the two great powers of Western Europe. The former would have no objections to acquiring the nearest portions of our territory as subject provinces; the latter, remembering our ancient strength, would never rest till we were broken into the smallest pieces. The Europeans have as yet only ventured to work indirectly by intrigue; they would then be emboldened to renew the Mexican experiment.

With all these agencies undermining our government, nothing short of a perpetual miracle could avert its destruction. The country would be *comminuted*. New England has homogeneousness enough to hold together, but all the territory west of the Hudson would be sundered into more fragments than there are states. The Southern pro-slavery portions of Pennsylvania, Ohio, Illinois, and Indiana, would separate from the Northern anti-slavery portions. The city of New York would break off from the state, the western counties from the eastern. Some of these fragments would probably be swallowed up by the Southern oligarchy or empire; the others, if they did not become European dependencies, would go on squabbling among themselves, with no better position in the world than the South American Republics or the petty German states.

The prospect is too terrible and melancholy to contemplate without a shudder, even in imagination; yet we must look at it, for the danger is here, imminent, right over our heads. A Republican Senate may delay it for two years, but from the time that an armistice is under way, from the time that it is *officially proposed* by us our ruin is certain; it may be delayed, but cannot be averted.

One would gladly disbelieve that men can be found so infatuated as to labor day and night for the very purpose of bringing about this catastrophe; but the fact is as undeniable as it is lamentable. They have been condemned too often out of their own mouths; and disagreeable as the investigation may be, the causes of their folly are, at least, not difficult to find.

In the first place, the copperhead is the mean white of the North. The Southern oligarch has established the same superiority over him as over his own plebeian neighbors. The copperhead is the slaveholder's servant, and in seeking to tear the country to pieces, he is only following his master's bidding. Secondly, he is inspired by an ever-craving lust for office and its emoluments, deprived of which, he rages like a beast deprived of its young. Certain politicians of the old Democratic party had come to consider the government of the country as their own property, which they, like the Aldermanic "Ring" of New York, could farm out for their sole personal advantage, and in which no outsider had any right to interfere.

Hence their blind fury against the Republicans, whom they regard as having robbed them of their own particular stealings. "We will never let a single Republican hold office again!" exclaimed a triumphant Western Copperhead, two years ago, when the elections seemed to promise a restoration of his party to power. That was his idea of sending his opponents to Tartarus! For vengeance these men will sacrifice anything. Earth and hell are alike ransacked; no ally is to be despised or unsought; Jefferson Davis, Louis Napoleon, the very English aristocracy whom they used to abuse — all these they beg, and beseech, and implore, and entreat and supplicate to come and help them ruin the country, so that only they may be revenged on those infamous Black Republicans, who have excluded them from the fat places which were their gods!

But General McClellan, it may be said, is not an old politician, or a "Peace-at-any-price" man. He explicitly declares that Union is the only possible basis of peace.

What then?

If we could take the General's letter by itself alone, "pure and simple," as the diplomatists say, then, without much coaxing, we might state the case thus: "The difference between Lincoln and McClellan is that the former wishes the Union restored without slavery, and the latter wishes it restored with slavery. Lincoln tried McClellan's plan for a year and a half, and then was obliged to give it up and adopt the more radical course as a military necessity. McClellan's election would, therefore, *put back* the war, and is so far to be deprecated; still, it does not necessarily involve absolute ruin."

But, alas! we can no more take the letter without the platform as an exposition of the party, than we can take Hebrews without John and James, or *vice versa*, as an exposition of the New Testament. The one complements the other, and it is too plain, on comparing them, that the letter was framed to catch one class of voters and the platform to catch another class, with directly conflicting views. And the comparison brings back to mind those twenty years of compromise and dishonesty, when every candidate was bound to be "available," and every declaration of principles to be Janus-faced; when the Presidents were miserable ciphers, the tools of their own cabinets; when politics were regarded as a mere knaves' scramble for office, and most persons considered government a mere superfluity — not a very ornamental one either — and the whole concern was driving to destruction in the merriest and pleasantest way imaginable.

But in those days there was something to be said for "going in on the general issue," as Seymour calls it. Though the practice was gradually eating away all political honesty and truth, its fatal effects were not yet clearly perceptible, and meanwhile the immediate questions before the people were not of a vital character. If a cabinet did split about a fiscal agent or an ad-valorem duty, nothing very terrible could come of it.

Such is not the case now. The issue between the two branches of the so-called Democratic party is as grave and as clearly drawn as that between death and life. "Immediate cessation of hostilities;" "Union as an indispensable condition of peace." It is no more possible to be in favor of *both* these than it is to serve God and Mammon; and an administration composed of war and peace men, *supposing them all to be in earnest,* would resemble a coach with three horses at each end.

Suppose McClellan elected. He must, according to all precedent, construct a Cabinet from both wings of his party. Then the President and half his Secretaries refuse to make peace except on the basis of Union. As Davis has spurned that condition in advance, they must go on with the war, in a slow, creepy, McClellanish sort of way, to be sure, but still go on with it somehow. But the other half of the Cabinet is, at least, equally earnest for an immediate cessation of hostilities. Will they not, therefore, do all in their power to block, and trammel, and hinder the war — to bring to a stand-still what was already retarded in its progress? *And is it not this exactly what "our adversaries" want?*

No, the alternative between the two candidates, Lincoln and McClellan, and the two parties, the Republican and the so-called Democratic, is *Peace and Union through the War,* or *Permanent separation, Dishonor, and Destruction.* Which will the American people choose?

Pamphlet 52

Joseph P. Thompson

Abraham Lincoln; His Life and Its Lessons. A Sermon, Preached on Sabbath, April 30, 1865. (Loyal Publication Society No. 85)

New York, 1865

[The assassination of Lincoln led to one last burst of Civil War pamphleteering. Eulogies and memorial addresses by the hundreds were delivered throughout the North, in many instances receiving circulation as pamphlets. Most of these not only praised Lincoln in almost Christlike terms but emphasized that the South must pay, and pay dearly, for his murder. These eulogies served a political purpose. Francis Lieber, President of the Loyal Publication Society, wrote to his Radical Republican friend, Senator Charles Sumner, "What is hellish treason in the mouth of a traitor, is true when it comes from loyal lips — it is well that it has happened. Lincoln could not die a more glorious death. It raises him high above others in our annals, and as for our cause — I remember your hasty lines of March 13, ending 'Alas! Alas!' We were fast drifting to namby-pambyism." It is not surprising that the Loyal Publication Society published one of the eulogies, pointing the moral of Lincoln's life and death. It had been preached by Joseph Parrish Thompson (1819–1879), a Congregationalist who from 1847 to 1871 was pastor of the Broadway Tabernacle in New York City. Thompson also for many years was one of the editors of Henry Ward Beecher's *Independent*. In the fall of 1862, he had written with impatience, "We are giving our most precious blood, and yet the President hesitates to use the negro!" [1]]

"The God of Israel said, The Rock of Israel spake to me, He that ruleth over men must be just, ruling in the fear of God: and he shall be as the light of the morning, when the sun riseth, even a morning without clouds; as the tender grass springing out of the earth by clear shining after rain." II. Samuel, XXIII. 3, 4.

[1] [Freidel, *Lieber*, 349, 360. Lieber also persuaded Levi P. Morton, owner of the American News Company, to publish a compilation of Lincoln's speeches, *The Martyr's Monument* . . . (New York, 1865). Another of the Rev. Thompson's sermons was published, *Memorial Services for Three Hundred Thousand Union Soldiers with the Commemorative Discourse* (Loyal Publication Society No. 88, New York, 1865).]

I COUNT it one of the noblest acts in the history of the race, an impressive proof of the progress of human society, that a nation has rendered its spontaneous homage — a tribute without precedent in its own annals, and hardly equalled in the annals of the world — to a man whom it had not yet learned to call great. It teaches us that there is something greater than greatness itself. No inspiration of genius had enrolled him among the few great names of literature; no feats of arms nor strategy upon the field had given him a place among military heroes; no contribution to the science of government, no opportunity of framing a new civil polity for mankind, had raised him to the rank of publicists, of philosophers, or of founders of states. Great he was in his own way, and of a true and rare type of greatness — the less recognized and acknowledged the more it is genuine and divine; — but the people had not begun to accord to him the epithet and the homage of greatness, nor is the loss of a great man to the world the chief calamity in his death. Not greatness, but *grandeur,* is the fitting epithet for the life and character of ABRAHAM LINCOLN; not greatness of endowment or of achievement, but grandeur of soul. Grand in his simplicity and kindliness; grand in his wisdom of resolve, and his integrity of purpose; grand in his trust in principle, and in the principles he made his trust; grand in his devotion to truth, to duty, and to right; grand in his consecration to his country and to God, he rises above the great in genius and in renown, into that foremost rank of moral heroes, of whom the world was not worthy.

Had the pen of prophecy been commissioned to delineate his character and administration, it must have chosen the very words of my text; "just," so that his integrity had passed into a proverb; "ruling in the fear of God," with a religious reverence, humility, and faith marking his private life and his public acts and utterances; bright "as the light of the morning," with native cheerfulness and the serenity of hope; and with a wisdom that revealed itself "as the clear shining after rain;" and gentle, withal, "as the tender grass springing out of the earth;" such was the ruler whose death the nation mourns.

> He hath borne his faculties so meek, hath been
> So clear in his great office, that his virtues
> Will plead like angels, trumpet-tongued, against
> The deep damnation of his taking-off:

And Pity — like heaven's cherubim, horsed
Upon the sightless couriers of the air,
Shall blow the horrid deed in every eye,
That tears shall drown the wind.

The life of Abraham Lincoln, the life by which he has been known to the people, and will be known in history, covers less than five years from the day of his nomination at Chicago, to the day of his assassination at Washington. Before this brief period, though he had been in posts of public life at intervals during thirty years, and had gained a reputation as a clear and forcible political debater, — evincing also a comprehensive faculty for statesmanship — he had done nothing, said nothing, written nothing, that would have given him a place in history or have caused him to be long remembered beyond the borders of his adopted State. And yet for that brief historical life which is now incorporated imperishably with the annals of the American Republic, and shall be woven into the history of the world, while human language shall remain, he was unconsciously preparing, during fifty years of patient toil and discipline.

Those seven years of poverty and obscurity in Kentucky, in which he never saw a church nor a school-house, when he learned to read at the log-cabin of a neighbor, and learned to pray at his mother's knee; those thirteen years of labor and solitude in the primeval forest of Southern Indiana, when the axe, the plow, and the rifle, trained him to manly toil and independence, when the Bible, Pilgrim's Progress, and Esop's Fables, his only library, read by the light of the evening fire, disciplined his intellectual and moral faculties, and a borrowed copy of "Weems' Life of Washington," acquainted him with the father of his country; and when the angel of death sealed and sanctified the lessons of her who taught him to be true and pure and noble, and to walk uprightly in the fear of God; that season of adventure in the rough and perilous navigation of the Mississippi, when the vast extent of his country, and the varieties of its products and its population, were spread out before his opening manhood; the removal to the fat bottom lands of the Sangamon, in the just rising state of Illinois, his farther discipline in farming, fencing, rafting, shop-keeping, while feeling his way toward his vocation in life; his patient self-culture by studious habits under limited opportunities; his observation of the two phases of emigration, northern and southern, that moved over the prairies side by side along different parallels, without mingling; his brief but arduous campaign in the Black Hawk war; his studies in law and politics, and his practical acquaintance with political and professional life; all this diverse and immethodical discipline and experience was his unconscious preparation for leading the nation in the most dark, critical, and perilous period of its history.

Abraham Lincoln was a "self-made man," but in just the sense in which any man of marked individuality is self-made. So far was he from affecting superiority to academic culture or independence of the schools, that it may be said of him as of his great counterpart in character, in aims, and in influence, the plebeian sovereign of England, RICHARD COBDEN, that while he was "a statesman by instinct," and was calmly self-reliant upon any question that he had studied or any principle that he had mastered, he always deferred greatly to those whose opportunities of information and means of culture had been better than his own. The true scholar is "self-made," for he is a scholar only so far as he has digested the works of others by his own processes of thought, and has assimilated the treasures of learning into the independent operations of his own mind. Whether his books or his teachers be few or many, whether his education be in professional schools or in the open school of nature and of practical life, he who would become a power, either in the world of opinion or in the world of action, must make himself a man by self-discipline and culture with such helps as are at his command. Mr. Lincoln made himself, not by despising advantages which he had not, but by using thoroughly such advantages as he had. He did not boast his humble origin, nor the deficiencies of his early education, as a title to popular favor, nor use these as a background to render the more conspicuous his native genius, or the distinction which he had achieved; but while he never forgot his birth, nor repudiated his flat-boat and his rails, nor divorced himself from the "plain people," he yet recognized the value of refinement in manner, and cultivated the highest refinement of feeling. When Mr. Douglas had recourse to personalities in political debate, Mr. Lincoln, in his rejoinder, said, "I set out in this campaign, with the intention of conducting it strictly as a gentleman, in substance, at least, if not in the outside polish. The latter I shall never be, but that which constitutes the inside of a gentleman,

I hope I understand, and am not less inclined to practise than others. It was my purpose and expectation that this canvass would be conducted upon principle and with fairness on both sides, and it shall not be my fault if this purpose and expectation are given up." [2] This self-made man, recognizing his lack of courtly breeding, so far from affecting indifference to good manners, studied to practise the truest gentility of speech and of feeling. Born in the cabin, reared in the forest, a hardy son of toil, whose early associations were with the rougher and coarser phases of life, he made himself a gentleman without even the "petty vices" that sometimes discredit the name; and when raised to the highest social position, proved that the heart is the best teacher of gentility. Never despising a good thing which he had not, he made always the best use of that which he had.

He himself has told how resolutely and thoroughly he sought to discipline his mind in later life by studies and helps of which he was deprived in youth. "In the course of my law-reading," said Mr. Lincoln to a friend,[3] "I constantly came upon the word *demonstrate,* and I asked myself, what do I do when I demonstrate more than when I reason or *prove?*" what is the certainty called demonstration? Having consulted dictionaries and books of reference to little purpose, "I said to myself, 'Lincoln, you can never make a lawyer if you do not understand what demonstrate means.' I had never had but six months' schooling in my life; but now I left my place in Springfield, and went home to my father's and stayed there till I could give any proposition of the six books of Euclid at sight."

Thus, at twenty-five years of age, Abraham Lincoln paid his honest tribute to that very means of mental discipline which experience has placed at the foundation of a college course. He "made himself" by using the same methods of training that Daniel Webster used as a student at Dartmouth, and Edward Everett, at Cambridge; and having determined upon the profession of law, he fenced in his mind to book-study with the same energy and resolution with which he had once split three thousand rails to fence in the fields for tilling. There is no royal road to learning, and Mr. Lincoln's success demonstrates anew the law that persevering labor conquers every obstacle. He did his utmost to repair the deficiencies of his youth in the only way in which they could be remedied, and

[2] Speech at Springfield, Ill., July 17, 1858.
[3] Rev. J. P. Gulliver, Norwich, Conn.

by that conquest over his own mind which was the key to all other victories, he showed himself a man. But for this, his mind would have remained a broad unfenced prairie, and he but a pioneer squatter, making no improvements, or at best a surveyor, staking out some general boundaries of knowledge, but holding no proper sense of ownership in the tract, or in the treasures that lay hidden beneath its surface.

I have thus sought to redeem from perversion that much-abused term, "the self-made man." None can quote Abraham Lincoln in justification of boorishness, of illiterateness, of opinionativeness, of uppishness, as prerogatives of a self-made man; nor can his name and life be used as in any sense an argument against that culture of society and of the schools of which he scarcely knew, until he had attained his majority. The unconscious plan of his life was none the less a *plan* of that Divine mind whose constant guidance he owned; and his first fifty years were a training school of Providence for the five that constitute his historical life.

An analysis of the mental and the moral traits of Mr. Lincoln, will show us how complete was his adaptation for that very period of our national history which he was called to fill, and which he has made so peculiarly his own. His mental processes were characterized by originality, clearness, comprehensiveness, sagacity, logical fitness, acumen, and strength. He was an original thinker; not in the sense of always having new and striking ideas, for such originality may be as daring and dangerous as it is peculiar and rare; but he was original in that his ideas were in some characteristic way his own. However common to other minds, however simple and axiomatic when stated, they bore the stamp of individuality. Not a message or proclamation did he write, not a letter did he pen, which did not carry on the face of it "*Abraham Lincoln,* his mark." He thought out every subject for himself; and he did not commit himself in public upon any subject which he had not made his own by reflection. Hence even familiar thoughts coming before us in the simple rustic garb of his homely speech, seemed fresh and new. He took from the mint of political science the bullion which philosophers had there deposited, and coined it into proverbs for the people. Or, in the great placer of political speculations, he sometimes struck a lode of genuine metal and wrought it with his own hands.

"The Union is older than the Constitution;" "The Union made the Constitution, and not the Constitution the Union."

"Can aliens make treaties easier than friends can make laws?"

"Capital is the fruit of labor, and could never have existed if labor had not first existed."

"In *giving* freedom to the *slave,* we *assure* freedom to the *free.*"

"Often a limb must be amputated to save a life; but a life is never wisely given to save a limb."

What volumes of philosophy, of history, of political economy, of legal and ethical science, are condensed into these pithy sentences, each bearing the mark of Mr. Lincoln's individuality. Much of this individuality of thought was due to the seclusion of his early life from books and schools, and to the meditative habit induced by the solitude of the forest.

To the same quality, and partly to the same cause, may be ascribed the clearness of his mental processes. Compelled in childhood to find out by observation, by experience, by meditative analysis, knowledge in which he had no teacher, and, for lack of external aids, thrown back habitually upon his own thoughts, he knew always the conclusions he had reached, and the process by which he reached them. If he must plunge into the depth of the forest, he took care to trace his path by blazing the trees with his mark; and if sometimes he seemed slow in emerging from the wilderness, it was because when a boy he had learned not to halloo till he was out of the woods. Deliberation and caution were qualities in which he was trained, when compelled to hew out a clearing for a home, within sound of wild beasts and of savage men; but because of these very qualities, he knew always where he stood and how he came there. That communion with nature which has taught Bryant such clear, terse, fitting words in rhythm with her harmonies, taught Abraham Lincoln clear, strong thoughts, whose worth he knew because he had earned them by his own toil.

I am not here dealing in conjecture. His own narrative, already quoted, informs us that when a boy, he used to get irritated when anybody talked to him in a way that he could not understand. "I don't think I ever got angry at anything else in my life; but that always disturbed my temper, and has ever since." Often, after hearing the neighbors talk in his father's house upon subjects he did not comprehend, he would walk up and down his room half the night, trying to make out the exact meaning of their "dark sayings." When once upon such a hunt after an idea, he could not sleep till he had caught it, and then he would "repeat it over and over, and put it in language plain enough for any boy to understand." This simplifying of thought was a passion with him; and in his own pithy words, "I was never easy until I had a thought bounded on the north, and bounded on the south, and bounded on the east, and bounded on the west."

How much the American people will hereafter owe to him for having staked out the boundaries of political ideas hitherto but vaguely comprehended. How conclusive against the right of secession is this clearly-bounded statement of the first inaugural:

> I hold that in the contemplation of universal law and of the Constitution, the Union of these states is perpetual. Perpetuity is implied, if not expressed, in the fundamental law of all national governments. It is safe to assert that no government proper ever had a provision in its own organic law for its own termination. Continue to execute all the express provisions of our national Constitution, and the Union will endure forever, it being impossible to destroy it, except by some action not provided for in the instrument itself.

The opening sentence of his Springfield speech, June 17, 1858, which was the foundation of his great debate with Douglas, bounded the question of nationalizing slavery so clearly and sharply, that Mr. Lincoln had only to repeat that statement from time to time, to clinch every argument of every speech: "A house divided against itself cannot stand. I believe this government cannot endure permanently half slave and half free. I do not expect the Union to be dissolved. I do not expect the house to fall; but I do expect it will cease to be divided. It will become all one thing or all the other."

Mr. Douglas's policy was fast making it "all one thing;" Mr. Lincoln lived to make it, and to see it "all the other!"

Imagination and a poetic sensibility were not wanting in a soul that could conceive the last inaugural or could indite the closing sentence of the first: "The mystic chords of memory, stretching from every battlefield and patriot grave to every living heart and hearthstone all over this broad land, will yet swell the chorus of the Union, when again touched, as surely they will be, by the better angels of our nature."

He was an ardent admirer of Burns, and a discriminating student of Shakespeare.

Enthusiasm was not lacking in a mind that, in the midst of a wasting civil war, could prophecy: "There are already those among us, who, if the Union be preserved, will live to see it contain two hundred and fifty millions. The struggle *of* to-day is not altogether *for* to-day; it is for a vast future also."

But neither enthusiasm nor imagination ever mastered that calm, clear judgment, trained to a cautious self-reliance by the early discipline of the forest-school.

Comprehensiveness was equally characteristic of Mr. Lincoln's views, upon questions where breadth was as important as clearness of vision. Those who have had occasion to consult with him upon public affairs have often remarked, that even in the course of protracted and able deliberations, there would arise no aspect of the question which had not already occurred to the mind of the President, and been allowed its weight in forming his opinion. His judgment was roundabout, encompassing the subject upon every side; it was circumspect — attending to all the circumstances of the case, and patiently investigating its minutiæ. He would not approve the finding of a court-martial without reading over carefully the details of the evidence, and hearing the pleas of the condemned and his friends; and this conscientious legal and judicial habit, applied to questions of state-policy, gave to his views a breadth and solidity beyond the grasp of the mere speculative politician. Hence came that reputation for sagacity and insight, which grew with our observation of the man and with the unfolding of events ratifying his judgment. How often where his seeming hesitancy had tried our patience, have we come to see that he had surveyed the whole question, had anticipated what lay beyond, and was biding his time. His studied silence touching his own intentions, in his replies to speeches of welcome along the route from Springfield to Washington in 1861, was dictated by this comprehensive wisdom. At every point he baffled curiosity and rebuked impatience by avowing his determination not to speak at all upon public questions, until he could speak advisedly. "I deem it just to you, to myself, and to all, that I should see everything, that I should hear everything, that I should have every light that can be brought within my reach, in order that when I do speak, I shall have enjoyed every opportunity to take correct and true grounds; and for this reason I don't propose to speak, at this time, of the policy of the government." [4] This was not the evasiveness of the politician, but the wise reserve of the statesman.

He maintained the same reticence upon the difficult problem of re-organization, which was the burden of his latest public utterance, after the fall of Richmond. His adroit substitution of a story or a witticism for a formal speech, at times when his words were watched and weighed, was but another illustration of this practical sagacity. And when the secret history of the dark periods of the war shall be disclosed, Mr. Lincoln will stand justified before the world, alike for his reticence while waiting for light, and for a policy guided by an almost prophetic insight, when, by patient waiting, he had gained clearness and comprehensiveness of view.

The mental processes of Mr. Lincoln were characterized, moreover, by a logical fitness, keenness, and strength. Not for naught did he master the science of demonstration. His speeches are a *catena* of propositions and proofs that bind the mind to his conclusions as soon as his premises are conceded. In his great debate with Mr. Douglas — a debate accompanied with all the excitements of a political canvass, and in which he was called upon to reply to his opponent in the hearing of eager thousands — it is remarkable that he never had occasion to retract or even to qualify any of his positions, that he never contradicted himself, nor abandoned an argument that he had once assumed. His caution and circumspection led him to choose his words and to state only that which he could maintain. His clear and comprehensive survey of his subject made him the master of his own position; and his calm, strong logic, and his keen power of dissection, made him a formidable antagonist. He who had such force of resolution, that in full manhood, after he had been a member of the State legislature, he could go to school to Euclid to learn how to demonstrate, was likely to reason to some purpose when he had laid down his propositions.

But it was mainly his adherence to ethical principles in political discussions that gave such point and force to his reasonings; for no politician of this generation has applied Christian ethics to questions of public policy with more of honesty, of consistency, or of

[4] Speech to the Legislature of New York.

downright earnestness. Standing in the old Independence Hall at Philadelphia, he said, "All the political sentiments I entertain have been drawn, so far as I have been able to draw them, from the sentiments which originated in and were given to the world from this hall. — I have never had a feeling, politically, that did not spring from the sentiments embodied in the Declaration of Independence." [5] But the sentiments of the Declaration which Mr. Lincoln emphasized are not simply political ideas — they are ethical principles. That "all men are *created* equal; that they are endowed by their Creator with certain inalienable rights; that among these are life, liberty, and the pursuit of happiness" — these are principles of natural ethics, sustained by the august sanctions of that God who is "no respecter of persons." And it was as truths of moral obligation that Abraham Lincoln adopted them as the rule of his political faith. He entered into public life, thirty years ago, with the distinct avowal of the doctrine whose final ratification by the people he has sealed with his blood — that "the institution of slavery is founded on both injustice and bad policy." [6] His whole life was true to that conviction. His great campaign for the senatorship, in 1858, was conducted throughout upon moral grounds. "I confess myself as belonging to that class in the country who contemplate slavery as a moral, social, and political evil, having due regard for its actual existence among us and the difficulties of getting rid of it in any satisfactory way, and to all the constitutional obligations which have been thrown about it; but nevertheless, desire a policy that looks to the prevention of it as a wrong, and looks hopefully to the time when as a wrong it may come to an end." [7] "If slavery is not wrong nothing is wrong." [8]

"One only thing," said he, in his speech at Cooper Institute, "will satisfy our opponents. Cease to call slavery *wrong*, and join them in calling it *right*. If our sense of duty forbids this, then let us stand by our duty, fearlessly and effectively. Let us be diverted by none of those sophistical contrivances wherewith we are so industriously plied and belabored — contrivances, such as groping for some middle ground between the right and the wrong, vain as the search for a man who should be neither a living man nor a dead man —

[5] Speech of 21st February, 1861.
[6] Protest in Illinois House of Representatives, March 3, 1837.
[7] Speech at Galesburgh, October 7, 1858.
[8] Letter to A. G. Hodges, Esq., of Kentucky.

such as a policy of 'don't care,' on a question about which all true men do care — such as Union appeals, beseeching true Union men to yield to disunionists, reversing the Divine rule, and calling, not the sinners, but the righteous to repentance — such as invocations of Washington, imploring men to unsay what Washington said, and undo what Washington did. Neither let us be slandered from our duty by false accusations against us, nor frightened from it by menaces of destruction to the government, nor of dungeons to ourselves. Let us have faith that right makes might; and in that faith, let us to the end, dare to do our duty, as we understand it."

Mr. Lincoln's logic was pointed with wit, and his ethical reasoning was often set home by a pithy story. The reputation of a story-teller and a jester was turned by his opponents to his disparagement; but his stories were philosophy in parables, and his jests were morals. If sometimes they smacked of humble life, this was due not to his tastes but to his early associations. His wit was always used with point and purpose; for the boy who committed all Esop's fables to memory, had learned too well the use of story and of parable to forego that keen weapon in political argument. The whole people took his witty caution "not to swop horses in the middle of the stream."

The base-born plea that social amalgamation would follow the emancipation of the negro, he met by a rare stroke of wit: "I do not understand that because I do not want a negro woman for a slave, I must necessarily want her for a wife. My understanding is that I can just let her alone. I am now in my fiftieth year, and I certainly never have had a black woman for either a slave or a wife. So it seems to me quite possible for us to get along without making either slaves or wives of negroes. I recollect but one distinguished advocate of the perfect equality of the races, and that is Judge Douglas's old friend, Colonel Richard M. Johnson." [9]

Yet Mr. Lincoln's wit was never malicious nor rudely personal. Once when Mr. Douglas had attempted to parry an argument by impeaching the veracity of a senator whom Mr. Lincoln had quoted, he answered, that the question was not one of veracity, but simply one of argument. "By a course of reasoning, Euclid proves that all the angles in a triangle are equal to two right angles. Now, if you

[9] Speech at Columbus, February, 1859.

undertake to disprove that proposition, would you prove it to be false by calling Euclid a liar?" [10]

II. Passing from the intellectual traits of Mr. Lincoln to his moral qualities, we find in these the same Providential preparation for his work, through long years of hardy training. He was of a meek and a patient spirit — both prime elements in a strong character. It might almost be said of him, as it was said of Moses, that "he was meek above all the men which were upon the face of the earth." The early discipline of poverty, toil, and sorrow, accompanied with maternal lessons of submission to God, had taught him to labor and to wait in the patience of hope. It was a household saying of his mother, when times were hard and days were dark, "It isn't best to borrow too much trouble. We must have faith in God." And so Abraham learned that "it is good for a man that he bear the yoke in his youth; and it is good that a man should both hope and quietly wait for the salvation of the Lord." And when the yoke of a nation's burdens and sorrows was laid upon his shoulders, his gentle, patient spirit accepted it without faltering and without repining. He did not borrow too much trouble, but had faith in God. Neither the violence of enemies, nor the impatience and distrust of friends, could irritate him; neither the threats of traitors, nor the zeal of partisans, could disturb his equanimity, or urge him faster than Providence, speaking through the logic of events, would seem to lead him. "Thy gentleness," said the Psalmist, "hath made me great;" and a certain divine gentleness had possessed and fortified the soul of Abraham Lincoln.

Cheerfulness was with him a moral quality as well as the native cast of his temperament. It sprang from the consciousness of sincerity, from good will toward men, and from habitual trust in God. His playful humor sometimes belied him; since no man was farther removed from levity and frivolity of mind. A thoughtful earnestness pervaded his being — an earnestness that sometimes verged upon sadness, yet never sank into moroseness. It was a cheerful earnestness: and while cheerfulness was the tone of his temperament, he cultivated this quality for the relief of his own mind, and for the stimulation of others against despondency.

I shall ever cherish among the brightest memories of life, an hour

[10] Speech at Charleston, September 18, 1858.

in his working-room last September, which was one broad sheet of sunshine. He had spent the morning poring over the returns of a court-martial upon capital cases, and studying to decide them according to truth; and upon the entrance of a friend, he threw himself into an attitude of relaxation, and sparkled with good humor. I will not repeat, lest they should be misconstrued, his trenchant witticisms upon political topics now gone by; yet one of these can wound no living patriot. I spoke of the rapid rise of Union feeling since the promulgation of the Chicago platform, and the victory at Atlanta; and the question was started, which had contributed the most to the reviving of Union sentiment — the victory or the platform. "I guess," said the President, "it was the victory; at any rate I'd rather have that repeated."

Being informed of the death of John Morgan, he said, "Well, I wouldn't crow over anybody's death; but I can take this as *resignedly* as any dispensation of Providence. Morgan was a coward, a nigger-driver; a low creature, such as you Northern men know nothing about."

The political horizon was still overcast, but he spoke with unaffected confidence and cheerfulness of the result; saying with emphasis, "I rely upon the religious sentiment of the country, which I am told is very largely for me."

Even in times of deepest solicitude, he maintained this cheerful serenity before others. It may be said of him, as of his great prototype, William of Orange, "His jocoseness was partly natural, partly intentional. In the darkest hours of his country's trial, he affected a serenity which he did not always feel, so that his apparent gayety at momentous epochs was even censured by dullards, who could not comprehend its philosophy. He went through life bearing the load of a people's sorrows upon his shoulders with a smiling face."

It is pleasant to know that what was, perhaps, the last official act of the President, before the fatal night, was performed in this spirit of joyousness. The Governor of Maryland called upon him with a friend late on Friday, and found him very cheerful over the state of the country; at the close of the interview, one of the visitors asked a little favor for a friend; the President wrote the necessary order, and said, "Anything now to make the people happy."

His kindness and sensibility were proverbial almost to a fault. Yet no other single trait so well exhibits the majesty of his soul; for it was not a sentimental tenderness — the mere weakness of a sympathetic nature — but a kindness that proceeded from an intelligent sympathy and good will for humanity, and a Christian hatred of all injustice and wrong. He once said in a political speech: "The Savior, I suppose, did not expect that any human creature could be perfect as the Father in heaven; but He said, As your Father in Heaven is perfect, be ye also perfect. He set that up as a standard, and he who did most towards reaching that standard attained the highest degree of moral perfection." With a noble contempt for political prejudices, and with a touching moral simplicity, Mr. Lincoln avowed this principle in his treatment of the negro: "In pointing out that more has been given you [by the Creator], you cannot be justified in taking away the little which has been given him. If God gave him but little, that little let him enjoy. In the right to eat the bread, without the leave of anybody else, which his own hand earns, he is my equal, and the equal of Judge Douglas, and the equal of every living man."

In his highest prosperity he never forgot his kindred with men of low estate. Amid all the cares of office, his ear was always open to a tale of sorrow or of wrong, and his hand was always ready to relieve suffering and to remedy injustice. I seem to see him now, leaning against the railing that divides the war-office from the White House, while the carriage is waiting at the door, and listening to the grievance of a plain man, then sitting down upon the coping and writing on a card an order to have the case investigated and remedied. An undignified position, do you say? It was the native dignity of kindness.

Sometimes a personal sorrow opens a little rift through which you can look down into the depths of a great soul. I once looked thus, for an instant, into the soul of RICHARD COBDEN. Having had some slight association with Mr. Cobden in England upon the question of common-school education, when he came here in 1859, I attended him to some of our public schools. On leaving the Thirteenth street school, I inquired if he would go over to the Free Academy. "No," said he, with a quick emphasis, "you must not take me to any more boys' schools — I can't bear it." The drop that trembled in his eye interpreted his meaning. Just before leaving home he had laid his only son, a bright lad of fourteen, in the church-yard where he himself now lies. Like Burke, "he had begun to live in an inverted order; they who ought to have succeeded him had gone before him." I had honored Mr. Cobden before, I have loved him since.

In the spring of 1862, the President spent several days at Fortress Monroe, awaiting military operations upon the Peninsula. As a portion of the cabinet were with him, that was temporarily the seat of government, and he bore with him constantly the burden of public affairs. His favorite diversion was reading Shakespeare, whom he rendered with fine discrimination of emphasis and feeling. One day (it chanced to be the day before the taking of Norfolk), as he sat reading alone, he called to his Aide in the adjoining room, "You have been writing long enough, Colonel, come in here: I want to read you a passage in Hamlet." He read the discussion on ambition between Hamlet and his courtiers,[11] and the soliloquy, in which conscience debates of a future state.[12] This was followed by passages from Macbeth. Then opening to King John, he read from the third act the passage in which Constance bewails her imprisoned, lost boy:

> (The king commands) Bind up your tresses.
> *Con.* Yes, that I will; and wherefore will I do it?
> I tore them from their bonds; and cried aloud,
> O that these hands could so redeem my son
> As they have given these hairs their liberty!
> But now I envy at their liberty,
> And will again commit them to their bonds,
> Because my poor child is a prisoner:
> .　　.　　.　　.　　.　　.　　never, never
> Must I behold my pretty Arthur more.
> 　　*K. Philip.* You are as fond of grief, as of your child.
> 　　*Con.* Grief fills the room up of my absent child,
> Lies in his bed, walks up and down with me,
> Puts on his pretty looks, repeats his words,
> Remembers me of all his gracious parts,
> Stuffs out his vacant garments with his form.
> Then, have I reason to be fond of grief.
>
> 　　✿　　✿　　✿　　✿　　✿
>
> O Lord, my boy, my Arthur, my fair son!
> My life, my joy, my food, my all the world!
> My widow-comfort, and my sorrow's cure.[13]

---

[11] Act ii. scene 2.
[12] Act iii. scene 1.
[13] Act iii. scene 4.

He closed the book, and recalling the words —

> And, father cardinal, I have heard you say
> That we shall see and know our friends in heaven:
> If that be true, I shall see my boy again ——

Mr. Lincoln said, "Colonel, did you ever dream of a lost friend, and feel that you were holding sweet communion with that friend, and yet have a sad consciousness that it was not a reality? — just so I dream of my boy Willie." Overcome with emotion, he dropped his head on the table, and sobbed aloud. Truly does Col. Cannon observe, that "this exhibition of parental affection and grief before a comparative stranger, showed not only his tender nature, but his great simplicity and naturalness — the transparency of his character. It was most suggestive." [14]

It was meet that Willie should be borne with him in his last long journey, to rest hereafter in the same tomb; for, believe me, he would have prized the love of his little Willie above all the homage of the nation's tears.

Akin to this kindliness and sensibility was his magnanimity of soul. "I would despise myself," said he in his debate with Douglas, "if I supposed myself ready to deal less liberally with an adversary than I was willing to be treated myself." And again he said: "If I have stated anything erroneous — if I have brought forward anything not a fact — it needed only that Judge Douglas should point it out, it will not even ruffle me to take it back. I do not deal in that way."

How magnanimously he disclaimed personal praise, and accorded honor to others. You will at once recall his letter to General Grant after the capture of Vicksburgh:

"I do not remember that you and I ever met personally. I write this now as a grateful acknowledgment of the almost inestimable service you have done the country. I write to say a word further. . . . When you took Port Gibson, Grand Gulf, and vicinity, I thought you should go down the river and join Gen. Banks, and when you turned northward, east of the Big Black, I feared it was a mistake. I now wish to make the personal acknowledgment, that you were right and I was wrong."

How gently he assuaged the tumult of party strifes by his tone of magnanimity toward his defeated opponent, in acknowledging a

[14] I am indebted for this incident to Col. Le Grand B. Cannon, then of Gen. Wool's Staff.

popular ovation rendered him upon his re-election to the Presidency.

Such was the whole spirit of his public life, culminating at last in an utterance which shall be immortal — "WITH MALICE TOWARD NONE, WITH CHARITY FOR ALL."

The inflexible integrity of Mr. Lincoln has imprinted itself upon the heart and the history of the American people, in that familiar but honorable epithet *"Honest* Abe." His was not simply a commercial honesty, in dollars and cents, but honesty in opinion, honesty in speech, honesty of purpose, honesty in action. "Always speak the truth, my son," said his mother to him, when in her Sabbath readings she expounded the ninth commandment. "I do tell the truth," was his uniform reply.

When Douglas attempted to impeach a statement of a brother senator, who was Mr. Lincoln's personal friend, Lincoln replied, "I am ready to indorse him, because, neither in that thing nor in any other, in all the years that I have known Lyman Trumbull, have I known him to fail of his word, or tell a falsehood, large or small:" and that to Abraham Lincoln was a certificate of character.

His integrity carried him through arduous political campaigns, without the shadow of deviation from principle. He adopted great principles and by these he was willing to live or to die. His debate with Douglas, as I before said, was throughout a struggle for principle — the principle that slavery was wrong, and therefore that the nation should not sanction it nor suffer its extension. "I do not claim," he said, "to be unselfish; I do not pretend that I would not like to go to the United States Senate; I make no such hypocritical pretence, but I do say to you that in this mighty issue, it is nothing to you, nothing to the mass of the people of the nation, whether or not Judge Douglas or myself shall ever be heard of after this night; it may be a trifle to either of us, but in connection with this mighty question, upon which hang the destinies of the nation perhaps, it is absolutely nothing."

When about to assume the grave responsibilities of the Presidency, he said to his fellow citizens, "I promise you that I bring to the work a sincere heart. Whether I will bring a head equal to that heart will be for future times to determine." [15] That his head was equal to his task all now agree; but it is far more to his honor that through all the temptations of office, he held fast his integrity.

[15] Speech at Philadelphia, February 20, 1861.

One who was much with him, testifies that "in everything he did he was governed by his conscience, and when ambition intruded, it was thrust aside by his conviction of right." What he said he did, "without shadow of turning." He was as firm for the right as he was forbearing toward the wrong-doer. How solemn his appeal to the seceders, at the close of his first inaugural: "You have no oath registered in heaven to destroy the government; while I shall have the most solemn one to preserve, protect and defend it." That oath he kept with all honesty and fidelity.

This honesty of principle inspired him with true moral heroism. Abraham Lincoln always met his duty as calmly as he met his death. He knew, at any time in the last four years, that to do his duty would be to court death; but in his first message he laid down the moral consideration that overruled all personal fears: "As a private citizen the Executive could not have consented that these institutions shall perish; much less could he, in betrayal of so vast and so sacred a trust as these free people had confided to him. He felt that he had no moral right to shrink, nor even to count the chances of his own life in what might follow. In full view of his great responsibility he has so far done what he has deemed his duty. Having thus chosen our course without guile, and with pure purpose, let us renew our trust in God, and go forward without fear and with manly hearts."

Bishop Simpson has quoted from a speech of Mr. Lincoln, in 1839, a declaration of the most heroic patriotism:

"Of the slave power he said, Broken by it? I too may be asked to bow to it. I never will. The probability that we may fail in the struggle, ought not to deter us from the support of a cause which I deem to be just. It shall not deter me. If I ever feel the soul within me elevate and expand to dimensions not wholly unworthy of its Almighty architect, it is when I contemplate the cause of my country deserted by all the world beside, and I standing up boldly and alone, and hurling defiance at her victorious oppressors. Here, without contemplating consequences, before high Heaven, and in the face of the world, I swear eternal fidelity to the just cause, as I deem it, of the land of my life, my liberty, and my love."

With what a lofty courage, too, did he stand by the rights and liberties of those to whom he was pledged by his proclamation of January 1, 1863.

What nobler words could be inscribed upon his monument than

these from his last message: "I repeat the declaration made a year ago, that while I remain in my present position I shall not attempt to retract or modify the emancipation proclamation. Nor shall I return to slavery any person who is free by the terms of that proclamation, or by any of the acts of Congress. If the people should, by whatever mode or means, make it an executive duty to re-enslave such persons, another, and not I, must be their instrument to perform it."

It was that decree of emancipation that inspired the hatred that compassed his murder. Yet from the day of his nomination he had been marked for a violent death; and knowing this, he had devoted his life to the cause of liberty. At Independence Hall, in Philadelphia, he said, in 1861, "Can this country be saved upon the basis of the sentiment embodied in the Declaration of Independence? If it can, I will consider myself one of the happiest men in the world, if I can help to save it. If it cannot be saved on that principle, it will be truly awful. But if this country cannot be saved without giving up that principle, I was about to say *I would rather be assassinated on this spot than surrender it.* I have said nothing but what I am willing to live by, and, if it be the pleasure of Almighty God, to die by."

A calm trust in God was the loftiest, worthiest characteristic in the life of Abraham Lincoln. He had learned this long ago. "I would rather Abe would be able to read the Bible than to own a farm, if he can't have but one," said his godly mother. That Bible was Abraham Lincoln's guide. Mr. Jay informs me, that being on the steamer which conveyed the governmental party from Fortress Monroe to Norfolk, after the destruction of the Merrimac, while all on board were excited by the novelty of the excursion and by the incidents that it recalled, he missed the President from the company, and, on looking about, found him in a quiet nook, reading a well-worn Testament. Such an incidental revelation of his religious habits is worth more than pages of formal testimony.

The constant recognition of God in his public documents shows how completely his mind was under the dominion of religious faith. This is never a common-place formalism nor a misplaced cant. To satisfy ourselves of Mr. Lincoln's Christian character, we have no need to resort to apocryphal stories that illustrate the assurance of his visitors quite as much as the simplicity of his faith; we have but to follow internal evidences, as the workings of his soul reveal themselves through his own published utterances. On leaving Springfield for the Capital, he said:

A duty devolves upon me which is, perhaps, greater than that which has devolved upon any other man since the days of Washington. He never would have succeeded except for the aid of Divine Providence, upon which he at all times relied. I feel that I cannot succeed without the same Divine aid which sustained him, and on the same Almighty Being I place my reliance for support; and I hope you, my friends, will all pray that I may receive that Divine assistance, without which I cannot succeed, but with which, success is certain.

He knew himself to be surrounded by a religious community who were acquainted with his life; and his words were spoken in all sincerity.

At Gettysburg, with a grand simplicity worthy of Demosthenes, he dedicated himself with religious earnestness to the great task yet before him, in humble dependence upon God. Owning the power of vicarious sacrifice, he said, "We cannot dedicate, we cannot consecrate, we cannot hallow this ground. The brave men, living and dead, who struggled here, have consecrated it far above our power to add or detract. The world will little note, nor long remember, what we say here, but it can never forget what they did here. It is for us, the living, rather, to be dedicated here to the unfinished work that they have thus far so nobly carried on."

We distinctly trace the growth of this feeling of religious consecration in his public declarations: "We can but press on, guided by the best light God gives us, trusting that in his own good time and wise way, all will be well. Let us not be oversanguine of a speedy, final triumph. Let us be quite sober. Let us diligently apply the means, never doubting that a just God, in His own good time, will give us the rightful result." [16] "The nation's condition is not what either party or any man desired or expected. God alone can claim it. Whither it is tending seems plain. If God now wills the removal of a great wrong, and wills also that we of the North, as well as you of the South, shall pay fairly for our complicity in that wrong, impartial history will find therein new cause to attest and revere the justice and goodness of God." [17] This devout feeling culminated at length in that sublime confession of faith, of hu-

[16] Letter to Kentucky.
[17] Letter to A. G. Hodges, April, 1864.

mility, of dependence, of consecration, known as his last inaugural. It is said, upon good authority, that had he lived, he would have made a public profession of his faith in Christ. But Abraham Lincoln needed no other confession than that which he made on the 4th of March last in the hearing of all nations.

A Christian lady, who was profoundly impressed with the religious tone of the inaugural, requested, through a friend in Congress, that the President would give her his autograph by the very pen that wrote that now immortal document, adding that her sons should be taught to repeat its closing paragraph with their catechism. The President, with evident emotion, replied, "She shall have my signature, and with it she shall have that paragraph. It comforts me to know that my sentiments are supported by the Christian ladies of our country."

His pastor at Washington, after being near him steadily, and with him often for more than four years, bears this testimony: "I speak what I know and testify what I have often heard him say, when I affirm the guidance and the mercy of God were the props on which he humbly and habitually leaned;" and that "his abiding confidence in God and in the final triumph of truth and righteousness through Him and for His sake, was his noblest virtue, his grandest principle, the secret alike of his strength, his patience, and his success."

Thus trained of God for his great work, and called of God in the fullness of time, how grandly did Abraham Lincoln meet his responsibilities and round up his life. How he grew under pressure. How often did his patient heroism in the earlier years of the war serve us in the stead of victories. He carried our mighty sorrows; while he never knew rest, nor the enjoyment of office. How wisely did his cautious, sagacious, comprehensive judgment deliver us from the perils of haste. How clearly did he discern the guiding hand and the unfolding will of God. How did he tower above the storm in his unselfish patriotism, resolved to save the unity of the nation. And when the day of duty and of opportunity came, how firmly did he deal the last great blow for liberty, striking the shackles from three million slaves; while "upon this, sincerely believed to be an act of *justice*, warranted by the Constitution (upon military necessity), he invoked the considerate judgment of mankind, and the gracious favor of Almighty God." Rightly did he regard this Proclamation as the central act of his administration, and the central fact of the nineteenth century. Let it be engraved upon our walls, upon our hearts; let the scene adorn the rotunda of the Capitol — henceforth a sacred shrine of liberty. It needed only that the seal of martyrdom upon such a life should cause his virtues to be transfigured before us in imperishable grandeur, and his name to be emblazoned with heaven's own light upon that topmost arch of fame, which shall stand when governments and nations fall.

> Moderate, resolute,
> Whole in himself, a common good.
> Mourn for the man of amplest influence,
> Yet clearest of ambitious crime,
> Our greatest yet with least pretence
> Rich in saving common-sense,
> And as the greatest only are,
> In his simplicity sublime.
>
> .   .   .   .
>
> Who never sold the truth, to serve the hour,
> Nor paltered with Eternal God for power
> Who let the turbid streams of rumor flow
> Thro' either babbling world of high and low;
> Whose life was work, whose language rife
> With rugged maxims hewn from life;
> Who never spoke against a foe.

And to this, borrowed of England's laureate, we add the spontaneous offering of our own uncrowned bard, the laureate of the people:

> Oh, slow to smite and swift to spare,
>   Gentle and merciful and just!
> Who, in the fear of God, didst bear
>   The sword of power, a nation's trust!
>
> In sorrow by thy bier we stand,
>   Amid the awe that hushes all,
> And speak the anguish of a land
>   That shook with horror at thy fall.
>
> Thy task is done; the bond are free;
>   We bear thee to an honored grave,
> Whose proudest monument shall be
>   The broken fetters of the slave.

Pure was thy life; its bloody close
Hath placed thee with the sons of light,
Among the noble host of those
Who perished in the cause of Right.

But this grand life imposes upon us lessons of duty as well as claims of honor. And we best honor the life itself by worthily fulfilling its lessons.

1. The life of Mr. Lincoln should incite us to unswerving fidelity to our institutions of civil government, as identified both with the existence of the nation and with the welfare of mankind. Standing by his grave we must renew for ourselves the vow which he made in our name by the graves of our dead at Gettysburgh — resolving that "the dead shall not have died in vain — that the nation shall, under God, have a new birth of freedom, and that the government of the people, by the people, and for the people, shall not perish from the earth."

In his first message, he taught us that on the side of the Union, the struggle was for "maintaining in the world, that form and substance of government, whose leading object is to elevate the condition of men, to lift artificial weights from all shoulders, to clear the paths of laudable pursuit for all, to afford all an unfettered start and a fair chance in the race of life — this is the leading object of the government for which we contend."

And again, in his second message, he showed that "the insurrection was largely, if not exclusively, a war upon the first principle of popular government — the rights of the people." We have saved that principle, not for ourselves alone, but for mankind.

To be true to Abraham Lincoln, is to be true to the American Union, as the inviolate and the inviolable heritage of freedom; true to that great idea of a nationality undivided, and of a sovereignty in the Nation above the State. In his own piquant words, we must put down effectually, "the assumed right of a State to rule all which is *less* than itself, and *ruin* all which is larger than itself." [18]

2. We must take measures for the utter extinction of slavery, by severing every tie of the slave-oligarchy to the polity and to the soil of the country. We must end this rebellion so effectually, that not a solitary root or fibre of it shall remain to plague us in the future. We owe it to ourselves, in view of all that we have done

---

[18] Speech to the Legislature of Indiana, 1861.

and suffered in the cause; we owe it to our dead, who gave themselves for our salvation; we owe it to our posterity, who shall reap
what we now sow; we owe it to mankind, to whom we should now
furnish an example of a free, just, and peaceful government; and
we owe it to the memory of the leader and martyr who hath consecrated our cause by his great sacrifice; that we guard effectually
against the recurrence of a war of opposing sections or civilizations.
And for this it is indispensable that we stamp this rebellion as a
crime, that we measure out to its sponsors and abettors appropriate
penalties, and that we root out the whole system of society by
which it was inspired, and for which it has been maintained — for
this conspiracy was a CRIME, without excuse on the part of its
leaders, whether of ignorance, of provocation, or of motive; without color or mitigation from beginning to end. It should be held
up as a crime to the execration of our children and of coming ages;
and to this end we must condemn the conspirators by a national
judgment that will ever after deter unprincipled and unscrupulous
demagogues from a like attempt. It is not enough that they who
have brought this terrible ruin upon the country be left simply to
share its natural consequences to themselves. There must be a
verdict against the crime, and a judgment upon the criminals that
shall stand as a warning, dark, frowning, terrible, to all agitators
and conspirators within the bosom of the Republic. No timid or
time-serving policy, no weak and sickly sentimentalism, no pity for
the criminals themselves, no good-natured forbearance toward a
section or class once courted with political favoritism, should be
suffered to restrain the judgment due to this stupendous crime.
Now since slavery inspired the rebellion, and since this was in turn
inspired by pride of social caste, and by lust of political domination, the axe should be laid at the roots of the system that gave to
the conspiracy its pretext and its vitality. The penalty of a voluntary and determined participation in the rebellion should be the
peremptory alienation of the estates of the conspirators, and the
perpetual disfranchisement of the conspirators themselves. This I
urge as the most radical and effective form of justice, and as indispensable to the peace of the country and to the safety of liberty.

Two popular cries, "Slavery is dead," and "Hang the traitors,"
are diverting the public mind from that broader and sterner justice
which is needed for the destruction of the conspiracy itself, and as

a warning against another such attempt, in after-times. Slavery is not dead. In two States it remains untouched by the Proclamation of Emancipation. In nearly the whole region of the rebellion the local laws which gave it life are unrepealed; and should the rebel States be restored to their status in the Union without the previous dispossession and disfranchisement of the rebels themselves, those laws would confront the Proclamation in the courts. The Constitutional Amendment prohibiting slavery is not yet sanctioned by the requisite number of States, nor even by all the Northern States. Southern planters professing loyalty to the Union have been known to boast that they would recover their slaves, and they would find politicians at the North ready to aid them, and to divide the country upon that issue. Slavery is not dead.

Now, hanging a few traitors will not kill slavery; and our danger is that slavery itself will slip through the noose, and that when it shall begin to revive from the shock, many who are now shouting "Hang the traitors," will take up the old familiar cry, "Hang the abolitionists." It is because of this now imminent peril, a peril that makes peace more threatening than war, that I would urge upon all who love Peace, Liberty, and Union, a measure dictated not by leniency toward criminals, but by the broadest considerations of justice and of public policy. As a help to the discussion of this measure, I submit the following propositions:

(1.) Capital punishment is the appropriate penalty for the crime of murder, and civil government is clothed with the sword for the punishment of crimes against the life of society.

(2.) The conspirators against the government of the United States should have justice meted out to them as criminals against society and the state.

(3.) Since the Constitution, which carefully defines the crime of treason, leaves it to Congress to declare its penalty, we are not shut up to any single form of penalty against these traitors; but should a capital indictment under the old law be waived, or should a jury fail of a capital conviction, the several damnatory acts of Congress during the Rebellion are still valid as penal ordinances.

(4.) There can be no doubt that the leading traitors deserve to forfeit their lives for their crime.

(5.) There can hardly be a doubt, that the execution of the leaders within ninety days after the conspiracy broke out, would have crushed the conspiracy by inspiring terror; but slavery would have remained intact, the mob by this time would have been at its old work of hanging negroes and abolitionists, and the seeds of rebellion would have ripened into another crop of traitors, nourished from the blood of men reputed martyrs for the South and its institutions.

(6.) The rebellion — which, at the outset, was simply a traitorous conspiracy — had grown to the gigantic proportions of a civil war, long evenly balanced in the scales of battle. The great powers of Europe recognised the rebels as belligerents, and we were compelled to an indirect recognition of them so far forth as the exchange of prisoners; and, moreover, our late President, with the Secretary of State, held informal consultations with their commissioners upon terms of peace. Now, there is a growing tendency in the civilized world to place political crimes in a different category from common crimes against person and life; and, in dealing with the rebel leaders, we must have due respect to the enlightened sentiment of Christendom, and be able to justify ourselves in the verdict of impartial history. The question is not simply what the traitors deserve, but, what form of penalty is now best for the safety of the country and for our good name in the coming centuries; and, therefore, not for their sakes but for our own, we can afford to let them live, seeing that we can inflict upon them a penalty more trenchant and more radical, dooming them to obscurity and ignominy, without exciting sympathy for them at home or abroad.

Moreover, since those who have been in arms against the government — which is the overt act of treason — are virtually set free of the gallows by the military action of the government itself, would it satisfy the claims of justice to hang the officials of the bubble Confederacy? and — what is of more consequence — would this break down effectually the spirit of the rebellion, and root out its motive and cause?

No doubt these conspirators richly deserve such a fate, and should it befall them I would accept it with becoming resignation. But the question is one of an enlightened and comprehensive policy for the nation. We must be careful to keep our hands clean of even the imputation of a passionate revenge; and we must be careful, also, to keep our soil clear of the seeds of rancor and of treason for the future. It is worthy of consideration, then, whether the mode of dealing with the traitors that I here propose, will not be more effectual than would be the capital execution of a few; for I take it that the public mind would soon be glutted with such executions, and then there might come a reaction of pity and of sympathy, that would allow the real authors of the conspiracy, as a class — the slaveocracy — to go unwhipt of justice. But, shall the way be open for Lee, or any of the paroled conspirators, to resume their citizenship within the Union they have labored to destroy?

I do not ask, could we *trust* them again in the places of power they once desecrated by perjury and treason. I do not ask could there be good fellowship with them again in the Senate? confidence in them in the Cabinet? I ask, is there nothing due to justice? Nothing due to the dignity of the nation? Nothing due to history? Nothing due to posterity? We must brand this monster crime with a penalty that will be felt, with an infamy that will never be forgotten at home or abroad.

Commonly, but not invariably, capital punishment is the most dreaded as well as the most ignominious form of penalty. But there are cases in which penalty comes in forms more dreadful and more ignominious than the scaffold. Our first feeling was one of regret that the murderer of the President was not brought to the gallows. But he would have then had the histrionic effect of a state trial, and perhaps a degree of pity, such as even the greatest criminal draws to himself after the first hideousness of his crime has passed. Now, what a fate was his! I shudder at the terrors of Divine retribution. In bodily anguish and tortured by fear, skulking from the view of men, with none daring to screen him nor to give him succor, dying daily a thousand deaths, tracked at length to his hiding place, smoked out like some noisome beast from his lair, and shot down without mercy, yet knowing his miserable fate, — the nerves of motion paralyzed, the nerves of feeling intensified, so that he begged for death as a relief from misery — and at the very time that the honored body of his victim was being borne through the land amid the mournful tributes of the whole people, his unpitied carcase, unshrouded and uncoffined, was carried out into the darkness, the stars forbearing to look upon it, the earth and the sea refusing it burial, while for every tear that dropped upon the bier of the martyr President, an execration fell upon the assassin, as he sank into the fathomless unknown. There may be a justice more terrible than the scaffold — or there may be a living infamy worse than death.

If now we strip all who have knowingly, freely, and persistently upheld this rebellion, of their property and their citizenship, they will become beggared and infamous outcasts; fleeing the country, not as hunted exiles courting sympathy abroad and creating sympathy at home, but like Cain, with the brand upon their foreheads, and with a punishment greater than they can bear. They will not dare to return to the South, for their wealth being gone, and their social and political power broken, they would find none so poor to do them reverence; nor would they risk their lives among the common people whom they had deceived and ruined. The landed aristocracy which had fostered slavery being thus evicted of the soil, and the political power that had upheld it being evicted of the state, slavery would die beyond the possibility of resuscitation. The Union people of the South, and the mass of the common people, won back by kindness, uniting with our veterans and Northern emigrants, would plant farms and villages upon the old slave plantations; and with our help in schools and churches, a new social order would arise upon the basis of freedom and loyalty, to be guaranteed by the institutions of education and religion, and by placing the ballot in the hands of every man who is known to be loyal, and who can read it.

All this must be a work of time; but the work is nothing less than to build up society and the state from the foundation, and this in the midst of chaos. There is now nothing of the old order of things that we can safely build upon, or that will serve as material for building. For, since the States rebelled in their organic character, they forfeited existence and lapsed into anarchy; every rebel then forfeited all his privileges as a citizen of the United States; so that, as I said at the opening of the war, there could be no question of *in* the Union or *out* of it, but the only alternative was *in* the Union, with full allegiance to its supremacy, or *under* it, subject to its authority, but debarred from all its privileges; and now from that chaotic territory, new States must arise under the tutelage of Congressional law. Our immediate danger is from the recognition of old State forms in the South and the rapid restoration of crude State governments. When you consider that except in the naturalization of foreigners, not Congress but the State fixes the condition of citizenship, you will see how great the danger is in readmitting to their status in the Union States scarce half purged of treason.

Loyal men in the South, having good means of information, estimate that seventy-five per cent. of the land in the Southern States is held by men who have been directly or indirectly in complicity with treason against the United States. If this tremendous political and social power be restored to these men by the mere fiction of an oath of allegiance, what shall hinder their imposing disabilities upon the colored race and the poor whites, that will virtually restore the old regime of the slave aristocracy? With land and legislation in their hands, they will again become the dictators of Southern sentiment, and by concentrating upon a common policy will make terms with political parties at the North for their own aggrandizement.

The time has fully come, when, as Mr. Lincoln significantly said in his first inaugural, we must "provide by law for the enforcement of that clause in the Constitution which guarantees that the citizens of each State shall be entitled to all the privileges and immunities of citizens in the several States." The time has fully come when we must make good his official declaration of July 30, 1863, that "it is the duty of every government to give protection to its citizens, of whatever class, color, or condition." The time is fully come when we must give vitality and practical effect to the fourth section of the fourth article of the Constitution, that "the United States shall guarantee to every State in this Union a republican form of government."

Mr. Lincoln has laid down with his usual clearness the principle that governs the case: "An attempt to guarantee and protect a revived State government, constructed in whole, or in preponderating part, from the very element against whose hostility and violence it is to be protected, is simply absurd. There must be a test by which to separate the opposing element, so as to build only from the sound." But just at the critical point of fixing the test, Mr. Lincoln's confiding kindness got the better of his good judgment. He did not make sufficient allowance for human depravity, nor for political chicanery; and his amnesty oath opens a wide door for perjured rebels to plot new mischief within the State.

But let us once clear the ground of the rebellious leaders, by unrelenting confiscation and disfranchisement, then let Congress fix the status of citizens, and these in due time frame a free State constitution, and all is clear and safe. Do you shrink from the time and cost of such measures? I grant it were easier and cheaper to hang a few rebels; but we should aim to destroy the rebellion, so that it shall have no issue and no successor. If true to Mr. Lincoln, we shall see that the work of emancipation is made sure, and we shall but follow his example by going beyond his own position, as the logic of events shall lead us forward. That the nation may live, slavery must utterly die.

3. Our last lesson from the life of Abraham Lincoln is that of unwavering confidence in God, for the guidance, the defence and the deliverance of the nation. Mr. Cobden was wont to say of men in public life, "You have no hold of any one who has no religious faith." Our hold upon Mr. Lincoln was in his character as a man of positive and earnest religious convictions; and his hold upon us and upon posterity is mainly through that character. He never distrusted God, and he was willing to follow implicitly the teachings of the Bible and of Divine Providence. His death has thrown us back once more upon God as our helper and our trust. In his own words, "I turn and look to the great American people, and to that God who has never forsaken them."

The historian of France has written, that when Louis XIV. died, "it was not a man, it was a world that ended." But with Abraham Lincoln a new era was born that is glorified and made perpetual through his death. He has told how once he was startled and terrified at being awakened at midnight to see the stars falling and to hear the cry that the end of the world had come. But he looked up to the Great Bear and the Pointers, and seeing them unshaken, he returned to his rest. And now that he has gone so calmly to his last rest, we look up through the cloud and see the steady pointers of the sky. A star of the first magnitude has fallen from the meridian; but the pole is unchanged, and the world holds on its course. Angel hands are only shifting the curtains of the sky for the dawn. The day is brightening; let us turn from this night of sorrow and of blood to welcome it with our morning hymn of hope and praise.

> O North, with all thy vales of green,
> O South, with all thy palms,
> From peopled towns and fields between,

Uplift the voice of psalms.
Raise ancient East, the anthem high,
And let the youthful West reply.

Lo! in the clouds of heaven appears
  God's well beloved Son;
He brings a train of brighter years —
  His kingdom is begun;
He comes a guilty world to bless
With mercy, truth, and righteousness.

O Father, haste the promised hour
  When at his feet shall lie,
All rule, authority, and power,
  Beneath the ample sky.
When He shall reign from pole to pole,
The Lord of every human soul.

When all shall heed the words He said
  Amid their daily cares,
And by the loving life He led,
  Shall strive to pattern theirs;
And He who conquered death shall win
The mighty conquest over sin.[19]

[19] Hymn by W. C. Bryant, read by Rev. S. Osgood, D.D., at the commemorative service in Union Square, April 25, 1865.

INDEX

INDEX

INDEX

INDEX

equally, 792; provision on desertion, 793; purchase of exemption from, 793

Conspiracy, Southern, 303, 1173

Constitutional Convention, U.S., 220, 223, 232, 243, 261, 406, 411; provision by for suspension of habeas corpus, 219; Committee of Detail, 222, 223, 229; Committee of Five, 225; Committee of Style and Arrangement, 225, 226, 229; meets, 827

Constitutional government: dissemination of documents, 543

Constitutional History of the United States, by George Ticknor Curtis, 525

Constitutional relations: between U.S. and its citizens, 487

Constitutional rights, 274, 1116; destroyed, 189–190; violated, 196; of rebels, non-existent, 486; invasions of, 745–755

Constitutional Union party, 86, 1077; consents to policy of non-coercion, 703; 1861 ticket of, 1076

Constitution, Confederate, 537–538, 835; Section IX. Article I., 640; based on inequality of races, 641; similarity to U.S. Constitution, 732

Constitution of Gt. Br., 220, 221, 223, 227, 260, 404, 441, 532, 754, 821; and habeas corpus, 208; and suspension of habeas corpus, 209, 210; changes in, 211–212; power of Parliament to suspend habeas corpus, 219; contrasted with U.S. Constitution in provision for habeas corpus, 229–230; distinction between common law and parliamentary practice, 259; judicial function of King, 281; spirit of, at war with Stuart family, 300; indemnity under, 533; inheritance laws under, 882

Constitutions, state; guarantees of freedom in, 288

Constitution, U.S., 181, 190, 223, 227, 255, 318, 376, 379, 380, 418, 419, 422, 448, 454, 477, 486, 498, 509, 514, 520, 530, 548, 557, 571, 572, 573, 600, 628, 645, 675, 677, 698, 728, 762, 845, 881, 931, 938, 983, 986, 994, 999, 1002, 1003, 1007, 1010, 1011, 1014, 1017, 1020, 1022, 1027, 1030, 1031, 1056, 1079, 1084, 1092, 1098, 1100, 1120, 1121, 1156; insolubility of, 20; on relations between federal government and the states, 20; Motley defends, 29; makes U.S. a nation, 31; is fundamental law of U.S., 32; empowered to act

directly on individuals, 33; supremacy of, 33, 67, 456, 832–833, 902; ordained and established by all the people, 34; permanence of, 35; established by people of the U.S., 38; language of is language of law, 39; perpetual, 39; no special provision against secession, 40; provision for amendment, 40–41, 67–68, 577; ratification of, 46–47, 57, 64–65, 79, 85, 828; effects of, 47–48; officials bound by solemn oath to maintain, 48; as compact, 64, 68–69, 71, 73–74, 79, 80, 883, 879–880, 894; strict construction of, 75, 920; Tenth Amendment of, 81; preamble to, 84, 480, 548, 577, 825, 828; revision of, by general consent, 126–127; nation is above, 154; Act of State of Va. adopting, 168; aim of, 181–182; stipulations cannot be executed, 188–189; amendment impossible, after secession, 189; violations of, 191, 517, 561, 576, 707, 1133; abolished, 186; presidential powers under, 218, 460; use of term insurrection, 221; position of amendments to, 229; principles of, 231; Section nine, first and second clauses, 244; provisions in executed without acts of Congress, 245–246; Congressional powers under, 246; above authority of Act of Congress, 249; Confederate view of, 253; articles of, 265; amendments to, 279; no executive prerogative under, 282; guarantees of freedom in, 288; duty of Americans to stand by it even in wartime, 294; on confiscation of property, 358, 358–359, 365; prohibits bills of attainder, 359, 360, 362; Fourth, Fifth and Sixth Amendments, 362; support for, 364; provision for punishment of crime, 365; war powers under, 365, 366, 378, 423, 468; aim of is good of whole, 405–406; administered for general good, 407; Bill of Rights, 411, 531; Article Four, 424; on Congressional power to call up militia, 425; subverted by Abolitionists, 437; loose and strict interpretations of, 446; Presidential power to subdue enemy under, 463; military power of President under, 463–465; no warrant for martial law under, 467, 470; as means of American freedom, 480; definition of treason under, 483, 741–742, 744–745, 885, 899, 1174; spirit of vs. letter of, 518; President's power extended be-

gressional control over, 818; views of
the Society for the Diffusion of Polit-
ical Knowledge on, 873; Lincoln's pol-
icy on, 898, 1125; aim of, 908; under
McClellan, 1126; question of, 1137
Red Bank: Negro soldiers at, 654
Reed, William Bradford, 856
Re-enslavement, 853, 854
Reform, right of, 62
Regulated servitude, 353, 354; proposed
by Emma Willard, 345; would place
Negroes in their true position, 350
Reign of Terror, France, 527, 738
Religion, freedom of, 406, 411, 726
Removal of the Deposits, 935
Rensselaer county, N.Y., 953
Renssalaer, Steven Van, see Van Renssa-
laer, Steven
Reparations: to South from North, 814–
815
Representation: three-fifths rule of, 731
Republican Congressional Committee, 13.
See also Union Congressional Committee
Republicanism: needs slavery, 132
Republican Party, 53, 333, 417, 545, 572,
703, 734, 981, 994, 1008, 1081, 1084,
1086, 1148; Pennsylvania State Central Committee, 6; determined to set
bounds to extension of slavery, 52;
ascendancy of, deplored, 99; Catholic
prejudice against, 142; success of, as
cause of Civil War, 296, 297, 302, 703;
position of, on slavery, 333, 1095–
1096; a Free Soil party, 334; alliance
with abolitionists, 638–639; organized
on anti-slavery basis, 702; doctrine of,
703–704; power of, 708–710; Convention of, New Hampshire, 903; platform
of, 1864, 1028, 1030, 1124; in majority
in Congress after secession, 1091; restoration of Union, inimical to, 1091–
1096; has thrived on Civil War, 1092;
opposition to Peace Convention, 1093;
secession of South advantageous to,
1093; wants complete emancipation as
condition of saving Union, 1096; not
alone in desiring end to slavery, 1097–
1098; Southern attitude toward, 1126;
fury of Democratic party at, 1147;
platform of, promulgated, 1162
Republican policies, 1862, 404
Republican publication societies, 3
Republicans, 302, 542, 890, 993, 1014,
1039; form Union Leagues and Loyal
Leagues, 2; found Loyal Publication

Society in New York City, 4; election
of impossible in reconstructed government, 301; the old set, 305–306; doctrine of universal compensated emancipation, 431; majority in Senate, 436;
in Congress, 439; in Ill. Senate, 610;
in North, press for enlistment of Negroes in Union army, 650; in Pa. legislature, 903; as Union Party, 1016;
solicit soldier vote, 1028; campaign
against Peace Democrats, 1135
Republicans, Black, 123, 1147
Republicans, French, 300, 308
Republicans, Moderate, 16
Republicans, Radical, see Radical Republicans
Republican State Central Committee of
Detroit, 14
Republican view: moderate, 914
Resolution of Independence, 839
Resolutions of '98, 834
Revenue laws, U.S., 592
Revenue, national: abolition would add
to, 970; portion collected from North,
1019
Revolution: peaceful, in U.S., 41, 47, 62;
Md. has no cause for, 91; to change
administration policy, 540; methods of,
dangerous, 541
    Right of, 62, 315, 426, 428, 759–
760; indisputable, 37–38; American,
38; belongs to individual not state, 63;
none in S.C., 316; resides in people,
529; upheld by Sons of Liberty, 1057.
See also American Revolution; French
Revolution
Reynolds: arrested for urging resistance
to Conscription, 1061
Rhetts, the, 581
Rhode Island, 417, 430, 725, 787, 789;
ratifies U.S. Constitution, 548; enlists
Negroes, mulattoes and Indians as soldiers, 653–654; Conscription Act vio-
lates Constitution of, 792; in Articles
of Confederation, 825; refusal to con-
fer powers on Congress, 826; Door
Constitution, 844; Savings Banks of,
956; Sons of Liberty in, 1046
Rhode Island, Battle of: Negroes in, 654
Rice, 444, 720, 963; production of, in
South, 60; as staple of Ga., 185
Rice, William A., 740
Richardson, W. A.: on re-election of Lin-
coln, 1025
Richmond, Bishop of, 142
Richmond Enquirer, 813, 1122; com-

THE JOHN HARVARD LIBRARY

*The intent of
Waldron Phoenix Belknap, Jr.,
as expressed in an early will, was for
Harvard College to use the income from a
permanent trust fund he set up, for "editing and
publishing rare, inaccessible, or hitherto unpublished
source material of interest in connection with the
history, literature, art (including minor and useful
art), commerce, customs, and manners or way of
life of the Colonial and Federal Periods of the United
States . . . In all cases the emphasis shall be on the
presentation of the basic material." A later testament
broadened this statement, but Mr. Belknap's interests remained constant until his death.*

*In linking the name of the first benefactor of
Harvard College with the purpose of this later,
generous-minded believer in American culture the
John Harvard Library seeks to emphasize the importance of Mr. Belknap's purpose. The John Harvard
Library of the Belknap Press of Harvard University
Press exists to make books and documents
about the American past more readily
available to scholars and the
general reader.*